The HEBREW BIBLE

The HEBREW BIBLE

A COMPARATIVE APPROACH

Christopher D. Stanley

FORTRESS PRESS
Minneapolis

THE HEBREW BIBLE
A Comparative Approach

Additional resources are available on the companion website, www.fortresspress.com/stanley.

Cover image: "Exodus" (1999, oil on canvas) by Richard McBee / Bridgeman Art Library / Getty Images.
Cover design: Christy J. P. Barker
Book design: James Korsmo

Library of Congress Cataloging-in-Publication Data

Stanley, Christopher D.
  The Hebrew Bible : a comparative approach / Christopher D. Stanley.
     p. cm.
  Includes bibliographical references.
  ISBN 978-0-8006-6347-6 (alk. paper)
  1. Bible. O.T.—Textbooks. 2. Palestine—Religion—Textbooks. 3. Judaism—History—To 70 A.D.—Textbooks. 4. Bible. O.T.—Comparative studies. I. Title.
  BS1194.S67 2009
  221.6—dc22

                              2008039758

The paper used in this publication meets the minimum requirements of American National Standard for Information Sciences—Permanence of Paper for Printed Library Materials, ANSI Z329.48-1984.

Printed in Canada.

13   12   11   10   09   1   2   3   4   5   6   7   8   9   10

CONTENTS

PART ONE: WHAT IS THE HEBREW BIBLE?

PART TWO: THE WORLD OF THE HEBREW BIBLE

PART THREE: THE RELIGION OF THE HEBREW BIBLE

A. Ideological Presuppositions

B. The Importance of Stories

INTRODUCTION FOR STUDENTS

You are about to embark on a journey to another world. This world is flat, not round like our own, and covered by a huge dome. Each day the sun, moon, and stars follow their regular paths across this dome. Beyond the dome are vast storehouses of water that break through from time to time in the form of rain. Beneath the ground lie similar pools that well up to the surface on occasion, producing massive floods. Even farther below is the realm of darkness where the dead live as empty shadows of their earthly selves.

The world that you are about to visit is inhabited by a variety of beings, both human and superhuman. For the most part, the humans live in small villages where they labor long and hard to provide the basic necessities of life for their families. Most are poor farmers and shepherds who struggle daily to make ends meet. Modern science and technology, including medical care, are unknown to them. Many of their women and children die in childbirth, and many of the children who survive the birth process lose their lives to disease or famine before they reach adulthood. Most of the residents of this world are illiterate, though they do possess a form of practical wisdom that is grounded in generations of observation and experience.

Alongside the humans live a host of gods and spirits whose actions determine much of what happens in this world. They shaped the world into its present form and control the forces of nature. Most of these beings are associated with a particular piece of territory, and many reside in special houses built for them by their human servants. Some oversee larger regions, while others are limited to smaller sites such as a river, a pool, or a grove of trees. Their power is especially evident in the unpredictable forces of nature. Rain and drought, heat and cold, wind and storm, even life and death are in their hands.

The supernatural residents of this world are not always friendly toward humans, and sometimes their actions seem unfair and unjust. They give aid to men and women whom they wish to succeed and rain hardships upon those whom they wish to bring down. Sometimes they use humans as pawns in their relationships with one another. But humans are not entirely helpless. Certain kinds of activities—prayers, sacrifices, ritual acts, expressions of loyalty—can earn them favorable treatment from the gods, while other deeds—chanting incantations, wearing amulets, avoiding certain places or acts—can help to protect them from the harmful actions of the deities. Much of what we would call religion centers on this question of how to ensure the favor of the gods and avoid their displeasure.

In the midst of this world lives a group of people who are dedicated to a god named Yahweh. Most of them reside in a small mountainous region that many regard as the center of the universe. Some of these people honor other gods alongside Yahweh, while others insist that their land belongs to Yahweh and that Yahweh alone should be worshipped if they are to enjoy divine protection and good harvests. Many believe that Yahweh lives among them in a special house that was constructed by one of their kings, while others insist that the deity roams freely about the land, appearing to its residents at a variety of locations. The followers of Yahweh tell stories of how the deity led their ancestors to this land and teach their children how they should live in order to enjoy Yahweh's blessings. They have no idea that many of their stories and beliefs will one day be written down and compiled into a book that will be read around the globe and shape the thinking of people in three major world religions.

THE PURPOSE OF THIS BOOK

This book is designed to introduce college and university students to a collection of books that scholars call the Hebrew Bible. This collection goes by different names in religious circles. For Jews, it is simply the **Bible**, a term that comes from the Greek word *biblia*, meaning "books." Today, many Jews prefer the more contemporary term, the **Tanak** (see chapter 3). Christians call it the **Old Testament** and include it as the first part of their Bible alongside the early Christian writings that they label the *New Testament*. Jews do not use the term *Old Testament* since they do not regard the New Testament as a sacred text. Muslims, too, view the Hebrew Bible as a source of truth, though they do not place it on the same level as the Qur'an. (For more on these issues, see chapter 2.)

This book does not presume that you are a religious believer or that you know anything about the Hebrew Bible. It also does not assume that you intend to study the Bible (or religion in general) as an academic major or career, though students who are moving in that direction will doubtless find it useful. It does presuppose that you have enough interest in the subject to wade through a significant amount of reading over the course of a semester. It also assumes that you are willing to come to the materials with an open mind and a sympathetic attitude so that you can imagine yourself into a world that is in many ways very different from our own.

But why should anyone wish to study the Hebrew Bible in the first place?

1. *Cultural understanding.* As a result of the social and political influence of Christianity and Judaism, the Hebrew Bible has permeated every aspect of Western culture. Much of the legal system of the West is based on principles derived from the Hebrew Bible. Many of its central ideas (concerning the supernatural world, the origin of the universe, the nature of human beings, and so forth) are taken for granted by people who know nothing about the origins of those ideas. Countless artistic and musical works have been inspired by its characters and stories. If we wish to understand Western culture, we need to know something about the Hebrew Bible.

2. *Religious insight.* The Hebrew Bible is part of the religious heritage of Jews and Christians, and to a lesser extent of Muslims. Students who belong to one of these traditions have a vested interest in learning more about its content. Those who stand outside of these traditions can also benefit from studying texts that have played such a vital role in the history of Judaism, Christianity, and Islam. At a minimum, they will gain a better sense of why Jews, Christians, and Muslims think and behave as they do. They can also learn why many people still feel com-

pelled to turn to the Hebrew Bible when working out their views on contemporary social and political issues.

3. *Cross-cultural experience.* The Hebrew Bible arose in a world that was very different from our own. The worldviews and lifestyles reflected in its pages often seem more like those of traditional African or Native American peoples than like the thought patterns of contemporary Jews or Christians. Studying the Hebrew Bible can give us valuable insights into the ways in which people in different cultures think and act. This ability to understand and relate to other cultures is crucial for success in a world where businesses and other organizations are increasingly acknowledging the importance of intercultural communication skills.

4. *Personal growth.* The Hebrew Bible contains ideas and insights that have proved both helpful and challenging to people across the centuries. The individuals who wrote and compiled these texts were struggling with many of the same questions that have perplexed humans in every era, including the meaning and purpose of life, the problem of evil, and the best way to live. Many people have found their answers to be helpful, while others have been troubled by their conclusions. While this book was not written to lead students into any kind of personal religious faith or activity, a close engagement with the Hebrew Bible will invariably challenge students to think seriously about some of the fundamental questions of human existence.

THE APPROACH OF THIS BOOK

As with any piece of literature, the Hebrew Bible can be studied from a variety of angles. The most common approach among biblical scholars is to situate the text within its historical context. Textbooks that follow this model are organized like history books, beginning with the historical origins of the people who produced these texts and tracing their social, political, and religious development throughout the period covered by the Hebrew Bible. Other scholars focus on the literary dimension of the text. Textbooks that adopt this approach usually introduce students to the books of the Hebrew Bible in their biblical order, though some follow other strategies such as examining the various types of literature that are found in the Bible. Still other scholars are interested in the religious and theological message of the text. Textbooks with a theological orientation typically focus on the central ideas that permeate the Hebrew Bible, with some authors attempting to trace the historical development of these ideas and others using a more topical approach.

The fundamental problem with all of these approaches is that they fail to do justice to the religious dimensions of the text. Religion is not the same as theology. Scholars who study the theology of the Hebrew Bible focus on the ideas and beliefs of the people who produced these texts. An examination of the religion embedded in the texts is much broader. It investigates not only the forms of religion that are prescribed by the Hebrew Bible but also the many and diverse ways in which religion was actually practiced in the ancient land of Israel, where the Hebrew Bible originated. It asks the same kinds of questions and relies on the same kinds of tools, categories, and insights that scholars use when studying other forms of religion such as Hinduism or Native American religions. Such a comparative approach calls attention to important issues that are frequently neglected in introductory textbooks, such as:

- Why are there so many stories in the Hebrew Bible? What role did stories play in the religious life of the people of ancient Israel?

- How was society structured in ancient Israel? Who had power and who did not? How was religion used to justify these structures?

- What is the underlying significance of the many religious rituals described in the Hebrew Bible? How do these compare with the rituals of other cultures?

- How were standards of behavior passed on from one generation to the next in ancient Israel? How were they enforced? To what extent was religion used to support these standards?

- How uniform or diverse was religious belief and practice in ancient Israel? How did people handle religious controversies?

- How do the religious beliefs of the people of ancient Israel compare with those of similar cultures at other times and places?

Unfortunately, our ability to answer these kinds of questions is limited by the fact that the Hebrew Bible represents only one slice of the religious life of ancient Israel. This does not mean that the authors agreed on every point; in fact, there is a surprising amount of diversity within the pages of the Hebrew Bible. But the people who wrote and edited these texts held certain common beliefs that informed all of their writings, and they frequently ignored or demonized the ideas and practices of people who held different views. Learning more about the diversity of religious life in ancient Israel can make it easier for us to see what is common and what is distinctive about the religious vision of the people who wrote and compiled these texts.

The task is harder than one might expect, however, since few writings other than the Hebrew Bible have survived from ancient Israel. Thus it is important that we learn how to read not only "with the grain" of the text (that is, hearing what it is saying on the surface) but also "against the grain" (that is, looking for data about beliefs and practices that the authors were trying to suppress) if we hope to develop a fully orbed picture of religious life in ancient Israel. The results will necessarily be limited and speculative, but with the help of archaeology and materials from similar cultures, we can develop a reasonable picture of how religion was practiced in ancient Israel, including but not limited to the people who produced the Hebrew Bible.

THE STRUCTURE OF THIS BOOK

The following overview of the structure of this book will help you to prepare for your journey through the Hebrew Bible.

1. The first section of the book (chapters 1–5) will introduce you to the academic study of the Hebrew Bible. Some of the issues to be explored in these chapters include the importance of Scriptures in world religions; the varied ways in which the Hebrew Bible has been used

by Jews, Christians, and Muslims; the origins and structure of the Hebrew Bible; and the methods employed by scholars in their study of the Bible.

2. The second part of the book (chapters 6–9) examines the historical claims of the Hebrew Bible. Chapter 6 explores how the events narrated in the text might have been influenced by the geography of the region. Chapter 7 lays out what scholars have learned about the daily lives of the people depicted in these texts. In both chapters the goal is to provide you with background knowledge about the culture that is taken for granted by the authors and editors of the Hebrew Bible. From here the discussion shifts to the narrative framework of the Hebrew Bible. Chapter 8 presents an overview of the story line that forms the backbone of the Hebrew Bible. Chapter 9 surveys the current scholarly debate concerning the historical reliability of these narratives. Much of the Hebrew Bible presupposes that readers are familiar with key stories about Israel's past, so it is important to have at least a general sense of the biblical story line in order to understand what the text is saying.

3. The remainder of the book (chapters 10–38) focuses on the religious life of the people of ancient Israel, with special attention to the beliefs and practices reflected in the Hebrew Bible. Chapter 10 explains how insights from the cross-cultural study of religion can help us to understand the religious vision embedded in the Hebrew Bible. The rest of the book aims to unpack the content of that vision. The analysis is divided into six sections.

(a) The first section (chapters 11–14) examines some of the central ideological presuppositions that run throughout the Hebrew Bible. Included here are beliefs about the nature of the universe, the supernatural realm, what it means to be human, and the relationship between the supernatural realm and humanity. These ideas are compared and contrasted with those of other people groups, including Israel's neighbors.

(b) The second section (chapters 15–21) investigates the role of stories in the Hebrew Bible. After an initial discussion of the role of stories in religious communities, the rest of the section looks at the meaning and purpose of some of the more significant stories in the Hebrew Bible. Special attention is given to stories about the origins of the universe and its inhabitants (including human

beings); the earliest ancestors of the people called *Israel*; the formation of Israel as a nation; and the subsequent history of the nation. Each chapter includes a summary of the debate concerning the historical reliability of these stories.

(c) The third section (chapters 22–24) looks at the various laws and regulations that were developed to guide the lives of the followers of Yahweh, the supreme deity of the people who produced the Hebrew Bible. As with the prior section, the discussion begins with a comparative examination of the role of ethical and ritual rules within religious communities, then moves into an analysis of the history and contents of the legal sections of the Hebrew Bible.

(d) The fourth section (chapters 25–30) examines some of the ways in which the people of ancient Israel sought to experience and address the supernatural world. The first chapter lays out some of the common features of human religious experience that have been identified by cross-cultural studies of religion. The ensuing chapters explore how these features come to expression in the Hebrew Bible and the culture from which it arose. Separate chapters investigate how religion was practiced within the extended family, the local community, and the state religious system.

(e) The fifth section (chapters 31–36) looks at the many books in the Hebrew Bible that contain sayings attributed to people known as prophets. The section begins with a study of the roles and activities of prophetic figures in other cultures, including their functions as social critics and reformers. This is followed by several chapters that explore the historical context and message of the various prophets whose sayings were eventually collected and edited for inclusion in the Hebrew Bible.

(f) The final section (chapters 37–38) examines the wisdom tradition of ancient Israel. The first chapter surveys the social context and purposes of wisdom instruction in traditional cultures, including ancient Israel. From here the discussion shifts to a review of several books in the Hebrew Bible that embody various forms of wisdom thinking. Special attention is given to the diversity of the ideas found in these books and the reasons for this diversity.

HOW TO USE THIS BOOK

Scattered throughout this book are Exercises that invite you to read selections from the Hebrew Bible and answer questions about what you have read. Many of these Exercises appear in the middle of a chapter. The purpose of these Exercises is to point you to passages from the Hebrew Bible that exemplify the ideas under discussion in the chapter. It is unlikely that your instructor will require you to do all of the written work indicated in these Exercises, but *it is important that you read the biblical texts listed in the Exercises even when no written work is required*. Reading the textbook alone will not help you to make sense of the Hebrew Bible on your own, nor is it sufficient to enable you to do well on an exam. The only way to learn to analyze and interpret the biblical text is to read it and think about it for yourself. The Exercises will help you to do that.

Another feature of the book that deserves explanation is the use of bold type on individual words throughout the text. The presence of bold type indicates that the word is defined in the Glossary at the back of the book. As a rule, words are only marked with bold type the first time they occur, so you will need to remember to consult the Glossary when you run into words that are unfamiliar to you. A wise reader will make regular use of it.

In the end, this book is meant to serve as a guide for reading the Hebrew Bible, not as a substitute. Students who read the textbook and ignore the biblical text are like armchair travelers who spend hours poring over glossy travel brochures and searching the Internet for information about an exotic vacation spot but never actually go to the trouble of traveling there. Their information might be accurate, but no description can replace the experience of actually visiting the site.

Of course, none of us will ever be able to visit and converse with the people of ancient Israel for ourselves. But students who make a serious attempt to understand the world of the Hebrew Bible may be surprised to learn that their imaginary journeys to the exotic land of the past can be as rewarding, and perhaps as life-changing, as an actual visit to a foreign country.

Bon voyage!

INTRODUCTION FOR TEACHERS

Writing an introductory textbook on the Hebrew Bible at a time when virtually every "assured result" of biblical scholarship is open for debate is a daunting enterprise. How can anyone hope to summarize the current status of the field in language that is comprehensible to the typical undergraduate student? The task seems hopeless. But perhaps this is the wrong question. Perhaps we should be asking instead, "Is this the only way to introduce students to the Hebrew Bible?"

This book was born out of a profound sense of frustration with the pedagogical approaches that dominate virtually every published introduction to the Hebrew Bible. The problem lies not with the quality of the scholarship, but with the manner in which it is presented. The nature of the problem can be seen by looking at two issues: the target audience of the textbooks and their institutional location.

1. Target audience. Most of the introductory textbooks currently on the market were written for students who have a general familiarity with the content and stories of the Bible and are eager (or at least willing) to learn more about the fascinating world of biblical scholarship. The primary goal of these textbooks is to lead students into a more critical understanding of the biblical text. This view of the pedagogical task shapes not only what is included in the book but also how it is presented. Much of the discussion revolves around the central critical questions that have engaged scholars since the rise of biblical criticism, such as the origins of the various books that make up the Hebrew Bible, the history of ancient Israel (including the historicity of the biblical narratives), the ideological orientations of the various biblical authors and editors, and the value of archaeology for understanding the biblical text. Some authors make an effort to engage students in careful literary readings of particular biblical texts, but the goal is the same: to lead students into a more nuanced, critical understanding of the Hebrew Bible.

So what is wrong with this approach? Nothing, as long as it is used with the proper audience. The tradi-

tional model has worked well for generations of students in both seminaries and undergraduate institutions. But times have changed, and fewer and fewer students are entering American colleges and universities with the amount of biblical literacy that these textbooks presuppose. In many parts of the country, the majority of students who sign up for an introductory course on the Hebrew Bible have only vague (and often incorrect) ideas about its content. Most are taking the course to satisfy a general education requirement, not to pursue a major in religious studies or theology. The needs and interests of these students are clearly different than those of their parents' generation. Yet instructors continue to use the same kinds of textbooks and methods to teach them about the Hebrew Bible. Is it any wonder that many of them find our courses to be boring, excessively difficult, or both?

2. Institutional location. The traditional approach to teaching the Hebrew Bible presumes that there is no need to justify the place of the subject in the curriculum. In other words, it assumes an institutional location that is sympathetic to the critical study of the Bible. This paradigm is still prevalent in seminaries and church-related colleges, but not in state universities and secular colleges. Faculty members in these institutions have increasingly been asked to defend the importance and validity of teaching courses in biblical studies. The traditional response has been to point out that these courses use critical methodologies and are fundamentally historical in orientation; that is, they do not concern themselves with questions about the relevance of these texts for contemporary believers. But the rhetorical weight of these arguments has been undermined in recent years by the rise of postmodern criticism that challenges the presumed objectivity of historical study while simultaneously calling attention to the inherently subjective nature of the educational process (and of religion in general). If courses in biblical studies are to survive the challenge of postmodernism, they must be justified along other lines.

One way to ensure a place for biblical studies in the curriculum is to employ the same methods for introducing students to the Bible that are used when studying other religions. In this approach, the Hebrew Bible would be treated not simply as a literary artifact of a particular religious community but also as a sample text (or better, a set of texts) through which students would learn the language and methods commonly used in the academic study of religion. When studying the narrative texts in the Hebrew Bible, for instance, students would learn to ask what kinds of religious purposes a story might have fulfilled in the lives of the people who created and/or preserved it. When looking at cultic texts, they would learn to talk about the symbolic and performative aspects of the various rituals and explore how the rituals in the Hebrew Bible compare with similar rituals in other cultures. When reading wisdom texts, they would learn about how wisdom traditions function in traditional societies, both among village cultures and among literate elites.

Framed in this way, the "Introduction to the Hebrew Bible" course could serve some of the same pedagogical functions as a more general "Introduction to Religion" course. The value of such a course would be clearer to scholars who are unfamiliar with the world of contemporary biblical studies, while the use of a common language could open up new channels for dialogue with colleagues in other fields. Such a cross-cultural approach might also prove more popular with students, since it coincides with the growing interest in other cultures on many college campuses. Students who enroll in a course of this type would learn less about professional biblical scholarship than those in traditional Hebrew Bible courses, but they would learn more about the breadth of human religious experience. Students who enjoyed such a course might be as likely to continue their studies with a course on Buddhism or Islam as with an upper-level course on the Hebrew Bible.

CHARTING A NEW COURSE

This book seeks to chart a new course for introducing students to the Hebrew Bible. What makes this book different is not the manner in which the biblical materials are interpreted but the way in which they are presented. Where others use the history of ancient Israel or the canonical books of the Bible as their organizing principle, this book is structured around an analytical framework derived from the comparative study of religion. (For an overview of the book's contents, see the "Introduction for Students.") This framework is most evident in the early chapters of the book, where the role of Scriptures in religious communities is discussed, and at the beginnings of each of the major sections, where comparative perspectives are used to shed light on a particular category of belief or practice. Much of the time, however, the comparative framework operates in the background, emerging from the shadows only when it promises to add substantially to the discussion.

The choice of a comparative approach reflects the intended audience of the book: freshmen and sophomores who are taking an introductory course on the Hebrew Bible either to fulfill a general education requirement or as an elective outside of their major. Students who are pursuing a major in religion/theology or who wish to take advanced courses in the Bible will find that the book provides an adequate foundation for further studies in the field, but no such intent is presumed. Because the book assumes no prior experience with the Hebrew Bible or the academic study of religion, it begins at a more basic level than most other introductory texts. Things that are taken for granted in other textbooks (familiarity with concepts, stories, characters, and so forth) are explained as though students are encountering them for the first time. Every effort has been made to ensure that the language of the book is accessible to the average student—the prose is simple, clear, and direct, and unnecessary technical terms and footnotes have been omitted. Some instructors may think that the book aims too low in its attempt to make the material available to students. But classroom testing has shown that students are able to learn more from a book like this than from those that target a higher level of biblical knowledge or reading ability.

Crafting a textbook that would introduce students not only to the Hebrew Bible but also to the academic study of religion has required many hard choices concerning the material to be included. Students can only learn a certain amount of material in a semester, so the addition of materials from the comparative study of religion has meant omitting certain issues normally covered in introductory textbooks and treating others more briefly than is customary. Yet a sympathetic reading of the entire book will show that in this case less truly is more. Too often the authors of introductory textbooks have failed to ask the most basic questions about what undergraduate students in a general education curriculum really need to know about the Hebrew Bible. Most books include far more information than students can possibly absorb in a semester, and many are so packed with details (especially about the history of ancient Israel) that students are apt to lose the forest in the trees. While a certain amount of detail is necessary to understand any subject, this book seeks to ensure that students grasp the big picture of contemporary biblical scholarship, even if it means sacrificing some of the details.

CRITICAL PERSPECTIVES

For the most part, this book presents mainstream scholarly views on the Hebrew Bible and comparative religion. No scholar will agree with every position that is taken here on the various points that are currently up for debate in both fields, but those who disagree should be able to recognize that the positions taken here are not idiosyncratic.

1. Hebrew Bible. With regard to the ongoing controversy over the historicity of the narrative books of the Hebrew Bible, this book follows a descriptive approach, laying out three broad schools of interpretation without endorsing any of them. The strength of this approach is that it allows instructors with widely differing views to use the book without feeling that their students are being misled. But it also means that students receive no clear answer to the question of whether it is possible to construct a well-rounded and consistent portrait of pre-exilic Israel from the narrative materials of the Hebrew Bible. Providing answers to that question is left to the instructor. This lack of a unifying historical center means that the depiction of Israel's past is more fragmentary and less coherent than in most other Hebrew Bible textbooks. But historical reconstruction is less central to this book

than to other introductory texts, so the absence of a clear stance on historical questions will have less impact on the learning experience than if the book were heavily historical in orientation.

A similar reticence will be observed concerning the Documentary Hypothesis and other source theories. Instructors who are accustomed to textbooks that devote considerable space to source theories (including tradition, form, source, and redaction criticisms) will be disappointed by the small amount of attention that these methods receive in the present volume. The decision to downplay source theories reflects an authorial judgment that the details of such theories are less important than other topics in a course geared toward general education students. Similar decisions have shaped the treatment of other issues throughout the book.

2. Comparative religion. Much of the comparative language employed in this book reflects a functionalist view of religion. Functionalism is employed here as a heuristic tool to describe how religion works. Its use should not be taken as an endorsement of the reductionism that too often accompanies functionalist interpretations of religion. In a similar way, the use of comparative materials and categories does not imply any judgment about the essential nature of religion or the degree of similarity or difference among various religions. The primary reason for including comparative materials is to demystify some of the beliefs and practices depicted in the Hebrew Bible, not to argue for any particular view of religion as a human phenomenon. A thoroughly comparative analysis would require more attention to holistic systems and more emphasis on differences than will be found in the present volume.

Those who have studied other religions will undoubtedly think of many other places where comparative perspectives might have been used to illuminate the biblical materials. In fact, the amount of comparative material included in the book is dwarfed by the space that is given to the standard questions of biblical scholarship. In addition, most of the comparative material that is included is rather general in nature, with only scattered references to specific religions. All of this is by design. Comparative insights are clearly useful when introducing students to the Hebrew Bible, but the inclusion of too many specific examples from other religions could distract students from their primary task of understanding the Hebrew Bible as a literary artifact produced by a particular ancient religious community. Instructors who would prefer to see more specific examples from other religions can always supplement the text with additional comparative materials.

HOW TO USE THIS BOOK

This book is designed to provide students with material that they can read and understand on their own so that the instructor does not have to spend every class session explaining or restating the textbook. This in turn can free the instructor to do more creative and interesting things in the classroom. Many will choose to spend their class time guiding students through focused analyses of particular biblical texts. Others might set up debates between teams of students or commission students to do artistic renditions of biblical stories. Still others might prefer to engage students in discussions of the theological and ethical questions raised by the texts. The key point is that a clear, readable textbook will make it easier for students to grasp essential concepts so that class time can be used to supplement rather than to rehash the content of the textbook.

No textbook, however, can replace a firsthand encounter with the biblical text. Most instructors recognize this and therefore assign readings from the Hebrew Bible to accompany the relevant chapters of whatever textbook they happen to be using. Such an approach assumes that students will recognize the links between the textbook and the biblical materials and integrate the two sets of readings into a coherent whole. In the eyes of students, however, the Bible and the textbook often seem like parallel and unrelated sets of readings, and their natural reaction is to focus on the textbook as in other classes. Unless they are required to write about the biblical readings, many (or even most) students will treat them as optional. Bright students who listen well and take good notes can sometimes go through an entire course on the Hebrew Bible without opening their Bibles.

To counter this problem, this textbook includes reading assignments and written exercises at key points in

every chapter. At the end of most of the major subsections, students are given a list of verses from the Hebrew Bible to read and a set of questions based on the readings. These exercises link the biblical readings to specific points in the textbook, creating a circular pattern of learning: the textbook prepares students to understand the biblical texts in the exercises, and the biblical texts reinforce what students have been reading in the textbook. But this only works if students do the exercises. It is therefore important that students be encouraged to read at least some of the biblical passages in each exercise (or others supplied by the instructor), even when they are not being asked to complete the assignment for a grade. This is especially true for the first fifteen chapters of the book, which do not focus on a particular book or set of texts from the Hebrew Bible. The exercises in these chapters are designed to give students a chance to apply what they are learning to specific biblical texts. A simple but effective way to motivate students to read the biblical passages is to divide the class into groups and require each group to write on one of the exercises and share their answers with the class. Another approach is to tell them that some of the questions from the exercises will appear on a quiz or exam. Reviewing some of the exercises in class, whether done by the instructor or by the students in small groups, can also help to underline the importance of the biblical readings.

Finally, a few comments are in order about the way in which the book is organized. The book was designed for a class that meets three times a week, with students normally reading a chapter for each class session. In most institutions, this will leave a few extra sessions that can be used either to focus more intensively on a few of the chapters (for example, looking more closely at some of the prophetic books) or to address issues that the instructor feels were not adequately treated in the book. For a course that meets only twice a week, some of the chapters could be doubled up or divided so that students will read one and a half to two chapters for each class session. The Web page for the textbook (www.fortresspress.com/stanley) contains sample syllabi showing how the readings can be allocated over different time frames.

Some instructors might be concerned about the apparent fact that students do not begin looking at specific biblical texts until chapter 15. But this is a misconception, as the exercises will have students reading and interacting with biblical texts from chapter 3 onward. Reading shorter texts with a particular question in mind is a more effective strategy for training students with no biblical background to make sense of the Bible than requiring them to read longer texts with little or no guidance. The readings in the exercises can then be used as the focal point of class discussion if the instructor so chooses.

The primary reason for postponing direct engagement with the biblical text until later in the book is to allow time for students to develop an academic mindset before sending them off to analyze texts on their own. For some, the world of the Bible is so foreign that they automatically import modern modes of thinking to help them make sense of the texts. Others come to the text with particular theological perspectives and agendas that shape their understanding of what they are reading. While it is certainly possible to address these issues inductively by reading the texts together in the classroom, it can be difficult to teach both content and critical methodology at the same time. The first fifteen chapters of this book are designed to address issues of methodology while simultaneously providing students with important background information that they will need to understand the biblical text. The overall purpose of these chapters is to help students develop a responsible historical imagination that will enable them to read these texts as the literary creations of authors and editors who lived and worked in a social, ideological, and literary world that was in many respects very different from our own. Experience with this approach has shown that it works in the classroom. Instructors who are accustomed to other approaches are encouraged to give it a try and see how it works for them and their students.

FINAL COMMENTS

Since textbooks typically go through multiple editions, instructors and students who think of ways in which this book might be improved are encouraged to send their comments and suggestions to the publisher, who will forward them to the author.

All quotations from the Hebrew Bible come from the New Revised Standard Version (1989 edition). Quotations from the Qur'an are taken from the contemporary translation of Majid Fakhry, *The Qur'an: A Modern English Version* (Reading, UK: Garnet, 1997).

PART ONE
WHAT IS THE HEBREW BIBLE?

Fig. 1.1. Scriptures vary widely in their format and appearance; clockwise from top left, a scroll of the Torah (Judaism), a copy of the Qur'an (Islam), an ancient Chinese sutra (Daoism), the *Rg Veda* (Hinduism), the *Gura Granth Sahib* (Sikhism), and an ancient Tibetan Buddhist text.

1

What Is Scripture?

Only be strong and very courageous, being careful to act in accordance with all the law that my servant Moses commanded you; do not turn from it to the right hand or to the left, so that you may be successful wherever you go. This book of the law shall not depart out of your mouth; you shall meditate on it day and night, so that you may be careful to act in accordance with all that is written in it. (Joshua 1:7-8)

All scripture is inspired by God and is useful for teaching, for reproof, for correction, and for training in righteousness, so that everyone who belongs to God may be proficient, equipped for every good work. (2 Timothy 3:16-17)

Then We [that is, God] gave Moses the Book, completing Our grace on him who would do good, making plain everything and serving as a guidance and mercy, so that they may believe in the encounter with their Lord. (Qur'an 6:154)

If there is one point on which Jews, Christians, and Muslims agree, it is that the **Hebrew Bible** is a **holy** book. The common term for a book that is viewed as holy by the members of a religion is **Scripture**, which comes from a Latin word that means "written." If we wish to understand the Hebrew Bible, we must first learn something about the role of Scriptures in religious communities.

THE STUDY OF SCRIPTURES

Most people who grew up around a synagogue, church, or mosque simply assume that all religions have books of Scripture that are fairly similar to their own. The truth is quite different. Not all religions have Scriptures, and those that do often view and use them in different ways. The reasons for these differences are complicated, reflecting the varied beliefs and histories of the individual religions.

Most religions that have Scriptures also have a class of scholars or other experts who study the Scriptures and apply them to the life of the community. Some of these scholars devote their entire lives to understanding the meaning and significance of the Scriptures. Because they know the Scriptures better than other people, they typically bear the responsibility for teaching the rest of the community about the Scriptures. In some groups they are also charged with enforcing obedience to the words of Scripture and punishing offenders.

The last few centuries have seen the rise of a different type of Scripture scholar, one who works within the walls of a university, not a religious community. Many of these scholars are members of religious groups, but many are not. Their goal is to advance human knowledge about religion, not to train religious believers. Often they ask hard questions about Scriptures that scholars within religious groups tend to avoid. Some of their findings agree with traditional understandings of Scripture, but many do not. Most are professors who pass on their methods and insights to college and university students in classrooms around the world. (For more on the differences between these two types of scholars, see chapter 5.)

The majority of these university-based scholars study the Scriptures of a single religion (Judaism, Christianity, Islam, Sikhism, Buddhism, and so forth). Some, however, have turned their attention to broader questions concerning the role of Scriptures within religious communities. Questions that they seek to address include:

- How does a book come to be regarded as Scripture within a religious community?
- How do the Scriptures of different religions resemble and differ from one another?
- What roles do Scriptures play in the lives of religious communities?
- How do religious people view and interpret Scriptures?

The remainder of this chapter will examine some of the answers that scholars have given to these questions.

DEFINING OUR TERMS

Perhaps the most fundamental question raised by the academic study of Scripture is this: What makes books of Scripture different from other books? The following definition provides a useful starting point for examining this question: *"Scripture is the writing accepted by and used in a religious community as especially sacred and authoritative."*[1] This definition is valuable because it highlights some of the chief characteristics of books that are regarded as Scriptures.

1. Scriptures are written.

The most fundamental requirement for the existence of Scriptures is the presence of people who know how to read and write. **Literacy** is a skill that is taken for granted by virtually everyone in the developed world today. For most of human history, however, the ability to read and write was limited to a small, elite class of people who could afford the time and expense of a formal education. In some cultures this included most of the members of the wealthy or ruling classes; in others, literacy was prevalent only among the **scribes**, **priests**, and scholars who kept records for the ruling **elites**. Some societies never developed a written language or the technology of book production.

Virtually all books of Scripture were written long ago in societies where the great majority of the population was illiterate. Like other works of literature, Scriptures were composed by members of the educated elite. The implications of this observation are profound. While religious people tend to think of their Scriptures as being universally valid (that is, relevant beyond their time and place of composition), the truth is that books of Scripture reflect the culture, beliefs, and biases of the people who produced them—usually upper-class males. Contemporary academic studies of Scripture have called attention to the effects of class and gender bias within books of Scripture. The presence of bias does not invalidate the message of the books, but it does mean that readers must be aware of the various ways in which elite biases might have affected the depiction of nonelites within the texts. Many books of Scripture express negative opinions about the religious beliefs and practices of the illiterate masses (including women) that may not have been shared by the majority of the population. In some cases the religious ideas and attitudes expressed in books of Scripture represent a minority viewpoint within the culture in which they arose.

In societies where literacy is limited or unknown, religious beliefs and practices are normally passed from generation to generation via **oral traditions**. Oral traditions serve many of the same purposes in the lives of illiterate people that books of Scripture do among the educated elites. For this reason some scholars have argued that the category of Scripture should be broadened to include oral materials. Most scholars have resisted this move, however, due to their conviction that the transition from oral traditions to written texts marks a fundamental change in the nature and history of a religious community, a change that often coincides with new developments in the organizational structure and thought-patterns of the group. This does not mean that having written texts makes the religions of literate cultures somehow better than those of illiterate cultures; the presence of technology says nothing about the relative merits or truthfulness of a society's ideas about the nature of reality. The chief difference is that writing tends to freeze the traditions at a particular stage in their development, whereas oral traditions can continue to evolve and change with the needs and insights of the culture.

2. Scriptures are accepted by and used in a religious community.

Literate societies produce a variety of written materials: financial records, stories, legal codes, poems, news reports, songs, historical works, and the like. In societies where religion plays a dominant role, as in virtually all cultures across human history, much of the literary output is tied directly to religion or reflects a religious outlook on life. Yet relatively few of these documents ever come to be regarded as Scripture. Why do some texts attain this status while others do not?

The elevation of a book to scriptural status reflects a judgment by the members of a particular religious group or culture that the book contains a classic statement of some of the central beliefs, values, and/or practices of the group. Sometimes this judgment is expressed through a formal vote or declaration by the members or leaders of the group, but usually the process is more gradual and

Fig 1.2. Ancient scribes copy texts onto scrolls in an Egyptian tomb painting.

informal. The process typically begins with the composition of a book that is copied and circulated among a small group of literate individuals. The author might be a well-known leader or teacher, a group of people charged with preserving the traditions of the group, or a complete unknown. Some of these early readers find the book useful and pass it on to others. Since books had to be copied by hand during the centuries when most books of Scripture were composed, the process of dissemination was often rather slow.

Once the book is placed into circulation, the process can move in a variety of directions. In some cases the book becomes so widely known and respected over time that it is incorporated into the cultural heritage of the group and passed on in families and schools over the generations. In other cases a book finds a place of honor within a narrower audience, as when a collection of ritual texts is deemed useful by the people who oversee the ritual life of the community. In still other cases a book is endorsed by the leaders of the group and thus becomes an official text of the community. Finally, many books are simply lost or never attain an elevated status within the community.

But this does not explain why people come to believe that certain books deserve a position of honor beyond other books that are known and used within a particular group or society. There is no single explanation that applies in every case. In cultures with a rich history of oral traditions, a book that renders those traditions faithfully into writing (especially the more important ones) might be seen as authoritative by people who know and respect the traditions. The same is true for books that summarize the group's time-tested wisdom for daily living. Books that express divine support for the present social order are always popular among the elites, while books that criticize the authorities are cherished by the followers of dissident leaders. Books that explain how religious **rituals** are to be conducted are likely to be honored by those who are charged with performing the rituals. Some books gain a following due to their literary qualities, especially poetic texts. Others are valued because they offer helpful observations about the nature of reality and the fundamental questions of human existence. Finally, some books earn respect due to their close association with the supernatural realm, whether because they claim to be divinely inspired or because they contain instructions for interacting with or manipulating superhuman powers.

3. Scriptures are viewed as especially sacred.

The word **sacred** means "set apart from the ordinary sphere of life." To call a book sacred is to suggest that it is different from other books, often through some sort of association with the supernatural realm. Religions differ in the way they define this association. Among Jews, Christians, and Muslims, the traditional view has been that the Scriptures are somehow inspired by the **deity**. To some people, this means that God dictated the words of Scripture directly to human authors, thus ensuring the truth of its contents. Others believe that the deity may have guided the production of the texts, but in a manner that respected the individuality and creativity of the human authors. Still others would limit the term **inspiration**

Fig. 1.3. Thoth, the Egyptian god of writing, dictates a text to a scribe.

to the belief that God speaks through the texts when they are read by people of faith.

The uniqueness of sacred texts is understood quite differently in the religious traditions of Asia (Hinduism, Buddhism, Taoism, and so forth). Most of the Scriptures in these religions are honored for the insights that they offer concerning the nature of ultimate reality (including the supernatural realm) and the way humans should live in light of that reality (both ethical and ritual conduct). These insights are credited to the wisdom of great teachers and holy people from the past, not to divine inspiration. Their ideas are regarded as sacred because people have found them to be uniquely valuable for making sense of reality and ordering their daily lives.

The sacredness of Scriptures can be exhibited in a variety of ways. In some religions, only certain people are allowed to touch or read from books of Scripture. In others, the use of the books is limited to particular religious settings. Some groups use special materials, special tools, and special forms of writing for copying or binding their Scriptures. Virtually all religions preserve their Scriptures in the original language in which they were written, and some use the books only in this form, even when most of the people in the group no longer understand the language. Where translations of the text are allowed, most religions still grant primacy to the original language of the text.

In most groups the physical books of Scripture are treated with special reverence. Official copies are often kept in special cases or wrappings when not in use. Sometimes the books are paraded in front of the followers, who are encouraged to touch them, kiss them, kneel before them, or otherwise express their respect for the holy books. Books of Scripture are frequently read aloud in public worship, accompanied by oral instruction regarding their meaning and application. In private homes, books of Scripture are often displayed in a position of honor and treated differently from other books.

Belief in the sacredness of Scripture also lies behind the common practice of using books of Scripture as channels of sacred power. People recite the holy words of Scripture in prayers, songs, chants, and incantations in order to open their minds to the supernatural realm and/or to call superhuman powers to their aid. Similar benefits are sometimes associated with studying or even touching the sacred books.

4. Scriptures are viewed as especially authoritative.

All religions recognize one or more sources of authority that serve to define and preserve their beliefs and practices over time. Common authorities include group leaders or institutions, religious experts, oral traditions, sacred texts, personal religious experience, and the conscience or reasoning capacities of the individual believer. Some groups hold one of these sources of authority in highest regard, while others honor multiple authorities.

To say that Scriptures are especially authoritative means that they are given more weight in determining and regulating the beliefs and practices of the religion than are other books that might be used from time to time within the group. Literate members of the group study the Scriptures in order to gain a better understanding of the nature of reality, the way the group should be organized, and the way individual believers should live. In some groups, the authority of the Scriptures is regarded as absolute: whatever the Scriptures say must be believed and obeyed without question. In other groups, the words of Scripture are open to criticism and must be confirmed, balanced, or interpreted by other authorities.

The list of books that are regarded as authoritative Scriptures within a religious community is called the **canon**. In some groups the canon includes only books that have been officially approved by the leaders of the group, while in others the canon is defined by custom, encompassing a variety of books that have gained the respect of the community over time. Religions also differ in the way they define the limits of their canons. In some groups the canon is considered closed, meaning that no new books can be added to the canon and no revisions can be made to the wording of the sacred texts. In other groups the list remains open, signifying that the individual books of Scripture can be revised and edited and the collection expanded or reduced over time.

Virtually all religions that have a closed canon went through a period when their canon was open. This is true even for a religion like Islam that insists that its sacred book (the **Qur'an**) was dictated directly by God to Muhammad: Muslims believe that the message was received over a period of twenty-three years and thus remained open to further additions and revisions until Muhammad's death. In most religions the existence of an open period is evident from the fact that their Scriptures contain books that were written at various times and places. Clearly the canon had to have been open

during the period when the books were being composed, a period that sometimes spanned centuries.

The move from an open canon to a closed canon is usually associated with some sort of crisis in the life of the community during which the Scriptures come to be seen as the primary guarantor of the group's identity in the face of external or internal threats. Many religious groups never faced such a threat or else responded to it in a different way; thus they never felt any obligation to close their scriptural canon. This does not mean that groups with an open canon think of their books of Scripture as less important or less authoritative than do groups with a closed canon. It simply means that they remain open to the creation or acknowledgment of additional books that might come to be regarded as sacred.

Fig. 1.4. (top) A Muslim engages in quiet reflection on the Qur'an; (bottom) a group of Jewish men celebrate the beginning of a new year of Torah readings.

VARIATIONS ON A THEME

While there are many similarities in the ways religions view and use Scriptures, there are also significant differences. Identifying these differences is important for understanding the nature of Scriptures.

1. Scriptures vary in number.

Jews, Christians, and Muslims are accustomed to thinking of Scripture as a single, unchanging book that is honored above all other books in their community. This view is fairly accurate for the Muslim Scriptures (the Qur'an), but not for Judaism and Christianity, whose "book" of Scripture is actually a collection of dozens of books that were composed at various times and places over the course of hundreds of years.

Most religions, in fact, honor multiple books of Scripture. Confucianism acknowledges five classic texts along with four supplemental books that are held in equally high esteem. Taoism employs two primary texts, the *Daode Jing* and the *Zhuangzi,* but Taoists have created hundreds of texts through the centuries that are valued as Scripture by different branches of the religion. Hinduism is grounded in a primary set of Scriptures called the Vedas, but in practice Hindus can choose from hundreds of books that are recognized as Scripture. Most Buddhists would accept the *Tripiṭaka* (a collection of Buddha's teachings) as sacred, but the religion includes many different schools that have their own canons of scriptural texts.

2. Scriptures contain different types of material.

The kind of material that one finds within books of Scripture varies widely from group to group. At one end of the spectrum are collections like the Jewish and Christian Scriptures, which contain books reflecting a broad range of literary styles: stories, songs, legal codes, letters, poems, historical narratives, theological treatises, **proverbs**, **apocalyptic** texts, and more. At the other end are books that contain only one or two types of literature. The *Ādi Granth* of Sikhism is made up almost exclusively of hymns, while the *Analects* of Confucius and the *Daode Jing* of Taoism consist primarily of sayings and dialogues (some situated within a narrative framework) that explain how people should live.

Among religions that recognize a large number of books as Scripture (Hinduism, Taoism, Buddhism, and so forth), one book will sometimes contain a single type of material and another book a different type, or else different types of literature might be segregated from one another within the same text. In Hinduism, for example, each of the four texts called the Vedas contains a section of hymns, a list of instructions for performing various rituals, a set of philosophical reflections on the meanings of the rituals, and a collection of dialogues between students and their masters, but each type of literature appears in its own section. Other Hindu Scriptures like the *Mahābhārata* and the *Laws of Manu* are more uniform, the former consisting mainly of ancient myths and legends and the latter of practical ethical instruction.

More often than not, the presence of diverse content within a set of sacred texts reflects a long history of development. As a result, it is not uncommon to find tensions and even contradictions within books of Scripture. Some religions freely acknowledge the presence of conflicting materials within their sacred texts, while others argue that such differences are more apparent than real. Often people within a religious tradition will disagree on this point, with the more liberal followers embracing the presence of diversity in their Scriptures and the more conservative members seeking to defend the unity of the texts.

One of the tasks of scholars in most religious traditions is to figure out how best to reconcile these differences within the sacred text. Sometimes this means finding a way to paper over apparent disagreements, as when scholars argue that certain texts pertain only to specific circumstances in the past while others are more universal in meaning. At other times a scholar might be charged with deciding which of several competing texts is relevant to a particular situation. Many of the conflicts that have arisen among religious people over the centuries can be traced to different ways of interpreting a common set of Scriptures.

3. Scriptures have varying degrees of authority.

Virtually all religions have certain books or passages of Scripture that are regarded as more important and authoritative than others. Often the followers of a religion will disagree about which texts should carry more weight in a particular situation. In some groups the dividing line between books of Scripture and other books is also rather vague.

For Jews, the **Torah** (the first five books of the **Bible**) is the most important part of Scripture. The remaining books of the Bible are viewed as extensions of the message of the Torah. The situation is complicated, however, by the existence of the **Mishnah** and the **Talmud**, later Jewish texts that discuss how the Torah should be applied to the daily lives of believers, as well as other ancient texts like the **midrashim** that seek to define the meaning and relevance of the Torah. Since these books are linked so closely to the Torah, many traditional Jews would view them as having more authority than some of the other books that are included in their canonical Scriptures. A similar view prevails among many Muslims concerning the *ḥadith*, collections of stories about the life and teachings of Muhammad that are used to interpret their sacred text, the Qur'an. Most Christians regard the later part of their Scriptures, the **New Testament**, as having more authority than the earlier part, the **Old Testament**, while some go further and privilege certain portions of the New Testament (for example, the words of Jesus or the teachings of Paul) over others. Hindus distinguish between Scriptures that they believe were revealed to ancient seers (*shrutis*) and texts that apply those early revelations to the circumstances of later societies (*smritis*). In principal, the earlier texts are the final authorities within Hinduism, but much of the language and content of these texts is incomprehensible to ordinary Hindus. As a result, those who read the Scriptures usually pay more heed to the later texts, especially those that pertain to their favorite god or goddess.

4. Scriptures are used in different ways.

Religions differ in the amount of weight that they grant to Scriptures in comparison with other aspects of their religion. In some groups, such as Judaism, Christianity, Islam, and Sikhism, Scriptures occupy a central place in the lives of both individuals and the group. The words of Scripture are read or recited routinely in public and private worship, and most of the beliefs and practices of the group are grounded in the teachings of Scripture. Ordinary believers turn to the Scriptures for guidance

Fig. 1.5. (top) A young Buddhist monk studies a book of Scripture as part of his training; (middle) a Christian minister quotes from the Bible while preaching a sermon; (bottom) a Jewish man carries an ornamented Torah scroll during a religious celebration.

concerning their daily conduct and ethical choices, while the leaders of the group study the Scriptures to learn how the group should be structured and how they should carry out their duties.

Other religions give their books of Scripture a less central position. Hindus acknowledge the value and importance of Scriptures, but most Hindus follow beliefs and practices that have been passed on orally for generations. Hindu Scriptures are often chanted in public and private worship, and many Hindu rituals follow patterns spelled out in the Scriptures. Nevertheless, few Hindus besides members of the priestly class or philosophers ever read or study the Scriptures for themselves, and even the experts no longer understand much of the language that is used in the foundational Hindu Scriptures, the Vedas. In a similar way, all Buddhists are familiar with the teachings known as the *Four Noble Truths* and the *Eightfold Path,* but they learn these teachings through oral instruction, not through reading Scriptures. Meditation and ethical conduct are more important to Buddhists than the knowledge of sacred texts, most of which are highly technical and studied only by monks and scholars.

CONCLUSION

The Hebrew Bible is a particular expression of a common human tendency to create and canonize a set of written texts to guide the life of a community. Not every religion has books of Scripture. Those that do have them vary greatly in the kinds of material that they include and the manner in which they view and use them.

Scriptures are not fundamentally different from other books: they are written and compiled by ordinary human authors and editors using the common language and images of their society, and they are copied and circulated and become popular in the same manner as other books within that culture. Like all literary works, they express the viewpoints and biases of their authors, which in ancient times usually meant the views of elite urban males.

What makes books of Scripture different from other books is not their mode of composition, but the fact that a particular religious community has decided that they are worthy of special respect. Such a decision reflects the group's judgment that these books are uniquely valuable for ordering the social, intellectual, ethical, or devotional life of the community. In some groups the human origin of the sacred books is either downplayed or forgotten, giving rise to stories that attribute the books to supernatural inspiration or to a group of supremely wise ancestors. By the time this happens, books of Scripture are usually well on their way to becoming a dominant source of religious authority within their community.

EXERCISE 1

Read these excerpts from the Scriptures of various religions and answer the following questions about each passage.

> (a) What kind of literature does the passage represent? Is it a story, a song, a law code, a poem, a letter, a historical narrative, a theological treatise, a collection of proverbs, an apocalyptic text, a piece of ethical instruction, or some other kind of literature?
>
> (b) What is the general subject matter of the text?
>
> (c) How do you think a text like this might have been used by followers of the religion? What leads you to this conclusion?

Qur'an 44:41-56 (Islam)

The tree of bitterness will surely be the food of the sinner,
Like molten lead, which boils in the bellies, like boiling water.
"Take him and thrust him into the pit of Hell.
Then pour over his head the agony of the boiling water,
Saying, 'Taste, you who are truly the mighty and noble one.
That is the punishment that you used to doubt.'"
However, the God-fearing are in a secure place, in gardens and well-springs.
They wear silk and brocade facing each other. Thus it will be.
And We gave them wide-eyed houris [female heavenly beings] in marriage.
They call therein for every fruit in perfect security.
They do not taste death therein, except the first death;
And he guards them against the punishment of Hell,
As a bounty from your Lord. That is the great triumph.

Mahābhārata: Astika Parva 18 (Hinduism)

Long ago, when the sea was still milk, Narayana said to the gods of heaven, "Churn the ocean, and she will yield amrita, the nectar of immortality, and precious gems, and all manner of illusion and revelation." So they placed the snow mountain Mandara in the middle of the milk sea. Its deep-striking roots rested on the ocean floor; its summit rose high above the surface. The great serpent Sesha, whose hood is an island of jewels, stretched himself across the sea, his body wrapped endlessly round the mountain in the center. On one shore his tail was held by the Asuras, the dark, olden gods; on the other shore his neck was held by the devas, the mortal gods of heaven. They each pulled in turn, so that the mountain spun first one way, then the other, while his trees and stones were thrown off into the foaming sea. First the mild Moon rose from the milk sea; then the Lady Lakshmi, bearing good fortune to men; then the smooth jewel adorning Narayana's breast; then Indra's elephant Airavata, white as clouds; then Surabhi, the white cow who grants any wish; then Parijata the wishing-tree of fragrance; then Rambha the nymph, the first Apsaras; and at last Dhanwantari the physician, robed in white, bearing a cup filled with amrita, the essence of life.

Hebrew Bible: Leviticus 6:8-13 (Judaism)

The LORD spoke to Moses, saying: Command Aaron and his sons, saying: This is the ritual of the burnt offering. The burnt offering itself shall remain on the hearth upon the altar all night until the morning, while the fire on the altar shall be kept burning. The priest shall put on his linen vestments after putting on his linen undergarments next to his body; and he shall take up the ashes to which the fire has reduced the burnt offering on the altar, and place them beside the altar. Then he shall take off his vestments and put on other garments, and carry the ashes out to a clean place outside the camp. The fire on the altar shall be kept burning; it shall not go out. Every morning the priest shall add wood to it, lay out the burnt offering on it, and turn into smoke the fat pieces of the offerings of well-being. A perpetual fire shall be kept burning on the altar; it shall not go out.

Analects 16.7-9 (Confucianism)

Confucius said, "There are three things which the superior man guards against. In youth, when the physical powers are not yet settled, he guards against lust. When he is strong and the physical powers are full of vigor, he guards against quarrelsomeness. When he is old, and the animal powers are decayed, he guards against covetousness."

Confucius said, "There are three things of which the superior man stands in awe. He stands in awe of the ordinances of Heaven. He stands in awe of great men. He stands in awe of the words of sages. The mean man does not know the ordinances of Heaven, and consequently does not stand in awe of them. He is disrespectful to great men. He makes sport of the words of sages."

Confucius said, "Those who are born with the possession of knowledge are the highest class of men. Those who learn, and so readily get possession of knowledge, are the next. Those who are dull and stupid, and yet compass the learning, are another class next to these. As to those who are dull and stupid and yet do not learn—they are the lowest of the people."

New Testament: 1 Corinthians 1:1-9 (Christianity)

Paul, called to be an apostle of Christ Jesus by the will of God, and our brother Sosthenes, to the church of God that is in Corinth, to those who are sanctified in Christ Jesus, called to be saints, together with all those who in every place call on the name of our Lord Jesus Christ, both their Lord and ours: Grace to you and peace from God our Father and the Lord Jesus Christ. I give thanks to my God always for you because of the grace of God that has been given you in Christ Jesus, for in every way you have been enriched in him, in speech and knowledge of every kind—just as the testimony of Christ has been strengthened among you—so that you are not lacking in any spiritual gift as you wait for the revealing of our Lord Jesus Christ. He will also strengthen you to the end, so that you may be blameless on the day of our Lord Jesus Christ. God is faithful; by him you were called into the fellowship of his Son, Jesus Christ our Lord.

Ādi Granth: Raga Bihagra, Mahala 5 (Sikhism)

Listen to my prayer, O my Lord and Master.
I am filled with millions of sins, but still, I am Your slave.
O Destroyer of pain, Bestower of mercy,
Fascinating Lord, Destroyer of sorrow and strife:
I have come to Your Sanctuary; please preserve my honor.
You are in all, O Immaculate Lord.
God hears and beholds all; He is with us,
The nearest of the near.

I was separated from Him, and now,
He has united me with Himself.
In the Saadh Sangat, the Company of the Holy,
I sing the Glorious Praises of the Lord.
Singing the Praises of the Lord of the Universe, forever sublime,
The blissful Lord is revealed to me.
My bed is adorned with God; my God has made me His own.
Abandoning anxiety, I have become carefree,
And I shall not suffer in pain any more.

Daode Jing 31 (Taoism)

Good weapons are instruments of fear; all creatures hate them.
Therefore followers of the Tao never used them.
The wise man prefers the left.
The man of war prefers the right.
Weapons are instruments of fear; they are not a wise man's tools.
He uses them only when he has no choice.
Peace and quiet are dear to his heart.
And victory no cause for rejoicing.
If you rejoice in victory, then you delight in killing;
If you delight in killing, you cannot fulfill yourself.
On happy occasions precedence is given to the left,
On sad occasions to the right.
In the army the general stands on the left,
The commander-in-chief on the right.
This means that war is conducted like a funeral.
When many people are being killed,
They should be mourned in heartfelt sorrow.
That is why a victory must be observed like a funeral.

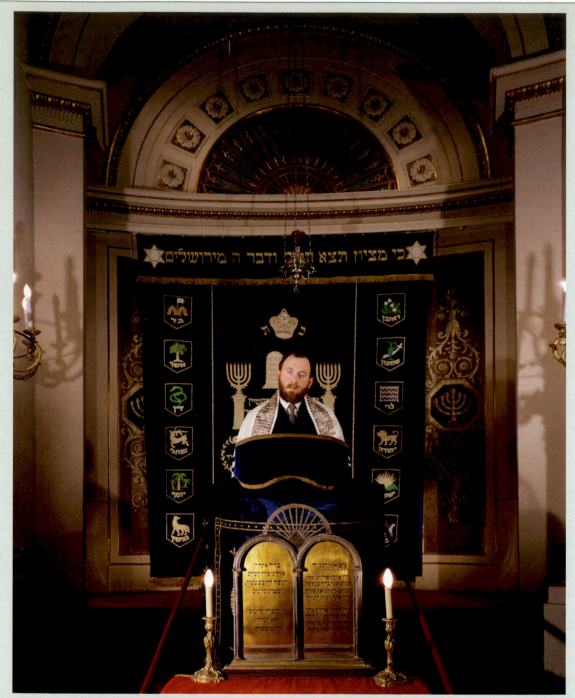

Fig. 2.1. A Jewish rabbi reads from a Torah scroll during a synagogue service.

Hebrew Bible or Old Testament?

This book of the law shall not depart out of your mouth; you shall meditate on it day and night, so that you may be careful to act in accordance with all that it written in it. For then you shall make your way prosperous, and then you shall be successful. (Joshua 1:8)

For whatever was written in former days was written for our instruction, so that by steadfastness and by the encouragement of the scriptures we might have hope. (Romans 15:4)

We have indeed given Moses the guidance and bequeathed to the children of Israel the Book, as a guidance and a reminder to people of understanding. (Qur'an 40:53-54)

The book that scholars call the Hebrew Bible is viewed as a sacred text by three major world religions: Judaism, Christianity, and Islam. Jews refer to it as the *Tanak* (or simply the Bible) and honor it as a witness to their religious history and a guide for contemporary living. Christians call it the Old Testament and interpret it as a record of how God worked in ancient Israel to prepare the way for the coming of the Messiah, Jesus of Nazareth. Muslims regard it as a corrupted edition of a revelation that God originally gave to Moses (the *Tawrat*) and David (the *Zabur*) and later restated with full clarity in the Qur'an. Because they have such different opinions about the overall meaning and purpose of the Hebrew Bible, it is not uncommon for Jews, Christians, and Muslims to disagree about the manner in which its content should be interpreted and applied. An examination of the way in which each of these groups views the Hebrew Bible will help us to understand some of the controversies and conflicts that have occurred among these three important religions.

BOOK OF THE COVENANT

From a historical standpoint, the Hebrew Bible is unquestionably a Jewish book. It was compiled and edited within the ancient Jewish community, and most Jews in antiquity were descended from the people whose story is told in its pages. The beliefs and practices of Judaism are deeply rooted in the Hebrew Bible and developed directly out of the religion that it depicts. Devout Jews recite the Hebrew Bible in their prayers and frame their lives around its laws. Its central message is that the Jewish people, by their familial descent from the people described in the Bible, have a special relationship with the all-powerful God who created and sustains the universe. It is no exaggeration to say that without the Hebrew Bible there could be no Judaism.

The most important part of the Hebrew Bible for most Jews is the collection of rules and regulations that occupies much of the first five books of the Bible. The Jewish term for these books is **Torah**, a Hebrew word that means "teaching" or "instruction." The reason that these materials are so important to Judaism is that they represent the terms of a special **covenant** (agreement or contract) that the creator of the universe, a deity named **Yahweh**, is said to have initiated with the ancient ancestors of the Jewish people. According to the Bible (Genesis 12:1—17:27), Yahweh (translated as "the LORD" in most English Bibles) chose a man named **Abraham** to enter into a unique relationship that would set him and his descendants apart from the people around them. Yahweh promised to protect and provide for Abraham and his descendants, and Abraham agreed to serve and honor Yahweh above all other gods.

The full terms of this relationship were spelled out at a later date in a long series of rules and regulations that Yahweh is said to have delivered to a man named **Moses** to pass on to the descendants of Abraham, whom the text now calls **Israel**. These **laws** fill most of the biblical books of Exodus, Leviticus, Numbers, and Deuteronomy. In these books, Yahweh assures the people of Israel that his covenant with Abraham is eternal and that he will never abandon them. But he also insists that the continuation of the **blessings** and protection that he promised them as his covenant people is contingent upon their obeying the laws that he gave to Moses. (For more on these concepts, see chapters 14 and 22.)

For most of Jewish history, this idea of a special covenant between Yahweh and his people has been central to Jewish identity. This explains why the books of Torah are so highly honored within Judaism. Jews across the centuries have been encouraged to study and obey the laws of Torah as a means of expressing their gratitude to the deity who chose them as his people and entrusted them with the knowledge of his will by giving them these rules for conduct. Even the Reform branch of Judaism, which views the laws of Torah more as spiritual guidelines than as binding obligations, respects the books of Torah, though the books of the **Prophets** also play an important role in their understanding of Scripture.

Over the centuries, many Christians have criticized this Jewish concern for living by the laws of Torah as a form of legalism. The term **legalism** refers to a belief that rigid obedience to a set of rules will earn God's favor and eternal rewards regardless of the feelings or attitudes that a person is harboring inside. This negative (and incorrect) view of Judaism, which can be seen in certain parts of the Christian New Testament, is rooted in a series of disputes that rocked the early Christian community. Christianity began as a sect of Judaism, so it was only natural that many of the early followers of Jesus would believe that Christians should follow the laws of Torah in order to demonstrate their loyalty to God. Christian leaders like the apostle Paul, on the other hand, argued that the death and resurrection of Jesus had initiated a new era

Fig. 2.2. The Tanak plays a vital role in Jewish rituals, including prayers (left), religious festivals (center), and public worship (right).

in which faith alone, not obedience to the Jewish Torah, was the way to receive forgiveness and blessing from God. Though Paul was speaking primarily about non-Jews, most Christians have understood him to be saying that faith in Jesus and obedience to the Jewish laws are mutually exclusive, even for Jews. This interpretation of Paul's letters led eventually to the belief that Jews who reject the Christian message about Jesus and continue to obey the laws of Torah are legalists who have turned from the way of faith and forfeited their position of favor with God.

Today, Jews and Christians hold a variety of positions on the relative merits of personal faith and obedience to the laws of Torah. But virtually all biblical scholars recognize that the common Christian stereotype of Judaism as an inherently legalistic religion represents a gross misunderstanding of Judaism. Studies of Jewish literature from the time of Jesus (as well as later periods) have shown that Judaism allows no disjunction between faith and obedience to the rules of Torah. Jews are told to obey the laws of Torah not as a mechanism for obtaining something from God but rather to express their profound love and gratitude for being chosen as his covenant partners. While legalists can be found in every religion, there is no reason to think that they are more numerous among Jews than among Christians, Muslims, or the followers of any other religion.

Next to the Torah, Jews have found their greatest inspiration from the book of **Psalms** (chapter 30) and the biblical books of the Prophets (chapters 31–35). Devout Jews read or recite prayers from the book of Psalms in their private worship, and selections from the Psalms play a central role in the weekly religious ceremonies of Jewish synagogues around the world. In a similar way, the sayings of the biblical prophets lie at the heart of Judaism's traditional emphasis on social justice. Again and again the prophets speak about the importance of treating the needy with justice and compassion and establishing societal structures that are fair and equitable for all. Many Jews have taken these words to heart and become leaders in movements for social and economic justice around the world.

Other books and themes from the Hebrew Bible have also influenced the beliefs and practices of Jewish communities across the centuries. During times of persecution, books like Esther and Daniel (discussed in chapters 21 and 36) have inspired people to stay faithful under trial by reminding the Jewish people how their ancestors survived earlier threats to their existence. In a similar way, books like Job and Ecclesiastes (chapter 38) have helped them to make sense of the ordinary troubles of life. Biblical stories telling how Yahweh gave the land of Israel to Abraham and his descendants, together with verses in the prophetic books speaking about the future return of the Jews to their land, led many Jews to work for the creation of a Jewish state in **Palestine** (realized in 1948) and later justified the construction of Jewish settlements in territory taken from the Palestinians in the war of 1967. Other verses from the prophets have led certain schools of Judaism to anticipate the coming of a person called the **Messiah** who will bring an era of peace, justice, and prosperity. Some have gone so far as to identify a particular person as the fulfillment of these hopes. All in all, it would be hard to overestimate the importance of Scripture to the religion of Judaism.

WITNESS TO THE GOSPEL

Christianity began as a sect of Judaism. As a result, its followers accepted the Jewish Scriptures as the words of God. Over the centuries, however, Christianity has had a love-hate relationship with the Hebrew Bible. On the one hand, Christians have historically claimed that God's covenant with the Jewish people, including the laws of Torah, was merely a prelude to the present era in which God offers people everywhere the chance to become part of God's covenant community through faith in Jesus Christ. To guide his people in this new era, God inspired a new set of Scriptures, the Christian New Testament, that describes the life of faith that God desires. The Hebrew Bible was renamed the Old Testament, a title that implies that God's earlier revelation is somehow outdated and no longer relevant. The choice of titles for the two books is significant: the term *testament* comes from the Latin word *testamentum*, which means "covenant," implying that Christians now share in a new covenant with God that transcends his old covenant with the Jewish people.

On the other hand, the fact that the early Christians adopted the Hebrew Bible as their own implies that they

Fig. 2.3. Like Jews, Christians interact with the Bible in a variety of settings, including personal prayers (below), study groups (bottom), and church services (right).

viewed its contents as both relevant and inspired. Over the centuries, Christians have incorporated the Old Testament into their ceremonies of worship, whether in their prayers, which often employ language from the book of Psalms, or in their readings and sermons, which regularly include selections from the Hebrew Bible. Christians also look to the Hebrew Bible for direction on moral issues. The same apostle Paul who insisted in his letters that the laws of Torah did not apply to non-Jews also referred repeatedly to the Hebrew Bible (including the Torah) to lend weight to his arguments and to provide guidance for Christian conduct. Jesus himself is quoted as saying that "not one letter, not one stroke of a letter, will pass from the law until all is accomplished" (Matthew 5:18). One of the central themes of early Christian preaching was that Jesus was the Jewish Messiah whose coming was anticipated by the Hebrew prophets. This belief led

Christians to find references to Jesus in every corner of the Hebrew Bible. From the earliest days to the present, Christian writers and thinkers have derived many of their key ideas from the Hebrew Bible, including their beliefs about the nature of God and humans, the origins of the universe, and God's role in human history.

The most common way of explaining this apparent discrepancy is to say that Christianity accepts the Hebrew Bible as divine revelation while simultaneously rejecting the laws of Torah as applying only to Judaism. In practice, however, Christian usage of the Hebrew Bible is more complicated. Christian leaders continue to look to the laws of Torah for guidance in handling moral and ethical issues such as abortion, gay rights, war, and capital punishment. Christian social activism has been inspired in part by the social justice themes that echo throughout the books of the prophets. Christians have also turned to the apocalyptic texts of the Hebrew Bible to help them date the end of the world and describe what will happen when the end takes place.

These and other examples show how thoroughly Christians have taken over the Jewish Scriptures as their own. Yet Christians remain divided over what this means for their attitudes and actions toward the Jewish people. Most Christians today would say that Jews should be respected due to their biblical status as God's chosen people. In the past, however, many Christians argued that Judaism had been replaced by Christianity in God's plans for humanity and that individual Jews deserved nothing but ill treatment for their rejection of Jesus and their acquiescence in his death. This line of thinking produced centuries of Christian anti-Semitism and oppression of Jews, and led ultimately to the horrors of the Holocaust. Clearly the way in which people interpret Scriptures can have far-reaching social consequences.

Jews, for their part, would disagree with many of the ways in which Christians have interpreted their sacred text. Jews can point to numerous verses in the Hebrew Bible that affirm the permanence of their special relationship with Yahweh and the laws that he gave to their ancestors. To say that this same deity has now rejected his people or is accepting non-Jews without requiring them to be **circumcised** and obey his laws makes no sense from a Jewish standpoint. Jews also insist that Christians are misinterpreting the words of the prophets and other biblical texts when they claim that the Jewish Bible predicted the coming of Jesus as a messiah. From the very beginning of the Christian movement, Jewish **rabbis** have pointed out that the biblical prophets were describing an earthly king who would lead Israel to victory over its enemies and introduce an era of peace, prosperity, and justice, a picture that does not fit the New Testament picture of Jesus. Today there are Jews who would honor Jesus as a Jewish rabbi or reformer, but few would take seriously Christian claims that Jesus was the Jewish Messiah or Son of God. On the whole, the fact that Jews and Christians share a common set of Scriptures has produced as much friction as agreement between the two communities.

FRACTURED REVELATION

The traditional Muslim view of the Hebrew Bible resembles that of Christianity, though in some ways it is even more dismissive of Jews and their Scriptures.

Fig. 2.4. Muslims, like Jews and Christians, rely on their sacred text for personal guidance (top), public instruction (middle), and the performance of rituals (bottom).

According to Islam, God has sent hundreds of prophets into the world at various points in history with the same message: humans should honor and serve the one true God by following proper forms of worship and living by a particular set of moral standards. Some of these prophets delivered their messages orally, while others were given books with which to communicate their message. Everywhere they went, the prophets met with a divided response, with some accepting and others rejecting their message.

The purpose of sacred books in this system was to preserve the teachings of the prophets so that people in future generations could follow the words of God after they were gone. Over time, however, all of these earlier books were corrupted as people lost or forgot portions of the original revelation, confused other parts, and added their own ideas to the text. Thus all of the books used by the various world religions (including Judaism and Christianity) contain mixtures of divine truth and human error. To remedy this problem, God sent the last and greatest prophet, a man named Muhammad, to speak the true, unadulterated revelation once again to humanity. This time God made sure that the message would be accurately recorded in a book called the Qur'an, and that it would be faithfully preserved across the generations. As a result, everyone now has a chance to hear and respond to the pure, uncorrupted message of God and thus to become part of God's people.

Among the prophets recognized by Islam are a number of characters from the Hebrew Bible, including Adam, Enoch, Noah, Abraham, Isaac, Jacob, Moses, Aaron, Elijah, Elisha, David, Solomon, and Ezra. The only people on this list whom the Qur'an associates with books are Abraham, Moses, and David. Muslims believe that the books of Abraham have been lost and the books of Moses (the Torah) and David (the Psalms) have been substantially corrupted over time. The remaining books of the Hebrew Bible were produced by authors whose names are not on the Qur'anic list of prophets, and many of them were writing about events that happened centuries before their own time. From a Muslim perspective, these facts indicate that the authors were writing without the assistance of divine revelation, which means that their texts should not be recognized as Scripture.

So how do Muslims know which parts of the Torah and Psalms represent the original divine revelation? The answer is simple: anything that agrees with the Qur'an is God's truth, while anything that contradicts or adds to the teaching of the Qur'an is the result of human additions or corruptions. The Psalms pose few problems on this score, though the fact that some of the psalms are credited to people other than David is sometimes cited as evidence of textual corruption. The Torah, on the other hand, contains large amounts of objectionable material. In particular, Islam rejects the Torah's teachings about an eternal covenant between God and the Jews, together with the majority of the laws associated with that covenant. Not surprisingly, these are the same issues that troubled the early Christians, though Christian authors resolved the problem by claiming that these materials were no longer relevant after the coming of Jesus rather than declaring them to be faulty human creations. Islam also rejects the biblical accounts of God giving the land of Palestine to the descendants of Abraham. The Qur'an is unclear about how these texts came to be corrupted: some verses claim that the corruptions arose out of arguments among the Jews, while others suggest that God gave laws to the Jews as a punishment for their rejection of Moses' original message.

In practice, Muslims make no direct use of the Hebrew Bible, even those parts that they approve, since they believe that they have the fullness of God's revelation in the Qur'an. This distinguishes them from Christians, who regard the Hebrew Bible as part of their Scriptures but interpret it differently than Jews do. Nevertheless, Muslims who study the Qur'an learn more about the Hebrew Bible than they realize. The Qur'an contains many stories about biblical characters that parallel stories in the Hebrew Bible, and many of the beliefs and practices that are affirmed in the Qur'an are essentially the same as those of Judaism, which in turn derived them from the Hebrew Bible. Included in this category are Muslim beliefs about the nature and character of God, the origins of the universe and human beings, the necessity of obeying the words of God, and most of their positions on specific moral and ethical issues. Scholars attribute these similarities to the time that Muhammad spent conversing with Jews and Christians while traveling across the

Middle East as a merchant and trader prior to becoming a religious leader. There is no evidence that Muhammad ever read the Hebrew Bible—in fact, Muslim tradition claims that he was illiterate—but he seems to have learned much about its content through oral channels. If this is true, then Islam is more indebted to Judaism and the Hebrew Bible than most Muslims recognize.

Jewish reactions to Muslim views of the Hebrew Bible are predictably negative. Sophisticated Jewish readers recognize that the Hebrew Bible was written by a variety of authors and editors over hundreds of years, but they see no connection between the lengthy development of the text and the truth-value of its message. Jewish scholars also point out that there is no textual evidence to support the Muslim claim that the Jews once possessed a simpler, purer book that was gradually corrupted to form the present version of the Hebrew Bible. Instead, Jews would argue that Muhammad drew many of his ideas and stories from oral traditions that he learned from the Jewish communities of Arabia and Palestine. In this view, it is the Qur'an that contains corrupted versions of the biblical stories and not the other way around.

From a traditional Jewish standpoint, both Christianity and Islam could be regarded as organized efforts to turn Judaism into a religion that is open to the masses without the duty of obeying the Jewish laws. Jews are happy to accept non-Jews into their religion as long as they are willing to embrace the laws that God delivered to their ancestors as part of their unique covenantal relationship with the deity. But they find it impossible to support any religious movement or teaching that claims to be able to bring people into a special relationship with the God of Israel without requiring them to obey the laws of Torah and unite themselves with the Jewish community.

WHAT'S IN A NAME?

Just as Jews, Christians, and Muslims differ over how the Hebrew Bible should be interpreted, so also they disagree about the name by which the deity should be called and the manner in which the passage of time should be marked. These differences have a direct bearing on the way they understand the Hebrew Bible.

The Names of God

As we will see in chapter 12, the principal deity of the people of Israel goes by many names and titles. Most are variations on the personal names Yahweh or **El**. The Hebrew Bible also frequently uses the title **Elohim**, the generic Hebrew word for supernatural beings (translated "gods" or "God," depending on the context), to refer to the covenant God of Israel. By the time of Jesus, virtually all Jews used titles such as *Elohim* or **Adonai** (the Lord) instead of personal names when speaking about the deity in order to avoid violating one of the **Ten Commandments** that says, "You shall not make wrongful use of the name of Yahweh your God" (Exodus 20:7). The Jewish followers of Jesus continued this practice, using the Greek words for "God" or "the Lord" in place of the personal names that appear in the Hebrew Bible.

A similar practice can be seen in Islam. The Arab world into which Muhammad brought the message of Islam in the early seventh century was polytheistic, meaning that people worshipped many different gods. Muhammad, by contrast, proclaimed that there was only one true god whom humans should worship and obey. According to the Qur'an, this is the same god who sent Abraham, Moses, Jesus, and other prophets on their missions. Muhammad called this unique deity Allah, the Arabic equivalent of the Hebrew word *Elohim*. (Arabic and Hebrew are closely related languages, much like Spanish and French.) Thus the term *Allah*, like *Elohim*, is a title rather than a personal name. The use of this title is not restricted to Muslims; Arab Christians have referred to their god as Allah since before Muhammad's time. The Qur'an also uses the title *Lord* repeatedly to refer to the deity, along with many other titles.

Academic scholars, by contrast, prefer to use the personal name Yahweh when referring to the God of the Hebrew Bible, since this is the term that was employed most often by the biblical authors and editors. (For more on the divine name, see chapter 12.) The frequency with which the name Yahweh appears in the biblical text is disguised in modern Bibles by the common editorial practice of inserting the title *the LORD* (in small capitals) in places where the personal name Yahweh (signified in Hebrew by the equivalent of the four letters YHWH) appears in the text. Now and then one hears about a Christian group that is trying to recover the use of the personal name for the deity, including some who misread the Hebrew name YHWH as *Jehovah* rather than *Yahweh*. On the whole, however, there is a serious gap between religious and academic usage at this point.

Marking Time

For most of human history, people in different parts of the world have used different calendars. Some cultures based their calendars on the twenty-nine- to thirty-day cycle of the moon, while others used a solar calendar that coincided with the earth's annual orbit around the sun. Ordinary people found the lunar cycle more useful than the solar cycle, since anyone could view the phases of the moon, whereas special training was required to determine precisely when a solar year had passed.

The problem with using the moon to mark time is that lunar months do not coincide with the seasonal cycles of the solar calendar, so that a particular lunar month might fall in the summer in one year and then shift gradually over a number of years to the fall or winter. Some societies simply ignored this discrepancy and used the lunar calendar for marking the dates of religious festivals and other special events. Others, including the people of ancient Israel, developed methods of reconciling the solar and lunar calendars so that religious festivals would fall at roughly the same point in the agricultural cycle each year. Usually this involved adding days, weeks, or months to the lunar calendar from time to time in order to keep the calendar aligned with the seasons.

Another calendar-related problem that every society must face is how to keep track of the long-term passage of time. Some cultures never developed a system of dating past events, while in others the system was known only to the educated elites. Those that worked out a way of counting the years usually start their enumeration with an important event in the past, whether real or imagined. For the Romans, the marking of time began with the founding of the city of Rome, which was thought to have occurred in the year known today as 753 B.C. For Jews, the system commenced with the creation of world, the date of which was calculated by adding up the ages of the characters in the early books of the Hebrew Bible until one reached Adam and Eve (3761 B.C. on our calendar). Muslims number the years from the date of Muhammad's move from Mecca to Medina, where Islam first gained a broad following (A.D. 622).

The "B.C./A.D." system of dating that is used by most of the world today was developed by a Christian monk in the sixth century. Until that time, Christians followed either the Jewish or the Roman dating system. Under this new system, dates prior to the birth of Jesus were marked as B.C. (before Christ) while dates after the birth of Jesus were labeled as A.D., an abbreviation for the Latin phrase *anno Domini*, which means "in the year of the Lord." Unfortunately, the monk who created the system had no way of knowing exactly when Jesus was born, and most scholars believe that he was off by a few years. Estimates for the actual date of Jesus' birth range from 6 B.C. to 4 B.C.

So how does any of this relate to the Hebrew Bible? In the first place, it helps us to understand the complex system of marking time that is presupposed in the Hebrew Bible. As we will see in chapter 7, the people whose lives are portrayed in the Hebrew Bible made their living by agriculture, which follows the annual cycle of the sun. Their religious calendar, however, was based on lunar months. Since their primary religious festivals were linked to the agricultural cycle, they were forced to add an extra month every few years to keep the calendars relatively consistent. Readers who know nothing about this calendar system will find it hard to understand some of the biblical passages that talk about the religious festivals of ancient Israel.

Even more important is the observation that the Hebrew Bible has no system of absolute dating. Some of the more important events are dated by reference to the year of a king's reign, but most of the stories are undated. The absence of a consistent dating system makes it difficult for scholars to figure out when many of the biblical stories are supposed to have occurred. It also raises questions about how much the people who composed the stories knew about the chronology of past events (see chapter 9).

Finally, the recognition that cultures use different calendars helps us to see the religious bias that is inherent in the Western system of dating events by reference to the birth of Jesus. The celebrated turn of the millennium in the year marked A.D. 2000 on the Christian calendar meant nothing on the Jewish calendar, where it overlapped the years 5760 and 5761, or the Muslim calendar, where it coincided with the years 1420 and 1421. Most Jews and Muslims use the Christian calendar alongside their own since it has become the world standard for marking time, but they are reminded every day of the fact that the calendar has a Christian bias.

To get around this problem, scholars who study the ancient world have created a more religiously neutral system of notation that preserves the accepted way of counting the years while eliminating the use of religious terminology. In place of A.D., scholars use the label C.E., which stands for "Common Era," while B.C. has been replaced by B.C.E., which means "Before the Common Era." The term *Common Era* refers to the era covered by the calendar that is in common use around the world today, specifically, the Christian calendar. Thus A.D. 2000 becomes 2000 C.E., while 652 B.C. is now 652 B.C.E.

Since this book will be used by people from a variety of religious traditions as well as people with no religious orientation, the scholarly system of notation will be used when referring to dates and events. People who are encountering this system for the first time should have little trouble learning to mentally convert B.C. to B.C.E. and A.D. to C.E.

CONCLUSION

Every reader brings a set of presuppositions and prior commitments to the reading and interpretation of a text. This is especially obvious when we look at how Jews, Christians, and Muslims view and interpret the Hebrew Bible. All three groups honor the Hebrew Bible as a holy book, but their views about which parts are most important and how the book should be understood are very different.

For Jews, the Hebrew Bible is a record of their special covenant relationship with the one true God who created and sustains the universe. Under this relationship, Yahweh promises to bless and protect the descendants of Abraham and they in return commit themselves to faithfully obey the laws of the covenant as contained in the first five books of the Bible. This covenant continues in force to the present day.

For Christians, the Hebrew Bible tells the story of how God was at work in the history of Israel to prepare humanity for the coming of the Messiah and Savior, Jesus of Nazareth. This story is continued in the New Testament, which explains how the death and resurrection of Jesus made it possible for all people, not just the Jews, to find a place among the people of God. The laws of Torah are no longer binding in this new age.

For Muslims, the Hebrew Bible is a corrupted edition of an earlier, simpler revelation that God sent to the Jewish people through a series of prophets, including Adam, Abraham, Moses, and David. This message told the Jews to honor the one God of the universe through proper forms of worship and to base their lives on God's moral and ethical standards. Elements of that original revelation can still be seen in the Hebrew Bible, but the full truth is contained only in the Qur'an.

At its core, then, each of these groups holds to beliefs that are fundamentally incompatible with the other two. Yet they also have much in common. Virtually all of the similarities among the three religions can be traced to their common origins in the ideas and language of the Hebrew Bible.

EXERCISE 2

Read the passages below and answer the following questions about each passage using the information that you learned in this chapter.

(a) In what book of Scripture do you think the passage is found—the Hebrew Bible (Judaism), the New Testament (Christianity), or the Qur'an (Islam)? What leads you to this conclusion?

(b) How does the passage fit with what you have learned about this group's view of the Hebrew Bible?

Passage 1

Mankind was one nation. Then God sent forth the prophets as bearers of good news and as warners. He sent them with the Book in truth, to judge between people regarding what they differed on. And none differed on it except those to whom it was given after clear proofs had reached them, out of envy for one another. God, by his will, guided those who believed to the truth on which they had differed. God guides whom he will to the right path.

Passage 2

When Abram was ninety-nine years old, the LORD appeared to Abram, and said to him, "I am God Almighty; walk before me, and be blameless. And I will make my covenant between me and you, and will make you exceedingly numerous." Then Abram fell on his face; and God said to him, "As for me, this is my covenant with you: You shall be the ancestor of a multitude of nations. . . . I will establish my covenant between me and you, and your offspring after you throughout their generations, for an everlasting covenant, to be God to you and to your offspring after you. And I will give to you, and to your offspring after you, the land where you are now an alien, all the land of Canaan, for a perpetual holding; and I will be their God."

Passage 3

For the promise that he would inherit the world did not come to Abraham or to his descendants through the law but through the righteousness of faith. If it is the adherents of the law who are to be the heirs, faith is null and the promise is void. For the law brings wrath; but where there is no law, neither is there violation. For this reason it depends on faith, in order that the promise may rest on grace and be guaranteed to all his descendants, not only to the adherents of the law but also to those who share the faith of Abraham (for he is the father of all of us, as it is written, "I have made you the father of many nations").

Passage 4

And when Abraham was tried by his Lord with certain commandments which he fulfilled, he [God] said, "I am making you a spiritual exemplar to mankind." Abraham said, "And what about my posterity?" He replied, "My covenant does not apply to the evil-doers."

Passage 5

It was not because you were more numerous than any other people that the LORD set his heart on you and chose you—for you were the fewest of all peoples. It was because the LORD loved you and kept the oath that he swore to your ancestors, that the LORD has brought you out with a mighty hand, and redeemed you from the house of slavery, from the hand of Pharaoh king of Egypt. Know therefore that the LORD your God is God, the faithful God who maintains covenant loyalty with those who love him and keep his commandments, to a thousand generations, and who repays in their own person those who reject him. He does not delay but repays in their own person those who reject him. Therefore, observe diligently the commandments—the statutes, and the ordinances—that I am commanding you today.

Passage 6

Then what becomes of boasting? It is excluded. By what law? By that of works? No, but by the law of faith. For we hold that a person is justified by faith apart from works prescribed by the law. Or is God the God of

Jews only? Is he not the God of Gentiles also? Yes, of Gentiles also, since God is one; and he will justify the circumcised on the ground of faith and the uncircumcised through that same faith. Do we then overthrow the law by this faith? By no means! On the contrary, we uphold the law.

Passage 7

And we have favored Moses and Aaron, and delivered them and their people from the great calamity. And we supported them, and so they were the victors. And we gave them both the clarifying Book. And we guided them unto the straight path. And we left with them both for later generations: "Peace be upon Moses and Aaron." Thus we reward the beneficent. They are indeed among our believing servants.

Passage 8

Then he said to them, "Oh, how foolish you are, and how slow of heart to believe all that the prophets have declared! Was it not necessary that the Messiah should suffer these things and then enter into his glory?" Then beginning with Moses and all the prophets, he interpreted to them the things about himself in all the scriptures.

Passage 9

And the LORD said to me: Conspiracy exists among the people of Judah and the inhabitants of Jerusalem. They have turned back to the iniquities of their ancestors of old, who refused to heed my words; they have gone after other gods to serve them; the house of Israel and the house of Judah have broken the covenant that I made with their ancestors. Therefore, thus says the LORD, assuredly I am going to bring disaster upon them that they cannot escape; though they cry out to me, I will not listen to them. Then the cities of Judah and the inhabitants of Jerusalem will go and cry out to the gods to whom they make offerings, but they will never save them in the time of their trouble.

Passage 10

And it was on account of the wrongdoing of the Jews that we forbade them certain good things which had been lawful to them; as well as on account of their frequent debarring of people from God's path—their taking usury, although they had been forbidden from doing it, and their devouring other people's wealth unjustly. We have prepared for the unbelievers among them a very painful punishment! But those firmly rooted in knowledge among them and the believers do believe in what was revealed to you and what was revealed before you. Those who perform the prayers, give the alms and believe in God and the last day—to these we shall grant a great reward!

Passage 11

For if that first covenant had been faultless, there would have been no need to look for a second one. God finds fault with them when he says: "The days are surely coming, says the Lord, when I will establish a new covenant with the house of Israel and with the house of Judah; not like the covenant that I made with their ancestors, on the day when I took them by the hand to lead them out of the land of Egypt; for they did not continue in my covenant, and so I had no concern for them, says the Lord. This is the covenant that I will make with the house of Israel after those days, says the Lord: I will put my laws in their minds, and write them on their hearts, and I will be their God, and they shall be my people. . . ." In speaking of "a new covenant," he has made the first one obsolete. And what is obsolete and growing old will soon disappear.

Passage 12

I will make a covenant of peace with them; it shall be an everlasting covenant with them; and I will bless them and multiply them, and will set my sanctuary among them forevermore. My dwelling place shall be with them; and I will be their God, and they shall be my people. Then the nations shall know that I the LORD sanctify Israel, when my sanctuary is among them forevermore.

What's in the Hebrew Bible?

All the people gathered together into the square before the Water Gate. They told the scribe Ezra to bring the book of the law of Moses, which the LORD had given to Israel. Accordingly, the priest Ezra brought the law before the assembly, both men and women and all who could hear with understanding. This was on the first day of the seventh month. He read from it facing the square before the Water Gate from early morning until midday, in the presence of the men and the women and those who could understand; and the ears of all the people were attentive to the book of the law. (**Nehemiah 8:1-3**)

And on the sabbath day they went into the synagogue and sat down. After the reading of the law and the prophets, the officials of the synagogue sent them a message, saying, "Brothers, if you have any word of exhortation for the people, give it." (**Acts 13:14-15**)

Many great teachings have been given to us through the Law and the Prophets and the others that followed them, and for these we should praise Israel for instruction and wisdom. (**Prologue to the book of Sirach**)

The Hebrew Bible is not a single book, but a collection of dozens of books that were written, compiled, and edited over the course of many centuries. These books include nearly every type of literature known to humanity. Because they were written by many people at different times and places, their ideas and viewpoints are not always consistent. The compilation of these diverse books into a single collection is the result of a gradual process of agreement within the Jewish and Christian communities that these books and no others would be regarded as Scripture.

THE STRUCTURE OF THE HEBREW BIBLE

For reasons that will be described more fully in chapter 4, the Jewish Bible and the Christian Old Testament are structured differently. In the Jewish version, the books are divided into three broad categories that reflect the process by which they came to be regarded as Scripture. In the Christian version, the books are organized under four headings based on the type of material that they contain. The early Christians also divided some of the longer Hebrew books into smaller units, leading to a larger number of books in the Christian canon. Finally, the list of books used by the Roman Catholic and Orthodox churches (Greek Orthodox, Russian Orthodox, and the like) contains a number of books that are not found in the Jewish Bible. Thus Jews and Christians disagree not only about how the Hebrew Bible should be interpreted but also about its contents.

The following chart shows the structure and contents of each group's version of the Hebrew Bible. Where possible, the book titles in each column have been arranged to show where they agree and where they differ.

JUDAISM	CHRISTIANITY		
Hebrew Bible	Catholic Bible	Orthodox Bible	Protestant Bible
Torah	*Law/Pentateuch*	*Law/Pentateuch*	*Law/Pentateuch*
Genesis	Genesis	Genesis	Genesis
Exodus	Exodus	Exodus	Exodus
Leviticus	Leviticus	Leviticus	Leviticus
Numbers	Numbers	Numbers	Numbers
Deuteronomy	Deuteronomy	Deuteronomy	Deuteronomy
Former Prophets	*Historical Books*	*Historical Books*	*Historical Books*
Joshua	Joshua	Joshua	Joshua
Judges	Judges	Judges	Judges
	Ruth	Ruth	Ruth
Samuel (1&2)	1 Samuel	1 Kingdoms (=1 Samuel)	1 Samuel
	2 Samuel	2 Kingdoms (=2 Samuel)	2 Samuel
Kings (1&2)	1 Kings	3 Kingdoms (=1 Kings)	1 Kings
	2 Kings	4 Kingdoms (=2 Kings)	2 Kings
	1 Chronicles	1 Chronicles	1 Chronicles
	2 Chronicles	2 Chronicles	2 Chronicles
		[*1 Esdras*]	
	Ezra	2 Esdras (=Ezra +	Ezra
	Nehemiah	Nehemiah)	Nehemiah
	Tobit	Esther *(longer)*	Esther
	Judith	*Judith*	
	Esther *(longer)*	*Tobit*	
	1 Maccabees	*1 Maccabees*	
	2 Maccabees	*2 Maccabees*	
		[*3 Maccabees*]	
		[*4 Maccabees*]	
Latter Prophets			
Isaiah			
Jeremiah			
Ezekiel			
The Twelve (Hosea, Joel, Amos, Obadiah, Jonah, Micah, Nahum, Habakkuk, Zephaniah, Haggai, Zechariah, Malachi)			

Hebrew Bible	Catholic Bible	Orthodox Bible	Protestant Bible
Writings	*Poetic Books*	*Poetic Books*	*Poetic Books*
Psalms (150)	Job	Psalms [151]	Job
Proverbs	Psalms (150)	[*Odes of Solomon*	Psalms (150)
Job		*(w/ Prayer of Manasseh)*]	
Song of Solomon	Proverbs	Proverbs	Proverbs
Ruth	Ecclesiastes	Ecclesiastes	Ecclesiastes
Lamentations	Song of Solomon	Song of Solomon	Song of Solomon
Ecclesiastes		Job	
Esther	*Wisdom of Solomon*	*Wisdom of Solomon*	
Daniel	*Sirach (Ecclesiasticus)*	*Sirach (Ecclesiasticus)*	
Ezra-Nehemiah		[*Psalms of Solomon*]	
Chronicles (1&2)			
(listed above under "Latter Prophets" or "Writings")	*Prophets*	*Prophets*	*Prophets*
	Isaiah	Hosea	Isaiah
	Jeremiah	Amos	Jeremiah
	Lamentations	Micah	Lamentations
	Baruch (including Letter of Jeremiah)	Joel	
	Ezekiel	Obadiah	Ezekiel
	Daniel *(longer)*	Jonah	Daniel
	Hosea	Nahum	Hosea
	Joel	Habakkuk	Joel
	Amos	Zephaniah	Amos
	Obadiah	Haggai	Obadiah
	Jonah	Zechariah	Jonah
	Micah	Malachi	Micah
	Nahum	Isaiah	Nahum
	Habakkuk	Jeremiah	Habakkuk
	Zephaniah	*Baruch*	Zephaniah
	Haggai	Lamentations	Haggai
	Zechariah	*Letter of Jeremiah*	Zechariah
	Malachi	Ezekiel	Malachi
		Daniel *(longer)*	

Note: Titles in *italic* type appear in Orthodox and Catholic Bibles but not in Jewish or Protestant Bibles; titles marked with [*italics*] appear only in Orthodox Bibles. Orthodox churches vary in the contents and order of their canons.

The Jewish Bible

The Jewish Bible is divided into three primary sections: the **Torah**, the **Prophets** (**Nevi'im**), and the **Writings** (**Ketuvim**). In recent years, many Jews have adopted the practice of referring to the Hebrew Bible by the name Tanak, a term derived from the first letters of the Hebrew titles of the three sections (TaNaK). Jews also employ Hebrew names for the various books of the Bible—for example, the book that Christians call Genesis is named *Bereshith*, which means "in the beginning" (the initial words of the book of Genesis), while the book of Isaiah is called *Yeshayahu*, the Hebrew name of the prophet whose name was shortened in English Bibles to Isaiah. To avoid confusion, the English names will be used throughout this book, even when referring to books in the Jewish Bible.

1. Torah. The Hebrew word *Torah*, which equates to the English word *teaching* or *instruction*, refers to the first five books of the Hebrew Bible (Genesis, Exodus, Leviticus, Numbers, and Deuteronomy). These books contain the foundational stories of the people of Israel, from the creation of the universe to the inauguration of Yahweh's covenant with Abraham to Yahweh's rescue of Abraham's descendants from **Egypt** under the leadership of Moses. The story ends with Abraham's descendants on the verge of reentering the promised land of Canaan where their ancestor Abraham had lived. The last four books contain hundreds of laws that Yahweh is said to have given to Moses and his followers after their departure from Egypt. A small religious group called the Samaritans, remnants of the people who once occupied the northern part of Israel,

use these five books alone as their Scriptures, though their version differs from the standard Jewish edition in certain places.

2. Prophets. The English title for this section is a straightforward translation of the Hebrew word *Nevi'im*, which means "prophets." A prophet in ancient Israel was someone who claimed to be receiving messages from Yahweh for delivery to his people. This section of the Hebrew Bible contains two types of material. The first part, called the **Former Prophets** (Joshua, Judges, Samuel, and Kings), tells the story of Abraham's descendants from the time they reentered the promised land until several hundred years later when they were conquered by armies from **Mesopotamia** and came under foreign rule. (The story is explained more fully in chapters 8, 9, and 19.) These books were included in the section called Prophets because they share the ideology and worldview of the prophets whose words were preserved in the Hebrew Bible.

The second section, called the **Latter Prophets**, consists of a series of books containing the sayings of men

Fig. 3.2. (above) A young man users a silver pointer to read from the Torah in a synagogue service; (right) a devout Jew wears a phylactery on his arm and hand while studying a printed copy of the Torah, as described in Deuteronomy 6:8.

who were regarded as prophets in ancient Israel (see chapters 31–35). In the Jewish Bible, these sayings are divided into four books. The first three books are named after the prophets whose sayings they preserve (Isaiah, Jeremiah, and Ezekiel). These books are arranged in chronological order according to when the prophet lived. The last book, called *The Twelve*, is a collection of sayings from twelve prophets who lived at different times and places spanning hundreds of years (Hosea, Joel, Amos, Obadiah, Jonah, Micah, Nahum, Habakkuk, Zephaniah, Haggai, Zechariah, and Malachi). These books are also organized in a rough chronological order, though some of them (including Joel, Obadiah, and Jonah) are out of place as a result of mistaken ideas about when they were composed.

3. Writings. The English title for this section is a translation of the Hebrew word *Ketuvim*, which means "writings." This category is made up of books that either did not fit readily under the headings of Torah or Prophets or were written after these two sections were considered closed. The material in the Writings is quite diverse, encompassing a variety of materials that came to be regarded as sacred in ancient Israel. The books of Psalms, Song of Solomon, and Lamentations are poetic compositions that were likely sung or chanted when they were in use. The books of Proverbs, Job, and Ecclesiastes are called **wisdom** books because they offer a series of wise observations about the meaning of life and how people should live. The books of Ruth, Esther, Ezra-Nehemiah, and Chronicles contain stories from Israel's past, much like the Former Prophets, though they were composed too late to be included in the Prophets section. Finally, the book of Daniel is a composite work, combining short stories about a heroic figure in Israel's past with a series of visions and dreams that recall some of the materials found in the prophetic books.

The Christian Old Testament

The Christian Old Testament contains most of the same material as the Jewish Bible, but the books are organized differently and additional books have been included in some versions. To understand why this happened, we must take a brief excursion into the history of the biblical text.

At the time when Christians took over the Jewish Bible as their sacred text, the content and order of the books in the collection were not yet settled. The five books of the Torah were considered a closed canon, but there was still a degree of fluidity in the section called the Prophets, and even more so in the Writings. In part this was due to the technology of the era, when most books were copied onto individual scrolls, making it difficult to talk about a fixed order or closed collection of texts. But it also seems that there was little interest among Jews in developing a standardized list of sacred texts. The fact that different Jewish groups used different books was apparently not viewed as a problem until perhaps the second century C.E., when the rabbis decided to settle the matter once and for all.

Thus the early Christians were simply following the practice of other Jewish groups when they included in their collection of sacred texts a number of Jewish books that the rabbis later excluded from the Jewish canon, such as Tobit, Judith, and the Wisdom of Solomon. In the fourth century C.E., a Christian scholar named Jerome labeled these books the **Apocrypha** (a Greek word meaning "hidden things," reflecting the belief by some that they should not be used in public worship) to distinguish them from the books that were included in the Hebrew canon, which had been settled by his time. These books were used in Christian churches until the sixteenth century, when Martin Luther and other Protestant Reformers argued that they should be excluded from the Christian Bible because they were not included in the Jewish canon. They reasoned that if the Jews did not regard books like Tobit, Judith, and the Wisdom of Solomon as inspired by God, then there was no reason for Christians to do so either.

Since that time, Christians have been divided over the contents of their Old Testament, with Protestants using a shorter list that coincides with the Jewish canon (though in a different order) and Roman Catholic and Orthodox churches retaining the longer canon that was adopted by the early church, with minor differences between the two groups. Catholics employ the term **deuterocanonical** (from a Greek expression meaning "second list") when referring to these books, reflecting their belief that these books represent a legitimate second part of the Christian canon even though they were not included in the Jewish Bible.

Fig. 3.3. A Bible is laid out on a podium for reading during a Christian worship service. The ornate design of the podium shows the special honor Christians give to its contents.

More radical was the decision by the early church to reorganize the books of the Jewish canon into four categories on the basis of content: the **Pentateuch**, the **Historical Books**, the **Poetic Books**, and the **Prophets**. The shift of the Prophets to the end of the collection was quite intentional, since it underlined the Christian belief that the Old Testament period ended with the prophets predicting the coming of Jesus. By this simple act of reorganization, the early Christians placed their distinctive stamp on the Hebrew Bible, signifying that the book belonged as much to them as to the Jews. To the

Jewish community, by contrast, this was yet more evidence of the Christians' willful disregard for the true meaning of the Jewish Scriptures.

1. Pentateuch. Christians vary widely in the titles they give to the first five books of the Hebrew Bible. Some use the Jewish name *Torah*, others the more generic term *Law* (translating the Greek word *nomos* that appears frequently in the ancient Greek versions of the Torah), and still others the descriptive label **Pentateuch**, which means "five scrolls." The latter is the most common term among Christian scholars. All Christian Bibles have the same contents in this section as the Jewish Torah.

2. Historical Books. Because of the gradual manner in which the Hebrew Bible was canonized, some of the books that narrate Israel's past were included in the Former Prophets and others among the Writings. Christian editors decided that it would be more useful to collect all of these books together immediately after the Torah in order to form a reasonably coherent narrative extending from the creation of the universe to the end of the biblical period. To do this, they inserted the narrative books from the Writings at the points where they belonged in the story line, ignoring the question of when the books were written. Thus the book of Ruth was placed after the book of Judges, since its story takes place during the era covered by that book, while the book of Chronicles was moved to a position following the book of Kings, since it covers much of the same territory as this earlier narrative.

Christian editors also divided some of the longer books into two parts at this time: the book of Samuel became the books of 1 Samuel and 2 Samuel, while the books of Kings and Chronicles were divided into 1 and 2 Kings and 1 and 2 Chronicles. The book of Ezra-Nehemiah was also split into two books at this time (though not in Orthodox churches), and a longer version of the book of Esther was adopted in place of the Hebrew version. Finally, Christian editors appended to the end of this section several Jewish narratives that were not finally included in the Hebrew canon (Tobit, Judith, 1 Maccabees and 2 Maccabees; the latter two books are placed in the Prophets section in some

Catholic Bibles). Many Orthodox churches also include other Jewish books such as 1 Esdras, 3 Maccabees, and 4 Maccabees in this section. None of these books appears in Protestant Bibles, which also use the shorter Jewish version of Esther.

Through these subtle acts of reorganization, the early Christians were able to create a relatively continuous narrative that runs from the book of Genesis through the books of the Maccabees, or from the creation of the universe to the second century b.c.e. In modern printed versions, these Historical Books make up over half of the Hebrew Bible. The net effect of all these changes was to underline the importance of history as the central element of the Hebrew Bible, replacing the Jewish emphasis on the laws of Torah. This shift in orientation reflects the Christian belief that the Old Testament should be viewed as the story of God's efforts to prepare humanity for the coming of Jesus. Jews, of course, would reject this interpretation of their holy text.

3. Poetic Books. Once the narrative books from the Writings were merged into the Historical Books and the books of Daniel and Lamentations were moved to the Prophets section (see below), all that remained of the Writings were books that could be described as in some sense poetic. The title *Poetic Books* (or *Poetry and Wisdom*, as used in some Bibles) was eventually adopted for this section, since most of the books that ended up here (apart from Ecclesiastes and portions of the books of Job and Sirach) follow the standard conventions of Hebrew poetry. The book of Psalms consists of songs and prayers that were used in the public worship of ancient Israel; the book of **Proverbs** is a collection of wise sayings framed in poetic verse; the books of Job and Song of Solomon are framed around a series of elaborate poetic speeches. These

are not, however, the only poetic books in the Hebrew Bible. Many other books and portions of books are written in poetic style, including most of the prophetic books, as we will see later in the chapter.

As with the Historical Books, the early Christians included in this section a number of Jewish texts that were ultimately excluded from the Jewish canon, including the Wisdom of Solomon and the book of Sirach. Many Orthodox churches also include the Odes of Solomon, the Psalms of Solomon, and the Prayer of Manasseh. Protestant Bibles omit all of these books. The resultant collection is more stylistically coherent than the mixed collection of texts that made up the Writings, but the range of ideas expressed in this section is more diverse than in any other part of the Bible.

4. Prophets. The final section of the Christian Old Testament, called the Prophets, includes all of the books that Jews call the Latter Prophets, though there are differences as well. In Christian Bibles, the books of Daniel and Lamentations were moved from the Writings to the Prophets due to perceived similarities with the other prophetic books, and the single Jewish book called *The Twelve* was divided into twelve different books, each containing the words of a different prophet and renamed "the **Minor Prophets.**" (Some Orthodox Bibles also arrange the books in a different order.) As with the other three sections, Christians also incorporated additional Jewish books into this section of the Bible (Baruch and the Letter of Jeremiah) and adopted longer versions of the books of Jeremiah and Daniel. (Protestant Bibles do not include these latter additions.) The impact of these changes is less pronounced than in the other sections of the Bible, but the outcome is the same: Christians use a different version of the Bible than do Jews.

EXERCISE 3

Look up the following books in the chart on pages 28–29 and indicate how each book is categorized by Jews, Catholics, Orthodox, and Protestants. If there is no difference, note that as well.

Exodus
2 Samuel
Nehemiah
Psalms of Solomon

Job
Amos
Daniel
Baruch

THE BIBLICAL STORY LINE

Though there are many differences between the Jewish and Christian canons of the Hebrew Bible, we must be careful not to overstate the gap between them. The Old Testament used by Protestant Christians is identical to the Jewish Bible except for the fact that the books are arranged differently. The Roman Catholic and Orthodox Bibles similarly incorporate the entire Jewish Bible into their canon, though they use longer editions of some of the books and include other books that are not recognized by Jews. More than 95 percent of the material found in the Roman Catholic and Orthodox Bibles appears also in the Jewish Bible.

The different versions of the Hebrew Bible also share a common story line. The story is presented in a more orderly fashion in Christian Bibles than in the Jewish Bible, but the overall narrative is the same (though the Catholic and Orthodox Bibles include books that extend the story beyond the events described in the Jewish and Protestant Bibles). This narrative functions as the backbone of the Hebrew Bible—everything else hangs from it. It is virtually impossible to understand what is going on in the Hebrew Bible without a general familiarity with its narrative framework.

An overview of the biblical story line as it unfolds in the narrative books of the Hebrew Bible can be found in chapter 8. In the meantime, a brief summary of the high points will help to provide a foundation for some of the materials that will be covered in the next few chapters. The question of how much history lies behind this narrative will be discussed in chapter 9.

The Hebrew Bible, like many other religious texts, begins with a series of stories narrating the creation of the universe and its inhabitants. Soon the focus narrows to a couple named Abraham and Sarah, whom a deity named Yahweh chooses out of all the people of the earth to be his partners in a special covenant relationship that will eventually extend to all of their descendants. At Yahweh's instigation, they move from Mesopotamia to the area that is today called Israel and settle there.

Much later, their great-grandchildren move from Israel to Egypt during a time of famine and remain there for several hundred years until the Egyptian **Pharaoh** begins to feel threatened by their growing numbers and places them under forced labor. Yahweh hears their cries for help and sends a man named Moses to rescue them from Egypt and lead them back to the land of their ancestors. This story is called the **Exodus**. On the way, they stop at **Mount Sinai**, where Yahweh appears to them and gives them a series of rules and regulations defining how they should act as his covenant people.

Because of their disobedience to Yahweh in the desert, the generation that came out of Egypt is cursed to wander there for forty years. Their children finally enter the land of Israel as an invading army and quickly conquer all of its inhabitants with the aid of Yahweh. Initially they set up a decentralized society that leaves them vulnerable to repeated attacks and conquest by their neighbors until Yahweh sends military leaders called **judges** to rescue them. Eventually they decide that they must rally around a king so that they can defend themselves against these attacks.

At first, Yahweh resists their call for a king as a rejection of divine rule. But he finally gives in to their appeals and appoints a man named Saul to rule over them. Saul is a capable military leader who unites the people behind him, but he disobeys Yahweh and is replaced by a young shepherd named David. Under David's rule, the armies of Israel conquer all of their neighbors and establish a sizable kingdom centered on the city of **Jerusalem**, which David has conquered and made his capital.

The kingdom of Israel reaches its pinnacle under David's son Solomon, who also builds a glorious temple for Yahweh in Jerusalem. After Solomon's death, the kingdom is divided between his son and a challenger, producing two kingdoms, one in the north that retains the name Israel and another in the south called **Judah**. The first king of Israel builds two worship centers for Yahweh in the north to cement the division. From that time forward, the kingdom of Judah is ruled from Jerusalem by the descendants of David, while the kingdom of Israel is ruled from the northern city of Samaria by a series of royal dynasties interrupted periodically by military coups.

Over the next few centuries, relations between the two kingdoms vary from close friendship to open war. Both kingdoms engage in sporadic conflicts with the nations around them, occasionally as allies but just as often on opposite sides. In both nations, the worship of Yahweh is increasingly supplemented by the worship of other deities. This arouses the anger of Yahweh, who sends prophets to warn them to worship and serve him alone or face judgment at the hands of foreign armies.

Eventually both kingdoms are faced with growing threats from the **Assyrians**, a powerful kingdom located to their north in Mesopotamia that is gradually expanding southward. The Assyrian armies finally conquer the kingdom of Israel and deport the survivors to Assyria, replacing them with people from other parts of their empire. The kingdom of Judah survives only by agreeing to pay tribute to the Assyrian king.

Not long afterward, the Assyrians are overthrown by the **Babylonians**, another Mesopotamian people whom they had incorporated into their empire. The Babylonians quickly move to conquer the lands controlled by the Assyrians. The kings of Judah form an alliance with Egypt to fend off the threat, but the Egyptians refuse to intervene and the kingdom of Judah is overrun by the Babylonians, who destroy their temple and devastate their land. The Babylonians carry the surviving elites away to Mesopotamia in an event known as the **Exile**. The poor remain in the land.

Eventually the Babylonians are conquered by their neighbors to the east, the **Persians**, whose king decrees that the people of Judah may return to their homeland if they wish. Some do so, but many others choose to remain in Babylonia. The Persians provide funds for those who return to rebuild their temple and eventually the city of Jerusalem as well. But they are not allowed to have a king—they remain under the rule of a Persian governor who is assisted by the Jewish **high priest**. The name *Jews*, a term derived from the name of their homeland, Judah, is first applied to them during this period.

The biblical narrative ends at this point, but the story of the Jews continues on. The Persians rule over Israel for two centuries until their empire comes to an end at the hands of Alexander the Great. After Alexander's premature death, his territories are divided among his Greek generals, whose descendants reign over Judah for another century and a half. At last the Jews succeed in regaining their independence in a war led by a group of brothers known as the **Maccabees**. They remain independent under the rule of kings from the line of the Maccabees until they are finally overcome by the Romans in the first century B.C.E. Apart from brief periods of freedom during ill-fated revolts in the first and second centuries C.E., the Jewish people remain under foreign domination until the formation of the state of Israel in 1948.

THE LITERATURE OF THE HEBREW BIBLE

No overview of the content of the Hebrew Bible would be complete without a brief discussion of the literary features of the text. From a literary point of view, the material in the Hebrew Bible is highly diverse, reflecting the pervasive influence of religion in the culture of the people who produced the texts. Virtually every type of literature known to contemporary scholars can be found within its pages. A few examples will suffice to show the literary diversity of the Hebrew Bible.

Historical Narrative

And in the ninth year of his reign, in the tenth month, on the tenth day of the month, King Nebuchadnezzar of Babylon came with all his army against Jerusalem, and laid siege to it; they built siegeworks against it all around. So the city was besieged until the eleventh year of King Zedekiah. On the ninth day of the fourth month the famine became so severe in the city that there was no food for the people of the land. Then a breach was made in the city wall; the king with all the soldiers fled by night by the way of the gate between the two walls, by the king's garden, though the Chaldeans were all around the city. They went in the direction of the Arabah. But the army of the Chaldeans pursued the king, and overtook him in the plains of Jericho; all his army was scattered, deserting him. Then they captured the king and brought him up to the king of Babylon at Riblah, who passed sentence on him. They slaughtered the sons of Zedekiah before his eyes, then put out the eyes of Zedekiah; they bound him in fetters and took him to Babylon. (2 Kings 25:1-7)

Song

It is good to give thanks to the Lord,
>   to sing praises to your name, O Most High;
to declare your steadfast love in the morning,
>   and your faithfulness by night,
to the music of the lute and the harp,
>   to the melody of the lyre.
For you, O Lord, have made me glad by your work;
>   at the works of your hands I sing for joy.
>   *(Psalm 92:1-4)*

Proverb

A soft answer turns away wrath,
>   but a harsh word stirs up anger.
The tongue of the wise dispenses knowledge,
>   but the mouths of fools pour out folly.
The eyes of the Lord are in every place,
>   keeping watch on the evil and the good.
A gentle tongue is a tree of life,
>   but perverseness in it breaks the spirit.
A fool despises a parent's instruction,
>   but the one who heeds admonition is prudent.
In the house of the righteous there is much treasure,
>   but trouble befalls the income of the wicked.
>   *(Proverbs 15:1-6)*

Legal Code

When you come upon your enemy's ox or donkey going astray, you shall bring it back. When you see the donkey of one who hates you lying under its burden and you would hold back from setting it free, you must help to set it free.

You shall not pervert the justice due to your poor in their lawsuits. Keep far from a false charge, and do not kill the innocent and those in the right, for I will not acquit the guilty. You shall take no bribe, for a bribe blinds the officials, and subverts the cause of those who are in the right.

You shall not oppress a resident alien; you know the heart of an alien, for you were aliens in the land of Egypt.
(Exodus 23:4-9)

Prophetic Oracle

Ah, you who make iniquitous decrees,
>   who write oppressive statutes,
to turn aside the needy from justice
>   and to rob the poor of my people of their right,
that widows may be your spoil,
>   and that you may make the orphans your prey!
What will you do on the day of punishment,
>   in the calamity that will come from far away?
To whom will you flee for help,
>   and where will you leave your wealth,
so as not to crouch among the prisoners
>   or fall among the slain?
For all this his anger has not turned away;
>   his hand is stretched out still.
>   *(Isaiah 10:1-4)*

Legend

When people began to multiply on the face of the ground, and daughters were born to them, the sons of God saw that they were fair; and they took wives for themselves of all that they chose. Then the Lord said, "My spirit shall not abide in mortals forever, for they are flesh; their days shall be one hundred twenty years." The Nephilim were on the earth in those days—and also afterward—when the sons of God went in to the daughters of humans, who bore children to them. These were the heroes that were of old, warriors of renown.
(Genesis 6:1-4)

Prayer

How long, O Lord? Will you forget me forever?
>   How long will you hide your face from me?
How long must I bear pain in my soul,
>   and have sorrow in my heart all day long?
How long shall my enemy be exalted over me?

Consider and answer me, O Lord my God!
>   Give light to my eyes, or I will sleep the sleep of death,
and my enemy will say, "I have prevailed";
>   my foes will rejoice because I am shaken.

But I trusted in your steadfast love;
>   my heart shall rejoice in your salvation.
I will sing to the Lord,
>   because he has dealt bountifully with me.
>   *(Psalm 13:1-6)*

Letter

Artaxerxes, king of kings, to the priest Ezra, the scribe of the law of the God of heaven: Peace. And now I decree that any of the people of Israel or their priests or Levites in my kingdom who freely offers to go to Jerusalem may go with you. For you are sent by the king and his seven counselors to make inquiries about Judah and Jerusalem according to the law of your God, which is in your hand, and also to convey the silver and gold that the king and his counselors have freely offered to the God of Israel, whose dwelling is in Jerusalem, with all the silver and gold that you shall find in the whole province of Babylonia, and with the freewill offerings of the people and the priests, given willingly for the house of their God in Jerusalem. With this money, then, you shall with all diligence buy bulls, rams, and lambs, and their grain offerings and their drink offerings, and you shall offer them on the altar of the house of your God in Jerusalem. *(Ezra 7:12-17)*

Funeral Dirge

Saul and Jonathan, beloved and lovely!
 In life and in death they were not divided;
they were swifter than eagles,
 they were stronger than lions.

O daughters of Israel, weep over Saul,
 who clothed you with crimson, in luxury,
 who put ornaments of gold on your apparel.

How the mighty have fallen
 in the midst of the battle!

Jonathan lies slain upon your high places.
 I am distressed for you, my brother Jonathan;
greatly beloved were you to me;
 your love to me was wonderful,
 passing the love of women.

How the mighty have fallen,
 and the weapons of war perished! *(2 Samuel 1:23-27)*

Love Poetry

As an apple tree among the trees of the wood,
 so is my beloved among young men.

With great delight I sat in his shadow,
 and his fruit was sweet to my taste.
He brought me to the banqueting house,
 and his intention toward me was love.
Sustain me with raisins,
 refresh me with apples;
 for I am faint with love.
O that his left hand were under my head,
 and that his right hand embraced me!
I adjure you, O daughters of Jerusalem,
 by the gazelles or the wild does:
do not stir up or awaken love
 until it is ready! *(Song of Solomon 2:3-7)*

Another important literary feature of the Hebrew Bible is the mixture of prose and poetry that it contains. Large portions of the Hebrew Bible are written in poetry, including most of the material in the books that Christians label **Poetic Books** and Prophets. The presence of poetry is easy to miss in our English translations, since Hebrew poetry lacks the elements of rhyme and

---

23 The LORD is my shepherd; I shall not want. [2]He maketh me to lie down in green pastures; he leadeth me beside the still waters. [3]He restoreth my soul: he leadeth me in the paths of righteousness for his name's sake.

23 Because the Lord is my Shepherd, I have everything I need! [2, 3]He lets me rest in the meadow grass and leads me beside the quiet streams. He restores my failing health. He helps me do what honors him the most.

23 [1]The LORD is my shepherd; I shall not want. [2]He makes me lie down in green pastures; he leads me beside still waters; [3]he restores my soul. He leads me in right paths for his name's sake.

Fig. 3.4. Different versions of the Bible present the lines of Psalm 23 verse by verse (the King James Version); as block paragraphs (the Living Bible); and set as verse (the New Revised Standard Version).

rhythm that English speakers are accustomed to using to identify poetry. Most modern printed editions of the Bible attempt to make poetry more visible by printing it in lines of varying length and leaving blocks of white space around the verses. Prose, by contrast, is usually printed in straight columns of equal width.

The most visible characteristic of Hebrew poetry is **parallelism**, the practice of using two or more lines to express a single thought. The precise relationship between the two lines varies. Sometimes the second line simply repeats the idea of the first line, while at other times it sets up a contrast with the first line. In still other cases the second line extends or completes the thought that was begun in the first line. This patterned use of language has the combined effect of emphasizing the point that the author is trying to make and leading the reader to reflect more carefully on what is being said. Consider the following examples.

> Contend, O Lord, with those who contend with me;
>> fight against those who fight against me!
>> *(Psalm 35:1)*

> A wise child makes a glad father,
>> but a foolish child is a mother's grief.
>> *(Proverbs 10:1)*

> For everything there is a season,
>> and a time for every matter under heaven.
>> *(Ecclesiastes 3:1)*

> Then the eyes of those who have sight will not be closed,
>> and the ears of those who have hearing will listen.
>> *(Isaiah 32:3)*

In many passages, particularly in the prophetic books, the standard two-line parallelism is extended to three or more lines. In these cases the parallel structure is typically more complex and harder to detect. The use of repetitive language is common in these more elaborate constructions.

> Have you not known? Have you not heard?
>> Has it not been told you from the beginning?
>> Have you not understood from the foundations of the earth?
> It is he who sits above the circle of the earth,
>> and its inhabitants are like grasshoppers;
> who stretches out the heavens like a curtain,
>> and spreads them like a tent to live in;
> who brings princes to naught,
>> and makes the rulers of the earth as nothing.
>
> Scarcely are they planted, scarcely sown,
>> scarcely has their stem taken root in the earth,
> when he blows upon them, and they wither,
>> and the tempest carries them off like stubble.
>> *(Isaiah 40:21-24)*
>
> Flight shall perish from the swift,
>> and the strong shall not retain their strength,
>> nor shall the mighty save their lives;
> those who handle the bow shall not stand,
>> and those who are swift of foot shall not save themselves,
>> nor shall those who ride horses save their lives;
> and those who are stout of heart among the mighty
>> shall flee away naked in that day, says the Lord.
>> *(Amos 2:14-16)*

Another common feature of Hebrew poetry that can be observed in English translations is the use of vivid imagery and symbolism. Much of this imagery reflects the agricultural and natural settings of ancient Israel, a fact that sometimes makes it difficult for modern city-dwelling readers to understand. (For more on this point, see chapter 6.) The following examples illustrate the richly figurative language that is so common in biblical poetry.

> The voice of the Lord is over the waters;
>> the God of glory thunders,
>> the Lord, over mighty waters.
> The voice of the Lord is powerful;
>> the voice of the Lord is full of majesty.

The voice of the Lord breaks the cedars;
    the Lord breaks the cedars of Lebanon.
He makes Lebanon skip like a calf,
    and Sirion like a young wild ox.

The voice of the Lord flashes forth flames of fire.
The voice of the Lord shakes the wilderness;
    the Lord shakes the wilderness of Kadesh.

The voice of the Lord causes the oaks to whirl,
    and strips the forest bare;
    and in his temple all say, "Glory!" *(Psalm 29:3-9)*

Many bulls encircle me,
    strong bulls of Bashan surround me;
they open wide their mouths at me,
    like a ravening and roaring lion.

I am poured out like water,
    and all my bones are out of joint;
my heart is like wax;
    it is melted within my breast;
my mouth is dried up like a potsherd,
    and my tongue sticks to my jaws;
    you lay me in the dust of death.

For dogs are all around me;
    a company of evildoers encircles me.
My hands and feet have shriveled;
I can count all my bones.
They stare and gloat over me;
they divide my clothes among themselves,
    and for my clothing they cast lots.

But you, O Lord, do not be far away!
    O my help, come quickly to my aid!
Deliver my soul from the sword,
    my life from the power of the dog!
    Save me from the mouth of the lion!

From the horns of the wild oxen you have rescued me.
    (Psalm 22:12-21)

A jealous and avenging God is the Lord,
    the Lord is avenging and wrathful;
the Lord takes vengeance on his adversaries
    and rages against his enemies.
The Lord is slow to anger but great in power,
    and the Lord will by no means clear the guilty.

His way is in whirlwind and storm,
    and the clouds are the dust of his feet.
He rebukes the sea and makes it dry,
    and he dries up all the rivers;
Bashan and Carmel wither,
    and the bloom of Lebanon fades.
The mountains quake before him,
    and the hills melt;
the earth heaves before him,
    the world and all who live in it.
    (Nahum 1:2-5)

Apart from sheer literary enjoyment, the main reason it is important to be able to distinguish between prose and poetry in the Hebrew Bible is to provide a check on potential misinterpretations of the text. Many misunderstandings have arisen over the centuries as a result of reading figurative poetic language as though it were prose, or interpreting prosaic statements as if they were written as poetry. When the psalmist implores God to "hide me in the shadow of your wings" (Psalm 17:8) or describes how God "sent out his arrows" against his enemies (Psalm 18:14), we should not conclude that the deity is in fact a winged archer. On the other hand, we cannot dismiss as mere poetry the biblical authors' prosaic narratives about Moses parting the Red Sea or the prophet Elijah flying off to heaven in a fiery chariot. We might conclude for other reasons that these stories should not be taken as factual accounts of real events, but it would be wrong to regard them as poetic texts that were never meant to be taken literally, since they are written in precisely the same kind of prosaic language as other biblical stories that contemporary readers find more credible.

CONCLUSION

From both a literary and a theological standpoint, the Hebrew Bible is not one book but many. Between its covers lie literally dozens of compositions from different periods representing a variety of literary styles and genres. The Jewish editors who compiled this collection into its present form used a three-part pattern of organization that gave pride of place to the Torah, the most important part of the Bible for Judaism.

When the early Christians made this collection the first part of their Scriptures, they reorganized the books into a four-part system that emphasized the historical and prophetic elements of the collection. In this way they expressed their belief that the true purpose of the Jewish Scriptures was to narrate what God had done in an earlier era to prepare the way for the coming of Jesus.

In the end, we must give due weight to both the similarities and the differences between the Jewish Bible and the Christian Old Testament. Though they contain much of the same material, the ways in which Jews and Christians understand and interpret their respective texts are so different that from a practical standpoint it sometimes appears as if they are reading two different books of Scripture.

EXERCISE 4

After this chapter, you will be asked to look up and read passages from the Hebrew Bible on your own. To do this, you will need to know how to locate verses in the Bible. You will also need to understand the system of notation that is commonly used when referring to biblical passages.

- Before you can look up a verse in the Hebrew Bible, you must first be able to locate the book in which the passage is located. The simplest way to do this is to look in the table of contents. After a while, however, this becomes rather tedious. A more helpful solution would be to set aside time now to memorize the books of the Hebrew Bible. To do this, simply locate the column in the chart on pages 28–29 that agrees with the Bible that you are using and then focus on memorizing one major section at a time. The effort that you put into memorizing the books of the Bible now will pay rich dividends in the years to come if you have any thought of using the Bible after you finish this book.

- In modern printed editions of the Bible, nearly every book is divided into larger units called chapters. These chapters are subdivided into smaller units called verses. Both the chapters and the verses are numbered in sequential order. (This numbering system is a modern invention—it did not appear in the original text.) The normal method of referring to a specific passage from the Hebrew Bible is to give the name of the book first, followed by the number of the chapter and the number of the verse. For example, Genesis 12:4 refers to verse 4 in chapter 12 of the book of Genesis. (Chapter and verse numbers are usually separated by a colon, though some publishers use a period for this purpose.) When referring to a passage that contains several verses, the verse numbers are separated by a hyphen. Thus, Isaiah 60:1-5 refers to the first five verses in chapter 60 of the book of Isaiah.

- Sometimes a passage will extend beyond the boundaries of a single chapter. In this case the beginning and ending verses of the passage are given, separated by a dash that indicates that all of the intervening verses should be read. Thus if you were asked to read Jeremiah 8:18—9:6, you would find chapter 8 in the book of Jeremiah and begin reading at verse 18, continuing through the end of that chapter and on into chapter 9, where you would stop after reading verse 6. To locate Exodus 21:1—22:15, you would turn to chapter 21 of the book of Exodus and begin reading with the first verse and keep reading until you reached verse 16 of chapter 22.

To help you become more comfortable looking up passages in the Bible, locate each of the following passages and identify what type of literature the passage represents, using the examples in this chapter as a guide. Then write a one- to two-sentence summary of the main point of each passage.

- Genesis 3:1-7
- Psalm 92:1-5
- Exodus 20:12
- 1 Chronicles 15:25—16:6
- Proverbs 23:29-35

- Isaiah 63:15—64:12
- Judges 9:7-15
- Nehemiah 2:1-6
- Hosea 4:1
- Daniel 10:4-9

Fig. 4.1. Statue of a seated scribe from ancient Egypt.

CHAPTER 4

Where Did the Hebrew Bible Come From?

Keep these words that I am commanding you today in your heart. Recite them to your children and talk about them when you are at home and when you are away, when you lie down and when you rise. Bind them as a sign on your hand, fix them as an emblem on your forehead, and write them on the doorposts of your house and on your gates. (Deuteronomy 6:6-9)

Let this be recorded for a generation to come, so that a people yet unborn may praise the LORD . . . so that the name of the LORD may be declared in Zion, and his praise in Jerusalem, when peoples gather together, and kingdoms, to worship the LORD. (Psalm 102:18, 21-22)

Now the rest of the acts of Jeroboam, and all that he did, and his might, how he fought, and how he recovered for Israel Damascus and Hamath, which had belonged to Judah, are they not written in the Book of the Annals of the Kings of Israel? (2 Kings 14:28)

The origins of the Hebrew Bible are shrouded in mystery. Our only evidence for the development of the collection, including the authorship and dating of individual books, comes from the texts themselves. Some of the books contain historical references or allusions that can be checked against the records of Israel's neighbors (the Assyrians, Babylonians, and Egyptians) in order to arrive at an estimated date of composition or editing. Others can be dated by correlating their contents with the more datable books. In the end, however, all that we have are inferences; there are no outside references to the authorship or dating of any of the books in the Hebrew Bible.

Because of the limited nature of the evidence, scholars have developed various theories about the origins and history of the biblical text. Some think that the Hebrew Bible contains materials that were composed fairly early in the history of the people of Israel (1000 B.C.E. or earlier), while others would date virtually all of the texts to the last few centuries before the Common Era (400–200

B.C.E.). Most of the arguments in this area are too technical for an introductory textbook. But it is important to have at least a general sense of the competing scholarly theories in order to understand why biblical scholars disagree so intensely about the nature of the Hebrew Bible and its reliability as a source for reconstructing the history of ancient Israel.

IN THE BEGINNING

Virtually all scholars agree that at least some of what eventually became the Hebrew Bible began as oral tradition, a term that refers to any kind of material that is passed on within a society by word of mouth. For example, people in every culture have a stock of traditional stories that they tell their children (and other adults) in order to keep alive the traditional beliefs and practices of the society. Other types of material that are commonly passed on in oral form include wise sayings about life (often called proverbs), songs, prayers, and rules of conduct.

Why do people pass on such important elements of their cultural legacy by word of mouth rather than in writing? The simple answer is that written texts are useless to people who cannot read. The evidence for literacy levels in ancient Palestine is sparse, but materials from similar cultures suggest that not more than 5 to 10 percent of the population would have been able to read or write at a functional level, and virtually all of these people would have lived in the cities. Public schooling was nonexistent

in ancient Israel; most children went to work in the fields or began training for a trade at a very early age in order to help the family survive. Formal education (including literacy training) was a luxury to which only the urban elites could aspire.

This does not mean, however, that the illiterate masses were ignorant. Cultures with low levels of literacy can pass on voluminous amounts of information by memory. In the Greek world, the *Iliad* and *Odyssey* were recited from memory for hundreds of years, and Jewish sources tell of rabbis who had memorized the entire text of the Torah.

These feats appear remarkable to us because we live in a literate society where accurate recollection is generally unnecessary and memory remains an undeveloped resource. In the ancient world, by contrast, memory was a vital tool for maintaining the heritage and vitality of the culture. Not everyone would have been capable of such prodigious feats of memorization, but examples like this remind us that we should be careful about making sweeping statements about what illiterate people might or might not have been able to pass on through oral tradition.

In societies where literacy is scarce, a variety of formal and informal institutions and activities work together to preserve the traditional beliefs, values, and practices of the culture. Parents tell their children the age-old stories of how the world reached its present form and where people like them fit into this world. Adults remind children about proper standards of conduct. Shepherds and farmers swap stories and songs around the campfire on a cold winter evening. Religious leaders recite stories, sing songs, offer prayers, and oversee the rituals that the group uses to curry favor with the supernatural forces that surround them. Many traditional cultures believe that accurate reci-

Fig. 4.2. Oral storytelling is still used today in many societies to communicate traditional beliefs and values from one generation to the next.

tation is vital to the success of their religious activities, so memorization is especially valued in this sphere.

So what parts of the Hebrew Bible might have originated as oral traditions?

1. Proverbs—short wise sayings about how to live—circulate orally in virtually every culture, even cultures with a high level of literacy (see chapter 37). Many of the sayings that were eventually collected into the book of Proverbs would have been recited orally among friends and families long before they were written down. The same can be said for proverbial sayings that appear elsewhere in the Hebrew Bible (for example, Ezekiel 12:22; 16:44; 18:2).

2. Virtually all of the songs and prayers that fill the book of Psalms are artful literary compositions that were created to be sung or recited orally in the worship of ancient Israel (see chapter 30). Most appear to have been composed in written form from the start, but some might have originated with the illiterate masses before they were taken up and crafted into their present form by the literate elites.

3. Most of the sayings in the books of the prophets represent excerpts from speeches that the prophets delivered orally to a public audience. Sometimes they addressed individuals or groups of people who gathered to hear them speak. At other times they simply shouted their message to anyone who happened to pass by on the street. Some of the prophets were consulted by kings and other high officials, while others were rejected and abused by people who felt threatened by their criticisms of the status quo. The biblical books that bear their names are essentially edited collections of snippets from their oral speeches. The process by which these oral sayings were converted into written texts is unclear—some may have been written down at an early date, while others were preserved in oral form by their disciples and others who heard them (see chapter 31).

4. Stories, like proverbs, play a crucial role in sustaining the beliefs and practices of an oral culture from generation to generation. Many scholars believe that the biblical narratives about the early days of the people of Israel (specifically, prior to the establishment of the monarchy around 1020 B.C.E.) were passed on orally for centuries before they were enshrined in books that became part of the Hebrew Bible. Some think that the stories had already been linked together into a **grand narrative** before they were written down, while others believe that the stories circulated independently until they were combined to form a coherent story line by the people who composed the biblical texts. Still others insist that most or all of the stories originated as written compositions late in Israel's history, so that there was no period of oral transmission.

Scholars are equally divided over the origins of the stories in the so-called Historical Books of the Bible. Many believe that these books were based on official records and other documents that were written close to the time of the events that they describe. The authors (or editors) may have exercised literary creativity in the way they told the stories, but their basic information came from written sources, not from oral tradition. Others point to evidence suggesting that the authors made use of both oral and written materials when composing their texts. Still others regard virtually all of the stories as literary fictions that made little use of earlier sources. Scholars who take this position disagree about how to handle outside materials that seem to corroborate the historicity of at least some of the characters and events narrated in these books (see chapter 9). On the whole, scholars are deeply divided over how much of the material in these books goes back to oral or written sources and how much should be credited to the literary creativity of a later author or editor.

5. The literary history of the legal materials in the Torah is largely a matter of conjecture. The Torah is a complex literary work that emerged out of a long history of compilation, revision, and editing (see chapter 22). In its present form it reflects the interests of the educated priestly elites who dominated the temple in Jerusalem. But scholars remain uncertain about how the laws of Torah developed. Most would agree that some of the laws originated among the illiterate masses while others were created and preserved among the priestly elites. Most also assume that members of the priestly class were functionally literate and thus capable of making written collections of laws. Yet evidence from other cultures suggests that most of the priests could have learned the laws that pertained to their duties (for instance, how to perform **sacrifices** and offerings) through oral instruction. In summary, it seems safe to say that at least some of the laws

that were finally incorporated into the Torah were transmitted orally for a lengthy period of time within limited segments of the Israelite populace. But the actual history that lies behind this admittedly general conclusion is difficult to uncover.

EXERCISE 5

Look up the following verses in your Bible and explain briefly how each of them might relate to the question of how oral traditions were passed on and used in ancient Israel.

- Exodus 12:24-27
- Deuteronomy 6:4-9
- Deuteronomy 6:20-25
- Psalm 78:1-8
- Psalm 145:3-7
- Ezekiel 2:3-7
- Proverbs 4:1-5

THE FIRST WRITINGS

So when and how were these scattered oral traditions converted into written texts that would eventually end up in the Hebrew Bible? The answer to this question is just as complex and uncertain as the previous one. According to the Torah, the earliest writing took place in the time of Moses, when Yahweh (or Moses?) inscribed the Ten Commandments onto two tablets made of stone (Exodus 24:12; 31:18; Deuteronomy 4:13). Later in the narrative, Yahweh tells Moses to write down some of the laws that he has received (Exodus 34:27; Deuteronomy 27:3; 31:24-26) and to record certain events for posterity (Exodus 17:14). Today only uncritical readers would take these statements seriously as history. Most scholars view them as an effort to place a stamp of legitimacy onto laws that were actually created at a much later date.

So what do scholars think really happened? The answer is different for each section of the Bible, and much remains uncertain. But one point is clear: all of the books were produced by people who could read and write. This simple observation is one of the keys to understanding the

Hebrew Bible. Only a small number of people in ancient Palestine would have been even moderately literate, and few of these would have had the necessary skills to compose or edit entire books of the type that we find in the Hebrew Bible. Most of the people who possessed these skills would have lived in one of the few larger towns or cities of Palestine, not in the villages where the bulk of the population resided. Most would have been males, and virtually all would have been members of the wealthy elite class that dominated the political and economic life of ancient Israel (see chapter 7). In short, the documents that make up the Hebrew Bible were written and edited by a small class of urban elite males.

This observation has profound implications for the way we understand the Hebrew Bible. The Hebrew Bible is not a neutral collection of documents that arose out of the ordinary religious life of the people of ancient Israel. It was produced by a small group of wealthy elite males, and its contents reflect their beliefs, interests, and biases. The ideas and experiences of women, poor people, and farmers (the vast majority of the population) are present only insofar as they were deemed interesting or useful by the elite male authors who compiled the texts. This does not mean that the Hebrew Bible is a chauvinistic propaganda piece; virtually all human literature was produced under similar conditions until fairly recent times. But it does suggest that we should be sensitive to the ways in which the authors' own backgrounds and biases might be reflected in the books that they produced. A significant amount of the material in the Hebrew Bible may have been derived from oral traditions that circulated for generations among the rural population of ancient Palestine. But these traditions were substantially revised and edited when they were converted into written texts. Much was added and much was lost in the process. The result is a set of texts that combines popular traditions with elite male perspectives. These texts present a rather one-sided picture of the religious life of ancient Israel. One of the tasks of contemporary biblical scholarship is to recover some of the voices that have been silenced in this process in order to develop a more balanced understanding of Israelite religion.

While much remains unclear about the early development and growth of written texts in ancient Israel, scholars

Fig. 4.3. (left) The learning and skills of professional scribes were highly valued in the ancient world, as depicted in this carving from an Egyptian tomb; (below) scribes continue to play a vital role in the Jewish community as copiers and interpreters of Scripture.

have some general ideas about how the process may have occurred.

1. The Torah in its present form includes material drawn from earlier collections of laws that were written down and compiled at various times in Israel's history. The earliest collections probably contained laws dealing with social relations (including but not limited to actions that were considered criminal offenses) and rules for the operation of the Jerusalem temple. It is probably no accident that the book of Deuteronomy, which appears to have been written during the time of the monarchy, focuses heavily on these issues.

2. The books of Psalms and Proverbs offer more explicit information about their prior history. In both cases the editors retained headings identifying the earlier collections that they incorporated into their books. (See the discussions in chapters 30 and 37.) The dates of these collections are uncertain, but some of their materials can be dated to the time of the monarchy based on their casual references to the conduct of the king. Since proverbs tend to circulate orally, we cannot be sure when the first written collection of proverbial sayings was compiled. In the

case of the psalms, on the other hand, it appears that most originated as literary texts. If this is true, then the psalms that mention kings are among the earliest datable written texts in the Hebrew Bible.

3. The effort to determine when the sayings of the prophets were first written down is fraught with problems. A number of passages in the prophetic books claim that Yahweh told the prophets to write down some of their sayings during their lifetime (Isaiah 30:8; Jeremiah 29:1-32; 30:1-2; 36:1-4; 36:27-32; Ezekiel 43:10-11; Habakkuk 2:2-3), and a few of the shorter books (Nahum, Obadiah, Habakkuk) may have been composed in written form from the start, though all show signs of later editing. For the most part, however, the evidence suggests that the present books of the prophets were compiled decades or even centuries after their deaths. Many scholars believe that the sayings were passed on orally during the intervening period, while others think that some of the prophets' words may have been written down by their disciples or other people who heard them speak. In some cases the materials are arranged in a topical manner that might point to the use of earlier collections. In the end,

much remains uncertain in this area. (For more on these questions, see chapter 31.)

4. The question of when the biblical stories were first written down is one of the most hotly debated topics in modern biblical scholarship. To begin with the stories in the Torah, the accepted view for nearly a century was that two different authors or editors who lived during the era of the Israelite monarchy (tenth to eighth century B.C.E.) had composed separate written accounts of the early history of the Hebrew people using stories and other materials that they knew from oral tradition. These two narratives were subsequently woven together and edited to form the basic story line of the Torah. In recent years, however, this view has been challenged by scholars who question the existence of these earlier sources, the dates of their composition, or both (see chapter 21). Most of the challengers agree that the people who composed the Torah narratives relied on written sources, but they think that the history of collection and editing was far more complex than the traditional view would allow. Some have even suggested that the whole idea of earlier written sources is a figment of the scholarly imagination. According to this view, the story line of the Torah was created late in Israel's history by the editors of the Torah and bears little or no relation to either oral tradition or history.

The situation is equally unclear for the stories in the so-called Historical Books. The books of Kings and Chronicles refer repeatedly to written sources from which they claim to have derived their information, and they suggest that the reader who wants to learn more about the lives and accomplishments of the kings whose stories they tell can consult these sources at their leisure. (For more on this point, see chapters 9 and 20.) Unfortunately, none of these outside sources has survived, so we do not know whether they contained the kind of extended stories that appear in the Hebrew Bible or simply the bare facts of each king's reign as recorded by a court archivist. Some scholars have suggested that the sources are entirely fictional, that is to say, that the references were made up by a storyteller who wanted to make the stories sound more credible. Even scholars who believe that the stories are based on historical records acknowledge that they were composed by an author or editor writing long after the

events, though it is possible that oral traditions may have been available to supplement the written records. The books that tell about the earlier history of Israel (Joshua, Judges, 1 Samuel, 2 Samuel) contain only a handful of references to outside sources (Joshua 10:18 and 2 Samuel 1:18 mention the "Book of Jashar"), so we can only speculate about whether they got their material from oral traditions, written sources, or the literary imaginations of the authors.

To sum up, during the period of the kings (late eleventh to early sixth century B.C.E.), the small number of people who could read might have been acquainted with written collections of laws, psalms, proverbs, prophetic sayings, and stories that were eventually incorporated into the Hebrew Bible. Some of these collections might have been shaped already into coherent literary works. But it is unlikely that any of these materials would have been regarded as Scripture by the people who read them, since written texts played little or no part in the religious life of the people of Israel during this period. The only materials that might have approached the status of Scripture were some of the legal texts that were used by the priests in the Jerusalem temple, but these resources would have been restricted to a small circle of people. Among the illiterate masses, religious belief and practice continued to be grounded in oral traditions that had been passed on for generations.

EXERCISE 6

Read the following passages and explain briefly how each of them might relate to the question of the origins and use of written texts in ancient Israel.

- Deuteronomy 31:19-22
- 1 Kings 2:1-3
- 2 Chronicles 31:3
- 2 Chronicles 35:25
- Psalm 102:18-22
- Proverbs 22:20-21
- Jeremiah 30:1-3
- Jeremiah 36:1-7

THE FORMATION OF THE CANON

If history had continued as it was going under the kings of ancient Israel, the Hebrew Bible might never have come into existence. The religious life of the people of Israel was framed around practice and ritual, not study or **doctrine**, and a book of Scripture would have been useless to the vast majority who could not read.

But major changes were in store for the people of Israel. Because of their strategic location between Egypt and Mesopotamia, the people of Palestine often found themselves caught in the middle of political, economic, and military rivalries between the great powers to their north and south (see chapter 6). For centuries, Israel's leaders found ways to adapt to the changing political climate and maintain a degree of freedom from outside domination. Finally their luck ran out. In 722 B.C.E. the Assyrian armies arrived from northern Mesopotamia (modern-day Iraq) and devastated the northern part of Israel, incorporating it into their empire. In 586 B.C.E. the Babylonians, another Mesopotamian people who had overthrown the Assyrians, did the same to the southern region. (For more on these events, see chapters 8 and 9.)

During the Assyrian invasion, many refugees were able to escape to the south, carrying with them their oral and written traditions. Some of these traditions may have been written down or edited soon afterward in order to preserve them from loss in a new environment. When the Babylonians invaded over a century later, some of the people once again succeeded in escaping to Egypt and other neighboring countries, but most of the elites who survived the conflict were shipped off to Babylon. In the process, they lost everything—their property, their wealth, their independence, their land, their temple.

Many concluded that Yahweh, the divine protector of Israel, had either rejected them or been defeated by the gods of the Babylonians. In either case, they would never see their homeland again. Others came to regard their circumstances as a punishment imposed by Yahweh as a result of their failure to faithfully obey the laws and traditions handed down by their ancestors.

Fig. 4.4. This image from the palace of the Assyrian king Sennacherib (eighth century B.C.E.) shows a group of Judeans being led away into exile after their city (Lachish) was conquered.

Some of the people in this latter group were members of the educated elite who took it upon themselves to collect and preserve the oral and written traditions of their ancestors and to compose narratives of their people's past that highlighted the events and practices that led to their downfall. These texts formed the nucleus of what would eventually become the Torah and the Prophets, including the stories that make up the Former Prophets. Others wrote new texts that expressed their anxiety about the current situation and their hopes that Yahweh would bring them through it. Some of these texts became popular among the elites and were eventually incorporated into the Writings. Still other people claimed to be receiving messages from Yahweh that resembled those that earlier prophets had spoken to them in their own land. Some of the sayings of these later prophets were preserved in books that found a place of honor in the community alongside the words of the earlier prophets. Slowly the idea of using a collection of written texts to regulate the life of the community began to emerge.

After several decades, the Babylonians were conquered by the Persians (modern-day Iran). The Persians permitted the people of Judah who had been taken to Babylonia (or more precisely, their children and grandchildren) to return to their homeland and rebuild their homes and their temple. Among the people who accepted this offer were priests and scribes who carried with them a budding collection of texts that had been compiled and edited in Babylonia. In the decades that followed, these texts became increasingly important as a source of guidance for the community. At some point a program of oral instruction was established to educate the masses about their content.

For a long time these texts remained open to further revision and editing (that is, the canon was still open). But after several generations they had achieved such a position of honor within the community that the idea of changing them in any way became unacceptable. In the case of the Torah, this closing of the canon seems to have occurred by the fourth century B.C.E. among most Jews, though for some it took longer. The books included in the Former Prophets also seem to have been closed at an early date since they do not narrate any events after the beginning of the time in Babylonia.

The final history of the books that were included in the Latter Prophets is more obscure. After the people returned to Judah, new prophets arose claiming to speak for Yahweh, and some of their messages were preserved in writing for the benefit of the community (Zechariah, Haggai, Malachi). At some point the books of the prophets were added to public recitations alongside the Torah, but their contents were still in flux as late as the first century B.C.E., as evidenced by two very different versions of the book of Jeremiah that were in use at that time. As the books of the prophets continued to be read and used within the community, people slowly came to regard

them as a second set of sacred texts alongside the books of Torah. By the late second century B.C.E., a Jewish author could refer without explanation to "the Law and the Prophets," implying that the Jews of his day honored a collection called "the Prophets" alongside the Torah. Precisely what texts he would have included in this section can no longer be determined.

The finalization of the category of texts called the Writings took even longer. Perhaps as early as the time in Babylonia, many of the psalms and proverbs that had been used in Israel were compiled into collections. In the years after they returned to Judah, Jewish authors produced a number of other books that earned the respect of their peers. Some of these books were copied and circulated so widely that they came to be regarded as Scrip-

Fig. 4.5. Contemporary Jews continue to study and debate the meaning and application of their sacred scriptures.

ture by educated Jewish leaders. Others were limited to a particular community or geographic area. In this way different Jewish groups came to use different books to guide their religious life alongside the accepted texts of the Torah and the Prophets. This was the situation when the Christian movement emerged out of Judaism in the first century C.E.

As far as we can tell, Jews felt no compulsion to define the boundaries of their growing canon until at least the late first century C.E. Jewish texts indicate that a group of rabbis spent time debating the contours of the canon around that time, but they had no authority to settle the question. Concerns were reportedly raised about four books that were eventually included in the Jewish canon: Ezekiel, because its vision of a future temple appeared to conflict with the one portrayed in the Torah; Ecclesiastes, because of its markedly pessimistic view of life; Esther, because it never mentions the name of God; and Song of Solomon, because of its highly erotic nature and its lack of reference to God. Scholars disagree about the historical reliability of this account, but evidence from other sources seems to indicate that the boundaries of the canon and the text of the books that were included in it had been largely finalized by the end of the first or the beginning of the second century C.E.

Why were the rabbis of the late first century concerned to define the limits of the canon when earlier Jews had apparently felt no such concern? Comparisons with other groups suggest that the formation of a fixed canon is usually a response to some kind of challenge or crisis within a religious community. In the case of the rabbis, that crisis was the devastation of Israel by the Romans (including the destruction of the city of Jerusalem and its temple) following the great Jewish revolt that took place from 66 to 73 C.E. With their temple gone and their social and religious system in tatters, the rabbis seem to have felt that it was crucial to rally their people around the one tangible thing that bound them together, their sacred Scriptures. This may have included coming to some kind of agreement about the precise content of the Scriptures.

Another key item on the rabbis' agenda was the establishment of schools where young men could be taught how to read and study the Scriptures. By training the next generation of religious leaders, they hoped to ensure that their ideas about the canon of Scripture (and many other things) would become accepted throughout Israel. Many of their oral teachings about the meaning and application of the Torah were later written down in the Mishnah (approximately 200 C.E.) and the Talmud (fourth to sixth centuries C.E.). Over time, many Jews came to revere the Talmud as having almost the same authority as the Bible.

CONCLUSION

The process by which the Hebrew Bible came into existence was long and tortuous. The final product was the result of numerous small decisions by countless unknown people over the course of several centuries. The collection was produced, compiled, and edited by the literate elites, who were also the only ones who were capable of reading and studying the texts on their own.

Once the texts began to be recited in public ceremonies, however, the masses became more aware of their content. Over time, Jews of every social level came to regard these books as sacred and authoritative for the life of the community—first the Torah, then the Prophets, and finally the Writings. Through this process Judaism became increasingly a "religion of the book," though it would be centuries before the masses were sufficiently literate to read the texts for themselves.

EXERCISE 7

Read the following passages from Jewish and Christian sources and explain how they relate to the previous discussion of when and how the content of the Jewish Scriptures was finalized. Pay special attention to the phrases marked in bold type.

(a) Prologue to Sirach (132 B.C.E.)

Whereas many great teachings have been given to us through **the law and the prophets and the others that followed them**, on account of which we should praise Israel for instruction and wisdom; and since it is necessary not only that the readers themselves should acquire understanding but also that those who love learning should be able to help the outsiders by both speaking and writing, my grandfather Jesus [in Hebrew, "Joshua"], after devoting himself especially to the reading of **the law and the prophets and the other books of our fathers**, and after acquiring considerable proficiency in them, was himself also led to write something pertaining to instruction and wisdom, in order that, by becoming conversant with this also, those who love learning should make even greater progress in living according to the law.

(b) 4QMMT 92-96 (second century B.C.E.)

And you know that we have segregated ourselves from the rest of the people and that we avoid mingling in these affairs and associating with them in these things. And you know that there is not to be found in our actions deceit or betrayal or evil, for concerning these things we give [*text missing*]; and further to you we have written that you must understand **the book of Moses and the words of the prophets and of David** and the annals of each generation.

(c) Philo, *On the Contemplative Life* 3 (30s C.E.)

And in every house there is a sacred shrine which is called the holy place, and the monastery in which they retire by themselves and perform all the mysteries of a holy life, bringing in nothing, neither meat, nor drink, nor anything else which is indispensable towards supplying the necessities of the body, but **studying in that place the laws and the sacred oracles of God enunciated by the holy prophets, and hymns, and psalms**, and all kinds of other things by reason of which knowledge and piety are increased and brought to perfection. . . . And the interval between morning and evening is by them devoted wholly to meditation on and to practice of virtue, **for they take up the sacred scriptures and philosophize concerning them**, investigating the allegories of their national philosophy, since they look upon their literal expressions as symbols of some secret meaning of nature, intended to be conveyed in those figurative expressions.

(d) Matthew 22:34-40 (mid-80s C.E.)

When the Pharisees heard that he [Jesus] had silenced the Sadducees, they gathered together, and one of them, a lawyer, asked him a question to test him. "Teacher, which commandment in the law is the greatest?" He said to him, "'You shall love the Lord your God with all your heart, and with all your soul, and with all your mind.' This is the greatest and first commandment. And a second is like it: 'You shall love your neighbor as yourself.' On these two commandments hang **all the law and the prophets**."

(e) Luke 24:25-27, 44 (mid-80s C.E.)

Then he [Jesus] said to them, "Oh, how foolish you are, and how slow of heart to believe all that the prophets have declared! Was it not necessary that the Messiah should suffer these things and then enter into his glory?" Then **beginning with Moses and all the prophets**, he interpreted to them the things about himself in all the scriptures. . . . Then he said to them, "These are my words that I spoke to you while I was still with you—that everything written about me **in the law of Moses, the prophets, and the psalms** must be fulfilled."

(f) Josephus, *Against Apion* 1.8 (mid-90s C.E.)

We do not possess myriads of inconsistent books, conflicting with each other. Our books, those which are justly accredited, are **but two and twenty**, and contain the record of all time. Of these, **five are the books of Moses**, comprising the laws and the traditional history from the birth of man down to the death of the lawgiver. This period falls only a little short of three thousand years. From the death of Moses until Artaxerxes, who succeeded Xerxes as king of Persia, **the prophets subsequently to Moses wrote the history of the events of their own times in thirteen books**. The **remaining four books contain hymns to God and precepts for the conduct of human life**. From Artaxerxes to our own time the complete history has been written, but has not been deemed worthy of equal credit with the earlier records, because of the failure of the exact succession of the prophets. We have given practical proof of our reverence for our own Scriptures. For, although such long ages have now passed, no one has ventured either to add, or to remove, or to alter a syllable; and it is an instinct with every Jew, from the day of his birth, to regard them as the decrees of God, to abide by them, and, if need be, cheerfully to die for them.

Fig. 5.1. The book display area at the annual meeting of the Society of Biblical Literature gives scholars an opportunity to review and purchase new books in their field.

Academic Study of the Hebrew Bible

The study of the history of Israel, even if it be confined to the political level, is now a complex discipline, involving a variety of interlocking skills, and it is no longer possible simply to regard it as a retelling of the Old Testament story with a few extra-biblical texts thrown in. . . . The Old Testament remains a prime source of historical knowledge; it is not in itself primarily a history book.[1]

No one disputes that most of the Bible was written as applied literature: as history, liturgy, laws, preaching, and the like. To read the Bible as literature means that we cease to consider it under the rubric [of] applied literature, and so no longer study it according to the procedures of rhetoric or history or theology; rather we take it as imaginative literature and begin to investigate it using the tools of literary criticism.[2]

Feminist biblical interpretation must therefore challenge the scriptural authority of patriarchal texts and explore how the Bible is used as a weapon against women in our struggles for liberation. . . . At the same time the Bible has served not only to legitimate the oppression of white women, slaves, native Americans, Jews, and the poor. It has also provided authorization for women who rejected slavery, colonial exploitation, anti-Semitism, and misogynism as unbiblical and against God's will.[3]

Students who did not grow up around a church or synagogue are often worried that their lack of background will place them at a disadvantage when taking a course on the Hebrew Bible. Many of these students are surprised to learn that their peers who were raised in religious homes also know little or nothing about many of the issues discussed in this book. The reason for this lack of knowledge is not hard to find. Many churches and synagogues are suspicious of modern academic study of the Bible because they fear that its methods and results will undermine the faith of their members. Others embrace the academic approach in theory but find it largely irrelevant to the needs and concerns of the people whom they are trying to teach. The result is that few people who attend churches or synagogues in America ever have a chance to learn what academic scholars are saying about the Hebrew Bible. Why is there such a gulf between academic and religious approaches to the Bible?

A BIT OF HISTORY

Until the last two centuries, most Jews and Christians would have considered it wrong and even sinful to raise questions about the Bible or to attempt to study it like any other piece of literature. If there was anything on which believers of every stripe agreed, it was that the Bible was the inspired word of God, a book like no other. Jews and Christians alike were aware that human authors actually wrote the books of the Bible (that is, the books didn't just drop out of heaven), but they were convinced that God had guided or superintended the process so as to ensure that its contents were true in every respect. Some even believed that God had dictated the words directly to the human authors so that their human minds played no role in the process.

Of course, this does not mean that believers saw no problems in the Bible. The ancient Jewish rabbis made a practice of highlighting and seeking explanations for biblical passages that seemed to contradict one another, and some of them wondered why certain stories and passages had been included in the Bible. Christian interpreters in the first few centuries questioned the morality of some of the statements that they found in the Jewish Scriptures, such as the passages where God commands the Hebrew people to slaughter all of the women and children among the people whom they were supposed to displace from their "promised land." Christians also struggled to find any abiding spiritual significance in the laws of the Torah. Yet behind all of these questions lay a fundamental assurance that the Bible was the word of God, which meant that there must be some kind of religious truth behind even the most troublesome of passages.

Among the Jewish rabbis, this confidence in the truthfulness of Scripture led to the development of a system of study that sought to find significance in every phrase, word, and letter of the Scriptures. Among Christians, the idea emerged that Scripture could be understood on many levels, so that a literal reading of a text was not always the best approach. Sometimes a more spiritual reading was needed to grasp the deeper truth of a passage. According to this view, for example, God's command to slaughter the women and children of Canaan might be interpreted as a call to put to death those sinful desires and passions that would distract a person from single-hearted devotion to God.

This fundamental trust in the reliability of Scripture was shaken by the rise of **biblical criticism** in Europe from the seventeenth century onward. (The word *criticism* here means "careful analysis and evaluation," as in the practice of literary criticism; it says nothing about the critic's attitude toward the Bible.) As early as the fourteenth century, the Renaissance had spurred a number of Christian scholars to learn Hebrew and Greek in order to study the Scriptures in their original languages, and by the

sixteenth century the Reformation was challenging many aspects of the traditional Roman Catholic approach to the Bible. Yet it was not until the appearance of the movement in the seventeenth and eighteenth centuries known as the **Enlightenment** that scholars began to talk openly about the need to study the Bible as a thoroughly human literary work. One of the key tenets of the Enlightenment was the belief that people should investigate everything for themselves rather than simply trusting what authorities told them. This meant that the Bible must be subjected to the same process of critical scrutiny as any other book. If it was found to contain errors or contradictions, or if it failed to support the traditional teachings of the church, then it was the duty of enlightened scholars to say so.

In the ensuing controversy, both the defenders and the challengers of traditional approaches to the Bible went to extremes to uphold the truth of their positions. People on both sides of the debate were forced out of positions in the churches and universities of Europe. By the nineteenth century, however, critical study of the Bible had gained a solid footing in Christian circles as Christian leaders came to realize that studying the Bible as a historical and literary work need not conflict with upholding its religious value. Many Christians discovered that historical and literary study could actually enhance their understanding of the Scriptures.

In Jewish circles, the tradition of critical analysis established by the early rabbis and the lack of any centralized authority to enforce uniformity made it easier for many people to accept the rise of biblical criticism. As early as the twelfth century, the renowned Jewish scholar Moses Maimonides was raising questions about the miracle stories in the Hebrew Bible and calling for a more philosophical approach to the interpretation of Scripture. Similar concerns led to the rise of Reform Judaism, a nineteenth-century movement that rejected (among other things) the necessity of obeying the ritual laws of the Torah and the biblical expectation of the coming of a messiah. The Reformists' liberal view of Scripture was strongly opposed by Orthodox Jews who sought to uphold traditional interpretations of the Bible.

Today the Roman Catholic Church, most of the major Protestant denominations, and two of the three major branches of Judaism have officially endorsed the practice of biblical criticism for use in their churches and seminaries. Pastors and other leaders in these groups are required to take courses in the critical study of the Bible as part of their seminary education, and a majority of the scholars who work on the issues addressed in this book belong to one of these traditions. Some of the less threatening conclusions of modern biblical scholarship have been incorporated into the educational programs of local congregations, primarily through programs that seek to explain the historical and social context of particular biblical books or stories. The more challenging aspects of biblical criticism, however, have been slow to trickle down to the ordinary members of Jewish and Christian congregations. This is especially true in more conservative forms of Christianity, such as the Orthodox community and most Protestant evangelical and fundamentalist churches. These churches tend to reject modern biblical scholarship on principle as an attack on the truth of Scripture, though many are willing to make use of studies that shed light on the historical context of the Bible.

IT'S ALL A MATTER OF PERSPECTIVE …

So what is it about critical or academic approaches to Scripture that makes many religious people uneasy? The problem goes beyond disagreements about the meaning of particular biblical texts. At its root are two fundamentally different ways of viewing and interpreting Scripture. A review of some of the key differences between the two approaches will help to illuminate the problem.

1. *Questioning versus trust.* Most Jews and Christians have been taught to trust the Bible even when they fail to understand it or see problems with what it says. For many people, questioning the Bible is the same as questioning God; to embark on this path is sheer arrogance. To critical scholars, by contrast, questioning is the first step to knowledge. Scholars devote their lives to understanding and explaining the biblical text, and not even a lack of data will prevent them from asking questions and seeking answers. Like good detectives, they gather evidence, attempt to make sense of it, and follow where it leads. Their tools are the ordinary methods of textual study, all

of which involve raising questions about the text. Their questioning does not grow out of a lack of respect for the Bible. In fact, many biblical scholars are active members of religious communities who regard their study as a deeply religious activity.

2. *Independence versus conformity.* Many Christian groups have a statement of faith or confession (whether formal or informal) that their members are expected to

Fig. 5.2. Religious people typically view Scriptures as a channel for communicating with God (above), while scholars regard Scriptures primarily as an object of study (below).

endorse. These statements summarize the central beliefs of the group as defined by its founders or other important leaders from its past. Most of these statements draw heavily on the language and ideas of the Bible. As a result, they serve to define and limit how people in the group should interpret the Bible. Academic scholars, on the other hand, work outside of these frameworks of interpretation. Their goal is to gain a better understanding of the biblical text, not to reinforce or undermine the teachings of a particular religious body. Not infrequently, their findings differ from the interpretations implied by a particular group's statement of faith. Many of the tensions that arise between academic scholars and religious communities can be traced to these kinds of differences.

3. *Diversity versus uniformity.* For the most part, Jews and Christians are taught to think of the Bible as a single, uniform book. Their leaders will often talk about what the Bible says or the biblical position on this or that issue. In many cases this way of thinking is linked to ideas about the inspiration of Scripture—the belief that God guided the minds of the biblical authors in such a way that they spoke the truth. People who hold this view insist that behind the obvious diversity of the Bible lies a single divine mind that gives a sense of uniformity and coherence to the whole. Academic scholars, by contrast, focus on the human dimensions of the text. Since most of the books were written and edited by different people at diverse times and places, scholars usually limit their attention to a single book or even a single strand of tradition within a book. Through careful examination of these smaller units, scholars seek to understand how the Bible developed and how the beliefs and practices of the people who used these texts changed over time. They also study how the various books work as literary texts. When they find points of unity amid all this diversity, they attribute it to historical, social, or literary factors, not to divine causality. Scholars do not attempt to determine what role any supernatural beings might have played in the production of these texts, since this question cannot be answered using the methods of academic scholarship.

4. *Understanding versus application.* People who use the Bible as members of a religious community generally believe that the Bible is true in its essential message, and many make a serious effort to live by what it teaches. Some insist that believers should study the Bible for themselves, while others prefer to trust what their leaders tell them about its contents. Much of the instruction that takes place in these groups is oriented toward applying the Bible (whether directly or indirectly) to the lives of their members. Among academic scholars, on the other hand, the goal is to understand the text as an entity in itself. The question of how that text might apply to the lives of believers lies outside their sphere of concern. Historical scholars focus on what the text meant in its original historical context, not what it means today. Literary scholars might reflect on the experience of the contemporary reader as part of their analysis, but their concern is to explain how the text works as a piece of literature, not to talk about how believers should live in light of its contents. The approaches used by religious people and biblical scholars are not mutually exclusive. Instead, each comes to the text with a different set of questions and interests that determines the kinds of insights that each will take away from the experience.

SO WHAT EXACTLY DO BIBLICAL SCHOLARS DO?

The academic study of the Bible is a highly diverse enterprise that involves thousands of scholars scattered all over the world. Historically, the field has been dominated by males of European descent, including many from the United States. In the last few decades, however, women and people from non-European backgrounds have become increasingly influential in shaping the direction and development of the field. Most biblical scholars serve as professors at colleges, universities, or seminaries, but some are employed at other types of institutions (including churches), and a few work as independent scholars. Some are deeply religious, while others are not. Within the academic arena, Jews and Christians work together with agnostics and atheists (and a smattering of people from other religious traditions) to advance their understanding of the Bible and the world in which it arose.

Fig. 5.3. A biblical scholar presents a paper to other scholars at the annual meeting of the Society of Biblical Literature.

Scholars share their work with one another by presenting papers at professional conferences and publishing books and articles.

Biblical scholars employ all of the methods developed by other disciplines for the study of ancient texts along with other approaches that are distinctive to the field of biblical studies. No scholar is an expert in all of the methods; most choose to specialize in one or a few modes of study. As a rule, scholars focus their efforts on a fairly limited set of materials or time period, such as the eighth-century prophets or the book of Psalms. Some devote their lives to studying the historical background of the Bible, especially the history and culture of Egypt and Mesopotamia. This process of specialization ensures that scholars have the training and skills that they need to carry out research and make reliable judgments in a particular area of study. It also means that scholars who work in a particular subfield must rely on the work of scholars in other areas to assist them in their work. Regular communication (via papers and publications) is essential for the advancement of knowledge in the field.

Most of the methods employed by contemporary scholars require knowledge of ancient languages and are therefore too technical for use in an introductory course. But the results of their studies can be understood by people with no technical background. All that is needed is a sense of curiosity about other cultures and a willingness to study and learn new material. Still, it can be hard to understand how scholars arrive at their results without at least a general awareness of the methods used in contemporary biblical scholarship.

THE THREE WORLDS OF BIBLICAL SCHOLARSHIP

In recent years it has become fashionable to speak about the three worlds in which biblical scholars operate. Some scholars study the world behind the text; others focus on the world within the text; still others explore the world in front of the text. Most of the methods employed by contemporary biblical scholars can be categorized under one of these three headings.

1. The World behind the Text

Since the earliest days of critical study of the Hebrew Bible, scholars have labored to relate the biblical text to its broader historical surroundings. Scholars who work in this area are concerned with understanding the world in which the Bible arose, which some call "the world behind the text." Three types of questions have guided most of their work.

(a) Where did the text come from? One issue that has engaged scholars since the beginning of biblical criticism is the history of the biblical text. Scholars who work in this area seek to determine why the texts were written (specifically, who wrote or edited them and when/where/why they carried out their work); what kinds of source materials the authors or editors might have used in preparing their texts (**source criticism, tradition criticism**); how these earlier materials might have been reworked as they were used by the people who passed them on (**form criticism**); and how the final authors or editors revised their source materials to integrate them into their own composition (**redaction criticism**). Also included under this heading are scholars who study how the text was passed on after being written (**textual criticism**) and how the final text was incorporated into the community's Scriptures (**canonical criticism**).

The central problem facing all of these methods of study is a shortage of outside evidence to confirm or disprove their conclusions. All scholarly theories concerning the origins and history of a particular book or passage are rooted in detailed studies of the biblical text, and scholars often disagree about how this evidence should be interpreted. Decades of scholarly debate have produced broad agreement on many of the key points concerning the origins of individual books and the Bible as a whole, but new theories continue to arise periodically to challenge the status quo. The highly speculative nature of much of the work in this area makes it one of the most controversial subfields within biblical scholarship.

(b) What really happened? Perhaps the earliest critical question to be raised about the Hebrew Bible was whether the events that it narrates really happened as described. Long before the rise of critical scholarship, Jews and Christians (and their detractors) were voicing concerns about some of the supernatural events depicted in the Bible. As archaeologists began to uncover records from the lands around Israel in the eighteenth and nineteenth centuries, further questions arose concerning various discrepancies between these records and the Bible. (For more on these points, see chapter 9.) Scholars who work on these kinds of issues use the standard methods of historical study to reconstruct what happened in the period covered by the biblical narratives. Some are archaeologists who dig up the hard data studied by historians, while others are textual scholars who labor to integrate the archaeological data with the literary records. Some historical scholars focus exclusively on the land of Israel, while others investigate the history of Israel's neighbors.

Historians encounter the same problems in this area as they do when studying other ancient civilizations: the fragmentary nature of ancient sources, the upper-class and masculine bias of most literary materials, the difficulty of relating archaeological finds to textual records, and so on. The religious content of the Bible also poses a challenge for historical scholars, as the methods of historical study require them to look for natural causes (social, political, economic, psychological, and the like) for the many events that the biblical authors attribute to divine action. Scholars have developed ways of working around these difficulties, but problems continue to plague efforts to reconstruct the history of the biblical period.

(c) What was life like in ancient times? While some historians labor to figure out how much of the Hebrew Bible is historical or how the biblical text reached its present form, others work on reconstructing the social life of the people of ancient Israel. Social historians aim to understand what it was like to live in the world depicted in the pages of the Bible. Some focus on the experiences of individuals—how they made their living, where they ate and slept, whom they married, how they trained their children, what they did with their dead, and so forth. Others look at the broader society—who had power over whom, how leaders exercised authority over the group, how violations and resistance were handled, how goods were distributed, how the group related to people around them, and the like. Some focus on a particular historical era, while others seek to trace changes over time. Social historians also seek to describe the religious beliefs and practices of the people whom they study at both the individual and the societal level. In this task they are assisted by theologians and historians of ideas who study how religious beliefs changed or remained the same over time.

Like others who have studied the history of ancient Israel, social scientists face the challenges of limited and biased materials, but they have the advantage of being able to draw on comparative materials from other cultures to serve as models to aid them in their reconstructions. Scholars debate whether some of these models are comparable enough to be relevant to the study of ancient Israel.

2. The World within the Text

In recent years many scholars have criticized the traditional historical approach for its failure to take seriously the literary character of the various books that are included in the Hebrew Bible. In their effort to reconstruct the world behind the text, historians usually end up dividing books into fragments and attributing various parts of their content to earlier sources. These fragmentary (and theoretical) sources then become the building blocks for a reconstruction of the history and society of ancient Israel.

No one would deny that historical studies of the Hebrew Bible have yielded useful results. Too often, however, historical scholars have ignored the fact that the biblical texts were written to be read as coherent literary works. One of the most consistent features of literature in every culture is that it creates a "world within the text," an imaginary space that the reader is invited to inhabit during the process of reading. Literary scholars seek to uncover and describe this world. Three types of questions guide much of the work of scholars who labor in this area.

(a) What does the text mean? Not all literature has a message; some is written simply to be enjoyed. But most of the literature that made it into the Hebrew Bible was preserved because it said something that people thought was important. One of the tasks of a literary scholar is to uncover and describe that core message. Some scholars believe that it is possible with careful investigation to arrive at the specific meaning that the author or editor intended when preparing the work. Others see this as a hopeless enterprise, particularly for works that have passed through as many editorial hands as the books of the Hebrew Bible.

At the most basic level, understanding the meaning of a text involves decoding the language in which it was written. The bulk of the Hebrew Bible was composed in the Hebrew language, but some of the later books include passages that were written in **Aramaic**, a related language that became the medium of international communication across the ancient Near East under the patronage of Assyrian and Babylonian rulers. Many Hebrew and Aramaic words and expressions have meanings that vary with the context, and a few words are so rare that their meaning remains uncertain. In some cases the meaning of the words is clear, but questions remain about how they fit together to form clauses and sentences. Answering these kinds of questions requires the skills of scholars trained in historical and comparative linguistics. Scholars who work in this area are required to master not only Hebrew and Aramaic, but also the closely related languages of Israel's neighbors. Contemporary theories of linguistics also play a vital role in their research. Despite their best efforts, uncertainties remain over the precise meaning of many verses in the Hebrew Bible.

(b) How does the text work? In recent years, many scholars have begun to apply the methods and perspectives of contemporary literary criticism to analyze the Hebrew Bible in the same manner as any other work of literature. When examining a story, for example, they might ask questions about the plot, the characters, the setting, the use of symbolism and imagery, the author's point of view, and other features commonly seen in stories. When studying a poem or song, they might highlight its structure, its mood, its use of language, and the various literary techniques that it uses to move the minds and emotions of the audience. When investigating a speech or other piece of persuasive literature, they might look at how the text is organized, how the argument unfolds, and what kinds of rhetorical devices are used to appeal to the intellect or emotions of the audience.

In all of these approaches, serious attention would be given to the experiential dimension of the text, specifically, how it appeals to the imagination of the reader in order to produce new insights and experiences. Questions about how the imaginary world created by the text might relate to the historical circumstances of the author and/or audience would be left to one side in an effort to describe and appreciate the literary artistry and beauty of the finished work. Scholars who apply literary methods to the Hebrew Bible often differ in their analyses of specific texts, but this is common to all forms of literary study, since no two people will ever read a literary text in precisely the same manner.

(c) How does the text relate to other texts? Every literary work is dependent to some degree on other works that have gone before it. Some literary scholars seek to uncover the links and resonances that exist between diverse pieces of literature. At the simplest level, this might involve tracing references and allusions to earlier literary works and identifying how those references serve to enhance the effectiveness of the work. At a more sophisticated level, it could mean looking for common patterns or structures that run through multiple pieces of literature or an entire literary tradition.

Yet another way of evaluating a piece of literature is to examine how it follows or diverges from the expectations of its genre. A **genre** is a culturally conditioned set of rules and conventions that serves as a guideline for the composition and interpretation of individual literary works. Examples of genres include short stories, poems, scientific treatises, and mystery novels. Genre analysis can help scholars to better appreciate the literary skills and artistry of the final author or editor as well as others who might have contributed to the text's creation. Genre analysis provides the big picture within which other forms of literary criticism operate.

3. The World in Front of the Text

Texts do not exist in a vacuum; a reader is needed to convert the black marks on the page into words and sentences that carry meaning. Until fairly recently, the activity of the reader in producing meaning out of written texts was largely ignored by biblical scholars. Today there are many scholars who seek to understand the role of readers in the interpretive process: this is "the world in front of the text." Their interests are diverse, but their studies, like the others, can be summarized under three broad headings.

(a) How do readers make sense of the text? Drawing meaning out of a text is the result of a complex and dynamic interaction between the psyche of a reader and the words and ideas that an author has encoded in ink marks on a page. All texts are open to multiple interpretations, and readers invariably bring different experiences and abilities to their encounter with the text. As a result, readers routinely derive different meanings from the same text.

Scholars who study the role of the reader use a wide variety of methods. Some conduct "close readings" of specific passages in order to identify places where the texts themselves are ambiguous and thus give rise to differing interpretations. Others seek to understand how gender, ethnicity, economic background, and similar factors influence the interpretive activity of readers. Still others focus on the underlying dynamics of the reading process, that is, how the human mind interacts with the subliminal structures of literature to produce meaning from written texts. A final group is concerned with the theoretical side of the reading process, including whether the meaning of a text is related to the intentions of the author or lies entirely within the mind of the reader. This area of biblical studies is highly diverse, with scholars using a variety of theories and methods in their work. As with literary criticism, their findings are as distinctive as their methods.

(b) How do readers evaluate the text? When the Bible is used in a religious setting, most Jews and Christians tend to accept what it says as both true and relevant to their lives. Even those who study the text with critical eyes tend to limit their concerns to particular issues or verses. Few believers are bold enough to raise questions about the fundamental beliefs and values embedded in these texts. Scholars, on the other hand, study the Bible as a product of its times, a historically conditioned book that reflects the thinking and values of a premodern society. Some of the beliefs and values expressed in the Bible have a timeless quality that makes them readily applicable to the modern world, but others conflict with contemporary ideas about the nature of the universe and human morality.

The task of sorting through the biblical materials and evaluating their relevance to the modern world is carried out by scholars known as theologians. Most theologians work within the context of a particular religious tradition, but this does not mean that they necessarily accept everything that their tradition (or the Bible) says. Some focus on the ideological dimensions of the Bible, exploring how biblical ideas about the nature of God or the origins of the universe might be brought into dialogue with the findings of modern science or the writings of contemporary philosophers. Others grapple with the moral and ethical problems raised by the Bible, such as the negative opinions of women and homosexuals and the positive views of war and violence that appear in many biblical texts. Theologians vary widely in the degree to which they are willing to challenge the biblical text, with some adopting a defensive posture and others rejecting much of what they find in the Bible. But virtually all theologians agree that the Bible must be subjected to critical scrutiny before it is applied to the contemporary world.

(c) How do readers use the text? For Jews and Christians, the Bible is not a book to be read once and discarded—it is a living text that deserves to be studied and applied to the lives of believers. Individuals rely on its words for inspiration and guidance in their daily affairs; groups use it to structure their worship, their teaching, their organizations, and their engagement with the world outside the group. Scholars may do any or all of these things as members of a religious community, but most do

not see this as a part of their role as scholars. Most would draw a sharp line between the scholarly activity of studying how religious people use the Bible in their daily lives and the personal activity of applying the biblical text to one's own life.

Some scholars, however, have argued that understanding cannot be divorced from action and that responsible scholarship should include practical engagement with the social message of the Bible. Many of these scholars are actively engaged in politics, where they use the Bible to support a variety of positions on such issues as abortion, economic justice, war, and gay rights. Outside the United States, the Bible has been cited by Christian leaders to motivate people to participate in both nonviolent and violent revolutions under a system of thought known as liberation theology. Scholars who regard advocacy as an element of scholarship argue that traditional scholars are abdicating their social responsibility in a misguided effort to maintain the scholarly illusion of being objective. In their view, there is no such thing as objectivity. All readers are subjective, and it is more honest and fruitful to acknowledge one's subjectivity and incorporate it into one's scholarly work. This view of scholarship has been resisted by most biblical scholars, but its influence has been growing in recent years.

PUTTING IT INTO PRACTICE: PSALM 137

Many students who are encountering biblical scholarship for the first time find themselves feeling confused and frustrated by the experience. What is the point of all these different approaches to the Hebrew Bible? Why not simply read the text and do what it says? The problem with such a simple reading of the Hebrew Bible is that it too often leads to misreading, misinterpretation, and misuse of the biblical text. The Hebrew Bible arose in a culture very different from our own, and much of what it says is clothed in language whose meaning is not immediately apparent to a modern reader. There is also much in the Bible that requires critical evaluation before it is applied to the modern world. The Hebrew Bible includes verses

that support such morally troubling practices as slavery, brutality in warfare, and the abuse of women, not to mention the use of capital punishment for such offenses as comitting adultery, following other religions, and refusing to obey one's parents. The work of biblical scholars is crucial for evaluating what the Bible says on these issues.

But biblical scholarship does more than simply protect against misuse of the biblical text. The methods used by biblical scholars also help us to understand the text better by raising questions that lead to insights that could easily be overlooked by an individual reader. A brief test case will offer a glimpse of the kinds of insights that can arise from a judicious application of biblical scholarship.

Psalm 137

1 By the rivers of Babylon—
    there we sat down and there we wept
    when we remembered Zion.
2 On the willows there
    we hung up our harps.
3 For there our captors
    asked us for songs,
    and our tormentors asked for mirth, saying,
    "Sing us one of the songs of Zion!"

4 How could we sing the LORD's song
    in a foreign land?
5 If I forget you, O Jerusalem,
    let my right hand wither!
6 Let my tongue cling to the roof of my mouth,
    if I do not remember you,
    if I do not set Jerusalem
    above my highest joy.

7 Remember, O LORD, against the Edomites
    the day of Jerusalem's fall,
    how they said, "Tear it down! Tear it down!
    Down to its foundations!"
8 O daughter Babylon, you devastator!
    Happy shall they be who pay you back
    what you have done to us!
9 Happy shall they be who take your little ones
    and dash them against the rock!

How would the three types of scholars described above approach this text?

1. Scholars who study the world behind the text (historians) would begin by looking for clues concerning when, where, and why the psalm was written. The reference to Babylon as a "devastator" in verse 8 indicates that the psalm was written at some point after the Babylonians had conquered the people of Judah in 586 B.C.E., while verses 1 and 4 imply that the author was one of the many people taken away to Babylonia after the conquest. The author's current location is unclear—the past tense in verses 1-3 seems to imply that the author has returned to Judah, while the poignant expressions of devotion to Jerusalem in verses 5-7 suggest that the city is still in ruins and the author is living in Babylon. If this is the case, it

Fig. 5.4. Jews today still gather to read Scripture and mourn on the anniversary of the destruction of the Jerusalem temple by the Babylonians in 586 B.C.E.

would mean that the text was written before the Persians conquered the Babylonians in 539 B.C.E. and allowed the exiled people of Judah to return to their land and rebuild their capital city. Historical scholars would also want to investigate how the Babylonians treated the people of Judah during their time in Babylonia (verse 3) and what the Edomites (a neighboring people) did to call forth the harsh sentiments expressed in verse 7. Minor points that might call for historical investigation include the musical practices mentioned in verses 1-3 and the practice of dashing babies onto rocks (common in ancient warfare) in verse 9. The psalm shows no clear signs of later editing, so the question of how the text reached its present form would probably not arise in this case. Since this is not a

narrative text, questions about historical accuracy would also be irrelevant, though scholars certainly would take note of the way the author's experience has shaped how he or she views and interprets the past.

2. Scholars who study the world within the text (namely, literary scholars) would observe that the text is a poem that can be compared with other poems in the Hebrew Bible. Careful examination would reveal that the kind of structured parallelism that characterizes most Hebrew poetry is less visible in this poem. This might be attributed to a lack of skill, but it could also be seen as an intentional literary device designed to create an impression of strong emotion. A literary scholar would work through the entire psalm line by line in an effort to show how the structure and language of the poem combine to communicate not only a set of ideas but also a profound sense of emotion. Points that might be deemed worthy of discussion include the vivid imagery that runs throughout the poem; the artificial quotations that appear in verses 3 and 7; the use of personification and apostrophe (direct speech to someone who is not present) in verses 5, 6, 8, and 9; the presence of repetition at key points in the psalm; the manner in which various characters ("we," the Babylonians, the Edomites, and God) are depicted in the poem; and the deeply emotive language that is employed throughout the psalm. A literary scholar would also investigate how these various literary devices work together to create the distinctive emotional tone of the poem.

3. A scholar concerned with the world in front of the text (that is, the role of the reader) might begin by noting how the poem offers only a rough sketch of the narrator's situation, leaving the reader to complete the picture through the use of imagination. In this way the text draws the reader into a profound encounter with the emotion of the text. Similar observations could be made about the way the text invites (or manipulates) the reader to adopt a particular view of the circumstances lamented in the poem. Questions could also be raised about some of the attitudes and moral perspectives implied in the poem. While it is easy to empathize with the deep expressions of pain and loss that are voiced in verses 1-7, a critical reader might feel compelled to ask whether the hateful prayers for vengeance in verses 7-9 and the associated image of a

deity who might answer those prayers represent a morally acceptable response to this or any situation. Some scholars would reject these attitudes as unwise, immoral, or inconsistent with moral standards expressed elsewhere in the Bible, while others would see in them an honest expression of an attitude that could motivate oppressed people to take action to liberate themselves from their oppressors. Still others might observe that the passage seems to call for the oppressed to leave their deliverance to God, thus encouraging people today to do the same. Finally, Jewish scholars might find this passage useful for motivating other Jews to remain loyal to Jerusalem and the Jewish people (verses 5-6). For some, this might be expressed in active support for the policies and actions of the state of Israel as a means of defending its population against similar sufferings in the future.

CONCLUSION

Contemporary scholars bring a wide range of methods to their study of the Hebrew Bible. Some work primarily on historical questions (the world behind the text), while others examine the literary dimensions of the text (the world within the text) or study the many ways in which the text is used by contemporary readers (the world in front of the text). Some of these scholarly methods have found their way into religious congregations—in fact, many biblical scholars are practicing Jews or Christians—while others have been greeted with skepticism or even hostility because of the challenges that they pose to traditional interpretations of the Hebrew Bible.

No scholar would claim that academic approaches to the Bible are infallible or that they represent the only way to study the biblical text. But all would agree that our understanding of the Hebrew Bible has been vastly enriched by the development and application of biblical criticism over the last two centuries.

EXERCISE 8

Read the following three passages in your Bible and think about how scholars using each of the three approaches described in this chapter might analyze the passage. Then choose one of the passages and write a three-paragraph report that summarizes your observations (one paragraph on each approach).

• Genesis 11:1-9
• Deuteronomy 22:13-21
• Zephaniah 1:14-18

PART TWO
THE WORLD OF THE HEBREW BIBLE

Fig. 6.1. The spring at Ein Gedi brings life-giving water to the barren wilderness near the Dead Sea.

The Importance of Geography

*When they had come to the land of Canaan, Abram passed through the land to the place at Shechem, to the oak of Moreh. At that time the Canaanites were in the land. Then the L*ORD *appeared to Abram, and said, "To your offspring I will give this land." So he built there an altar to the L*ORD*, who had appeared to him. From there he moved on to the hill country on the east of Bethel, and pitched his tent, with Bethel on the west and Ai on the east; and there he built an altar to the L*ORD *and invoked the name of the L*ORD*. And Abram journeyed on by stages toward the Negeb.* (Genesis 12:5-9)

When Saul had taken the kingship over Israel, he fought against all his enemies on every side— against Moab, against the Ammonites, against Edom, against the kings of Zobah, and against the Philistines; wherever he turned he routed them. He did valiantly, and struck down the Amalekites, and rescued Israel out of the hands of those who plundered them. (1 Samuel 14:47-48)

*O children of Zion, be glad and rejoice in the L*ORD *your God; for he has given the early rain for your vindication, he has poured down for you abundant rain, the early and the later rain, as before. The threshing floors shall be full of grain, the vats shall overflow with wine and oil. I will repay you for the years that the swarming locust has eaten, the hopper, the destroyer, and the cutter, my great army, which I sent against you. You shall eat in plenty and be satisfied, and praise the name of the L*ORD *your God, who has dealt wondrously with you.* (Joel 2:23-26)

Most people who use the Hebrew Bible in a church or synagogue know little or nothing about the geographic environment in which these texts arose. As a result, they miss much of the richness and depth of the biblical narratives. Many of the stories in the Hebrew Bible assume that the reader is familiar with the physical world in which the stories take place. Most of the key developments in the political history of Palestine can be traced in part to its strategic geographic location. Virtually every aspect of the social and economic life of the people who produced these texts was influenced by the physical environment in which they lived. The more we know about the geography of the land of Palestine, the better we will understand the history, culture, and literature of the people whose lives are depicted in the Hebrew Bible.

THE LAND OF PALESTINE

The people who wrote and edited the Hebrew Bible lived in a small territory at the eastern end of the Mediterranean Sea known today as Israel. The name Israel is used in at least three different senses in the Bible: (a) as a *geographic* term, referring to the general region in which many of the stories of the Bible are said to have taken place; (b) as an *ethnic* term, identifying a particular group of people who lived in this region; and (c) as a *political* term, designating a kingdom that occupied the northern part of this region for more than two hundred years. This ambiguity has led many biblical scholars to employ other terms besides *Israel* when speaking about the geographical territory associated with the Hebrew Bible.

But other names are also problematic. In ancient times the territory was known as **Canaan**, but the precise identity of the geographical region covered by this term is unclear. The name Palestine is similarly ambiguous. The word comes from the name of a non-Hebrew people group that lived along the southern coast, the **Philistines**. It was used by the Greeks as a geographic designation for the general area, and later by the Romans as the name of a political province that included modern Syria. The name continued to be used, sometimes officially and sometimes unofficially, from the Roman period until the creation of the state of Israel in 1948, though the borders of the lands encompassed by that term changed repeatedly. The non-Jewish people known today as Palestinians are the descendants of people who lived in this area during the centuries prior to the formation of the state of Israel.

Thus it appears that none of the names in common use is really accurate when referring to the geography of the region. But the term *Israel* appears so frequently with different senses in the Hebrew Bible that many biblical

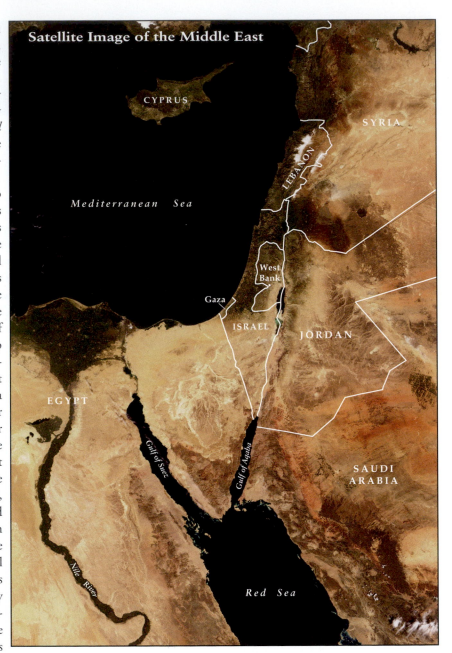

Fig. 6.2. This satellite map shows the location of the contemporary nation of Israel and its immediate neighbors.

scholars prefer to use the term *Palestine* (or ancient Palestine) when referring to the geographic region in which the kingdoms of Israel and Judah were situated.

Between a Rock and a Hard Place

Palestine is part of the region commonly known as the Middle East. (When discussing the period covered by the Hebrew Bible, scholars usually call this region the *ancient Near East*.) The Middle East extends southward from modern-day Turkey to Egypt and eastward to include the lands of Iran and Saudi Arabia.

The satellite photo on the previous page reveals the stark topography that characterizes the region around Israel and the political boundaries of the modern countries that occupy this region. Notice where the modern state of Israel appears on the photo—it occupies one of the few green spots on the photo. From space, most of the region looks like a barren desert.

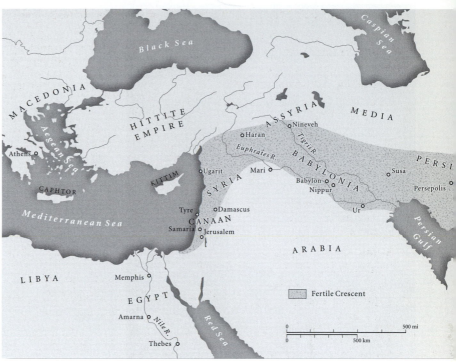

Fig. 6.3. The ancient Near East. Note the location of the Fertile Crescent, the band of territory that has enough water for permanent human habitation.

In reality, the area is not as barren as it appears. The lightest areas in the photo are indeed deserts, but much of the area has enough resources to support human life. The most precious resource throughout the region is water. It is no accident that the great civilizations of the Middle East arose in areas that had stable water supplies—Mesopotamia (modern-day Iraq), watered by the great Tigris and Euphrates rivers; Egypt, blessed by the consistent flooding of the Nile River; and Palestine, where rains spawned by the Mediterranean Sea soak the region often enough to support a culture based on farming and herding. For this reason the strip of territory that extends from Mesopotamia through Palestine to Egypt is called the *Fertile Crescent*. Even in areas where water is scarce, humans have been able to eke out a living by migrating with the limited rainfall and congregating around the many oases (natural springs) that dot the region.

The uneven distribution of water across the Middle East helps to explain why Palestine has been a crossroads of civilization and a sphere of conflict since the beginning of recorded history. Palestine occupies a key position between two other well-watered regions, Mesopotamia and Egypt, where major civilizations arose. To the west

is the Mediterranean Sea, while much of the land to the east is desert. If the residents of Mesopotamia or Egypt wanted to move goods or armies across the region, the easiest route ran along the coast of Palestine (a road called the Way of the Sea). Another major route (the King's Highway) crossed its eastern perimeter. Thus the rulers of Mesopotamia and the Egyptian Pharaohs both believed that it was important for them to control the strategic land bridge of Palestine. Sometimes they used armies to achieve their goals, while on other occasions they simply threatened or entered into alliances with the local rulers of Palestine, including the kings of Israel and Judah.

From time to time the kings of Mesopotamia and Egypt encountered troubles that hindered their ability to control the region (for example, when they were engaged in wars with their neighbors or squabbling over succession to the throne). During these periods the residents of Palestine were able to assert their independence and build up armies of their own to defend their control of the region. Eventually, however, one or the other of the great powers would succeed in resolving its problems

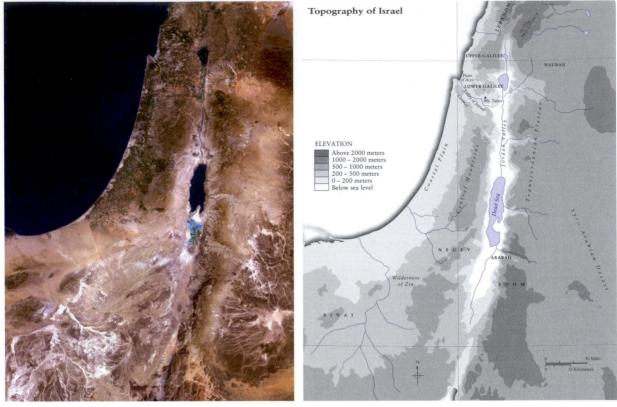

Topography of Israel

ELEVATION
- Above 2000 meters
- 1000 – 2000 meters
- 500 – 1000 meters
- 200 – 500 meters
- 0 – 200 meters
- Below sea level

Fig. 6.4. (left) A satellite image of the land of Palestine; (right) a topographic map showing the major elevation changes in this narrow strip of land.

and would move once again to assert its dominance over the region, and the cycle would begin anew. Many of the battles that are described in the Hebrew Bible took place during one of these periods. By the end of the biblical period, a series of kings from the north—first the Assyrians, then the Babylonians, then the Persians—had conquered this strategic territory and incorporated it into

their empires. (For more on the political history of the region, see chapters 8 and 9.)

Good Fences Make Good Neighbors

For a land that receives so much attention in the news, Palestine is surprisingly small. The Hebrew Bible defines

Fig. 6.5. (left) A village in Upper Galilee; (right) the mountains of southern Lebanon.

the territory of Israel as extending from Dan in the north to Beersheba in the south, a distance of approximately 155 miles. The distance from the Jordan River in the east to the Mediterranean Sea in the west averages forty-five miles. Thus the land of Palestine is about the size of the state of Vermont. People in the ancient world could have walked across the entire territory from east to west in two to three days, or from north to south in a little over a week.

The land of Palestine is marked off from the surrounding territories by a series of natural borders that played a key role in the social, economic, and political history of the region. To the north are mountains; to the east, the Jordan River valley; to the south, the desert; and to the west, the sea. None of these boundaries is rigid, but together they served to distinguish the residents of Palestine from their immediate neighbors.

The satellite photo on the previous page shows what the land of Palestine looks like from space. From here the physical barriers between Palestine and the neighboring territories do not seem particularly formidable. The map on the right highlights the key physical features of the region. Here the elevation differences can be seen more clearly.

To the north. The mountains that occupy the northern end of the land of Palestine (called Upper Galilee) are not especially tall, averaging 3,000–4,000 feet in elevation, but they are fairly dense and rugged. The mountains farther north (labeled *Lebanon* and *Anti-Lebanon* on the map) are much taller, averaging 6,000–8,000 feet above sea level, with one peak reaching more than 10,000 feet in elevation. The photos in figure 6.5 show typical scenes from these regions.

To the north of these mountains lies the territory of Phoenicia, a land of city-states that dominated the Mediterranean sea trade for much of the period covered by the Hebrew Bible. The biblical authors usually refer to this region by the names of its two primary cities, Tyre and Sidon. The Phoenicians established trading posts and colonies all around the Mediterranean basin, from which they eventually created a vast sea-trading empire. But they made no effort to incorporate their neighbors to the south into that empire; instead, they formed alliances. Geography played a key role in this decision. The mountains that divided Phoenicia from Palestine posed a significant barrier to the movement of ancient armies, and the Palestinian coastline was virtually devoid of natural harbors that could be used by Phoenician ships. Phoenician traders, on the other hand, did not need wide roads to transport their wares by animal caravan through the maze of valleys that cut across the mountains. Through trade and political alliances, Phoenician goods and coins found their way into Palestine on a regular basis. Thus geography helped to protect the people of Palestine from domination by their neighbors to the north and led to a more cooperative relationship between the peoples of Phoenicia and Palestine.

To the east. The land of Palestine is marked off from the territories to its east by a great rift valley that extends southward from Syria through the Red Sea and across the continent of Africa to the nation of Mozambique. This valley, which averages ten miles wide in the vicinity of Palestine, marks the place where two of the earth's tectonic plates meet. Much of the northern end of this valley is traversed by the Jordan River, a fairly narrow and winding stream whose elevation drops dramatically from 300 feet above sea level in the Huleh Valley in the north of Palestine to more than 1,300 feet below sea level at the

Fig. 6.6. (left) The Jordan River brings life to the barren rift valley that separates Israel from Jordan; (right) a view across the Dead Sea to Jordan.

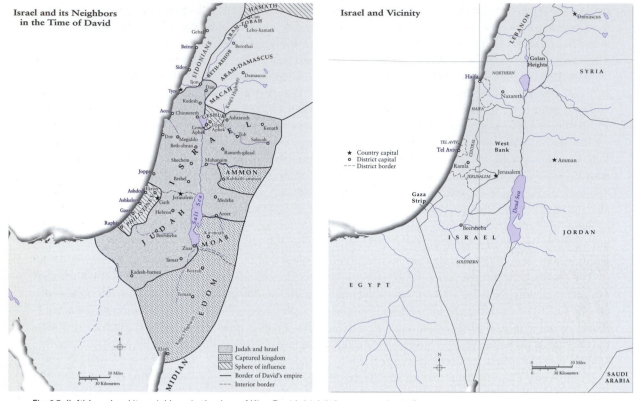

Fig. 6.7. (left) Israel and its neighbors in the days of King David; (right) the same region today.

shores of the **Dead Sea** in the south, the lowest point on the surface of the earth.

For much of its length, the rift valley poses a significant barrier to travel and commerce. The channel carved by the Jordan River averages half a mile wide and a hundred feet deep, and its banks were covered in biblical times with thick brush that was nearly impenetrable in places and populated by wild animals. The valley is also quite hot in the summer, with daytime temperatures reaching 120°F (49°C). Away from the river, the valley is surrounded by steep cliffs that had to be traversed or bypassed in order to reach the plateaus where the people lived. None of these factors would have deterred a determined army or trade caravan; in fact, there were several trade routes that crossed the valley. But the geography of the region did make ordinary interchange between people on each side of the river more difficult.

Deep river valleys and gorges also divided the eastern bank of the Jordan River into several distinct regions with their own peoples and cultures. In the Hebrew Bible these

territories are known (running from north to south) as Bashan, Gilead, Ammon, **Moab**, and **Edom**. Today these areas are included in the kingdom of Jordan, as shown on the maps in figure 6.7.

In ancient times these areas were linked by a road called the King's Highway that served as the major inland route between Mesopotamia to the north and Egypt and Arabia to the south (see figure 6.7). Like the people of Palestine, the residents of these areas often found themselves caught in the middle of the political and economic competition that characterized relations between their neighbors to the north and south. As their fortunes alternated between eras of subservience and periods of independence, so also their interactions with the inhabitants of Palestine varied from cooperation to conflict. Several biblical narratives portray the residents of these regions as distant relatives of the people of Israel, signifying that at least some of the residents of Palestine viewed the people across the Jordan more favorably than the distant powers of Mesopotamia and Egypt. But the Bible also includes many stories of tension and warfare between them, suggesting that relations between people on each side of the Jordan were more often characterized by suspicion and hostility.

To the northeast of Palestine lies the nation of Syria, or Aram as it is known in the Hebrew Bible (see figure 6.7). Because there were fewer geographic barriers to travel and trade in this area, the kings of Israel had a vested interest in the affairs of Syria/Aram. The rift valley is relatively narrow and shallow here, and the passes through the mountains are broad enough to have accommodated one of the two major trade routes that linked Mesopotamia and Egypt, "the Way of the Sea." Because of its proximity to Mesopotamia, Syria was the first to feel the pressure when the rulers of the various Mesopotamian kingdoms felt the urge to expand their territory southward to tighten their control over the trade routes. But Syria also experienced periods of independence and military success when the Mesopotamian kings were weak or distracted. During these times they frequently came into conflict with the kings of Israel, sometimes as a result of territorial disputes and sometimes at the instigation of one of their neighbors. At the peak of their power, the armies of Syria controlled the coastal plain of Palestine and much of the territory east of the Jordan River.

But the relatively low physical barriers between Mesopotamia, Palestine, and Syria, together with the strategic value of the trade routes that crossed the region, made it inevitable that the kings of Mesopotamia would seek to dominate the affairs of the nations to their south.

To the south. During the biblical period the northern two-thirds of Palestine was covered by forests, farmland, and pasture. In the southern region, called the **Negev**, however, the land receives only enough rain to support grasslands (used for grazing) and limited forms of agriculture. Even these minimal activities are difficult to sustain in the harsh and inhospitable desert called the Sinai, as shown in the photos in figure 6.8.

Bedouin shepherds have grazed their herds in the Negev region for millennia, but permanent habitation has been limited mostly to sites with wells or oases. The bulk of the Sinai Desert would have been virtually uninhabited in ancient times, providing a natural buffer between the people of Palestine and the people of Egypt to

Fig. 6.8. Scenes from the Negev Desert at the southern end of Palestine.

the southwest. This buffer was by no means impassable; several well-worn trade routes (including the Way of the Sea) allowed traders and armies to move freely across the desert. But the sheer distances that were involved (as many as 150 miles each way, requiring ten days of difficult travel) helped to reduce the amount of contact between the two regions and to promote the development of distinct cultures in Palestine and Egypt. Nevertheless, Egypt did have an effect on Palestine by two primary means: the regular exchange of trade goods between the two areas and the influence of Egyptian armies that were sent from time to time to protect the trade routes or to halt an invading army that threatened Egypt. The fact that Egypt had a steady source of water in the Nile River also made it a popular destination for people from Palestine seeking food during times of famine.

To the west. The western border of Palestine is the Mediterranean Sea. The coast of Palestine has almost no natural harbors, making it harder for seafaring peoples to threaten the inland residents of Palestine. This lack of harbors also discouraged the residents of Palestine from developing a fishing or sea-trading industry of their own. But the presence of a watery border did not provide complete protection from their neighbors to the west. In the twelfth century B.C.E., a group known as the Sea Peoples moved into the eastern Mediterranean region, probably from Greece or western Turkey, and built settlements in some of the coastal areas. One group, called the Philistines, took over the southern coastal region of Palestine, the area known today as the Gaza Strip. To protect themselves, they erected a number of fortified cities that became the focal points of a distinctive Philistine culture. They also built up a strong army that enabled them to extend their power farther inland, where a strip of rich farmland called the **Shephelah** became an inviting target as their numbers increased. The Hebrew Bible tells many stories of battles between the Philistines and the people who lived in the nearby mountains (the area later called Judah) over this territory. When the mountain dwellers finally grew strong enough to drive the Philistines out of the Shephelah, they built a number of fortified cities in this area to protect themselves against the Philistine threat. These same cities played a major role in their defense against later invaders.

EXERCISE 9

Read the following passages from the Hebrew Bible, paying attention to the places and peoples that they mention. Then use the maps in this chapter to locate as many of these sites as possible. Finally, choose three of the texts and write a paragraph explaining how they relate to this chapter's discussion of the ways in which geographical factors affected relations between the residents of Palestine and their neighbors.

• Genesis 42:1-17
• Judges 3:12-30
• 2 Samuel 5:17-25
• 1 Kings 5:1-12
• 2 Kings 17:1-6
• 2 Kings 25:1-12
• 2 Chronicles 12:1-9

Getting the Lay of the Land

Geography also played a major role in shaping the way people lived and the events that took place within the natural borders of the land of Palestine. Some areas receive enough rain to produce a wide variety of agricultural crops, while others are barren desert. In some places the soil is deep and rich, while in others it is shallow and rocky. Some parts of the land are relatively flat and easy to travel; others are rugged and nearly impassable.

The territory where most of the residents of Palestine lived can be divided into three major regions: the Galilee, the Central Highlands, and the Coastal Plain. (Two other geographic regions on the perimeter of Palestine, the rift valley and the southern deserts, were discussed earlier.) A brief overview of each of these areas will shed light on the lifestyles and history of the people whose lives are depicted in the Hebrew Bible.

The Galilee. The name **Galilee** is used seven times in the Hebrew Bible to refer to the northernmost region of Palestine. The origin of the name, which comes from a Hebrew word meaning "circle" or "circuit," is obscure. The whole of Galilee is covered by mountains, but the northern portion (Upper Galilee) is rugged and forested,

Fig. 6.9. (top) Most of the mountains in Upper Galilee would have been heavily forested in biblical times; (bottom) one of the many broad and fertile valleys in Lower Galilee.

agriculture during the biblical period. To the south, a steep vertical slope averaging 1,500–2,000 feet in height cut it off from the trade routes of Lower Galilee. Traders moved through its narrow valleys ferrying goods to and from the cities of Phoenicia, but the bulk of its permanent residents were scattered among a handful of small villages. Cities (actually little more than large towns) were found only along the eastern rim of the region, near the Jordan Valley and the inland extension of the Way of the Sea. Geography played a key role in their location: the cities were situated where they could defend and collect revenue from the trade route. It is no accident that these cities appear in the Hebrew Bible primarily in stories of conflict.

The landscape of Lower Galilee is quite different. Here the steep hillsides of the north give way to rolling hills averaging 1,500–2,000 feet in elevation and broad valleys that contain some of the best farmland in Palestine. The amount of rain is less than in Upper Galilee, but the precipitation is sufficient and reliable enough to support a wide range of crops for both local use and export. Olive trees and grapes were planted on the terraced hillsides, while wheat and barley flourished in the valleys. In addition to its obvious agricultural value, Lower Galilee was important as a thoroughfare for trade and transportation. The Plain of Megiddo and the Jezreel Valley served as the primary channels for the Way of the Sea as it turned inland from the coast on its way to Syria and Mesopotamia (see figure 6.7). Thus the broad plains of Lower Galilee had a strategic value not only for the people of Palestine but also for the great powers to their north and south who regularly shipped goods and armies along this route. Fortified cities like Megiddo and Jezreel were built on the summits of key hills from which they could survey the

while the southern part (Lower Galilee) contains more valleys and farmland, as can be seen in the photos above.

Because of its rugged topography and its distance from the central mountains where most of the people depicted in the Hebrew Bible lived, the region called Upper Galilee does not play a significant role in the biblical narratives. The area is scenically attractive and receives more rain than other parts of Palestine, but its heavy forestation and mountainous terrain (including steep hillsides leading to peaks that average over 3,000 feet) made it ill-suited for

Fig. 6.10. Wooded mountains and occasional fertile valleys characterize the Central Highlands.

called Israelites whose story is narrated in the Hebrew Bible. This territory, called the **Central Highlands**, is a subsystem of a broader range that extends from Lebanon in the north to the tip of the Sinai Peninsula in the south. Some of the mountains in this region are nearly as tall as those in Upper Galilee, with peaks averaging 2,500–3,000 feet in height, but the elevation changes are more gradual, making the area more suitable for agriculture and grazing, as can be seen in the photos on the left.

Because this region is more mountainous than the territories to the east and west, the major trade routes bypassed the highlands in favor of the smoother terrain along the Coastal Plain (the Way of the Sea) or the plateau east of the Jordan River valley (the King's Highway). As a result, the people who lived in the Central Highlands gained less from the international trade that passed through their region, but they also escaped the attention of the foreign armies that moved periodically across the Coastal Plain and the lands east of the Jordan River. Only when they tried to extend their control from the mountains into the Coastal Plain or the region east of the Jordan River did they come into conflict with other nations who had strategic interests in the area.

In the prebiblical period, the Central Highlands were heavily forested and thus poorly suited for agricultural use. Most of the residents of Palestine lived in the valleys and lowlands, where they were ruled by a series of independent (and often warring) cities located at strategic points around the region. This pattern began to change in the twelfth century B.C.E. when archaeological surveys show a large increase in the population of the Central Highlands (see chapter 20). From this time onward the mountains were gradually deforested and a common mode of agricultural production was established across the region, with terrace farms dominating the hillsides and shepherds grazing their flocks in the rockier areas. Roads were carved

route and sound the alarm in case of invasion. Apparently they served their purpose well, since the Hebrew Bible tells of many battles that took place in this region. During times of peace, however, the local economy would have benefited handsomely from the presence of the trade route. This was especially true for the fortified towns, whose leaders would have attempted to collect tolls on goods that moved across the area.

The Central Highlands. Directly south of the Galilee and west of the Jordan River valley lies a strip of mountainous territory roughly eighty miles long and fifteen miles wide that was the historic heartland of the people through the mountains to facilitate trade between the new settlements, including a major north-south route that bisected the region. Towns, and later small cities, sprang up at strategic points along these roads.

By this process the residents of the Central Highlands developed a common culture and sense of identity that were both similar to and different from those of the people in the lowlands. These are the people whom the Hebrew Bible calls "the people of Israel," "the people of Judah," or occasionally "the Hebrews." Like most people, the biblical authors took their own culture for granted, so they say little about how geographical factors helped to shape the culture and identity of the people whose story they narrate. But contemporary scholars can point to many ways in which geography influenced the history and destiny of the residents of the central mountain region.

The Coastal Plain. Along the western coast of Palestine lies a strip of relatively flat land roughly ten miles wide that is known as the **Coastal Plain**. On its eastern edge, the plain transitions into a series of rolling hills that rise fairly quickly into the Central Highlands. The transition is more abrupt in the north and more gradual in the south, where the hilly area called the Shephelah was one of the first areas that the residents of the mountains sought to colonize. Unfortunately for them, the area was also coveted by their Philistine neighbors along the southern coast, and the armies of the Egyptians and the Mesopotamian kings also passed through this territory from time to time. It is thus no surprise that the Hebrew Bible tells of many battles that took place in this area.

In ancient times, much of the seacoast was cut off from the interior by dense forests and swamps in the north (the area called the Plain of Sharon) and by shifting sand dunes and rugged cliffs farther south. Virtually all of the towns and cities of the Coastal Plain, along with the major road through the area (the Way of the Sea), were located several miles inland rather than on the coast. The coastline was fairly straight and unbroken, with only a few sites in the north that could harbor even small fishing boats. This explains why, despite their lengthy frontage on the Mediterranean Sea, the residents of Palestine never developed a sea-fishing industry or a network of sea trade like the Phoenicians.

Away from the seashore, the Coastal Plain is a rich and fertile region that receives ample rain from storms that arise out of the Mediterranean Sea, though the amounts become less toward the south. As a result, this area was settled and farmed from an early period. The presence of the Way of the Sea made it easy for the residents to ship their excess agricultural products to Egypt

Fig. 6.11. (top) A fertile field along the Coastal Plain; (bottom) a harvest scene from the Shephelah region.

or Mesopotamia. On the other hand, their proximity to

the primary trading route meant that the residents of the Coastal Plain had to put up with the sporadic incursions of foreign armies battling for control of this strategic region. The political situation of the area was in constant flux, with one set of rulers being replaced periodically by another. Other than the Philistines, however, none of these outside parties made any effort to settle their own citizens in the area. Even the people of the nearby Central Highlands did not move in large numbers to the Coastal Plain during times when they exercised political control over the region. Geography might have played a role in this decision as well, since the farming methods that were used in the Coastal Plain were different from those employed in the hills and valleys of the highlands, while the grapes and olives prized by the hill dwellers did not grow well in the Coastal Plain.

THE MEANING OF THE LAND

In virtually every culture where people rely on agriculture for their daily lives, the religious belief system includes stories about the land and deeply held convictions concerning its value. Common to most of these cultures is the belief that the territory that they inhabit is in some sense the center of the universe, the place by which all other places on earth are measured and found wanting. One way of expressing this belief is through stories that narrate how this plot of land was the first to appear at the time of creation and/or how the first living things (or the first humans) emerged from its soil. Another type of story tells how the people's ancestors were placed in this territory by a deity who had a special interest in this particular piece of turf. In still other cases the land is valued because it

Fig. 6.12. In a dry land like Palestine, the provision of water was seen as one of the primary duties of the supernatural realm.

provides a spiritual link with the ancestors who continue to reside in the land and watch over its residents even after death. All of these stories seek to forge a link between the people's place of residence and their core religious beliefs.

At a minimum, such stories serve to inculcate an attitude of love and respect for the land and its inhabitants (usually the other members of the **tribe** or group). In some cases the stories carry the additional burden of explaining why the people live in this territory and not some other place. Stories of this type are especially common among groups that have moved from another location or taken their present homes by force from another group.

People who live close to the land also have a deep sense of its power. Prior to the modern era, humans lacked a scientific understanding of how the natural world operates, including such simple matters as how seeds grow, how the weather works, and the nature of disease. They knew a lot about the practical aspects of caring for their land and animals, but they knew little about the environmental forces that shaped their destiny. As a result, it was common for them to attribute vast powers to the earth itself or to spirits that were believed to reside at a particular geographical site. In most cases this included the idea that proper conduct (whether moral or ritual) was necessary to ensure a successful farming season. When the crops grew well, it was seen as a mark of divine blessing or attributed to the proper conduct of rituals; when the crops failed, or when they were destroyed by drought or insects, it was charged to the activity of an evil spirit or the consequences of a moral or ritual failure.

The people of Palestine shared these kinds of beliefs and attitudes toward their land. From the scanty literary remains that have survived outside the Hebrew Bible, scholars know that the traditional religious beliefs and practices of Palestine centered on a series of nature deities who were believed to control the forces with which they were associated, including the sun, the moon, the winds, and the storm (see chapter 12). Lesser spirits exercised power over smaller areas, such as a spring, a grove of trees, or a mountain. All of these deities were closely linked to the land. When one entered a deity's territory, one was expected to pay honor to that deity; when one left the area, that duty came to an end, since one was now out-side the deity's sphere of influence. The principal means by which people sought to gain the favor of the deities and avert their displeasure was the performance of rituals, including sacrifices (normally animals, but occasionally humans as well). Appeals to the gods could never replace the practical aspects of farming, but they were clearly necessary if one was to enjoy a good harvest.

The Hebrew Bible contains a number of stories and beliefs about the land that both resemble and differ from what we find in other forms of Palestinian literature. The fact that the Hebrew Bible was compiled over such a long period makes it difficult to know when some of these ideas arose and how widely they were held, but we can be certain that they represent a pattern of belief that was held by important sectors of both the elites and the common people.

At the core of the Hebrew Bible lies the belief that the land of Palestine is ruled not by a series of nature deities but by a single god, Yahweh, who exercises all of the powers that others attributed to the traditional gods of the land. When the rains arrive at the proper time, when the seeds grow up into healthy plants, when the season yields a bountiful harvest—all of the credit goes to Yahweh. When the rains fail to come, when the young sprouts wither under the blistering heat, when the mature crops are eaten by a horde of invading locusts—this, too, is the work of Yahweh. Yahweh is lord over all; no other deities can challenge his will.

When we ask what determines whether Yahweh blesses or curses the crops, the answer is less clear. According to one important school of thought, the central issue is the proper performance of rituals. Yahweh has spelled out a set of rituals by which the people should express their devotion, and a failure to perform these rituals can cause the deity to turn against them. Other voices in the Hebrew Bible insist that rituals are effective only when accompanied by proper moral conduct, particularly the promotion of social justice. Still others claim that rituals must be done with an attitude of personal devotion in order to be acceptable to Yahweh, who will respond by blessing the crops and protecting the worshipper from harm. Finally, some question whether humans can ever really understand or influence the plans of Yahweh. These ideas are not mutually exclusive, but their diversity suggests that the people who produced the Hebrew Bible struggled mightily to make sense of the physical world in which they lived and to find some way of controlling the often unpredictable forces of nature.

The belief that Yahweh exercised sovereignty over the land of Palestine did not originally include the idea that Yahweh ruled over the entire universe (see chapter 12). The Hebrew Bible contains many expressions of uncertainty about whether Yahweh can hear cries for help from a distant land. Gods in the ancient world were normally linked to specific territories, so it was only natural that the followers of Yahweh would believe that they had left Yahweh's presence and entered the realm of other deities when they left the land of Palestine. This belief posed special problems for the people of Israel and Judah when they were carried off to live in Mesopotamia after being conquered by the Assyrians and Babylonians, since the normal practice in antiquity was to worship the gods of the territory where one was residing. One of the central hopes of the biblical prophets was that Yahweh's scattered children would one day return to their land, since only here could they know the full joy of Yahweh's presence.

For those who followed Yahweh, the belief that the deity had special ties to the land of Palestine carried with it the conviction that the presence and power of Yahweh could be experienced through the physical features of the land. Certain places were thought to be especially sacred to the deity, and people traveled to these sites when they wanted to ask Yahweh for help or give thanks for a favorable response to their prayers. Often these sites were associated with prominent locations such as hilltops or groves of trees. Special value was given to places where stories indicated that one of their ancestors had met with Yahweh. Some of these sacred sites evolved into regional worship centers with special buildings, altars, and personnel to assist the worshippers in bringing their prayers to the deity. Others remained unmarked. All of the sites were chosen because people believed that Yahweh was uniquely present at this particular geographic location. (These issues will be explored more fully in chapters 25–28.)

Among the narratives linking the people to the land are a set of stories about the purported ancestors of the people of Israel that scholars call the **ancestral narratives** (chapter 17). These stories, recorded in the book of Gen-

esis, tell how Yahweh came to a man named Abraham and told him to leave his home in Mesopotamia and travel to the land of Palestine, which Yahweh promised to give to Abraham and his descendants as their eternal possession (Genesis 12:1-3; 13:14-17; 15:12-21; 17:1-8). Since the territory was occupied by other people at the time, Yahweh's promise implied that Abraham's descendants would one day displace these people, whether by conquest or by slaughter. This implication becomes explicit in the book of Exodus, where Abraham's descendants are commanded to enter the land and drive out the current residents in order to cleanse Yahweh's territory of their evil practices (Exodus 23:20-33; 33:1-3; 34:10-16; see chapter 15). The books of Joshua and Judges narrate the execution of this divine command. But the promise of the land is not absolute. As long as the people faithfully serve Yahweh, the land will yield plentiful harvests and they will be victorious over their enemies. But if they turn away from Yahweh and follow other gods like the prior inhabitants of the land, then they, too, will be cast out of Yahweh's territory (Leviticus 18:24-28; 26:3-45; Deuteronomy 4:23-31; 8:10-20; 28:1-68).

Regardless of what we conclude about the historicity of these stories and when they arose (see chapter 9), they clearly underscore the close link between religion and land in the minds of the biblical authors. The land does not belong to the people, but to Yahweh, and the success of their agricultural labors (along with their continued residence in the land) is determined by their level of faithfulness to the deity. But the stories serve another purpose as well—to justify the dominance of one group of people over others who occupied the same territory. Behind the stories of Abraham and the subsequent conquest of Palestine lies a cultural memory that the people who told these stories had gained and maintained control over the land by force. By attributing their success to Yahweh, they were able to justify to themselves and others their position of dominance over those whom they identified as the descendants of the people whom their ancestors had displaced. This is precisely the kind of story that social elites and conquerors use to rationalize and defend their power. It is therefore no surprise to see stories of this type embedded in religious texts that were produced and preserved by the elites of ancient Israel.

How widely the ideas in these stories were known and shared by the broader populace is unknown. Probably most people would have been aware of the claim that the land of Palestine was a gift of Yahweh to the deity's followers and the related belief that Yahweh was the source of its fruitfulness. Some would have accepted these claims while others would have rejected them as too exclusive, since they left no room for the traditional deities of the land. Eventually the question of whether one should look to Yahweh alone or to some combination of deities in order to assure a fruitful harvest divided the people of ancient Palestine into competing camps. Echoes of that debate can still be seen in the pages of the Hebrew Bible, especially in the books of the prophets (discussed in chapters 31–35) and Deuteronomy (chapter 19).

CONCLUSION

Understanding the geography of Palestine is crucial to making sense of many of the stories and other materials that appear in the Hebrew Bible. The people who wrote and edited these documents took this knowledge for granted, since this was the world in which they lived. Readers who know nothing about the geographical background of the Hebrew Bible invariably miss much of the richness and depth of the biblical text.

Contemporary readers approach the Hebrew Bible as outsiders who grew up in a different time, place, and culture. Not only are we unfamiliar with the many places named in the Hebrew Bible, but most of us also know little or nothing about the world of agriculture, especially as it was practiced in the ancient world. Our thinking about the forces of nature is shaped by the ideas of science; few of us are inclined to look for deities in the sun, moon, wind, or rain, or to engage in religious rituals in an effort to influence the weather.

Because we live in a different world than the people of the Bible, serious study is required if we wish to understand how they viewed reality and the role that religion played in their lives. Understanding the physical world in which they lived is a vital step along this path.

EXERCISE 10

Read the following passages from the Hebrew Bible, paying attention to what each text says about the way the authors viewed the land of Palestine and its relation to Yahweh. Then choose three of the passages and write a paragraph on each, explaining how their ideas resemble and differ from those of people in contemporary American society.

• Exodus 23:20-33
• Leviticus 26:3-45
• Psalm 104:1-18
• Isaiah 55:6-13
• Joel 2:18-27
• Amos 4:6-12

Fig. 7.1. These contemporary Israeli agricultural workers look strikingly similar to the people who worked the fields in biblical times.

Everyday Life in Biblical Times

One day Elisha was passing through Shunem, where a wealthy woman lived, who urged him to have a meal. So whenever he passed that way, he would stop there for a meal. She said to her husband, "Look, I am sure that this man who regularly passes our way is a holy man of God. Let us make a small roof chamber with walls, and put there for him a bed, a table, a chair, and a lamp, so that he can stay there whenever he comes to us." (2 Kings 4:8-10)

Be dismayed, you farmers, wail, you vinedressers, over the wheat and the barley; for the crops of the field are ruined. The vine withers, the fig tree droops. Pomegranate, palm, and apple—all the trees of the field are dried up; surely, joy withers away among the people. Put on sackcloth and lament, you priests; wail, you ministers of the altar. Come, pass the night in sackcloth, you ministers of my God! Grain offering and drink offering are withheld from the house of your God. (Joel 1:11-13)

They hate the one who reproves in the gate, and they abhor the one who speaks the truth. Therefore because you trample on the poor and take from them levies of grain, you have built houses of hewn stone, but you shall not live in them; you have planted pleasant vineyards, but you shall not drink their wine. (Amos 5:10-11)

The Hebrew Bible was written by and for people who shared a common culture and way of life. As a result, the authors took for granted vast amounts of knowledge about daily affairs, including where people lived, how families operated, what people did to put food on the table, who held power over whom, how the economy worked, and so on. This presents a problem for contemporary readers, since most people today know little or nothing about the social realities that are presupposed by the biblical authors. People who participate in a church or synagogue sometimes gather bits and pieces of information about the world of the Bible through sermons and religious education classes, but their knowledge remains fragmentary at best. In the absence of reliable historical data, modern readers invariably make faulty assumptions about the people depicted in the Hebrew Bible, usually by presuming that people in ancient times lived and thought

as we do today. This can lead to serious misunderstandings of the text.

The best way to overcome this problem is to learn more about the daily lives of the people whose experience is reflected in the biblical text. The principal resources for this task are the Hebrew Bible and the findings of archaeologists. Additional insights can be gleaned from studies of the surrounding cultures (primarily Mesopotamia and Egypt) and comparisons with similar cultures at other times and places. Fortunately, the daily lives of people in traditional agricultural societies tend to remain fairly stable over time, so questions about the dating and historical reliability of some of the biblical stories (as discussed in chapter 9) need not interfere with our efforts to reconstruct the everyday experiences of the people of ancient Palestine. Even if a particular narrative should prove to be unreliable, the social world reflected in the biblical documents and the findings of archaeologists cohere well enough to give scholars a general idea of the way people lived in ancient Palestine.

FAMILY STRUCTURES

In traditional agricultural societies such as we see in ancient Palestine, people define their identity by reference to groups—first the extended family, then the **clan** or tribe. The high value that modern societies place on self-discovery, self-expression, and individual rights is foreign to these kinds of cultures. Children are raised to respect and preserve the traditional ways of the family and the society. Independence and novelty are discouraged as threats to the survival of the culture.

In ancient Palestine, the most important family unit was not the nuclear family, but the extended family. Most people lived in simple stone houses where up to three generations of the same family crowded together at night with their livestock and the rest of their personal property. Few adults survived beyond the age of forty, so three-generation families would have existed for only short periods of time (while the grandchildren were young), though individuals could live to as much as seventy years of age. The oldest male ancestor of the family (the grandfather or father) functioned as the head of the family group. Everyone else in the household, from children to married adults, was expected to submit to his authority. Men also held authority over women within the family, though in reality many women exercised significant influence with their male relatives. The oldest son had a special place of honor in the family, since he was the one who was expected to take over when the current head of the family died. Property was passed through the male line unless there were no male heirs.

As in virtually all traditional cultures, certain types of work were typically performed by men and others by women. In rural areas, men spent most of their days laboring in the fields (plowing, seeding, weeding, harvesting, and the like) or tending the family's flocks of sheep and goats. Women generally worked closer to home, but they, too, helped in the fields when more hands were needed. Only men were trained to use weapons, whether for hunting or for defending their flocks or family. Men performed craftwork that pertained to farming or herding (building terraces, making plows and other implements, and so forth), while women engaged in domestic craftwork (spinning thread, weaving cloth, making baskets and pottery, and the like). Women also did most of the labor associated with providing meals for the family, including building and maintaining the cooking fire; drawing and transporting water; tending a garden; feeding and milking domestic animals; grinding flour for bread; and cooking food over an open fire or in a clay oven. Children helped with all of these tasks.

Births, marriages, and deaths caused frequent fluctuations in the number of people in the family household. Since women typically married in their early teens, those who survived the perils of multiple childbirths would have spent most of their lives either pregnant or nursing young children. Women who were unable to bear children labored under a social stigma, since popular belief held that the failure to produce children was the fault of the woman. Children (especially boys) were highly prized for the help that they could offer on the farm and the support that they could give to their parents in old age. Since women probably nursed their babies until they were two or three years old, the natural contraceptive effect of nursing would have prevented most of them from having more than five or six children (if they lived long enough). Only half of these children would have reached adulthood due to the high levels of infant mortality and the prevalence of disease.

As a rule, people were expected to marry within their own clan in order to ensure that land and movable property stayed within the family. **Genealogies** (lists of ancestors) were important for keeping track of the members of the clan. Fathers were expected to guard the virginity of their daughters until they were married. No such duty applied to their sons. Marriages were arranged by the male heads of families, whose chief concern was the good of the family, not the desires of their children. The groom's family normally paid a bride price to the family of the bride in order to compensate them for the loss of their daughter's labor and to formalize the new economic relationship between the two families. Sons brought their new wives to live with their extended family when they married, making the bride a member of the husband's family.

Men were allowed to have multiple wives (**polygamy**), though the practice was probably uncommon due to the financial demands that it placed on the family. Men could also engage in sexual liaisons with unmarried prostitutes, but not with the wives of other men. Women, on the other hand, were limited to one husband, and any form of sexual activity outside of marriage was forbidden. Economics played a role in this dual standard: if women were allowed to have sex with a variety of men, there would be no way of knowing who had fathered their children and thus no way to be sure which man bore financial responsibility for the children or whose land they would inherit. Divorce was permitted, but it was probably uncommon due to the value placed on family life and the need for workers to carry out the tasks of the family.

Most of the care of young children was provided by the mother. As they grew older, children were educated within the home by both parents. Education consisted of learning the group's traditions via oral instruction and gaining skills in performing the ordinary tasks of living (running a farm, performing a trade, and the like). Only the wealthiest families could afford to have a tutor to teach their children how to read and write. Once the children were old enough to work, the daughters normally assisted their mothers in their daily labors while the sons worked with their fathers.

Death could occur at any age. While painful for the family, it was viewed as a normal part of life. The oldest son was responsible for the burial and care of the dead. Funerals included professional mourners (usually women) who were paid to **lament** the dead. Death without proper burial brought disgrace to both the dead person and the family. Normally people were buried on the day they died; cremation was rare. Some people were

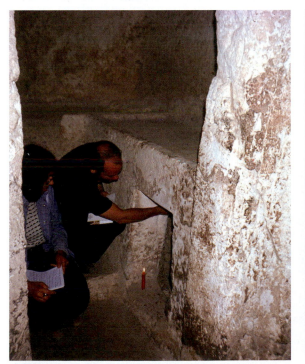

Fig. 7.2. (left) A common type of Israelite tomb—the body was placed on the flat shelf until decomposition, at which time the bones were moved to the opening below; (right) a hoard of gold jewelry found in an Israelite tomb.

buried in single graves, while others were interred in family tombs where the bodies were laid out on benches or in special niches carved out of the rock. In the case of family tombs, the bones were usually collected after a year and placed in a pile with others in order to make room for more bodies. In the Hebrew Bible, this is called being "gathered to the ancestors." Most burials also included objects from everyday life, including pottery vessels, oil lamps, figurines, and jewelry. The significance of these objects is unclear, though they may have been intended for use after death. The family was responsible to care for the tomb after the person's death. For some, this probably included bringing food to the burial site to nourish the deceased.

When the head of the family died, his place was normally taken by the oldest son, though the land could also be divided among the sons, creating several extended families out of one. Widows and widowers were free to remarry. Those who did not marry usually stayed in the household where they had lived when married, though childless widows were sometimes sent back to their parents' family. Orphans were raised by the extended family, though they remained vulnerable to neglect and abuse until they reached adulthood. Inability or failure to care for the members of one's extended family was considered a sign of disgrace.

EXERCISE 11

Read the following passages from the Hebrew Bible and list some of the features of family life that you see reflected in each passage.

- Genesis 24:1-67
- Ruth 1:1-18
- Psalm 128:1-6
- Proverbs 4:1-27
- Proverbs 31:10-31

RURAL HOUSING PATTERNS

Though most of the residents of ancient Palestine engaged in agriculture, they typically lived together in small villages rather than in individual houses on their own plots of land. The men went out to work in the fields (whether their own or those of a landlord) during the daytime, while the women usually remained in the village. In the mountainous regions, villages were normally located on hilltops, requiring the residents to climb up and down the hillside whenever they wished to go anywhere. Many of the men had to walk a considerable distance from the village to reach their plots of land.

Fig. 7.3. (top) A modern reconstruction of an ancient Israelite well; (right) an ancient stairway leading to a reservoir beneath the city of Beer-Sheba in southern Palestine.

The availability of a stable water supply was one of the key factors that determined the location of a village. The climate of Palestine is dry for most of the year, and there are virtually no lakes or year-round streams to provide water for drinking or crops. Fortunately, the porous limestone that lies beneath the surface holds water well, and the land is dotted with small springs where the water table reaches the surface. In places where there are no springs, wells frequently yield water, though the process of drilling a well shaft through the rocky soil of Palestine without modern tools was a tedious and backbreaking enterprise. Most towns and villages were located near a spring or well, with plastered **cisterns** (artificial reservoirs) being used to collect rainwater during the rainy

season. Villages were close together by modern standards, with a village every couple of miles in the more hospitable parts of the hill country.

Most villages were small, containing perhaps fifteen to thirty houses with one hundred to three hundred residents. Houses were packed tightly together, often sharing common walls as in a modern condominium building. Many were arranged in a circular pattern around a central courtyard. There were no formal roads between the houses, only footpaths that led from the center of the village to the fields. Most of the residents would have been related to one another, some more closely than others. The experience of living in such close proximity to kin would have created a strong sense of community within

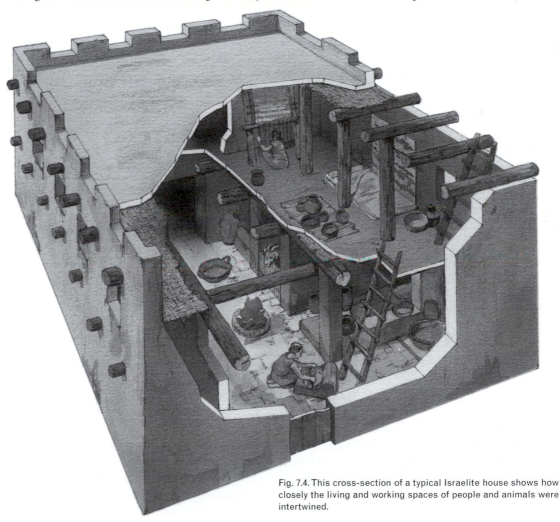

Fig. 7.4. This cross-section of a typical Israelite house shows how closely the living and working spaces of people and animals were intertwined.

the village. Most people probably lived their entire lives in the same village.

Because they were so small, villages had no formal government or police force. Instead, problems were handled through the extended family system. If a person was harmed, it was the duty of the nearest male relatives to confront the offender, establish the facts of the case, and inflict punishment upon the guilty party. Disputes that could not be settled in this way were brought before the oldest male residents of the town or village, known as the elders, for judgment. The process was highly informal, with the village's open-air threshing floor serving as a temporary courtroom. The elders had no power to enforce their rulings; their chief role was to serve as mediators and prevent vengeance from spiraling out of control. In general, it seems that their decisions were respected and followed. The elders also met as needed to discuss problems facing the village and to provide guidance for the community in times of crisis. They could also recommend that the men of the village take collective action to deal with a problem.

Within the village, most houses followed a common pattern that archaeologists call the *four-room house*. Houses were small; the living space was about the size of a modern one-bedroom apartment. Most were made of stone, though mud bricks were also used along the Coastal Plain and in the valleys where clay was plentiful. Walls were thick by modern standards (eighteen to twenty-four inches), providing a measure of insulation on hot days and cold nights. The ground floor of the house was usually divided into four rooms, with three rooms running parallel to one another and a fourth in the back running perpendicular to the others, as indicated in figure 7.4.

The two side rooms in the front section were probably used to house and feed the family's domestic animals at night. The central room was used to prepare food for both animals and people, while the back room was reserved for storage. All of the floors were made of packed earth. The family slept together on the second floor or on the flat roof that framed the top of the house. The roof, reached by an internal ladder or an external staircase, was especially welcome on hot summer nights. Since there were usually no doors within the house, privacy was virtually nonexistent.

Because of the heat (and the absence of glass), houses had very small windows, leaving the inside of the house fairly dark most of the time. Oil-burning lamps made of clay were used to light the house at night, but most people rose and slept with the sun, making illumination less important. On cold evenings, an open fire was lit in the central room to heat the house. The odors of the domestic animals and the unwashed human bodies, together with the smoke from the fire pit, would have made the house smell rather foul to modern noses.

Most families owned little or no furniture—people slept on mats and sat on the floor or on flat stones. Food and drinks were stored in large pottery jars, and pottery bowls and cups were used for eating. Most of the cooking was done over an open fire in the courtyard outside the house, though some houses had a baking oven on the first floor. The proximity of the food preparation areas to the spaces used by the animals would have made food-borne diseases fairly common.

LIFE ON THE FARM

Since most people in ancient Palestine made their living directly or indirectly by farming or shepherding, the practice of agriculture was a vital part of children's education. Even the wealthy gained much of their income from the ownership and management of large estates. The Hebrew Bible abounds in agricultural imagery because this is the world in which the people who produced these texts lived.

The practice of agriculture in ancient Palestine was heavily dependent on environmental factors. The climate of Palestine is subtropical, which means that it has only two seasons: a rainy season from October through April and a dry season from May through September, when virtually no rain falls. More than 70 percent of the rain comes in the months from December through February. The amount of rain varies widely across the region, from approximately twenty-eight inches per year in Upper Galilee (about the same as the American plains) to four inches per year around the Dead Sea (similar to Las Vegas). In general, the amount of rain decreases as one moves from north to south and from west to east across the region, with the eastern edge (near the Jordan River) and the southern

Fig. 7.5. (top) Olive trees were a vital crop in ancient Palestine, producing both food and the oil burned in lamps; (bottom) hillside terraces are still used in Israel to capture precious rainwater for agricultural use.

the *latter rains* in the Hebrew Bible) that would boost the crops to maturity. Unfortunately, this ideal pattern occurs only a third of the time. Another third of the time the weather alternates between wet and dry spells, while in other years the rains that are needed to prepare the earth for planting or to mature the plants never arrive, causing the crops to be late or spindly or to dry up entirely. Crop diseases and insect infestations (especially locusts) also conspired to make the life of the Palestinian farmer precarious. The Hebrew Bible contains many references to famines and starvation that resulted from crop failures (Genesis 12:10; Ruth 1:1; 2 Samuel 21:1; Joel 1:1-20; Amos 4:6-9).

As long as the rains came, most of the land could produce the primary staples of the Palestinian diet. Olives and grapes were important where the climate was suitable, while wheat and barley were grown throughout the land. Other common food crops included figs, lentils, chickpeas, cucumbers, onions, and garlic. Specialized crops such as dates and pomegranates were grown in limited areas. Most agricultural products were eaten in the area where they were grown, though some were traded with other regions or exported. Excess crops were dried and stored in large underground silos.

rim (the Negev) receiving too little rain for agriculture and some areas too little for shepherding. The most productive farmland is located in the valleys of Lower Galilee and the strip of land that runs from north to south between the mountains and the Coastal Plain. The construction of terraces (low stone walls designed to retain soil and rainwater) made the hillsides in the Central Highlands suitable for growing many but not all crops.

The first seeds were normally planted in October after the early rains softened the surface of the ground that had been hardened by the heat and dryness of summer. In a good season, the seeds would receive enough rain over the next three months to nurture them into full-size plants, followed by a final burst of showers in February (called

Areas where the land was unsuitable for farming or lying unplanted for a time were used for grazing sheep and goats. Sheep were raised primarily for their wool, which the women spun into thread for clothing. Goats were the chief source of milk; cattle were ill suited for the broken terrain and dry conditions of ancient Palestine. On the estates of wealthy landlords, sheep and goats were also raised for meat and for use in sacrifices. Ordinary farmers ate meat only rarely, since this meant reducing the size of the herd that provided them with the necessities of wool and milk.

Shepherds normally stayed with their herds in the daytime and brought them back to the village at night. In the dry season, however, they frequently had to travel far from home to find suitable pasturage and water, since sheep have a tendency to overgraze the land and destroy pastures. Much of the routine tending of the animals was

Fig. 7.6. (top) A shepherd tends his sheep in green pastures; (bottom) a woman cards wool to turn it into thread.

neighbors (pottery, baskets, furniture, and the like), but their opportunities were limited by a general lack of marketplaces and the fact that most people made their own household goods. Those who could not earn enough to live were forced to beg, rely on other family members, or sell their children or themselves into slavery. There was no governmental safety net.

EXERCISE 12

Read the following passages and list some of the features of everyday rural life that are mentioned in each text.

- Deuteronomy 28:1-48
- Ruth 2:1-23
- Psalm 23:1-6
- Isaiah 5:1-7
- Joel 1:1-12

TOWNS AND CITIES

Scattered among the small villages where the majority of people lived were a number of larger towns and a handful of cities where life both resembled and differed from the daily routine of the villages. As with the villages, towns and cities in the mountainous regions were built on hilltops, with buildings sprawling down the hillsides as the tops became too crowded. The number of people who lived in these larger regional centers is hard to determine, but they were clearly small by modern standards. A typical town probably had fewer than a thousand residents, while the population of most cities would not have exceeded a few thousand. Only the two royal capitals, Jerusalem and Samaria, might have contained as many as ten thousand to twenty thousand residents at their peak—still little more than large towns by modern standards. By contrast, the cities of Nineveh and Babylon, the capitals of Assyria and Babylon, had perhaps one hundred thousand to two hundred thousand inhabitants (the size of a modest American city), while Damascus, the capital of neighboring Aram (modern Syria), might have been half that size.

done by older children, though some adults also worked full-time as herders. Children in the ancient world did not have the luxury of leisurely summer days filled with play; everyone had to work to provide for the needs of the family. Shepherding could be dangerous work, since predatory animals (primarily lions and wolves) would periodically attack the flock in order to secure food. Slings, clubs, and stones were the primary weapons for protecting the herd. Dogs were not normally used in ancient shepherding, since most dogs were semi-wild scavengers.

In a society that depended so heavily on agriculture, families that lost their land due to poor crops, ill health, or bad management were left in a precarious state. Some would have found work as day laborers on the farms of wealthy landowners who paid them poorly and often mistreated them. Others crafted items for sale to their

Housing in the towns and cities followed the same basic patterns as in the villages, though the presence of wealthy elites meant that some of the houses were larger and more ornate than others. Houses were packed together in irregular patterns separated by alleyways and shared courtyards. Only the largest cities had anything like an organized street plan. Wealthier homes were typically located on the western side of town where the prevailing westerly winds provided a measure of relief from the hot sun and the odors of the open sewage that ran through the streets of the poorer areas. Scattered courtyards might have been used for markets or as sites of public assembly.

One of the features that distinguished many towns and cities from villages was the presence of protective walls that guarded them against marauding invaders. Walls were made of stone or mud brick and could be as much as twenty to thirty feet high and fifteen to twenty feet thick. Some towns had solid walls, while others were surrounded by two parallel walls that were separated by a space large enough to house a narrow row of homes, shops, or storage areas. The space between the two walls could be filled in with stones to make a solid wall in case of an invasion. Additional fortifications were often set up inside and outside the walls to keep them from being undermined or battered down. The fact that many towns and cities were situated on hilltops made it difficult for invaders to attack them without suffering heavy losses from arrows and stones launched from the walls above. The Hebrew Bible contains many stories of armies attacking and besieging walled towns and cities, sometimes successfully and sometimes not (Deuteronomy 3:3-7; 2 Samuel 11:18-25; 20:14-22; 2 Kings 6:24—7:20; 18:13—19:37; 25:1-21).

The presence of walls meant that towns and cities had to have heavily fortified gates leading into and out of the enclosed area. Everyone who wanted to enter or leave the security of the walls, including farmers who went out to work in the fields each day, had to pass through these gates. As a result, the open courtyard just inside the gates became a popular meeting place for the community. Merchants, craftsmen, and farmers brought their wares to this area in an effort to find buyers. Larger gate structures also contained several side chambers with built-in benches where smaller groups could meet. When a dispute arose between two people from the local community, the elders

of the town or city sat in these chambers to hear the case and mediate the dispute. The gate was also the place where contracts were formalized through public statements of mutual promises. Promises made in this area were witnessed not only by the elders of the community but also by the deity, whose guardian presence was commonly marked by a religious **shrine**. A familiarity with the special role of the gate area enhances our understanding of many passages in the Hebrew Bible where such

Fig. 7.7. (top) A contemporary hilltop village with farming terraces running across the side of the hill; (bottom) the remains of an ancient hilltop city in southern Palestine.

knowledge is taken for granted (Deuteronomy 21:18-21; 25:5-10; Joshua 20:4-6; Ruth 4:1-12; 2 Samuel 15:1-6; Proverbs 1:20-23).

Yet another factor that made towns and cities different from villages was the presence of wealthy elites. In the village, virtually everyone was a small farmer whose labor yielded barely enough for the family to survive, so any disparities in income or wealth were minor. Life was regulated by custom, and there was no formal system of government. In the towns and cities, by contrast, a handful of families controlled a disproportionate share of the resources and dominated the affairs of the community, whether as formal representatives of the ruling authorities or through the informal influence that wealth invariably commands. Money and connections were often more important than age and wisdom in this kind of society. Farmers and artisans were effectively disempowered and became targets of abuse by the wealthy. The spirit of cooperation that was vital to village life was replaced by social divisions rooted in wealth. The gap between rich and poor widened with the passage of time.

The presence of wealthy elites in the towns and cities also affected the types of architecture found there. In addition to the bigger and more ornate homes of the rich, the larger towns and cities contained many types of buildings that were not normally present in a village, including agricultural processing facilities, warehouses, military quarters, palaces, and temples. Industrial production in the ancient world was small-scale and primitive by modern standards, but archaeologists have unearthed complexes that produced olive oil, wine, pottery, linen, and other items in large enough quantities to be shipped beyond the local area. Military quarters, including stables for horses, were required to house the soldiers who were stationed at key sites to protect the land from invaders. Palaces were constructed to serve as temporary or permanent homes and offices for high officials. Temples served as places of worship that ensured the favor and protection of the deity. All of these buildings would have been built and managed by the elites using labor supplied by the nonelites.

The elites also developed new forms of culture and entertainment that both resembled and differed from those that prevailed among the ordinary residents of the community. The difference was somewhat similar to the

Fig. 7.8. (top) Horse troughs from the royal stables at the fortress of Megiddo; (bottom) fortified walls from the ancient city of Samaria.

distinction between high culture and popular culture today. The stories and traditions used by the rich and the poor would have been alike in many respects, but the versions told by the elites may have been more complex (since they could write them down) and slanted toward their own interests. The artistic styles and products of the elites were more refined, since they could afford the best materials and workmanship and were able to import luxury goods from foreign lands. The elites also had servants (or slaves) to handle their daily chores, giving them ample leisure time to indulge in music, drinking, and revelry. Rich and poor wore similar kinds of clothing, but the wealthy dressed in finer materials and wore more ornaments, perfumes, and jewelry. The wealthy also ate better food, including meat, a rarity in the diet of the poor.

TRAVEL AND TRADE

By tradition, the people who lived in villages sought to be self-sufficient both as individuals and as a community. Unless there was a reason for specialization (the presence of unusually good clays for pottery, for example), village residents made and used what they needed locally and thus had little motivation to engage in trade. When a family needed something that they could not produce, they swapped a proportionate amount of goods with another family (a practice known as **barter**). Money was unknown in these settings until fairly late in the biblical period.

Villages that were located close to towns or cities, on the other hand, were invariably drawn into the political and economic orbit of the neighboring community. Governing officials from the urban areas forced villagers to pay taxes (calculated as a certain amount of grain, wine, or olive oil) and to provide laborers for their building projects (usually one or more healthy sons). This meant that farmers had to grow and harvest more crops with fewer workers. In bad crop years, wealthy landowners from the towns and cities would lend food items or seed to struggling farmers who signed over their land as collateral. If the problem persisted, the landowner would seize the land in payment of the debt and combine it with other parcels to form large estates to produce goods for trade. Villagers who lost their land often had to leave their village and move to the nearest town or city in order to find work as day laborers or to find buyers for their craft goods. The effect of these developments was dramatic: while the bulk of the population struggled to stay alive, the elites grew increasingly wealthy and enjoyed lives filled with luxury and ease. Many of the prophets whose sayings are recorded in the Hebrew Bible spoke out forcefully against the unfairness of this system, but their calls for change went largely unheeded.

Since the elites could not use all of the agricultural goods that were produced by the farms under their control, they developed networks of trade that allowed them to exchange their excess goods for other assets that were not available locally, including silver or gold, which served as a substitute for money. Most roads were little more than dirt paths cleared of large stones, bushes, and other impediments to travel. Trade goods were normally carried on the backs of pack animals or in carts pulled by donkeys, mules, or oxen. Camels and horses would have been uncommon on the roads of ancient Palestine, since camels were used primarily for desert travel and horses were reserved for military use. Travel was slow—a person on foot could cover perhaps twenty miles in a day, while a loaded caravan of animals and carts moved even more slowly due to the poor condition of the roads.

Eventually the excess goods made their way by land to the larger cities of the region, where they were either sold for local use or shipped to more distant markets by land or sea. Imports followed the reverse path, with traders passing through the major cities of Palestine selling vital materials like gold, silver, iron, tin, lead, and copper, as well as luxury items such as ivory, jewels, spices, perfumes, and rare dyes and fabrics. Local officials imposed tariffs and tolls on trade caravans as they passed through their lands in order to earn money from the trading enterprise. This invariably increased the price of imported goods, but the elites had more than enough money to pay.

EXERCISE 13

Read the following passages and list some of the features of town or city life that are mentioned in each passage.

- 1 Kings 10:14-29
- 1 Kings 21:1-16
- Job 29:1-25
- Isaiah 5:8-17
- Micah 6:9-16

THE PLACE OF RELIGION

No examination of the daily lives of the people of ancient Palestine would be complete without a discussion of the role of religion in their day-to-day experience. Since most of the rest of this book is devoted to exploring this topic, a few cursory observations will suffice for now.

Many people today think of religion as an activity that is distinct from the ordinary affairs of life. Some associate the term with groups of believers gathering together for worship; others regard it as a private matter that involves the innermost recesses of one's being. Neither of these definitions of religion would have made sense to the average person in ancient Palestine. Sometimes an individual might travel to a holy site in order to request help from a deity or give thanks for special favors, but there were no churches or synagogues where people met together on a regular basis to worship. Most people probably prayed or sang to a deity from time to time, but these activities took place in the context of public rituals, not private spirituality. In fact, the whole idea of religion as a spiritual quest or an avenue for personal growth would have seemed rather odd to most of the residents of ancient Palestine. Religion centered on the group's relationship to the god(s); personal spiritual experiences were secondary if they occurred at all. Individuals had a role to play in maintaining the favor of the deity, but only as members of a family or clan, not as isolated spiritual seekers. Family metaphors were also used to describe the group's relationship with the deity.

The practical consequence of this way of thinking is that most of what we would call religion was incorporated into the daily life of the family. The precise form that it took depended on the deities that the family wanted to honor. (For more on what they did, see chapter 26.) Some people kept small shrines in their homes that held statues or images of one or more deities. The function of these shrines is unclear, though it seems likely that people made some kind of daily or periodic offerings in front of them. Additional rituals were performed at specific times of the year in conjunction with the agricultural cycle.

But the influence of religion reached well beyond these momentary ritual acts. Rules, traditions, and taboos guided many aspects of daily life. Among the rules that were eventually included in the Torah are regulations prescribing the kinds of food that people should eat and the way it was prepared, the types of clothing that they should wear, the way they should treat their family members and animals, the proper channels for sexuality, and many other aspects of daily life. Other regulations explained what to do in less common situations such as the birth of a child, the death of a family member, or the causing of harm to another person. Families that followed a different set of gods or traditions would have had their own rules concerning these issues. When people followed these rules, they were doing their part to uphold the family's relationship with the patron deity and thus to procure the deity's favor or blessings upon the family. If they refused to obey the rules, they could face ostracism for causing harm to the family. In this way the extended family served not only as the primary sphere for expressing religious devotion but also as its principal enforcer.

Fig. 7.9. Luxury goods of the ancient Israelite elites. On the left, gold and silver jewelry; on the right, ivory image of a supernatural creature.

CONCLUSION

Studying the Hebrew Bible is a cross-cultural experience. The people whose lives are reflected in these documents lived in a world that was very different from our own. Their daily activities and mode of thinking were more like those of a poor third world country than those of contemporary American Jews or Christians. Similarities that might be noted include the central position of agriculture in the local economy; the vast gulf between a small group of wealthy urban elites and the rest of the population who struggled to survive; the emphasis on family and male-dominated gender roles; the close-knit village culture; and the infusion of religion into every aspect of life.

If we hope to understand the Hebrew Bible, we must approach it with the same kind of cross-cultural sensitivity and empathy that an anthropologist brings to a study of other societies. This includes not only learning all that we can about their beliefs and practices, but also refraining from judgment about those elements of the culture that seem strange to us. This does not mean that we have to approve of everything that we encounter in the biblical texts, but it does mean that we should make a serious effort to see the world from their point of view. In short, we must become good listeners. Only when we have truly heard and understood their point of view can we decide which parts we will embrace and which parts we will reject.

EXERCISE 14

Imagine that you are a typical villager from ancient Palestine who has been transported by time machine into twenty-first-century America. Excluding the obvious differences in technology, what are some of the things that you would notice about American culture that differ from the world in which you grew up?

Fig. 8.1. The ceiling of the Sistine Chapel in Rome, painted by Michelangelo, is covered with images from biblical stories.

The Grand Narrative

I will recount the gracious deeds of the LORD, the praiseworthy acts of the LORD, because of all that the LORD has done for us, and the great favor to the house of Israel that he has shown them according to his mercy, according to the abundance of his steadfast love. (Isaiah 63:7)

I will open my mouth in a parable; I will utter dark sayings from of old, things that we have heard and known, that our ancestors have told us. We will not hide them from their children; we will tell to the coming generation the glorious deeds of the LORD, and his might, and the wonders that he has done. (Psalm 78:2-4)

Remember the days of old, consider the years long past; ask your father, and he will inform you; your elders, and they will tell you. (Deuteronomy 32:7)

One of the central questions that has vexed scholars over the last two centuries is how far the biblical narratives can be trusted as historical documents. The first half of the Hebrew Bible (Genesis through Esther in Christian Bibles) presents a relatively continuous story that extends from the creation of the universe to the formation of the people called Israel to their dramatic downfall at the hands of invaders from the north and their subsequent efforts to rebuild their communal and religious life under foreign rule. The story is interrupted in places by other material (primarily the lists of laws in the Torah narratives) and the continuity of the narrative breaks down toward the end (the books of Ezra and Nehemiah), but the thread of the story is never lost. Evidently the people who put together the Hebrew Bible felt that it was important to formulate a coherent grand narrative that would make sense of their people's past. The success of their efforts can be gauged by the fact that Jews and Christians over the centuries have taken this story as a factual account of the way things really happened.

Contemporary scholars have found ample reason to question the historicity of this narrative, though they disagree about how much of the material in these books is historical and how much should be viewed as **myth** or legend (see chapter 9). One point on which all would agree, however, is that it is impossible to grasp the message of the Hebrew Bible without a general familiarity with the biblical story line. This chapter offers a book-by-book overview of that story.

GENESIS

The Hebrew Bible begins with one of the most famous narratives in Western civilization, the story of how God created the universe and its inhabitants. The story quickly descends into tragedy, however, as the first humans, **Adam** and **Eve**, are cast out of their idyllic garden home for disobeying God's instructions and eating from a forbidden tree. The tragedy deepens when their descendants become so intent on evil and violence that the deity decides to send a massive flood to obliterate all but one man, Noah, and his family. After the flood, the plotline veers upward again as the earth is populated with Noah's descendants, who become the ancestors of the various people groups that were known to the biblical storytellers. Yet even here

Fig. 8.2. Images from the story of Abraham's near-sacrifice of his son Isaac (Genesis 22), one of several panels cast in bronze by Lorenzo Ghiberti in the fifteenth century on the door to the baptistery of the cathedral in Florence, Italy.

the hopeful tone is mingled with tragedy as God acts to confuse the languages of humans in order to prevent them from becoming too unified and powerful.

From here the story narrows to a single family, a man named Abram (later changed to Abraham), his wife, Sarai (later Sarah), and their descendants.

The story of Abram begins when he is commanded by a deity named Yahweh to leave his home in Mesopotamia and travel with his family to an undisclosed location that Yahweh will show him. The destination turns out to be the land of Canaan, or Palestine. Yahweh promises to bless Abram and to make his descendants into a mighty nation who will rule over the land to which Yahweh is leading him. This presents a problem for Abram and Sarai, since they have no children and Sarai is too old to become pregnant. Finally, they arrive at a solution: Sarai gives her servant Hagar to Abram, and Hagar produces a male heir whom they name Ishmael.

Several years pass before an angelic visitor arrives to inform them that Yahweh intends to enable Sarai herself to become pregnant and bear a child. This child, named **Isaac**, quickly displaces Ishmael in the affection of his parents. In fact, Isaac becomes so dear to Abram that Yahweh decides to test his loyalty by commanding him to kill Isaac as a human sacrifice on a mountaintop altar. At the last moment Yahweh intervenes to stop the sacrifice and commends Abram for his unwavering devotion to the deity.

At this point the story shifts briefly to the adult Isaac, who marries and produces twin sons named Esau and **Jacob**. The rivalry between these two sons forms the focal point of the central chapters of Genesis. Jacob, the younger of the twins, tricks his older brother, Esau, out of his inheritance rights and then flees to Mesopotamia to escape his brother's wrath. Here he finds work with his uncle Laban, who proves to be as much of a trickster as Jacob himself. While living in Mesopotamia, Jacob marries Laban's two daughters, Leah and Rachel, who over time give birth to twelve sons and a daughter. Finally, Jacob decides to return home and mend his relationship with his brother, Esau. Along the way he encounters a strange man (probably an angel) who wrestles with him all night and then changes his name to *Israel* (meaning "one who wrestles with God"), a name that is later applied to his descendants. In this way Jacob's twelve sons come to be known as the ancestors of the twelve tribes of Israel.

The latter chapters of Genesis tell the story of Jacob's favorite son, Joseph. As a young man, Joseph is sold into slavery in Egypt by his jealous brothers. After several years as a slave, including a stint in prison based on a false accusation, Joseph is unexpectedly elevated to high office after he interprets several dreams which had been disturbing the Pharaoh (the king of Egypt). Joseph rightly identifies these dreams as the voice of God warning of a coming famine. When the famine strikes, Joseph's brothers travel to Egypt to buy food, but they do not recognize their brother. For a while Joseph tests his brothers to see if they have changed. Finally, he reveals his identity to them and invites his entire family to move to Egypt for the duration of the famine.

EXODUS

The book of Exodus begins in Egypt, several generations after Joseph, with the rise of a new Pharaoh who feels threatened by the increasing numbers and power of Jacob's descendants, who are now known as Hebrews or Israelites. To keep them under control, the Pharaoh first places them under forced labor, then commands that all of their newborn sons should be killed. In an ironic twist of fate, one of these Hebrew boys winds up being raised in the Pharaoh's own household after his daughter finds the baby floating in a reed basket in the Nile River. The child is given the name of Moses.

As an adult, Moses flees from Egypt after killing an Egyptian whom he caught beating one of his fellow Hebrews. Forty years later, Yahweh tells him to return to Egypt and lead his people back to Canaan. At this point the story turns into an epic battle of wills between Moses and the Pharaoh. Again and again Moses goes to the Pharaoh and demands that the Hebrews be allowed to leave Egypt, adding threats of supernatural punishment if his request is denied. Again and again the Pharaoh refuses. After each refusal Yahweh responds by sending a terrible **plague** against the Egyptians (the Nile River turning to blood, locusts destroying the crops, and similar disasters). As the Pharaoh continues to resist Moses' demands, Yahweh informs Moses that he intends to send one last plague: the angel of death will pass through the land and kill the oldest male child in every house that is not marked with the blood of a sacrificial lamb (the basis for the Jewish feast of **Passover**). After this plague, the Pharaoh finally relents and allows the Hebrews to leave. Once they have left, however, he changes his mind once again and sends his soldiers to pursue them. The Hebrews escape by a miracle: Yahweh splits the sea before them and then closes it over the heads of the Egyptian armies.

After several weeks of traveling through the desert under divine protection, the escapees arrive at Mount Sinai, the place where Moses had first heard Yahweh telling him to return to Egypt. Here they witness the awesome power of Yahweh: the earth shakes, the mountain is covered by a thick cloud of smoke, and the air resounds with flashes of lightning, rolling thunder, and the blast of trumpets. Out of the dark clouds comes a majestic voice pronouncing the words known as the Ten Commandments. As the people cower in fear, Moses draws closer to the voice, which recites to him a series of laws designed to regulate the social and religious life of Yahweh's people.

Fig. 8.3. Lucas Cranach the Elder, *Closing of the Red Sea*

Yahweh then invites Moses to climb the mountain, where he stays for forty days and nights. Here he receives additional instructions about the design and operation of the special tent (called the **tent of meeting**) where Yahweh plans to visit his people and receive their worship while they are in the desert.

Eventually the Israelites grow tired of waiting for Moses to return, so they turn to Moses' brother, Aaron, for leadership. Aaron's first act is to forge a golden statue of a calf to represent the presence of Yahweh among the people. Yahweh is angered by this attempt to identify him with a physical image, so he sends Moses back down the mountain to punish the people. At Moses' urging, the men of the tribe of Levi kill three thousand of their fellow Hebrews. But even this does not assuage Yahweh's anger. Yahweh orders them to leave his holy mountain. Only Moses' intense pleading induces Yahweh to go with them and protect them through the remaining desert. The book ends with a long and detailed account of the construction and dedication of the special tent that Yahweh had instructed Moses to build for him.

LEVITICUS

The book of Leviticus consists primarily of a series of laws that Moses is said to have received from Yahweh in the tent of meeting while the people were camped at the foot of Mount Sinai. Most of these laws concern matters of ritual **purity** (see chapter 23). The only narrative material appears toward the middle of the book, where a description of the formal installation of Aaron and his sons as priests is followed by a handful of short tales about faithful and unfaithful priests.

NUMBERS

The book of Numbers is more disjointed than the previous books, as the flow of the narrative is repeatedly disrupted by lengthy sets of divine instructions. The book opens with Yahweh telling Moses to take a census of the various clans of the Hebrews (over six hundred thousand males!), followed by a long description of their camping and travel arrangements. The ensuing chapters contain assorted laws and stories that pertain mostly to the organization and conduct of worship at the tent of meeting.

The thread of the narrative finally resumes when the tent of meeting is taken down and the Hebrews leave Mount Sinai to continue their journey to Canaan. As they travel, the people begin complaining about the lack of food in the desert, but Yahweh performs a series of miracles to meet their needs. When they finally draw near to the territory of Canaan, Moses sends twelve spies to scout out the land. Ten of the spies report that the inhabitants of Canaan are too strong to be overcome. When the people hear this, they rebel against Moses for bringing them out into the desert to die. At this point Yahweh declares that this generation will indeed die in the desert and their children will enter the land.

The next few chapters contain a series of loosely connected stories in which various people complain about Moses' leadership and are promptly punished by Yahweh. The stories are interspersed with lists of laws that Moses is said to have received from Yahweh during this period.

Toward the end of the section, Moses himself is informed that he will not be allowed to enter Canaan after he fails to do exactly as Yahweh had commanded when performing a miracle designed to give water to the people.

The plot does not begin to move forward again until the generation that came out of Egypt has died off in the desert and their children start advancing toward the land of Canaan, still under Moses' leadership. Along the way they encounter several kings on the eastern side of the Jordan River who attempt to stop them from passing through their territory. Some of these encounters lead to battles in which the Hebrews are always victorious. Stories of their progress toward Canaan are intermingled with more laws that Moses is said to have received during this period. The book concludes with a series of instructions concerning the conduct of sacrificial offerings and various rules for the division and settlement of the land on both sides of the Jordan River.

DEUTERONOMY

Most of the book of Deuteronomy consists of a long speech that Moses is said to have given to the Hebrew people just before they crossed the Jordan River to enter the land of Canaan. Forty years have passed since Moses led their parents out of Egypt. As they face this crucial moment of transition, Moses reminds them how they reached this point, then proceeds to restate and reframe many of the laws that Yahweh had given to their parents to guide their individual and communal lives. The primary speech takes place on a single day, so it does little to advance the plot. The same is true for a shorter speech at the beginning of the book. Only near the end of the book does the story begin to move forward. Upon concluding his speech, Moses writes down the laws of Yahweh and then gives them to the priests with instructions that they should be read aloud to the people annually. Then he commissions his longtime assistant Joshua to succeed him and recites a lengthy song that foreshadows the future trials of the people of Israel. The book closes with Moses pronouncing blessings on each of the twelve tribes of Israel, then climbing a mountain from which he can glimpse the territory of Canaan. After this he dies, without setting foot in the land toward which he had been traveling for much of his adult life.

JOSHUA

The book of Joshua begins with Yahweh giving instructions to Joshua about how to prepare the people for the coming invasion of Canaan. As before, they send spies into the land, but this time the spies return with a message of certain victory. As they prepare to cross the Jordan River and launch their invasion, the waters miraculously part, allowing them to walk through on dry land.

From here the action becomes swift and furious as the Hebrew people, led by Joshua, sweep across the land of Canaan in a series of armed battles that bring the bulk of the territory under their control. Most of the fighting is initiated by the Israelites. Their usual practice is to surround and attack one of the walled Canaanite cities, then kill all of the inhabitants. In a few cases they engage in defensive actions against kings who hear about their military success and send armies to stop them. Several times they are aided by miraculous events that show clearly that Yahweh is fighting on their side. Their only defeat occurs when one of their soldiers violates Yahweh's command to offer all of the spoils of battle to him, causing Yahweh to give the victory to their enemies. Still, their success is not absolute. The story names a number of areas from which they were unable to dislodge the **Canaanite** inhabitants. Some of the cities in these areas were never conquered, while in others the inhabitants were put to forced labor.

Fig. 8.4. James Tissot, *The Seven Trumpets of Jericho*

The latter half of the book describes in detail the territories that Joshua allotted to each of the twelve tribes of Israel. When the distribution is complete, Joshua delivers a farewell address in which he calls on the people to renew their commitment to serve Yahweh alone. The people respond by swearing eternal loyalty to Yahweh. The book ends with a brief note stating that the Israelites served Yahweh faithfully as long as that generation lived.

JUDGES

The book of Judges begins somewhat awkwardly: Joshua is dead in the first chapter but alive in the second. The first chapter recounts a series of victories won by the Israelite armies after Joshua's death, followed by a long list of cities that they were unable to conquer. The second chapter reports Joshua's death then summarizes the narrative pattern that will dominate the remainder of the book: (a) the Israelites turn away from Yahweh to follow other gods; (b) Yahweh allows their enemies to conquer and oppress them; (c) Yahweh sends a leader (called a *judge*) to rescue them from their oppressors; (d) the people serve Yahweh during the life of the judge; and finally (e) the judge dies and the people return to their old ways.

The book of Judges depicts the exploits of a dozen of these judges. The coverage is uneven: some receive only cursory treatment, while others are given several chapters (Gideon, Jephthah, Samson). Most of the stories focus on a single episode in which a judge leads the armies of Israel to victory over their enemies and frees the people for a time from foreign domination. As a rule, the judges are men, but the book also includes a lengthy story about a female judge named Deborah who directs the Israelite army into battle and shares credit for the victory with another woman named Jael who kills the enemy commander in his sleep.

Despite their military successes, many of the leading characters are depicted as flawed: Gideon and Barak are afraid to lead their armies into battle; Abimelech kills all of his brothers in a bid to become king; Jephthah makes a rash promise that leads to the death of his daughter; Samson uses his God-given strength to satisfy his passing whims and passions.

The book concludes with a gruesome tale of a war that begins when an unnamed religious official, in an effort to save his own life, abandons his mistress to be gang-raped and murdered by a mob in the territory of Benjamin. The ensuing war of revenge leaves the tribe of Benjamin near extinction. To repopulate the tribe, the male leaders of the other tribes arrange for hundreds of unsuspecting Israelite women to be kidnapped and forcibly married to the surviving men of Benjamin. In the eyes of the storyteller, this episode illustrates the chaos that inevitably arises when there is no central authority to keep the people in line and punish their offenses.

1 SAMUEL

The primary concern of 1 Samuel is to describe how and why the people of Israel made the transition from a loose confederacy of twelve tribes to a unified nation ruled by a king named David. The first few chapters center on a man named Samuel. Samuel is a transitional figure: though he is called a judge, there are no accounts of him leading an army or winning a military victory. Most of the narratives depict him as a religious leader. Sometimes he acts as a priest, but more often he is portrayed as a prophet who receives messages from Yahweh to deliver to the Israelites. After Samuel's time, the governing function of the judges passes to the king, while priests and prophets take over the religious aspects of Samuel's activities.

According to 1 Samuel, the decision to choose a king was prompted by the poor behavior of Samuel's sons who had replaced him as judges when he grew old, together with the people's desire to be like the nations around them that had kings to lead them into battle. At first Samuel seeks to dissuade them by describing the many burdens that kings invariably impose upon their subjects, but the people continue to demand a king. Finally, Samuel gives in to their demands after Yahweh gives his grudging approval. At Yahweh's instigation, Samuel chooses a man named Saul to serve as Israel's first king. Saul quickly reveals his skills as a battle captain when he leads the Israelite armies to victory over several of their foes. Just as quickly, however, Saul finds himself rejected by Yahweh after he fails to obey Samuel's instructions concerning the conduct of his

battles. Saul continues to rule as king until the end of the book, though he slowly sinks into madness.

The remainder of 1 Samuel centers on a young shepherd boy named David whom Samuel, following Yahweh's guidance, chooses to be the future king of Israel. The story takes many twists and turns before David finally ascends the throne. The twists begin when Saul, unaware of Samuel's action, makes David a member of his court. The book gives two conflicting accounts of how this happened. In the first, David's reputation as a musician leads Saul to invite him to the court to play for him and soothe his troubled mind. In the second, David attracts Saul's attention when he kills a giant named Goliath who had been taunting the Israelite armies. Whatever the cause, David soon wins the heart of Jonathan, Saul's son, in friendship and the hand of Michal, Saul's daughter, in marriage. Appointed a commander in Saul's army, David moves from victory to victory and is acclaimed throughout the land for his military prowess. Saul grows increasingly jealous. Finally, he decides that he must remove David as a threat to his power.

For the next several chapters, Saul and his army pursue David across the land of Israel in an effort to capture and kill him. David, for his part, seeks only to preserve his own life; his respect for the king remains unwavering despite Saul's murderous intentions. Finally, David is forced to take refuge with the Philistines, Israel's enemies, where he works for several years as the leader of a mercenary band. The book ends on a tragic note as Saul, dispirited and fatally wounded, takes his own life to avoid being carried away as a trophy by the Philistines at the end of a losing battle.

2 SAMUEL

Second Samuel tells the story of the rise and fall of King David. Soon after Saul's death, David is proclaimed king by the members of his own tribe, Judah. This leads to a long war between David's forces and the supporters of Saul's son Ishbaal. Finally, Ishbaal is assassinated by his own captains and David is declared king over all Israel.

David establishes his capital at Jerusalem, a city that had remained under the control of the Canaanites until it was conquered by David's warriors. One of his first acts is to build a tent in the city to house the holy implements that had been kept in the tent of meeting since the time of Moses. Yahweh, pleased at being given priority in David's plans, promises that David's descendants will rule over Israel forever. With Yahweh's help, David defeats all of the neighboring peoples and subjects them to Israelite control, enriching Jerusalem with the spoils.

At the height of his success, however, David commits a serious sin that leads to his downfall. Spying a beautiful woman from the roof of his palace, he commands that she be brought to him for his sexual pleasure. When he learns

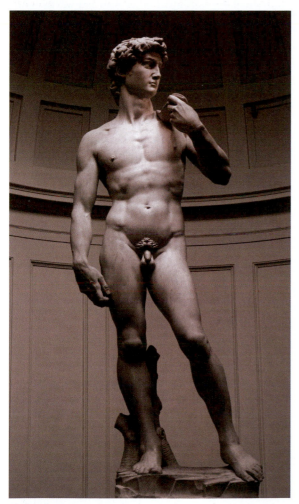

Fig. 8.5. Michelangelo, *David*

that she is pregnant with his child, he has her husband killed in battle. Though he repents of his sinful actions when challenged by one of his advisers, David's world soon begins to fall apart. First, Amnon (one of David's sons) rapes Tamar, his half sister. Then another of his sons orders the rapist killed in order to avenge his sister. This second son, Absalom, leads an armed revolt against his father that forces David to flee from Jerusalem until his army succeeds in defeating Absalom and his supporters. Later a man from outside his family leads a second uprising that results in the bulk of Israel rejecting David's rule until he, too, is defeated.

The book ends with David incurring Yahweh's anger once again by taking a census of his people. (Why this act makes Yahweh angry is never explained.) As punishment, Yahweh sends a pestilence upon the land that kills seventy thousand people in three days. The pestilence ends when David constructs a special altar to Yahweh and offers sacrifices to appease his anger.

1 KINGS

First Kings opens with the death of David, who despite his flaws is honored as the greatest king in Israel's history, and ends with the death a century later of another king, Ahab, who is depicted as one of the worst kings in Israel's history. Most of the stories in 1 Kings focus on the actions of kings and their associates, though prophets also play an important role in the second half of the book.

The book begins with a battle for the succession to the throne in light of David's impending death. The winner is David's son Solomon, who is renowned in the Hebrew Bible for his wisdom and his vast wealth. Much of the narrative about Solomon's reign centers on his construction of a spectacular temple for Yahweh in Jerusalem to replace the tent shrine that was erected there by his father. Solomon is also remembered for organizing a centralized bureaucracy to govern the land and for developing lucrative trade relationships with the surrounding peoples. But Solomon's success finally leads to his undoing: in order to carry out his construction projects, Solomon imposes forced labor and heavy taxation upon his people, leading some to compare his actions to the burdens inflicted by the Egyptians upon their ancestors. To maintain friendly relations with other nations, he enters into political marriages that lead to the introduction of non-Israelite gods into the royal court. The latter years of his reign are marked by several attempted revolts that are said to have been instigated by Yahweh.

Upon Solomon's death, the throne passes to his son Rehoboam, who rejects the people's call to relax the burdens that Solomon had placed upon the nation. Frustrated by his intransigence, the ten northern tribes rebel and choose their own king, a former official of Solomon named Jeroboam. The rebellion is explicitly approved by Yahweh through the mouths of two different prophets. From this time forward the Hebrew people are divided into two nations, Israel in the north and Judah in the south.

The remainder of the book weaves together the stories of the two nations under their first several kings, with the bulk of the attention going to the northern kingdom, Israel. Jeroboam, the first king of Israel, becomes the prototypical "bad king" after he decides to build two new worship centers in the northern kingdom so that his subjects will not have to travel to Jerusalem to offer sacrifices to Yahweh. Not only did these centers pose a com-

petitive threat to the temple in Jerusalem, but each also contained a golden calf (probably a miniature statue of a bull) that was supposed to represent the divine presence. Though the narrative implies that the new temples were dedicated to the worship of Yahweh, the biblical storyteller condemns them as centers of **idolatry**, the worst sin that an Israelite could commit. All of the kings who follow Jeroboam on the throne of Israel, even the ones who are portrayed as capable military and political leaders, are judged to be failures in Yahweh's eyes because they did not remove the calf shrines of Jeroboam. In a similar way, the kings of Judah are judged according to how they viewed the worship of other gods and whether they tried to centralize the worship of Yahweh in the Jerusalem temple. The few who attempted to repress other forms of worship are honored, while the rest receive only qualified endorsement or are rejected as unfaithful to Yahweh.

In the southern kingdom of Judah, the office of king remains within the family of David throughout the narrative. Even when a king acts in ways that are contrary to the will of Yahweh, he is always succeeded by one of his sons, except for a single episode in 2 Kings 11 when the king's mother seizes the throne and reigns for a few years. In the kingdom of Israel, by contrast, the reins of power shift repeatedly from one family to another through a series of military coups. Several of the kings reign for only a short while before they are deposed and murdered. The pattern continues until the coming of Ahab, whose rule occupies the last third of the book.

Ahab is portrayed as a witless tool in the hands of his Phoenician wife, Jezebel, who engages in a campaign to destroy all of the prophets of Yahweh and promote the worship of her own god, **Baal**, in Israel. Jezebel is opposed by the prophet Elijah, whose pronouncements are accompanied by supernatural events that demonstrate the power of Yahweh over the forces of nature that Baal was presumed to control. In one dramatic episode, Yahweh sends fire from heaven to consume the sacrifices that Elijah had laid out on a water-drenched altar after the prophets of Baal proved unable to move their own deity to perform a similar act. Soon other prophets join with Elijah in announcing Yahweh's coming judgment upon the royal pair and their followers. The story ends with Ahab being killed in battle after ignoring the words of a prophet who predicted that he would not come home alive.

Fig. 8.6. Jean-Honoré Fragonard, *Jeroboam Sacrificing to the Golden Calf*

2 KINGS

Second Kings continues the story of the downward spiral of the kingdoms of Israel and Judah. The first ten chapters extend the narrative of the contest between Elijah, Ahab, and Jezebel. The book begins with Elijah announcing Yahweh's judgment against the new king, Ahab's son, for maintaining the religious policies of his parents. Soon afterward, Elijah is taken up to heaven in a fiery chariot. He is succeeded by his assistant Elisha, who takes over as head of the group of prophets that had congregated around Elijah. Like his mentor, Elisha performs a series of miracles, though most of his supernatural acts are done to help or harm individuals rather than to assert Yahweh's preeminence over Baal. Unlike Elijah, Elisha is willing to help the king of Israel, another son of Ahab and Jezebel, on occasions when the nation is threatened by foreign invaders.

The era of Ahab and Jezebel finally comes to an end when Yahweh tells Elisha to take word to an Israelite army commander named Jehu that Yahweh has chosen him to execute his judgment against Ahab's line. Jehu then stages a bloody coup that leads to the brutal murders of the kings of Israel and Judah, the queen mother Jezebel, Ahab's seventy sons, the rest of Ahab's relatives, and all of the prophets and worshippers of Baal. Following Jehu's turbulent reign, the remaining kings of Israel (nine in the space of ninety years) receive only cursory attention until the moment when the nation is conquered by the Assyrians, who had been expanding their rule south and west from their homeland in Mesopotamia. The narrator pauses at this point to explain that the Assyrians overcame Israel not because of their superior military prowess but because Yahweh had decided to punish his people for ignoring his warnings to stop following other deities and worship him alone. The story of the northern kingdom concludes with a brief postscript that tells how the Assyrians deported the surviving Israelites to Mesopotamia and replaced them with people from other parts of their empire who proceeded to add Yahweh to the **pantheon** of deities that they worshipped.

The story of Judah takes a more circuitous path. Events in Judah receive little attention during the stories of Elijah and Elisha, Ahab and Jezebel, and their sons.

The royal house of Judah had intermarried with the family of Ahab and Jezebel during this period, so its kings (and one queen) are condemned in the same breath as the northern kings. Following Jehu's coup, the southern kings are presented in a more positive light, but they still receive only cursory treatment apart from a few brief scenes. Once Israel is conquered, however, the spotlight shifts squarely to Judah and its kings. From here to the end of the book, the nation faces continual challenges from internal corruption (primarily the worship of gods other than Yahweh) and external enemies (Assyrians, Egyptians, and eventually Babylonians). Two kings, Hezekiah and Josiah, are depicted favorably as a result of their efforts to purge the nation of improper forms of worship and bring the nation back to Yahweh. The narratives of their reigns are considerably longer than those of other kings, despite the fact that neither deals effectively with the threat of foreign invasion. The remaining kings are condemned for tolerating or even encouraging forms of religious expression that the narrator regards as contrary to the will of Yahweh. Their reigns are described rather briefly, using stereotyped language that focuses on their

Fig. 8.7. Assyrian armies conquered numerous cities across the ancient Near East, as depicted in this ancient image of their sacking of the Elamite city of Susa.

religious failings. The eventual fall of Judah is attributed to their faulty religious practices.

As the narrative winds down, Judah once again finds itself caught in the middle of political and military conflicts between the great powers to its north and south. First the Egyptians and then the Babylonians depose the king of Judah and replace him with a king of their own choosing. Finally, Zedekiah, the last king of Judah, rebels against the Babylonians, who respond with a full-scale invasion that quickly overruns the territory of Judah and devastates the city of Jerusalem. The walls of the city are torn down, the vessels and implements of the temple are removed, the temple is burned, and a number of the leaders are ritually executed, together with the king's sons. All of the survivors, apart from some poor farmers who are left to till the land, are taken away to Babylonia. The land of Judah is incorporated into the Babylonian Empire.

Fig. 8.8. This model from the Pergamon Museum in Berlin shows the main route into the city of Babylon through which the exiled people of Judah would have been led by their captors.

INTERLUDE: THE UNTOLD STORY OF THE EXILE

One of the most surprising features of the Hebrew Bible is the absence of any coherent narrative about what happened to the people of Judah in the decades following the Babylonian invasion in 586 B.C.E. According to 2 Kings 24–25, the great majority of the people who survived the destruction of Jerusalem were taken away to Babylonia. Later generations, viewing these events through the eyes of those who eventually returned from Babylonia, called this period the Babylonian exile, or more simply, the Exile. The Hebrew Bible says little about the experiences of the exiles who lived for the next several decades in Babylonia and nothing at all about the people who remained in the land of Judah during this time. The story resumes only after the Persians conquer the Babylonians in 539 B.C.E. and announce that the exiles (or their descendants) may return to Judah if they wish. This gap of several decades echoes the narrator's treatment of the residents of Israel who were taken away to Assyria in 722 B.C.E. Nothing is said about these people after they are deported from their land; they simply disappear from the narrative, never to be seen again.

Scholars have been able to piece together some of what happened during the Exile from bits of information contained in the Hebrew Bible and other sources. But the gap in the biblical narrative is still puzzling, especially when we consider that the Exile led to notable changes in the social and religious lives of the people of Judah, including the composition and editing of some of the books that eventually became part of their Scriptures (see chapter 4). Clearly the people who produced these books were more concerned with making sense of their nation's past than with recording their observations about their present circumstances (see chapter 19).

The Hebrew Bible does contain a few narratives about events that supposedly took place in Assyria or Babylonia, but all were written long after the events that they report, and none includes anything like a coherent narrative of the period as a whole. (For a discussion of the contents and historical validity of these books, see chapter 21.)

(a) The book of Tobit, which does not appear in Jewish or Protestant Bibles, recounts a legend about two families who were supposedly deported from Israel at the time of the Assyrian conquest. The story revolves around a series of personal trials and tribulations encountered by the main characters. Nothing is said about the history or experience of the broader Israelite community in Assyria.

(b) The book of Daniel contains a series of loosely related stories about a man named Daniel who was reportedly one of the early deportees from Judah to Babylonia. The stories are presented in chronological order and cover the entire period of the Exile, but they center on Daniel's interactions with the various kings of Babylon and include few references to the larger community of exiles in Babylonia.

(c) The book of Esther is set in Persia during the period after the Persians conquered the Babylonians. The story revolves around a plot by one of the king's high officials to destroy the Jewish community that is scattered across the Persian Empire. All of the events narrated in the book take place in the upper echelons of the Persian administration during a period of not more than a few years. Other than this episode, the book contains no information about events involving the people of Judah in Persia.

EZRA

The grand narrative of the Hebrew Bible resumes in the books of Ezra and Nehemiah, though the continuity of the narrative is not as clear as in the earlier books. The two books tell overlapping stories about the restoration of social and religious life in Judah following the end of the Exile. Both claim to be based on eyewitness records: two of the ten chapters of the book of Ezra include a narrator who uses the first-person pronoun *I*, while most of the book of Nehemiah is framed in first-person language.

The book of Ezra begins with an edict by King **Cyrus** of Persia, whose army has recently conquered the Babylonians, encouraging the exiled people of Judah to return to their homeland and rebuild the temple of Yahweh at the king's expense. Roughly fifty thousand people are said to

have returned to Judah at this time, carrying with them the vessels and implements that the Babylonians had removed from their temple. Upon arriving in Jerusalem, they erect a new altar and reinstate the regular offering of animal sacrifices on the former site of the temple. Then they set out to rebuild the temple.

Fig. 8.9. Stone relief from the palace of Cyrus, sixth century B.C.E., Pasargadae, Iran.

Some of the people who had remained in the land during the Exile offer to help with the construction of the temple, but they are rebuffed by the returning exiles, so they begin looking for ways to stop the project. Eventually they succeed in persuading the new king of Persia to order a halt to the construction in order to prevent Jerusalem from becoming a center of resistance to the Persians. The chronology of the book is confused at this point, but the narrative implies that work on the temple stops for several years until two prophets, Haggai and Zechariah, begin calling on the people to resume their efforts. The local Persian officials send a letter to the new Persian king asking what they should do about the renewed building program. When the Persian king learns that the temple project had been initiated by one of his royal predecessors, he orders his officials to support its

Fig. 8.10. The Persian king Darius I receives one of his officials in this relief from the royal palace at Persepolis. His son, the future king Xerxes I, stands behind him.

construction from the royal treasury. Eventually the work is completed and the temple is dedicated to the worship of Yahweh.

From here the story shifts to a later period when a priest named Ezra returns to Judah at the head of another group of exiles who bring with them more royal funds to support the temple in Jerusalem. Ezra is a scribe—an expert in the laws of Torah—who has been commissioned by the Persian king to teach these laws to the people of Judah and appoint officials who will enforce them. Upon arriving in Judah, Ezra calls upon the men of the community to renew their covenant with Yahweh, an act that includes divorcing the wives that many of them have taken from among the people who had remained in the land during the Exile. The book closes with the people agreeing to follow Ezra's advice in an effort to avoid Yahweh's anger.

NEHEMIAH

The book of Nehemiah tells the story of a man of Judah named Nehemiah who at the beginning of the book is serving as a cupbearer to the Persian king. Upon receiving a report about the awful conditions faced by the residents of Judah, Nehemiah asks the king to allow him to return to his homeland and rebuild the city of Jerusalem. The king not only agrees to his request but also grants him the resources that he needs to carry out his task.

Upon arriving in Jerusalem, Nehemiah inspects the fallen walls of the city and begins making plans to rebuild them. Once the construction begins, however, some of the local officials attempt to hinder his efforts, even threatening to attack the builders while they are working. To stop them, Nehemiah stations guards on the walls for the remainder of the building program. Finally, the walls are completed.

Following an account of Nehemiah's efforts to protect the poor during a time of famine, the book gives a lengthy description of a national covenant renewal ceremony that is led by the scribe Ezra. At a time when the people of Judah are gathered together in Jerusalem from their various towns and villages, Ezra begins to read aloud from the book of Torah. Upon hearing the contents of the book, the people begin to weep and mourn over their failure to abide by the terms of Yahweh's covenant. After the people have confessed their sins and the sins of their ancestors, the leaders enter into a written agreement to obey all of the laws of Torah and to provide everything that is needed for the operation of the temple. The people then cast lots to decide which of them will move to Jerusalem and repopulate the city.

Fig. 8.11. Nehemiah inspecting the walls of Jerusalem; a nineteenth-century woodcut by Gustav Doré.

The final chapters of the book contain assorted stories describing other actions that Nehemiah carried out during his term as governor. These include dedicating the new city wall; appointing officials to manage the affairs of the temple; removing foreign people and practices from the community of Judah (including wives and children); and closing shops and markets that were selling goods on the **Sabbath**. The book ends with a short prayer in which Nehemiah asks Yahweh to remember the many good works that he has done on Yahweh's behalf.

CONCLUSION

The people who cast the Hebrew Bible into its present form placed a high value on stories from the past. But they were not mere preservationists—they labored with great care to shape the traditional stories of their people into a grand narrative that would serve as a national epic

for future generations. The resultant story, which fills nearly half of the Hebrew Bible, does not attempt to offer an objective account of past events. Instead, it presents an interpretation of the past that the editors hoped would prove useful to people in their own time as well as the future.

Behind all of their efforts to make sense of the past lay the conviction that their god Yahweh, the creator of the universe, had been working throughout human history to create a people who would be dedicated to his service. This belief guided every phase of their activities: the stories that they decided to include; the way they told the stories; the amount of space they devoted to particular characters or episodes; the manner in which they combined the stories into larger narrative units; and the overarching themes that they embedded in the narrative. The result is a narrative that is so sweeping in its scope and so insistent in its message that many Jews and Christians today still regard it as a reliable account of human history.

EXERCISE 15

Below is a list of people and events that are part of the grand narrative of the Hebrew Bible. The order in which they are listed, however, is incorrect. Your task is to place them in their proper order by placing a "1" next to the earliest item, a "2" next to the second earliest, and so on. When you are done, look back through the chapter and check your answers. Repeat the exercise until you can arrange all of the items in their correct order. Learning the order of the major biblical events and characters at this point in the course will make it easier for you to understand the materials that will be presented later in the book.

Note: Placing events in their proper order will be easier if you recall what is included in each of the major sections of the biblical narrative.

- Torah   From creation through the end of the Exodus period
- Joshua/Judges   From the entry into Canaan through the period of the judges
- 1 & 2 Samuel   From Samuel through the early kings (Saul and David)
- 1 & 2 Kings   From Solomon through the end of the monarchy

_____ The Exile	_____ The period of the judges
_____ Ahab and Jezebel	_____ The divided kingdom
_____ Abraham and Sarah	_____ Judah conquered by the Babylonians
_____ Noah and the flood	_____ Hezekiah and Josiah
_____ David's reign	_____ The construction of the first temple
_____ The rebuilding of the temple	_____ The Hebrews enter Canaan
_____ The Exodus from Egypt	_____ Jacob and Esau
_____ Ezra teaches the Torah	_____ The creation of the universe
_____ Solomon's reign	_____ The giving of the Torah
_____ Israel conquered by the Assyrians	_____ Samuel and the first king, Saul

Fig. 9.1. Volunteers work at an archaeological dig at Megiddo in northern Israel.

Narrative and History

Why should verification be a prerequisite for our acceptance of a tradition as valuable in respect to historical reality? Why should not ancient historical texts rather be given the benefit of the doubt in regard to their statements about the past unless there are compelling reasons to consider them unreliable?[1]

Despite the overriding theological agenda of the final editors of the Hebrew Bible, both the basic framework of the narrative and many of the original sources that lay behind the final redaction may be regarded as "historical," at least within the parameters of the history-writing that prevailed in the ancient world generally. That is all that we can expect, since it is unreasonable to demand that the ancient writers should have been modern, scientific, and academic historians, or that they should have written the history we want.[2]

The Israel found on the pages of the Old Testament is an artificial creation which has little more than one thing in common with the Israel that existed once upon a time in Palestine, that is, the name. Apart from this not absolutely insignificant element, the Israelite nation as explained by the biblical writers has little in the way of a historical background. It is a highly idealized construct created by ancient Jewish scholars in order to legitimize their own religious community and its religio-political claims on land and religious exclusivity.[3]

Now that we have examined the broad story line of the Hebrew Bible, we can turn our attention to what is undoubtedly the most difficult and controversial set of questions raised by academic study of the Hebrew Bible: How reliable is the biblical narrative? Should it be regarded as history, legend, or some combination of the two? What did the authors and editors of this narrative think they were producing? How much can we know about what really happened in ancient Israel?

THE NATURE OF THE EVIDENCE

As we noted in chapter 5, serious historical investigation of the Hebrew Bible did not begin until the rise of biblical criticism in the eighteenth century. Prior to that time, most Jews and Christians simply assumed that the Bible offered an accurate account of past events. People were aware that the Bible did not report everything that had happened in the ancient world (for example, it did not talk about the history of Greece or Rome), but their fundamental trust in the words of the Bible led them to accept as historically true all that it said about the past, just as they trusted what it said about the nature of God, humans, and the physical world.

Problems arose, however, as soon as critical scholars began to put the biblical stories to the test. Some of these problems were identified through careful study of the Bible itself, while others were discovered by comparing the text of the Bible with external sources.

Problems within the Text

1. Discrepancies and contradictions. One of the earliest problems noted by critical scholars was the presence of discrepancies and contradictions within the biblical story line. Contradictions can be found throughout the Hebrew Bible, including conflicting statements about how many of each type of animal God told Noah to take into the ark before the Flood (Genesis 6:19-20 vs. Genesis 7:2-3); disagreements between Joshua and Judges over who conquered various cities and when the conquests occurred (Judges 1 vs. Joshua 10); divergent testimony concerning who killed King Saul (1 Samuel 31:4-6; 2 Samuel 1:8-10; 2 Samuel 21:12; 1 Chronicles 10:14); and contrary reports about whether certain kings removed the **high places** from the land of Judah (Jehoshaphat: 1 Kings 22:43 vs. 2 Chronicles 17:5-6; Asa: 1 Kings 15:14 vs. 2 Chronicles 14:3-5). Discrepancies are especially common where numbers are involved, as with the length of the Hebrews' stay in Egypt (Genesis 15:13 vs. Exodus 12:40); the number of fighting men enrolled in David's census (2 Samuel 24:9 vs. 1 Chronicles 21:5); the ages of Ahaziah and Jehoiachin when they became kings over Judah (2 Kings 8:26 vs. 2 Chronicles 22:2; 2 Kings 24:8 vs. 2 Chronicles 36:9); and the number of people from various families who returned to Judah after the Exile (Ezra 2; Nehemiah 7).

The Hebrew Bible also contains a number of **doublets**, duplicate stories of the same event that disagree at many points. Obviously the two conflicting accounts could not both be historically correct. Examples include the two creation stories in Genesis 1 and 2 (see chapter 16); two accounts of the changing of Jacob's name to Israel (Genesis 32:22-28; 35:9-10); two stories of the Hebrews crossing the Jordan River under Joshua's direction (Joshua 3–4); and two reports of the slaying of the giant Goliath (by David in 1 Samuel 17:41-51; by Elhanan in 2 Samuel 21:19).

These and many similar examples have led most scholars to conclude that the biblical narratives were constructed out of diverse materials whose contents were not always in agreement. The fact that the contradictions were not eliminated during the editorial process suggests that the people who compiled the Hebrew Bible were more interested in preserving the content of their sources than in formulating a historically coherent narrative.

2. The question of sources. Further questions arise when scholars begin to ask where the authors of the biblical stories got their information. Apart from a few scattered references to materials that are no longer available (Numbers 21:14; Joshua 10:12-13; 2 Kings 14:28; 15:6, 11; and others), none of the narrative books in the Hebrew Bible mentions any specific sources that the authors or editors might have consulted when preparing their stories about Israel's past. As a result, it can be difficult to know when the storytellers are relying on earlier material and when they are simply using their imaginations. Scholars have developed a variety of techniques for identifying earlier source material in the biblical narratives, but there are many stories whose origin and development remain unknown. Some might have been derived from royal chronicles or oral traditions that were passed down over time, but this is unlikely for many stories and impossible for others. Even when scholars succeed in isolating earlier materials, it is often difficult to evaluate the reliability of the sources.

Similar problems surround the colorful details and lively dialogue that adorn many of the biblical stories. The ancient world simply did not have the technology to record precisely what was said and done on a particular occasion, and the bulk of the population was illiterate in any case. While it is certainly possible that someone might have memorized the exact words that a person spoke in a given situation, the idea that these words could have been passed on accurately for centuries before they were written down in the books of the Bible defies all probability, particularly for words that carry little weight in the narrative. Even more problematic are stories that claim to report things that were said outside the hearing of the Hebrew people (Exodus 1:8-10; Joshua 10:3-4; Judges 15:6-7; 2 Samuel 6:20-22) or words that a character spoke or thought to himself (Genesis 27:41; 32:20; Judges 16:20; 1 Samuel 16:6-7; 1 Kings 12:26; Esther 6:6). In a few cases the narrator even claims to report the thoughts of Yahweh or the words that Yahweh spoke to the heavenly hosts (Genesis 1:26; 6:3; 11:6-7; 17:17-18).

All of these facts point to the inevitable conclusion that much of the dialogue and colorful detail in the biblical narratives was created by the narrator to fill out the stories and make them more interesting, not recorded at the moment the events occurred. If this is true, then these elements of the stories cannot be taken seriously as history.

3. The presence of the supernatural. Historians have long been troubled by the pervasive presence of the supernatural in the biblical stories. Questions were raised in ancient times about some of the more flamboyant miracles that appear in the Hebrew Bible, such as the ten plagues that God sent against the Egyptians (Exodus 7:14—12:32); the splitting of the Red Sea (Exodus 14:15-29) and the Jordan River (Joshua 3:7—4:24); the sudden collapse of the walls of Jericho (Joshua 6:1-21); and the sun's standing still for a time so that Joshua could chase down his enemies (Joshua 10:12-14).

Fig. 9.2. Raphael, *Joshua Causes the Sun to Stand Still*

With the coming of the Enlightenment, many intellectuals began to challenge the idea that the deity had performed such spectacular feats in biblical times because they saw nothing like this in their own day. In support of their position, they pointed to the work of scientists whose studies had demonstrated that the universe operated according to a series of mathematical laws. The discoveries of science led many thoughtful people to reject as ludicrous the idea that God might have interfered with the clockwork activity of the cosmos in order to help a particular group of people to escape from trouble.

Similar challenges arose from the world of philosophy, whose most influential figures rejected on principle the idea that humans could know and communicate with the supernatural realm in the manner depicted in the Hebrew Bible. Around the same time, comparative studies of stories told by the "uncivilized" peoples who were being conquered by the nations of Europe convinced many people that belief in miracles and personal interaction with supernatural forces were signs of a primitive worldview that should be rejected by modern thinkers.

As a result of these developments, scholars began to look for naturalistic or psychological explanations for events that were depicted as miracles in the Hebrew

Bible. For example, some explored the terrain and climate around the Red Sea and the Jordan River in hopes of identifying a natural occurrence that might have given rise to exaggerated tales about the supernatural splitting of the two bodies of water. Implicit in their efforts was the assumption that the biblical stories were based on actual events that had been exaggerated or corrupted over the centuries, leaving scholars the task of uncovering the historical truth that lay embedded in the biblical narratives.

Eventually scholars came to recognize that stories about supernatural activity and interactions with the divine realm did not have to be grounded in actual historical events in order to have validity within a religious community. Even fictional narratives can convey valuable insights into the nature of reality and the way humans should live their lives. This insight opened up new and fruitful avenues of investigation as scholars shifted their attention from determining what historical events (if any) gave rise to the biblical miracle stories to exploring what the stories tell us about the religious mind-set of the people who created and used them. Whether any of the miracle accounts reflect actual experiences of supernatural activity is impossible for historians to say—the answer lies beyond the sphere of historical investigation.

As a rule, however, historians tend to ignore references to the supernatural when analyzing the historical dimension of the biblical narratives.

4. The effects of bias. In recent years scholars have become acutely aware that many of the biblical narratives have a theological or social agenda that affects the way the stories are told. The biblical authors and editors were not simply reporting events that happened in the past; they were interpreting the past through a religious lens. This is especially apparent in passages where characters or actions are judged to be good or evil. The standard of judgment is invariably religious; specifically, was the behavior consistent with the will of Yahweh as understood by the people who told or edited the story? Other standards of evaluation (economic or military success, political influence, recognition by future generations, and so forth) become irrelevant once it is determined that a person was unfaithful to Yahweh.

Religious judgments can be expressed in various ways. Sometimes the judgment is stated explicitly by the storyteller, as in the repeated refrain, "He [the king] did what was evil in the sight of the LORD, walking in the way of Jeroboam and in the sin that he caused Israel to commit" (1 Kings 15:34; compare 1 Kings 15:26; 16:13, 19; 2 Kings 14:24; 15:28), or in the less common evaluation, "He [the king] did what was right in the sight of the LORD" (1 Kings 15:11; 2 Kings 12:2; 15:3, 34). On other occasions evaluative comments are placed in the mouth of Yahweh or another character in the story (Numbers 12:5-9; 2 Samuel 12:1-14; 2 Kings 20:1-7; 21:10-15). In still other cases the narrator's judgment is seen in the outcome of the story—people who behave properly experience positive outcomes, while people who act badly bring doom upon themselves and others.

The criteria by which characters and actions are evaluated are fairly consistent throughout the grand narrative of the Hebrew Bible. (For more on these criteria, see chapters 19 and 20.) Scholars believe that these criteria reflect the values and concerns of the people who edited the stories into their present form. This is especially obvious in stories that serve to reinforce the social or religious status quo, as when Yahweh is shown making women subordinate to their husbands (Genesis 3:15) or declaring his support for the royal dynasty of David (2 Samuel 7:8-17; 1 Kings 3:10-14; Psalm 89:20-29). Elsewhere the effect is subtler, as in the story of the giving of the laws on Mount Sinai, where a series of awesome supernatural events underlines the importance of faithfully obeying the laws of Torah (Exodus 19:9-24). Stories are also recited to encourage the audience to follow a particular set of moral or religious values, such as refraining from the worship of other gods (1 Kings 11:1-25; 18:20-40), circumcising male children (Genesis 17:1-27; Exodus 4:24-26), or resisting the temptations of adultery (Genesis 39:1-20; 2 Samuel 11:1—12:23). Stories such as these are told not merely to communicate information about the past but also to motivate people to live by a particular set of behavioral standards.

The presence of bias in the biblical narratives does not mean that the stories have no historical value. But it does mean that historians must be aware of the many ways in which the social or theological agenda of the authors and editors might have influenced their decisions about what kinds of stories were and were not included in the Hebrew Bible and how those stories were told.

Problems with External Sources

1. The results of archaeology. While some scholars were highlighting problems and contradictions within the biblical stories, others were looking for evidence from outside the Bible that might indicate whether the stories were reliable. Much of this external evidence came from the findings of archaeologists. The Middle East is covered with mounds and ruins that mark places where people lived in ancient times. Formal exploration of these sites began in the 1800s. The earliest excavations involved moving huge quantities of earth in an effort to uncover monumental buildings such as palaces and temples. Vast amounts of material were lost or destroyed in the process. Since there was no reliable system for dating the finds, excavators linked their findings to the stories in the Hebrew Bible. Many claimed that their discoveries either supported or refuted the historical veracity of the Bible. Later excavations showed that many of these early claims were unfounded.

Not until the twentieth century did scholars develop scientific methods for identifying sites, excavating them, and analyzing their contents. Today, archaeologists, aided by an army of volunteer helpers, methodically sift through every inch of ground in a carefully monitored effort to uncover every possible piece of evidence about how people lived at a given site during the centuries or even millennia when it was occupied. Decades of comparative studies have enabled archaeologists to develop a system for dating their discoveries with a fair degree of precision. Contemporary excavations use computers and a variety of sophisticated technical equipment, together with the skills of experts from a variety of fields, to analyze their findings.

Along with these changes in method has come a change in mind-set. Most contemporary archaeologists are seeking to understand the history of a particular site, including how people lived there at various times in the past, not to prove or disprove the Bible. As a result of their work, we now have a much better understanding of the social world that is presupposed by the biblical narratives (see chapter 7). But there are still many scholars who refer to archaeological findings when arguing for or against the historical reliability of the biblical narratives. For example, some scholars have argued that the discovery of ash layers (the product of massive burning) in several Canaanite cities at excavation levels associated with the twelfth and thirteenth centuries B.C.E. confirms the biblical accounts of the conquest of Canaan by Joshua and the Israelites. Others have argued that these ash layers actually come from a variety of time periods and that many of the towns and cities that Joshua is supposed to have conquered were either empty or untouched during the time when the Israelites are said to have invaded Palestine. (For more on these points, see chapter 18.) Similar arguments have been raised concerning the size and significance of the kingdoms of Saul and David, as well as many other points in the biblical narratives.

The central problem with using **archaeology** to support or refute the biblical narratives is that it requires interpretation. No one will ever uncover a sign indicating that a particular biblical event happened at this or that site, and the dating system used in archaeology is rarely precise enough to establish solid links between an archaeological discovery and a particular story from the Hebrew Bible. Moreover, archaeologists have excavated only a tiny fraction of the available sites, and there are many

Fig. 9.3. (top) Volunteers work at an archaeological dig at Kinnereth in northern Israel; (bottom) a collection of pottery vessels waiting to be excavated.

gaps and uncertainties in the chronology of the sites that have been excavated. In the end, the fragmentary remains uncovered by archaeologists stand mute without some kind of interpretive framework. Models from the social sciences provide guidelines for describing how people might have lived at a given site, and materials from the surrounding cultures can be used to determine how the site relates to the broader history of the region. But when it comes to reconstructing the history of a site, scholars have to come to terms with the Hebrew Bible, since it is the only written text from antiquity that offers a coherent account of events in the land of Palestine. The question of whether and how the biblical narratives should be used

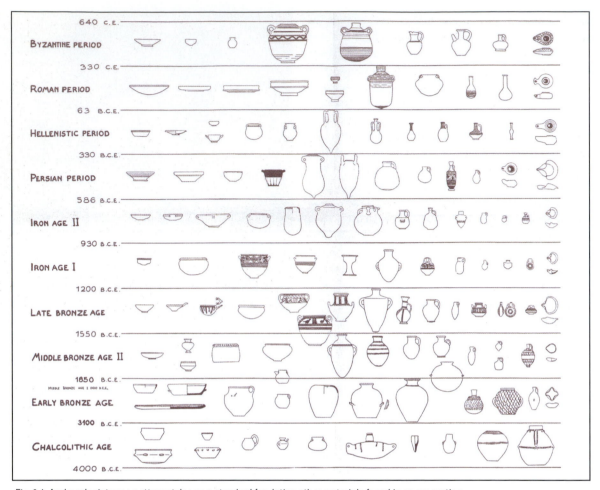

Fig. 9.4. Archaeologists use pottery styles as a standard for dating other materials found in an excavation.

to interpret the findings of archaeology is one of the most difficult and contentious issues in contemporary biblical scholarship.

2. Nonbiblical written materials. Among the ruins of houses, shops, palaces, and temples, archaeologists have occasionally found documents or inscriptions that shed light on the historicity of the biblical narratives. Some of these writings carry dates, while others can be linked to a particular period using the standard methods of dating archaeological discoveries. Most have no direct links to the Hebrew Bible; their value lies in what they tell us about the times and culture in which they were produced. A few, however, have proved useful for evaluating the historicity of the biblical story line.

Among the most beneficial findings have been lists containing the names of the kings who ruled over the kingdoms of Mesopotamia during the period covered by the grand narrative of the Hebrew Bible. Prior to these discoveries, scholars had only a rough idea of when the events narrated in the Hebrew Bible might have occurred, since the stories contain no absolute dates. The discovery of the Assyrian and Babylonian king lists enabled scholars to determine when the various kings of Israel and Judah ruled, which in turn made it possible to date other stories. The lists also showed that some of the biblical narratives contained accurate information about the surrounding nations, while others, such as the books of Daniel and Ezra, included errors (see chapter 21). Additional benefits have resulted from comparisons with records found in Egypt, which include the earliest datable reference to the people of Israel, an inscription known as the **Merneptah Stela**. This inscription has proven crucial in recent debates about the origins of Israel (see chapter 18).

Other important texts provide information about the world in which the biblical stories are set. The discovery of a large number of texts during the excavation of a city named Ugarit on the Mediterranean coast of Syria vastly expanded our knowledge of the religious beliefs and practices of the people of Palestine, providing a balance to the negative depictions of non-Yahwistic religions in the Hebrew Bible. The unearthing of tablets containing ancient Mesopotamian creation and flood stories that predated the biblical accounts likewise enabled scholars to trace the historical development of the versions found in the Hebrew Bible.

Occasionally archaeologists uncover textual materials that pertain directly to characters or events mentioned in the Hebrew Bible. Assyrian and Babylonian records include references to a number of Israelite kings, including a stone obelisk that depicts King Jehu of Israel bowing before the Assyrian King Shalmaneser III. In a similar way, a ninth century B.C.E. **stela** (commemorative pillar) from Moab tells the Moabite version of the wars between Judah and Moab narrated in 2 Kings 3:4-27, including references to king Omri and his son and possibly to king David.

Other Mesopotamian texts that pertain to events narrated in the Hebrew Bible include a series of a wall engravings depicting the siege of Lachish, a fortress in western Judah that was conquered in 701 B.C.E. during the Assyrian invasion of Judah (see 2 Kings 18:13-14) and a clay prism that gives the Assyrian perspective on the siege of Jerusalem that is described in 2 Kings 18:17—19:36. One clay tablet, called the Babylonian Chronicles, describes Nebuchadnezzar's attack on Jerusalem roughly a century later, an event narrated in 2 Kings 24:1-20. From a still later period in the biblical narrative, the Cyrus Cylinder talks about the Persian king Cyrus's policy of returning people who had been displaced by the Babylonians to

Fig. 9.5. (left) The Black Obelisk shows the Israelite king Jehu kneeling before the Assyrian king Shalmaneser III (see p. 260); (right) a tablet from the Babylonian Chronicles describes the fall of the Assyrian capital of Nineveh, which is also celebrated in the biblical book of Nahum.

their native lands and rebuilding the sanctuaries of their gods, a policy echoed in the royal decree found in Ezra 1:1-4. In virtually all of these examples (and many others that could be cited), the external records contain material that both supports and raises problems for the historical reliability of the biblical narrative.

In summary, scholars remain deeply divided over the relevance of archaeology for the historicity of the biblical narratives. Everyone would agree that the labors of archaeologists have enriched our understanding of the world that is presupposed by the authors and editors of the Hebrew Bible. Yet few of their findings can be tied to any particular biblical story, and those where a connection might be discerned can be interpreted in different ways. Archaeologists have uncovered materials that suggest that the people who crafted the biblical narratives had access to historically accurate information when formulating their accounts, but they have also dug up materials that have undermined the reliability of the biblical stories. The complexity of the evidence suggests that we should refrain from making broad statements about the extent to which archaeology supports or undercuts the biblical story line. Every proposed point of contact must be evaluated on its own merits.

THE LIMITS OF HISTORICAL STUDY

In light of these difficulties, how can we know what really happened in ancient Israel during the period covered by the biblical narratives? The simple answer is that we cannot. Historians are limited in what they can accomplish, especially when dealing with events as distant as the ones depicted in the Hebrew Bible. At least three problems hinder any attempt to develop a reliable picture of the history of ancient Israel.

1. The nature of the materials. Few significant written texts have survived from ancient Israel apart from the Hebrew Bible. The people who crafted the stories in this collection might have gathered some of their material from oral or written records, but they possessed neither the resources nor the motivation to check the accuracy of their sources. They wrote not simply to record events in the history of Israel but to offer a religious interpretation of their people's past. Their decisions about what materials to include or exclude and how to tell the story were driven not by historical interests but by religious concerns. They shaped their narratives with considerable literary artistry, especially when speaking about the distant past, where their stories frequently include colorful characters, extended dialogue, dramatic plots, and supernatural interventions. Distinguishing between fact and fiction in these kinds of narratives is a perilous enterprise that requires a substantial amount of guesswork.

2. Methodological problems. Scholars have developed a variety of methods to assist them in tracing the historical development of the biblical materials, but some of these methods are controversial and yield inconsistent results (see chapter 5). Scholars who rely on traditional methods of historical investigation continue to disagree about how to integrate the findings of archaeology with the biblical narratives. Scholars also bring their own presuppositions and biases to their work, and these invariably affect what they see in the texts and how they evaluate what they are reading. As a result, equally skilled scholars can produce very different reconstructions of the history of ancient Israel.

3. Limits of the discipline. All historians recognize that the study of the past is an inherently uncertain enterprise. Some events are documented in multiple sources and can be reconstructed with a fair degree of confidence. More often, however, historians end up working with fragmentary, biased, and/or conflicting materials that are open to multiple interpretations. As they sort through these materials, historians have to make reasoned judgments about many points for which certainty is impossible. Historians also seek to uncover the factors that contributed to particular actions or events and how those factors relate to one another. All of these tasks are highly subjective, requiring the disciplined application of professional skills, expert knowledge, and sound judgment. As a result, historians often arrive at conflicting interpretations of the same material, producing spirited debates about whose interpretation best fits the evidence. Thus the depiction of history as a set of facts is misleading. In reality, the study of history is an inexact science that relies heavily on interpretation and argumentation to determine the relative probability of different scholarly interpretations of the past. Establishing with absolute certainty what really happened is beyond the scope of the historian. This is as true for the biblical narratives as for any other set of documents from the past.

MAKING SENSE OF ISRAEL'S PAST

Scholars who have studied the historicity of the biblical narratives have come to widely varying conclusions about their reliability as historical sources. The differences are so profound that it has become virtually impossible to sketch a coherent portrait of the history of ancient Israel that most scholars would accept. Some believe that events unfolded much as they are described in the Hebrew Bible. Others insist that the biblical narratives must be critically sifted to produce a more accurate historical account. Still others argue that the story line of the Hebrew Bible is a work of fiction that shows little awareness of the actual history of Palestine during the period in question. A review of these three options will suffice to show the breadth of opinion that can be found among contemporary biblical scholars regarding the historical validity of the grand narrative of the Hebrew Bible.

Conservative Interpretations

Conservative scholars aim to "conserve" as much history as possible from the biblical narratives. Most adhere to traditional ideas about the divine inspiration of the Bible and therefore believe that the Bible should be trusted as a historical source. Some regard the Bible as inerrant, meaning that it contains no factual errors of any type, while others accept the possibility that there might be occasional inaccuracies in the biblical text. Virtually all **conservatives** believe that the biblical narratives should be presumed accurate unless solid evidence can be brought forward to the contrary.

Conservative scholars have devoted substantial effort to uncovering data about the historical and cultural environment of the ancient Near East that might shed light on the meaning and reliability of the biblical narratives. Many are driven by a concern to make the Bible come alive to contemporary Jews or Christians by explaining the significance of unusual customs and practices that are mentioned in the Hebrew Bible. Others work to develop solutions to problems that have been noted by scholars who question the historicity of the biblical story line. Some in this group seek to reinforce the credibility of the narrative as a whole by highlighting points from archaeology or the records of the surrounding nations that support the biblical record. Others focus on particular stories or episodes, marshalling evidence in support of their historicity and challenging the arguments of those who question their reliability.

Since conservative scholars regard the biblical narratives as historically accurate, their efforts at historical reconstruction are mostly limited to resolving discrepancies in the biblical story line and relating the grand narrative of the Hebrew Bible to the broader history of the ancient Near East. Some might wonder whether the first eleven chapters of Genesis (from the creation stories to the calling of Abraham) should be considered history in the same sense as the narratives about the kings of Israel and Judah, but few would ever voice such doubts in print, since this could open the door to questioning other biblical stories as well. From a conservative standpoint, this is a path to be avoided, since questioning the trustworthiness of Scripture could lead people to doubt God and ultimately to abandon their faith. This concern for the souls of their followers serves as a strong incentive for conservative scholars to defend the historical accuracy of the biblical narratives.

Maximalist Interpretations

Mainstream critical scholars do not share their conservative colleagues' concern to defend the Bible against historical challenges. In their view, personal religious beliefs should not interfere with historical research, nor should the findings of historians shake an individual's religious faith. Faith and historical study represent two different ways of using the biblical text: historians mine the Hebrew Bible for data about the history of ancient Israel, while believers seek to understand and follow the religious message of the text. Most critical scholars respect the Hebrew Bible—indeed, many are believers themselves—but they recognize that the biblical narratives contain factual errors and biases and so require critical scrutiny before they can be used fruitfully as historical sources.

Until rather recently, most critical scholars believed that generations of research had produced a fairly reliable picture of the history of ancient Palestine and the growth of the biblical literature. Today, however, virtually every aspect of that picture is open to question as a result of protracted debates between two groups of scholars commonly known as **maximalists** and **minimalists**. Neither group is entirely happy with these titles, but no other terminology has found broad acceptance. Both groups agree that the biblical narratives were produced long after the events that they narrate and that critical sifting is required before they can be used as historical sources. But they differ widely in their estimates of how much historical material the stories contain. Maximalists believe that the majority of the stories are based on earlier oral or written traditions that contained significant amounts of historically trustworthy data. Minimalists, on the other hand, regard the biblical narratives as largely fictional works composed in the **postexilic** period to forge a common past for a group of people who were seeking to assert their claims to control the land of Palestine. The ideas of the minimalists will be discussed further below.

Maximalists cite four lines of evidence in support of their position. The first is archaeology. While many important sites remain unexcavated, maximalists can point to numerous cases in which the findings of archaeology lend an aura of credibility to the broad contours of the biblical narrative and sometimes even to individual stories. Examples can be found in the discussions of the primary narratives in chapters 18–21.

The second type of evidence cited by maximalists is correlation with external sources. As we saw earlier, materials from surrounding cultures refer repeatedly to the kings and people of Israel and Judah from at least the time of the monarchy. The broad story line of the Hebrew Bible also coincides at many points with what we know about the history of the ancient Near East from other sources. Some of the individual stories show familiarity with cultural practices that had changed or died out by the time of the final editors. These kinds of evidence undermine the minimalist view that the people who produced these texts knew little about the true history of ancient Palestine.

The third line of argument concerns the use of earlier written sources. Source critics and redaction critics look for evidence within the narratives to indicate that the present text is based on earlier written materials (breaks in the story line, differences in style, duplicate accounts of the same event, and the like). Most of their work is too technical for an introductory textbook, but their studies have led many scholars to conclude that the present grand narrative of the Hebrew Bible is based on earlier narratives that were composed during the times of the kings. If this is true, it would mean that the biblical narratives contain material that was written down closer to the time when the events are supposed to have occurred, thus making it more likely that they include reliable information. Supporters of this view point to a number of places where the authors of the biblical narratives name texts where their readers can learn more about the events that they are reporting, including "the book of the annals of the kings of Israel" (cited twenty times), "the book of the annals of the kings of Judah" (fifteen times), "the book

of the kings of Israel and Judah" (seven times), and "the book of Jashar" (Judges 10:13; 2 Samuel 1:18). (For more on these materials, see chapter 20.) Many maximalist scholars believe that these references indicate that the authors used official court documents that were written close to the time of the events, though they acknowledge that the present narratives have been substantially elaborated by the art of the storyteller.

Finally, supporters of the maximalist position point to comparative studies of oral traditions in other cultures. These studies suggest that in cultures where the bulk of the population is illiterate, as in ancient Israel, oral traditions can preserve genuine historical memories for generations or even centuries, as discussed in chapter 4. This does not mean that all oral narratives are based on historical occurrences, nor that oral traditions are capable of preserving minute historical details with accuracy. But it does serve to lessen the problem of the temporal distance between the composition of the biblical narratives and the events that they claim to narrate.

On the whole, maximalist scholars believe that historians should evaluate each story on its own merits, weighing and sifting the evidence for and against its reliability while avoiding sweeping judgments about the reliability or unreliability of the narrative as a whole. They recognize that different scholars will read the evidence differently, but they insist that consistent and rigorous application of traditional methods of historical analysis will produce agreement on the main lines of the history of ancient Israel.

As a result of their studies, most maximalist scholars feel confident that the stories depicting the era of the monarchy (specifically, from Saul and David onward) contain substantial amounts of historical material. Their reconstructions of the history of this period do not stray far from the biblical story line, though they discount many of the details of particular episodes. For the period prior to Saul and David, their conclusions are more diverse, since evidence that might confirm or refute the biblical narratives is sparse. Some maximalists believe that the earlier stories are mostly fiction, since they show more signs of the storyteller's art and share many features with the myths and legends of other cultures: characters who engage in dialogue with the deity, unlikely heroes, divinely aided victories, miraculous occurrences, and so forth. Others insist that there must be a historical basis for some of the stories since they match up fairly well with what we know about the times and places in which they were supposed to have taken place. Many in this group believe that the book of Judges preserves reliable information about the structure of Israelite society prior to the rise of the monarchy and possibly about some of the events and characters of the period. Most also think that the Exodus story has some kind of historical basis—even if the actual events have been exaggerated by generations of storytellers—since they find it hard to understand why the Israelites would have created a fictional story about their ancestors being enslaved in a foreign country. Fewer believe that historical events lie behind the narrative of the conquest of Canaan as narrated in the book of Joshua or the stories of Abraham, Isaac, and Jacob and their families. Virtually none would argue for the historicity of any of the stories prior to Abraham (Genesis 1–11).

Minimalist Interpretations

Minimalist scholars, like maximalists, are a diverse group, but most hold similar views of the origins of the Hebrew Bible that shape their opinions about the historicity of the biblical narratives. Minimalists begin with the fact that the Hebrew Bible did not reach its present form until well after the Babylonian exile. But where maximalists see the postexilic era as a time when earlier oral and written traditions were edited to form a coherent story line, minimalists believe that virtually the entire content of the grand narrative was created for the first time during this period. Most think that the story was formulated by a group of elites who wanted to justify their claims to dominate the social, political, and religious institutions of Palestinian society in the postexilic period. Some of its contents may have originated as late as the second or first century B.C.E. In other words, the narrative is a pious fiction that bears little relation to the actual history of Palestine during the period it purports to narrate.

Minimalists cite at least three lines of argument in favor of their position. The first, like that of the maximalists, is archaeology. According to minimalist scholars, the archaeological record undercuts the biblical narratives at key points. For example, the Hebrew Bible depicts David and Solomon as important regional rulers who controlled not only Palestine but also most of the surrounding territories. But the archaeological record offers little support for this contention. According to the minimalists, Jerusalem did not become a major political center until the ninth century B.C.E. or later, a full century or more after the time of David and Solomon. The kingdoms of Israel and Judah, if they existed at all, were small, isolated, and insignificant within the broader landscape of the ancient Near East. Minimalists also contend that there is no evidence outside the Hebrew Bible to indicate that the people who lived in the towns and villages of Palestine thought of themselves as members of a single people called Israel. The neighboring peoples rarely use this name, and the few places where it does occur only confirm the existence of a small state called Israel, not the united ethnic, political, and religious community that is depicted in the Hebrew Bible. In general, minimalists accuse other scholars of relying too heavily on the Bible when trying to make sense of archaeological remains and thus distorting the historical evidence.

The second argument concerns the availability of early source material. To minimalist scholars, the time gap between the events in the biblical story line and the late postexilic period—several hundred years at a minimum—is simply too great to think that it could have been bridged by oral traditions. The only reason that they can see for proposing such a process is to salvage the historicity of the biblical narratives, a task that they believe misrepresents the true history of the region. Viewing the stories as works of fiction created for a particular purpose in the late postexilic period removes the need for such a face-saving expedient.

The third and most important line of argument concerns the purpose of the narrative. Most maximalist scholars believe that the grand narrative of the Hebrew Bible was created to answer important questions that were raised by the Babylonian conquest of Judah and the deportation of its citizens to Mesopotamia. The underlying message of the narrative is that these events occurred because Yahweh was punishing his people for their sins. Minimalists, on the other hand, see the **exilic** orientation of the story as part of a fictional illusion created by the authors. As they see it, the entire story of Israel and Judah was formulated to serve the purposes of a group of elites who had little or no information about the actual history of the two minor Palestinian states that bore these names.

Minimalists have differing ideas about when these elites lived and what they were trying to accomplish. At one end are scholars who trace the composition of the narrative to an ill-defined group that sought to gain control over the city of Jerusalem and its institutions in the late sixth or early fifth century B.C.E. by insisting that they were descended from the original inhabitants of the land of Judah. In reality, few of these people had any previous connection with Jerusalem or Palestine; they were united only by a common story and a common desire for power. At the other end are scholars who would date the story much later (second to first century B.C.E.) and attribute it to one of the parties in the protracted power struggles that marked the Jewish community during this time. Though they disagree about the specifics, minimalist scholars agree that the biblical narratives were created as ideological weapons and therefore should not be taken seriously as historical texts.

What, then, do minimalists say about the actual history of ancient Palestine? In general, they argue that much of the history of the region is beyond recovery. But this does not mean that the effort is worthless. Archaeological excavations reveal how the people of Palestine lived at various times and places. Careful correlations of data from different archaeological sites can enable scholars to construct a skeletal history of the region. Studies of geography and climate provide information that can be useful for explaining changes in habitation patterns and economic activities. References to the people of Palestine in the documents of Mesopotamia and Egypt offer further bits of information that can be used to illuminate particular periods. Through it all, scholars must resist the temptation to use the biblical narratives as a framework for organizing their historical observations, since this invariably leads them to misread the evidence. This shortage of historical information about ancient Israel and Judah does not pose a serious problem for minimalist scholars, since they believe that the biblical narratives were designed to speak to a later period for which we have better historical sources.

SO WHO IS RIGHT?

Many students are troubled to hear that scholars have raised so many questions about the historicity of the biblical narratives because the idea conflicts with much of what they have been taught in their church or synagogue. Most want someone to tell them which theory is correct. Unfortunately, there is no objective basis for answering this question. Instead, each approach has its strengths and weaknesses.

1. Conservatives can be commended for wanting to take the Hebrew Bible seriously as a historical source. They recognize that the people who produced these texts believed they were writing about the history of their people, regardless of the validity of their sources. On the other hand, conservative scholars often overlook the difficulties associated with preserving and reporting past events in the ancient world. The value of their approach is also limited by their consistent reticence about accepting historical evidence that runs contrary to their fundamental beliefs about the Bible. As a result, their reconstructions of the history of ancient Israel include substantial amounts of questionable material and ignore or suppress important historical evidence.

2. Maximalists are known for their careful historical research and their judicious application of the standard methods of critical **historiography** to the biblical narratives. Most are intimately familiar with the intricacies of the archaeological, linguistic, and textual evidence that relates to the historicity of events in the ancient Near East. As a result, their historical reconstructions are usually thoughtful and well reasoned within the parameters of their method. On the other hand, maximalists have been criticized for practicing outdated methods of historiography that pay too little attention to the biases inherent in their materials, including the biblical narratives. Maximalists have also been accused of giving too much credit to the Hebrew Bible as a historical source, leading to historical reconstructions that include too much unreliable material.

3. Minimalists have contributed to the discussion by highlighting the creative role of the people who cast the biblical texts into their present form. By situating the

books in a postexilic context, they have raised important questions about the agendas that shaped the biblical narratives and the amount of historical information that might have been available to the people who formulated the stories. Their skepticism toward traditional approaches has also led them to recognize problems with the methods and conclusions of maximalist scholars, including their tendency to rely too heavily on the biblical narratives as historical sources. On the other hand, minimalist scholars have been criticized for misreading the archaeological evidence and failing to take seriously important materials from outside the Hebrew Bible that support the historicity of the biblical narratives. Opponents have also challenged their apparent presumption that the presence of an agenda somehow negates the possibility that a narrative might be rooted in genuinely historical materials.

In light of the many questions that remain unanswered concerning the historicity of the biblical narratives, this book will not attempt to offer a coherent reconstruction of the history of ancient Israel. Instead, evidence concerning historicity will be presented in conjunction with the analysis of individual episodes in chapters 18–21. The resultant discussion will no doubt seem rather fragmented and open-ended, but that is all that can be reasonably attempted at this point in the debate.

Fortunately, the method of this book does not require a clearly defined and coherent historical reconstruction. Since we are concerned primarily with the value of these texts to the people who produced and used them, what matters for our purposes is how ancient audiences might have understood the stories, not what contemporary scholars believe about the history that lies behind them. Apart from a few minimalists, scholars agree that the people who told and passed on these narratives, whether orally or in writing, thought that they were recounting actual events from their people's past. As far as they were concerned, Abraham was the physical and spiritual ancestor of their people, Yahweh delivered the Torah to Moses on Mount Sinai, the Israelites conquered the Canaanites and settled in their land, and the prophet Elijah once called down fire from heaven to demonstrate that Yahweh was the genuine god of Israel. As long as ancient audiences accepted these stories as true, their value for sustaining faith was the same whether or not

the events happened exactly as narrated. (The significance of stories for religious believers will be discussed further in chapter 15.)

CONCLUSION

Critical scholars have identified many reasons to question the historical validity of the biblical narratives: the presence of contradictions and discrepancies within the stories; uncertainty over the sources that were used in constructing the narratives; the inclusion of improbable supernatural events; the distorting effects of authorial bias; and conflicts with archaeological data and other external sources. Scholarly studies have also uncovered many forms of evidence that can be cited in support of the narratives, including external materials that coincide with some of the biblical stories and signs that earlier oral and written sources were used in the composition of the narratives.

Scholars vary widely in the amount of weight that they give to these lines of evidence in reconstructing the history of ancient Israel. Conservatives believe that the biblical accounts should be trusted unless conclusive evidence can be brought forward to disprove them. Maximalists insist that each narrative must be evaluated on its own merits using the standard methods of critical historiography. Minimalists claim that the stories are basically propaganda pieces that contain little reliable historical information about ancient Israel and Judah. Each position has its strengths and weaknesses that must be considered when weighing its methods and results.

In the end, the data are simply too fragmentary and biased and the methods of historiography too limited to allow us to be certain about much of the history that lies behind the biblical texts. But there is still significant value in weighing the evidence to determine which interpretations are more probable than others. For the people who created these narratives, on the other hand, it was the religious message and not the bare historical data that ultimately mattered.

EXERCISE 16

Below are translations of two important external sources that pertain to the history of ancient Israel. Beneath the title of each text is a reference to a biblical passage that coincides with the external source. Read the external source first, then the biblical passage, noting the similarities and differences between them. Then choose one of the passages and write a couple of paragraphs summarizing the relation between the two passages, including (a) specific points at which they agree and disagree; (b) possible explanations for their differences; and (c) the implications of your observations for the historicity of the passage.

(a) The Mesha Stela (830 B.C.E.) (compare with 2 Kings 3:4-27)

I am Mesha, the son of Kemosh[-yatti], the king of Mesha, the Dibonite. My father was king over Moab for thirty years, and I was king after my father. And I made this high-place for Kemosh in Karchoh, . . . for he has delivered me from all kings (?) and because he has made me look down on all my enemies. Omri was the king of Israel, and he oppressed Moab for many days, for Kemosh was angry with his land. And his son succeeded him, and he said—he too—"I will oppress Moab!" In my days did he say [so], but I looked down on him and his house, and Israel has gone to ruin, yes, it has gone to ruin forever! And Omri had taken possession of the whole land of Medeba, and he lived there (in) his days and half the days of his son, forty years, but Kemosh restored it in my days. And I built

Baal Meon, and I made in it a water reservoir, and I built Kiriathaim. And the men of Gad lived in the land of Ataroth from ancient times, and the king of Israel built Ataroth for himself, and I fought against the city, and I captured it, and I killed all the people [from] the city as a sacrifice (?) for Kemosh and for Moab, and I brought back the fire-hearth of his Uncle (?) from there, and I hauled it before the face of Kemosh in Kerioth, and I made the men of Sharon live there, as well as the men of Maharith. And Kemosh said to me: "Go! Take Nebo from Israel!" And I went in the night, and I fought against it from the break of dawn till noon, and I took it, and I killed [its] whole population, seven thousand male citizens (?) and aliens (?), and female citizens (?) and aliens (?), and servant girls; for I had put it to the ban for Ashtar Kemosh. And from there, I took thence the vessels of YHWH, and I hauled them before the face of Kemosh. And the King of Israel had built Jahaz, and he stayed there during his campaigns against me, and Kemosh drove him away before my face, and I took two hundred men of Moab, all its division (?), and I led it up to Jahaz. And I have taken it in order to add it to Dibon.[1]

(b) Sennacherib's Prism 3:18-49 (689 B.C.E.) (compare with 2 Kings 18:13—19:36)

As for Hezekiah, the Judean, I besieged forty-six of his fortified walled cities and surrounding smaller towns, which were without number. Using packed-down ramps and applying battering-rams, infantry attacks by mines, breeches, and siege machines, I conquered (them). I took out 200,150 people, young and old, male and female, horses, mules, donkeys, camels, cattle, and sheep, without number, and counted them as spoil. He himself, I locked up within Jerusalem, his royal city, like a bird in a cage. I surrounded him with earthworks, and made it unthinkable for him to exit by the city gate. His cities which I had despoiled I cut off from his land and gave them to Mitinti, king of Ashdod, Padi, king of Ekron and Sillibel, king of Gaza, and thus diminished his land. I imposed dues and gifts for my lordship upon him, in addition to the former tribute, their yearly payment. He, Hezekiah, was overwhelmed by the awesome splendor of my lordship, and sent me after my departure to Nineveh, my royal city, his elite troops (and) his best soldiers, which he had brought in as reinforcements to strengthen Jerusalem, with 30 talents of gold, 800 talents of silver, choice antimony, large blocks of carnelian, beds (inlaid) with ivory, armchairs (inlaid) with ivory, elephant hides, ivory, ebony-wood, boxwood, multicolored garments, garments of linen, wool (dyed) red-purple and blue-purple, vessels of copper, iron, bronze and tin, chariots, siege shields, lances, armor, daggers for the belt, bows and arrows, countless trappings and implements of war, together with his daughters, his palace women, his male and female singers. He (also) dispatched his messenger to deliver the tribute and to do obeisance.[2]

1. Translation by K. A. D. Smelik, "The Inscription of King Mesha," in *The Context of Scripture*, ed. William W. Hallo and K. Lawson Younger (Leiden: Brill, 2000), 2:137–38.

2. Translation by Mordechai Cogan, "Sennacherib's Siege of Jerusalem," in *The Context of Scripture*, ed. William W. Hallo and K. Lawson Younger (Leiden: Brill, 2000), 2:302–3.

PART THREE
THE RELIGION OF THE HEBREW BIBLE

Fig. 10.1. A Torah scroll is displayed at a former synagogue in Cologne, Germany.

The Hebrew Bible as a Religious Text

Religion is a seeking and responding to holiness through acts of devotion, through proclamation and reflection, and through membership in holy communities with those who share common beliefs, concerns, ceremonies, and traditions.[1]

Religion is a system of symbols which acts to establish powerful, pervasive, and long-lasting moods and motivations in men by formulating conceptions of a general order of existence and clothing these conceptions with such an aura of factuality that the moods and motivations seem uniquely realistic.[2]

Religion is the state of being grasped by an ultimate concern, a concern which qualifies all other concerns as purely preliminary and which itself contains the answer to the question of the meaning of our life.[3]

All books of Scripture are rooted in a historical context, so any attempt to understand their content requires at least a general familiarity with the history of the people who produced them. This is especially true for a collection like the Hebrew Bible, where virtually every book either narrates or refers to events that the authors believed took place in the times of their ancestors.

But the people who wrote, compiled, and edited these texts were not simply recording the past for posterity. The Hebrew Bible is a collection of religious texts, not a history book. When it speaks about the past, its vantage point is invariably religious—the people who produced it believed that the events of history were determined not by social, economic, or political causes, but by the will and actions of Yahweh their god. Thus even the so-called Historical Books of the Hebrew Bible were written to communicate a religious message.

When we turn to the other books in this collection, the religious orientation becomes even more apparent. References to the supernatural world appear on nearly every page, and much of their content revolves around the question of how the people of Yahweh should express their devotion to the deity.

As we turn to investigate what these books tell us about the religious beliefs and practices of the people who produced them, however, problems arise. Two issues in particular must be addressed before we can proceed with our investigation of the religious dimension of the Hebrew Bible: (a) What do we mean by *religion*, and (b) what is the relation between religion and books of Scripture?

THE HEBREW BIBLE AND RELIGION

The Hebrew Bible contains many passages whose link to religion is not at all apparent to contemporary readers. Consider the following passages.

Whoever kidnaps a person, whether that person has been sold or is still held in possession, shall be put to death. *(Exodus 21:16)*

You shall not let your animals breed with a different kind; you shall not sow your field with two kinds of seed; nor shall you put on a garment made of two different materials. *(Leviticus 19:19)*

A single witness shall not suffice to convict a person of any crime or wrongdoing in connection with any offense that may be committed. Only on the evidence of two or three witnesses shall a charge be sustained. *(Deuteronomy 19:15)*

When you sit down to eat with a ruler, observe carefully what is before you, and put a knife to your throat if you have a big appetite. Do not desire the ruler's delicacies, for they are deceptive food. *(Proverbs 23:1-3)*

How sweet is your love, my sister, my bride! how much better is your love than wine, and the fragrance of your oils than any spice! Your lips distill nectar, my bride; honey and milk are under your tongue; the scent of your garments is like the scent of Lebanon. *(Song of Solomon 4:10-11)*

While it might be possible to guess at the religious significance of some of these verses, the issues that they address do not sound particularly religious to a modern ear. In other passages the link to the supernatural world is clear, but a contemporary reader might wonder how such an issue came to be included in the sphere of religion in the first place. The following passages could be said to fit this category.

This is my covenant, which you shall keep, between me and you and your offspring after you: Every male among you shall be circumcised. You shall circumcise the flesh of your foreskins, and it shall be a sign of the covenant between me and you. Throughout your generations every male among you shall be circumcised when he is eight days old, including the slave born in your house and the one bought with your money from any foreigner who is not of your offspring. *(Genesis 17:10-12)*

When a person has on the skin of his body a swelling or an eruption or a spot, and it turns into a leprous disease on the skin of his body, he shall be brought to Aaron the priest or to one of his sons the priests. The priest shall examine the disease on the skin of his body, and if the hair in the diseased area has turned white and the disease appears to be deeper than the skin of his body, it is a leprous disease; after the priest has examined him he shall pronounce him ceremonially unclean. *(Leviticus 13:2-3)*

If anyone of the house of Israel or of the aliens who reside among them eats any blood, I will set my face against that person who eats blood, and will cut that person off from the people. For the life of the flesh is in the blood; and I have given it to you for making atonement for your lives on the altar; for, as life, it is the blood that makes atonement. *(Leviticus 17:10-11)*

Still other texts express divine approval for ideas and actions that run counter to the values of many contemporary readers. The passages below should be sufficient to indicate the nature of the problem.

But if the slave declares, "I love my master, my wife, and my children; I will not go out a free person," then his master shall bring him before God. He shall be brought to the door or the doorpost; and his master shall pierce his ear with an awl; and he shall serve him for life. *(Exodus 21:5-6)*

The LORD spoke to Moses, saying: Speak to Aaron and say: No one of your offspring throughout their generations who has a blemish may approach to offer the food of his God. For no one who has a blemish shall draw near, one who is blind or lame, or one who has a mutilated face or a limb too long, or one who has a broken foot or a broken hand, or a hunchback, or a dwarf, or a man with a blemish in his eyes or an itching disease or scabs or crushed testicles. No descendant of Aaron the priest who has a blemish shall come near to offer the LORD's offerings by fire; since he has a blemish, he shall not come near to offer the food of his God. *(Leviticus 21:16-21)*

If a man meets a virgin who is not engaged, and seizes her and lies with her, and they are caught in the act, the man who lay with her shall give fifty shekels of silver to the young woman's father, and she shall become his wife. Because he violated her he shall not be permitted to divorce her as long as he lives. *(Deuteronomy 22:28-29)*

If you do not diligently observe all the words of this law that are written in this book, fearing this glorious and awesome name, the LORD your God, then the LORD will overwhelm both you and your offspring with severe and lasting afflictions and grievous and lasting maladies. He will bring back upon you all the diseases of Egypt, of which you were in dread, and they shall cling to you. Every other malady and affliction, even though not recorded in the book of this law, the LORD will inflict on you until you are destroyed. *(Deuteronomy 28:58-61)*

Clearly the people who wrote, compiled, and edited the Hebrew Bible had a different understanding of religion than is common in modern Western societies. In some ways their ideas and practices are more like those of traditional Native Americans or African tribal groups than like contemporary Judaism, Christianity, or Islam. If we wish to understand the religious dimension of the Hebrew Bible, we must be willing to lay aside our own cultural ideas and value judgments and enter imaginatively into the mind-set of people who viewed the world very differently than most of us do today. If we cannot do this, the world of the Hebrew Bible will remain forever closed to us.

WHAT IS RELIGION?

Religion is a notoriously difficult term to define. Like obscenity, most people probably believe that they know it when they see it—until they come face to face with a religious system that differs markedly from their own. Scholars of religion, by contrast, are more attuned to the richly variegated forms of religious expression that can be seen around the globe. Despite repeated efforts, they have found it difficult to formulate a definition of religion that could apply to them all.

Most scholars now recognize that any definition that would be broad enough to encompass every form of religion in the world today would be so general and abstract that its value would be minimal. Instead, scholars prefer to look for common features or patterns of religion that recur across different cultures. One system of analysis that many scholars have found helpful identifies six dimensions, or categories, of religious life that can be seen in virtually all forms of religion.[4]

1. *The mythological dimension.* Every religion relies on stories to transmit its beliefs and values from one generation to the next. The content of religious stories varies widely from group to group, but certain issues attract the attention of storytellers in every culture, including the

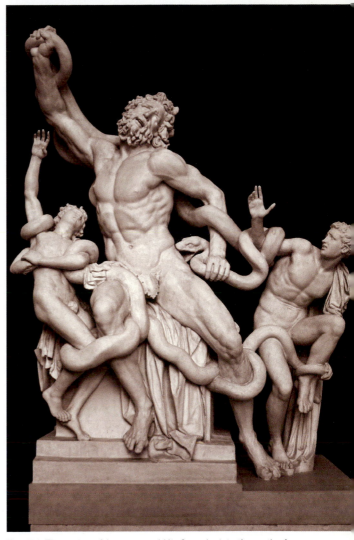

Fig. 10.2. The statue of *Laocoon and His Sons* depicts the myth of the strangulation of a Trojan priest and his family by snakes sent by gods who favored the Greeks in the Trojan War.

origins of the universe and its inhabitants, the history of their people, the lives of great leaders from the past, the activities of the supernatural world, and so forth. Some of these stories might be grounded in history, while others are clearly framed as fiction or fantasy. Scholars often use the term **myth** to describe both fact-based and fictional stories, since they are concerned primarily with the way the stories function within the religious community, not with their factuality. The term *myth* does not imply any judgment about the truth value of the stories.

Fig. 10.3. The Pope plays a central role in defining the doctrines of the Roman Catholic Church.

informally (often through stories) and taken for granted within the group.

3. *The ethical dimension.* Questions about proper and improper conduct are vital to every religion. Religions vary in the answers that they give to these questions, but there are certain points on which virtually all would agree, such as encouraging love and peace and discouraging harm to others. Disagreements can usually be traced to differences in their histories or patterns of belief. Some religious groups have lists of laws or rules that define good and bad conduct, while others limit their instruction to broad moral principles and leave it to individual believers to apply these principles to their own lives. Many also offer moral guidance for the broader society in which they are embedded. Religions frequently reinforce their ethical

Fig. 10.4. The issue of gay marriage is an ethical question that has engaged the minds of many religious people in recent years.

teachings with promises of future rewards and punishments, whether in this life or beyond. Ethical instruction usually begins in childhood and continues throughout the life of the believer.

2. *The doctrinal dimension.* Every religion has a set of beliefs about the ultimate nature of reality and the place of human beings in the cosmos. Most religions claim that there is more to reality than the visible universe, but their beliefs about the nature of the unseen world vary widely. Some groups attribute their beliefs to the insights of a wise teacher or leader from the past, while others follow the distilled wisdom of generations of ancestors. Religious beliefs do not have to be systematically organized or internally consistent to be accepted by a religious group, but they do have to be coherent enough to make sense to the followers of the religion. In cases where greater consistency is desired, religions often delegate the task to individuals who have special expertise in theological reflection. Some groups enshrine their most important beliefs in a formal **creed** or statement of belief, but most religious ideas are passed on

4. *The ritual dimension.* Rituals are formalized actions by which religious people seek to encounter, manipulate, or respond to the supernatural world. Rituals presume familiarity with the central stories and beliefs of a religion; indeed, most rituals can be interpreted as symbolic enactments of key beliefs. People who do not share the group's beliefs will not comprehend the meaning of much that is done in a ritual context. Some acts might even seem nonsensical or irreligious to an outsider. Rituals can be as simple and spontaneous as prayers before a meal

or as elaborate and orchestrated as a multiday religious festival. Most groups distinguish between rituals that are used in public settings and rituals that may be performed in private by individuals. Some limit the performance of certain rituals, particularly those that involve the manipulation of supernatural powers, to trained specialists (priests, monks, shamans, and the like).

5. *The experiential dimension.* All religions believe that there is some kind of invisible reality that stands behind the visible order. Most contend that humans can experience this reality through the use of special techniques or rituals. Some believe that experiences of the supernatural are open to anyone who seeks them, while others insist that certain kinds of experiences are available only to trained experts or figures from the past. Religious

experience is closely tied to beliefs. Religious beliefs not only tell believers what is out there to be experienced but also help to define and explain the experiences that group members report. Since religions have different beliefs, each religion has its own ideas about the kinds of experiences that believers should seek, the means by which these experiences can be achieved, the effects of religious experiences, and the relation between experience and other aspects of religious life. Some religions place more emphasis on group experiences, while others emphasize the private and personal nature of human encounters with the supernatural realm.

Fig. 10.6. A Buddhist meditates before a statue of the Buddha as a means of opening his mind to a religious experience.

Fig. 10.5. A spirit house in Thailand where worshippers come to make ritual offerings to supernatural beings.

6. *The social dimension.* Religions are by definition communal enterprises. Like other groups, they require organization and direction. Most have some sort of formal or informal organizational structure that designates certain individuals or classes of people as leaders and others as followers. Religious leaders fulfill a variety of roles, including defining and defending the beliefs and practices of the group; educating and disciplining group members; overseeing group activities; representing the religion to outsiders; and ensuring the continuation of the religion to the next generation. Not all religions hold regular public meetings, but most have some type of system by which members can interact with one another on a periodic basis, thus promoting a sense of group identity.

Fig. 10.7. The Japanese Shinto ceremonies have a distinctly social dimension.

very far toward understanding it. The chief value of these categories lies in the way they help us to recognize and make sense of the breadth and diversity of the cultural systems that we call religion.

People who know little about other religions have a tendency to interpret and judge them in the light of their own. By paying careful attention to these six dimensions of religion, we can learn to overcome this natural bias and allow ourselves to appreciate the richness, complexity, and uniqueness of the religious systems that come to expression in the pages of the Hebrew Bible.

> ## EXERCISE 17
>
> Read the following passages from the Hebrew Bible and see how many examples of the six dimensions of religion you can find in each passage.
>
> • Exodus 24:1-18
> • Nehemiah 8:1-18
> • Psalm 135:1-21
> • Jeremiah 7:1-29

Many have rituals that can only be conducted in a group gathering. Most religions also encourage their members to give material and emotional support to one another, especially during times of crisis. Some also seek to influence or improve the society around them, while others do not see this as their responsibility.

These six dimensions of religion—the mythological, the doctrinal, the ethical, the ritual, the experiential, and the social—have been identified in virtually every religious group that scholars have studied, so there is ample reason to think that they will be useful in our study of the religion of the Hebrew Bible. There is nothing magical about the categories, however: simply pinning labels onto the various elements of a religion does not take us

SCRIPTURES AND RELIGION

As we noted in chapter 4, the creation of Scriptures requires literacy. During the time when most contemporary books of Scripture were being composed, this skill was limited to a small class of elite males. These people invariably left their mark on the contents of the books. Not only did they determine what kinds of material would be included and excluded, but they also shaped how the material would be presented. Usually this meant highlighting the beliefs and practices with which they agreed and belittling or ignoring competing ideas. This process of selection, composition, and editing helped to determine which elements of a diverse religious tradition would be preserved and which would be suppressed or lost. Unless their competitors had their own writings or other means of preserving their traditions, their voices and ideas eventually disappeared.

When scholars study books of Scripture, they have to decide whether they want to focus on the form of religion that is affirmed in the texts (the religious vision of the final editors) or to use the texts as a resource for uncovering how the religion was practiced at some earlier point in the history of the community. Both approaches are legitimate as long as one is clear about the task that one intends to pursue.

In the case of the Hebrew Bible, the second approach is complicated by the long and convoluted history of the text. The Hebrew Bible is a collection of documents that were written and edited by a long series of mostly unknown people over the course of centuries. Many of these books passed through multiple stages of editing before they reached their present form. No one is sure when the collection was last touched by an editor. Materials from different times and places are mingled together so thoroughly that scholars find it difficult to reconstruct how individual books developed or to single out a specific stage for attention.

Over the last century, scholars have developed a variety of methods for detecting the presence of editorial layers within particular books. But many problems remain.

1. For those who choose to focus on the finished text, the primary problem is the diversity of the collection. Scholars can usually identify the editorial viewpoint of an individual book without much difficulty, but it is harder to decide whether a common perspective underlies the entire collection. There are enough disagreements among the books to raise serious doubts about whether the final edition reflects a consistent point of view or whether a variety of editors with different viewpoints worked independently on the individual books. The presence of similar ideas and themes across the collection can be taken as evidence for a broad-based editorial agenda or as a sign that the authors came out of a common **Yahwistic** tradition. The evidence is ambiguous enough that scholars can argue intelligently on both sides of the issue.

Scholars who choose to study the religious vision of a single book also face the daunting task of determining which parts of the book reflect the thinking of the editors and which represent ideas that were already present in their sources. They also have to decide whether the editors intended to endorse all of the views that they inherited from the tradition or whether some traditions were so well known and established that they could not easily be left out or changed. The results of these investigations are invariably quite speculative, but when handled carefully they can produce valuable insights into the beliefs and practices of the people who compiled and edited the biblical texts.

2. Scholars who seek to describe how religion was actually practiced in ancient Palestine also face problems. In addition to deciding which layers of the text belong to which period, scholars have to sift through the one-sided and biased information that appears in the Hebrew Bible. On the one hand, the texts refer again and again to people whose beliefs and practices differed markedly from those of the biblical authors. Some of these people were followers of Yahweh, while others honored other deities alongside or instead of Yahweh. From this we can infer that the religious life of ancient Israel was more diverse than the views represented by the biblical authors. On the other hand, the texts cast virtually everyone who disagreed with the biblical authors in a negative light. No texts from these other traditions have survived to balance out the negative biblical images—no hymns to Yahweh and Asherah, no sayings from the prophets of Baal, no ritual texts explaining how to conjure up the spirits of the dead. This means that most of what we know about these alternate expressions of religion comes from the scattered comments of their Yahwistic opponents. These limited and biased materials offer little insight into what people were actually thinking and doing in these other groups. They also tell us little about the relative popularity of various forms of religion (including the forms upheld by the biblical authors) at different times in Israel's history.

Scholars who wish to uncover the diversity of religious life in ancient Palestine have to learn to read against the grain of the biblical texts in order to develop a more balanced understanding of the beliefs and practices that are criticized by the biblical authors. Information gleaned from textual studies can be supplemented by materials from archaeology and the records of surrounding cultures. Data from similar cultures at different times and places can sometimes be helpful in guiding scholarly speculation where materials are lacking. Integrating these diverse and fragmentary materials into a coherent picture is not an easy task, and scholars disagree about many issues. But the results of this line of research—a more balanced depiction of religious life in ancient Israel—are sufficient to justify the effort.

A MIDDLE PATH

Deciding which of these two approaches to follow is difficult, since both have their strengths and weaknesses. Ideally, students should learn how to read the Bible from both perspectives. For that reason the following chapters aim to strike a balance between the two approaches.

1. The analysis of the biblical material is divided into six sections that focus on various aspects of the religion of the Hebrew Bible. Some of these categories coincide with the major types of literature in the Hebrew Bible, while others do not. Each of these sections is introduced by a chapter that presents a cross-cultural analysis of the phenomenon in question. As will be seen, the material in these chapters is rooted in our discussion of the six dimensions of religion, but it would be wrong to associate each section with a particular dimension.

2. Since the chief goal of this book is to introduce students to the Hebrew Bible, the bulk of the attention in each section will be given to the religious vision of the biblical authors and/or editors. Where possible, this vision will be linked to the social and historical context in which the authors or editors lived. Here and there students will be asked to think critically about how the process of transmission and editing might have affected the content and viewpoint of the biblical books.

3. Since we cannot hope to understand the biblical text without reference to its cultural and religious context, most chapters also include a section that compares the religious vision of the biblical authors and/or editors with what we can know about the way religion was actually practiced during the era when the texts were written. Some chapters give more attention to this question than others. Through this process we can see more clearly what is common and what is distinctive about the religious vision that guided the biblical authors. The inclusion of competing views also serves to highlight the diversity that characterized religious life in ancient Palestine throughout the period covered by the Hebrew Bible. This in turn can make it easier for us to recognize the one-sided and polemical nature of some of the biblical materials.

CONCLUSION

The academic study of religion provides a variety of tools and methods for analyzing the different forms of religious life depicted in the Hebrew Bible. The model that will be used in this book focuses on six dimensions of religion—the mythological, the doctrinal, the ethical, the ritual, the experiential, and the social. This simple model can help us to understand and appreciate the diverse religious systems that were present in ancient Palestine.

Our analysis is complicated, however, by the fact that our primary source of information, the Hebrew Bible, favors one system of belief and practice over others and portrays alternative systems in a negative light. If our aim is to develop a balanced view of religious life in ancient Palestine, we must learn to recognize—and then compensate for—the social and religious agendas of the biblical authors and editors. This includes learning to read against the grain of the texts in order to gather information about beliefs and practices that the authors rejected. If done with care, this process can also help us to better understand what the biblical authors and editors were hoping to accomplish in their writings.

EXERCISE 18

Read the following passages from the Hebrew Bible and pay attention to how the author depicts competing forms of religion. Then choose one of the passages and answer the following questions.

(a) What kinds of beliefs and practices does the author criticize?
(b) What does the author say is wrong with these competing beliefs and practices?
(c) What is the author's attitude toward people who follow these beliefs and practices?

- Deuteronomy 7:1-11
- 2 Kings 21:1-15
- Jeremiah 44:1-28
- Ezekiel 8:1-18

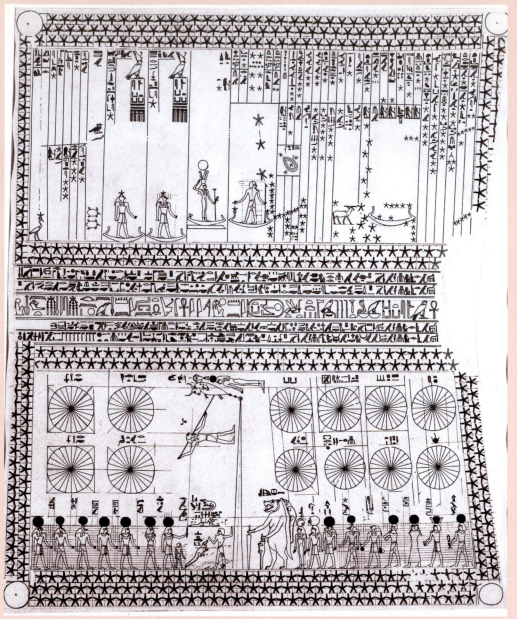

Fig. 11.1. A chart of the heavens found on the ceiling of the tomb of Senenmut, an Egyptian government official who lived in the sixteenth century B.C.E.

The Nature of the Universe

By the word of the LORD the heavens were made, and all their host by the breath of his mouth. He gathered the waters of the sea as in a bottle; he put the deeps in storehouses. Let all the earth fear the LORD; let all the inhabitants of the world stand in awe of him. For he spoke, and it came to be; he commanded, and it stood firm. (Psalm 33:6-9)

And God said, "Let there be a dome in the midst of the waters, and let it separate the waters from the waters." So God made the dome and separated the waters that were under the dome from the waters that were above the dome. And it was so. God called the dome Sky. And there was evening and there was morning, the second day. And God said, "Let the waters under the sky be gathered together into one place, and let the dry land appear." And it was so. God called the dry land Earth, and the waters that were gathered together he called Seas. And God saw that it was good. (Genesis 1:6-10)

God thunders wondrously with his voice; he does great things that we cannot comprehend. For to the snow he says, "Fall on the earth"; and the shower of rain, his heavy shower of rain, serves as a sign on everyone's hand, so that all whom he has made may know it. . . . By the breath of God ice is given, and the broad waters are frozen fast. He loads the thick cloud with moisture; the clouds scatter his lightning. . . . Whether for correction, or for his land, or for love, he causes it to happen. (Job 37:5-7, 10-11, 13)

Every religion—indeed, every person—has a set of beliefs about the nature of reality that shapes the way one makes sense of the world. These beliefs are so fundamental to the thought processes of groups and individuals that they are usually taken for granted by the people who hold them. Examples include the belief that the earth revolves around the sun (or the sun around the earth); that the universe operates according to natural laws (or by the arbitrary whims of the gods); that humans have free will and can control their destinies (or live under the bondage of fate); that the future will be better than the past (or the world is in decline); and so forth.

As these examples suggest, beliefs about the nature of the universe can help people to make sense of reality even when they are not literally true according to the canons of science. As long as people are willing to order their lives according to a set of beliefs, these ideas offer them the same benefits as the findings of science do for people raised in our own era.

Scholars use a variety of terms to describe these fundamental beliefs that people have about the nature of reality. Some prefer the term *social constructions of reality*; others speak of people living in a *symbolic universe*. A simpler and more common term is **worldviews**. Worldviews include the beliefs about reality that are taken for granted within a culture as well as any ideas that people develop on their own. Since each person is unique, scholars sometimes say metaphorically that individuals live in different worlds even when they reside in the same territory. To understand what they mean by this and why it is important, we need to learn more about the origins, nature, and power of worldviews.

THE NATURE OF WORLDVIEWS

Unlike animals, humans are born incomplete. We cannot rely on our instincts to tell us what to do; we must learn from others how the universe works and how to live in it. Parents and other relatives give us our initial orientation to reality. As we grow older, the influence of family members is supplemented by other institutions such as schools, religious groups, and social organizations. Together these institutions instill in us an understanding of reality that is rooted in the collective observations and wisdom of past generations. Personal experience and reflection also play a role in our growing understanding of the world around us.

Humans also have no innate social organization. We do not instinctively form herds or hives in which all of the members know their roles and fulfill them to the best of their ability. Consequently, all of our social institutions are human creations. Since humans have no innate drive to follow a particular social system, individuals must be trained to support the prevailing system. Thus every form of social organization includes some sort of program for teaching participants how the system works and what they must do to maintain it. Often these programs include statements linking the structures of society to key elements of the group's view of reality (that is, its worldview). Virtually all include some sort of disciplinary apparatus to punish those who refuse to cooperate with the system.

Worldviews and social systems do not exist in a vacuum. Every society faces challenges to its beliefs as a result of contact with other groups that have differing views of reality and/or different social systems. Some groups respond to these challenges by incorporating elements of the competing system into their own worldview in a process called **syncretism**. Others seek to isolate their members from the competing views, often through regulations that limit contact with outsiders. This practice is known as **separatism**. Still others develop arguments that aim to show the weaknesses of the other group's views and the strength of their own beliefs and practices. Scholars label this response **apologetics**. The nature of the group's response depends partly on the inherent content of the competing worldviews and partly on the power relationships between the two groups.

THE POWER OF RELIGIOUS WORLDVIEWS

Throughout recorded history, religion has been an important tool for defining how humans view reality and motivating them to support societal institutions. Before the development of modern science, virtually everyone attributed the unpredictable and uncontrollable elements of life to supernatural forces. Stories were told to explain how these forces worked, and rituals were created in an effort to manipulate or appease them. Moral guidelines were reinforced by claims that disobedience would upset the balance of the universe. Children were trained from infancy to embrace this view of reality. As a result, everyone who belonged to a particular tribe or group (except for an occasional deviant) viewed the world in the same way. Religion was central to their understanding of reality.

Religion also played a vital role in defining and defending societal institutions. For most of human history, religion has centered on the group, not the individual. The religious activities of individuals were prescribed and regulated by leaders who sought to protect the group's interests. Religious beliefs and practices were grounded in stories that explained how the group came into being and how they entered into their present relations with the supernatural world. Rituals were conducted and prayers offered on behalf of the group and its leaders. Societal hierarchies and duties (particularly those related to gender and class) were regarded as embodiments of the supernatural order. The present distribution of power, resources, duties, and obligations within the group was likewise attributed to the gods. The entire social organization was regarded as a static system to be upheld and defended against change.

Thus it happened that religion became one of the central forces shaping the way in which people everywhere interpreted their experiences and organized their social interactions until fairly recent times. Similar processes can be observed in groups that followed widely divergent beliefs and practices. From this we learn that the content of a worldview is less important than the fact that people regard it as true. Virtually any set of beliefs can be used to make sense of life and organize society as long as there are people who are willing to view the world through their lens. In cultures where a single view of reality predominates, the idea that anyone would question the accepted beliefs is so unthinkable that people who do so are often regarded as insane. Those who take the added step of challenging the prevailing social system are accused of resisting the divine order and subjected to severe punishment.

Most Americans and Europeans find it hard to imagine a society dominated by religious worldviews because it differs so markedly from their own societies. Religious worldviews have lost much of their power over the last few centuries due to the rise of modern science, which offers an understanding of the universe that undermines many traditional religious views. Most religious groups have reformulated their worldviews to take into account the findings of science, but there are still large numbers of people (sometimes called **Fundamentalists**) who continue to resist scientific conclusions or theories that conflict with their religious beliefs. Other factors that have weakened the power of religious worldviews include the steady move toward separation of church and state and the growing acceptance of secularism and pluralism in Western nations. These developments have led most religious people to abandon any effort to justify the institutions of society on religious grounds, though many still use religious arguments to defend their positions on public policy issues.

Despite these challenges, religion remains a powerful force in the lives of hundreds of millions of people around the globe. Polls show that huge majorities of people claim to be religious on a personal level, and many of these people continue to embrace traditional religious views of reality. In some parts of the world, commitment to a religious worldview has led people to look for ways to resist the influx of Western secularism. Some have even turned to violence to protect their traditional ways. The belief that societal institutions and practices should be guided by religion also remains strong in many countries. This view is especially common in Islamic nations, but

it can be observed in other parts of the world as well. Even in societies where religion has lost its influence in the public sphere, religious people continue to use their beliefs to define and defend the structures of their own group. Thus we should not be surprised when we learn how much power religion held over the lives of people in the ancient world.

Fig. 11.2. (top) Hindus gather at a temple complex at Har Ki Pauri, India, to take a ritual bath in the Ganges River; (bottom) Roman Catholics fill St. Peter's Square in Vatican City to hear the Pope speak.

EXERCISE 19

Review the following statements and think about which ones reflect your own worldview. For those that do not, write a one-sentence summary of your own view of the issue.

(a) The universe came into existence through divine action.

(b) The universe is a closed system of cause and effect; true miracles are impossible.

(c) The universe is directed by a God who has my best interests at heart.

(d) On the whole, life seems to make little sense.

(e) Human nature is basically good.

(f) Humans have free will and can determine their own destinies.

(g) The scientific method is the only path to true knowledge.

(h) God directs the events of human history.

(i) The present life will be followed by a divine judgment.

(j) Technology will eventually solve all of the world's problems.

RELIGIOUS WORLDVIEWS IN ANTIQUITY

Worldviews are developed to address questions that people in every generation have asked about the nature of the universe and human existence. Every society (and to some degree, every individual) provides different answers to these questions, but the range of options is not unlimited. People today know far more about the universe than their ancestors did, but our basic mental equipment has not changed significantly over the last few millennia. Our understanding of how the body works has likewise grown exponentially in recent years, but our physical makeup is no different than it was in ancient times. We have learned to control our environment in ways that ancient people could never have imagined, but the universe that we seek to understand is the same one that they experienced. People today are touched by many of the same joys and sorrows that humans have encountered since the earliest days of civilization. These similarities help to explain why the answers that ancient people gave to the pressing questions of human existence continue to hold meaning for people today.

Among people who live in the same area around the same time, the similarities in experience and worldviews are even more profound, especially when there has been a regular interchange of goods and ideas between them. Ancient Palestine did not exist in a vacuum; the people who wrote and edited the Hebrew Bible were well aware of the diversity of beliefs and practices that prevailed in their own land and the nations around them. In some instances they embraced ideas that originated elsewhere, while in other cases they rejected alternate views. But the basic questions that they struggled to answer were the same ones that troubled everyone in the ancient Near East. These questions can be summarized under four broad headings.

(a) *The natural world.* What is the shape and structure of the physical universe? How did it come into being? Why do the forces of nature behave as they do? Can anything be done to influence or control these unpredictable forces?

(b) *The supernatural world.* What kinds of supernatural powers are present in the universe? What role do supernatural beings play in the operation of the natural world and the lives of humans? What can humans do to affect their actions?

(c) *The nature of humanity.* Why do humans behave as they do? What is the place of humans within the natural and supernatural worlds? What happens to humans after they die?

(d) *The chosen people*. How did we (specifically, the people who are answering the question) come to be favored by the supernatural realm? What obligations does this special status impose upon us? What potential costs and benefits does it bring?

Of course, the people of antiquity did not frame their questions in these precise terms, nor would they have organized their questions under these particular headings. But much of what we would define as their worldview is the result of an implicit attempt to answer these kinds of questions. As we will see, the answers that people gave to the first set of questions were fairly similar throughout the ancient Near East, whereas their answers to the other three sets of questions were more diverse. An examination of the biblical authors' views on these subjects will help us to understand the worldviews that guided their thinking throughout their writings. The first set of questions will be examined in the present chapter. The other three will be explored in the next three chapters.

THE NATURE OF THE UNIVERSE

The division of reality into the physical or natural world and the spiritual or supernatural world is a modern invention. For people in the ancient Near East, as for most other traditional cultures, what we call the supernatural was just as real and present as the natural. The gods lived and worked among human beings; there was no separation between the two realms. From time to time one of the gods might even take on human form. The presence and power of the gods were especially strong at certain geographic sites; lesser deities were often thought to be restricted to a particular site. Some of the gods also watched over humans from the sky in the form of the sun, moon, and stars. Many gods lived in temples that humans built for them, often channeling their power through an image that had been erected to represent them. Gods and other spiritual powers managed those aspects of life that were beyond human control, directing the forces of nature and helping or hurting humans (whether as groups

or individuals) as they saw fit. Stories were told about the spectacular deeds of the gods, but these were not regarded as miracles in the modern sense, since there was no concept of natural law that the gods might choose to violate on special occasions. The gods were active in every aspect of human affairs; some of their activities were simply more obvious than others.

This belief in the interpenetration of the supernatural and the natural did not stop the ancients from studying the physical world. But their information was limited to what they could observe with the naked eye and what they learned from people who had traveled to distant lands. Like virtually everyone before the invention of modern transportation, the people of the ancient Near East had a fairly realistic understanding of the lands and peoples close to them, but their knowledge declined significantly as the distance from their homes increased. The same is true for their understanding of the heavens. Careful observation of the sun, moon, and stars led them to recognize regular patterns in the motions of the heavenly bodies, but the mechanisms that gave rise to those regularities were beyond their ability to discover. In both cases the gaps in their knowledge were filled by fantasy. Everyone in antiquity had heard stories about the strange and wild

Fig. 11.3. (top) The Canaanite god Baal, lord of the storm, prepares to launch a thunderbolt; (bottom) the Egyptian god Hapy, ruler of the Nile floods, carries a platter dripping with life in the form of three *ankhs*.

creatures that lived on the far borders of civilization and the great monsters that filled the seas. Distant lands were depicted as places of great wonders and riches, but they also housed many evils and dangers.

Based on what they had observed and heard, the ancients developed an understanding of the physical world that captured the imaginations of people throughout the ancient Near East. The diagram below shows how they envisioned the universe.

To the naked eye, the earth appears to be relatively flat except for the mountains and valleys. As a result, virtually everyone in the ancient Near East envisioned it as a rather lumpy disk resting on a massive series of underground pillars surrounded by a vast sea. Above this disk

was the dome of the sky, across which the sun, moon, stars, and planets made their regular paths. Around the edges of the disk stood enormous pillars that supported the dome. Beyond these pillars lay the great ocean and the gates through which the heavenly bodies entered and left the sky each day.

Above the dome was a massive reservoir whose waters passed through the dome from time to time bringing rain (or less often, hail or snow) to the earth. Below the flat disk of land lay huge pools of water that occasionally burst open, causing devastating floods. In the lowest depths, far beneath the ground, lay the realm of the dead, where those who had passed from this life kept up a shadowy form of existence. Those who had not been buried or whose families failed to care for them properly after death were doomed to roam the world above the ground as ghosts.

Within this broad framework, each culture developed additional variants that explained the origins and prominent features of the local landscape. In every case the formation of the universe was traced to the actions of deities who were worshipped by the people telling the story. Often the land where the storytellers lived was depicted as the first piece of earth to emerge from the primal waters or chaos. Sometimes the initial emergence was narrowed to a particular tract of land, typically the site of an important religious shrine.

When describing the land itself, special attention was devoted to its vital water resources, which were invariably associated with the gods. In Egypt, the central focus was the Nile River, the divine source of all life, whose dependable waters enabled the Egyptians to maintain a thriving agricultural society in the midst of a blazing desert. The Tigris and Euphrates rivers played a similar role for the residents of Mesopotamia. In Palestine, by contrast, the life-giving waters flowed not from rivers but from the sky. Life depended upon the timely arrival of the rainy seasons each winter and spring. It is no accident that a number of the poetic texts in the Bible picture Yahweh as a storm-god riding on the clouds of heaven to rescue or punish humans (Job 36:26-33; 37:2-18; Psalm 68:4-9; Isaiah 28:2;

The Ancient Pictorial View of the Universe

1. The waters above (and below) the earth
2–4. Chambers of hail, rain, snow
5. The firmament with its "sluices"
6. The surface of the earth
7. The navel of the earth: "fountain of the great deep"
8. The mountain pillars supporting the firmament
9. Sweet waters (rivers, lakes, seas) on which the earth floats
10. Sheol, the realm of death (the "pit")

Fig. 11.4. A common ancient view of the universe.

Joel 2:22-26). One of the central functions of the gods in the ancient Near East was to provide the water that was so vital to the continuation of life; a shortage of water was inevitably viewed as a divine curse (Exodus 9:33; Deuteronomy 11:11-17; 28:22-24; Jeremiah 14:22; Amos 4:6-8).

EXERCISE 20

Read Genesis 1:1—2:3 and Job 38:1-38, paying attention to what is stated or implied about the nature of the physical world in each passage. Make a list of points where the two authors agree or disagree with the standard ancient Near Eastern view outlined above.

THE UNIVERSE ACCORDING TO THE HEBREW BIBLE

The Hebrew Bible contains relatively few statements indicating how its authors viewed the physical makeup of the universe. The scarcity and brevity of the comments suggest that the authors had little new to offer in this area. The few references that do appear agree closely with what we know about the views of other people in the ancient Near East. This is noteworthy in light of the fact that the authors consciously rejected many of their neighbors' beliefs about the nature of humanity and the supernatural world. It seems as though they were saying, "Your science is fine, but your **theology** needs to be corrected."

A brief review of some of the passages that refer to the physical structures of the universe will show how closely the views of the biblical authors resemble those of other people in the ancient Near East and how far they diverge from our own ways of thinking.

Genesis 1:1—2:3

As the story opens, God (whose existence is simply taken for granted) is named as the creator of "the heavens and the earth," a term that encompasses the entire visible world. Faced with a watery chaos, God simply speaks and brings order to the universe. From the beginning of the narrative we see parallels with the stories told by other people in the ancient Near East. (For more on this point, see chapter 16.) Creation accounts from Mesopotamia, Egypt, and Canaan tell how a deity framed the present universe out of a preexisting sea, whose ever-shifting waters make it a symbol for chaos and resistance to the will of the deity. The order in which things are created in Genesis 1 also follows the order in the Mesopotamian stories, even when it sounds illogical to modern ears (for example, night and day being divided [vv. 4-5] and plants yielding fruit [vv. 11-12] prior to the creation of the sun [vv. 16-18]). In verses 6-10 we read about the creation of the sky dome that separates the waters into two parts, those above and those below the dome, along with the emergence of land from the waters beneath the dome. The image of the physical world implied here is identical to what we see in the surrounding cultures. The portrait becomes complete with the placement of the sun, moon, and stars in the dome in verses 14-18, just as in the Mesopotamian story. The many similarities are noteworthy when we consider that the Genesis story diverges markedly from the other stories in the way it depicts the supernatural world and the nature of humanity (chapters 12 and 13). The creation story in Genesis 1 describes the creation of the world as it appeared to people in the ancient Near East, not the world that we know from modern science.

Job 38:1-38

The speech in Job 38 is the first part of a lengthy poetic monologue by Yahweh that fills four chapters of the book of Job. The speech consists of a series of rhetorical questions in which Yahweh celebrates the marvels of the universe while highlighting Job's ignorance concerning the nature and extent of the world and its inhabitants. The speech presumes an understanding of the universe that agrees precisely with the view that was popular across the ancient Near East. According to Yahweh, the earth rests on a foundation (v. 4) that has bases and a cornerstone (v. 6). Fixed boundaries and gates keep the waves of the sea from overwhelming the land (vv. 8-10). The sea arises out of springs located far below the earth (v. 16).

Beneath the sea lies the realm of the dead (v. 17). Both light (specifically, the sun, moon, and stars) and darkness have dwellings where they stay when out of human sight (v. 19). Beyond the sky are storehouses in which snow, hail, and wind are kept ready for the times when they are needed (vv. 22-24, 37). The sky is also marked with channels through which the rain and lightning flow, bringing storms to water the earth (vv. 25-27). Ice and frost also have their places in the sky (heaven) (vv. 29-30). Behind all of this lies the power of Yahweh, the deity who created and rules over all of these natural wonders.

Other Passages

Most of the references to the nature and structure of the universe in the Hebrew Bible are brief and allusive. The passing nature of the references shows that the authors were operating from a common understanding of the physical world that they expected their readers to share. A cursory review of some of these verses will show how closely their ideas resemble those that prevailed elsewhere in the ancient Near East. Points of similarity are marked by **bold type**. Note that the same Hebrew word is trans-

Fig. 11.5. This sketch from a tenth-century B.C.E. mummy coffin shows how the Egyptians viewed the cosmos.

lated as "heaven" or "heavens" in some verses and "sky" in others.

> In the six hundredth year of Noah's life, in the second month, on the seventeenth day of the month, on that day all the **fountains of the great deep** burst forth, and the **windows of the heavens** were opened. The rain fell on the earth forty days and forty nights. *(Genesis 7:11-12)*

> He raises up the poor from the dust; he lifts the needy from the ash heap, to make them sit with princes and inherit a seat of honor. For the **pillars of the earth** are the LORD's, and **on them he has set the world**. *(1 Samuel 2:8)*

> Who has resisted him, and succeeded?—he who removes mountains, and they do not know it, when he overturns them in his anger; who shakes the earth out of its place, and its **pillars** tremble; who commands the sun, and it does not rise; who **seals up the stars**; who alone **stretched out the heavens** and **trampled the waves of the Sea**; who made the Bear and Orion, the Pleiades and the **chambers of the south**; who does great things beyond understanding, and marvelous things without number. *(Job 9:4-10)*

> The **pillars of heaven** tremble, and are astounded at his rebuke. By his power he **stilled the Sea**; by his understanding he struck down Rahab. *(Job 26:11-12)*

> Then the **channels of the sea** were seen, and the **foundations of the world** were laid bare at your rebuke, O LORD, at the blast of the breath of your nostrils. *(Psalm 18:15)*

> In the heavens he has set a **tent for the sun**, which comes out like a bridegroom from his wedding canopy, and like a strong man runs its course with joy. Its rising is from the **end of the heavens**, and its circuit to the end of them; and nothing is hid from its heat. *(Psalm 19:4-6)*

> By the word of the LORD the heavens were made, and all their host by the breath of his mouth. He **gathered the waters of the sea** as in a bottle; he **put the deeps in storehouses**. *(Psalm 33:6-7)*

> When the earth totters, with all its inhabitants, it is I who keep its **pillars** steady. *(Psalm 75:3)*

> I am counted among those who go **down to the Pit**; I am like those who have no help, like those forsaken among the dead, like the slain that lie in the grave, like those whom you remember no more, for they are cut off from your hand. You have put me **in the depths of the Pit, in the regions dark and deep**. Your wrath lies heavy upon me, and you overwhelm me with all **your waves**. *(Psalm 88:4-7)*

> The LORD by wisdom **founded the earth**; by understanding he **established the heavens**; by his knowledge **the deeps broke open**, and the clouds drop down the dew. *(Proverbs 3:19-20)*

> Whoever flees at the sound of the terror shall fall into the pit; and whoever climbs out of the pit shall be caught in the snare. For the **windows of heaven** are opened, and the **foundations of the earth** tremble. *(Isaiah 24:18)*

Another way in which the authors of the Hebrew Bible shared the worldview of their neighbors was in their belief that the affairs of nature are guided and directed by supernatural powers. The biblical authors believed that their god, Yahweh, ruled over every aspect of the natural world; their neighbors divided the task among a variety of deities. Similar ways of viewing the operation of the universe were held by virtually every human society until the rise of modern science. People in antiquity did not limit the hand of the gods to the unusual events of life that might be regarded as miracles. Even the most mundane and recurring events of nature were dependent on divine activity, as can be seen in the following examples from the Hebrew Bible.

> Listen, listen to the thunder of his voice and the rumbling that comes from his mouth. Under the whole heaven he lets it loose, and his lightning to the corners of the earth. After it his voice roars; he thunders with his majestic voice and he does not restrain the lightnings when his voice is heard. God thunders wondrously with his voice; he does great things that we cannot comprehend. For to the snow he

says, "Fall on the earth"; and the shower of rain, his heavy shower of rain, serves as a sign on everyone's hand, so that all whom he has made may know it. Then the animals go into their lairs and remain in their dens. From its chamber comes the whirlwind, and cold from the scattering winds. By the breath of God ice is given, and the broad waters are frozen fast. He loads the thick cloud with moisture; the clouds scatter his lightning. They turn round and round by his guidance, to accomplish all that he commands them on the face of the habitable world. Whether for correction, or for his land, or for love, he causes it to happen. *(Job 37:2-13)*

By your strength you established the mountains; you are girded with might. You silence the roaring of the seas, the roaring of their waves, the tumult of the peoples. Those who live at earth's farthest bounds are awed by your signs; you make the gateways of the morning and the evening shout for joy. You visit the earth and water it, you greatly enrich it; the river of God is full of water; you provide the people with grain, for so you have prepared it. You water its furrows abundantly, settling its ridges, softening it with showers, and blessing its growth. You crown the year with your bounty; your wagon tracks overflow with richness. The pastures of the wilderness overflow, the hills gird themselves with joy, the meadows clothe themselves with flocks, the valleys deck themselves with grain, they shout and sing together for joy. *(Psalm 65:6-13)*

If you will only heed his every commandment that I am commanding you today—loving the LORD your God, and serving him with all your heart and with all your soul—then he will give the rain for your land in its season, the early rain and the later rain, and you will gather in your grain, your wine, and your oil; and he will give grass in your fields for your livestock, and you will eat your fill. Take care, or you will be seduced into turning away, serving other gods and worshiping them, for then the anger of the LORD will be kindled against you and he will shut up the heavens, so that there will be no rain and the land will yield no fruit; then you will perish quickly off the good land that the LORD is giving you. *(Deuteronomy 11:13-17)*

More will be said in the next chapter about the role of Yahweh and other gods in providing or withholding the blessings of fertility for the earth and its people. For now it is enough to note how this belief affects the way the biblical authors viewed the world around them. For them, there is no such thing as dead matter or mechanistic laws of nature. Everything that happens in the physical world is evidence of the presence and power of God. The rising of the sun and the coming of the rains are as much divine acts as the splitting of the Red Sea. Once we grasp this point, we can better understand why the ancients refused to divide life into separate sacred and secular spheres. If every moment and every place are infused with the presence of the supernatural, it would be the height of folly to think that one could ignore these powerful forces at any point in one's life. To follow this path is to incur divine displeasure and flirt with disaster.

CONCLUSION

Every society and every individual has a worldview, a set of fundamental beliefs about the nature of reality that guides the way they interpret the world around them and the experiences that they encounter. Worldviews also influence the manner in which societies are structured. Worldviews are passed from generation to generation through family training, educational programs, and other societal institutions. In this way they become so deeply ingrained in people's minds that they attain the status of self-evident truths that are beyond question.

Religion has played a central role in the development and maintenance of worldviews for most of human history. Religious worldviews make sense of human experience by relating it to a supernatural world that lies beyond the ordinary reach of human senses. Religious traditions claim to offer insight into the nature and operation of both the natural and the supernatural worlds. Most insist that the key to human happiness lies in maintaining a proper balance between the two worlds.

The authors and editors of the Hebrew Bible shared certain elements of their worldview with other residents of the ancient Near East even as they diverged from them in other areas. One area in which they largely agreed with their neighbors was their conception of the nature and structure of the physical universe. Apparently the biblical authors saw no conflict between the view of the natural world that they took over from their neighbors and the Yahwistic faith that they were seeking to promote. It was enough for them to rewrite the ancient traditions in such a way that Yahweh became the chief actor behind the forces of nature.

EXERCISE 21

Read the following passages from the Hebrew Bible and make a list of the things that they say or imply about the nature of the physical world and Yahweh's role within it.

- Deuteronomy 28:1-24
- Job 37:1-13
- Psalm 104:1-30
- Proverbs 8:22-31

Fig. 12.1. Canaanite deities mentioned in the Hebrew Bible include (clockwise from top left) El, Asherah, Baal, and Astarte.

The Supernatural World

*In the year that King Uzziah died, I saw the Lord sitting on a throne, high and lofty; and the hem of his robe filled the temple. Seraphs were in attendance above him; each had six wings: with two they covered their faces, and with two they covered their feet, and with two they flew. And one called to another and said: "Holy, holy, holy is the L*ord *of hosts; the whole earth is full of his glory." The pivots on the thresholds shook at the voices of those who called, and the house filled with smoke. And I said: "Woe is me! I am lost, for I am a man of unclean lips, and I live among a people of unclean lips; yet my eyes have seen the King, the L*ord *of hosts!"* (Isaiah 6:1-5)

*The L*ord *descended in the cloud and stood with him there, and proclaimed the name, "The L*ord*" [Yahweh]. The L*ord *passed before him, and proclaimed, "The L*ord*, the L*ord*, a God merciful and gracious, slow to anger, and abounding in steadfast love and faithfulness, keeping steadfast love for the thousandth generation, forgiving iniquity and transgression and sin, yet by no means clearing the guilty, but visiting the iniquity of the parents upon the children and the children's children, to the third and the fourth generation."* (Exodus 34:5-7)

*Then Micaiah said, "Therefore hear the word of the L*ord*: I saw the L*ord *sitting on his throne, with all the host of heaven standing beside him to the right and to the left of him. And the L*ord *said, 'Who will entice Ahab, so that he may go up and fall at Ramoth-gilead?' Then one said one thing, and another said another, until a spirit came forward and stood before the L*ord*, saying, 'I will entice him.' 'How?' the L*ord *asked him. He replied, 'I will go out and be a lying spirit in the mouth of all his prophets.' Then the L*ord *said, 'You are to entice him, and you shall succeed; go out and do it.'"* (1 Kings 22:19-22)

Virtually every religion insists that there is some kind of invisible reality behind, above, or beyond the present visible world and that humans should orient their lives toward this unseen realm. Some, like Buddhism or Confucianism, offer only vague hints concerning the nature of this ultimate reality; others, such as Hinduism or Islam, have highly developed notions of the nature of the invisible world. Some believe that the supernatural world is populated by a host of gods, angels, spirits, demons, and other superhuman entities. Others insist that there is only one supreme being beyond the human level. Still others conceive of the unseen reality as a dimension of existence or an impersonal mind or force rather than a place where supernatural beings dwell.

The residents of ancient Palestine held a variety of beliefs about the nature and content of the supernatural world. The people whose ideas are recorded in the Hebrew Bible were an important subset of this population, though their numbers and political strength varied greatly over the years. Their beliefs centered on a god named Yahweh whom they regarded as the sole legiti-mate deity of the people of Israel. Their views on the nature of Yahweh and Yahweh's relation to other spiri-tual forces evolved over time, and their writings include significant variations and even disagreements. If we hope to understand the Hebrew Bible, we need to develop a clear understanding of the way the authors envisioned the supernatural world.

GRASPING AFTER SHADOWS

The belief that there is another reality beyond the vis-ible order is rooted in our human need to understand the world in which we live. Throughout human his-tory people have raised questions about the origins and nature of the universe. Since the creation and operation of something so vast could not possibly be the work of humans, most have concluded that some sort of superhu-man beings or forces must have been at work. Humans have also labored to make sense of unusual experiences that seemed to have no evident explanation, from inex-plicable cures to bouts of mental illness to vivid dreams to strange feelings at a particular geographical location. Here, too, the most common solution has been to credit supernatural powers.

When it comes to defining the nature of those super-natural powers, however, people have developed many different answers. Most can be catalogued under a few broad headings.

1. *Animism*. Probably the oldest way of defining the supernatural, **animism** envisions the entire physical world as being alive (animated) with spiritual power. Animals, trees, rocks, wind, rain—everything is thought to have a spiritual essence in the same manner as humans. Some of these spiritual entities are friendly toward humans, while others are harmful. Specially trained people are able to interact with the good spirits and motivate them to help humans while keeping the evil spirits at bay. Rit-uals and magical spells play a similar role for ordinary individuals.

2. *Polytheism*. **Polytheism**—the belief in many gods—is similar to animism in the way it associates supernatural beings with the forces of nature. But where animists see

nature itself as alive, polytheistic systems claim that the universe is ruled by a number of personal deities whose existence is independent of particular physical phenom-ena. Individual deities might bear responsibility for a spe-cific aspect of nature, such as the wind or the sea, but nature is one of their tools, not their essence. In most cases the gods are related to one another in a social system that resembles the society of the people who serve them. Usually this includes some form of hierarchy. Polytheistic systems of ritual and worship are usually more developed than animistic systems, but their goal is the same—to motivate the gods to act favorably toward humans and to keep away harmful forces.

3. *Pantheism*. Where animism and polytheism envi-sion personal beings at work behind the forces of nature, **pantheism** sees a higher unity that transcends the lim-its of personality. The word *pantheism* comes from two Greek words that together mean "everything is divine." Pantheism agrees with animism that the universe is per-meated by a spiritual presence, but pantheism defines this presence in impersonal terms. According to pantheism, everything that exists in this world is simply a manifesta-tion of a single cosmic mind or presence that is the only true reality. The entire universe is divine, and all of life is sacred. Rather than trying to control the forces of nature, true pantheists seek to become one with nature through a program of mental discipline and reflection that trains them to see the universe as it really is.

4. *Monolatry*. **Monolatry** is the practice of serving and honoring a single deity without negating the reality or value of other gods. Monolatry resembles polytheism in its belief that the forces of nature are controlled by a series of personal deities, but it insists that one deity is more powerful or more worthy of service than others. Various reasons are given that explain this belief, includ-ing tradition (following the same god whom the ances-tors served); geographical location (honoring the deity who rules over a particular region); power (forging an alliance with a deity who can control the other gods); and societal need (serving the god who can provide the material benefits that the group needs to survive). Mono-latry typically requires special acts of devotion toward the guardian deity. It may or may not exclude the worship of other gods.

5. *Monotheism.* **Monotheism** is the belief that there is only one divine being in the universe. Implicit in monotheism is the claim that other deities are figments of the human imagination; the various forces of nature that polytheists see as the activity of many gods are in reality the work of one supreme deity. This does not mean that the deity necessarily controls everything that happens, but it does mean that there are no other forces capable of hindering or frustrating the divine will. Monotheism does not exclude the existence of lesser supernatural entities in the universe (for example, angels and demons), but it insists that they are only servants of the deity, not deities themselves. To offer worship or obedience to these creatures—or to anyone other than the one true deity—is to engage in idolatry, the wrongful worship of false gods.

6. *Dualism.* **Dualism** agrees with monotheism in asserting that there is only one supernatural being who is working for the good of the universe. But dualists refuse to believe that all of the pain and suffering in the world can be attributed to a single good god or goddess. Instead, they posit the existence of a second supernatural being whose purposes run counter to those of the primary deity. The universe is the battleground for these two powerful beings, and humans must choose which of the two they will serve. Most forms of dualism believe that the good deity will ultimately win the battle, but in the short run humans can benefit from allying themselves with either power.

Not all of these views of the supernatural realm are represented in the Hebrew Bible. The authors and editors of the biblical texts were generally either monolatrous or monotheistic, but their writings indicate that polytheism also played a prominent role in the religious life of ancient Palestine. Whether animistic beliefs and practices were present in ancient Palestine is unclear, but elements of dualism can be seen in some of the later apocalyptic texts of the Hebrew Bible. Only pantheism is entirely absent from the Hebrew Bible, as it is incompatible with the belief in personal deities that dominated the ancient Near East.

GODS OF THE ANCIENT NEAR EAST

The world in which the Hebrew Bible arose was polytheistic. Every culture in the ancient Near East honored a pantheon of greater and lesser deities who directed the affairs of the universe. Most were associated with a particular aspect of nature, such as the sun, moon, sea, or storm. Each culture also had a supreme deity who ruled over the council or family of the gods. All of these deities had names, though the names and duties of the gods and goddesses varied from culture to culture.

For the most part, the gods were envisioned as being tied to a particular territory and having a special relationship with its inhabitants. Humans were expected to honor the gods of the land by performing required rituals of worship and obeying the wishes of the gods. The gods in turn were responsible for maintaining the fertility of the land and protecting the people from their enemies. Devotion to the gods was not exclusive; when a person was traveling through the territory of other deities, it was expected that the traveler would honor the local gods.

Like their neighbors, many of the residents of ancient Palestine worshipped multiple gods. The nature of the familial relationships among the gods varied from region to region, but the chief deities were El, the creator of the universe; Asherah, the earth goddess; Baal, the storm-god who was commonly depicted as the leader of the gods; Astarte, the goddess of sex and fertility; Anath, the goddess of war; Yam, the god of the sea and one of Baal's chief enemies; and Mot, the god of death and the underworld. Dozens of other supernatural beings filled the legends and lore of Palestine. Some of the gods were honored with special places of worship, while others were addressed primarily at special times of life such as pregnancy or death.

With the rise of Yahweh as the supreme god of Israel, the traditional deities lost some of their influence, though they continued to play an important role in the religious life of Palestine throughout the biblical period. Several of the major deities acknowledged by the people of Palestine are mentioned in the Hebrew Bible, but the authors offer little specific information about them, since they assumed that their readers already knew about the traditional gods.

WHO IS LIKE YAHWEH?

The people whose traditions are reflected in the Hebrew Bible honored a single god as their protector and ruler, one who stood supreme over all other deities. By the time the Hebrew Bible was being written, this deity bore the name Yahweh, though the text also includes materials that use the name El (or Elohim). The fact that the god of Israel has a name is obscured in most English Bibles, where the names Yahweh and El/Elohim are translated as "the Lord" (sometimes written in capital letters) and "God," respectively, following ancient Jewish customs that considered the name of the deity too holy to pronounce. In ancient times, El and Yahweh were two separate deities, but their identities were merged together fairly early in Israel's history. El was originally the god of the sky as well as the creator god in the Canaanite pantheon. But the name El is also the generic word for "god" in Hebrew (that is to say, it can refer to any deity), so it was easy for the followers of Yahweh to argue that El was simply another name for Yahweh, especially when both were regarded as creators in their respective traditions. The title Elohim is technically the plural of El, though when applied to Yahweh it probably means something like "the god of gods" or "the supreme god."

The personal name Yahweh comes from the Hebrew verb meaning "to be," though its precise meaning is unclear. Common suggestions include "the [only?] one who exists" and "the one who causes [other things] to exist." The former translation underlines the uniqueness of Yahweh; the latter emphasizes Yahweh's role as creator. Both ideas are important to the authors of the Hebrew Bible. A story from the book of Exodus gives an explanation of the name that might reflect ancient traditions. In this story, a man named Moses hears a voice calling to him out of a bush that is burning in the desert. The voice identifies itself as "the God of your father, the God of Abraham, the God of Isaac, and the God of Jacob" (Exodus

3:6). The voice tells Moses to go to Egypt and free the Hebrew people from Egyptian oppression and lead them to the land of Canaan that was promised to their ancestors. Moses asks the voice how the people will know that he is speaking for their god. The voice responds by telling Moses the name that stands behind the voice.

> But Moses said to God, "Who am I that I should go to Pharaoh, and bring the Israelites out of Egypt?" He said, "I will be with you; and this shall be the sign for you that it is I who sent you: when you have brought the people out of Egypt, you shall worship God on this mountain."
>
> But Moses said to God, "If I come to the Israelites and say to them, 'The God of your ancestors has sent me to you,' and they ask me, 'What is his name?' what shall I say to them?" God said to Moses, "**I AM WHO I AM.**" He said further, "Thus you shall say to the Israelites, '**I AM** has sent me to you.'" God also said to Moses, "Thus you shall say to the Israelites, '**The LORD [Yahweh], the God of your ancestors, the God of Abraham, the God of Isaac, and the God of Jacob**, has sent me to you': This is my name forever, and this my title for all generations." *(Exodus 3:11-15)*

The god of the Hebrew Bible resembles the gods of the ancient Near East not only in having a name, but also in having a gender. Throughout the Hebrew Bible,

Fig. 12.2. An Israelite drawing from the eighth century B.C.E. that includes a reference to "Yahweh and his Asherah"; scholars disagree whether the drawing depicts Yahweh with a female consort.

the masculine pronoun is used when referring to Yahweh, and the majority of the images by which Yahweh is described (father, king, warrior, judge, and so on) are derived from the sphere of male activities. Archaeological and literary evidence suggests that Yahweh was sometimes accompanied by a female consort, though the editors of the Hebrew Bible firmly rejected this view. On the other hand, the Hebrew Bible never mentions Yahweh having genitals or engaging in any kind of sexual activity, unlike other male deities in the ancient Near East. The Hebrew Bible also contains a number of passages in which Yahweh is portrayed using feminine imagery (mother, midwife, brood hen, and others), though these are vastly outnumbered by the masculine images. In a few places, Yahweh's gender is cloaked in ambiguity. In the creation story in Genesis 1 (perhaps originally a story about El), the man and woman together are said to reflect the **image of God**, yet the deity is described using the masculine pronoun: "So God created humankind in his image, in the image of God he created them; male and female he created them" (Genesis 1:27).

Perhaps the best that can be said is that whereas Yahweh is technically depicted as a male deity, the masculine element has been suppressed in comparison with other male gods of the ancient Near East. The reason for this difference is unclear: it might represent the beginnings of an effort to depict a deity who is above gender, but more likely it signifies a rejection of the sexual motifs and the accompanying standards of sexual morality that characterized ancient Near Eastern mythology. The use of the masculine pronoun for Yahweh in this book reflects a concern to accurately represent the language and ideas of the ancient authors even when they diverge from modern ways of thinking.

WHERE DID YAHWEH COME FROM?

The origins of Yahweh as a deity are shrouded in mystery. The Hebrew Bible makes no attempt to answer the question: as far as its authors are concerned, Yahweh existed before the creation of the universe, and that is all that matters. This approach sets them apart from the surrounding cultures, which have many stories explaining how the gods originated. The silence of the Hebrew Bible on this point cannot be accidental. Most likely it represents an attempt to assert the uniqueness of Yahweh in comparison with competing deities who originated out of the material substance of the universe or through sexual generation.

But this does not explain how a god named Yahweh came to be honored as the supreme deity by a particular group of people who resided in ancient Palestine. The biblical authors claim that humans learned about Yahweh through divine revelation. The Hebrew Bible contains numerous stories in which Yahweh appears and speaks to human beings from the time of Adam and Eve onward. The narrative places special emphasis on Yahweh's encounters with a man named Abraham and his descendants, the people who later came to be known as Israelites. According to the Hebrew Bible, Yahweh gradually led this small group of people to a fuller understanding of his divine nature and its implications for their conduct. This revelation was summed up in the laws of Torah that Yahweh gave to Moses on Mount Sinai. Later Yahweh sent prophets to tell his people what he thought about their failure to live up to these standards.

Scholars, on the other hand, look for more mundane explanations for the rise of new ideas. Unfortunately, the evidence in this case is so scanty that all answers must be regarded as speculative. Many scholars have thought that the ancestors of the people called Israelites must have migrated to Palestine from a region where a deity named Yahweh was already enrolled in the pantheon of gods and that they subsequently came to believe that this (possibly minor) deity was uniquely interested in their welfare. The proposal sounds plausible, but there is no extrabiblical evidence to indicate that a deity named Yahweh was worshipped anywhere in the ancient Near East prior to the rise of Israel and Judah, with the possible exception of a handful of older materials from Syria whose meaning and relevance are disputed.

Within the Hebrew Bible, a number of texts link Yahweh with Edom (Judges 5:4; Isaiah 63:1; Habakkuk 3:3; Zechariah 9:14), a territory south of Palestine that figures in some of the stories about Israel's early ancestors, or with **Midian**, a region farther to the southeast. (For the locations of Edom and Midian, see the map on p. 74.)

According to Exodus 3:1, the famous Mount Sinai (also called **Horeb**), where Moses reportedly received the Ten Commandments, was located in Midian, and Moses is said to have lived for many years in Midian with a father-in-law who is called "the priest of Midian" (Exodus 2:16; 3:1; 18:1). The deities whom his father-in-law served are never identified, though he does offer **praise** and sacrifices to Yahweh at one point in the story (Exodus 18:9-12). Moses also follows his father-in-law's advice concerning the importance of delegating authority (Exodus 18:13-27). Since both Edom and Midian are depicted as Israel's enemies later in the biblical narrative, some have argued that the Israelite storytellers would not have associated these people with Yahweh without due cause. To this point, however, no evidence has been found outside the Hebrew Bible to indicate that Yahweh was known and worshipped in either Edom or Midian. Without such evidence, the idea that Yahweh could have been adopted from one of these areas remains only a tantalizing hypothesis.

Comparisons with other cultures suggest that we should not discount the possibility that one or more of the ancestors of the people known as Israel and Judah could have had some kind of profound religious experience that they viewed as the revelation of a new deity. Many new religious movements have begun with similar claims. In the end, however, scholars know little more about the origins of Yahweh worship than parents who are forced to respond to the age-old children's question, "Where did God come from?"

YAHWEH AND THE GODS OF PALESTINE

The relation of Yahweh to the other gods who were worshipped in ancient Palestine was understood differently by different people. Many found a place for Yahweh in the list of deities whom they honored with special rituals as they sought to ensure the health and safety of their families, animals, and crops. Some of these people even gave Yahweh a place of preeminence among the gods, possibly in conjunction with a female consort, Asherah. Smaller numbers rejected Yahweh entirely in favor of one or more competing gods, particularly Baal. Still others honored Yahweh as the patron deity of Israel and Judah

while allowing for the possibility that there might be other gods for other nations. Not until late in the biblical era (that is, during or after the Exile) did many people come to see Yahweh as the one and only god of the universe and to regard all other deities as human creations.

The position of the biblical authors within this environment of religious diversity is ambiguous. On the one hand, they are unanimous in their belief that Yahweh is the only deity worthy of worship by the descendants of Abraham. There are no stories or other texts in which the worship of Baal or Asherah is regarded as acceptable and many in which it is condemned. On the other hand, there are statements in the Hebrew Bible that do not accord well with traditional definitions of monotheism. At least three broad tendencies can be discerned within the texts.

1. One group of texts exhibits a strong **absolutist** attitude concerning Yahweh's status. These passages insist

Fig. 12.3. (top) A shrine from Hazor in northern Palestine—the stones may represent different deities worshipped at this site; (bottom) the innermost court of the temple at Arad in southern Palestine, where Yahweh was apparently paired with another deity—note the two standing stones with altars.

that Yahweh is the only true god and that all other deities are the creations of human minds and hands. Most of these texts are highly critical of the worship of other gods, mocking those who honor them and pronouncing Yahweh's judgment upon the deities and their followers. Many verses claim that Yahweh is the sovereign ruler and judge not only of Israel but also of the surrounding nations. The following texts exemplify this attitude.

> Thus says the LORD [Yahweh]: Do not learn the way of the nations, or be dismayed at the signs of the heavens; for the nations are dismayed at them. For the customs of the peoples are false: a tree from the forest is cut down, and worked with an ax by the hands of an artisan; people deck it with silver and gold; they fasten it with hammer and nails so that it cannot move. Their idols are like scarecrows in a cucumber field, and they cannot speak; they have to be carried, for they cannot walk. Do not be afraid of them, for they cannot do evil, nor is it in them to do good. There is none like you, O LORD; you are great, and your name is great in might. *(Jeremiah 10:2-6)*

> Thus says the LORD [Yahweh], the King of Israel, and his Redeemer, the LORD of hosts: I am the first and I am the last; besides me there is no god. Who is like me? Let them proclaim it, let them declare and set it forth before me. Who has announced from of old the things to come? Let them tell us what is yet to be. Do not fear, or be afraid; have I not told you from of old and declared it? You are my witnesses! Is there any god besides me? There is no other rock; I know not one. All who make idols are nothing, and the things they delight in do not profit; their witnesses neither see nor know. And so they will be put to shame. *(Isaiah 44:6-9)*

While most modern readers presume that this is the viewpoint of the entire Hebrew Bible, the reality is that relatively few texts adopt such an absolute position, and most of these were written late in the biblical period. Eventually this view became the standard position within Judaism, but it would be wrong to think that this is the dominant view of Yahweh throughout the Hebrew Bible.

2. More common is an **exclusivist** attitude toward deities other than Yahweh. This position does not deny the existence of other gods, but it considers Yahweh to be greater than and different from all other deities. It also insists that the people of Israel and Judah should worship and serve Yahweh alone. According to this view, Yahweh is a jealous god who will not allow any other deity to share either the responsibility or the credit for his actions. When his people worship other gods alongside him, they place him on the same level as other deities and fail to acknowledge him as their lord and provider. This is deeply offensive to Yahweh, who expects complete loyalty from his people. This view of the deity can be seen in the following passages.

> Take care not to make a covenant with the inhabitants of the land to which you are going, or it will become a snare among you. You shall tear down their altars, break their pillars, and cut down their sacred poles (for you shall worship no other god, because the LORD [Yahweh], whose name is Jealous, is a jealous God). You shall not make a covenant with the inhabitants of the land, for when they prostitute themselves to their gods and sacrifice to their gods, someone among them will invite you, and you will eat of the sacrifice. And you will take wives from among their daughters for your sons, and their daughters who prostitute themselves to their gods will make your sons also prostitute themselves to their gods. *(Exodus 34:12-16)*

> Then the Israelites did what was evil in the sight of the LORD and worshiped the Baals; and they abandoned the LORD [Yahweh], the God of their ancestors, who had brought them out of the land of Egypt; they followed other gods, from among the gods of the peoples who were all around them, and bowed down to them; and they provoked the LORD to anger. They abandoned the LORD, and worshiped Baal and the Astartes. So the anger of the LORD was kindled against Israel, and he gave them over to plunderers who plundered them, and he sold them into the power of their enemies all around, so that they could no longer withstand their enemies. Whenever they marched out, the hand of the LORD was against them to bring misfortune, as the LORD had warned them and sworn to them; and they were in great distress. *(Judges 2:11-15)*

Passages such as these do not question the existence of other gods; what they reject is the worship of these other gods by the people of Yahweh. People who cannot remain loyal to Yahweh arouse Yahweh's anger and eventually suffer punishment.

3. Less obvious but equally important are passages that display a **syncretistic** attitude toward other deities. Syncretism involves combining elements from two or more religions to form a new system. The Hebrew Bible contains many passages that silently incorporate elements of non-Yahwistic polytheism into their images of Israel's god. In a few passages, Yahweh (or Elohim) is depicted as the chairman of a council of supernatural beings, similar to a pantheon of deities, who serve as a sounding board for his actions (Genesis 1:26; 1 Kings 22:19-23; Psalm 82:1; Jeremiah 23:18-22). Other verses assert that Yahweh is supreme over other gods, implying that other deities may indeed exist (Exodus 15:11; Psalms 89:5-7; 95:3; 97:7-9; 138:1). Many of the stories about divine messengers and their activities resemble the depictions of lesser deities in other cultures (Genesis 31:11-13; Exodus 23:20-21; 2 Samuel 24:16-17; 2 Kings 19:35; Psalm 78:49). The same is true for the handful of references to the **Satan** (that is, the "adversary"), whom the Hebrew Bible depicts as a supernatural being who converses with Yahweh in heaven, not as a devil who rules over hell (Job 1:6-12; 2:1-7; Zechariah 3:1-2; 1 Chronicles 21:1).

Elsewhere Yahweh is portrayed in language normally associated with the gods of Canaan. Many verses describe Yahweh as a storm-god like the Canaanite deity Baal, who seems to have been Yahweh's chief competitor for the position of ruler of Palestine. Other verses identify Yahweh as the deity who brings fertility to the land, replacing the Canaanite goddess Asherah. In a few passages Yahweh is even credited with acts that Canaanite myths attribute to their own deities, such as the conquest of monsters with names like Leviathan, Rahab, Yam (sea) and Mot (death) (Job 7:12; 26:12-13; Psalms 74:13-14; 89:9-10; Isaiah 27:1; 51:9). Most prominent is the equation of Yahweh with El, the Canaanite creator god. Dozens of passages in the Hebrew Bible call the deity *El*, and much of the imagery with which Yahweh is clothed recalls depictions of El in Canaanite mythology. Even the name Israel is derived from the divine name El, not Yahweh, leading many scholars to suspect that El was the original god of

the people called Israel and their loyalty to Yahweh was a later development.

On the whole, the biblical authors offer a mixed picture of the relationship of Yahweh to the other gods of Palestine. Most scholars think that this diversity of ideas reflects changing beliefs about the supernatural in ancient Palestine, with polytheistic thinking giving way gradually to monotheism. Others attribute the diverse views to different social classes, religious groups, or geographic regions. Virtually all would agree that the depiction of Yahweh in the Hebrew Bible is the product of a long history of engagement—both positive and negative—with the beliefs and stories of polytheistic Canaanite religion.

EXERCISE 22

Read the following passages and indicate in each case whether you think that their view of the relationship between Yahweh and other deities is absolutist, exclusivist, or syncretistic.

- Exodus 23:31-33
- Leviticus 20:1-5
- Deuteronomy 13:1-5
- Joshua 24:14-24
- Psalm 89:5-13
- Psalm 97:7-9
- Psalm 115:1-8
- Isaiah 40:18-25
- Isaiah 45:20-22
- Habakkuk 2:18-20

THE CHARACTER OF YAHWEH

Since Yahweh is depicted as a personal being, it is only natural to ask what kind of character the biblical authors assign to the deity. Fortunately, Yahweh's character remains fairly constant throughout the Hebrew Bible, though some texts place more emphasis on one characteristic or another. A survey of some of the key terms that are used to describe Yahweh's character and activities can give a sense of the way in which the biblical authors conceived of the deity. Some of these terms overlap in meaning, but each has distinctive elements as well.

1. *Holy.* The word **holy** refers to a person or object that has been "set apart" for a special purpose. To call Yahweh holy is to say that Yahweh is fundamentally different, set apart from the ordinary world of humans and other gods. This does not mean that Yahweh is entirely unlike other deities—we have already seen that this is not the case—or that Yahweh has no human characteristics. It means rather that Yahweh is unique, existing in a class of his own beyond all other beings (scholars sometimes use the phrase "wholly other"), and is therefore worthy of special honor and respect.

The concept of Yahweh's holiness often includes the idea that Yahweh is morally pure and perfect and therefore unable to do anything wrong. This characteristic sets Yahweh apart from the other gods of Palestine, whose actions and commands are often derided as immoral by the followers of Yahweh, as well as from humans, whose sinfulness is generally assumed by the biblical authors. Humans who encounter the holy presence of Yahweh (an experience that modern scholars call a **theophany**) are often overcome by a deep sense of their own frailty and sinfulness. Those who wish to enjoy the protection and care of such a holy being must strive to keep themselves holy, that is, set apart from the practices of the surrounding nations. Passages where the idea of Yahweh's holiness receives special attention include Exodus 19:9-25; Leviticus 11:43-47; Psalm 99:1-9; Isaiah 6:1-7; Ezekiel 36:21-24.

2. *Glorious.* The Hebrew Bible contains many verses that insist that Yahweh cannot be represented by any physical image. This belief, enshrined in the second of the Ten Commandments (see chapter 24), sets Yahweh apart from other deities whose presence was routinely marked by some sort of physical symbol, whether a carefully crafted statue or a simple stone pillar. The idea is not that Yahweh is formless, but that the brilliant light and power associated with his presence (sometimes called his glory) would overwhelm and possibly kill any human who viewed him in his full majesty.

The Hebrew Bible does include a few stories of people who claim to have seen Yahweh and lived. Most describe him as a shining figure seated upon a throne

Fig. 12.4. (left) A stained glass window by Marc Chagall depicting the prophet Isaiah's awesome encounter with Yahweh and his angels in Isaiah 6; (right) a painting by Gérard de Lairesse (*Abraham and the Three Angels*) showing Abraham entertaining angels who come to him in human form, one of whom appears to be Yahweh (Genesis 18).

and surrounded by a host of angels and other super-human figures (Exodus 24:9-11; Isaiah 6:1-4; Ezekiel 1:26-28; Daniel 7:9-10; Amos 9:1). Occasionally Yahweh is shown taking the form of a human or angel and walking among humans (Genesis 3:13-18; 16:7-13; 18:1-3; Judges 6:11-18; 13:1-22). Apparently some of the biblical authors believed that Yahweh could veil his glory enough to allow humans to see at least a semblance of his form when he wished. Passages that depict the glorious presence of Yahweh include Leviticus 9:23-24; Numbers 16:41-45; 2 Chronicles 7:1-3; Psalm 29:1-9; Isaiah 4:5-6; Ezekiel 10:1-22.

3. *Righteous.* The word *righteous* is used to describe someone who lives up to the terms or expectations of a relationship—someone who does right by other people. The range of meaning extends from being a faithful friend to fulfilling social obligations to obeying the dictates of the law. To call Yahweh righteous is to say that Yahweh is committed to doing what is morally and relationally right in every situation, including his interactions with humans. When he makes a promise, he will fulfill it.

Yahweh exhibits his **righteousness** in a variety of ways, including giving laws that reveal what he regards as the proper forms of human conduct; rescuing people who are loyal to him from danger or oppression; and executing judgment upon those who violate his norms of rightness. Some of the biblical authors suggest that the very idea of what is right can be derived from Yahweh's character: because Yahweh is by definition righteous, anything that Yahweh does is right, even when it might not seem so to humans. Passages that emphasize the righteousness of Yahweh include Job 34:16-28; Psalm 97:1-6; Isaiah 45:21-25; Daniel 9:7-14; Zephaniah 3:5-7.

4. *Faithful.* To be faithful is to be dependable or trustworthy in a relationship. The idea of Yahweh's faithfulness is similar to Yahweh's righteousness when it is used to refer to Yahweh standing by his people in times of trouble and rescuing them from danger. In this setting, it means that Yahweh can be counted on to be there when he is needed and not to abandon those who are loyal to him.

A similar idea lies behind the many references to Yahweh's "steadfast love" or "covenant loyalty" toward his people. Because he loves the descendants of Abraham, he remains committed to them even when they are unfaithful to him. Like a parent, he sometimes has to discipline his people, but his anger is only temporary; he never turns his back on them. Yahweh is forever committed to his people, and he shows it by his actions. Passages where Yahweh's faithfulness is highlighted include Genesis 9:12-17; Psalms 36:5-10; 145:13-16; Isaiah 54:6-10; Lamentations 3:21-33.

5. *Mighty.* Throughout the Hebrew Bible, Yahweh is depicted as holding vast power over the forces of nature, the affairs of nations, and the lives of human beings. Though there are a few passages that seem to acknowledge the possibility that other deities might also exercise a measure of power within the universe, the Hebrew Bible shows a strong tendency to attribute all acts of supernatural power to Yahweh. Other beings are allowed to perform works of power on Yahweh's behalf (mostly heavenly messengers, sometimes called angels, though the book of Job also places "the Satan" in this category), but no other being is capable of resisting Yahweh's might.

Some of Yahweh's displays of power relate to the physical world or humanity in general, but the deeds that capture the attention of the biblical authors are the ones that affect Yahweh's people, Israel. Many of Yahweh's mighty acts are done to protect and provide for his people, but he also uses his power to punish humans who refuse to do what he wants. Stories tell of Yahweh sending plagues and famines upon their crops, commanding foreign armies to pillage and destroy their land, and even striking people dead on occasion. Passages that underline Yahweh's power include Exodus 15:6-13; Deuteronomy 7:17-23; Job 12:13-25; Psalm 44:1-8; Isaiah 29:5-8.

6. *Knowing.* Yahweh's knowledge of the universe is extensive, but not unlimited. As the divine creator, he knows all about the physical world and how it works. He also keeps close tabs on what transpires in the world of humans, peering down at them from his throne in the sky. He keeps a special watch on Israel, but he knows about events in other nations as well, including things that will occur in the future. He is even capable of probing into the secret places of human hearts.

Yet there are also passages in the Hebrew Bible that suggest that that Yahweh does not know everything. In several places Yahweh is shown asking humans to tell him what has happened or what they intend to do. Many of the psalms presume that Yahweh is unaware of the painful sufferings that the speaker is experiencing and needs to be informed. Often Yahweh is shown giving choices to humans and spelling out the consequences in a manner that suggests that Yahweh is unsure what they will choose. Sometimes Yahweh's predictions about things that will occur in the future do not take place as stated, and there are several passages where Yahweh is said to have changed his mind in response to seemingly unforeseen human actions. Passages that celebrate the vastness of Yahweh's knowledge include Genesis 15:12-21; Joshua 1:1-6; Psalms 33:13-19; 139:1-18; Isaiah 29:15-24; 48:3-8.

7. *Compassionate.* Though many people think of the God of the Hebrew Bible as a harsh and angry judge, the biblical texts go to great lengths to emphasize the loving, compassionate, gracious side of Yahweh. Many passages speak of Yahweh lavishing tender care upon the world that he created, providing food for the wild animals and sun and rain for the plants. Yet his compassion is most fully revealed in his love for humans. Yahweh knows that humans are weak and prone to sin, yet he loves them anyway. His compassion leads him to treat them far better than they deserve.

Yahweh is particularly devoted to the people of Israel and Judah, whom he selected out of all the nations of the earth to be the recipients of his compassion and devotion. Like a loving parent, Yahweh teaches, trains, protects, and provides for his people, while overlooking and forgiving their faults and failures. When he is finally forced to discipline them, his goal is restoration, not revenge. Passages that focus on Yahweh's compassion include Psalms 103:8-18; 106:44-47; Isaiah 49:13-18; Hosea 11:8-11; Zechariah 10:6-12.

8. *Merciful.* The Hebrew Bible tells a tragic story of human failure. Despite Yahweh's best efforts, humans repeatedly choose to ignore or resist his wishes and commands. Yahweh cannot allow this rejection to go on indefinitely or humans will conclude that there is no justice or order in the universe. Yet time and

time again he chooses the path of mercy instead of judgment.

Yahweh gives his people laws so that they will know how they should live and thereby avoid his judgment. When he sees them going astray, he sends his prophets to warn them to turn around before he has to discipline them. He bears patiently with the wayward members of his people for the sake of those who remain faithful. No matter how bad things get, he always holds out the possibility of mercy for those who decide to turn from their sinful ways. When at last he decides that punishment is the only way to get their attention, he stands ready to forgive and comfort his people as

Fig. 12.5. A painting from a medieval copy of the book of Psalms showing God responding to the cries of his people.

soon as they return to him. Passages that describe the merciful side of Yahweh include Nehemiah 9:26-31; Psalm 51:1-9; Isaiah 55:6-7; Micah 7:8-10; Zechariah 1:12-17.

PERSONIFICATIONS OF YAHWEH

In addition to the many adjectives that they used to describe Yahweh, the biblical authors and editors drew on a rich stock of images and analogies from ordinary life to express their beliefs about the deity. Since Yahweh was regarded as a personal being, most of their images came from the human sphere, but they also used metaphors taken from the animal world (brooding mother hen, lion, bear) and the physical environment (rocky crag, raging storm, earthquake, sun, fire, and so forth). Figures from the world of work were especially popular: Yahweh is depicted at various points as a shepherd, a potter, a carpenter, a baker, a midwife, a warrior, and a ruler. Parental images drawn from both genders are also common.

Though Yahweh is never envisioned as having a physical body, various texts refer metaphorically to his face, mouth, arms, and hands, along with the armor, shield, and weapons that he wears when fighting. They also credit him with a broad range of human emotions, including love, anger, regret, pride, happiness, disappointment, jealousy, hatred, and more. Some of the authors even show Yahweh having human thought processes—the deity reasons with himself, asks for advice, makes decisions, plans, and changes his mind.

Within this wealth of images and metaphors, a few stand out because they are used so often to describe the deity.

1. *King.* In a world where power is associated with kings and their courts, it seems inevitable that one deity will be designated the supreme ruler who holds final authority over the affairs of the universe. Like an earthly monarch, this deity is charged with maintaining order in the realms of nature, humans, and gods, as well as keeping the forces of chaos at bay. For the biblical authors, this role was filled by Yahweh. With regard to the physical world, Yahweh fulfills his kingly role by keeping the forces of nature working as they should. Everything that people today would attribute to natural laws was viewed as an act of Yahweh; the sun, moon, and stars behave as

Fig. 12.6. Altarpiece by Jan van Eyck from the cathedral in Ghent, Belgium, showing God as king over all of humanity.

they do because they obey the commands of their king. The same is true for supernatural beings like angels, who are depicted as perfectly obedient servants and messengers of Yahweh. Humans, by contrast, are less consistent about obeying the divine will.

To call Yahweh "king" over the world of humans is to assert that people should do what he says instead of following their own selfish desires. A similar idea is present when Yahweh is designated as "lord," a term that refers to a master who rules over his servants. The expectation that humans should obey their divine ruler applies above all to the people of Israel, but the Bible contains texts that call on other nations to submit to Yahweh as well. Israel's failure to obey Yahweh does not prevent him from exercising his royal authority; he is quite capable of using other nations to achieve his ends, including enacting judgment against Israel. Passages that portray Yahweh as a mighty king include 1 Chronicles 16:28-33; Psalms 9:1-5; 97:1-9; Isaiah 40:21-23; Ezekiel 1:26-28.

2. *Creator*. The idea of Yahweh as the creator of the universe and its inhabitants is less prominent in the Hebrew Bible than many people think. Apart from the Genesis creation stories, this aspect of Yahweh's character is celebrated primarily in the book of Psalms and Isaiah 40–66, though it is mentioned often enough elsewhere to suggest that it was known to most of the biblical authors and editors.

The Hebrew Bible does not limit Yahweh's creative activity to the beginning of the universe; Yahweh is a deity who acts in creative ways throughout human history. From the formation of Israel (and other nations) to the creation of individual human beings, everything new is attributed to Yahweh's creative power. The depiction of Yahweh as creator enabled people to make sense of many features and events in the physical world that could not be explained in other ways. Passages that highlight the creative aspects of Yahweh's activity include Genesis 2:4-23; Job 38:1-38; Psalm 33:6-9; Proverbs 8:22-31; Isaiah 51:12-16.

3. *Savior*. According to the biblical authors, Yahweh is not a distant deity who is uninvolved in human affairs. Though his throne is in the heavens (the same word that is translated "the sky"), he also lives and acts in the world of humans. His presence is especially strong in the land of Palestine, since he has made a commitment to defend Israel and Judah from their enemies and to rescue them from trouble. Some believe that Yahweh watches over them from the temple that Solomon built in Jerusalem; others insist that Yahweh listens to his people from a variety of sites around the land.

When Yahweh acts to defend and rescue his people from trouble, the biblical authors refer to him as their "savior." (The idea of God saving people from sin so that they can spend eternity in heaven is a Christian concept that does not appear in the Hebrew Bible.) The image of Yahweh as a victorious warrior is also common in these texts. Yahweh's commitment to rescue his people is not unconditional; only those who adhere to Yahweh's standards of conduct can be confident that Yahweh will save them from trouble. Many passages in the Hebrew Bible, especially in the book of Psalms, are concerned with explaining why Yahweh has failed to act as savior in a particular situation. Passages where Yahweh is celebrated as the savior of his people include Exodus 3:7-10; 2 Samuel 22:1-4; Psalms 25:1-22; 34:15-22; Isaiah 43:1-7.

4. *Judge*. As a righteous king, Yahweh expects his commands to be obeyed. In cases where human disobedience is flagrant and/or ongoing, the image of Yahweh as judge comes to the forefront. Sometimes Yahweh is portrayed as calling together his heavenly court and initiating a lawsuit against the violators. More often he serves as judge, jury, and executioner, with the act of punishment receiving primary emphasis.

Yahweh's role as judge applies primarily to the people of Israel, but other nations can also experience his judgment, particularly those that attack and harm his people. Judgment scenes involving individuals are less common, though the book of Psalms resounds with calls for Yahweh to judge the wicked, who can be either individuals or nations. The books of the prophets are likewise filled with threats of divine judgment. Ordinarily, Yahweh's judgments involve the imposition of earthly sufferings: social humiliation, disease, famine, military defeat, and the like. The idea that Yahweh might issue rewards and punishments beyond this life appears only in a few late texts. Passages that depict Yahweh as a judge include Genesis 3:14-24; Psalms 7:6-13; 75:1-8; Isaiah 13:9-13; Micah 6:1-5.

THE DARK SIDE OF YAHWEH

While there is broad agreement throughout most of the Hebrew Bible concerning the central elements of Yahweh's character, the canon also includes texts that challenge some of the popular beliefs about Yahweh. Contemporary scholars have also voiced discomfort with some of the ways in which Yahweh is portrayed.

Most of the questions raised by the biblical authors center on the way in which Yahweh manages human affairs. Some were disturbed by the rampant injustice that they observed in their society. Wherever they looked, they saw disparities in wealth, bribery and dishonesty in the courts, corrupt business practices, violence against the poor, and other forms of social injustice (Job 24:1-25; Psalm 73:1-12; Ecclesiastes 4:1-4; Habakkuk 1:1-4, 13-17). If Yahweh was truly holy and righteous and exercised sovereign power over the universe, why did he not act? Similar questions were voiced by individuals who were experiencing personal sufferings (social rejection, disease, unfair treatment, and so forth) despite their record of loyalty to Yahweh (Ruth 1:19-21; Job 29:1—31:40; Psalms 10:1-13; 35:17-25; 88:1-18). If Yahweh was committed to protect his loyal followers, why had these troubles come upon them? Why didn't Yahweh take them away? Where was Yahweh's love and compassion? The questioning was especially acute when Israel was defeated by foreign foes

who honored gods other than Yahweh (Psalms 74:1-11; 79:1-10; 80:8-19; Lamentations 5:1-22). How could Yahweh allow his people to be conquered by a nation that was more sinful than they?

Behind these questions lay a recognition that the traditional teachings about Yahweh's character did not always match people's observations about the way the world works. Could it be that the traditional beliefs were wrong? Some of the authors who were unhappy about what they saw explored the possibility that Yahweh might have a "dark side." Perhaps Yahweh isn't always righteous in his actions, they said; perhaps Yahweh is fickle or selective in his love and can't be trusted; perhaps Yahweh is not strong enough to protect or rescue his people; perhaps Yahweh falls asleep from time to time or is too far away to hear, so that he doesn't always know when his people are suffering; perhaps Yahweh even takes pleasure in

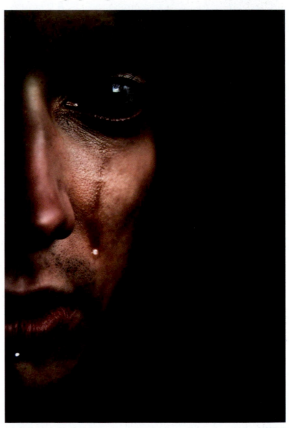

Fig. 12.7. Experiences of tragic loss are compounded by the sense that one has been dealt an injustice.

tormenting people and watching them suffer. How many people were troubled by such questions is impossible to say. But it is easy to see why some might have found these ideas attractive, since they not only explained many of the dark experiences of life but also coincided with the way many other gods were viewed at the time. Why should Yahweh be any different?

For most of the followers of Yahweh, however, such

sense within the context of their traditional beliefs. The most popular explanation for the pain and suffering that affected everyone from time to time was to regard them as punishments inflicted by a righteous deity in response to people's sins. This explanation made it easier for many sufferers to accept their fate, since it transferred the blame from Yahweh to themselves. But the solution was far from perfect—it did not explain the sufferings of the righteous, nor did it account for the continued success of those who flagrantly violated Yahweh's standards. It also fostered a "blame the victim" mentality that many contemporary scholars find distasteful.

A different solution was developed to address these concerns. This position, too, absolves Yahweh from blame by criticizing the questioners—their thinking is too short-sighted or too limited to grasp what Yahweh is doing. Humans must give Yahweh time to work out his purposes. At the proper time, the wicked will be

Fig. 12.8. An Assyrian deity, symbolized by a winged disk, watches over the Assyrian king Ashurbanipal as he meets with one of his officials.

ideas would have been unthinkable, since to accept them would have required a radical reorientation of their worldview. Instead, they searched for answers that made

brought down and the righteous will be rewarded for their sufferings. Those who wait patiently will see the judgments of God. The problem with this explanation, of course, is that many people die before they witness the promised reversal of fortunes. Some of the biblical authors resolved this problem by asserting that Yahweh would punish or bless the children of those who died unrewarded. Others concluded that the universality of death made it impossible for humans to comprehend how Yahweh would accomplish his plans. All that humans could do was trust that it would work out in the end.

Not until the end of the biblical period did people begin to voice the solution that would have the most enduring impact. According to this view, the righteous character of Yahweh requires that there be some kind of final judgment in which the wicked are punished and the righteous are rewarded, but it need not occur within the parameters of history. Some thought that it would take place immediately after death, while others placed it in a future era. The beauty of this solution is that it postpones the resolution of the problem beyond the lives of the questioners. It gained adherents because it allowed believers to accept the sufferings and injustices of life while simultaneously maintaining their traditional beliefs about the noble character of Yahweh. Its usefulness is apparent from the fact that it eventually became the standard position in most forms of Judaism, Christianity, and Islam.

In addition to the concerns that were voiced by ancient authors, contemporary scholars have identified other problems in the biblical portrait of Yahweh that suggest that the deity has a "dark side." Some are bothered by the biblical notion that Yahweh sends suffering upon human beings in order to uphold and defend an abstract system of righteousness, since it conflicts with their belief that love is the central element of God's character. Others are troubled by the thought that Yahweh would punish his people for using their God-given minds and freedom of will to explore non-Yahwistic religious ideas and practices, actions that the biblical text condemns as idolatry. Most disturbing are the many verses in which the biblical authors claim divine support for actions and institutions that would be considered oppressive and abusive by modern standards. For example, the assertion that Yahweh instituted (or at least approved of) an absolute monarchy in ancient Israel (1 Samuel 8:22; 2 Samuel 7:1-17; Psalm 72:1-19; 89:19-37) places Yahweh squarely on the side of the ruling political authorities. In a similar way, the fact that Yahweh regulates but does not criticize the practice of slavery (Exodus 21:2-11, 20-21, 26-27; Leviticus 19:20-22) implies that Yahweh has no problem with humans

owning other humans. The same difficulty can be seen in verses that show Yahweh choosing only males to serve him as priests (the "sons of Aaron," as in Exodus 28:1, 40-43; Leviticus 21:1-15), which paint the deity as a male chauvinist, and passages where Yahweh orders his people to slaughter the wives and children of their enemies when attacking their cities (Deuteronomy 7:1-6; 20:16-18; Joshua 10:40; 1 Samuel 15:1-3), which cast him as a heartless bigot.

Some of these concerns are offset by other texts that insist that Yahweh stands on the side of the poor and oppressed. But this does not make the troubling passages go away. None of these problems is noted by the biblical authors, so we can assume that they saw no difficulty with any of the ideas cited here. The reason for their silence is not hard to guess—all of the verses in question support the interests of the male elites who wrote and edited the texts. Like many other humans before and after them, they were convinced that God was on their side. As a result, they gave little thought to the consequences of their beliefs for people outside of their community who experienced the "dark side" of Yahweh at their own hands.

CONCLUSION

The religious environment of ancient Palestine was far more complex than the views that are endorsed by the biblical authors and editors. Traditional polytheism was practiced throughout the biblical period, and many polytheists had no trouble finding a place for Yahweh in their pantheon of deities. Many of those who honored Yahweh as the chief deity of Israel and Judah were willing to acknowledge the existence of other gods, even as they tried to discourage people from worshipping them. The number of people who regarded Yahweh as the only true god was fairly small until late in the biblical period. In the meantime, Yahweh picked up many of the characteristics of the gods whom he displaced.

Because Yahweh is a personal deity, the biblical authors and editors depicted him with many of the features of a human personality. On the one hand, Yahweh is portrayed as a holy, awesome, and righteous deity who possesses tremendous (though not unlimited) power and knowledge and insists upon absolute loyalty on the part of his people. On the other hand, Yahweh relates to humans with faithfulness and love, tempering all of his actions with compassion and mercy. The complexity of Yahweh's character is reflected in the diversity of images employed to describe him, including king, creator, savior, and judge.

Most of the biblical authors and editors were content to affirm traditional beliefs about Yahweh without question, but some were troubled by the discrepancies between what they had been taught about Yahweh and what they observed in the world around them. Their varied efforts to resolve these tensions add richness and diversity to the biblical portrait of Yahweh, the god of Israel.

EXERCISE 24

Read the following passages from the Hebrew Bible that illustrate the "dark side" of Yahweh. What does each passage say or imply about Yahweh? Why do many modern readers find these passages disturbing?

• Genesis 6:1-7
• Genesis 11:1-9
• Leviticus 21:16-34
• Numbers 5:11-31
• Deuteronomy 28:15-37
• Joshua 11:1-15
• 2 Samuel 6:1-11
• 2 Samuel 24:1-25
• Amos 4:6-13
• Ezekiel 16:1-43

Fig. 13.1. This Egyptian stela shows how virtually everyone in the ancient Near East viewed the place of humans in the cosmos, with men and women engaging in social activities under the oversight of the gods.

On Being Human

Then God said, "Let us make humankind in our image, according to our likeness; and let them have dominion over the fish of the sea, and over the birds of the air, and over the cattle, and over all the wild animals of the earth, and over every creeping thing that creeps upon the earth." So God created humankind in his image, in the image of God he created them; male and female he created them. (Genesis 1:26-27)

I praise you, for I am fearfully and wonderfully made. Wonderful are your works; that I know very well. My frame was not hidden from you, when I was being made in secret, intricately woven in the depths of the earth. Your eyes beheld my unformed substance. In your book were written all the days that were formed for me, when none of them as yet existed. (Psalm 139:14-16)

For the fate of humans and the fate of animals is the same; as one dies, so dies the other. They all have the same breath, and humans have no advantage over the animals; for all is vanity. All go to one place; all are from the dust, and all turn to dust again. Who knows whether the human spirit goes upward and the spirit of animals goes downward to the earth? (Ecclesiastes 3:19-21)

When the authors and editors of the Hebrew Bible wrote down their ideas about the nature of the supernatural world and its inhabitants, they were not engaging in idle philosophical speculation. They knew that what people believe about the character of the universe carries direct implications for the way they understand their own place in the cosmos, including the way they live their lives and organize their society.

The same is true for their beliefs about what it means to be human and the way humans should relate to the deity. Here and there one of the biblical authors/editors says something explicit about these matters, but most of the time their beliefs operate at the subconscious level as part of their worldview. Consequently, we have to infer what they believed from the many stories, laws, songs, sayings, and prophecies that make up the Hebrew Bible. Fortunately, the ideas that emerge from these writings are

consistent enough to allow us to compile at least a broad outline of their thinking in this area. By comparing their ideas with the beliefs of people in other cultures, including the ancient Near East, we can identify what is common and what is distinctive about their views.

FRAMING THE QUESTION

Throughout the millennia, humans have struggled to understand their place in the universe. Virtually all of the answers that have arisen from this quest have placed humans and their concerns at the center of the universe. Cultures differ, however, in the way they frame their questions and the answers that they propose.

In the industrialized Western world, people tend to look at reality through an individualistic lens. Most of the questions that they ask concern matters of personal identity and destiny: "Who am I? Why am I here? Why does the universe treat me as it does? Where am I going?" In traditional agrarian societies, by contrast, people are oriented toward the group. Individuals derive their sense of identity and worth from their role in important social groups (family, clan, tribe, and so forth). Personal quests for meaning and significance are usually discouraged. Questions about life are framed not in singular but in plural terms: "Who are we (referring to the people or group)? Why are we here? Why does life treat us as it does? Where are we going?"

Much of this difference can be traced to the fact that groups play a much larger role in the social, economic, and political life of traditional cultures than they do in the industrialized West. The thought patterns of people in traditional cultures are shaped by the realities of daily life in an agricultural economy. In the ancient Near East, most families lived close to the subsistence level, and every member had to work together to enable the family to meet its basic needs. Life in the towns and villages also required a high level of mutual support and cooperation. Individuals were taught from childhood to sublimate their wishes and dreams to the needs of the group and to devote their energies to ensuring the group's success. All of these forces led people to value the good of the group over personal freedom and self-realization. This in turn affected the way they thought about the universe and their place in it.

As a rule, peasants and farmers who struggled to make ends meet had little time or energy to devote to abstract questions like the nature and purpose of human existence. Most of them probably accepted without question the answers that were given to them by the oral traditions of their culture. Only the elites could afford the luxury of reflecting independently on the "big questions" of life and recording their thoughts in writing. But they, too, operated within the dominant thought patterns of their culture. As a result, their reflections on the character of human existence tend to emphasize the group over the individual and are consistently religious in character.

WHAT DOES IT MEAN TO BE HUMAN?

Beliefs about the nature of human existence and the place of humans in the universe seek to address three related questions:

(a) What is the essential nature of the human individual? (Who am I?)
(b) What makes our group different from others? (Who are we?)
(c) What is our relation to people outside our group? (Who are they?)

The answers that people give to these questions are closely linked to their overall view of the universe, that is, their worldview.

1. In **animistic** societies, people believe that the lives of humans, animals, and spirits are intimately intertwined. Many believe that living beings can transform from one of these states to another. Human nature is perceived as fluid; even death is simply a transition from a physical to a spiritual mode of existence within the society. Human existence is precarious, since humans are surrounded by spiritual forces that are not always friendly and cannot always be controlled. The tribe or clan plays a dominant role in shaping individual identity. Stories depict their group and their locality as the focal point of the universe. Outsiders are often regarded as hostile or even subhuman.

2. In **polytheistic** societies, humans are typically viewed as servants of the gods who rule over them in a well-defined hierarchy. Humans who fulfill their duties to the gods can expect to be protected from many of the harmful possibilities of life. But the gods are not always trustworthy, and the ebb and flow of alliances and conflicts among them can have an unpredictable effect on human affairs. As a result, human experience is characterized by uncertainty. Beliefs about what happens to humans after death vary widely, ranging from a disembodied ghostly presence to reincarnation in another body. Most polytheistic groups believe that their community has a special relationship with a particular set of deities that sets them apart from neighboring groups, who have similar relationships with their own gods. Interactions between

Fig. 13.2. Followers of polytheistic religions often bring food offerings to the gods in an effort to gain or hold onto their favor, as in this engraving of worshippers approaching a statue of the Greek goddess Demeter.

Fig. 13.3. In pantheistic religions, meditation is a vital path for individuals to realize their union with the divine.

groups involve not only their human representatives but also their respective gods. The formation of a new alliance might be marked by marriages among their deities, while victory in battle is a sign that the gods of the conquerors have overcome the gods of the defeated group.

3. In **monolatrous** societies, the view of humans is similar to that of polytheistic societies, since both systems think of humans as being surrounded by multiple deities whose acts can affect humans individually and collectively. But monolatrous societies offer more security to their members, since they regard themselves as living under the watchful care of a deity who is supreme over all others. In return for this protection, the deity requires loyalty and service from the group. This expectation typically leads to a strong sense of group identity, since the members of the group are bound by their collective obligation to the deity who watches over them, a relationship that sometimes extends beyond the grave. Attitudes toward people outside the group can vary from hostility to acceptance.

4. In **pantheistic** societies, humans are regarded as inherently divine. Like other living things, humans are an expression of a single cosmic presence or consciousness that permeates the entire universe. The common belief that humans are superior to other beings is a false perception that must be overcome through mental and spiritual discipline. Most versions of pantheism believe that personal identity is a temporary state that can be transcended after death by merging into the divine essence, whether immediately or after many reincarnations. In principle,

pantheistic worldviews place all humans on an equal footing in relation to the supernatural, making group identities obsolete. But even pantheistic societies can take pride in the belief that their group is supremely enlightened, leaving room for individuals to derive at least part of their identity from membership in a particular group.

5. In **monotheistic** societies, humans are commonly seen as the objects of special divine attention, and therefore as beings who have dignity and worth. But they remain limited and frail creatures, not divine beings themselves. Most monotheistic systems believe that humans have free will to choose between good and evil. Some claim that humans have an inherent tendency to choose evil, a tendency that must be overcome by self-discipline. Others insist that humans are morally neutral or even inclined toward the good. Monotheistic systems vary widely in their ideas about human survival after death. Like pantheism, monotheism implicitly undercuts group identities by giving all humans equal access to the supernatural realm. But history shows that monotheists in fact have a strong tendency to view themselves as the sole possessors of truth

and to look down on people who follow other systems of belief.

6. In **dualistic** societies, humanity is regarded as fundamentally divided. Some humans are on the side of the good force, while others are on the side of the evil force. Many dualists believe that individual humans are divided within themselves between good and evil tendencies and that they have the freedom to choose which side to join. Others insist that membership in the two camps is predetermined. Dualistic societies typically have a strong sense of group identity, since they view themselves as the allies of the good force and those outside the group as servants of the powers of evil. Their views about individual existence after death vary widely.

> ## EXERCISE 25
>
> Try to imagine yourself living in a time and place before the rise of modern science and technology. Which of these six ways of making sense of human existence do you think might seem most plausible to you under those circumstances? Why?

HUMANS IN THE HEBREW BIBLE

Since the authors and editors of the Hebrew Bible were mostly monolatrous or monotheistic in their thinking, their views of the human condition are similar to those of other monolatrous and monotheistic societies. But every society has its own way of framing the issues, and the same is true for the people who created the Hebrew Bible. An examination of the answers they might have given to the three questions cited above will help us to understand the various elements of their view of human existence. The first question—Who am I?—will be treated in this chapter. The other two questions (Who are we? and Who are they?) will be examined in the next chapter.

Human Origins

Since they did not perform autopsies, the people of ancient Palestine knew little about the inner workings of the human body, and even less about the relation between the bodily organs and the inner self or personality. Most of their ideas were rooted in naïve observations and personal experience. For example, they seem to have thought that pregnancy resulted entirely from the man's life-giving "seed" being implanted in the "field" of the woman's body. The woman's body added nothing to the conception process; she was simply a receptacle for the man's seed. Similar views were held by virtually everyone in the ancient world. The formation of the man's seed into a child, on the other hand, required the personal intervention of the deity, who thus "knew" every child from before its birth (Job 31:15; Psalm 139:13-16; Ecclesiastes 11:5; Isaiah 44:2; Jeremiah 1:5).

Since every individual was regarded as a unique creation of God, it was only natural to conclude that humans have inherent value and dignity that place them above the animals in the created order. The creation account in the book of Genesis depicts humans as the pinnacle of God's creation, describing both man and woman as being made "in the image of God" (Genesis 1:27). The meaning of this expression is unclear; scholars have suggested that it might refer to the humans' lofty position of authority over God's creation (Genesis 1:28); their ability to create like God; their capacity to have a personal relationship with the deity; their power to reason or to love; or various other ideas. At a minimum it suggests that humans are qualitatively different from God's other creatures about which no such statement is made. The idea that humans are somehow godlike is not restricted to the Hebrew Bible; other ancient Near Eastern cultures tell stories of humans being created out of some kind of divine substance, which is another way of making the same point.

The Genesis creation account also shows God delegating to humans both the right and the responsibility of directing and caring for the created order (Genesis 1:28; 2:15). This vision of humans as God's vice-rulers over creation distinguishes Genesis from other ancient Near Eastern texts, where humans are commonly depicted as slaves of the gods who are charged with satisfying the needs and whims of their divine rulers. But this does not mean that Genesis gives humans the right to do whatever they wish with God's creation. At first they are allowed

Fig. 13.4. Lucas Cranach the Elder, *Adam and Eve in the Garden of Eden*

to eat only fruits and vegetables (Genesis 1:29), and they are prohibited from eating the fruit of one particular tree (Genesis 2:16). Eventually God does give them permission to kill and eat the meat of animals, but first they must drain the animal's life-giving blood (Genesis 9:3-4). Still later in the narrative God gives laws that seek to ensure the humane treatment of both animals and land (Exodus 23:5, 10-12; Leviticus 22:27; 25:4-7; Deuteronomy 22:4, 6-7, 10; 25:4), though many people today would question how the practice of animal sacrifice could be described as humane. (For more on the duty to sacrifice animals to the deity, see the discussion in chapter 29.)

Mind and Body

Like many other people in the ancient world, the biblical authors believed that life was a gift of God that was closely associated with blood (Leviticus 17:11-14; Deuteronomy 12:23). This belief probably arose from the common observation that the life of a human or animal quickly ebbs and then ceases when blood flows unchecked from a bodily wound. As the carrier of life, blood was thought to possess awesome power, and special provisions regulated how it should be handled, whether it came from animals or humans (see chapters 23 and 29).

People also thought of breath as a vital force that sustained life. Anyone could see that breathing was a necessary part of life and that the end of breathing was a sign of death. So it was only natural for them to conclude that breath was a powerful, God-given force that kept people and animals alive (Genesis 1:30; 2:7; 1 Kings 17:17-23; Job 12:10; 34:14-15; Psalm 104:29; Ecclesiastes 3:19; Ezekiel 37:4-10).

A careful study of the Hebrew words for "life" (*nephesh*) and "breath" (*ruach*) shows that the biblical authors used

Fig. 13.5. William Blake, *Elohim Creating Adam*. The painting illustrates Genesis 2:7, where the deity literally breathes the breath of life into the first human.

both words in a similar way to refer to an invisible power that energizes the physical body and keeps it operating. Confusion arises from the fact that our English Bibles often translate these two words as **soul** and **spirit**. In Western thought, the terms *soul* and *spirit* usually refer to an immortal personal essence that gives people a sense of self while they are alive and bears their identity to a different plane of existence after death. This way of viewing the self, which arose out of Greek philosophy and was extended further by Christian theologians, is virtually absent from the Hebrew Bible.

As a rule, the biblical authors use the words *soul* and *spirit* in a sense that resembles our modern concepts of "consciousness" or "mind." Like modern humans, they were aware of the presence of an inner self that appeared to direct and control the actions of the body, but they did not regard this inner self as immortal. Instead, they seem to have envisioned the soul or spirit as being inextricably linked to the physical body, so that when the body died, the soul/spirit also ceased to exist. Interestingly, this view is somewhat similar to the ideas of modern neuroscience, which tells us that the experience of consciousness

is rooted in the electrochemical activities of the brain and ceases when the brain is severely damaged or when the body stops functioning.

Of course, people in antiquity knew nothing about the relation between the mind and the brain. Most of the time they seem to have associated thoughts and feelings with the heart, the kidneys, or the intestines, whether because these organs are located deep inside the body or because strong emotions are sometimes accompanied by pains in the abdomen. This is exactly what we find in the Hebrew Bible, though this reality is often obscured in English translations that use modern psychological categories to translate ancient language that links mental states with parts of the body. In the Hebrew Bible, for example, intentions commonly reside in the heart, while deep feelings arise out of the bowels. But the language is not consistent; none of the biblical authors seems to be following any systematic theory that links mental and emotional states with particular parts of the body. What they do have in common is a desire to tie the inner self closely to the physical body. All of the biblical authors and editors seem to regard humans as unitary beings—embodied souls or ensouled bodies—and not as internally divided entities made up of a mortal body and an immortal soul. The terms *body* and *soul* (or *spirit*) are simply two ways of looking at the same being, with one focusing on the external features and the other the internal features of the person.

So where does this leave the body? Until fairly recently, the Western intellectual tradition was dominated by Greek philosophical thinking that viewed the body as the troublesome source of all kinds of physical desires that distracted the eternal soul from its true purpose and destiny. Plato traced the problem to the fact that the body is made up of earthly matter that serves as a snare (or even a prison) for the eternal substance of the soul. Like the Greek view of the soul, however, this pattern of thinking is foreign to the Hebrew Bible. None of the biblical authors or editors voices any negative opinions about the material universe or the physical body. In the creation story of Genesis 1, God repeatedly declares the various parts of the created order to be good, and the biblical authors show no embarrassment about depicting Yahweh as the one who formed the physical world and its inhabitants (Deuteronomy 4:32; Psalms 89:11-12; 94:9; 148:1-6; Proverbs 8:27-31; Isaiah 45:18; Zechariah 12:1), including the bodies of humans (Genesis 2:7; Job 10:8-11; Psalm 139:13-16; Isaiah 49:5). A few stories even show Yahweh himself taking on human form (Genesis 3:13-18; 18:1-3; 32:22-30; Judges 6:11-18; 13:1-22). In the book of Psalms, the people of Yahweh are repeatedly encouraged to worship the deity with their bodies by singing, dancing, shouting, clapping, raising hands, kneeling, and so on. Nothing about the human body makes it an unfit instrument to honor the deity. The body is sometimes described as frail and weak because of its vulnerability to sickness and death, but it is never depicted as a channel of temptation or sin. Instead, both the physical world and the human body are portrayed as gifts from God to be enjoyed.

On the other hand, enjoyment does not mean doing whatever one pleases. The body is also the primary channel through which humans engage in relationships with one another and with God. In the view of the biblical authors, humans do not exist in a vacuum; relationships are fundamental to their identity. These relationships carry with them certain obligations and duties, some of which limit what humans can do with their bodies. For example, the Torah prohibits eating certain kinds of food, having sex with certain individuals, and engaging in certain activities that would use the body to cause harm to others, such as physical assault and murder. The body is not itself a source of temptation or sin, but if left unregulated it can become a channel through

which sinful and harmful actions are carried out. This is one of the primary reasons why Yahweh gives laws to his people—to let them know what kinds of bodily actions are pleasing to Yahweh (and beneficial to others) and what kinds of actions offend him (and cause harm to others).

Freedom to Choose

Implicit in this last statement is another important fact about the biblical authors' view of human nature—their belief that humans have the freedom to choose what they

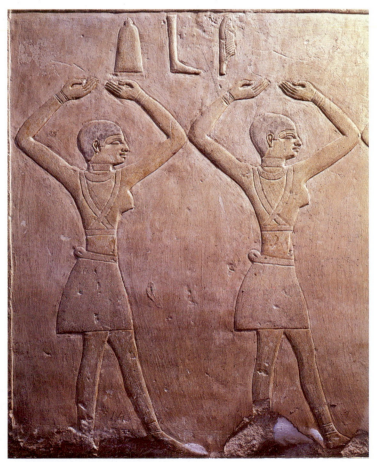

Fig. 13.6. Physical activities such as dancing and raising one's hands, as depicted in an Egyptian relief, played a vital role in the worship of Yahweh as portrayed in the book of Psalms (see chapter 30).

will do with their lives. Unlike many forms of Christianity, the Hebrew Bible contains no doctrine of **original sin**, the belief that human nature has been corrupted from its original state so that humans now have an inherent tendency to resist the will of God. The passage that is cited most often in favor of this position, Genesis 3, indicates only that sinful human choices brought suffering and death into the world. It says nothing about any change in the essential nature of humans (see chapter 16). The handful of verses that speak of humans being sinful from birth or childhood (for example, Genesis 8:21 and Psalm 51:5) are describing situations in which evil has become particularly rampant. They should not be generalized into universal statements of belief.

The authors and editors of the Hebrew Bible consistently assume that humans have the freedom to choose to do good or evil, to follow Yahweh or other deities. Yet they also recognize that humans can get locked into patterns of behavior that make it difficult for them to change, as seen in texts like Isaiah 6:9-13 and Ezekiel 2:3-8. In a few cases this "hardening of the heart" is attributed to divine action (Exodus 4:21; 7:3; 14:4, 17; Deuteronomy 2:30; Joshua 11:20; Isaiah 63:17). On the whole, the biblical authors show a thoughtful awareness of the complexity and ambiguity of human motivations, but they still presume that humans have the inherent freedom and ability to choose how they will live their lives.

The Hebrew Bible also insists that humans are responsible for the consequences of their choices. Some kinds of choices are right and others are wrong, and each leads to particular kinds of outcomes. While some texts seem to imply that actions are linked to consequences by a natural moral law that is embedded in the universe, more often the results are attributed to divine action. Those who choose to do what is good and right will be rewarded by Yahweh, while those who choose the path of evil will be punished. For the most part, the biblical authors believe that the consequences of human actions will be realized in this life; only in the latest biblical writings do we see any hint of a belief in rewards and punishments after death (see chapter 21).

Life after Death?

The ultimate fate of the human individual is never clearly addressed in the Hebrew Bible. Most of the time the authors seem to assume that death is the end of human existence; all that remains of a person after death are the children whom one left to carry on the activities of the family and the good or bad impressions that one made on other people during one's life—that is, one's reputation (Job 14:7-12; 17:11-16; Psalm 49:10-14; Ecclesiastes 9:1-6). On the other hand, there are a number of passages that point to a popular belief that some kind of faint, disembodied shadow of the person (a ghost?) passes downward through the earth after burial until it reaches a nebulous realm called **Sheol** (Isaiah 14:9-11; Ezekiel 32:17-32; 10:19-22; 38:16-17; Ezekiel 26:19-21). Some English translations obscure this point by inserting the generic term *the grave* in place of the Hebrew word *Sheol*.

The conditions of existence in Sheol are never discussed, but there is nothing to suggest that it includes either rewards or torments. A few verses imply that the dead are cut off from contact with the deity, since Sheol is located deep beneath the earth and Yahweh lives high above the clouds (the literal meaning of *heaven*) (Psalms 6:4-5; 30:8-9; 88:3-12; Isaiah 38:18). The dead are also separated from the land of the living, though there were people with special skills (called *mediums* or *necromancers*) who were said to be able to bring the ghosts of the dead back to earth for consultations (1 Samuel 28:4-20; 2 Kings 21:26; 23:24; Isaiah 8:9; 19:3; 29:4; see chapter 27). This kind of activity was soundly rejected by the people who compiled the Hebrew Bible (Leviticus 19:11; 20:6, 27; Deuteronomy 18:11; 2 Kings 23:24).

A handful of verses from the end of the biblical period hint at the rise of new modes of thinking that anticipated a future **resurrection** of the dead or the transition of the soul to heaven after death (see chapter 36). Unfortunately, the Hebrew Bible offers no coherent depiction of what these people expected to happen, and the few references that do appear are sketchy at best (Daniel 12:1-3; Isaiah 26:19; Ecclesiastes 3:21; 12:7; compare Job 19:25-27; Psalm 49:15; Hosea 13:14). Over time, these new ideas about life beyond the grave came to dominate most forms of Judaism, Christianity, and Islam. But this way of envisioning the future fate of humans would have been foreign to most of the authors and editors of the Hebrew Bible.

CONCLUSION

Unlike the teachers of Buddhism or Hinduism, the authors and editors of the Hebrew Bible offer little systematic reflection on the nature of human existence. But their writings do contain enough hints and allusions to suggest that their views of reality included many common assumptions about human nature.

At the heart of their thinking was the belief that humans are integrated, holistic beings who occupy a position of honor and dignity above Yahweh's other creatures. In their view, the body is just as vital to human existence as the inner self—humans are fundamentally ensouled bodies or embodied souls. The mysterious life force that energizes the body takes physical expression in the blood that flows through its veins and the breath that fills its lungs.

Humans were made to live in bodily relationships with God and others, not in isolation or self-centered independence. But humans are also free to choose whether to live their lives as the deity intended, and their choices carry genuine consequences. In general, the biblical authors believed that these consequences would be realized in the present life, since most of them believed that human existence ceases with death. Some may have believed in various forms of afterlife, but the belief in heavenly rewards and punishments finds no clear expression in the Hebrew Bible.

EXERCISE 26

Read the following passages from the Hebrew Bible, then choose any three of them and summarize what each passage states or implies about the author's beliefs concerning what it means to be human. Keep in mind the various points that were raised in this chapter.

- Genesis 1:26-30
- Genesis 2:15-25
- Joshua 24:14-24
- Psalm 16:7-11
- Psalm 49:5-15
- Psalm 88:3-12
- Psalm 139:13-18
- Isaiah 59:1-8

Fig. 14.1. This ninth-century B.C.E. tablet shows the Babylonian king (right) making a land grant to one of his officials under the watchful oversight of the gods, as symbolized by the images in the upper panel.

The Ideal Society

I will establish my covenant between me and you, and your offspring after you throughout their generations, for an everlasting covenant, to be God to you and to your offspring after you. And I will give to you, and to your offspring after you, the land where you are now an alien, all the land of Canaan, for a perpetual holding; and I will be their God. (Genesis 17:7-8)

Know therefore that the LORD your God is God, the faithful God who maintains covenant loyalty with those who love him and keep his commandments, to a thousand generations, and who repays in their own person those who reject him. He does not delay but repays in their own person those who reject him. Therefore, observe diligently the commandment—the statutes, and the ordinances—that I am commanding you today. (Deuteronomy 7:9-11)

Yes, thus says the Lord GOD: I will deal with you as you have done, you who have despised the oath, breaking the covenant; yet I will remember my covenant with you in the days of your youth, and I will establish with you an everlasting covenant. . . . I will establish my covenant with you, and you shall know that I am the LORD, in order that you may remember and be confounded, and never open your mouth again because of your shame, when I forgive you all that you have done, says the Lord GOD. (Ezekiel 16:59-60, 62-63)

In this chapter we continue our examination of the central ideas that shaped the personal and religious identity of the followers of Yahweh in ancient Palestine. Where the previous chapter focused on the way the individual is defined in the Hebrew Bible (Who am I?), the present chapter will explore the theoretical framework that shaped the biblical authors' vision for their society (Who are we?), including their relations with people outside the group (Who are they?). Toward the end of the chapter we will examine how this theoretical outlook compares with what we know about real-world social conditions in ancient Palestine.

THE ROOTS OF SOCIAL IDENTITY

As we have noted on several occasions, people in traditional societies derive much of their sense of identity from their membership in various social groups. The most basic identity group is the extended family. Here children are trained to accept the group's understanding of who they are as individuals, their role within the family, and the way they should relate to people within and outside the group.

Above the family in most traditional societies stands the clan, a grouping that includes several extended families and frequently the tribe, a unit consisting of several related (or sometimes unrelated) clans. Relationships among group members are less personal and immediate at this level, but the ideals and expectations associated with these larger groups still play a vital role in defining the identity and obligations of the individuals and subgroups that make up the society.

Fig. 14.2. Both Hasidic Jews (top) and Sikhs (bottom) wear special clothing to mark their ethnic and religious identity.

The broadest identity group is the people (that is, the ethnic group), a nebulous entity whose influence on individual members can vary from symbolic identification to totalitarian control. Members are taught from an early age that loyalty to their own people is crucial to the survival of the group, especially in times of conflict with outsiders. In many societies this message is reinforced by a conviction that the people have a special relationship with the gods. This belief is then celebrated in public rituals that remind members of the importance and uniqueness of their group.

In addition to orienting the individual toward his or her rank and duties within the society, most such groups develop a set of identity markers that define who is and is not a member of the group. Almost any distinguishing feature can serve as a marker of group identity: physical features, records of family descent, modes of speech, styles of dress or behavior, social or religious customs, and so forth. The practical significance of this division of the world into "us" (the in-group) and "them" (the out-group) varies from culture to culture. In some cases the distinction is benign and inclusive: the in-group provides psychological and material resources for the individual while simultaneously encouraging a positive attitude toward people outside the group. In other cases the in-group becomes the breeding ground for **exclusivism**, intolerance, and even organized attacks against outsiders. Most groups fall somewhere between these extremes.

Because traditional societies view reality through a religious lens, they invariably develop religious explanations for the existence and expectations of the society and its subgroups. Often these explanations are passed on through stories about the group's past. Some of these stories have historical foundations, while others do not. Their purpose is the same in either case: to instill in members an idealistic vision of how the group should operate by pointing to special times and people in the past where the vision was supposedly defined or realized. The same thing happens in our own day when politicians tell stories about the Founding Fathers in an effort to garner support for their ideas about what the country ought to be like. Of course, stories are not the only means of communicating these ideals; the same vision can be passed on through poems, songs, rituals, codes of conduct, and other modes of societal instruction.

To be effective, a religious interpretation of society must be able to capture the imaginations of the people who direct the social, political, and religious institutions of the society. A vision for society that fails to gain their approval will either die out or fragment the society into competing subgroups. Other factors that can interfere with the success of a particular vision for society include the presence of ideas or practices that differ significantly from the accepted traditions; the absence of a reliable means of transmitting the vision; and the potentially divisive effects of social, ethnic, or religious rivalries within the leadership or the group as a whole.

THE IDEA OF COVENANT

When we ask whether the Hebrew Bible offers any kind of overarching religious vision for the society in which it was produced, one answer stands out clearly: the idea of covenant. A covenant is an agreement or contract that defines the relationship between two parties. In the ancient Near East, people and nations sometimes entered into covenants that spelled out how the two parties were supposed to act toward one another. An analogous situation arises today when nations ratify treaties or individuals sign a loan contract. Most covenants entailed an exchange of mutual promises, though the obligations could also be entirely one-sided. In cases where the two parties were social equals, the terms and conditions of the covenant were usually negotiated. In other cases (for example, alliances between stronger and weaker nations or individuals), the party with the greater power or social standing dictated the terms of the covenant.

Depending on the nature of the relationship, the duties of the covenant partners could be spelled out in great detail, as in a loan agreement, or framed in more general terms, as in marriage vows. Most covenants included severe penalties for anyone who violated their conditions. Sometimes these penalties were judicial in nature, but more often they took the form of **curses** to be inflicted by the gods, who were regarded as witnesses and enforcers of the covenant. As a rule, the establishment of a covenant was accompanied by some kind of ritual or other symbolic act—a sacrifice, an oath, an exchange of gifts, a meal.

Since the biblical authors viewed Yahweh as a personal being, it was only natural that they should turn to the metaphor of a covenant when describing the way in which Yahweh relates to his people. The covenant idea was attractive because it combined the legal notions of promise and obligation with the more personal images of

faithfulness and loyalty to a covenant partner. Again and again the biblical authors insist that the covenant between Yahweh and his people must be viewed not as a set of legalistic duties but as a deeply personal relationship based on mutual love and commitment. Some of the prophets go so far as to depict Yahweh's covenant with Israel as a marriage and to condemn Israel's violations of the covenant as a form of adultery.

The importance of the covenant image to the biblical authors is apparent from the frequency with which it appears in the Hebrew Bible. The word *covenant* is used more than 250 times to describe agreements between Yahweh and humans, and the concept is often presupposed even when the term is absent. The idea is prominent in all three sections of the Hebrew Bible. The laws of Torah are

Fig. 14.3. (top) A Canaanite stela of two men settling a contract; (bottom) an ancient contract engraved on a stone tablet.

presented as the terms of a special covenant relationship between Yahweh and his chosen people. The prophets condemn the people of Israel and Judah for not living up to their side of the divine covenant. The narrative books attribute the military defeats of Israel and Judah to their unwillingness to abide by the terms of their covenant with Yahweh. The psalms honor Yahweh as the covenant deity of Israel and plead with him to assist his people as an expression of his loyalty to the covenant. Only the wisdom books make little use of the covenant image (see chapter 37). Virtually all scholars would agree that the idea of covenant lies at the heart of the social and religious vision of the Hebrew Bible.

While there are stories that speak of Yahweh having a covenantal relationship with an individual or family, the majority of the references to covenant in the Hebrew Bible concern Yahweh's relationship with the descendants of Abraham. This relationship sets the people of Israel apart from every other people group on earth. Nations that stand outside of this covenant are not condemned by Yahweh, but neither are they his people. This privilege is reserved for Israel alone.

From time to time Yahweh uses other nations to carry out his purposes for his covenant people. Many verses speak of Yahweh sending foreign armies to punish his people for violating his covenant (Deuteronomy 28:49-57; Joshua 7:10-13; Judges 2:10-23; 2 Kings 17:16-23; Isaiah 8:5-10; Jeremiah 4:5-18) or to conquer their oppressors and free them from bondage (Isaiah 45:1-8; Jeremiah 50:1-5; Zephaniah 2:13-15). Yet never does Yahweh enter into a covenant with any of these nations. Instead, once they have fulfilled their purpose, he pronounces judgment against them for the harm that they have done to his people (Isaiah 10:12-34; 47:1-15; Jeremiah 50:8—51:58; Nahum 1:12-13). At best these other nations have a temporary role in Yahweh's plan.

A few passages suggest that Yahweh's ultimate intention is to incorporate all of humanity into his covenant people (Genesis 12:3; Psalm 87:4; Isaiah 42:6-7; 49:6; 56:3-7; Micah 4:1-4), but this is not a central theme in the Hebrew Bible. Not until the rise of Christianity (and later Islam) did the idea of a universal people of God become an integral part of the Western tradition.

A STORY OF COVENANTS

The idea of covenant is central to the narrative books of the Hebrew Bible. The story is structured around a series of covenants that Yahweh is said to have made with humans. At the heart of this narrative lies the covenant that Yahweh established with the people whom he rescued from Egypt, the ancestors of the people known as Israel. As the narrative progresses, the people of Israel and Judah (especially their kings) are evaluated according to their faithfulness to the terms of the covenant. Eventually they are punished for their failure to live up to their side of the covenant. A brief overview of the way in which the concept of covenant is developed in the narrative books will demonstrate the centrality of this idea to the authors and editors of the Hebrew Bible.

1. The idea of a covenant between Yahweh and humans is probably implied in the creation story in Genesis 2–3, where Yahweh commands the first human to tend the garden and to refrain from eating the fruit of a particular tree. No penalty for violation is stated, but the first man and woman are cursed by the deity when they fail to follow his commands (see chapter 16). Curiously, Yahweh's obligations are never identified; perhaps we are to assume that he has already fulfilled his side of the relationship by providing a perfect place for the man and woman to live.

2. The earliest explicit use of the term *covenant* appears in the flood story in Genesis 6–9 (see chapter 16). In Genesis 6:18, God says that he intends to establish a covenant with Noah, the only person out of the entire human race who has remained faithful to God. In Genesis 9, this covenant is extended to include every living thing on earth, for all time. The covenant appears to be one-sided: God promises never again to flood the earth (Genesis 9:8-17) while laying no obligations upon Noah. The fact that Noah is described as "a righteous man, blameless in his generation" who "walked with God" (Genesis 6:9) seems to suggest that no conditions were required because Noah was already living the kind of life that God desires.

3. The story of Abraham and Sarah (Genesis 12–23) marks the first instance of a covenant that involves only a limited portion of the human race (see chapter 17). The

covenant is instituted in three stages over a fourteen-year period of Abraham's life: its content is foreshadowed in Genesis 12:2-3, formalized in Genesis 15:7-21, and confirmed in Genesis 17:1-14. As with Noah, the covenant is heavily one-sided. Yahweh promises to make Abraham's descendants into a great nation and to give them the land in which Abraham is currently dwelling, and he assures them that he will be their God and they will be his people forever. All other nations will be judged according to the way they treat Abraham and his descendants.

Abraham's side of the covenant is framed in very general terms: "Walk before me [Yahweh], and be blameless" (Genesis 17:1). These words recall the language that was used in Genesis 6:9 to describe Noah's character. Elsewhere the author states that Abraham's "trust" in Yahweh's promises was the basis for Yahweh regarding him as "righteous" (Genesis 15:6). The passage seems to suggest that Yahweh did not need to spell out the terms of the covenant because he knew that Abraham would uphold his end of the relationship. Abraham does receive one instruction from Yahweh: he and his descendants are to circumcise all of their male children as a sign of the covenant (Genesis 17:10-14). But this act only marks Abraham's descendants as members of the covenant people; it does not say what Yahweh expects from them under the covenant. A similar lack of specificity concerning the human side of the covenant can be seen in the passages where Yahweh confirms his promises to Abraham's son Isaac (Genesis 26:1-5) and his grandson Jacob (Genesis 28:13-15; 35:9-13).

4. The most important covenant in the Hebrew Bible—if we judge by the amount of attention that it receives in the biblical narrative—is the one that Yahweh makes at Mount Sinai with the people whom he had recently rescued from Egypt (Exodus 19–24). This covenant differs from the earlier ones in several ways: (a) it involves a group of people from the start, not an individual and his family (Exodus 19:3-5; 24:1-7; Deuteronomy 4:9-14; 5:1-31; 29:1-15); (b) it includes a long list of rules that the human participants are expected to follow in order to express their devotion to Yahweh and his covenant (as spelled out in the books of Exodus, Leviticus, Numbers, and Deuteronomy); (c) it makes human obedience a condition for receiving the blessings of the covenant (Exodus 19:5; 23:22; Leviticus 26:3; Deuteronomy 4:40; 6:1-3; 7:12-16; 28:1-14); and (d) it includes an explicit list of penalties for violation (Leviticus 26:14-45; Deuteronomy 28:15-68).

Fig. 14.4. Raphael, *The Presentation of the Tablets of Law to the Hebrews*

When these differences are taken into account, we find an understanding of covenant that places substantially more responsibility on the human participants than the others that we have encountered. Despite the fact that the covenant is framed as an agreement between Yahweh and his people as a whole, the majority of its regulations are directed toward individuals. Obedience to these guidelines is necessary for Yahweh's people to be assured of the deity's blessings and to avoid his curses. Implicit in this interpretation of covenant is the conviction that Yahweh cares as much about the mundane activities of ordinary individuals—what they eat, who they marry, how they treat their animals, and so forth—as he does about the specialized deeds of priests and rulers. Everyone's actions matter; everyone is responsible for upholding the covenant.

Today, of course, many people would resist such a notion of a deity who seeks to control every aspect of life, since it runs counter to modern ideas of personal freedom and autonomy. Yet for the predominately peasant population to whom these commands were addressed, such a vision of Yahweh's relationship with his people could have served to enhance their sense of personal identity and self-worth, since it elevated their daily activities to the level of divine service. They, like the priests, could do things that would bring divine blessing upon the nation. This belief that the deity cares as much about the actions of ordinary peasants as about the deeds of the religious and political elites distinguished the biblical system of laws from many other religious systems of its day. It would be wrong, however, to regard this as a democratization of religion, since the laws still came to the peasants through the hands of the religious elites who maintained control over their content (see chapter 22).

Who were the individuals to whom this understanding of covenant was addressed? On the narrative level, the Exodus covenant pertains most immediately to the generation that ratified it in the desert (Exodus 24:1-8). Only in the book of Deuteronomy do we see clear references to the covenant being binding on their descendants (Deuteronomy 4:37-40; 6:1-2; 10:14-15; 12:28; 29:29; 30:6, 19; 32:46). When we turn to the books of the prophets and the psalms, on the other hand, we find dozens of verses that presuppose that the Exodus covenant is relevant to the entire people of Israel and Judah. Many of these verses contain fierce condemnations of people whom the authors believe are not living up to the terms of the covenant (Psalm 50:16-23; Isaiah 24:4-13; Jeremiah 11:1-11; Ezekiel 44:5-9). Passages such as these show clearly that there were people in ancient Palestine who believed that the story of the Exodus covenant presented an attractive social and religious vision that could serve as a framework for reforming their society (including the behavior of individual members) in troubled times. The identity and social location of these people cannot be determined from the narrative itself, but other verses in the Hebrew Bible might help us to identify them more closely (see below).

5. The other major covenant in the Hebrew Bible is the one that Yahweh is said to have made with David, the great king of Judah, and his descendants (2 Samuel 7). This covenant is important not because it is mentioned often by the biblical authors (it is not), but because it provided religious justification for the ongoing rule of the Davidic dynasty and later became the basis for speculation about the coming of an ideal king from the line of David, sometimes called the Messiah. Like the other covenants that Yahweh made with individuals, this one consists primarily of divine promises with no clear list of obligations on the part of the human partner.

According to 2 Samuel 7, Yahweh promised to bring honor to David's name and to maintain his family on the throne of Judah forever. Yahweh would treat the kings of Judah as his sons, loving and protecting them but also correcting them when they do wrong. This prophetic oracle served two purposes at once in the biblical narrative: it legitimized David's shaky claim to the throne (a claim resisted by the sons of Saul, his predecessor) and protected his heirs against subsequent challenges. The passage also sets up a close link between the family of David and the Jerusalem temple by showing Yahweh authorizing the construction of the sanctuary by David's son and successor, Solomon. This link was then used to justify royal control over the temple and to elicit priestly support for the kings. It is no accident that a number of the psalms that were recited in the Jerusalem temple celebrate the king's special covenant with Yahweh (Psalms 2:1-9; 18:46-50; 21:1-7; 45:1-9; 72:1-17; 78:70-72; 89:19-37; 132:10-18).

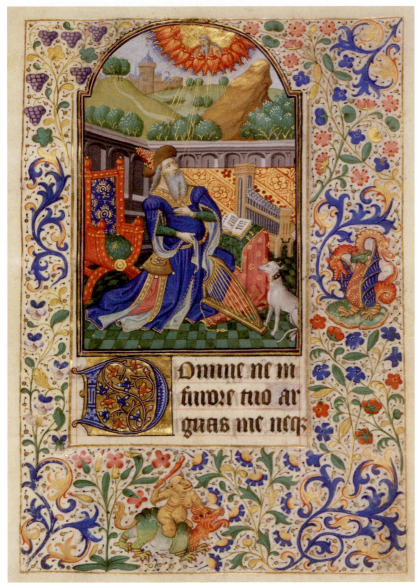

Fig. 14.5. King David converses with God about the covenant God promised to establish with his family in this image from a sixteenth-century monastic prayer book.

statutes and ordinances for them." The passage says nothing about what this covenant might have entailed, though it suggests that the materials that Joshua gave to the people were incorporated into the laws of Torah. On the other hand, it might simply be referring to a covenant renewal ceremony of the type that we find in several other texts that speak of people making a covenant with Yahweh (2 Kings 11:17-18; 23:1-3; 2 Chronicles 15:10-15; 29:8-10). A similar idea can be seen in a handful of verses that speak rather loosely of people making a covenant when they promise to do something that they believe Yahweh wants from them in a particular situation (Ezra 10:1-4; Jeremiah 34:8-18). Finally, we should note a few passages that allude to a belief that Yahweh has a special covenant with the families whose members were chosen to serve as priests and **Levites** (priestly assistants) at the Jerusalem temple (Numbers 25:10-13; Nehemiah 13:29; Jeremiah 33:20-22; Malachi 2:4-8). The Torah contains several texts that describe the selection of the priestly families (Exodus 28–29; Leviticus 8–9; Numbers 18), but the term *covenant* is used in none of them, so it is hard to be sure precisely what the people who referred to such a covenant had in mind.

6. The Hebrew Bible also refers to several other covenants that humans are said to have made with Yahweh. Most are mentioned only once, and few offer any details about what the author had in mind in crafting the passage. According to Joshua 24:25, Joshua "made a covenant with the people" on Yahweh's behalf and "made

7. The idealistic quality of the covenant idea comes through clearly in several passages from the books of the prophets that speak of a future era when Yahweh will establish a new covenant or a covenant of peace with his people. These verses add a note of hope to the often critical words of the Hebrew prophets. This hope for a new

Fig. 14.6. Robert Walker Weir, *The Embarkation of the Pilgrims from Delfthaven in Holland*. The Pilgrims were one of many Christian groups who believed they had a special covenant with the God of the Bible.

covenant proved useful during the Exile, when the people of Judah were questioning whether Yahweh still cared for them in light of their devastating defeat at the hands of the Babylonians. In this context, the words of the prophets offered a comforting vision of the social, psychological, and spiritual renewal of the people of Judah. They spoke of a future time when Yahweh would rescue Judah (and Israel?) from foreign domination and restore the people's independence, possibly under the leadership of an ideal Davidic king (Isaiah 9:1-7; 11:1-16; 16:5; Jeremiah 23:5-8; 30:8-11; 33:12-26; 50:4-5; Ezekiel 34:20-31; 37:15-28; Hosea 3:4-5). At this time Yahweh would enter into a new covenant with his people. The content of this covenant is described in relational terms: Yahweh will forgive his people, watch over them, and bless them with peace and prosperity, and they will love, honor, and obey him with wholehearted devotion (Isaiah 55:3-5; 59:21; 61:7-9; Jeremiah 31:31-34; 32:36-41; Ezekiel 16:59-63;

34:25-31; 37:26-28; Hosea 2:16-23). Never again will Yahweh have cause to hand his people over to judgment; this new covenant will truly last forever.

The value of such a vision for a group of people laboring under the physical and psychological burdens of military defeat and foreign rule is obvious. The dissolution of their national identity posed tremendous threats to the personal identities of the people of Judah. If they were to avoid losing their collective identity, a new social vision was needed. To gain acceptance, however, this vision had to be consistent with the beliefs that they already held. The idea of a new covenant was well suited for this purpose, since it drew upon a theme that was familiar in at least some Yahwistic circles. In the hands of the prophets, it took on a nearly irresistible appeal, since it promised the exiles that their world would one day be as it had been, only better. This message was perfectly suited for encouraging a disheartened people to hold on to their national and ethnic identity at a time when the future of their nation and people appeared bleak.

Buried within this expectation of a new covenant was an implicit call for religious reform and renewal: those who hoped to enjoy the benefits of the new era must be prepared to serve Yahweh without reservation when the time arrived. This included setting aside the worship of other gods. For those who had not previously served Yahweh in this manner, the prophets' vision of a new covenant included a demand for a profound change of identity. If they persisted in honoring other deities alongside or instead of Yahweh, they would be relegated to the status of outsiders and excluded from the community. Some of the laws of Torah even called for their religion to be suppressed and their families killed (Exodus 23:23-24; Leviticus 20:1-8; Numbers 25:1-5; Deuteronomy 4:15-28; 7:1-6; 12:1-4). Clearly this vision of a new covenant would not have been welcomed by everyone in ancient Palestine.

EXERCISE 27

Read the following passages and notice what each one says or implies about the nature and meaning of covenant in the Hebrew Bible. Then summarize any common themes that you see recurring across the various passages.

- Genesis 9:8-17
- Genesis 17:1-14
- Deuteronomy 5:1-22
- Psalm 89:19-37
- Jeremiah 31:31-37

PEOPLE OF THE COVENANT

Once we see how well this vision of a new covenant works to encourage a dispirited group of exiles to maintain their faith in Yahweh, we begin to notice a similar pattern in other passages that employ the covenant metaphor. In the story of Noah, the audience is told that God expects them to live righteous and obedient lives even when everyone around them follows a different standard. In the story of Abraham, they are reminded that they are a special people, chosen by Yahweh out of all the nations of the earth to follow his ways. Both stories implicitly challenged the people of Judah to hold on to their traditions and resist the temptation to adopt the culture and values of their Babylonian and Persian overlords. The story of the Exodus covenant told them how to do this. This story claimed that Yahweh had given their ancestors a series of rules and regulations that showed them how Yahweh wanted them to live. Following these rules would help them to remain separate from the people and cultures around them and so preserve their identity. It would also ensure that they stayed in Yahweh's good graces and avoided displeasing him. In time, their faithful behavior would motivate Yahweh to rescue them from their foreign oppressors. The story of the Davidic covenant would have added further fuel to their hopes for the future restoration of their nation.

The fact that the covenant ideal speaks so eloquently to the needs of the people of Judah under Babylonian and Persian rule has led some scholars (the group known as minimalists; see chapter 9) to suggest that the idea of covenant was created precisely for this purpose. Scholars who follow this view dismiss the stories of Noah, Abraham, and Moses as pious fictions created to communicate a religious vision to the people of Judah in a time of trouble. As they see it, nothing in these stories has any historical value, including the idea of a **preexilic** covenant between Yahweh and the ancestors of the people of Israel and Judah. References to the covenant in the Psalms and Prophets are editorial additions or generic references that say nothing about any earlier belief in a covenant between Yahweh and Israel or Judah.

The chief problem with this interpretation is that it fails to explain why such a novel concept would have been embraced by the people for whom it was supposedly created. While it is true that crises can give rise to radical new ideas, most groups and individuals turn to the security of established traditions to carry them through difficult times. As a new idea, the claim that Yahweh had established a covenant with Judah's ancestors would have raised more questions than it answered, since anyone could see that Yahweh had not protected Judah from foreign conquest. Why then should they believe that Yahweh would assist them in the future? The frequent use of covenant language in the Psalms and Prophets is also an embarrassment to this position. The effort to dismiss all of these verses as later additions falls apart under scrutiny.

The best way to make sense of the popularity of the covenant idea in the Hebrew Bible is to presume that the idea had a significant history in Yahwistic circles prior to the Babylonian conquest. This belief would have been shaken by events surrounding and following the Exile. Those who adhered to the idea would have felt compelled to defend Yahweh against charges of unfaithfulness or impotence. To do this, they had to show how the past, present, and future made sense when interpreted through the lens of covenant. To explain why these tragic events had come upon the people of Judah, they constructed a narrative that charged their ancestors with being unfaithful to the covenant and thus incurring Yahweh's judgment. To show what their compatriots should do now, they compiled a collection of laws that spelled out how the people of Yahweh should live in order to fulfill their side of the covenant. To assuage people's doubts about the future, they pointed to sayings of the prophets that anticipated the coming of a future era, including a new covenant, when all of their current troubles would come to a resounding end. In short, they took the materials and traditions that they had inherited from the past and reshaped them into a collection of texts that would address the needs of their own day. These texts became the heart of the collection that we now call the Hebrew Bible.

Apparently their efforts were successful, since the idea of a covenant between Yahweh and his people, embodied in the laws of Torah, was one of the central concepts that defined the identity of the people of Judah in the postexilic period. Not everyone accepted the idea; the Hebrew Bible indicates that there were people who continued to worship other gods alongside or instead of Yahweh through the end of the biblical era (see chapters 21 and 35). But the very popularity of the notion shows that there were many people who found the idea of covenant

useful for making sense of the world and their place in it. In this concept they found a vision for social and individual life that gave them answers to the classic questions asked by people everywhere: Who am I? Who are we? Who are they?

The impact of this concept on the history of Western civilization has been vast. The idea that God has entered into a special covenant with a group of humans became a dominant theme in the history of Judaism and Christianity, and to a lesser extent Islam. Through their influence it shaped the thinking of other groups who believed that they were the recipients of such a covenant, such as the American Puritans. In a similar way, the vision of a future era of peace and plenty has been appropriated by countless apocalyptic groups over the centuries who expected this hope to be realized during their lifetime. Finally, the belief that the king has a special covenant with God became the basis for the medieval idea of the divine right of kings that was used to justify the rule of monarchs until fairly recent times. The scribes and scholars who framed this idea in ancient Palestine had no idea how powerful their vision would prove to be.

CONCLUSION

The biblical authors and editors were neither philosophers nor social theorists, but their writings contain serious reflections about the nature of human society. Since they were writing from a Yahwistic perspective, it was inevitable that their vision for the ideal society would be framed in religious terms.

At the heart of their thinking was the belief that Yahweh periodically entered into special covenants with individuals and groups whom he chose to favor with his affection. The terms of these covenants were dictated by Yahweh, but it was presumed that both parties would abide by their conditions. Faithfulness to the covenant led to material success for Yahweh's human partners, while repeated violations could bring divine judgment. People who accepted the covenant idea tended to interpret significant events as the acts of a deity who was seeking to further the purposes of the covenant.

The most important covenant in the Hebrew Bible is the Exodus covenant that called for obedience to the laws of Torah. The early history of this particular model of covenant can no longer be traced, but it seems to have been known in some form during the era of the prophets. Its popularity increased after the Babylonian conquest, when it helped many people to make sense of the troubling events that had befallen them and restored their hope for the future. Its chief value lay in the way it linked the ordinary activities of individuals with the identity and survival of the group.

EXERCISE 28

Read the following passages that speak of Yahweh's covenant with Israel and think about how each passage might have spoken to the needs and concerns of people affected by the physical, psychological, and religious trauma of the exilic and postexilic periods.

- Genesis 15:1-21
- Deuteronomy 30:1-10
- Psalm 111:1-10
- Jeremiah 11:1-8
- Ezekiel 37:15-28
- Hosea 2:16-23

Fig. 15.1. Storytellers play a vital role in virtually all traditional societies, as represented here by a Native American storyteller.

CHAPTER 15

Stories and Faith

Give ear, O my people, to my teaching; incline your ears to the words of my mouth. I will open my mouth in a parable; I will utter dark sayings from of old, things that we have heard and known, that our ancestors have told us. We will not hide them from their children; we will tell to the coming generation the glorious deeds of the LORD, *and his might, and the wonders that he has done.* (Psalm 78:1-4)

When your children ask you in time to come, "What is the meaning of the decrees and the statutes and the ordinances that the LORD *our God has commanded you?" then you shall say to your children, "We were Pharaoh's slaves in Egypt, but the* LORD *brought us out of Egypt with a mighty hand. The* LORD *displayed before our eyes great and awesome signs and wonders against Egypt, against Pharaoh and all his household. He brought us out from there in order to bring us in, to give us the land that he promised on oath to our ancestors. Then the* LORD *commanded us to observe all these statutes, to fear the* LORD *our God, for our lasting good, so as to keep us alive, as is now the case.* (Deuteronomy 6:20-24)

Listen to me, you that pursue righteousness, you that seek the LORD. *Look to the rock from which you were hewn, and to the quarry from which you were dug. Look to Abraham your father and to Sarah who bore you; for he was but one when I called him, but I blessed him and made him many.* (Isaiah 51:1-2)

Anyone who picks up a copy of the Hebrew Bible and thumbs through it for a few minutes will be struck by the number of stories that it contains. A careful reader will notice that the entire first half of the book is structured as a relatively continuous narrative that reaches from the creation of the world to the Babylonian exile. Christian Bibles extend the initial narrative through the restoration of Judah under Persian rule. This grand narrative is itself made up of hundreds of shorter stories. Some of these stories serve to advance the developing plot of the larger narrative, while others seem more like detours. Most have a common literary style. Many seem designed to teach a lesson or communicate a message to the audience. All are marked by the beliefs and values of the people who told them.

The origins of most of these stories are unclear. In their current form, they echo the interests and concerns of literate male elites who sought to promote the worship of Yahweh in ancient Palestine. Little insight is required, however, to see how many of these stories are rooted in the daily lives and concerns of the common people. This is to be expected, since stories are the primary means used by illiterate people in every society to pass on their beliefs and practices from generation to generation. Some of the stories that made their way into the Hebrew Bible could have been recited orally around campfires and in family gatherings for decades or even centuries before they were written down in their present form.

The next few chapters will explore the role of stories in the Hebrew Bible. The present chapter examines what scholars have learned about the purpose and functions of stories in traditional cultures around the globe. This is followed by a survey of some of the ways in which contemporary literary criticism can enhance our ability to make sense of the many stories that fill the Hebrew Bible. The value of literary approaches will become clear once we start looking more closely at specific stories. The next five chapters will explore the religious significance of five major blocks of story material in the Hebrew Bible: the creation stories, the ancestral narratives, the Exodus saga, the Deuteronomistic narrative, and a selection of post-exilic texts.

IN THE BEGINNING WAS THE STORY

The practice of telling stories is as old as the human ability to communicate. Every society has its collection of ancient tales that have been passed on orally for generations. Some are familiar to everyone in the culture, while others are limited to people of a particular clan, social group, or geographic area. Children hear the time-honored stories again and again as they grow up. In some groups the most important stories are passed on through a formal system of education. Occasionally this includes a provision that the stories be memorized in a certain form. Those who are especially adept at memorizing and reciting the stories are often given special honors for their role in preserving the traditions of the ancestors.

Tracing the history of these stories is notoriously difficult. Most offer few clues as to their origins, and their content invariably changes over time, with materials being dropped and added along the way. The process of evolution continues even after the stories are written down, as witnessed by the presence of multiple written versions of the same story. Scholars have labored mightily to discover patterns of development in stories and to relate passing references to historical events in their efforts to retrace the history of particular stories. But their reconstructions always include a fair amount of guesswork.

STORIES AND COMMUNITIES

Fortunately, we do not need to know how a story developed in order to examine the role that it might have played within a given community. The simple fact that a story was deemed important enough to pass on over time suggests that it spoke to a particular need or concern within the group. In situations where members of the community are available for consultation, scholars can ask what the story means to them and how it is used. Information gleaned from this process can then be compared with similar responses from other cultures. Repeated studies of this type have shown that stories fulfill a number of important functions within traditional societies.

Fig. 15.2. Images depicting the creation stories of the Mayan (above) and Haida (below) peoples.

1. *Explaining the nature of reality.* Traditional societies are keenly aware of the dangers and uncertainties of life. They know how easily bad weather or disease can ruin their crops, leaving them on the brink of starvation. They know how quickly a pack of wild animals can wipe out their herds or kill their families. They know how perilous is the process of childbirth and how powerless they feel when death takes their young animals and children before they reach maturity. They know that there are many forces in the world that they can neither control nor understand.

The thought of living with so much uncertainty and chaos would drive many modern people to despair. Fortunately, humans seem to have an innate drive to find meaning in the world around them and to interpret it as an orderly and friendly place. Contemporary Western cultures use the abstract language of science, philosophy, and theology to frame their explanations of the universe. Traditional cultures prefer the more concrete approach of stories. Stories provide answers to a wide range of human questions and concerns, including the origins of the universe and its inhabitants, the operation of the natural world, the reasons for pain and suffering, and the way people should live in order to maximize the benefits and minimize the sorrows of life. Stories help to domesticate the uncontrollable elements of human experience by placing them within a cosmic framework in which most events make sense. Typically this includes some kind of belief in an unseen reality that gives order and meaning to the complexity of human experience. In short, stories help humans to make peace with the difficulties and uncertainties of life and get on with their lives without being paralyzed by feelings of fear, longing, and regret.

On a more mundane level, stories are used to explain why things are the way they are. Some focus on the physical world—the origins of a constellation, an unusual landform, a favorite crop, a particular animal. Others explore human nature—why humans have the kinds of bodies that they do, why people are greedy or murderous, why women or men act in certain ways, why people have to die. Still others seek to explain a particular social custom—why people get married, why certain individuals or clans are designated as leaders, why a religious ritual is performed in a certain way, why particular crops are raised as they are. Names are also a popular topic—how a particular person, place, or object came to be given the name that it holds. Virtually anything that calls for explanation in a traditional society can give rise to a story.

2. *Defining and preserving group identity.* Traditional societies are not known for their acceptance of diversity. Most have a strong sense of group identity that marks some people as *us* and others as *them*. These distinctions are typically reinforced by stories that explain how the group telling the stories is related to those outside the group. Often these stories portray the *us* group as the first humans. In some stories they are the only humans, with all others being categorized as subhuman. Behind all such stories lies the assumption that distinctions between groups were established in the hoary past and cannot be changed. In this way stories help to preserve the identity of the group and protect it from change.

Fig. 15.3. (above) Statue depicting the legendary founder of Rome, Romulus, and his brother Remus being suckled by a she-wolf; (below) the heroes Arjuna and Hanuman join in battle in a scene from the Indian epic the *Mahabharata*.

Stories also maintain group identity by preserving a record of the group's past. The past is vitally important to traditional societies. Where modern people believe in progress and expect that things will be better in the future, traditional societies often tell stories of a golden age in the remote past from which humans have subsequently declined. These kinds of stories lead people to

Fig. 15.4. (top) Ancient Egyptian stories that placed the Pharaoh among the gods helped to legitimate his rule; (below) stories of gods and heroes like Herakles served to reinforce the ideals of masculinity within ancient Greek culture.

value the past more than the future and to focus on preserving the ways laid down by the ancestors rather than promoting change. Whether the stories about the group's past are historically true is irrelevant—as long as members are willing to accept them, stories that trace the group back to ancient times provide an aura of permanence and stability. This is especially important for groups that have

faced challenges or hardships that posed a threat to their survival. Stories that can incorporate these experiences into a meaningful pattern often play a vital role in helping group members to maintain or recover their sense of identity and security in difficult situations.

3. *Justifying and defending societal institutions and practices.* Every society has a set of institutions and norms that define how power is to be assigned and exercised, how economic goods are to be allocated, how men and women are to relate to one another, how societal problems are to be addressed, and so forth. Since a different system can always be envisioned, those who benefit from the current arrangement have a strong interest in justifying its existence and defending it against challenge. Stories about the past play a vital role in this process, especially in traditional societies. Most traditional societies have stories that relate the existing social institutions and practices to the fundamental nature of the universe. Some trace the current system to the actions or commands of the gods in the distant past. Others portray the earthly society as a mirror image of the system that governs the divine realm. Still others attribute the organization of society to distant ancestors who had more wisdom than people in the present day. The actual historical process by which the prevailing institutions arose is invariably obscured by such narratives. As long as people are willing to accept these stories, the current social arrangement is rendered virtually invincible. Who would dare to question the ways of the gods or the wisdom of the ancestors?

Stories also help to define how the various participants in the social system should conduct themselves. Many societies have stories about ideal kings, priests, warriors, and other leaders who are offered as role models for the current holders of these positions. Most also include stories that depict the evils that can arise when ordinary people refuse to accept the direction of their leaders. Stories that reinforce traditional male-oriented gender roles are especially common. Stories such as these help to motivate people to support the status quo and maintain the values of the society over time.

4. *Passing on beliefs and values to the next generation.* The training of children is a vital concern of every human society. Unless a society can pass on its core beliefs and

values to the next generation, it will lose its essential character. Societies differ widely in the things that they seek to teach their children, but they invariably use stories as a key part of their instructional program. Stories achieve their effect by appealing to the imagination and emotions rather than directly to the reasoning faculties. Children who would resist or fail to understand more didactic modes of instruction are always willing to listen to entertaining anecdotes that make the same point. In this way they are subtly socialized to accept the beliefs and values of their society. Narratives that offer role models of proper and improper behavior are especially useful in teaching children the expectations of their society.

But the social value of stories is not limited to children. In traditional societies, storytelling is a popular form of entertainment for adults. Some cultures have people who are specially trained to sing or recite well-known stories during social or religious gatherings. Stories are also recounted among friends or family while sitting around a campfire or traveling long distances by foot. As the ancient tales are told and retold, adults are reminded of the core beliefs and values that bind them together as a society. Stories learned in childhood take on deeper meaning when they are reviewed with the mind of an adult. In this way, narratives help to ensure that adults remain faithful to the traditions and pass them on accurately to their children.

EXERCISE 29

Look up the following passages and figure out how each story relates to the four functions of stories outlined above. Look for evidence of multiple functions for each account.

- Genesis 11:1-9
- Exodus 18:1-27
- Job 1:1-22
- Daniel 1:1-21

THE POWER OF STORIES

Why are stories so popular? Where do they get their power? How is it that a narrative—even a blatantly fictitious one—can speak to people in a way that other forms of communication cannot? Some of the answers have been mentioned already. Stories are easy to remember, making them well suited for cultures with low levels of literacy. Stories are entertaining and thus more likely to hold the attention of children (and adults) than other forms of instruction. Stories propose answers to fundamental questions about the nature of the universe and the meaning of life. The ones that do this especially well come to be valued for the psychological benefits that they bring to those who accept them. Finally, stories reinforce beliefs and values that people already hold for other reasons. Stories are valued because they give implicit support to the tenuous identities that people create for themselves and their societies.

But the real power of narrative lies at a deeper level than these initial observations would suggest. Stories arise from the human imagination, and they wield power by appealing to the imaginations of those who hear them. They create imaginary worlds in which the ordinary rules and limits of human existence are often suspended. In the world of fairy tales, for instance, animals can talk, magic is an ordinary occurrence, and everyone lives happily ever after. Even stories that use the real world as their model often include elements that lie beyond ordinary human experience, such as the ability to know what characters are thinking.

Stories draw the audience into this world by sketching only the most relevant features of the scenery and characters and leaving the rest for the audience to fill in. In this way the audience becomes emotionally invested in the narrative as cocreators of the world in which it takes place. Stories also invite people to identify with the characters and to imagine how they might handle the complications that arise in the course of the story. Through this leap of imagination, the audience is given a vision of what life might look like through the eyes and feelings of someone other than themselves. As the plot unfolds, the audience is led to explore ways of thinking and acting that might not occur to them in their ordinary lives. The process engages their emotions as well as their reason. Out of such vicarious experiences can come new insights that can have a profound impact on the way people live in the real world.

This revelatory quality is what gives stories their power to shape the lives of people who hear them. It also helps to explain why they are so important in religious communities. Virtually all religions claim to offer some type of insight into a reality beyond the visible world. Some seek to lead people into direct experiences of this world through prayer, meditation, ecstatic dance, rituals, hallucinogenic drugs, and other practices. Others work on training people to think differently about the world around them through programs of education, counseling, and self-discipline. A good story has the ability to access both of these channels at once by leading the hearer into imaginary experiences that produce valuable new insights.

Once they become familiar, of course, narratives can lose their power to enlighten. But the same can be said for any other channel of religious experience. The fact that stories are repeated again and again among people who know them by heart suggests that their value is not exhausted with the first encounter. Many tales have survived for generations or even centuries through oral recitation alone. This would not have happened unless people continued to hear them speaking with a fresh voice to each new generation. Some stories are so profound and universal in their implications that they retain their revelatory character even when transposed to a new cultural context (for example, the use of stories from the Hebrew Bible in Christianity and Islam). In short, stories possess a power that frequently transcends their simple and beguiling form.

INTERPRETING STORIES

Analyzing a story is a bit like conducting an autopsy—it yields many insights into the way the subject operates, but it can never replace a direct encounter with the living original. Literary analysis is useful for highlighting the artistry of a narrative and showing why it works as it does. Sociological analysis can point out some of the purposes that the story might have served within the group that preserved it. But analytical studies alone can never lead us into a full and rich understanding of a story. The only way to grasp the full significance of a narrative is to give ourselves the time and emotional freedom to enter into it and experience it firsthand. The next few chapters will give you many opportunities to do this with biblical narratives.

The problem with this approach, of course, is that everyone experiences stories differently. Stories are inherently ambiguous and subject to multiple interpretations. Even the most detailed narrative leaves much to the imagination of the audience, and many tales presume that the hearers will be able to supply substantial information about the beliefs and practices of the culture in which they arose. Few narratives offer any explicit declaration of their intent; virtually all require the audience to infer meaning from the way the story develops.

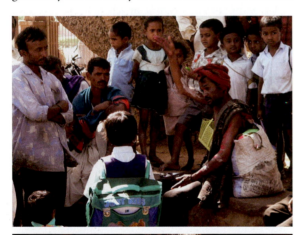

Fig. 15.5. Traditional storytellers in India (top) and Africa (bottom) continue to pass on the time-honored stories of their culture to new generations of children.

Further ambiguities arise from the diversity of the audience. Each person who encounters a story is a unique individual who brings a distinct personality and a life full of experience to the task of interpreting the account. When they reach a gap in the story, people make different decisions about what kind of material to supply. Some of these differences are trivial (for example, what color robe the main character was wearing), but some are significant enough to produce different understandings of the essential point of the story. All of these observations point to the same conclusion: there can never be only one correct interpretation of a story.

On the other hand, the range of possible interpretations is not unlimited. The language in which a story is told places broad limits on the ways in which it can be understood, and some interpretations are arguably more consistent with the details of the narrative than others. Nevertheless, we cannot escape the fact that meaning, like beauty, is in the eye of the beholder. This is true for religious stories as much as for any other kind of narrative. There is no method or system that one can follow in order to arrive at the "correct" meaning of a story in the Hebrew Bible.

The discipline of literary criticism is devoted to analyzing and discussing the form and content of works of literature, including stories. Through careful study of works from different eras, literary scholars have discovered that narratives have many common features that appear to transcend time and culture. These features work together to communicate the meaning of the story. Experience suggests that close attention to some of these features can help readers to identify clues that point to possible meanings for the story. The most important factors to be examined are the setting, the characters, and the plot of the narrative.

1. *Setting.* Most people think of the setting of a story as the time and place in which the narrative takes place. These factors make up the *physical setting* of the story. Some stories describe these elements in great detail, while others leave them largely to the imagination of the reader. In addition to enhancing the aesthetic value of the story, the physical setting often plays a role in advancing the plot.

Another aspect of setting that is most important when analyzing stories from the ancient world, including those in the Hebrew Bible, is the *cultural setting*. The cultural setting refers to the beliefs, values, and practices that are taken for granted by the storyteller. In ancient societies, stories were told within a cultural framework that was familiar to everyone in the audience. There was no need for the storyteller to spell out the meaning of cultural references within the story, since the audience could easily supply the missing information. Modern readers, on the other hand, lack that cultural knowledge. For some narratives this is unimportant, since the cultural context is merely incidental. For others, however, a familiarity with the original culture is necessary in order to grasp the essential point of the story. In these cases interpretation becomes a cross-cultural experience that requires the reader to learn more about ancient cultures in order to make sense of the narrative. Without this information, the reader is left to fill in the gaps with modern cultural information or simply guess at how an ancient audience might have understood the story. This is a common experience for readers who are encountering the stories of the Hebrew Bible for the first time.

2. *Characters.* Characters are vital to every story, but the manner in which characters are depicted and used varies from culture to culture. Contemporary narratives make a serious effort to portray characters as well-rounded, realistic individuals who grow and change through their fictional experiences. In the ancient world, however, this was uncommon. Characters were usually depicted in flat, one-dimensional terms with little or no sense of personal development. Many are little more than cultural stereotypes or role models. Glimpses into their inner life are brief and limited to the point at hand. Motives and intentions, when mentioned at all, are usually framed in simplistic terms. Contemporary readers who attempt to imagine themselves into the minds and lives of such characters often find it difficult to understand their motives and actions, since the characters do not conform to modern literary expectations.

Fortunately, the ancient storytellers often include clues that enable us to test the validity of our interpretations of their characters. The most common way of voicing a positive or negative judgment on a character is by showing where the person's actions lead. Ancient storytellers are fond of painting bad endings for characters whose actions they disapprove and happy endings for those whom they wish to commend. In other cases the storyteller will allow one character to make statements that evaluate the actions of other characters, though it is not always clear which characters' words can be trusted. Occasionally the narrator will break into the story and pass judgment directly on a character's actions. But there remain many cases in which characters are ambiguous enough to support multiple interpretations of their nature and actions. Sometimes the choices that one makes among the competing options can have a serious impact on the way one understands an entire story.

3. *Plot.* Most stories revolve around some kind of conflict in which one or more characters are put to a test. Sometimes the test comes through other people, while at other times the characters are forced to do battle with the forces of nature, oppressive social institutions, or the dark forces that haunt the human psyche. The ways in which the characters respond to this challenge make them role models—sometimes positive, sometimes negative—for audience members who might face similar problems.

Authors use a variety of plot devices to engage the minds and emotions of the audience and draw them into the story. Common plot devices include suspense (uncertainty about the outcome of the conflict); surprise (unexpected twists in events); dialogue (conversations among the characters that reveal their thoughts, feelings, and intentions); and dramatic irony (information given to the audience that is hidden from the characters). Most of the stories in the Hebrew Bible are heavily plot-driven. Some of the longer stories have plots that are as subtle and complex as anything in modern literature. Many have happy endings, but the Bible contains its share of tragedies, too. Careful attention to the manner in which the plot unfolds through the various scenes can yield insight into the storyteller's point of view and help the reader to make sense of subsidiary elements in the plot. In the end, however, the plots of biblical stories are similar to other narratives in containing ambiguities that can be resolved in different ways by different readers.

Even skilled readers who are attentive to the issues raised in this brief summary will disagree about the meaning of many stories. Nevertheless, those who pay careful attention to these factors will find it easier to discuss with others the reasons for their differing interpretations. This is especially important when dealing with stories from another culture like the ones in the Hebrew Bible. The next four chapters offer many opportunities for learning to make sense of the biblical narratives.

STORIES AND FAITH

Before leaving the subject of stories, we need to look briefly at the relation between stories and religious faith. Some people worry that analyzing the biblical narratives as stories rather than as historical documents will undermine the faith of religious believers. This is an understandable concern for people who believe that a genuine faith must be grounded in real historical events. In this case, however, the concern is misplaced. When we examine the biblical narratives through the lens of literary analysis, we are not passing judgment on the historicity of the stories. The question of historicity is simply left to the side. Literary analysis is not interested in determining whether the events really happened as narrated; its goal is to uncover what the stories tell us about the literary creativity and religious faith of the people who told them.

A trip to a contemporary religious bookstore will show beyond doubt that faith can be expressed through many different literary media. This is exactly what we find in the diverse collection of books that we call the Hebrew Bible. Apparently the people who used and compiled these books did not think that history was the only form of narrative that could be used to express their message. Contemporary readers should be careful about coming to ancient narratives with rigid expectations that the authors had no intention of fulfilling.

CONCLUSION

Stories play an important role in virtually all religious traditions. They are used to explain the nature of reality, to define and preserve group identity, to justify and defend social institutions and practices, and to pass on beliefs and values to the next generation. Their popularity can be traced in part to their entertaining and memorable format. But their real power comes from their ability to transport their hearers into an imaginary world where they are able to try out new ways of thinking and acting. In this way stories become vehicles of revelation and transformation.

Interpreting stories—especially stories from another culture—is a painstaking process that requires careful study and attention to detail. The process is complicated by the inherent ambiguity of stories and the diverse backgrounds and outlooks that readers bring to the task of interpretation. Readers will never agree on every element of their interpretation of a story, but a familiarity with literary criticism can help them to approach the process in a focused and disciplined manner.

EXERCISE 30

Read the following stories from the Hebrew Bible and think about how each one attempts to draw you into the narrative. Then choose one of them and write a short commentary describing the way in which the story uses (a) setting, (b) characters, and (c) plot developments to create an imaginary world that engages your mind and emotions. Finish with a couple of sentences summarizing what you see as the central message or primary effect of the story.

• Genesis 38:1-26
• Judges 4:1-24
• 1 Kings 21:1-28

Fig. 16.1. Giovanni di Paolo, *The Creation*

Stories of Origins

In the beginning when God created the heavens and the earth, the earth was a formless void and darkness covered the face of the deep, while a wind from God swept over the face of the waters. Then God said, "Let there be light"; and there was light. (Genesis 1:1-3)

By the word of the LORD the heavens were made, and all their host by the breath of his mouth. He gathered the waters of the sea as in a bottle; he put the deeps in storehouses. Let all the earth fear the LORD; let all the inhabitants of the world stand in awe of him. For he spoke, and it came to be; he commanded, and it stood firm. (Psalm 33:6-9)

For thus says the LORD, who created the heavens (he is God!), who formed the earth and made it (he established it; he did not create it a chaos, he formed it to be inhabited!): I am the LORD, and there is no other. (Isaiah 45:18)

Virtually all religions have stories that tell how the universe and its inhabitants came into being and how human society reached its present form. The universe that they were seeking to explain, of course, is not the one revealed by modern science but the commonsense world that their ancestors—the creators of the stories—saw and experienced every day (see chapter 11). Many of their explanations were rooted in careful observations of the physical world and thus contain elements of a primitive form of science. But they did not have the tools of modern science to explain and test their observations. Instead, they turned to religion to make sense of their findings. In most cases this led to the creation of stories that credited the origins of the universe to the activity of supernatural forces. Some of these tales were eventually incorporated into Scriptures.

The Hebrew Bible begins with a series of narratives that describes the origins and early history of the universe and its inhabitants. Jews and Christians have traditionally regarded these stories as accurate and reliable reports of actual events. Over the last couple of centuries, however, large numbers of people in both religions have come to accept scientific theories about the origins of the universe and to deny any historical value to these stories. For these people, the accounts provided by science (a Big Bang followed by biological evolution over vast expanses of geological time) make better sense of the evidence than traditional religious stories. On the other hand, there are many Jews and Christians (commonly called *literalists* or *fundamentalists*) who continue to believe in the literal truth of the biblical accounts while rejecting scientific explanations of the universe.

Surprisingly, both sides have a similar understanding of the religious message that is embedded in these biblical stories of origins. In fact, many people who see no historical or scientific value in the biblical accounts are willing to accept the ideas that they present concerning the nature of God, humanity, and the physical world. As we noted in the last chapter, stories can serve as channels for profound religious insights regardless of whether they are grounded in history. Centuries of reading experience have shown this to be true for the Genesis creation stories. Thus, whatever we believe about the origins of the universe, there is much to be gained from investigating these stories as religious narratives that reflect the worldview and insights of a group of people in ancient Palestine, just as we would study the stories of any other religion. That at any rate is the approach that we will follow in the present chapter.

EXPLAINING THE UNIVERSE

The belief that the universe reached its present form through the activity of supernatural powers is a vital part of the worldview of nearly every culture known to historians. This does not make the belief true; it simply underscores the vital role that religion has played in helping humans to make sense of reality. Humans everywhere have felt that the existence of the universe cries out for an explanation. Most have concluded that something as vast and orderly as the world around them required a supernatural cause. Similar reasoning led them to propose a supernatural origin for human beings and other forms of life, including their diversity and geographic distribution.

Since the question of origins concerns events in the past, it was only natural that people would choose to communicate their beliefs in the form of stories. The actual content of these stories varies widely from culture to culture, reflecting differences in their underlying worldviews. Some have elaborate stories about the way in which the physical world came into existence; others focus on the origins of their own place of residence and say little about the rest of the universe. Some include stories about the origins of the gods, while others ignore this question. Some go on at length about the origins of animals and plants, especially those that were important for the livelihood of the people who told the stories. Others move directly from the formation of the earth, sky, and water to the emergence of the first humans. Some portray the first people as the ancestors of all humanity, while others focus their attention on a specific branch of the human family tree. Some have a relatively continuous narrative that unites their stories of origins into a coherent whole, while others are content with a loose collection of stories that lacks a consistent story line. Many groups have multiple stories that offer competing explanations of the origins of

various aspects of reality. A few groups, as in some forms of Hinduism and Buddhism, claim ignorance about the details of creation.

The people of ancient Palestine also told stories about the origins of the world and its inhabitants. Some of these stories arose locally, while others were variations of stories that were known across the ancient Near East. Stories from Mesopotamia were especially popular, since the people of Palestine had long-standing ties to Mesopotamia as a result of migration, trade, and political alliances. The influence of Mesopotamian models can be seen in several of the narratives that found their way into the Hebrew Bible.

When the Hebrew Bible was compiled, the editors made the decision to begin their collection with a set of stories about the origins of the universe and its inhabitants before narrowing their focus to the ancient ancestors of Israel and Judah (as described in chapter 17). The narrative that they constructed can be found in Genesis 1–11. The purpose of these chapters was to explain the major elements of the physical and social world of ancient Palestine through the lens of a Yahwistic faith. The remainder of this chapter is devoted to exploring the religious significance of some of the key stories in this section of the Hebrew Bible.

EXERCISE 31

Read Genesis 1–11 in one sitting and make a list of the various features of the physical and social world (both large and small) that these chapters seek to explain.

PARADISE LOST (GENESIS 1:1—3:24)

Virtually everyone in the Western world knows at least the broad outlines of the creation story narrated in Genesis 1–3—how God made the world and its inhabitants in seven days by speaking everything into existence; how God placed the first man and woman in a beautiful garden and commanded them not to eat of a certain tree under pain of death; how a talking serpent enticed first the woman and then the man to violate God's command; and how God subsequently pronounced curses upon the man and woman for their disobedience and threw them out of the garden.

Fig. 16.2. Lucas Cranach the Elder, *Paradise*

This tragic tale has been celebrated, debated, and lamented by artists, musicians, and theologians for centuries. Ordinary Jews, Christians, and Muslims (the latter using the Qur'anic version of the story) have returned to this narrative again and again for spiritual inspiration and theological reflection. The two themes that most readers have identified as central to the story are the power and goodness of God and the painful consequences of human sin. The narrative has also been used throughout the Western world to justify male control of women on the grounds that the story depicts women as second-rate creatures and weak-willed temptresses whose disobedience was the source of all human sin. Upon closer study, however, we find that the story is more complex and ambiguous than many traditional interpretations allow.

One Story or Two?

Scholars have long known that the first two chapters of Genesis contain not one continuous creation narrative but two apparently unrelated stories that differ in their setting, characters, and plot. A careful comparison of Genesis 1:1—2:3 with Genesis 2:4-25 will make these differences apparent.

1. Differences in setting. The story in Genesis 1 begins on a watery earth that is described as "a formless void" (1:2). The scenery changes with each step in the seven-day creation. Nothing is said about where the humans settle or where the final divine speech to the humans takes place (1:28-30). In Genesis 2, by contrast, the story begins on a piece of earth that is devoid of plant life but watered periodically by streams that well up from below the ground (2:5-6). The existence of the earth is taken for granted; nothing is said about its formation. After the first human is formed "from the dust of the ground" (2:7), the scene shifts to a garden that the deity plants "in the east" (2:8-14). Most of the action takes place here. The story ends with the main characters, Adam and Eve, being thrown out of the garden into an unidentified place on the earth (3:23-24).

2. Differences in characters. In the first story, the man and woman are unnamed, and they do nothing except listen to the deity's final speech (2:28-30). The plot centers on the actions of the deity, not the humans. In the second story, the first being is nameless (*Adam* is the generic Hebrew word for human) until it is separated into male and female (2:21-22). At that point the woman is named *Isshah* (the Hebrew word for woman, 2:23), later changed to Eve (3:20), while the man comes to be known as Adam (compare 4:1).

The chief character in both narratives is the divine creator, though he is called by different names in the two passages. In Genesis 1, his name is Elohim, the generic Hebrew term for a deity (translated "God" in English versions). Beginning in Genesis 2:4, the name changes to Yahweh Elohim. English Bibles commonly render this title as "the Lord God," but it could also be translated as "the god Yahweh." The manner in which the deity is depicted also differs markedly between the two passages. In Genesis 1, the creator stands above and apart from the physical universe. His power is astounding; he simply speaks and things come into existence. He works according to a master plan and is clearly pleased with the results,

Fig. 16.3. Contrasting depictions of God in the two creation stories: (left) William Blake, *The Ancient of Days*; (right) Jacob de Backer, *Garden of Eden.*

declaring each act of creation to be good. Everything is under his control.

In Genesis 2 and 3, by contrast, the deity works entirely within the created order. He forms Adam, the plants, and the animals out of the ground (2:7, 9, 19); he plants (not "creates") a garden for Adam (2:8); he personally leads the animals before Adam to be named (2:19); he performs surgery on Adam's body to form the woman (2:21-22); he goes out for an evening stroll in the garden (3:8); he slaughters some of his own animals to make clothes for the man and woman; and so forth. The god depicted in Genesis 2–3 is clearly powerful, but he has limitations. He does not understand at first that the man needs a woman, not an animal, for a companion (2:18-23); he has to ask where Adam and Eve are hiding (3:8-9); he knows nothing about the humans' act of disobedience and seems genuinely surprised that they would disobey him (3:11-13); and he is even disappointed with the serpent, whose negative potential he apparently did

not recognize (3:14-15). His morals are also not above suspicion. He told the man that he would die if he ate from the tree (2:17), though this did not actually happen (implying that the serpent told the truth in 3:4-5); he pronounces curses on the man and woman that seem disproportionate to their crime (3:14-19); and he throws the man and woman out of the garden from fear that they might become like him (3:22). In short, the character of the deity in Genesis 2–3 is more like one of the ancient Greek or Roman gods than like the deity who appears in most of the rest of the Bible.

3. Differences in plot. In the first story, the creation takes place in an orderly fashion over the course of seven days. The second story contains no time references and the action seems rather haphazard. The first story narrates the separation of land, sea, and sky and the creation of the heavenly bodies (1:1-10, 14-19). The second story says nothing about these matters; the earth is fully formed (though unpopulated) when the story begins (2:5-6). In

Genesis 1, the plants and animals are created prior to the human beings, and the man and woman are created together (1:20-27). In Genesis 2, there are no plants on the earth when the man is formed (2:5; compare 2:8), and the animals and the woman are created after the man (2:19-22). Some translations seek to obscure this latter point by inserting the word *had* before the main verb in 2:8 and 2:19, but the addition has no basis in the Hebrew text.

The most important plot difference, however, is that the first story has a happy ending while the second story ends on a tragic note. In Genesis 1, God's speech to the humans explaining how to care for the created order is followed by the words "and it was so" (1:28-30), suggesting that the humans subsequently obeyed God's commands. The story closes with God himself taking a rest on the seventh day, just as Jews do on the Sabbath. This ending implies that the characters all lived happily ever after. The second story, by contrast, ends with the humans (and the serpent) standing outside the garden under the curse of God with their future clearly in doubt. The second story also includes many plot features that are not present in the first story: the placing of the man in the Garden of Eden (2:8-15); the command not to eat from the tree of the knowledge of good and evil (2:16-17); the quest for a partner for the man (2:18-25); and of course, the story of the eating of the forbidden fruit and its aftermath (3:1-24). The plotline moves upward until the formation of the woman and the institution of marriage (2:23-25), then shifts onto a steady downward path. The ending indicates clearly that the story is to be read as a tragedy.

Fall or Progress?

The classic interpretation of Genesis 3 sees it as an explanation for the presence of sin and evil in the world. According to this view, God made everything perfectly good and therefore cannot be blamed for the present corrupt state of the world. The fault for that lies with humans, who willfully chose to disobey God and thereby brought sin and suffering into the universe. Christians derived from this story the doctrine of **original sin**, which claims that the essential nature of humans was utterly corrupted at this time. As a result, humans are incapable of living as God desires, leaving them hopelessly guilty before God (and thus in need of a savior). Jews and Muslims, by contrast, find no evidence for such a belief in this story.

Fig. 16.4. Contrasting endings of the two creation stories: (left) *The Creator's Rest*, a medieval mosaic from the Duomo of Monreale, Italy; (right) a painting by Cavalier d'Arpino (Giuseppe Cesari), *Expulsion of Adam and Even from Paradise*.

Fig. 16.5. Two images by Jan Breughel the Elder highlight different aspects of the biblical creation stories: the one on the left (*Earthly Paradise*) emphasizes the peace, harmony, and beauty of God's creation, while the one on the right (*Garden of Eden*) draws attention to the human corruption of God's ideal world.

In recent years, many interpreters have come to question this interpretation of the passage. They admit the tragic nature of the story, but they view it as an effort to explain particular problems that plagued the people of ancient Palestine—the presence of dangerous snakes, the threats posed by frequent pregnancies, the ongoing struggles between men and women, the inevitable growth of weeds, the reality of death—and not as an abstract statement about human sin and the presence of evil in the world. In this view, the perfect garden of Genesis 2–3 is a literary fantasy that offers an ideal toward which humans should strive, not a lost world that they can never recover.

Even the story about the eating of the forbidden fruit is given a positive spin by many interpreters. The newer readings point out that it was the serpent, not God, who told the truth about the effects of eating the fruit, and that God himself finally admits the benefits that humans will receive from being able to distinguish between good and evil (3:22). In this view, the humans emerge as heroes for having discovered the good that had been hidden from them, while Yahweh comes across as a liar and bully who exacts a terrible vengeance upon the man and woman once his deception is found out. Such an interpretation of the story would clearly offend many religious believers, but it finds support in many of the details of the narrative. In the end, both approaches represent selective readings of the text.

Women as Inferior?

Over the centuries, male interpreters have turned to these stories again and again as evidence for their contention that women are inferior and need to be dominated by men. Three arguments have been cited in support of this view.

1. The creation of the woman appears to be an afterthought—she came into existence only because the man needed a "helper" (2:18). She was also crafted out of the man's body. Only the man received the "breath of God" when he was created (2:7).

2. It was the woman, not the man, who was tricked by the serpent into eating the fruit (3:1-6). The serpent apparently knew that the woman would be easier to deceive than the man (perhaps because she possessed weaker reasoning capabilities or a more pliable will) and that she was also capable of enticing her husband to follow her into sin (see 3:17, where the man is rebuked for listening to his wife).

3. When God punished the woman for her violation, he stated clearly that she was to be ruled by her husband (3:16). Like the other curses, this statement applies to the real world, not the ideal world of the garden.

All of these points have been challenged in recent years by interpreters who note that the traditional view misreads many elements of the story and ignores others.

1. In both stories, the first human is described in gender-neutral terms. Both narratives use the generic

Fig. 16.6. Contrasting views of the role of the woman in the two creation stories: (left) a scene from the ceiling of the Sistine Chapel, painted by Michelangelo; (right) William Blake, *Eve Tempted by the Serpent*.

Hebrew word for "human" rather than the word for "male" when describing the first created being (1:27; 2:7). Both indicate clearly that this term includes the female, the first by creating a poetic parallel between "human" and "male and female" (1:27; see also 5:12) and the second by having the female formed out of the body of the first being (2:21-22). The first story also states that the woman, like the man, was made "in the image of God" (1:27). The fact that the woman is described as a "helper" for the man in the second story (2:18) is not a mark of inferiority. The Hebrew word used here always refers to an equal or a superior (including God) in the Hebrew Bible, never an inferior. The idea of equality is also embedded in the Hebrew word rendered as "partner" in 2:20, a word that signifies that the woman and the man constitute two halves of a whole. Finally, there is nothing in the story to suggest that being formed out of the man's body makes the woman inferior. In fact, one could argue that the woman was actually made of better material than the man, who was formed from the dirt (2:7). In short, the language of both stories suggests that the authors viewed women as the natural equals of men, not as their inferiors.

2. The story of the serpent and the woman in Genesis 3 contains no hint that the serpent viewed the woman as inferior or easy to deceive. In fact, the woman is depicted as a thoughtful dialogue partner who initially defends God's command even though she was not present to hear it. Only after she recognizes the value of wisdom does she

makes the conscious choice to eat the forbidden fruit in order to obtain that which it promised (3:6). Moreover, nothing is said about the woman tempting or enticing her husband. In fact, this was unnecessary, since the story suggests that Adam was present throughout the entire exchange (3:6). Once their actions are uncovered by Yahweh, the woman can at least protest that she was deceived by the trickery of the serpent (3:13); the man can only acknowledge that he ate the fruit when his wife offered it to him (3:12). Contrary to traditional interpretations, the woman comes across as the stronger and more admirable character in this story.

3. The meaning of the statement in Genesis 3:16 about the man ruling over the woman remains problematic. Since the rest of the curses seem designed to explain the way life actually operates (as viewed through the eyes of ancient Palestinian farmers), the verse in question probably seeks to justify a patriarchal understanding of marriage in which men wield primary authority within the household. Whether the man's rule applies to all aspects of life or only to the woman's sexual activity (as might be implied by the first part of the verse) is unclear. Neither of these readings is consistent with the language of Genesis 2, where emphasis is placed on the equality of the genders within marriage (2:18, 24). The fact that women and men are portrayed as equals in the ideal world of Genesis 2 suggests that even the supporters of the patriarchal status quo could envision a better world in which

women and men functioned as equals. Certainly there is nothing in Genesis 3:16 that suggests that the woman is any way inferior to the man in her essential makeup

THE STORY CONTINUES

The stories in Genesis 4–11 narrate what happened to Adam and Eve and their descendants after they were expelled from the garden. These chapters serve to bridge the gap between the two most important creation stories in the Hebrew Bible, the creation of humans in Genesis 1–3 and the creation of the people of Yahweh that begins with Abraham and his family in Genesis 12. Along the way, the stories seek to answer many questions about the physical and social world that might have occurred to ancient Palestinian farmers and herders, including the origins of human civilization. A few of the stories make significant points about religious beliefs and values. A brief review of the major stories will show why each story was included in the Hebrew Bible and the meaning that it held for later generations.

The Origins of Civilization (Genesis 4:1—5:32)

The first two chapters after the expulsion from the garden depict the expansion of the human community from a family of four to perhaps thousands. Genesis 4 tells about the descendants of Cain, the firstborn son of Adam and Eve, while Genesis 5 lists the descendants of Seth, their third child. The question of where Cain and Seth got their wives was debated by later commentators, but the ancient storytellers apparently did not share our concern for narrative consistency.

Scattered throughout this narrative are brief comments that seek to explain the origins of some of the positive and the negative aspects of human civilization. On the positive side, the story mentions the commencement of such vital social institutions as farming and shepherding (4:2, 20), cities (4:17), music (4:21), and metalworking (4:22). The story also depicts the first human expressions of religion, including both personal prayer (4:26; 5:24) and ritual sacrifice (4:3-5). On the negative side, the text explains how human relationships were first infected by

jealousy (4:5), murder (4:8, 23), and the drive for vengeance (4:15, 23-24). The story of the conflict between Cain and Abel could also be taken as an effort to explain the perennial tensions between farmers and shepherds, with shepherds apparently holding the advantage (4:4, 20). The incredible life spans of the people mentioned in chapter 5, like the idealized garden in chapters 2–3, resemble stories from other cultures that depict the era of the earliest ancestors as a time when things were far better than they are now.

The Judgment of Civilization (Genesis 6:1—9:17)

Genesis 6–9 recounts the famous story of Noah and the flood. Stories about great floods were common in the ancient world, reflecting the anxieties that arose whenever the powerful storms of the rainy season caused the riverbeds to overflow with torrents of raging water. The version that appears in Genesis has remarkable parallels with a Mesopotamian tale called the Epic of Gilgamesh, a fact that has led most scholars to conclude that the biblical story was derived from older Mesopotamian narratives.

The present version of the story of Noah was formed by weaving together two earlier stories whose origins are obscure. Most likely they were preserved in different groups or geographic regions. A careful reading shows that the editor has attempted to preserve as much as possible from the earlier stories, even when it leads to the peculiar result of events being narrated twice. Examples of this phenomenon include the initial announcement of the flood (6:17 and 7:4); the instructions about bringing animals into the ark (6:19-21 and 7:2-3; note the difference in the number of animals); the coming of the flood (7:6 and 7:11); the entry of Noah, his family, and the animals into the ark (7:7-9 and 7:13-16); and the coming of forty days of rain (7:12 and 7:17). As in Genesis 1–2, the duplications coincide with the use of different names for the deity.

At its core, the flood story is a narrative about judgment and salvation, both of which are important themes throughout the Hebrew Bible. As in Genesis 3, the story depicts Yahweh as being surprised at how corrupt humans have become and even voicing regret at having made them (6:3, 5-7). The judgment that he finally imposes appears

Fig. 16.7. The flood story has been a popular theme for artists throughout the ages. (top) Edward Hicks, *Noah's Ark*; (bottom) Antonio Carracci, *The Flood*.

even harsher than the curses of Genesis 3, since nothing is said about humans receiving any guidance or warning prior to the coming of the flood (6:3-7). Apparently Yahweh agrees, since he promises at the end of the story never to flood the earth like this again (8:21-22; 9:15-16). The association of this promise with rainbows (9:13-16) is more than a quaint explanation of a natural phenomenon; it also expresses the relief that ancient people felt when the rainstorms ended and a rainbow appeared.

The other key theme that emerges from this story is the supreme importance of righteous living and obedience to the deity. Unlike the similar Mesopotamian story, the Genesis version carries a strong moral tone: the victims are punished because they have become "evil" (6:5), "filled with violence" (6:11), and "corrupt" (6:11-12), while the

hero is kept safe because he is "righteous" and "blameless" (6:9; 7:1), not because the deity made an arbitrary choice to preserve his life. Noah and his family are preserved only because Noah "did all that God commanded him" (6:22; 7:5, 16). The first thing he does when he comes out of the ark after the flood is to offer sacrifices to God (8:20-22). In every respect Noah stands as a role model for the audience of the story.

The Restoration of Civilization (Genesis 9:18—11:9)

The expulsion of Adam and Eve from the garden was followed by a shocking violation (the murder of Abel) that elicited a divine curse (the failure of crops, 4:12), leading to a great division among humans (the sons of Cain and Seth) and eventually another divine judgment (the flood). The story of what happens after the flood follows a similar pattern (9:11—11:9).

Modern readers find it hard to understand why the fact that Ham "saw the nakedness of his father" (9:22) should evoke such a harsh punishment, and some have speculated that the storyteller is alluding to some kind of illicit sexual activity. But the people who told these stories would not have been surprised at this development, since their culture regarded looking at the naked body of one's relatives as a shameful act, presumably because it could lead to incest (note the prohibitions in Leviticus 18 and 20). The equally harsh condemnation of Ham's son Canaan and his descendants to lives of slavery (9:25-27) would also have been comprehensible in a culture where many people believed that the deity punished children for the sins of their parents (Exodus 20:5; 34:7; Numbers 14:18; Deuteronomy 5:9; Jeremiah 32:18; Ezekiel 18:2). The full meaning of this latter curse only becomes clear in chapter 10, where we learn (as the ancient audience would have known already) that the descendants of Canaan are the various people groups whom Yahweh later commands the people of Israel to exterminate as they move into the land of Canaan at the end of the Exodus story (10:15-19; see Exodus 23:22-24; 34:11-14; Deuteronomy 7:1-6; 20:16-18; Joshua 11:16-20). Later we hear that some of these groups were enslaved rather than being destroyed (Joshua 9:20-27; 16:10; 17:12-13; Judges 1:27-35). In short, the primary purpose of the "curse of Ham" story is to justify the conquest and subjugation of the Canaanites by the people of Israel and Judah, whose lineage is incidentally traced to Noah's son Shem (9:26; see also 10:21-31; 11:10-26). This association with Shem explains why Jews are called *Semites* and why people who are biased against them are called *anti-Semitic*, though the latter term is a modern invention.

Behind the lengthy genealogy in chapter 10 lies a concern to explain the origins of the various people groups who were known to the authors and editors of the Hebrew Bible. Since the chapter uses ancient names to identify the groups, the purpose of the list is invariably missed by modern readers, whereas ancient readers would have had no trouble understanding its intent. Pride of place in the list goes to the peoples of the western Mediterranean, including Greece (10:1-5); the people to the north and south of Palestine, including Egypt, Ethiopia, and Mesopotamia (10:8-14); and the inhabitants of Palestine itself (10:15-31).

The final story in this collection seeks to explain how the various groups listed in chapter 10 came to speak different languages when they were all descended from the first man and woman (11:1-9). As in the earlier story in the garden, Yahweh's action is depicted as a preemptive effort to keep humans from attaining powers similar to his own (11:6-7). Apparently ancient audiences were not disturbed by these repeated depictions of Yahweh as a jealous and fearful bully.

SEEING THE BIG PICTURE

The people who compiled the narrative of Genesis 1–11 drew their material from a variety of sources whose earlier history is largely lost to us. But they did not simply throw the stories together; they combined them into a coherent narrative with a number of recurring themes. Most of these themes are religious in character, implying that the editors were seeking to communicate a distinctive religious vision. A brief summary of some of the major themes that run through the narrative will serve to underline the religious perspective of the text.

1. The physical world is characterized by both order and disorder. Order was embedded in the universe from the beginning by the careful planning of the almighty creator. It can be seen most clearly in the everyday operation of the forces of nature. But disorder, too, is inherent in the universe, as evidenced by the daily troubles that humans face as they seek to raise enough food to keep themselves and their families alive. These ordinary struggles are only intensified when the deity decides to use the powers of nature to bring judgment upon his creatures.

2. The world is governed by a deity who is far more powerful than humans and not always predictable. His intentions toward his creation are generally good, but his knowledge is limited, and he sometimes acts against humans out of fear or jealousy of what they might do, or to punish them for wrongful acts. As lord of the universe, he expects humans to obey his commands and live righteous lives. He sends suffering upon those who disobey him and protects those who are faithful to him. In the end, however, his judgment is limited by his mercy and his concern for his creatures.

3. Humans are the pinnacle of the created order, with a God-given duty to care for the world that the deity has entrusted to them. Humans derive their life force from God, and like their creator they have the power to bring order and life or disorder and death to the world. Humans are also relational beings who were made to live in loving relationships with God and others. Unfortunately, humans do not always live as God desires. When they fail, they can inflict terrible harm upon one another and incur the wrath of the deity. Viewed from this angle, much of human suffering is self-inflicted.

WHY THIS STORY?

Now that we have a better understanding of the creation narratives, we are in a position to ask where these stories came from and why the authors framed them as they did. The fact that many of these stories have parallels in Mesopotamian legends has led most scholars to conclude that the narrative in its present form was crafted during the period of the Babylonian exile (586–539 B.C.E.), though it is possible that it was written later under the influence of Mesopotamian models. The message of the texts also fits well into this period. In fact, much of the richness of the stories only becomes apparent when they are read in dialogue with their Mesopotamian counterparts. This suggests that the narrative may have been composed to give the exiled community a Yahwistic alternative to the stories that were popular in Babylon during the time of the Exile.

A couple of examples will show how this may have worked. The Mesopotamian story that bears the closest resemblance to the Genesis 1 creation story is called **Enuma Elish**, after the initial words of the poem in Akkadian. (Modern translations can be found on the Internet; the creation is described in Tablets IV–VI.) This story, composed in the twelfth century B.C.E. from earlier traditions, tells of a colossal battle that erupts among the gods when Tiamat, goddess of the waters, sets out to obtain vengeance for the death of her hus-

Fig. 16.8. A tablet from the Epic of Gilgamesh that contains part of the Babylonian flood story.

band. When she proves too powerful for the other gods, a god named Marduk, the chief deity of Babylon, arises to fight against her on the condition that he be granted supreme authority over the universe if he prevails. The other gods agree, and Marduk succeeds in defeating Tiamat and is named ruler of the gods. Out of the body of the defeated goddess he forms the physical world, following the same basic order of creation as we see in Genesis 1. (Note the repeated mention of "waters" in Genesis 1:1-13.) Finally he creates humans out of the blood of a god named Kingu who is charged with initiating the rebellion. They are given the task of serving the gods by building them houses (temples) and bringing them food (sacrifices).

Though this story obviously differs markedly from the Genesis 1 account, the similar order of creation in the two stories suggests that the author of Genesis 1 may have

known the Mesopotamian legend or another one like it and crafted a story that would serve as an alternative to it. Viewing the story in this way sheds new light on some of the special emphases of the Genesis story. For example, Genesis 1 depicts a deity who is so powerful that he can simply speak and the physical world comes into existence. No conflict is required; everything unfolds in a serene and orderly manner. This is the polar opposite of the chaotic struggles that characterize the Mesopotamian story. The same is true for their respective views of humankind. The Genesis 1 story asserts that humans, both male and female, have an inherent dignity as creatures who bear the image of the supreme god. The Enuma Elish, by contrast, depicts humans as an afterthought in the divine conflict, lowly beings formed out of the blood of a rebel god to care for the needs of the gods so that they could rest (as in Genesis 2:2-3). The Genesis picture of a single deity ruling unchallenged over an orderly universe and having a special concern for his creatures would have brought comfort to a group of exiles from Judah surrounded by a Babylonian culture that viewed the universe as a more chaotic and less friendly place.

Similar observations can be made about the two cultures' flood stories. The **Epic of Gilgamesh**, a hero legend known in a variety of forms throughout ancient Mesopotamia, contains a flood story that agrees at so many points with the Genesis narrative that virtually all scholars agree that the Genesis version is based on this story or the traditions that lay behind it. (Modern translations can be found on the Internet; the flood story appears in Tablet XI.) But there are notable differences as well. In the Mesopotamian story, neither the coming of the flood nor the warning that is given to the hero, Utna-pishtim, has any cause except for the will of the gods. When the flood finally does come, the storm is so terrible that even the gods cower in fear. Once the flood is over, one of the gods who was involved in the decision to send the flood flies into a rage because a human survived the deluge. This same deity makes the survivor and his wife immortal and removes them to a distant land on the edge of the world.

A careful review of the differences between the two stories shows that the moral element is much stronger in the biblical story than in the Mesopotamian tale. Instead of a host of gods who scheme against one another and bring suffering upon humans for no apparent reason, the Genesis story depicts a single almighty god who controls all of the forces of nature and decrees judgment against humans only when their wickedness has grown too great to bear. Similarly, the man who is saved from the flood was protected because of his righteous con-duct, not because he happened to be a favorite of one of the gods. The message of the Genesis story is clear: the universe operates according to a fixed moral order under the rule of a mighty but just god who judges the wicked and protects the righteous from danger. Similar messages can be seen in other narratives that originated during the exilic period (see chapter 21). In the face of a Babylonian culture that constantly belittled and marginalized their beliefs, this rewriting of a well-known Mesopotamian narrative would have served to remind the exiles of Judah that their present suffering was part of a broader divine plan that included protection for those who lived righteously before their god.

CONCLUSION

One of the most common uses for stories is to explain how the world came to be the way it is. Some stories are meant to answer the big questions that every culture asks about the nature of the universe, while others aim to explain particular aspects of the physical and social world as experienced by the people who told the stories.

The stories in Genesis 1–11 represent an elaborate attempt to answer some of the questions that people in ancient Palestine raised about the world as they saw it. The story line is based on a series of traditional narra-tives from various sources (including Mesopotamian leg-ends) that the editors revised and crafted together into a relatively coherent whole. In the process, they infused the narrative with a distinctive religious vision that was rooted in their own Yahwistic faith. This vision affirmed the inherent goodness and order of the natural and super-natural worlds while also offering an explanation for the presence of disorder and evil in the universe.

While some of the stories in Genesis 1–11 are based on ancient traditions, the narrative as a whole was prob-ably formulated during the Exile, since its vision of God, humans, and the universe accords well with what we see in other documents from this period. But the sto-ries apparently proved useful to people in later periods as well, since the entire unit was eventually incorporated into the Scriptures of Judaism.

EXERCISE 32

Most of the stories in Genesis 1–11 are not mentioned anywhere else in the Hebrew Bible. This suggests that they were either not well known or were created later than most of the other biblical materials. The Hebrew Bible also contains references to the origins of the universe that differ substantially from the Genesis stories.

Read the following passages and make a list of the things that they say happened at the time when God created the universe. When you are done, go back over the list and mark which items seem to agree with the Genesis 1–2 creation story and which ones differ. Then see if you can construct an alternate story of creation from the events that do not appear in the Genesis creation story.

- Job 9:4-14
- Job 26:7-14
- Job 38:1-11
- Psalm 8:1-9

- Psalm 104:1-9
- Psalm 136:1-9
- Proverbs 8:22-31

Fig. 17.1. József Molnár, *The March of Abraham*

Ancestral Narratives

*Now the L*ORD *said to Abram, "Go from your country and your kindred and your father's house to the land that I will show you. I will make of you a great nation, and I will bless you, and make your name great, so that you will be a blessing. I will bless those who bless you, and the one who curses you I will curse; and in you all the families of the earth shall be blessed." So Abram went, as the L*ORD *had told him.* (Genesis 12:1-4)

*The L*ORD *appeared to Isaac and said, "Do not go down to Egypt; settle in the land that I shall show you. Reside in this land as an alien, and I will be with you, and will bless you; for to you and to your descendants I will give all these lands, and I will fulfill the oath that I swore to your father Abraham. I will make your offspring as numerous as the stars of heaven, and will give to your offspring all these lands; and all the nations of the earth shall gain blessing for themselves through your offspring, because Abraham obeyed my voice and kept my charge, my commandments, my statutes, and my laws."* (Genesis 26:2-5)

God appeared to Jacob again when he came from Paddan-aram, and he blessed him. God said to him, "Your name is Jacob; no longer shall you be called Jacob, but Israel shall be your name." So he was called Israel. God said to him, "I am God Almighty: be fruitful and multiply; a nation and a company of nations shall come from you, and kings shall spring from you. The land that I gave to Abraham and Isaac I will give to you, and I will give the land to your offspring after you." (Genesis 35:9-12)

Every culture has its stories of great heroes from the past. Some are remembered for their role in the founding of the people or culture; others are celebrated as warriors or statesmen; still others are honored as exemplary leaders or models of virtue. Some of these people were real historical characters, while others are clearly mythical. Often the line between history and legend is blurred in these stories, especially in the ancient world. People whom scholars believe may have existed are shown doing supernatural acts and engaging in regular dialogue with the gods, who watch over them with special care. Sometimes the legendary element becomes so strong that it is hard to be certain whether the person was a real historical character or originated as a figment of the cultural imagination.

The stories in Genesis 12–50 are the biblical equivalent of these stories of great heroes from the past. People like Abraham and Sarah, Isaac and Rebekah, Jacob and Rachel, and Joseph and his brothers are portrayed as the direct physical ancestors of the people of Israel and Judah. This emphasis on common ancestry helped to forge a sense of ethnic unity among the people who valued these stories. But the people who crafted the stories and told them to their children were not concerned primarily with narrating dry facts about the past. All of the characters in Genesis 12–50 are presented as positive or negative role models whose words and deeds reveal how the deity wants his people to live. Whether the stories are historically accurate, or whether the characters existed at all, was irrelevant to their purpose. They were effective as long as the people who used them took them seriously as narratives about their honored ancestors.

This chapter will explore the historical background and religious value of some of the key stories in this important section of the Hebrew Bible. The first part of the chapter provides a broad overview of the story line that runs through Genesis 12–50. This is followed by an examination of some of the questions that scholars have raised about the historical value of these stories. The chapter ends with a discussion of what these stories might have meant to the people who told them, including their religious value.

THE PLOT OF GENESIS 12–50

The stories in Genesis 12–50 tell about the first four generations in the lineage of Abram, a man from Mesopotamia whose name was later changed to Abraham. These stories are often called the ancestral narratives because the Hebrew Bible claims that the main characters were the ancient ancestors of the people of Israel and Judah. While the primary spotlight is on the male characters (traditionally called the **patriarchs**), the female characters (matriarchs) also receive more attention in these chapters than women elsewhere in the Hebrew Bible.

Act I: Abraham and Sarah

The story begins with Abram being called by Yahweh to leave his homeland and travel with his family and herds to Canaan, the land later called Palestine (Genesis 12:1-3). The author does not explain how Abram, who presumably worshipped many gods while living in Mesopotamia, knew the identity of the deity who spoke to him; he simply does what he is told and asks no questions. The words that Yahweh speaks to Abram in this scene, together with a similar promise after his arrival in Canaan (Genesis 12:7), foreshadow events that will require several

books and many generations to reach their fulfillment. To ensure that the audience grasps the importance of these words, the author repeats them with variations in Genesis 15:12-20; 17:4-8; and 22:15-1 and reaffirms them to Abram's descendants in Genesis 26:1-5, 24; 28:13-15; 35:9-12; and 48:4 (see also 27:28-29; 28:3-4; 32:12).

In these texts, Yahweh promises to bless Abram by making his descendants into a great nation that will possess the entire land of Canaan. This promise is fulfilled in the books of Joshua and Judges when the children of the Exodus generation invade and conquer Canaan under the leadership of Joshua (see chapter 20). Yahweh also promises to bless or curse other nations based on how they treat Abram. The Hebrew Bible contains many stories of Yahweh acting on this promise. Similar ideas can be seen in the books of the prophets, who pronounce Yahweh's blessings or curses upon Israel's neighbors based on their treatment of Israel (see chapters 31–35).

From the beginning of the story, Abram is presented as a model of obedience. Following the command of Yahweh to leave his homeland, he travels to Canaan, then to Egypt, then back again to Canaan, where he wanders from place to place seeking fresh pasture in the manner common to all shepherds. His travels are punctuated by a series of visits from Yahweh, who repeatedly acknowledges and rewards Abram's faithful and righteous conduct.

The bulk of the narrative focuses not on Abram's travels but on events within his family. The central problem around which the plot revolves is the inability of Abram's wife, Sarai, to become pregnant. In a world where children were prized for their ability to help with the work of the family and maintain the family line, sterility was a terrible disgrace that fell chiefly on the woman—in this case, Sarai. In desperation, Sarai gives her slave Hagar to Abram to bear him children in her place, leading to the birth of a son named Ishmael. At the story level, there is nothing wrong with Sarai's act—polygamy is viewed as normal in these narratives, and Hagar, as a female and a slave, has no say in the matter. But Yahweh has other plans: through heavenly messengers he tells Abram (now renamed Abraham) that his wife, Sarai (now called Sarah), will have a son in her old age, a prediction that is fulfilled with the birth of their son, Isaac.

Fig. 17.2. (left) Matthias Stomer, *Sarah Bringing Hagar to Abraham*; (right) Michelangelo Caravaggio, *The Sacrifice of Isaac*

After some initial conflicts between Hagar and Sarah over their respective sons, Hagar and Ishmael drop out of the narrative, since the storyteller does not regard them as part of the ancestral line of Israel and Judah. (The Qur'an, by contrast, adds many more stories about Abraham, Hagar, and Ishmael at this point, since Muslims regard Ishmael as the son through whom God's purposes are realized.) Sarah also disappears from the story, presumably because she has fulfilled her assigned role of giving birth to the promised child and ensuring that he stands unchallenged as his father's heir. Her death is mentioned only in passing, overshadowed by a story about Abraham's successful efforts to buy a plot of land in which to bury her.

Abraham, on the other hand, faces one last challenge before he can exit the scene: he is commanded to offer his precious son Isaac as a human sacrifice to Yahweh. Even in the face of this extreme situation, however, Abraham remains a model of obedience and faith. At the last moment Yahweh intervenes to prevent the slaughter, satisfied that Abraham will do whatever he asks. Having passed the test, Abraham disappears from the narrative as the storyteller's focus shifts to his descendants. His death and burial receive only cursory mention; by then the plot has left him far behind.

EXERCISE 33

Read the following stories from the life of Abraham, paying attention to the way the character of Abraham is depicted in each passage. In what ways is Abraham presented as a role model for others to follow? How might you explain the apparent flaws or weaknesses in Abraham's character?

- Genesis 12:1-20
- Genesis 16:1-16
- Genesis 18:1-15
- Genesis 22:1-19

Act II: Isaac and Jacob

Where Abraham is depicted as a man of action, his son Isaac is a passive character who appears primarily in scenes dominated by others. When his father ties him up and lays him on the altar to be sacrificed to the deity, he offers no complaint. When the time comes for him to be married, he waits at home while his father sends a servant to find him a wife. When he moves for a time to the land of the Philistines, he lies about his marriage in order to protect himself from harm. Even after he has grown wealthy and powerful, he gives way repeatedly to a petty king who fears his growing power. In the twilight of his life, he discovers that he has been tricked by his wife into pronouncing a blessing on his younger son rather than the older one as he intended. When he finally dies, his death is mentioned only in passing.

Long before Isaac's quiet death, the story has moved on to the next generation, with the majority of the attention going to Isaac's younger son, Jacob. Jacob is a classic trickster whose behavior recalls similar characters in many other cultures around the globe. Tricksters enhance the entertainment value of the stories in which they appear, but they also play a more serious role by highlighting ambiguities or tensions in the value systems of a given society. From the day of his birth, Jacob is shown striving to get ahead, often at the expense of other people. Twice he takes advantage of family members in moments of weakness—first his brother, Esau, then his father, Isaac. For a while it appears that he has met his match in his uncle Laban, another trickster who traps Jacob into marrying both of his daughters when he had intended to marry only the younger one. Laban's daughters, Leah and Rachel, also reveal trickster qualities as they scheme to find ways to produce male heirs for their husband. In the end, Jacob and his wives are too much for Laban. After using a form of folk magic to increase his herds at the expense of his uncle, Jacob sneaks away

with his uncle's household idols hidden away in his baggage, courtesy of Laban's younger daughter, Rachel.

Until this point the narrative follows a conventional trickster plot. But the story takes an unexpected turn when Jacob decides to return home and face his brother, Esau, whom he had deceived out of his inheritance rights when both were younger. Ever the trickster, Jacob sends lavish gifts ahead to his brother in an effort to appease him before he arrives. The night before they meet, however, Jacob encounters a mysterious being with whom he wrestles until morning, an experience that leaves him lame. The scene ends with Jacob as a new man—humbled but blessed by the deity. He also has a new name that will be used to identify his descendants forever: *Israel*, meaning "one who struggles with God." From this point forward, Jacob's life takes a more positive turn as he finds forgiveness from his brother and becomes a devoted follower of Yahweh, the god of his fathers. The dramatic reversal in his life makes him a role model of a different sort than his grandfather Abraham.

Once he has been transformed, Jacob moves to the sidelines and becomes a bit player in a narrative that revolves around the actions of his sons. Toward the end of the story, he reemerges as a prophet who pronounces divine blessings upon his grandsons and foretells the

Fig. 17.3. (left) Jan Victors, *Isaac Blessing Jacob*; (right) Eugène Delacroix, *Jacob Wrestles with the Angel*

future of his sons and their families (Genesis 48–49). He dies a beloved character, lamented by all who knew him.

Act III: Joseph and His Brothers

The final episode in the saga of Abraham's family centers on a man named Joseph, the eleventh of Jacob's twelve sons. Jacob's other sons are mostly ignored by the story-teller. Only two, Judah and Joseph, play leading roles in the story, and only Joseph receives any extended attention. Four other sons have minor acting and/or speaking parts; the other six are known only by their names. This unequal treatment is surprising, since Jacob's sons are identified near the end of the story as the ancestors of the twelve tribes of Israel. On this basis we might have expected the biblical authors to include stories about all of the tribal ancestors in order to satisfy the interests of their supposed descendants.

On closer inspection, however, we discover that the selective treatment of Jacob's sons is no accident. The two characters who receive the most attention, Joseph and Judah, are depicted in later narratives as the ancestors of the people of Israel and Judah respectively. Two other sons who play minor roles, Simeon and Benjamin, represent tribes whose lands were eventually absorbed into Judah. The other son who puts in a brief appearance, Levi, is valued as the ancestor of the priestly class in Israel. In short, the only sons of Jacob who receive significant attention are the ones whom the tradition regards as the ancestors of the dominant social and political groups in ancient Palestine. If the tribal system has any historical validity (see chapter 20), the stories of the other tribal ancestors must have been intentionally suppressed or ignored when the documents were compiled.

The story of Joseph begins by depicting Joseph as a naïve young man who brags to his family about two recent dreams in which his father, mother, and brothers all bowed down before him. As the narrative progresses, we learn that these dreams foreshadow events that will indeed come to pass later in the story. To Joseph's brothers, however, these visions reflect sheer arrogance. Their resentment is intensified by the attitude of their elderly father, Jacob, who dotes on Joseph as his favorite son. Finally, the brothers hatch a plot to kill Joseph and blame his death on a wild animal. At the last minute, however, they have second thoughts and decide to sell him instead to some passing traders, who in turn sell him as a slave to one of Pharaoh's officers in Egypt.

Fig. 17.4. Friedrich Overbeck, *Joseph Being Sold by his Brothers*

In Egypt, Joseph proves to be a model worker, and soon he is given charge over all of his master's property, which prospers under his care. But his good fortune does not last. After he repeatedly resists the efforts of his master's wife to seduce him, she falsely accuses him of attempted rape and he is sent away to prison for several years. While in prison, Joseph becomes known among the inmates for his ability to interpret dreams that foreshadow the future. When Pharaoh has a dream that seems to bode ill for his people, he calls for Joseph and learns from him that God is warning him about a great famine that will soon come upon the land of Egypt. Pharaoh, impressed by Joseph's abilities, names him his second-in-command and places him in charge of gathering and storing food to be used during the famine.

Fig. 17.5. Peter Cornelius, *The Recognition of Joseph by his Brothers*

When the famine arrives, the people of Egypt have plenty to eat, while the people of the neighboring lands, including Canaan, are soon on the brink of starvation. As Canaanites had done for centuries, Jacob sends his ten oldest sons to Egypt to buy grain. When they are brought before Joseph, they do not recognize him, but he knows who they are. Joseph decides to test his brothers to see if they have changed since the time they sold him into slavery. Accusing them of being spies, Joseph imprisons one of his brothers as a hostage and sends the others back to Canaan to retrieve their youngest brother,

Benjamin, who also happens to be Joseph's only full brother.

When Benjamin arrives, Joseph secretly plants a silver goblet in his baggage, then accuses him of theft. Instead of abandoning Benjamin, Judah begs to be allowed to take his half brother's place so that Benjamin can return home safely to his father. At these words, Joseph breaks down and tells his brothers who he is and invites them to bring their families, including his father, Jacob, to Egypt for the duration of the famine. Later, after Jacob has died, Joseph assures his brothers that he has no desire to take revenge on them, since God has used their evil actions to bring about good for the people of Egypt and Canaan. From here the story skips to Joseph's deathbed, where he requests that his body be taken back to Canaan when his family returns there after the famine. He has no way of knowing that it will be several generations before his request is fulfilled at the time of the Exodus.

EXERCISE 35

Read the following stories from the life of Joseph, paying careful attention to the way his character is depicted. To what extent is Joseph presented as a role model for others to follow? How does his character compare with that of his ancestors Abraham, Isaac, and Jacob?

- Genesis 37:1-28
- Genesis 39:1-23
- Genesis 41:1-49
- Genesis 42:1-24
- Genesis 44:1—45:15
- Genesis 50:15-21

HISTORICAL CONSIDERATIONS

Was there really a historical person named Abraham, or should we view him as a mythical founder of the race such as we find in many other cultures? What about his family? Does Genesis 12–50 narrate actual events in the lives of the early ancestors of Israel and Judah, or are these stories more like the legends of great heroes from a hazy past that many cultures tell around the campfire at night?

Despite rigorous investigation and debate, scholars remain deeply divided over these questions. Conservative scholars, who prefer to trust the Bible wherever possible, believe that the stories offer credible historical accounts of the people whose lives they narrate. They support their position by pointing to evidence suggesting that many of the customs presupposed in the stories agree with what we know about the times and places in which the stories are said to have taken place. Examples include the special ceremonies used when making covenants; the practice of adopting a male heir when a family has no sons; the use of slaves as surrogate mothers for sterile women; and the

types of burial practices depicted in the narrative. Conservatives also insist that the events described in these stories comport well with what we know about the history of Mesopotamia, Palestine, and Egypt during the period when the stories are supposed to have occurred (perhaps 1800–1600 B.C.E.). In particular, they associate the wanderings of Abraham with reports of major migrations from Mesopotamia to Canaan during this period and the rise of Joseph with the openness of Egypt to foreign influences in the middle of the second millennium B.C.E.

More critical scholars, on the other hand, question the historical value of most or all of the stories in the ancestral narratives. Many claim that conservative scholars have distorted the historical evidence to fit their preconceived beliefs about the historicity of the Bible. Others note that many of the customs that conservatives cite in support of their position were practiced at other times in the history of the region and thus are useless for dating or confirming the narratives. But critical scholars have been unable to reach agreement as to how far one should go in discounting the stories.

Maximalist scholars acknowledge that the narratives contain many fictional elements that were added to make them more interesting and entertaining, including conversations between the characters and details of the plot. But many still believe that the stories are rooted in genuine historical memories about real people who bore the names of the characters who appear in the stories. The chief question for these scholars is whether the present narrative is based on memories of an actual multigenerational family of ancestors or whether Abraham, Isaac, and

Fig. 17.6. (top) A cuneiform tablet referring to the Apriu (or Habiru), a term some scholars associate with the name *Hebrews* that is applied to Abraham and his descendants in the Hebrew Bible; (bottom) a mural from a nineteenth-century B.C.E. Egyptian tomb showing Semitic herdsmen entering Egypt, as at the end of the story of Joseph.

Jacob were the ancestors of different tribal groups that banded together in an alliance and subsequently wove their ancestral legends together into a single narrative in order to create a mythical history for the newly united people. Most maximalists believe that the present version of the narrative was written fairly late in the history of Israel (during or after the Exile) using stories that had previously circulated as isolated units. This suggests that the overarching plotline of the ancestral narrative, along with many of the details of the individual stories, is a late creation and thus historically unreliable.

Scholars who adopt a minimalist position view the ancestral narratives as part of a great foundation myth that was formulated at a time when the actual history of the region was long forgotten. In their view, the stories of Abraham, Isaac, Jacob, and their families were created out of thin air by storytellers seeking to forge a common past for the people of Palestine during the Persian period (that is, after the Exile) or even later. They find it incredible that anyone could believe that these stories were passed on orally for over a millennium and still preserve any accurate memories of the past. They also point to anachronisms in the stories that they say reflect the circumstances, beliefs, and practices of later periods. In their view, the stories make more sense when viewed as part of an effort by a particular set of religio-political leaders to gain support for their program to unite a divided and dispirited people under their own leadership. Nothing in these stories should be taken seriously as history.

Evaluating these alternatives is difficult, and firm conclusions are impossible in light of the heated debates that continue to rage among proponents of the competing views. Minimalists are accused of ignoring archaeological and historical evidence that lends support to the ancestral stories; maximalists are criticized for placing too much trust in the biblical narratives. The very fact that these disputes are taking place with such fervor suggests that the storyteller has done a superb job of creating a realistic world within the text for the characters to inhabit. This is especially significant when we note that the stories also contain many elements that are commonly associated with fantasy: people talking with supernatural beings; a ninety-year-old woman having a baby; fire and brimstone falling from the sky to destroy a city; and similar events.

Here we see the nub of the problem: the stories are realistic enough to remove them from the realm of pure fantasy, yet they contain enough fantastic elements to raise questions about their relation to actual history. Evidence from archaeology and other historical sources is less helpful for these stories than for later narratives, since there is little in these stories about wandering herdsmen and their families that would have left any lasting mark on the landscape. Information from the surrounding cultures is also inconclusive, since scholars have pointed to evidence that supports both early and later dates for the stories. In the end, all we can say with certainty is that the ancestral narratives are religious stories whose relation to actual past events remains unclear.

THE ANCESTRAL NARRATIVES AS RELIGIOUS STORIES

To raise questions about the historical reliability of the biblical narratives is a modern way of thinking that would not have occurred to the people who told and used these stories in ancient Palestine. As far as they were concerned, the stories recounted their people's past, and their worldviews and actions were shaped by this belief. Most scholars think that the stories of the patriarchs and matriarchs were told and retold orally in various forms over many generations before they were finally included in the Hebrew Bible. This suggests that the stories about Abraham, Isaac, Jacob, and their families spoke to the needs and concerns of people in many different times and places.

While we cannot be sure what forms the stories took during this oral phase, it seems likely that many of the themes that appear in the present version of the stories were present in the oral traditions. What kinds of messages might the followers of Yahweh have drawn from these stories?

1. The "chosen people." At the core of the ancestral narratives is the conviction that Yahweh has chosen a particular group of people out of all the nations of the earth to be his special covenant partners (see chapter 14). This belief that a specific people group stands at the center of the universe is called **ethnocentrism**. Similar concepts can be seen in virtually all traditional cultures, though they use different language to express it. The primary purpose of ethnocentric stories and language is to create or reinforce a sense of group identity and cohesiveness: *we* are special, so *we* should stick together and support one another. This feeling of ethnic pride can be a source of tremendous strength and unity for a group whose members are willing to embrace the identity that it offers them.

But there is also a dark side to ethnocentric thinking. Those who are not part of *us* are frequently viewed with suspicion and hostility; some groups even regard outsiders as subhuman or unworthy of life. In this form, ethnocentrism has led to all kinds of repressive and violent actions by one group against another. Ethnocentrism can also lead to ostracism or punishment of group members who are perceived as being insufficiently loyal to the group or overly sympathetic to outsiders.

The ancestral narratives are part of a broader story that portrays the people of Israel and Judah as the physical descendants of Abraham, Isaac, and Jacob, and thus as the ultimate beneficiaries of the patriarchs' special covenant with Yahweh. For those who accepted it, this vision of their identity offered substantial psychological and social benefits, whether they lived under the monarchy or during or after the Exile.

On the psychological side, the stories gave them a sense of ethnic identity that distinguished them from the other residents of Palestine. According to the ancestral narratives, they originated not in Palestine but in Mesopotamia, the intellectual and cultural center of the region. In this way they laid claim to a lofty heritage that belied their often humble appearance. The stories also reminded them that they lived under the watchful care of a powerful deity who was intensely concerned about their welfare. This knowledge could have helped to calm their fears and anxieties as they faced the many uncertainties and troubles of everyday life in ancient Palestine.

On the social side, the ancestral narratives claimed that the people of Israel and Judah shared common ancestors and were thus part of a single great family. This belief, regardless of its validity, would have created feelings of mutual obligation and support among people in both nations who viewed themselves as the descendants

of Abraham. The stories also helped to define how these people should relate to others outside their Abrahamic family. Yahweh's repeated promises to bless those who helped them and curse those who tried to harm them clearly justified the pursuit of ethnic self-interest. Finally, the ancestral narratives asserted the right of these people to rule over the land of Canaan and to drive out or repress people who did not share their ethnic heritage. This claim no doubt helped to salve their collective conscience when they reflected on the way they had treated the other residents of the land both past and present.

2. The importance of loyalty. Though the ancestral narratives are heavily plot-driven, they also portray various characters as positive and negative role models. The character quality that receives the most consistent attention in the narratives is loyalty. In a traditional society, loyalty to the clan and the family is one of the chief values that must be taught to each new generation if the group is to survive. Adults, too, must be reminded periodically of the need to place the good of the group above personal gain. Virtually all of the characters in the ancestral narratives demonstrate by their actions the importance of maintaining loyalty to fellow group members, and by extension to Yahweh as well.

On the positive side, the most prominent examples of loyalty are Abraham and Joseph. Abraham's entire life is characterized by unerring devotion to Yahweh. When Yahweh speaks, Abraham obeys. He remains loyal even when he is told to slaughter his son Isaac as a sacrifice to Yahweh, a command that clearly contradicted the deity's earlier assurances that he would have countless descendants through Isaac. Abraham is not above raising questions about Yahweh's intentions from time to time, but he always obeys in the end. In his absolute obedience to Yahweh, Abraham stands as a model for Yahwists in a later day whose religious consciousness was framed around obedience to God-given laws.

In Joseph's case, on the other hand, it is loyalty to human authorities that is implicitly commended. The story begins with Joseph violating the norms of familial loyalty by flaunting two dreams that showed his parents and brothers bowing down to him. Once he arrives in Egypt, however, Joseph becomes a model of loyalty to ruling authorities. His loyal service causes him to be elevated to higher and higher positions of responsibility, first in his master's household, then in the prison where he is sent after refusing to violate his allegiance to his master, and finally over the whole of Egypt. In his role as overseer of the collection and distribution of food during the famine, Joseph always acts in the best interests of Pharaoh. In the end, he demonstrates the loyalty that he had earlier denied to his family by forgiving his brothers and arranging for their families (including his father) to receive food and pasture in Egypt for the duration of the famine. The social harmony and material blessings that result from Joseph's loyalty to authority serve as a subtle incentive for later audiences to adopt a similar attitude toward their own authorities.

Between these two positive examples of loyalty stand a number of stories that show the negative consequences that result when people fail to abide by the common standards of loyalty in relationships. Given the choice of any part of Canaan in which to graze his herds, Abraham's nephew Lot chooses the best land for himself rather than leaving it for his uncle. As a result of this choice, he eventually loses all that he has, including his wife, and subsequently becomes the ancestor of two of Israel's perennial enemies, the Moabites and Ammonites (Genesis 13:1-13; 19:1-29).

Fig. 17.7. (top) Pieter Pietersz Lastman, *The Dismissal of Hagar*; (bottom) Raphael, *The Brothers [of Joseph] Explain Their Dreams*

Later in the story Abraham, faced with competing loyalties to his wife, Sarah, and her slave Hagar, allows Hagar to be abused by Sarah until she is finally rescued by Yahweh. In the end he decides to send Hagar away for good in order to put an end to the rivalries between the two women, an action that also costs him his son Ishmael (Genesis 16:1-16; 21:1-21).

The pattern continues with Abraham's children and grandchildren. Despite cultural norms that give primary inheritance rights to the oldest son, Rebekah favors her younger son, Jacob, and devises a scheme to obtain Isaac's

blessing for Jacob in place of Esau, the older son who was Isaac's favorite. The family is split apart by the deception. Esau marries a Canaanite woman in order to spite his parents, and his descendants become the Edomites, who appear later as a threat to Judah. Jacob spends most of the next two decades in Mesopotamia, afraid to return home to his family and face his brother's reprisals (Genesis 27:1—28:9; 29:1—33:20). While away from home, Jacob himself becomes a victim of relational disloyalty when his uncle Laban, after promising to give his younger daughter, Rachel, to Jacob in marriage, violates his oath by sending his older daughter, Leah, to Jacob's tent on the wedding night instead of Rachel. Though Laban clearly benefits from this disloyal act in the short run, he finally loses the best of his herds, his daughters, and even his gods to Jacob (Genesis 29:1—31:55). All of these stories employ negative examples to underline the vital importance of loyalty in relationships, one of the chief values of virtually all traditional societies.

3. The transforming power of Yahweh. One of the most endearing features of the ancestral narratives is the true-to-life quality of their characters. None of them is depicted as a saint; even the best of them have flaws and make unwise decisions. Abraham shades the truth concerning his relationship with Sarah (Genesis 12:10-20; 20:1-18) and treats Hagar like a disposable sex object (Genesis 16:1-6; 21:9-19). Sarah manipulates Abraham into getting rid of Hagar (Genesis 16:5-6; 21:9-14) and lies to Yahweh about laughing when he promised that she would have a son in her old age (Genesis 18:1-15). Virtually all of the characters in the Jacob narrative are selfish, conniving, and untrustworthy, though most have a few redeeming qualities as well. Even Joseph brags about his future greatness (Genesis 37:5-11) and deceives his brothers several times before revealing his identity to them (Genesis 42:1—45:8).

But this is only part of the story. By the end of the narrative, several of the key characters have been transformed by the power of Yahweh. Abraham's doubts about Yahweh's plans for his posterity (Genesis 15:1-6; 17:17-18) are overcome when he shows himself willing to sacrifice the very one through whom Yahweh had promised that his plans would be fulfilled (Genesis 22:1-19). Jacob's self-reliance is shattered when he fails to overcome the mysterious stranger who wrestles with him at night and dislocates his hip, leaving him lame (Genesis 32:22-32). Joseph's pride is humbled as he learns to accept his lowly state and faithfully serve those whom Yahweh has placed over him (Genesis 39:1-6, 19-23; compare 41:37-40). Judah, who joined in the conspiracy to get rid of Joseph and later refused to fulfill his familial obligations to his widowed daughter-in-law (Genesis 38:1-26), finally sees the error of his ways and offers to become a slave himself in order to save his younger brother Benjamin (Genesis 44:18-34).

Difficult circumstances also yield repeatedly to the power of the deity, who is clearly in control even when matters appear otherwise. The advanced age of Abraham and Sarah presents no obstacle for Yahweh's plan to give them a child of their own. In fact, Yahweh waits until both become so old that the idea is ludicrous before carrying out his plan. Similarly, the blatant favoritism exhibited by Sarah, Rebekah, and Jacob toward their children does not interfere with Yahweh's purposes. Both the sons that they favored and the ones whom they rejected are eventually blessed by Yahweh; all will be the fathers of tribes and nations. The same is true for the heartbreaking story of Leah and Rachel competing to bear sons for Jacob and so earn his affection: out of their efforts come sons who will be the ancestors of the twelve tribes of Israel (Genesis 29:31—30:24). Yahweh's sovereign control over circumstances is especially evident in the story of Joseph, where his brothers' plot to rid themselves of Joseph's boasting initiates a series of divinely guided twists and turns that eventually leads to the preservation of the very brothers who had betrayed him. Joseph's words to his brothers after their father's death sum up this vital theme: "Even though you intended to do harm to me, God intended it for good, in order to preserve a numerous people, as he is doing today" (Genesis 50:20).

The chief value of these stories lies in their insistence that Yahweh is always at work in the circumstances of his people, despite the vagaries of human behavior and the threats posed by uncontrollable events. No situation or individual lies beyond the transforming and redeeming power of Yahweh. Sometimes Yahweh acts in ways that are immediately apparent, but more often he uses the choices and actions of ordinary human beings to carry out his purposes, making his presence known only in hindsight. A true follower of Yahweh will remain loyal whatever the circumstances, even when Yahweh's intentions are difficult to discern.

While this message has provided comfort to Jews and Christians in a variety of situations, it would have been especially helpful to people in ancient Palestine whose lives were punctuated by unpredictable and often unpleasant occurrences, whether caused by humans or natural forces. Stories such as these assured them that there is a meaning and purpose in the apparently chaotic events of life, even though this fact is often obscured from human view. Nothing—not even the stubborn resistance of those who questioned or rejected the will of Yahweh—could prevent Yahweh from carrying out his good intentions for those who remained loyal to him. Those who embraced this message would have found in it a valuable source of psychological and emotional strength during times of hardship and suffering.

CONCLUSION

The ancestral narratives in Genesis 12–50 are similar to stories that we see in many cultures about ancestral heroes whose actions defined the identity of the people and set them on their current path. Whether the characters portrayed in these stories really existed or were created by storytellers can no longer be determined with clarity.

Most scholars would agree that at least some of the stories were passed on orally for generations among the followers of Yahweh before they were finally included in the Hebrew Bible.

The chief value of these stories lies in their ability to forge a sense of ethnic and religious unity among the followers of Yahweh by linking them to a common set of ancestors. The ancestral narratives distinguish these people from their neighbors by insisting that they are the heirs of a special covenant relationship that Yahweh initiated with their ancestors. This covenant bound them together as a community and justified their efforts to exercise control over the entire land of Canaan at the expense of people who were not members of their group.

The stories also helped to define and regulate the conduct of Yahweh's covenant people by setting forth a series of positive and negative role models for their instruction and guidance. This strategy of depicting revered ancestors as moral examples served to enhance the likelihood that the moral values presented in the stories would be accepted and followed by people who regarded themselves as the heirs of Yahweh's covenant.

EXERCISE 36

For Americans, stories about the Founding Fathers serve many of the same purposes that the stories of Abraham, Isaac, and Jacob did in ancient Palestine. Think back on the things that you have learned about these men (and occasionally women) during your years of schooling and answer the following questions.

(a) How would you evaluate the historical reliability of the stories that you were told? Would you trust some of these stories more than others? Why?

(b) How balanced and realistic was the information that you were given about these people's lives and characters? What kinds of points were emphasized? What might have been left out?

(c) Why do you think that these people's personal lives and accomplishments receive so much attention in the American educational system? What do these stories do for the people who hear them? Whose interests do the stories serve?

Fig. 18.1. The Negev Desert, one of the areas where the Israelites are said to have wandered for forty years according to the Exodus narrative.

CHAPTER 18

The Exodus Narrative

Then Joseph died, and all his brothers, and that whole generation. But the Israelites were fruitful and prolific; they multiplied and grew exceedingly strong, so that the land was filled with them. Now a new king arose over Egypt, who did not know Joseph. He said to his people, "Look, the Israelite people are more numerous and more powerful than we. Come, let us deal shrewdly with them, or they will increase and, in the event of war, join our enemies and fight against us and escape from the land." Therefore they set taskmasters over them to oppress them with forced labor. (Exodus 1:6-11)

God also spoke to Moses and said to him: "I am the LORD. I appeared to Abraham, Isaac, and Jacob as God Almighty, but by my name 'The LORD' [that is, Yahweh] I did not make myself known to them. I also established my covenant with them, to give them the land of Canaan, the land in which they resided as aliens. I have also heard the groaning of the Israelites whom the Egyptians are holding as slaves, and I have remembered my covenant. Say therefore to the Israelites, 'I am the LORD, and I will free you from the burdens of the Egyptians and deliver you from slavery to them. I will redeem you with an outstretched arm and with mighty acts of judgment. I will take you as my people, and I will be your God. You shall know that I am the LORD your God, who has freed you from the burdens of the Egyptians. I will bring you into the land that I swore to give to Abraham, Isaac, and Jacob; I will give it to you for a possession. I am the LORD.'" (Exodus 6:2-8)

At midnight the LORD struck down all the firstborn in the land of Egypt, from the firstborn of Pharaoh who sat on his throne to the firstborn of the prisoner who was in the dungeon, and all the firstborn of the livestock. Pharaoh arose in the night, he and all his officials and all the Egyptians; and there was a loud cry in Egypt, for there was not a house without someone dead. Then he summoned Moses and Aaron in the night, and said, "Rise up, go away from my people, both you and the Israelites! Go, worship the LORD, as you said." (Exodus 12:29-31)

As we saw in the last chapter, most societies tell stories about heroic ancestors or other characters from the past whose actions helped to define the identity of the people and set them on their current path. But many cultures also have additional stories that celebrate a particular moment or event in the group's past that proved to be crucial to their development as a people. Some of these stories are rooted in historical reality, like accounts of the American or French Revolutions. Others are clearly non-historical by modern standards, such as the emergence of the Hopi people from underground caves or the founding of Rome by the wolf-raised twins, Romulus and Remus. In still other cases a possibly historical event has been so thoroughly encrusted with legend that it is virtually impossible to figure out what really happened, as with the ancient Greek tales of the Trojan War or the legends of Arthur and the Knights of the Round Table.

The question of historicity was not a major concern for the people who preserved and used these stories. The simple fact that the stories came to them hallowed by time was enough to ensure their acceptance by each new generation. People knew them so well that they could refer to a particular element of a story in passing and presume that they would be understood. Since the stories usually depicted a time when the group was in its prime, people often used them as a standard for judging the society of their own day or arguing for a particular course of societal action.

When a single story or cycle of stories comes to be so widely revered that it exercises a dominant influence over the way people think about their society, it is said to be *paradigmatic* for that society. (The word *paradigm* refers to an ideal model.) The Hebrew Bible contains one story that functions in such a paradigmatic manner, the lengthy narrative called the Exodus story. Not only does the story occupy 80 percent of the Torah (the books of Exodus, Leviticus, Numbers, and Deuteronomy), but its influence can be seen throughout the Hebrew Bible. This chapter will explore the content of this story and its central position in the thinking of the people who edited the Hebrew Bible.

THE PLOT OF THE EXODUS STORY

Unlike the patriarchal narratives, the plot of the Exodus story does not develop in a simple linear pattern. But the story does have major turning points. Viewed as a drama, the plot can be divided into three acts. The first act, which tells how Yahweh used a man named Moses to rescue his oppressed people from their Egyptian masters, unfolds in a sequential manner except for a long digression on Passover rituals near the end of the section. The second act is more disjointed, consisting of a series of smaller narrative episodes interspersed with large chunks of material detailing the laws and regulations that Yahweh is said to have given to his people at Mount Sinai in the desert. Tracing a consistent plotline through these sections can be difficult, though the story does reach a clear turning point when Yahweh declares that the generation whom he led out of Egypt will die in the desert because of their refusal to trust him. The final act narrates the next generation's move from the desert region to the borders of the land of Canaan. This section, too, is broken up in places by large sections of legal material, but on the whole the plot flows more continuously than in the previous section. The story concludes with a long speech that Moses delivers to the desert generation just before they enter Canaan. This speech, which fills most of the book of Deuteronomy, takes place on a single day, so it does not notably advance the plot. The actual ending of the story (namely, the entry into Canaan) is narrated in the books of Joshua and Judges. Since the story enters a new phase at that point,

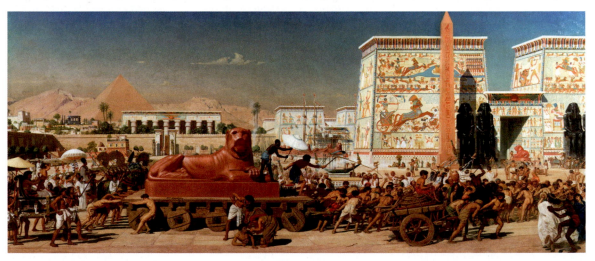

Fig. 18.2. Edward Poynter, *Israel in Egypt*

Fig. 18.3. (left) Domenico Fetti, *Moses and the Burning Bush*; (right) James Tissot, *Moses Speaks to Pharaoh*

this part of the narrative is normally treated separately from the Exodus story and labeled the *conquest narrative* (see chapter 20).

Act I: Yahweh to the Rescue (Exodus 1:1—15:21)

The first part of the Exodus story picks up where the patriarchal narratives left off, with Jacob's family living happily in Egypt. But the story quickly turns dark when a new ruler (called by his official title, Pharaoh, not by his name) comes to the throne. Fearful of the rapidly growing numbers of Jacob's descendants (now called *Israelites* or *Hebrews*), Pharaoh compels them to serve as laborers on his building projects. Later he orders that all of their male children be killed at birth, but the Hebrew midwives courageously find ways to avoid obeying this rule.

At this point the spotlight shifts to an unnamed Hebrew woman who tries to preserve her baby boy's life by placing him in a watertight basket in the reeds along the banks of the Nile River. In one of the many ironies pervading the Exodus narrative, the boy is found by the Pharaoh's daughter, who names him Moses and adopts him as her son, then unknowingly hires his mother to care for him. The acts of these unnamed women ultimately prove to be Pharaoh's undoing.

Years later this same Moses, now a young man, is forced to flee from Egypt after killing an Egyptian overseer who was beating one of his fellow Hebrews. He ends up in a territory northeast of Egypt called Midian, where he becomes a shepherd. While herding sheep one day in the desert near a mountain called Horeb, Moses encounters a marvelous sight: a bush that is covered with flames yet not burning up. A voice from the midst of the flames tells Moses that Yahweh has heard the cries of his oppressed people and has chosen Moses to lead them out of Egypt and bring them to the land of Canaan, where their ancestors Abraham, Isaac, and Jacob had once lived. Moses protests that he is not fit for the job and insists that no one will follow him. Yahweh overcomes his objections by performing several miracles that he promises to repeat later to convince the Hebrew people to accept Moses. He also refers obliquely to other miracles that he will do to motivate the Egyptian Pharaoh to let his people go. When Moses protests that he is a poor speaker, Yahweh sends his brother, Aaron, to help him with the mission.

Emboldened by Yahweh's promise, Moses goes first to the Hebrew leaders and then to Pharaoh. At first he meets with failure on both fronts: Pharaoh refuses his demand to let the Hebrew people go and makes their work even harder, which in turn leads the Hebrews to reject him as well. Moses is understandably disheartened by this experience. But Yahweh reassures him that his power will win the day. From here the story depicts

Fig. 18.4. Andrea Previtali, *Crossing of the Red Sea*

a series of ten mighty plagues that Yahweh sends upon Egypt in an effort to motivate Pharaoh to let his people go. In most cases the plagues are preceded by a scene in which Moses asks Pharaoh to let the Hebrews leave Egypt and warns of a dreadful divine punishment if he refuses. Many of the judgments that Yahweh inflicts sound bizarre to a modern reader, including turning the Nile River into blood; filling the land with swarms of frogs, gnats, and flies; and blotting out the sun with darkness for three days. Others represent more extreme versions of ordinary natural disasters, such as diseases that attack the bodies of animals and humans, or hail and locusts that destroy all the crops of Egypt. Most of the plagues involve objects that were commonly associated with Egyptian divinities. In this way Yahweh demonstrates that he is more powerful than any of the Egyptian gods.

Despite these afflictions, Pharaoh refuses to let the Hebrew people go. The narrator attributes Pharaoh's refusal to a hardened heart, though the text vacillates over whether this hardening is produced by Yahweh or by Pharaoh himself. At last Yahweh announces his last and greatest plague—the death of the oldest male child of every human and animal in the land of Egypt. The chil-

dren of the Hebrews will be "passed over" in the coming judgment (as they were in the earlier ones) as long as the adults mark their doorposts with the blood of a sacrificial lamb. This episode is symbolically reenacted each year in the Jewish celebration known as Passover. Following this dreadful event, Pharaoh finally agrees to allow the Hebrew people to leave his country with all their possessions.

But the story is not yet finished. Recognizing that the land cannot bear the loss of so many workers, Pharaoh changes his mind and rides out with his soldiers to bring the Hebrew people back to Egypt. Soon Pharaoh has them trapped against the shore of the Red Sea (or possibly the Sea of Reeds). As the Egyptian army approaches, however, Yahweh blinds them with a thick cloud and sends a powerful wind that splits the sea, creating a dry path for the Hebrews to pass through. When Pharaoh and his soldiers attempt to pursue them, the sea comes crashing down on them and all are killed. The first act of the Exodus story ends on a note of exuberant joy as the Hebrews celebrate Yahweh's mighty victory over their former oppressors.

been laced with yeast to make it rise. (The use of **unleavened bread**—a flat bread made without yeast—in the Jewish Passover ceremony recalls this detail of the story.) It is therefore no surprise that once the initial joy of their escape had passed, they began to grumble about the lack of food and water in the desert. This is the first of many episodes in which the people complain against Yahweh (and Moses) for bringing them out into the desert to die. Most of the stories follow a similar pattern: the people complain to Moses; Moses reports their complaints to Yahweh; Yahweh tells Moses what he is going to do; and Yahweh acts to address the situation. (Incidentally, conversations between Moses and the deity are considered entirely normal throughout the Exodus narrative.) In each case Yahweh provides what the people need, though he often complains about their attitude.

At the heart of this second act of the Exodus narrative lies the story of the giving of the Torah at Mount Sinai, (called Horeb earlier in the narrative) (Exodus 19:1—33:6). Three months after leaving Egypt, Moses leads the people to the site where he had first met Yahweh in the

Act II: The Great Test (Exodus 15:22—Numbers 14:45)

According to Exodus 12:39, the Hebrew people left Egypt so suddenly that they had no time to gather the food they would need for their trip to Canaan. All that they took with them was bread made from dough that had not yet

Fig. 18.5. Cosimo Rosselli, *Tables of the Law with the Golden Calf*

burning bush. This time he climbs the mountain to talk with Yahweh, who informs him that he wishes to speak to him from the mountain in front of the entire people so that they will know for certain that Yahweh is with him. In preparation for this event, the people are to cleanse themselves and engage in two days of purification so that Yahweh can appear among them. If they do not, Yahweh's holy presence will destroy them.

On the appointed day, the top of the mountain is covered with fire and smoke and the air resounds with the peals of trumpets and thunder. At last a voice booms forth from the mountain, uttering the words that have come to be known as the Ten Commandments (see chapter 24). The people are so overwhelmed with fear upon hearing Yahweh's voice that they insist that Yahweh should speak to Moses alone. So Moses goes up the mountain to receive the words of Yahweh. Soon he returns with a long list of laws that Yahweh has given him to direct their social and religious conduct (Exodus 20:22—23:33). The people agree to implement Yahweh's laws and engage in a covenant-making ceremony to formalize their commitment. Then Moses returns to the mountain for another forty days, where he receives a long list of additional regulations that spell out how and where Yahweh desires to be worshipped (Exodus 25:1—31:18).

After a while the people decide that Moses is not coming back, so they ask Aaron, Moses' brother, to make them a god to lead them in his absence. Aaron fashions a golden statue of a bull calf to represent Yahweh (Exodus 32:4), and the people engage in a religious festival in honor of the calf deity. (Bulls were a common symbol of power in the ancient Near East and often served as visible representations of a particular god.) Upon seeing this, Yahweh orders Moses to return to the people and put a stop to this violation of his honor before he destroys them in his anger. When Moses arrives and sees what is going on, he smashes the stone tablets upon which Yahweh had written the Ten Commandments and orders his associates, the Levites, to go on a killing spree that leaves three thousand people dead (Exodus 32:25-29). Then Yahweh orders them to leave his holy mountain (Exodus 33:1). Only after much cajoling does Moses succeed in convincing Yahweh to accompany them to the land of Canaan. Before

they depart from Mount Sinai, Yahweh gives Moses another copy of the Ten Commandments to carry with him, along with instructions for building an elaborate tent (called the tent of meeting or the **tabernacle**) with special furnishings where Yahweh will meet with them as they travel.

At this point the flow of the narrative is disrupted by a long series of laws and regulations that Yahweh is said to have given to Moses at various times marked only by vague statements like "Yahweh spoke to Moses." (For more on these laws, see chapters 23 and 24.) The laws that Yahweh supposedly dictated during this period appear in the book of Leviticus. Apparently the narrator imagined these laws being given during an extended stay at the foot of Mount Sinai, since the book begins with Yahweh speaking to Moses from the tent of meeting about the proper methods of sacrifice and ends with the statement, "These are the commandments that the LORD gave to Moses for the people of Israel on Mount Sinai" (Leviticus 27:34).

The plotline reemerges in the book of Numbers. The book begins with a long discussion of the logistics of moving more than six hundred thousand men and their families through the desert (Numbers 1:46; 2:42). Not until chapter 10 do the people actually leave Mount Sinai and set out for Canaan. The trip has hardly begun before the people once again start to complain. At first the complaints center on food, but they promptly escalate into direct challenges to Moses' authority as leader. This time Yahweh is less patient than before. Upon hearing their complaints, Yahweh afflicts them with repeated bouts of sickness (Numbers 11:33; 12:10; 14:37; 16:46) and sends fire upon their camp (Numbers 11:1; 16:35). Yahweh's actions result in thousands of deaths.

The low point of the narrative comes in Numbers 13–14, where the people finally come close enough to Canaan to send in spies to survey the land. As with the story of the golden calf, the attention that is lavished on this episode underlines its importance to the narrative. Of the twelve spies who are sent to examine what lies before them, ten bring back pessimistic reports about powerful giants and fortified cities that can never be defeated. The other two insist that the power of Yahweh is sufficient to enable them to overcome these obstacles and conquer the land. As might be anticipated, the people believe the pessimistic reports and decide to choose another leader and return to Egypt. At this point Yahweh has had enough. He appears above the sacred tent in dazzling light and tells Moses to get out of the way so that he can destroy the people. Once again Moses convinces him to refrain. This time, however, Yahweh declares that because they failed to trust him at this key moment, the present generation will never see the land of Canaan. They will wander in the desert for forty years until they die. But Yahweh has not abandoned his people. Despite his anger with them, he promises that he will eventually bring their children back to the land of their ancestors.

Once the people realize the seriousness of their situation, they acknowledge that they were wrong and they begin to make plans to invade the land as the two spies had encouraged them to do. Moses warns them to refrain from the attack because Yahweh will not go with them into battle, but they go anyway and are soundly defeated. The second act of the Exodus story ends on a heavy note of despair.

EXERCISE 38

Read the story of the golden calf (Exodus 32:1—34:10) and the story of the spies (Numbers 13:1—14:45). Note the similar ways in which Yahweh, Moses, and the people are depicted in the two passages. How do these depictions compare with what you saw in the earlier chapters of the Exodus story?

Act III: The Final Advance (Numbers 15:1—Deuteronomy 34:12)

The final act of the Exodus story begins on the same note of testing as the second act. In fact, one could just as easily end the second act with Numbers 17 (or even Numbers 20:13) as with Numbers 14. This time, however, it is Moses who is tested and fails.

Throughout the entire Exodus story, Moses' loyalty to Yahweh has been tested again and again, and each time he has come through unscathed. In fact, Moses comes across as more reasonable and self-controlled than

Fig. 18.6. Palma Giovane, *The Brazen Serpent* (see Numbers 21:3-9)

Yahweh on several occasions. This pattern continues in Numbers 16–17, where more than 250 leaders of the community rise up to challenge Moses' authority over the people. Once again Yahweh threatens to destroy the

Fig. 18.7. Jacopo Tintoretto, *Moses Striking the Rock*

entire people, and once again Moses intercedes with Yahweh to limit his judgment to the men who had sought to overthrow Moses. This time the earth opens up and swallows the challengers and their families.

When the people complain to Moses and Aaron about what Yahweh has done, Yahweh sends a plague upon the camp that kills nearly fifteen thousand people. Then he sets up an ordeal to put an end to all of these rivalries for leadership. Twelve sticks are placed in the sacred tent overnight, one for each of the twelve tribes of Israel. Aaron's name is written on the stick denoting his tribal ancestor, Levi. By the morning, Aaron's stick has sprouted buds, blossomed, and produced ripe fruit! This miraculous event is taken as a sign that Yahweh's favor rests on

the family of Aaron (and by extension on his brother, Moses), and the stick is preserved as proof.

Just when it looks like Moses is secure, however, he suffers a tragic fall. When the people complain once again about the lack of water in the desert, Moses goes to Yahweh for help with the problem. This time Yahweh tells Moses to take up Aaron's stick that had budded (as a sign of authority?) and speak to a nearby rock, and water would come gushing forth from it. Instead of following Yahweh's instructions to the letter, Moses strikes the rock twice with the stick while rebuking the people in words that seem to suggest that it is he and Aaron who are providing the water, not Yahweh (Numbers 20:10). Yahweh's judgment is swift: despite their long and faithful service, neither Moses nor Aaron will be allowed to enter the land of Canaan. Nothing is said about their response, though Aaron dies soon afterward.

From here the plot begins to move upward as the people start advancing toward Canaan. (Presumably the former generation has died off by now, but the narrator never mentions this vital fact.) The narrative includes two more episodes of testing that result in divine punishment (Numbers 21:4-9 and 25:1-9), but most of the stories are positive in nature, including several that show the Hebrews winning military victories against nations that stand in their way. The longest such story tells how the king of Moab, on the eastern side of the Dead Sea, hired a professional prophet named Balaam to place a curse on the Hebrews so that his people would be able to defeat them (Numbers 22–24). Much to the king's dismay, Yahweh intervenes to prevent Balaam from pronouncing anything but blessings upon his people. Among other things, Balaam's blessings point ahead to the many victories that the Hebrews will win under the rule of an unnamed king who will one day arise to lead the people of Israel (Numbers 24:7-9, 17-19).

The ending of the Exodus story is anticlimactic. Most of the final scenes serve to prepare the people (and the reader) for the next phase in the narrative, the conquest of Canaan (see chapter 20). Moses passes the baton of leadership to his assistant Joshua; plans are made for the division of the land after it is conquered; rules of inheritance are clarified; and warnings are issued about the dangers of following the social and religious customs of the residents of Canaan.

The story concludes with a book-length speech given by Moses to the people just before they enter the land. This speech occupies the entire book of Deuteronomy. After reviewing and commenting on some of the key events that had transpired since the people left Mount Sinai, Moses proceeds to remind them of the laws that Yahweh gave to their parents in the desert. The legal material in these chapters actually differs in many respects from the material presented in the earlier episodes of the Exodus narrative, but the speech describes it as a simple restatement. (For more on this point, see chapter 19.) Throughout the speech, Moses issues warnings and predictions about things that will occur once the people have settled in the land of Canaan.

After he finishes his speech, Yahweh allows Moses to climb one of the mountains that overlooks the land of Canaan so that he can see from a distance the land that he has been trying to reach for more than forty years but will never be allowed to enter. Soon afterward, Moses dies at the age of 120 years. Thus, the Exodus narrative ends on a bittersweet note, with a crucial phase in the story of the Hebrew people coming to a close and a new one ready to begin.

Fig. 18.8. The view from Mt. Nebo, where Moses is said to have viewed the Promised Land before dying (Deuteronomy 31:1-4).

EXERCISE 39

Read the story of Balaam in Numbers 22–24. Why do you think this story receives such an extended treatment in the Exodus narrative? What are some of the messages that it conveys?

HISTORICAL CONSIDERATIONS

What are we to make of this narrative? Is it history or legend, or perhaps some combination of the two? For the people who compiled the Hebrew Bible, the answer was clear: the story recounted the sequence of events by which their ancestors became a free people united under the laws of Torah, much as stories about the Revolutionary War explain how the American colonists gained their freedom from foreign rule and framed their own Constitution. The story of the exodus from Egypt is celebrated in poems and songs throughout the Hebrew Bible, and the books of the prophets refer repeatedly to this narrative when offering criticism or encouragement to their people in a later era. Nothing in the Hebrew Bible suggests that the authors or editors thought of the Exodus story as a fictional or mythical account. Whenever they refer to the story, they seem to presuppose that something like this really happened.

Contemporary scholars, on the other hand, have arrived at widely differing judgments concerning the historicity of the Exodus narrative. Conservative scholars, whether Jewish or Christian, view the story as a generally reliable account of actual events. Many acknowledge that there are problems here and there with the narrative, but their overall attitude of trust in the Bible leads them to accept the story as it stands. Maximalists tend to agree that there is a historical core to the narrative, but they insist that the events upon which the story is based have become so encrusted with layers of myth and legend that it is difficult to know what really happened. Using the tools of historical scholarship, they seek to uncover the facts that might have given rise to the present version of the story. Minimalists, by contrast, believe that there is little or no historical content in the story. In their view, the Exodus story is a piece of religious fiction created to give a mythical sense of identity to a group of people

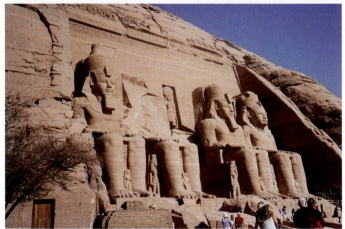

Fig. 18.9. (top) An Egyptian tomb painting (fifteen century B.C.E.) shows men working on a building project; (bottom) the temple of Pharaoh Ramses II at Abu Simbel, Egypt, marked by four giant seated images of the Pharaoh.

from diverse backgrounds who lived in Palestine during the Persian period or later.

How can scholars come to such differing conclusions about such an important biblical story? As with the patriarchal narratives, a number of factors contribute to their varied evaluations of the material. The most important of these factors are the shortage of outside material by which to test the story (external evidence); the difficulty of dating the materials on which the narrative appears to be based (internal evidence); and the heavy supernatural coloring of the story.

External Evidence

Scholars who believe that the Exodus story is rooted in real events disagree about what actually happened and when the events took place. The biblical account contains no dates, and Egyptian records make no mention of any of the events depicted in the Exodus narrative, so scholars are left to piece together bits of information from various sources in their efforts to figure out the most likely time frame for the Exodus story. An Egyptian inscription called the Merneptah Stela, written around 1210 B.C.E., identifies Israel as one of several people groups in Canaan that had been defeated by Pharaoh's armies. This implies that the Exodus story, if rooted in history, would have had to occur sometime before 1210 B.C.E. Fixing a more precise date is difficult due to a lack of evidence. One biblical passage (1 Kings 6:1) sets the date of the Exodus at 480 years prior to the fourth year of King Solomon's reign, or 1446 B.C.E. But virtually all scholars agree that the Exodus story does not fit what we know about conditions in Egypt in the mid-fifteenth century B.C.E., so the date given by this passage appears to be faulty.

The most popular theory associates the story of the Hebrews' forced labor in Egypt with the massive building campaigns of a Pharaoh named Ramses II, who ruled from 1279 to 1212 B.C.E. Ramses is known to have employed foreign workers (mostly prisoners of war) in his projects, and many of his construction projects took place in the Nile delta region where the Bible says the Hebrew people lived. If this association is correct, the events underlying the Exodus story would have taken place sometime in the thirteenth century B.C.E. The story of Moses, whose name is clearly Egyptian, being taken into Pharaoh's palace as a child also fits well into this period, since there is evidence of children from Canaan and other areas living in the royal court during this time.

Scholars also debate the geography of the Exodus. Those who believe that the story of the miraculous parting of the Red Sea reflects memories of a real his-

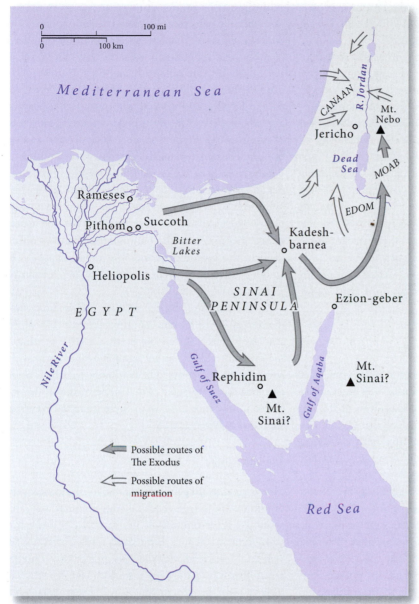

Fig. 18.10. Scholars have proposed different routes for the Exodus and the migration into Canaan of groups who became part of Israel.

unclear: the biblical text could be rendered either "Red Sea" or "Sea of Reeds." The main body of the Red Sea is too far south to suit the narrative, so most of the scholarly proposals have focused on smaller bodies of water on the eastern border of Egypt where some sort of natural disturbance (winds, tides, earthquakes, or other phenomena) might have caused a body of water to recede for a time while a group of people passed through.

The route followed by the Hebrews as they traveled from Egypt to Canaan is also a matter of debate. The narrative gives the names of numerous sites where the people are supposed to have passed by or camped, but few of these places are known today. Even the location of Mount Sinai is uncertain. Several sites have been suggested, but the evidence for all of them is many centuries later than the supposed time of the Exodus. Surface surveys of the region have turned up no evidence that such a large number of people (six hundred thousand men and their families according to Exodus 12:37) camped for forty years in the desert. In an area where a single Bedouin encampment can leave marks for centuries, the absence of any signs of major habitation along any of the proposed routes presents a serious problem for the historicity of the narrative. This has led many Exodus supporters to suggest that the narrative is based on a story of a much smaller group of people who traveled fairly rapidly from Egypt to Canaan and

torical event have proposed several sites where it might have taken place. The Hebrew Bible gives the names of three nearby towns (Exodus 14:2, 9), but their locations are uncertain. The identity of the body of water is also then settled for a time at one of the desert oases such as Kadesh-Barnea (Numbers 13:26; 20:1, 14-16), where evidence of habitation is more common.

On the whole, the best that can be said about the external evidence is that it is ambiguous. Some aspects of the story seem to fit with what we know about Egypt and Canaan in the thirteenth century B.C.E., and there is inscriptional evidence that a group named Israel was present in Canaan by the end of this period. But the lack of any reference to Moses or the Exodus event in the Egyptian records and the absence of any physical evidence for a period of wandering in the desert pose serious problems for the biblical narrative as it stands. These omissions are serious enough to lead many scholars to the view that the Exodus story is a fictional creation of an Israelite storyteller who knew enough about Egypt and the desert to forge a credible setting for his tale. Others continue to believe that there is at least some historical basis to the narrative.

Internal Evidence

As we will see in chapter 22, the Torah is a composite text that was constructed out of earlier oral and written materials. Since the Exodus story spans four of the five books of the Torah, scholars recognize that it, too, was compiled from earlier sources. Unfortunately, the process by which this happened is shrouded in mystery. Scholars have developed a variety of methods for identifying the presence of earlier sources in the Torah, but their efforts to date these materials and retrace the stages of composition have proven less reliable. Scholars disagree about the nature and extent of the sources and whether they were preserved in oral or written form. They also differ over how to date the sources and when they were put together. Some believe that the present text is the result of a long process of collection and revision carried out over many centuries by a series of unknown editors. Others believe that the Torah was formed into a coherent work fairly late in Israel's history (that is, during or after the Exile).

These disagreements have serious implications for the historicity of the Exodus narrative. If the Torah (including its narrative content) was compiled gradually over time,

or if some of its sources were written down at an early date, then the basic story line could be fairly ancient. This does not guarantee that the narrative is historically accurate, but scholars generally presume that older texts are more likely to be reliable than later ones. If on the other hand the first extended narrative of the Exodus event was created by an editor working a thousand or more years after the supposed date of the Exodus, then the likelihood of historical reliability is small. A later written account could still be based on reliable oral and written traditions, but the chances of foreign elements creeping into the stories and new stories being created over time are very high under this scenario. In addition, the editor would have had to rely heavily on his imagination to link the materials together into a continuous narrative and to create the dialogue that gives these stories their timeless appeal. The amount of factual content preserved in such a narrative would probably be fairly low.

In the end, the absence of clear information about the history of the Exodus narrative makes it difficult for scholars to reach agreement about the relative value of the internal evidence as an argument for or against the reliability of the stories. The one point on which nearly everyone seems to agree is that none of the stories was placed into writing close to the time when the events are supposed to have occurred.

The God Factor

Even more than the patriarchal narratives, the Exodus story overflows with the presence of the supernatural. Yahweh is a primary actor throughout the narrative, and much of what occurs in the story is the direct result of divine intervention. Moses talks with the deity as if he were a human acquaintance, and the legal material in the Torah is said to have been dictated to Moses by Yahweh. Events that modern people would regard as miracles play a vital role in the narrative; in fact, they happen so often that they lose their shock value. Some of the miracles could be viewed as extreme versions of natural phenomena that are known to occur in the region where the story takes place, such as the swarms of gnats and locusts that Yahweh sends against Egypt (Exodus 8:16-18; 10:13-15) or the appearance of flocks of quail near the seashore for food (Numbers 11:31-32). Many, however, involve events that are fundamentally supernatural in character, such as the simultaneous deaths of all of the firstborn children and animals in Egypt, the bush that glows with fire but is not consumed, and the writing of the Ten Commandments onto stone tablets by the finger of Yahweh (Exodus 31:18).

As we observed in chapter 9, historians do not include "God" as a causal factor when reconstructing events in the past. They can speculate about why people attributed a particular event to divine causality and examine what this tells us about the beliefs of people in the past, but the methods of historiography prohibit them from saying that a deity caused this or that to happen. When a narrative includes references to divine activity, historians have two primary options: to classify the story as a legend that has no basis in historical reality, or to investigate whether the story might be based on actual historical events that were subsequently interpreted as the acts of a deity. Those who take the first approach believe that the supernatural elements are so integral to the Exodus narrative that they cast a shadow of doubt over the historicity of the entire story. Scholars who follow this view claim that efforts to uncover a historical core behind the Exodus story are as useless as trying to locate the land of Oz on a map or investigating the historical basis of the Cinderella story. Historians can legitimately ask when and how such a story might have arisen and what purposes it might have served for the people who preserved it, but they should not waste their time trying to distinguish between history and legend, since the story is a legend from beginning to end.

Scholars who believe that the Exodus story has a historical foundation simply ignore the story's references to divine activity and apply the same methods that they would use with other stories to reconstruct a plausible sequence of events that can be explained by natural or human causes. Some in this group believe that the Exodus story has become so enshrouded in legend that a responsible historian can only affirm the broad outlines of the story, namely, that a group of forced laborers (slaves?) escaped from their oppressive Egyptian overlords through a series of events that they regarded as orchestrated by Yahweh and made their way to the land of Canaan after a trip through the Egyptian desert. Others think that some of the more significant details of the narrative might have a historical basis (for example, the references to Moses as the leader of the group or the route followed by the escapees), even though the present version has been heavily shaped by the art of the storyteller and the faith of the people who preserved the stories. Still others insist that most or all of the stories contain valid recollections of actual historical events. Some in this group would propose alternative explanations for the supernatural elements in the narrative, while others would insist that historians should not in principle reject the possibility of divine activity.

In the end, the pervasive presence of the supernatural casts a cloud over all attempts to determine the historical reliability of the Exodus narrative. Historians are inherently skeptical of stories that speak of miracles and other forms of divine activity because they run counter to the naturalistic explanations required by the historical method. The historical method has no criteria for evaluating claims that a deity was active in a given situation. Historians can explore why the people who composed these stories came to believe that Yahweh was at work in the events of their past, but they cannot determine whether those beliefs are valid. Only believers can make those judgments.

THE RELIGIOUS SIGNIFICANCE OF THE EXODUS STORY

The Exodus story is the most important narrative in the Hebrew Bible. Its centrality is apparent not only from its length, which far surpasses that of any other cycle of stories in the Hebrew Bible, but also from the frequency with which episodes or ideas from the story are mentioned outside of the Torah. Only the creation account rivals the Exodus narrative for the amount of attention that it receives elsewhere in the Hebrew Bible, and most of the references to this story center on Yahweh's role as creator of the heavens and the earth (Job 38:1-38; Psalm 33:6-9; Proverbs 8:22-31; Isaiah 51:12-16). Allusions to other parts of the story are uncommon: Adam's name appears only twice in the Hebrew Bible outside of Genesis 1–3, and Eve's not at all.

The patriarchs are also named fairly often outside the Torah, but the range of material covered by these references is narrow. The only episode that receives repeated attention is the scene in which Yahweh establishes the covenant with Abraham and his descendants. Some of the personal names from the ancestral narratives (Jacob/Israel, Esau, Jacob's twelve sons) are used elsewhere to identify people who are alleged to be their descendants, but references to particular stories in which these characters appear are few and brief. Sarah, Rachel, Leah, and Ishmael are mentioned only once or twice outside the Torah, and Hagar and Rebekah not at all.

The Exodus story, by contrast, is cited literally hundreds of times outside the Torah. Most of the attention centers on Yahweh's rescue of his people from Egypt and the reception of the Torah at Mount Sinai, but other episodes are mentioned here and there as well. The sheer breadth of the references suggests that the Exodus narrative was well known in ancient Palestine, whether as a unified epic like Homer's *Iliad* or as a series of loosely related tales like the Hindu *Mahābhārata*. At a minimum we can be sure that the story was important to the final editors of the Hebrew Bible.

Whatever we conclude about the historical reliability of the Exodus narrative, it is important to keep in mind that the story was not written simply to preserve a record of the past. The presence of so many direct and indirect references to the Exodus story in the Hebrew Bible indicates that the narrative played a crucial role in defining and maintaining the religious worldview and practices of at least some of the residents of ancient Palestine. Apparently the people who told and retold these stories viewed the Exodus narrative as a paradigm for their own relationship with Yahweh. A review of the principal themes in the present version of the Exodus story together with an examination of how the story is used elsewhere in the Hebrew Bible can give us a fairly good sense of what these people thought was important about the Exodus story and how they used it to guide their lives.

1. *Celebrating the greatness of Yahweh.* Virtually all of the references to the Exodus story in the Hebrew Bible lay special emphasis on the character of Yahweh. This is not surprising, since the story claims that it was through the Exodus that the Israelites came to know and understand the character of their deity. Of course, this was not their first introduction to Yahweh: the text calls him "the god of your fathers" (Exodus 3:6, 13-16; 4:5) and "the god of the Hebrews" (Exodus 3:18; 5:3; 7:16), and his decision to rescue them from Egypt is grounded in his covenant with their ancestors Abraham, Isaac, and Jacob (Exodus 2:24; 3:6-8; 6:3-8). But the narrative contains a number of verses that insist that the Israelites came to know Yahweh through the events of the Exodus in a manner that transcended all previous revelations of his character (Exodus 3:13-15; 6:3-5; 24:9-11; 33:17—34:7). At a minimum this suggests that the people who cherished these stories regarded them as a fruitful source of information about the nature of their deity.

The portrait of Yahweh that emerges from the Exodus story is similar to what we find elsewhere in the Hebrew Bible (see chapter 12). Features that receive special attention include Yahweh's awesome power over the world of nature and humans; his deep and abiding concern for his covenant people; his unfailing commitment to act in a righteous manner; his patience with the failings of his people; and his utter holiness. The Exodus story also contains some less attractive glimpses into Yahweh's character that are often overlooked by later interpreters. Included here are episodes in which Yahweh comes across as petty, irritable, unfair, cruel, and intolerant. The reason these aspects of Yahweh's behavior are commonly ignored is obvious: they do not coincide with the view of God that is held by most Jews and Christians today. The fact that these images were included in the Torah suggests that a more complex image of the deity was either deeply embedded in the ancient traditions or important to the people who compiled the present version of the story.

2. *Defining the identity of the people of Israel.* Every nation or people group needs a story that explains why they regard themselves as a single people, distinct from those around them. Such stories do more than define who counts as a member of the group; they also help to create a sense of unity and loyalty among the various individuals and subgroups that make up the group. The

Exodus story served this purpose for a group of people in ancient Palestine. The ancestral narratives were important for explaining where they came from, but the ancestors were still little more than an extended family when they went down to Egypt. By the time they left, they had become so numerous that they needed some sort of authority structure beyond the family to regulate their lives together. They had become a people.

Implicit in the Exodus story is the claim that the identity of this people is to be found not in a centralized government or other societal structures, but in the laws of Torah. Of course, the narrative depicts Moses, and later Joshua, as strong leaders, and the Torah clearly presupposes the existence of institutions like courts and (in the book of Deuteronomy) a king. But the Exodus story insists that Yahweh's people are united by more than a common set of societal and governmental institutions. Yahweh is their ruler, and his laws are their constitution. As long as they obey Yahweh's laws, they will remain under his care as his special covenant people. Obedience to the Torah will also set them apart from the people around them, thus helping them to preserve their distinctive identity. Disobedience, on the other hand, will lead to conquest and exile, events that threaten their continued existence as a people.

Whether this message had a more precise significance depends on when it arose. If themes like these were already embedded in the Exodus tradition during the time of the monarchy, they might have functioned as implicit criticisms of a growing tendency to rely on centralized governments and royal authority as the basis for national identity in Israel and/or Judah. More likely, however, the message reflects conditions during or after the Exile, when the governmental and societal institutions of the monarchy no longer existed and the identity of those who had survived the Babylonian onslaught was in need of reconstruction.

3. *Motivating proper forms of conduct.* The Exodus narrative is filled with stories of people who serve as models of proper and improper behavior. The narrator's opinion of the characters' conduct is usually quite obvious, whether it is expressed directly by the mouth of Moses or Yahweh or indirectly by the results of the characters' actions. Stories depicting the punishment of bad behavior

are more common than accounts of good behavior being rewarded. A similar pattern can be observed outside the Torah, where a significant percentage of the references to the Exodus narrative recall episodes of divine punishment. This is especially true in the books of the prophets, where the Exodus story is cited again and again to demonstrate how the people of the prophet's day have failed to live up to their covenant with Yahweh and to remind them of how Yahweh punishes people who persistently or flagrantly flout his will (see chapters 31–35). Apparently the people who preserved these traditions believed that threats were an effective way to motivate people to behave in the desired manner, which of course meant doing what Yahweh said.

The story of the giving of the Torah serves a similar purpose. As we will see in chapter 22, there is ample evidence to indicate that the individual laws of Torah were created over a period of centuries in response to the concrete needs of people who used them to guide their lives. The Exodus narrative obscures this process of development and change by insisting that Yahweh revealed the entire body of laws to Moses and Aaron during their forty years of wandering in the desert, primarily when they were camped at the foot of Mount Sinai. This claim effectively elevates the laws of Torah to a place beyond question or challenge. All that humans can do is obey these God-given laws. A similar strategy can be seen in the many passages in which Yahweh describes the rewards and punishments that will come upon those who obey or disobey his laws (Leviticus 26:1-45; Deuteronomy 11:13-28; 28:1-68; 29:18—30:10). Why would anyone willfully choose to disobey such a deity?

Taken together, the stories and speeches in the Exodus narrative provide ample incentive for people to follow the laws of Torah regardless of whether they understand or agree with everything that the laws require. Such a call for unquestioning obedience would have been useful for socializing children and maintaining discipline among the followers of Yahweh at any time from the monarchy to the postexilic period.

4. *Justifying societal institutions and practices.* The laws that Yahweh is said to have given to Moses at Mount Sinai contain a blueprint for society that both justifies and critiques the social institutions of ancient Israel. The social

vision that lies behind these laws will be discussed in chapter 24. The narrative also contains a number of episodes that seek to explain particular aspects of the social and religious life of the people who produced the texts. The most obvious example is the feast of Passover, which seems to have originated as an agricultural festival but was later associated with the story of the Hebrews' sudden departure from Egypt when the death angel killed all of the firstborn sons of the Egyptians and spared the sons of the Hebrews. Linking this festival to such an important narrative not only gave it a lofty origin but also made it one of the major religious events on the Hebrew calendar.

Another example can be found in the stories about the tabernacle that the people carried with them during their time of wandering in the desert. The tabernacle was a large, multilayered tent where Yahweh rested whenever the people stopped to camp. Moses also went to this tent when he wanted to speak with the deity. The layout of the tabernacle closely resembles the pattern of the temple in Jerusalem where Yahweh was said to dwell during the period of the monarchy. While the biblical narrative suggests that the Jerusalem temple was modeled on the Mosaic tabernacle, many critical scholars believe that the opposite was the case: the description of the tabernacle was based on what the authors knew about the Temple in Jerusalem (see chapter 28). According to this view, the tabernacle is a literary fiction designed to lend a sense of antiquity to the Jerusalem Temple in order to reinforce its claim to be the central site for the worship of Yahweh. Such a story would have been highly useful to the political and religious leaders of Judah who periodically sought to elevate the Jerusalem temple above the many local shrines where people in the countryside preferred to express their devotion to Yahweh (see chapter 27).

Yet another example concerns the question of who could serve as priests of Yahweh. A number of passages outside the Exodus story suggest that priestly duties were carried out by a variety of people in ancient Israel, including a group called the Levites (depicted in the Exodus story as the priests' assistants), the king, and in some cases the head of a household (see chapters 26–28). Two stories in the book of Numbers, reinforced by a number of legal passages, seek to counter this practice by limiting the priesthood to a particular group of families and dis-

suading others from challenging their claim to the office. In Numbers 16–17, a group of 250 tribal leaders come before Moses and contest the restriction of priestly duties to Moses and Aaron (16:10, 40). Yahweh responds by destroying all of the leaders of the rebellion. To forestall future challenges, Yahweh then uses a miraculous sign to indicate that Aaron's descendants alone are to come before him as priests (17:8-10). In a later story, the priestly line is narrowed further to the descendants of Aaron's son Phinehas, who demonstrated his devotion to Yahweh by executing a couple who were engaged in inappropriate sexual activity (Numbers 25). These stories, together with similar verses in the legal sections of the Torah, gave divine approval to a particular family's claims to the priesthood while discouraging potential challengers. It is no accident that the priests who served in the Jerusalem temple claimed to be descended from Aaron and Phinehas. The claim that Yahweh had chosen their family alone to serve as his priests clearly reinforced their efforts to centralize the worship of Yahweh in the Jerusalem temple.

CONCLUSION

The Exodus story is the most important narrative in the Hebrew Bible. Both its length and the frequency with which it is mentioned in other books testify to the value that people placed on this tradition. While the present version was composed fairly late in the history of Israel, there is ample reason to think that earlier versions of many of the stories were passed on orally for some time before they were written down.

Since the Exodus narrative is mentioned often outside the Torah, we can develop a fairly clear picture of what people thought was important about these stories and the role that they played in the social and religious lives of the people who preserved them. The Exodus story presents a paradigmatic vision of the past, present, and future of the people of Israel. This vision is fundamentally religious, centering on Israel's collective relationship with a deity named Yahweh whom the story claims rescued their ancestors from the oppressive rule of the Egyptians. This same deity gave their ancestors a series of instructions about how their society should be ordered and how they should live as individuals. Their future fate as a people depended on how faithfully they complied with these instructions.

Of course, not everyone accepted this vision. Some resisted its exclusive focus on Yahweh, while others held differing ideas about how their society should be organized or the proper standards for individual and social conduct. But the basic story of how Yahweh acted to rescue their ancestors from oppression in Egypt seems to have been widely known and celebrated among those who acknowledged Yahweh as their primary deity. In this way the Exodus story provided a common sense of identity for the followers of Yahweh even when they disagreed about the practical implications of their faith.

EXERCISE 40

Read the following passages that contain references to the Exodus story. As you read, make note of (a) which elements of the Exodus narrative are explicitly mentioned and (b) what kinds of messages or lessons are derived from the narrative.

- Deuteronomy 7:17-26
- Nehemiah 9:6-37
- Psalm 78:12-55
- Psalm 135:1-14
- Ezekiel 20:1-38

Fig. 19.1. Assyrian warriors scale the walls of Lachish. The Assyrian king Ashurbanipal decorated his palace in Ninevah with bronze reliefs depicting his victory.

chapter 19

The Deuteronomistic Narrative:
Overview

The LORD said to Moses, "Soon you will lie down with your ancestors. Then this people will begin to prostitute themselves to the foreign gods in their midst, the gods of the land into which they are going; they will forsake me, breaking my covenant that I have made with them. My anger will be kindled against them in that day. I will forsake them and hide my face from them; they will become easy prey, and many terrible troubles will come upon them. In that day they will say, 'Have not these troubles come upon us because our God is not in our midst?' On that day I will surely hide my face on account of all the evil they have done by turning to other gods." (Deuteronomy 31:16-18)

Then the Israelites did what was evil in the sight of the LORD and worshiped the Baals; and they abandoned the LORD [Yahweh], the God of their ancestors, who had brought them out of the land of Egypt; they followed other gods, from among the gods of the peoples who were all around them, and bowed down to them; and they provoked the LORD to anger. They abandoned the LORD, and worshiped Baal and the Astartes. So the anger of the LORD was kindled against Israel, and he gave them over to plunderers who plundered them, and he sold them into the power of their enemies all around, so that they could no longer withstand their enemies. Whenever they marched out, the hand of the LORD was against them to bring misfortune, as the LORD had warned them and sworn to them; and they were in great distress. (Judges 2:11-15)

This occurred because the people of Israel had sinned against the LORD their God, who had brought them up out of the land of Egypt from under the hand of Pharaoh king of Egypt. They had worshiped other gods and walked in the customs of the nations whom the LORD drove out before the people of Israel, and in the customs that the kings of Israel had introduced…. Therefore the LORD was very angry with Israel and removed them out of his sight; none was left but the tribe of Judah alone…. The LORD rejected all the descendants of Israel; he punished them and gave them into the hand of plunderers, until he had banished them from his presence. (2 Kings 17:7-8, 18, 20)

In the previous chapter we left the Hebrew people standing on the banks of the Jordan River ready to cross into the land of Canaan. According to the narrative, this is the land that Yahweh had promised to their ancestors centuries earlier when he entered into a covenant with Abraham, Isaac, and Jacob (Deuteronomy 30:20; 34:4; compare Genesis 15:18-21; 26:4; 28:13-14; Exodus 3:16-17; Numbers 32:11-12).

The story of what happened to the people after they entered the land is told in the books that Jews call the *Latter Prophets* (Joshua, Judges, Samuel, and Kings) and Christians label the *Historical Books* (Joshua, Judges, Ruth, 1 Samuel, 2 Samuel, 1 Kings, 2 Kings). A broad overview of the story line of these books was presented in chapter 8. Scholars disagree about how much of this material should be regarded as historical, but the narrative covers nearly seven centuries in the life of the Hebrew people, from the thirteenth-century B.C.E. invasion of Canaan by Joshua's forces to the sixth-century B.C.E. conquest of Judah by the Babylonians.

The plot of this story is too long and complex and the characters too numerous to examine in any detail in an introductory textbook. Even a cursory review will require two chapters. The present chapter will explore how and when this extended narrative came into existence and the purposes that it may have served in the lives of the people who produced it. Special attention will be given to the many similarities between this narrative and the book of Deuteronomy, the last book of the Torah. The study will continue in chapter 20 with a closer look at the individual books that make up the narrative. In this chapter we will examine the ongoing debates over the historical reliability of these books and their religious message.

THE STORY BEHIND THE STORY

The books of Joshua, Judges, Samuel, and Kings tell the story of the rise and fall of the Hebrew people in the land of Palestine. The plot is a classic tragedy: it begins with the children of the Exodus generation invading and conquering the land where Abraham and his family had once lived and ends centuries later with their descendants being conquered by invaders from the north and forcibly removed from their land. The story line flows fairly smoothly from book to book, suggesting that the entire narrative was composed or edited as a single unit. (The book of Ruth interrupts the flow of the story in Christian Bibles, but it was placed in its present position long after the other books were completed and will therefore be discussed in chapter 21.) The continuity of the story line suggests that the books were put together by someone who was skilled at crafting large-scale narratives. But who did it, and why?

As with most stories from the ancient world, the people who composed and edited this epic narrative did not sign their work or spell out their intent. But the story contains enough clues to give us a rough idea of their identity and purposes. We can presume that the authors and/or editors were members of the elite class of ancient

Israel and/or Judah, since they were the only ones who would have been able to read and write. This explains the attention that is given to the actions of kings and other high officials throughout the narrative. Scholars also agree that the final stages of composition and editing occurred during or after the Exile, since the plotline ends soon after the people of Judah are deported to Babylon. A similar date must be presumed for the final editing of the Torah narratives, since the book of Joshua picks up precisely where the book of Deuteronomy (the last book of the Torah) leaves off.

What might have motivated someone at this late date in Israel's history to compose such a sweeping narrative? The novelty of this kind of literary exercise is commonly overlooked by modern readers, who view history books as a standard part of every people's cultural heritage. In the ancient world, however, people did not normally think of time advancing in a straight line as we do today. Instead, they envisioned time as revolving in a cyclical pattern like the seasons. The idea of history as a continuous narrative of events leading up to the present day was simply not part of the ordinary person's mind-set. Stories about the past tended to focus on people or episodes that were regarded as especially significant by those who told about them. Bards recited sagas about great heroes or events from a golden era; families told stories about their distant ancestors; scribes or engravers praised the accomplishments of a king's reign. Royal **annals** might list the events of several kings' reigns in succession, but this is a far cry from the kind of continuous and unified narrative of past events that we find in the Hebrew Bible.

The earliest parallel to the biblical story of Israel's past appears in the writings of the Greek author Herodotus (ca. 484–432 B.C.E.), who is sometimes called the Father of History. Herodotus wrote about the intense and bloody war between the Greeks and Persians that ended around the time he was born. He consulted a variety of sources to collect data for his narrative, including both oral interviews and written materials. His purpose in writing, however, was not simply to record the past. The Greeks had just become involved in another war, and Herodotus seems to have hoped that they might learn something from a look at their prior experience. Whether the authors and editors of the biblical narrative might have been influenced by Herodotus

Fig. 19.2. An ancient bust of the Greek historian Herodotus.

and his successors is impossible to say, since scholars disagree about when the biblical story line was put together. But it seems clear that they shared Herodotus's overarching concern to describe a traumatic event in the recent past in a way that would speak to the needs of their contemporaries.

The fact that the biblical narrative of Israel's past ends during the Exile is no accident. The events surrounding the forced deportation of the elites of Judah to Babylonia were deeply distressing to those who survived the experience. Not only had they lost friends and family members in the war, but the defeat of their armies, the devastation of their land, and especially the destruction of the Jerusalem temple raised fundamental questions about the viability of their religious faith and their future as a people. This was especially true for those who honored Yahweh as the principal deity and protector of Judah. Where was Yahweh when the Babylonians came? Why had he not led their armies to victory? How could he have allowed his temple to be destroyed? Had he abandoned them in their hour of need? Had he been too weak to resist the gods who aided the Babylonian armies? Could he hear their cries for help now that they were so far from their native land? Similar questions arose when they considered their future. Would they ever be able to go home to Judah? Should they adapt to the ways of the Babylonians, or should they distance themselves from the surrounding culture in an effort to retain their distinctive beliefs, customs, and practices? Should they continue to honor Yahweh as their primary deity, or should they pay tribute to the ever-present gods of the Babylonians, following the standard practice of people who traveled from place to place in the ancient Near East?

Fig. 19.3. During the Exile, the people of Judah would have been surrounded by symbols of the power of Babylonia such as these images from the Ishtar Gate, the primary entrance into the city of Babylon.

As they struggled to answer these questions, some of the literate followers of Yahweh seem to have concluded that the answer lay in a careful review of their past. In their view, the victory of the Babylonians over Judah did not mean that Yahweh had turned his back on his people or that he had been too weak to defend them against the gods of the Babylonians. In fact, the opposite was true: the entire sequence of events, along with the earlier conquest of the northern kingdom by the Assyrians, had been orchestrated by Yahweh in order to discipline his people for their disloyalty to him, especially their worship of other deities.

This interpretation of the past offered two important benefits. First, it enabled the followers of Yahweh to hold on to their faith, including their belief in Israel's special covenant relationship with Yahweh, despite the painful events of their recent past. By describing Yahweh's active involvement in his people's history, the story suggested to the readers that their present circumstances also had meaning and purpose. Second, the narrative implied a course of action for the future. If Yahweh had brought them to this point because they and their ancestors had been unfaithful to him, then the exiles should make a serious effort to discover what Yahweh wanted from them in the present and commit themselves to serving him alone. In practical terms, this meant collecting and editing the laws of Torah and the sayings of the prophets and striving to create a community that relied on Yahweh's words to guide their individual and collective lives.

The social and religious importance of this narrative cannot be overstated. Prior to the Exile, only a minority of the population of Judah would have thought that there was anything wrong with honoring other gods alongside or instead of Yahweh. Even fewer would have accepted the claim that Yahweh required his people to carefully obey a set of rules designed to regulate their social and religious behavior (see chapter 22). In the aftermath of the Exile, however, it appears that a group of devoted Yahwists saw an opportunity to win others over to their side by showing how their viewpoint could make sense of all that had happened to them as a people. The result of their labors (after later editing) is the narrative that fills the books of Joshua through Kings.

Though they might have had access to a certain amount of historical material (see chapter 20), the people who prepared this narrative were not writing simply to record events in the past. Their goal was to convince others to accept their beliefs and embrace their fundamentally conservative vision for maintaining their people's identity in the midst of a foreign culture. At the heart of this vision lay a call to live by a set of laws that the authors claimed Yahweh had given to their ancestors and to keep away from Babylonian influences. Apparently they succeeded, since the Jewish community in Babylonia became one of the primary centers for the study and interpretation of the laws of Torah in the ensuing centuries.

READING BETWEEN THE LINES

The people who composed this narrative were clearly thoughtful and creative individuals. The presence of supernatural elements and frequent dialogue distinguishes their accounts from modern works of history, but there are still many sections that read like straightforward, objective descriptions of past events. Upon closer study, however, it becomes obvious that the narrative is both selective and biased. The selectivity of the story is evident in the way it focuses on military and political leaders to the exclusion of ordinary people. Selectivity is also apparent in the varied amounts of attention that the story gives to people who occupy similar positions—some are honored with multiple chapters while others are dismissed in a few verses. The biased nature of the narrative can be seen in the way the societal leaders are described and judged. Few are depicted in neutral terms; virtually all are judged positively or negatively by the narrator.

The special attention given to societal leaders throughout the story is more than a by-product of the authors' upper-class background. It grows out of their conviction that Yahweh judges his people according to the conduct of their leaders. This belief shapes the manner in which the characters are portrayed. From beginning to end, the leaders of Israel and Judah are judged on the basis of their religious behavior. Comparatively little is said about their social, economic, or political accomplishments. What matters to the authors of this story is whether a leader was sufficiently devoted to Yahweh and his temple in Jerusalem. This viewpoint can be seen clearly in the editorial comments that accompany their depictions of the kings of Israel and Judah. Those whose deeds show a suitable degree of devotion to Yahweh are judged to be good kings whose actions caused the deity to shower blessings upon the nation. Those who honored other gods or condoned worship at religious centers other than the Jerusalem temple are regarded as bad kings whose deeds stirred up Yahweh's displeasure and eventually led to the downfall of the nation.

Sometimes this interpretive principle leads to curious interpretations of history. On the one hand, King Solomon, who built the temple of Yahweh in Jerusalem and was by all accounts one of the most effective rulers in the history of Israel, is ultimately condemned by the narrator for joining his foreign wives in the worship of other deities besides Yahweh. The partition of Israel into two kingdoms following Solomon's death is interpreted as Yahweh's judgment against this religious failure (1 Kings 11:1-13). By contrast, Josiah, a king who died at a young age in an unnecessary battle that left Judah under the control of Egypt, receives more praise than any king since David for leading a religious revival among his people and destroying all of the religious shrines outside Jerusalem (2 Kings 22:1-2; 23:25-35). In fact, Josiah is portrayed in such a favorable light that many scholars believe that an earlier version of the narrative might have ended with his reign.

Of course, the people who formulated this narrative were not so naïve or biased as to suppose that all of the blame for the fall of Israel and Judah lay with their leaders. At key points in the story, they include summary statements that accuse the people as a whole of religious violations that served to stir up Yahweh's anger against his people. As with the rulers, the violations center on the worship of other gods, an act that the authors regard as disloyalty to Yahweh.

> Then the Israelites did what was evil in the sight of the LORD and worshiped the Baals; and they abandoned the LORD [Yahweh], the God of their ancestors, who had brought them out of the land of Egypt; they followed other gods, from among the gods of the peoples who were all around them, and bowed down to them; and they provoked the LORD to anger. They abandoned the LORD, and worshiped Baal and the Astartes. *(Judges 2:11-13)*

> They went after false idols and became false; they followed the nations that were around them, concerning whom the LORD had commanded them that they should not do as they did. They rejected all the commandments of the LORD their God and made for themselves cast images of two calves; they made a sacred pole, worshiped all the host of heaven, and

served Baal. They made their sons and their daughters pass through fire; they used divination and augury; and they sold themselves to do evil in the sight of the LORD, provoking him to anger. *(2 Kings 17:15-17)*

Thus says the LORD, I will indeed bring disaster on this place and on its inhabitants—all the words of the book that

Fig. 19.4. (top) Mattia Preti, *Solomon Offering Incense to Pagan Gods*; (bottom) William Hole, *King Josiah Cleansing the Land of Idols*

the king of Judah has read. Because they have abandoned me and have made offerings to other gods, so that they have provoked me to anger with all the work of their hands, therefore my wrath will be kindled against this place, and it will not be quenched. *(2 Kings 22:16-17)*

The punishment for these violations is the same in every case: raids or attacks by armed enemies. Clearly the authors intended to draw a parallel between events in their nation's past and the conquest of Judah by the Babylonians.

So the anger of the LORD was kindled against Israel, and he gave them over to plunderers who plundered them, and he sold them into the power of their enemies all around, so that they could no longer withstand their enemies. Whenever they marched out, the hand of the LORD was against them to bring misfortune, as the LORD had warned them and sworn to them; and they were in great distress. *(Judges 2:14-15)*

The LORD rejected all the descendants of Israel; he punished them and gave them into the hand of plunderers, until he had banished them from his presence. *(2 Kings 17:20)*

The LORD said, "I will remove Judah also out of my sight, as I have removed Israel; and I will reject this city that I have chosen, Jerusalem, and the house of which I said, My name shall be there." *(2 Kings 23:27)*

In summary, all of the evidence suggests that the artful narrative that fills the books of Joshua through Kings was not composed as an objective record of past events, but rather as an extended religious tract that used materials from the past to deliver a message to the present. The narrative is dominated by a concern to make sense of the Babylonians' conquest of Judah and the ensuing transfer of the survivors to Babylonia through the lens of a Yahwistic faith. In the eyes of the people who crafted this story, it was Yahweh, not the military might or deities of Babylonia, who had caused these unhappy events. Yahweh had sent foreign armies against his people because he was angry over their persistent disloyalty to him, as evidenced primarily in their worship of other gods. This problem,

which involved both the rulers and the ordinary people of Israel and Judah, had been brewing for centuries while Yahweh had borne patiently with them and held his wrath in check. Eventually, however, the violations became so persistent and so blatant that Yahweh was forced to act to bring his covenant people back into line.

EXERCISE 41

Read the following passages from the Hebrew Bible and note how they link the social, economic, and political events of Israel and Judah with the religious actions of their rulers and/or people. Who receives the credit or blame in each case? What do they do that incurs Yahweh's favor or judgment?

• Judges 2:6-23
• 2 Samuel 24:1-25
• 2 Kings 17:1-23
• 2 Kings 18:5-8, 17-25; 19:1-7, 35-37

THE INFLUENCE OF DEUTERONOMY

How did the people who crafted this story come to believe that the Babylonian conquest of Judah and the ensuing exile represented Yahweh's punishment for the sins of their ancestors? One possible influence is the sayings of the preexilic prophets (see chapters 32–33). Prophets were individuals who claimed that Yahweh had given them messages (via dreams, visions, voices, and so forth) to deliver to the people of Israel or Judah. Many of their sayings were eventually collected and edited to form the books known as the Latter Prophets in the Hebrew Bible.

Messages of judgment are common among the sayings of the prophets who lived before the Exile. Several of them are said to have announced that Yahweh would send foreign armies against his people unless they turned from their sinful ways and devoted themselves fully to Yahweh. The similarity between these sayings and the viewpoint of the Historical Books has suggested to many scholars that the latter books were written or edited by people who had come to believe that the earlier prophets, who were mostly rejected in their own lifetimes, had in fact spoken the truth. Their intention was to write a prophetic history of Israel and Judah that would show their peers how the words of the prophets had eventually come to pass.

Partial support for this theory can be found in the way prophets are portrayed in the narrative books of the Hebrew Bible. Prophets appear at key points in the story to pronounce words of judgment—or occasionally hope—concerning the future of Israel or Judah. Prophets who challenge the religious failings of the kings of Israel and Judah are consistently depicted in a positive light. The messages attributed to the prophets also agree closely with the viewpoint of the narrator. All of these points suggest that the people who composed the narrative viewed the prophets in a favorable light. The presence of such a sympathetic attitude toward the prophets represents a marked shift from the preexilic period, when the literate elites seem to have regarded the prophets as cranks and social misfits (see chapters 32–33).

The problem with this explanation is that the sayings of the prophets were not compiled into books and placed into circulation until at least the time of the Exile, and there is no way to be sure how widely their words were known prior to this time. Some scholars even think that the prophetic sayings that speak of Yahweh judging his people by sending foreign armies against them were created by the people who composed the narratives and are not part of the original prophetic message. Moreover, prophets do not play the dominant role in the biblical story line that we might have expected if the sayings of the prophets had been a dominant influence on the thinking of the authors. In fact, there is no mention of any of the prophets whose books predict the judgment of Judah by the hand of the Babylonians (Micah, Jeremiah, Habakkuk, Ezekiel), apart from a brief statement attributed to Isaiah over a hundred years before the event took place (2 Kings 20:16-18). If the authors were seeking to vindicate the words of the prophets, they certainly could have made their intentions more obvious.

A more likely source for the authors' ideas about the meaning of the Exile is the book of Deuteronomy, the last book of the Torah. Unlike the sayings of the prophets, this book (or at least an early version of it) would have been available to the literate elites for several decades prior

to the Exile, if the story in 2 Kings 22–23 can be trusted. According to this account, young King Josiah (640–609 B.C.E.) sent workers to carry out repairs on the temple of Yahweh in Jerusalem. During the course of the repairs, the high priest reported that he had found a "book of the law" in the temple (2 Kings 23:8). Upon hearing this book read aloud, Josiah began tearing his clothes and lamenting the judgment that he concluded would soon come upon the people of Judah because they had failed to obey the laws prescribed in this book during the decades when his father and grandfather had promoted the worship of other deities. In an effort to avert that judgment, Josiah gathered the people together and solemnly renewed their covenant with Yahweh. Then he proceeded to suppress and destroy every place of worship in the land except for the temple in Jerusalem—even sites that were devoted to Yahweh. Once this was finished, he led the people of Judah in a massive celebration of the Passover festival.

EXERCISE 42

Read the story of Josiah and his family in 2 Kings 21:1—23:35 and answer the following questions.

(a) What did Manasseh (Josiah's grandfather) do that was so displeasing to Yahweh?

(b) What does Josiah fear in 2 Kings 22:11-13? Why? Is he right?

(c) How does the description of Josiah's actions in 2 Kings 23 compare with those of Manasseh in 2 Kings 21?

(d) How does Yahweh respond to Josiah's actions?

While the identity of the "book of the law" that sparked this religious revival is not specified in the text, scholars have long noted that the actions that Josiah is said to have taken after reading it correspond precisely with the prescriptions of the book of Deuteronomy. One of the central points of Deuteronomy is that there is only one place where Yahweh is to be worshipped.

When you cross over the Jordan and live in the land that the LORD your God is allotting to you, and when he gives you rest from your enemies all around so that you live in safety, then you shall bring everything that I command you to the place that the LORD your God will choose as a dwelling for his name: your burnt offerings and your sacrifices, your tithes and your donations, and all your choice votive gifts that you vow to the LORD. And you shall rejoice before the LORD your God, you together with your sons and your daughters, your male and female slaves, and the Levites who reside in your towns (since they have no allotment or inheritance with you).

Take care that you do not offer your burnt offerings at any place you happen to see. But only at the place that the LORD will choose in one of your tribes—there you shall offer your burnt offerings and there you shall do everything I command you. *(Deuteronomy 12:10-14)*

This restriction of sacrificial worship to a single site is accompanied by repeated commands to destroy all places of worship except for "the place that the LORD your God will choose as a dwelling for his name" (Deuteronomy 12:11, later understood as a reference to the temple in Jerusalem).

When the LORD your God brings you into the land that you are about to enter and occupy, and he clears away many nations before you . . . this is how you must deal with them: break down their altars, smash their pillars, hew down their sacred poles, and burn their idols with fire. *(Deuteronomy 7:1, 5)*

The images of their gods you shall burn with fire. Do not covet the silver or the gold that is on them and take it for yourself, because you could be ensnared by it; for it is abhorrent to the LORD your God. *(Deuteronomy 7:25)*

You must demolish completely all the places where the nations whom you are about to dispossess served their gods, on the mountain heights, on the hills, and under every leafy tree. Break down their altars, smash their pillars, burn their sacred poles with fire, and hew down the idols of their gods, and thus blot out their name from their places. You shall not worship the LORD your God in such ways. But you shall

seek the place that the LORD your God will choose out of all your tribes as his habitation to put his name there. *(Deuteronomy 12:2-5)*

The language of these verses from Deuteronomy is echoed throughout 2 Kings 23, which describes Josiah's vigorous efforts to eliminate all of the shrines, images, and other objects of worship from the territories of Israel and Judah except for the temple in Jerusalem. Many of Josiah's actions target practices specifically prohibited in the book of Deuteronomy, including worshipping at high places throughout the land (2 Kings 23:5, 8, 9, 13, 15, 19, 20; see Deuteronomy 33:29); using carved objects (pillars, poles, stones, and so forth) as aids to worship (2 Kings 23:14; see Deuteronomy 7:5; 12:3; 16:21-22); making offerings to the heavenly bodies (2 Kings 23:5, 11; see Deuteronomy 4:19-20; 17:2-5); engaging in ritual prostitution (2 Kings 23:7; see Deuteronomy 23:18); and consulting the dead (2 Kings 23:24; see Deuteronomy 18:11). In a similar way, much of the language used to describe Josiah's covenant renewal ceremony in 2 Kings 23:1-3 is taken from Deuteronomy 30:1-10, a text that explains what the people of Israel should do when they decide to return to Yahweh after a period of divine judgment.

In short, the language of 2 Kings 22–23 seems to imply that the "book of the law" that Josiah used as the basis for his religious revival was the book of Deuteronomy, or at least an early version of it. If this is correct, then the people who compiled the biblical narrative many decades later would have been familiar with Deuteronomy and might have been influenced by its ideas.

The significance of this observation becomes clear when we note the ideological similarities between the two sets of material. At the heart of the book of Deuteronomy is the belief that the people of Israel stand in a covenant relationship with Yahweh that requires them to be devoted to Yahweh alone and to avoid all other gods. If they are faithful to this covenant, Yahweh will reward them with material blessings, granting them success in all that they do and protecting them from foreign armies. If they violate the terms of the covenant, on the other hand, Yahweh will rain a series of curses upon them. Scholars call this belief system **Deuteronomic theology**. The ultimate curse is for Yahweh to remove his protective presence and allow them to be conquered by invading armies and carried away to a foreign land.

> When you have had children and children's children, and become complacent in the land, if you act corruptly by making an idol in the form of anything, thus doing what is evil in the sight of the LORD your God, and provoking him to anger, I call heaven and earth to witness against you today that you will soon utterly perish from the land that you are crossing the Jordan to occupy; you will not live long on it, but will be utterly destroyed. The LORD will scatter you among the peoples; only a few of you will be left among the nations where the LORD will lead you. *(Deuteronomy 4:25-27)*

> If you do forget the LORD your God and follow other gods to serve and worship them, I solemnly warn you today that you shall surely perish. Like the nations that the LORD is destroying before you, so shall you perish, because you would not obey the voice of the LORD your God. *(Deuteronomy 8:19-20)*

> The LORD will cause you to be defeated before your enemies; you shall go out against them one way and flee before them seven ways. You shall become an object of horror to all the kingdoms of the earth. Your corpses shall be food for every bird of the air and animal of the earth, and there shall be no one to frighten them away. . . . The LORD will scatter you among all peoples, from one end of the earth to the other; and there you shall serve other gods, of wood and stone, which neither you nor your ancestors have known. Among those nations you shall find no ease, no resting place for the sole of your foot. There the LORD will give you a trembling heart, failing eyes, and a languishing spirit. Your life shall hang in doubt before you; night and day you shall be in dread, with no assurance of your life. *(Deuteronomy 28:25-26, 64-66)*

This is precisely what the authors of the biblical narrative saw happening in their own day: Judah's defeat and exile at the hands of the Babylonians were the direct result of their ancestors' disloyalty to their covenant with Yahweh. The close ideological and linguistic ties between the book of Deuteronomy and the narrative books of the Hebrew Bible have led scholars to coin the term

Deuteronomistic History to refer to the story that begins in the book of Deuteronomy and continues through the book of Kings. (The related term **Deuteronomistic narrative** is preferred in this book, since it leaves open the question of the historicity of the materials.) Most scholars think that the influence actually moved in both directions: the authors of the narrative books not only relied on Deuteronomy for the ideological framework of their story but also edited the narrative sections of Deuteronomy (and perhaps other parts as well) to tie the book more closely to their own work. In the process, they incorporated the book of Deuteronomy into a narrative that would ultimately run from the creation of the world in Genesis to the coming of the Exile in the book of Kings.

WHY DEUTERONOMY?

This lengthy historical excursion has left one question unanswered: How could the author(s) of Deuteronomy have anticipated the kinds of events that would happen centuries later to the nation of Judah? To formulate an answer to this question, we must dig deeper into the history of the book of Deuteronomy. Most scholars believe that the legal sections of the book of Deuteronomy originated in the northern kingdom of Israel and were set down in writing (or edited from earlier texts) by priests who escaped to Judah prior to the devastation of Israel by the Assyrians in 722 B.C.E. and the subsequent deportation of much its population. Those who survived this disaster were faced with the same kinds of questions that troubled the exiles of Judah many decades later. As they struggled to understand what had happened to their nation, some of the survivors of Israel recalled the age-old tradition that Yahweh had established a special covenant with their ancestors that required faithfulness to a set of God-given laws. The historical origins of this idea can no longer be determined with certainty (see chapter 14), but the prophets of the eighth century B.C.E. (Amos and Hosea in the north, Isaiah and Micah in the south) seem to presuppose its existence, so it did not originate with the people who crafted Deuteronomy.

Scholars have often observed that the book of Deuteronomy seems to follow the common pattern of an ancient Near Eastern treaty between states of unequal power. Some have suggested that these treaties may have provided the model for the biblical notion of a covenant between Yahweh and his people. Like other ancient treaties, the book of Deuteronomy spells out the obligations of the lesser partner (Israel) under the covenant and concludes with a list of curses, or divine punishments, that the deity is supposed to impose upon the lesser party if they should fail to live up to the terms of the agreement (Deuteronomy 28:15-68). One of the curses commonly associated with violations of ancient treaties is the withdrawal of protection by the superior covenant partner (and the deity), leaving the lesser party vulnerable to military conquest and exile by foreign armies. No great imagination is required to see how the authors of Deuteronomy might have concluded that the defeat of their armies by the Assyrians was one of the curses of the covenant that Yahweh had imposed upon the people of Israel in return for persistent violations of their covenant with the deity, including their worship of other gods.

Decades later, when the exiled elites of Judah faced a similar situation, some of them apparently turned to the book of Deuteronomy for help in making sense of their sufferings. In Deuteronomy's covenant theology they found an interpretive principle that explained their recent experience as the inevitable result of their failure to live up to the terms of their relationship with Yahweh. As they pursued this line of thought, they began to discern a meaningful pattern in the diverse oral traditions and written records that they had brought with them from Judah. Some of them used these new insights to reframe the story of their past into the epic saga that we now call the Deuteronomistic narrative. This saga became an important tool for communicating to their peers their understanding of what had happened to their nation.

The narrative that they created may have been edited further during the postexilic period, but it was not long before their account of their people's past came to be regarded as the authoritative interpretation of Israel's historical experience. Over time, it became the structural backbone of the community's collection of Scriptures. Because of its position of honor in the biblical canon, Jews and Christians through the centuries have viewed the Deuteronomistic narrative as a reliable account of the history of Israel and Judah. Not until the rise of modern historical scholarship did scholars recognize that the narrative was rooted in a specific theological agenda.

MULTIPLE AUDIENCES

The Deuteronomistic narrative is not the only set of stories in the Hebrew Bible that was written for an audience who lived long after the events that it narrates. As we saw in chapter 4, most of the books that were eventually included in the Hebrew Bible passed through multiple stages of editing before reaching their present form. At each stage in the editing process, the editors labored to make the texts speak more directly to their own day. Sorting out the contributions of the various compilers and editors is a painstaking process requiring keen linguistic and literary skills and a fertile historical imagination, and even the best of scholars disagree on many points.

Yet there is nothing to prevent even a novice reader from learning how to ask the right questions about the historical purposes of the biblical stories. Most contemporary readers know little or nothing about the historical origins of the biblical narratives, so they limit their attention to the surface level or plotline of the stories. Depending on what they believe about the supernatural, they either take the stories at face value as historical accounts or view them as myths or legends to be interpreted in a nonliteral fashion or ignored. What is missing from these approaches is a recognition that the biblical narratives were created to address the questions and concerns of people who lived long after the events that they purport to narrate. When we neglect these later people and their interests, we miss much of the richness and depth of the stories and become preoccupied with questions like whether individual stories are historically accurate or whether they offer lessons that can be applied to the lives of people today.

Many of the biblical narratives are based on historical materials, but they are not fundamentally historical documents. They are religious texts whose full significance cannot be grasped without reference to the audience(s) for which they were created. A sound understanding of the biblical narratives requires that we learn to ask questions not only about the story line but also about the people who told and used the stories. The value of this approach will become apparent in the next chapter when we look at specific episodes from the Deuteronomistic narrative.

CONCLUSION

The creation of the Deuteronomistic narrative was one of the key literary events in the history of ancient Israel, and perhaps in the history of Western civilization. Its vision of a supreme deity who directs the affairs of nations and holds both rulers and ordinary people accountable for their actions has shaped the way Jews and Christians interpret historical events from ancient times to the present.

The central purpose of the Deuteronomistic narrative was to help the defeated exiles of Judah make sense of the suffering and humiliation that they had endured at the hands of the Babylonians. By insisting that Yahweh had in fact orchestrated these events as punishment for their sins, the people who crafted this narrative found a way to integrate their painful experience with their beliefs about Yahweh. Otherwise they might have been tempted to abandon their traditional forms of religion and shift their allegiance to the gods of Babylonia.

At the heart of the narrative was a critique of the past behavior of the people of Israel/Judah and their leaders that included implicit recommendations for their future conduct. These recommendations, which centered on loyalty to Yahweh and obedience to his Torah, were vital to the future development of Judaism. In this way the story of Israel's past came to serve as both a warning and a guide to future generations.

EXERCISE 43

Read the following passages from the Hebrew Bible and summarize what each passage says or implies about the relationship between faithfulness to Yahweh and his covenant and the events of social and political history. What do you think of their position?

- Deuteronomy 28:1-68
- Joshua 23:1-16
- 1 Samuel 12:1-25
- 2 Kings 24:18—25:12
- 2 Chronicles 36:11-21

Fig. 20.1. King Jehu of Israel bows before the Assyrian king Shalmaneser III on a ninth-century B.C.E. column called the Black Obelisk.

CHAPTER 20

The Deuteronomistic Narrative: *Individual Stories*

But Joshua said to the people, "You cannot serve the LORD, for he is a holy God. He is a jealous God; he will not forgive your transgressions or your sins. If you forsake the LORD and serve foreign gods, then he will turn and do you harm, and consume you, after having done you good." And the people said to Joshua, "No, we will serve the LORD!" Then Joshua said to the people, "You are witnesses against yourselves that you have chosen the LORD, to serve him." And they said, "We are witnesses." (Joshua 24:19-22)

And Samuel said to the people, "Do not be afraid; you have done all this evil, yet do not turn aside from following the LORD, but serve the LORD with all your heart; and do not turn aside after useless things that cannot profit or save, for they are useless. For the LORD will not cast away his people, for his great name's sake, because it has pleased the LORD to make you a people for himself. . . . Only fear the LORD, and serve him faithfully with all your heart; for consider what great things he has done for you. But if you still do wickedly, you shall be swept away, both you and your king." (1 Samuel 12:20-22, 24-25)

The LORD said by his servants the prophets, "Because King Manasseh of Judah has committed these abominations, has done things more wicked than all that the Amorites did, who were before him, and has caused Judah also to sin with his idols; therefore thus says the LORD, the God of Israel, I am bringing upon Jerusalem and Judah such evil that the ears of everyone who hears of it will tingle. I will stretch over Jerusalem the measuring line for Samaria, and the plummet for the house of Ahab; I will wipe Jerusalem as one wipes a dish, wiping it and turning it upside down. I will cast off the remnant of my heritage, and give them into the hand of their enemies; they shall become a prey and a spoil to all their enemies, because they have done what is evil in my sight and have provoked me to anger, since the day their ancestors came out of Egypt, even to this day." (2 Kings 21:10-15)

In the previous chapter we examined the historical circumstances under which the stories that make up the so-called Historical Books of the Hebrew Bible (Joshua through Kings) and the book of Deuteronomy were forged together into a coherent narrative. (For an overview of the story line of this narrative, see chapter 8.) In this chapter we will look more closely at some of the issues surrounding the individual books that make up this collection and sample a few of the key stories in each book. Since the bulk of the narrative centers on the

actions of political and religious leaders, special attention will be given to the way in which leadership is defined and evaluated within the various books.

THE BOOK OF JOSHUA

The book of Joshua, though not part of the Torah, serves as the climax and conclusion of the Exodus narrative. In fact, some scholars have argued that the book was originally composed as part of the Exodus story and only later became part of the Deuteronomistic narrative. Whatever its origins, the book was clearly edited at some point in its history to serve as a transition between these two major narrative units of the Hebrew Bible.

The story begins with Yahweh appointing Joshua, Moses' assistant, to succeed Moses as leader of the Israelites after Moses' death, which was narrated at the end of Deuteronomy. The next eleven chapters show the Israelites, assisted by the power of Yahweh, crossing into Canaan from the desert and swiftly conquering virtually all of the kings and cities of the land. From here the story shifts to a detailed account of the division of the conquered territory among the twelve tribes of Israel, a narrative that fills ten chapters. The book concludes with a farewell address by Joshua and a covenant renewal ceremony in which the people dedicate themselves to follow Yahweh alone.

The historicity of this account has been hotly debated among scholars in recent years. Since the Exodus story seems to presuppose a date in the late thirteenth century B.C.E., the battles narrated in the book of Joshua must have taken place in the late thirteenth or early twelfth century B.C.E. if they are indeed historical. This date finds a measure of support in the Merneptah Stela, an Egyptian victory monument that names Israel as one of the people groups living in Canaan around 1210 B.C.E., though the stela says nothing about who these people were or how they got there.

On the other hand, excavations of many of the sites that Joshua is said to have conquered raise serious problems for the biblical account. A handful of sites show signs of destruction and resettlement around this time, but the excavations offer few clues as to the identity of the conquerors. Canaanite cities sometimes fought

MERNEPTAH STELA

Translation of the final part of the Merneptah Stela where Israel is mentioned:

The (foreign) chieftains lie prostrate, saying "Peace."
No one lifts his head among the Nine Bows.
Libya is captured, while Hatti is pacified.
Canaan is plundered, Ashkelon is carried off, and Gezer is captured.
Yanoam is made into non-existence;
Israel is wasted, its seed is not;
And Hurru is become a widow because of Egypt.
All lands united themselves in peace.
Those who went about are subdued by the king of Upper and Lower Egypt . . . Merneptah.[1]

Fig. 20.2. The Merneptah Stela, which commemorates Pharaoh Merneptah's victories over various neighboring peoples, mentions "Israel" as one of the people groups that resided in the land of Canaan.

among themselves, and Egyptian armies also passed through this area from time to time. Most of the sites either show no signs of disruption or were uninhabited during this era, including the cities of Jericho and Ai, which play a vital role in the conquest narrative. Supporters of the biblical story argue that battles for control of a town or city would not necessarily leave any lasting marks in the archaeological record. But one would still expect to see signs of cultural change if the cities had been taken over by people from outside the region. Most archaeologists have concluded that such evidence is lacking.

Fig. 20.3. Archaeological excavations of the city of Jericho indicate that the site was probably unoccupied when, according to the book of Joshua, Yahweh caused the city walls to fall down.

On the other hand, the archaeological evidence does show a rather sudden and sharp increase in the number of small, unfortified settlements in the hill country of Canaan during the thirteenth and twelfth centuries B.C.E. Nearly all were built on sites that were previously uninhabited, and most are located far from Canaanite cities. The growth of the population during this period (a fourfold increase over roughly a century) suggests that the new residents migrated from outside the area. But scholars disagree about their place of origin. Some argue that they were nomads who moved here from the fringes of the desert and adopted a more settled agricultural lifestyle. Others see them as poor peasants who were seeking refuge from the turmoil and oppression that characterized life in the Canaanite cities during this period. Still others believe that people may have converged on this sparsely populated region from a variety of directions around the same time, perhaps including a group that claimed to have been liberated from forced labor in Egypt. Whatever their origins, the residents of these new hill towns appear to be the people who later came to be known as Israelites.

Apart from conservative scholars who are committed to defending the biblical stories, contemporary historians seem to be divided between maximalists, who think that the conquest story is a legendary exaggeration of a less dramatic historical event (the settlement of a small group of Egyptian refugees in the hill country of Canaan), and minimalists, who view the entire narrative as a fictional account composed centuries later to provide a common mythical history for a group of people from diverse backgrounds who were being encouraged to think of themselves as a single people called Israel. The fact that the book has been edited to fit into the Deuteronomistic narrative shows that it did not reach its present form until at least the time of King Josiah, and probably not until the exilic period, that is, six to seven centuries later than the events that the book claims to narrate. This fact, together with the archaeological problems noted earlier, suggests that the conquest story may tell us more about the concerns and interests of the exilic period than about the events of Joshua's day, though some scholars believe that the tribal boundaries spelled out in the latter half of the book might go back to ancient times. Little imagination is required to see how the image of Yahweh leading his people from victory to victory in battles against the followers of other gods would have proved inspiring to the Babylonian exiles who had experienced little but defeat and disgrace at the hands of pagan powers.

EXERCISE 44

Read Joshua 2:1—6:27 and 23:1—24:33 and answer the following questions about each passage.

(a) What parts of the Exodus story are mentioned in these passages? What parts are left out? What does this say about the viewpoint of the people who told the story?

(b) Summarize what both passages say about the relationship between Yahweh and Israel. How does this compare with what you learned in chapter 19 about the viewpoint of the Deuteronomistic narrative?

(c) What is Joshua like as a leader in the two passages?

THE BOOK OF JUDGES

The book of Judges explains what happened to the Hebrew people between the time they entered Canaan and the establishment of the monarchy. The book is framed around the stories of twelve charismatic military leaders called *judges* whom Yahweh raised up from time to time to rescue the Israelites from foreign oppression. The term *judge* refers to the fact that some of these individuals are described as judging the people of Israel for the remainder of their lives after their victories. Most likely this entailed serving as arbiters of disputes, since there was no formal court system during this time.

If we add up the number of years that Israel is said to have been oppressed and the number of years that each judge is said to have exercised authority after freeing the people from oppression, the total comes to exactly four hundred years. A comparison with other records shows that this is historically impossible: there is no way to fit a period of this length into the years between the Exodus event (late thirteenth century B.C.E.) and the beginning of the monarchy (middle of the eleventh century B.C.E.). Either the events and characters are entirely fictional or the editors have created an artificial (and inac-

curate) chronological framework to tie together a series of traditional stories about ancient Israelite heroes and leaders who lived prior to the monarchy. The choice of a round number for the duration of the period (four hundred years) and the inclusion of twelve judges (a symbolic number in the Hebrew Bible, as in the "twelve tribes of Israel") add to the impression that the chronological framework is a later addition to the story.

But why create such a framework at all? The answer can be found in several verses that reflect the viewpoint of the Deuteronomistic editors. The key passage is Judges 2:10-23, which spells out the pattern that dominates the rest of the book: the people abandon Yahweh and worship other gods; Yahweh hands them over to foreign rulers; Yahweh pities his people and sends a judge to rescue them; the people return to their old ways; and the cycle starts over again. The language of this passage is echoed in the introductions to the individual stories. Again and again we read, "The Israelites did what was evil in the sight of the LORD, and the LORD gave them into the hand of [a foreign people or ruler]" (Judges 3:7-8, 12; 4:1-2; 6:1; 10:6-8; 13:1). This is followed by a statement saying that the Israelites cried out to Yahweh for help and Yahweh sent them a deliverer (Judges 3:9, 15; 4:3; 6:7-8; 10:15-16).

As the plot unfolds, however, the critique extends beyond the misbehavior of the people to include the judges themselves. Several of the later judges are depicted in less than flattering terms (Gideon, Jephthah, Samson). By the end of the book, the narrative has made its point that the system of intermittent judges is incapable of ensuring the peace and stability of the people, whether against outsiders or against one another. For this, a monarchy is needed (Judges 17:6; 21:25). In this way, the artfully structured story line of the book of Judges prepares the way for the establishment of the monarchy in the book of Samuel.

So what are we to think about the historical reliability of the individual stories? As we saw in chapter 9, conservative scholars defend the historicity of the characters and events depicted in the Hebrew Bible, while minimalist scholars regard the entire Deuteronomistic narrative as a fictional composition designed to create a heroic past for a group of people who lived a millennium or more after the events that it purports to describe. Maximalist scholars are more diverse in their views, but most seem to think that the stories are rooted in historical reality, even if their present form owes much to the creativity of the storyteller's art. In fact, many would argue that the poem in Judges 5 celebrating Deborah's victory over the king of Hazor is one of the oldest passages in the Hebrew Bible.

Why do maximalists believe that much of the material in the book of Judges is ancient? Some of the evidence is linguistic—the book contains language that many scholars believe is archaic, reflecting an earlier stage in the development of Hebrew. The descriptions of societal institutions and practices in Judges also seem to fit the era before the rise of the monarchy and not later periods. Finally, there are a number of places where Judges stand at odds with other books in the Hebrew Bible, a fact that suggests to many scholars that the editors were working with ancient traditions that they did not feel free to change. Among the many examples that could be cited are conflicts with the book of Joshua over when and how various cities were conquered (Judges 1); differences with other books over the names of the tribes of Israel (Judges 5:13-18); uncritical depictions of people using private shrines and images to worship Yahweh (Judges 17:1-13; compare 8:22-27); and even a story that seems to condone the practice of human sacrifice (Judges 11:32-40).

The process by which these ancient heroic tales were combined into a coherent narrative is difficult to discern. Many of the stories bear the marks of oral storytelling, and some may even have originated among the illiterate masses as a form of religious entertainment. Most contain messages that could be applied to virtually any period in ancient Israel. The book seems to have passed through several stages of editing, with shorter collections being expanded over time until the Deuteronomistic editors added their own characteristic touches and incorporated the book into their epic account of the history of Israel and Judah. Their interpretive comments are subtle and scattered, but their observations were clearly adequate to enlist these traditional narratives into the service of the **Deuteronomic** message.

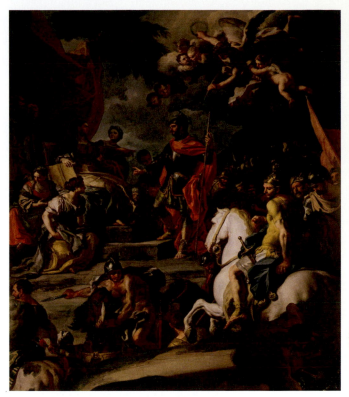

Fig. 20.4. Francesco Solimena, *Barak and Deborah*

EXERCISE 45

Read Judges 6:1—7:25 and 19:1—21:25 and answer the following questions about each passage.

(a) What would you say is the central message of the story? What purposes might this story have served for the people who preserved and used it in ancient Israel?

(b) Both stories contain plot elements that seem strange or even offensive to modern readers. What do you think is the purpose of these odd developments? How do you think they might have been perceived by an ancient audience?

(c) How does each passage depict the leadership of Israel during the Judges period?

THE BOOK(S) OF SAMUEL

The book of Samuel is divided into two parts in Christian Bibles, but it was originally composed as a single book, as can be seen from the way the story flows without interruption from 1 Samuel to 2 Samuel. The book is framed around a series of episodes from the lives of three important leaders of ancient Israel: Samuel, Saul, and David. Together, their lives span roughly a century. Saul and David receive more ink than any other characters in the Hebrew Bible besides Moses, and the story of David is even more intimate and detailed than that of Moses.

Nevertheless, it would be wrong to think of the book of Samuel as a biographical text. As an integral part of the Deuteronomistic narrative, its chief concern is to explore the ups and downs of the people's relationship with Yahweh. At the heart of the book is a concern to describe the process by which the people of Yahweh became a nation ruled by kings who were not always faithful to the will of Yahweh. Along the way, the book continues the implicit critique of national leadership that commenced in the book of Judges. On the one hand, all three of the leaders depicted in the book can boast great accomplishments: Samuel oversees the introduction of the monarchy and installs the first two kings into office; Saul ensures the lasting independence of Israel through his military victories; David forges the people into a unified nation and brings peace by conquering and ruling over all of their neighbors. Yet, on the other hand, all three have tragic flaws that limit their effectiveness: Samuel appoints his corrupt sons to serve as judges in his place; Saul resists following Samuel's instructions and sinks into a paranoia that causes him to chase David, his best military commander, all over the land in an effort to kill him; David abuses his power at the height of his rule and endures rebellion and war for the remainder of his kingship. The message is clear: the monarchy may be an effective military and political system, but placing so much power in the hands of one person leads inevitably to pride, corruption, and divine judgment.

As with the book of Judges, the Deuteronomistic editors inserted statements at key points in the narrative to ensure that their readers recognized and understood their critique of the monarchy. In 1 Samuel 8:1-18, the elders of Israel ask Samuel to appoint a king to lead their armies and rule over them, presumably so that they can escape the insecurity and instability that characterized the existing system of intermittent judges. Yahweh interprets this request as a rejection of his own rule over the people and tells Samuel to describe to the people the heavy burdens that kings will impose upon them and their children. According to this passage, there is something fundamentally wrong with the entire institution of monarchy.

Yet the picture is not entirely negative. Yahweh does accede to their request—in fact, he chooses the first king himself—and a few chapters later we hear Samuel telling the people that Yahweh will bless them and their kings as long as they obey the words of Yahweh. Following the Deuteronomistic pattern, however, Samuel also states that Yahweh will turn against his people if they or their kings refuse to do what he says (1 Samuel 12:13-15, 20-25). This message is quickly underlined when Samuel declares that Yahweh has rejected Saul and his descendants because of Saul's unwillingness to follow his (and Yahweh's) instructions (1 Samuel 13:5-14; 15:10-31). Similar ideas can be seen in the other main passage in the book of Samuel that relates to the establishment of the monarchy (2 Samuel 7:1-17). In this story, Yahweh informs David through a prophet that he intends to preserve David's dynasty forever. Yet Yahweh also threatens to use other people (foreign nations?) to punish David's descendants if they sin against him. By the end of the Deuteronomistic narrative, this is exactly what has happened.

Taken together, these verses suggest that Yahweh stands behind the institution of monarchy despite its obvious potential for abuse, though his treatment of individual kings (and their subjects) depends on the kings' behavior. This is precisely the kind of interpretation that we might expect from a group of religious elites who were trained to respect the monarchy but who felt disempowered and disillusioned by the conduct of their rulers and the ensuing consequences (specifically, the Babylonian exile). Similar views can be seen in the accounts of the later rulers of Israel and Judah in the book of Kings.

What does the presence of a Deuteronomistic viewpoint say about the historicity of the narrative? As usual, conservative scholars defend the accuracy of the narrative while minimalists disparage it. Minimalists argue that there is no evidence outside the Bible to confirm the existence of any of the characters in the book of Samuel, including Samuel, Saul, and David. Their reading of the archaeological materials suggests that there were no organized political centers in Palestine until the ninth century B.C.E. in the case of Israel and the seventh century B.C.E. for Judah. This view received a serious blow in 1993 with the discovery of a ninth-century B.C.E. inscription at Tell Dan in northern Israel that appears to mention the house of David. Maximalist scholars have argued that the minimalists have ignored or misread other parts of the archaeological record as well. In the end, it appears that the archaeological data from the era when Saul and David are supposed to have lived are too skimpy or unclear to lend much support to either position.

On the literary side, careful investigations have convinced a majority of scholars that the Deuteronomistic editors used earlier materials when composing their narrative. Several scholars have pointed to evidence that suggests that two lengthy sections of the book (1 Samuel 16—2 Samuel 5 and 2 Samuel 9–20 plus 1 Kings 1–2) are based on stories that may have been written down during the early years of the monarchy. Others have noted features in the text that suggest that the authors may have had access to the royal chronicles of Israel and

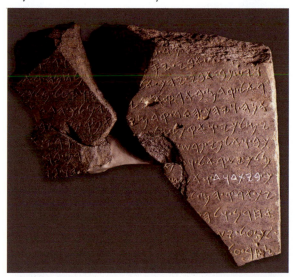

Fig. 20.5. This inscription from Tel Dan in northern Israel appears to provide evidence of the existence of the royal House of David as early as the ninth century B.C.E.

Judah. These arguments are disputed by scholars who view the entire book of Samuel as a work of fiction. Most, however, still believe that the book is rooted in genuine historical memories that have been enhanced by the storyteller's art.

EXERCISE 46

Read 1 Samuel 15:1-35 and 2 Samuel 11:1—12:25 and answer the following questions about each passage.

(a) How do Saul and David resemble one another in the two passages? How do they differ?

(b) What do these passages say about Yahweh and his relationship with the king?

(c) Why do you think the editors chose to include these negative episodes in their story rather than painting the early kings of Israel as perfect heroes and role models for later kings?

THE BOOK(S) OF KINGS

Like Samuel, the book of Kings was originally composed as a single book that was later divided into 1 Kings and 2 Kings. The continuity is even more apparent here than in the book of Samuel, since the break occurs in the middle of a series of stories about the prophet Elijah's interactions with the kings of Israel.

The book begins with the accession of Solomon as David's successor and ends with the people of Judah being taken away to exile in Babylonia, a period of roughly four hundred years. Once the kingdom is divided under Solomon's son Rehoboam in 1 Kings 12, the narrative alternates between stories about the kings of Israel and stories about the kings of Judah until Israel is conquered by the Assyrians in 2 Kings 17. From then on, the story focuses exclusively on the kings of Judah.

The kings are introduced in the order in which they come to the throne, even when this violates the alternating literary structure of the narrative, as when the king of one nation outlives two or more kings from the other nation (as in 2 Kings 15). During the era of the two kingdoms, the reign of each new king is dated by reference to the king of the other nation (for example, "In the twenty-third year of King Joash son of Ahaziah of Judah, Jehoahaz son of Jehu began to reign over Israel in Samaria; he reigned seventeen years"; 2 Kings 13:1). This recurring pattern suggests that the people who compiled the story used as one of their sources a list that coordinated the reigns of the kings of Israel with those of Judah. Similar lists are known from Mesopotamia.

Apart from these few references, the chronology of the narrative is often unclear. The book contains no absolute dating system and gives few details about when most of the events are supposed to have occurred. In addition, some of the numbers pertaining to the duration of the kings' reigns do not add up properly, though it is possible that the Hebrew numbers may have been corrupted through centuries of copying. Whether the people who crafted the story lacked information about the dating of events or were unconcerned about strict chronology is impossible to say.

The book of Kings refers to three other sources that the editors claim to have used in the composition of their narrative: "the book of the annals of the kings of Israel" (mentioned twenty times), "the book of the annals of the kings of Judah" (fifteen times), and "the book of the

Fig. 20.6. (above) This cuneiform tablet from the royal annals of the Assyrian king Tiglath-Pileser I (twelfth to eleventh century B.C.E.) narrates some of the key accomplishments of his reign; (right) this clay prism contains a royal inscription by the Assyrian king Sargon II (eighth century B.C.E.) describing his military victories.

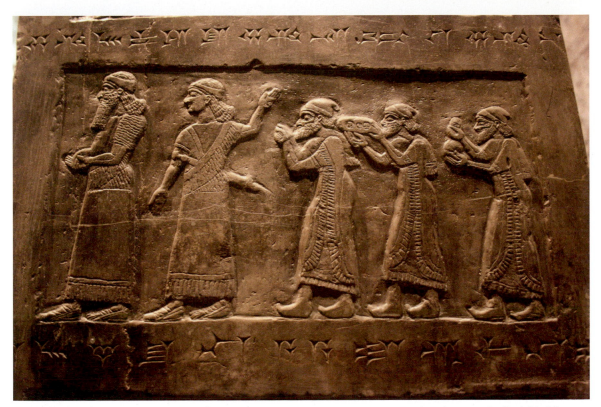

Fig. 20.7. Israelites bring tribute to the Assyrian king Shalmaneser III on a ninth-century B.C.E. column known as the Black Obelisk.

kings of Israel and Judah" (seven times). Most scholars presume that these were official records maintained by royal administrators; similar materials have been found in the surrounding nations. If the editors were in fact able to consult such records, the case for the historical reliability of many of the stories in the book of Kings would be substantially strengthened.

Still, there are problems with this theory. The most obvious is that the royal chronicles of Israel and Judah are unlikely to have been available in Babylonia during the Exile, when the Deuteronomistic narrative was being composed. This fact has led many scholars to suggest that the present book of Kings is based on an earlier edition that was created during the period of the monarchy when official records would have been readily available. Minimalist scholars remain unconvinced by this explanation. As they see it, all of these references to outside sources are fictional literary devices inserted into the narrative to lend credibility to the book.

Further reasons for believing that the book of Kings is based on historically credible sources were cited in chapter 9: references to biblical characters and events in the records of Assyria, Babylonia, and Egypt; accurate reporting of events involving the surrounding nations; archaeological discoveries that seem to agree with portions of the biblical record; and so forth. On the other hand, the book also contains statements that conflict with what we know from other sources. For example, 2 Kings 19:35-36 claims that the Assyrian king Sennacherib lifted his siege of Jerusalem after an angel killed 185,000 of his soldiers in one night. Assyrian records, by contrast, say that Sennacherib withdrew after King Hezekiah agreed to pay a heavy tribute. Many other cases could be cited where the authors embellish their sources with the storyteller's art. This is especially obvious in passages where the narrator claims to report what Yahweh or other people were thinking or feeling in the privacy of their own minds (for example, 1 Kings 3:10; 11:9; 14:22; 2 Kings 5:11,

20; 13:3-4; 20:19). Thus, while there is ample reason to think that the book of Kings includes significant amounts of historical material, we must be careful about making blanket statements about the historicity of the book as a whole. Every story must be evaluated on its own merits.

Even a cursory reading of the book of Kings shows that it does not pretend to offer a balanced, objective account of events in ancient Israel and Judah. As we saw in chapter 19, all of the kings are judged by the standards of the Deuteronomistic editors, with the kings' religious activities taking precedence over all of their other actions. The narrative also gives disproportionate attention to certain kings while virtually ignoring others. The activities of Solomon, David's successor, fill ten chapters of the present text (1 Kings 1:28—11:43), followed by Ahab with six (1 Kings 16:29—22:40), Hezekiah with three (2 Kings 18:1—20:21), and Josiah (2 Kings 22:1—23:20) and Jeroboam (1 Kings 12:1—14:20) with two each. By contrast, the reigns of eight kings are described in the span of two chapters in 1 Kings 15–16, while seven kings fill a single chapter in 2 Kings 15. Not surprisingly, the kings who receive the most ink are the ones whose actions relate most directly to the concerns of the Deuteronomistic editors. Solomon establishes the temple of Yahweh in Jerusalem as required by the book of Deuteronomy; Jeroboam builds two calf shrines at Dan and Bethel in clear violation of the prohibitions of Deuteronomy; Ahab promotes the worship of other gods and winds up on the losing end of a lengthy contest with the prophet Elijah, who upholds the "Yahweh-only" viewpoint found in Deuteronomy; Hezekiah and Josiah lead religious revivals that center on obedience to the provisions of the Deuteronomic code.

In the end, even the kings who are viewed positively in the book of Kings are corrupted by their power, echoing the critical attitude toward the monarchy that we saw in the books of Judges and Samuel. Solomon imposes forced labor on his people and begins to worship other gods under the influence of his foreign wives; Hezekiah shows off his wealth to a delegation from the king of Babylonia and is rebuked by the prophet Isaiah; Josiah leads the armies of Judah into an unnecessary battle and leaves his people under the domination of Egypt. The message is clear: even the best of the kings did things that contributed to the conquest of Judah by the Babylonians. Once again we see how the Deuteronomistic editors selected and shaped their materials to create a story line that would explain how their people ended up in Babylonia.

One final place where the Deuteronomistic viewpoint comes bubbling to the surface is in the attention given to prophets. Stories about the prophet Elijah and his successor, Elisha, fill fifteen chapters of the book of Kings (1 Kings 17—2 Kings 9), where they appear as champions of the true faith of **Yahwism** and opponents of the worship of other gods. Prophets also play a vital role in advancing the plot elsewhere in the book, including Solomon's selection as David's successor (1 Kings 1:1-53); Jeroboam's plot to break away from Solomon's rule (1 Kings 11:29-39); Jehu's revolt against Joram, king of Israel (2 Kings 9:1—10:29); and Hezekiah's perseverance against the Assyrian siege of Jerusalem (2 Kings 18:1—19:37). Scattered throughout the narrative is a series of stories about mostly unnamed prophets who issue predictions about the future (usually words of judgment) that invariably come true (1 Kings 13:16; 14:7-8; 16:1-13; 20:35-43; 22:10-38; 2 Kings 3:9-20), including announcements of the coming exile (1 Kings 14:6-16; 2 Kings 17:13-18; 21:10-15; 22:14-20; 24:1-4). These positive depictions of the prophets represent a marked departure from the attitude of critical disdain that characterized the preexilic era (see chapters 32–33). Perhaps the authors were seeking to rehabilitate the image of the

---

EXERCISE 47

Read 1 Kings 18:1—19:18 and 2 Kings 18:13—20:19 and answer the following questions.

(a) What is the relationship between the prophet and the king in each passage? How might you explain the differences?

(b) What does each passage say about the political and religious leadership of Israel and Judah?

(c) What would you say is the message of each passage?

prophets so that their compatriots would take seriously the words of the prophets that were being compiled into books in their own day.

CONCLUSION

The books of Joshua, Judges, Samuel, and Kings present a continuous story of Israel's past that extends from the conclusion of the Exodus saga to the coming of the Babylonian exile. Scholars disagree about how much historical material these books contain, though most would agree that the level of uncertainty increases the further one goes back in time. To limit one's attention to historical questions, however, is to miss the point of the narrative, since none of these books was written primarily to provide an objective account of the past. Each book is a creative literary work that uses the art of the storyteller to enliven and enrich earlier source material in an effort to communicate a specific theological message to the people of the authors' day.

Though all of the books show signs of repeated editing, the experience of the Babylonian conquest and exile seems to have played a decisive role in shaping them into their present form. Each book aims to show how Yahweh has been at work in the events of Israel's past, even in the suffering that they experienced at the hands of the Assyrians and Babylonians. Their successes as well as their troubles are interpreted as Yahweh's responses to the moral and religious conduct of his people and their leaders. This view of the past is characteristic of the Deuteronomistic editors who were seeking to make sense of the Babylonian exile and to point the way toward a more prosperous and peaceful future.

EXERCISE 48

Read the story of Solomon's dedication of the Jerusalem temple in 1 Kings 8:1-66, paying special attention to the content of his prayer.

(a) What elements of the Deuteronomistic viewpoint can be seen in Solomon's prayer?

(b) What kind of future does Solomon's prayer envision for the people of Israel?

(c) What kind of message does this passage offer to people living during or after the Babylonian exile?

Fig. 21.1. A frieze from the palace of the Persian king Darius shows a group of Persian lancers (sixth century B.C.E.).

Postexilic Narratives

In the first year of King Cyrus of Persia, in fulfillment of the word of the Lord *spoken by Jeremiah, the* Lord *stirred up the spirit of King Cyrus of Persia so that he sent a herald throughout all his kingdom and also declared in a written edict: "Thus says King Cyrus of Persia: The* Lord *[Yahweh], the God of heaven, has given me all the kingdoms of the earth, and he has charged me to build him a house at Jerusalem, which is in Judah. Whoever is among you of all his people, may the* Lord *his God be with him! Let him go up."* 2 Chronicles 36:22-23)

"Now therefore, our God—the great and mighty and awesome God, keeping covenant and steadfast love—do not treat lightly all the hardship that has come upon us, upon our kings, our officials, our priests, our prophets, our ancestors, and all your people. . . . Here we are, slaves to this day—slaves in the land that you gave to our ancestors to enjoy its fruit and its good gifts. Its rich yield goes to the kings whom you have set over us because of our sins; they have power also over our bodies and over our livestock at their pleasure, and we are in great distress." (Nehemiah 9:32, 36-37)

Nebuchadnezzar said to them, "Is it true, O Shadrach, Meshach, and Abednego, that you do not serve my gods and you do not worship the golden statue that I have set up?" . . . Shadrach, Meshach, and Abednego answered the king, "O Nebuchadnezzar, we have no need to present a defense to you in this matter. If our God whom we serve is able to deliver us from the furnace of blazing fire and out of your hand, O king, let him deliver us. But if not, be it known to you, O king, that we will not serve your gods and we will not worship the golden statue that you have set up." (Daniel 3:14, 16-18)

The creation of the Deuteronomistic narrative was a landmark in the literary and religious history of the people of ancient Israel. The fact that it was preserved and used by the postexilic community suggests that its vision of Israel's past was well received by its intended audience. The fact that it was eventually combined with other books to form the grand narrative that became the backbone of the Jewish Scriptures indicates that its message also proved valuable to later generations.

The production of religious narratives did not end, however, on the day when the descendants of the first generation of Babylonian exiles were allowed to return to Palestine. The postexilic period witnessed a flowering of narrative literature within the Yahwistic communities of Judah, where they became the dominant party, as well as in the surrounding nations, where they remained a minority. Some of these narratives gained enough popularity and respect to warrant inclusion in the Hebrew Bible, while others were incorporated into non-Hebrew canons of Scripture (Greek, Latin, Coptic, and Ethiopic) or remained outside the canon altogether. Even the ones that failed to make their way onto anyone's list of canonical texts (including some that were written too late to be considered) must have been valued by at least a segment of the literate population or they would not have been preserved.

This chapter provides a brief orientation to some of the more important narrative texts from the postexilic period. The bulk of the chapter is devoted to books that were eventually included in the Hebrew Bible; others receive more cursory attention. The discussion follows the order in which scholars believe the books were written. Primary attention is given to the historical, literary, and religious questions that have arisen in relation to each book. Sample passages are provided for the major books, but these are not meant to substitute for a reading of the actual texts.

CHRONICLES

Like the books of Samuel and Kings, the book of **Chronicles** was composed as a single work and only later divided into two books. The book is essentially a selective retelling of the narrative of Samuel and Kings from a different angle. As with other books, locating the perspective from which the story is told can help us to grasp the concerns and interests of the people who produced the text.

The book of Chronicles begins with nine chapters of genealogies (lists of family members across several generations) that rely heavily on the earlier narrative books

for their content. The genealogies begin with Adam and eventually subdivide to cover the twelve tribes of Israel. For some tribes, the list of names is short, while others extend as far as the Babylonian exile and beyond. The longest is the genealogy of David's family, which continues for seven generations after the last king of Judah, or well into the postexilic period (1 Chronicles 3:1-24). The list of returning exiles in 1 Chronicles 9 also points to a postexilic date for the book, as does the royal decree in 2 Chronicles 36:22-23 allowing the people of Judah to return to their homeland. Most scholars date the book around 400 B.C.E.

The story line begins in 1 Chronicles 10 with the death of Saul and the rise of David to the kingship. The picture of David in Chronicles differs markedly from the way he is portrayed in 2 Samuel, where the overlap of the two books begins. Most of the stories in 2 Samuel center on the troubles that David experienced as a result of his violation of Bathsheba (2 Samuel 11). The book of Chronicles, by contrast, includes only one story that might reflect negatively on David and his reign (1 Chronicles 21), and even here David ultimately does the right thing. In Chronicles, David is portrayed as a devoted servant of Yahweh who spends his last days making plans for the temple that his son Solomon will build for Yahweh

Fig. 21.2. Luca Giordano, *The Building of the Temple*

in Jerusalem. The description of David's plan for the temple fills several chapters, implying that the temple was a major concern for the people who composed the book of Chronicles. A similar preoccupation can be seen in the description of Solomon's reign, where six of the nine chapters relate to Solomon's construction and dedication of the temple. Like David, Solomon is depicted as an ideal king who is thoroughly committed to Yahweh. Nothing is said about the worship of foreign gods that leads to his downfall and the division of his kingdom in 2 Samuel.

The remainder of the book includes many of the same stories found in Samuel and Kings, but the narrative centers on the southern kingdom of Judah, the land ruled by David's descendants. The northern kingdom is mentioned only when its kings are engaged in alliances or warfare with the kings of Judah. Along the way, Chronicles adds new material about several of the kings of Judah that details their attitudes and actions toward Yahweh and his temple. Some of the kings are depicted more favorably than in the book of Kings, while others are painted in darker colors.

One of the kings who receives a more positive treatment in Chronicles is Abijah, who is portrayed as a bad king in 1 Kings 15:1-8 but whom Chronicles presents as a staunch defender of Yahweh and his temple (2 Chronicles 13:1-22). A different kind of reversal can be seen in the case of Manasseh, who is characterized as the worst of the bad kings in the Deuteronomistic narrative (2 Kings 21:1-18) but who in Chronicles repents of his evil ways and tears down the images of foreign gods that he had set up around Jerusalem, including some that he had placed in the temple (2 Chronicles 33:10-20). Hezekiah similarly receives glowing reviews for removing unclean objects from the temple and restoring the pure worship of Yahweh as prescribed by King David (2 Chronicles 29:1—31:21). Kings who are portrayed more negatively in Chronicles than in Kings include Joash, whom Chronicles shows turning to the worship of other gods after acting earlier in his reign to restore the temple (2 Chronicles 24:1-27; compare 2 Kings 12:1-21), and Azariah (also called Uzziah), whose pride leads him to enter the temple and offer incense to Yahweh, a task reserved for the priests (2 Chronicles 26:16-21; compare 2 Kings 15:1-7). In nearly every case it is the kings' treatment of the Jerusalem temple that determines how they are evaluated in the book of Chronicles.

The historicity of the book of Chronicles has long been debated by scholars. The book refers again and again to outside sources where the reader can learn more about the various kings that it describes: "the records of the seer Samuel," "the records of the prophet Nathan," "the records of the seer Gad," "the prophecy of Ahijah the Shilonite," "the visions of the seer Iddo," "the records of the prophet Shemaiah," "the book of the kings of Judah and Israel," "the annals of Jehu son of Hanani," and so forth. Only one of these sources, "the book of the kings of Judah and Israel" (cited with a slightly different title in Kings), is mentioned elsewhere in the Hebrew Bible. Many scholars believe that the names were created by the author to lend an air of credibility to the account, since it is highly unlikely that so many materials recorded centuries before the Exile would have survived into the postexilic era and then been lost forever after the book of Chronicles was written. In reality, most of the stories in Chronicles seem to have been taken from the books of Samuel and Kings, so its reliability depends heavily on that of the earlier books. But Chronicles also includes materials that do not appear in the earlier books. In these cases it is possible that the authors had access to other historical sources, but each story must be evaluated on its own merits.

Several themes emerge from Chronicles' account of Israel's past. The depiction of David as the ideal king fits well with the postexilic hope, grounded in the words of the earlier prophets, that Yahweh would one day send another king like David to rule over his people with righteousness and compassion (Isaiah 9:6-7; 16:5; Jeremiah 23:5-6; 30:8-9; 33:14-26; Ezekiel 34:22-24; 37:15-28; Amos 9:11-15; Zechariah 12:7-9). The book's emphasis on guarding the purity of the Jerusalem temple also echoes a central concern of the postexilic period, when purity laws and temple worship became more crucial to the religious life of the people of Yahweh (see chapter 23). The consistent focus on the southern kingdom reflects this same mind-set, since the temple of Yahweh was located in the territory of Judah. The role of prophets as messengers who deliver the word of Yahweh is even more visible in Chronicles than in Samuel and Kings, reflecting the growing importance of the prophetic books in the postexilic Yahwistic community.

At the most basic level, however, the message of Chronicles is similar to that of Samuel and Kings: Yahweh blesses and protects his people when they are loyal to his covenant and his temple, and he punishes them when they reject him and follow other gods. In this sense the book remains firmly rooted in the Deuteronomic viewpoint.

EXERCISE 49

Read 1 Chronicles 28:1—29:20 and 2 Chronicles 29:1-36 (two of the passages added by the author of Chronicles) and answer the following questions.

(a) How does each passage depict the kings of Judah? What similarities and differences do you see in the two accounts?

(b) Where in each passage do you hear echoes of Deuteronomic theology?

EZRA-NEHEMIAH

The books known today as Ezra and Nehemiah form a single book in the oldest Hebrew manuscripts. In this case, however, the transition between the two books is not smooth; the book now known as Nehemiah marks a new beginning, interrupting the story of Ezra until it commences again in Nehemiah 8.

The book of Ezra-Nehemiah tells a series of stories about events that are said to have occurred in Palestine in the postexilic period. The plotline is not continuous—it jumps from episode to episode, and some of the events may be out of order. The book begins with the Persian king issuing a decree allowing the exiles to return to Judah and rebuild their temple (539 B.C.E.). The first part of the book (Ezra 1–6) tells what happens when they try to implement this decree. For two decades they encounter opposition from "the adversaries of Judah and Benjamin" (Ezra 4:1), identified here as people of the

northern kingdom who remained in Palestine during the Exile (Ezra 4:2). Eventually they succeed in completing and dedicating their new temple (515 B.C.E.). The story then skips ahead several decades (to 458 B.C.E. or 398 B.C.E., depending on how one views the history behind the narrative) to the coming of Ezra the scribe, who leads another group of returning exiles to Palestine (Ezra 7–8). Upon his arrival, Ezra challenges the earlier group of returnees to divorce their foreign wives and restore the purity of Yahweh's people (Ezra 9–10).

The next part of the book (Nehemiah 1–7) centers on a man named Nehemiah, a member of the exile community who served as cupbearer to the Persian king around 445 B.C.E. Upon hearing that Jerusalem remains defenseless, Nehemiah seeks and receives the king's permission to return to the land of Judah and repair the walls of the city. For the next twelve years, he serves as the Persian governor of Judah. Like the first group of returning exiles, he encounters opposition but eventually succeeds in his mission. The completion of the city walls is followed by an account of Ezra the scribe teaching the people from "the book of the law of Moses" and leading them in a formal renewal of their covenant with Yahweh (Nehemiah 8–10). The last three chapters (Nehemiah 11–13) contain a series of unrelated and undated stories describing the resettlement of Jerusalem, the formal dedication of the restored city walls, and a series of rulings that Nehemiah issues to enforce obedience to the laws of Torah.

The book of Ezra-Nehemiah is clearly a composite work that drew its material from a variety of sources. Since the book was probably written within a few decades of the latest events that it narrates (sometime in the fourth century B.C.E.), most scholars believe that it contains a substantial amount of reliable historical information. Much of the book of Nehemiah (1:1—7:73; 12:27-43; 13:4-31) and portions of the book of Ezra (7:27—9:15) are written in first-person language, implying that they offer eyewitness accounts of the events that they narrate. Some scholars have argued that the stories were framed in this way to lend an air of credibility to the narrative, but most think that these parts of the book are based on the actual personal memoirs of Ezra and Nehemiah. Scholars have also found little reason to question the validity of the long lists of personal names from the postexilic community (Ezra 2:1-70; 8:1-14; 10:18-44; Nehemiah 7:6-73; 10:1-27; 11:3-36; 12:1-26), some of which the authors claim to have copied from written records (Ezra 8:1; Nehemiah 7:5; 9:38—10:1). At a subtler level, the credibility of the book is enhanced by the absence of stories depicting miracles and conversations with the deity such as we find in other parts of the Hebrew Bible.

Fig. 21.3. The so-called Cyrus Cylinder, a sixth-century B.C.E. cuneiform text, describes how the Persian king Cyrus allowed the peoples conquered by the Babylonians to return to their homelands and rebuild their temples.

On the other hand, not everything in Ezra-Nehemiah has survived critical scrutiny. Scholars have mixed opinions about the historicity of the letters to and from the kings of Persia that appear in the book of Ezra (1:2-4; 4:9-22; 5:6-17; 6:2-12; 7:11-26). Some view them as authentic, while others regard them as loose summaries of genuine documents or as wholly fictional creations. The third-person narrative sections are also problematic, since they appear to contain inaccuracies at certain points, including the chronological relationship between Ezra and Nehemiah (see Nehemiah 8). Perhaps the best that can be said is that the book of Ezra-Nehemiah contains a significant amount of reliable information about the life of the postexilic community, but not everything in the book can be taken as historically valid.

Like the other narrative books, Ezra-Nehemiah was not written simply to record events of the past. The book offers a view of the postexilic period that would not have been shared by everyone in the authors' time. Not only was the return from Babylonia more complicated and gradual than the book suggests, but the book's insistence that the returning exiles are the only true people of Yahweh is a one-sided assertion that flies in the face of the evidence. Those whom the book depicts as their opponents were mostly descended from people who had remained in their homeland during the Exile. These people understandably resented the intrusion of a group of outsiders from Babylonia who claimed the right to dominate the social and religious life of Judah. The problem was intensified by the returnees' attitude of superiority and their rejection of all offers of help from those whom they labeled as enemies.

Since they were convinced that Yahweh was on their side, anyone who interfered with their work was by definition an enemy of Yahweh and his people. This explains why marriages to people outside the group of returned exiles (specifically, those labeled "foreign women") are prohibited in Ezra-Nehemiah, as well as why so much stress is placed on obedience to the laws of Torah, many of which have a segregationist tone.

In short, the book of Ezra-Nehemiah is the product of a particular group within the postexilic community that was committed to promoting faithful observance of the laws of Torah that they had compiled during their time in Babylonia. Again and again these laws told them to avoid becoming entangled with people outside the group who had different ideas about what it meant to follow Yahweh (or other gods). Members of the community who read this book would have been encouraged to think of themselves as the only true followers of Yahweh and to look down on people outside the group as irreligious or even enemies of Yahweh. Once again we see how a seemingly objective account about Israel's past can serve to advance the social or theological agenda of a particular group within ancient Palestine.

RUTH

The book of Ruth is a delightful story that centers on the efforts of two women, Ruth and Naomi, to survive in a world dominated by men. The story is set during the time of the judges, roughly a century before King David's rise to power. The narrative begins with a brief preface that describes how Naomi and her family moved from Bethlehem to the neighboring land of Moab during a time of famine. Sometime later, Naomi's husband and sons died, leaving her and her two Moabite daughters-in-law, Ruth and Orpah, to fend for themselves. Naomi decides to return home to the land of Israel. Ruth insists on going with her, despite the hard life that awaits them there as unmarried women.

Like other poor women, Ruth goes to the field of a local farmer to pick up stalks of grain that had been dropped on the ground during the harvest so that she can make bread to eat. The landowner, a wealthy man named Boaz who is much older than Ruth, takes an interest in her and tells his workers to intentionally leave extra grain for her to gather. After several weeks of this kindness, Naomi decides that the time has come for Ruth to act. She tells Ruth to dress up in her finest clothes, then go to where Boaz is sleeping and lie down at his feet in order to demonstrate her interest in him. The text does not say whether the encounter leads to sex, but Boaz clearly appreciates the attention.

The next day Boaz announces his intention to purchase a piece of land that had belonged to Naomi's dead husband, Elimelech, an arrangement that carries with it the duty to marry Ruth and produce an heir so that the property will stay in Elimelech's family. First, however, he

Fig. 21.4. Thomas Matthews Rooke, *The Story of Ruth: Ruth and Naomi, Ruth and Boaz, Ruth and Obed*

has to fend off another relative whose claim to the land is higher than his. In the end, he succeeds in obtaining the land and takes Ruth as his wife. The story ends with Ruth giving birth to a son, Obed, who turns out to be the grandfather of King David.

Dating the book of Ruth is difficult, since there are few clues to indicate when or why it might have been written. Much of the discussion has centered on the fact that Ruth, a non-Israelite, is depicted as the great-grandmother of King David. Since the Moabites appear often as Israel's enemies in the biblical narratives (Numbers 22:1—25:5; Judges 3:12-30; 1 Samuel 14:47; 2 Kings 3:4-27), it is difficult to understand what might have motivated someone to craft such a story during the preexilic era when David's descendants occupied the throne of Judah. Even if the genealogical link to David is a later addition as some scholars believe, the story's positive attitude toward the inclusion of a Moabite woman into the people of Israel cries out for an explanation. One popular theory places the origin of the story in the postexilic period as an effort to counter the views expressed in the book of Ezra-Nehemiah, where marriages to foreign women are condemned as a sign of unfaithfulness to Yahweh (Ezra 9:1—10:17; Nehemiah 13:1-3; 15:23-27). Other scholars date it to sometime during the monarchy when members of the elite class might have wanted to encourage positive relations with foreigners in general or Moabites in particular. Whenever it was written, most scholars agree that the book is a work of fiction similar to a modern short story, so questions of historical reliability do not come into play.

One of the most intriguing aspects of the book is the attention that it gives to the viewpoints and experiences of women. From beginning to end, the book paints a bleak and realistic portrait of the precarious status of unmarried women in a male-dominated society. Yet the female characters are by no means helpless. Though men clearly hold the reins of social and economic power in the world of the story, it is the women whose careful planning and bold actions eventually bring them to a place of security. Even the kindly Boaz is manipulated by Ruth and Naomi into doing their bidding. Through this story we see that women may have wielded more informal authority in ancient Israelite society than is apparent from the male-oriented texts that dominate the Hebrew Bible.

The idea that Yahweh works through the actions of faithful humans lies at the heart of the book of Ruth. In the early part of the story, Yahweh's character is cast into doubt by the experience of Naomi, whose losses have caused her to regard Yahweh as a bringer of misfortune and suffering (1:13, 20-21). As the story progresses, however, we see that Yahweh is indeed at work in the circumstances of Naomi and Ruth, though his involvement is hidden behind seemingly chance occurrences: Ruth happens to end up gathering grain in the field of Naomi's near relative Boaz; Boaz happens to come walking through the field and catch sight of Ruth on her first day there; Naomi's other near relative happens to walk by the city gate at precisely the moment when Boaz is sitting there waiting for him; and so on. But human effort and risk-taking also have a role to play in the fulfillment of Yahweh's purposes: Naomi leaves her life in Moab to return to her homeland in search of food; Ruth abandons her family and their gods to follow Naomi and Yahweh; Ruth goes into the fields to gather grain despite the potential for abuse by male field workers; Ruth places her reputation and her future at risk by lying down with Boaz at night; Boaz initiates the purchase of Elimelech's property in the knowledge that he could lose Ruth in the process; Boaz takes Ruth as his wife and, despite his age, produces a male heir who becomes the grandfather of King David.

In short, the story suggests that Yahweh has good intentions toward his people, but humans must also do their part before Yahweh's purposes can be fulfilled. At this level of generality, the message could be applied to virtually any time or place. What makes the story unusual is the fact that it is a foreigner, Ruth of Moab, who is shown doing what Yahweh wishes and receiving Yahweh's blessings in return. Even more surprising is the inclusion of this non-Israelite among the ancestors of the mighty King David. This inclusive attitude toward foreigners is the polar opposite of what we saw in Ezra-Nehemiah, where non-Israelites are flatly rejected by Yahweh. While the date of the book remains uncertain, it is easy to see why many scholars have concluded that the book was written in the postexilic period to counter the harshly negative view of outsiders that permeates Ezra-Nehemiah.

Fig. 21.5. Bernardo Cavallino, *Esther before Ahasuerus*

EXERCISE 51

Read the book of Ruth and answer the following questions.

(a) What words might you use to describe how the various characters relate to one another in this story?

(b) Identify all of the passages where Yahweh is mentioned in the book. What do these passages (and the story as a whole) say about the character and actions of Yahweh?

ESTHER

Like the book of Ruth, the book of Esther tells about a female character who is caught in a difficult situation in a world dominated by men. The characters and setting, however, could hardly be more different. Esther is one of many beautiful girls who is brought to the palace of the king of Persia to be evaluated as a possible replacement

for a wife whom the king had divorced for refusing to obey his command to dance in front of a drunken crowd of nobles. When the time comes for Esther to spend a night with the king, he is captivated by her beauty and chooses her to be his queen. What the king does not know is that Esther is a Jew, one of the exiles who had been carried away to Babylonia prior to the destruction of Jerusalem.

Esther has an uncle named Mordecai who uncovers a plot against the king and saves the king's life. Soon afterward, Mordecai's own life is threatened when he runs afoul of Haman, the king's new prime minister, by refusing to bow down and honor him. To rid himself of Mordecai, Haman bribes the king to issue an edict ordering his people to kill all of the Jews in Persia. When Mordecai hears of this, he asks Esther to intercede with the king, telling her, "Perhaps you have come to royal dignity for just such a time as this" (4:14).

Esther is worried about being rejected by the king, so she invites him and Haman to two successive banquets until the king volunteers to give her whatever she wants. At this point she identifies herself as a Jew and explains Haman's plot against her and her people. The king immediately calls for Haman to be hanged and appoints Mordecai to take his place. But the king's decree cannot be changed. Instead, he orders Mordecai to draft a new edict giving his Jewish subjects the right to defend themselves by arms and to plunder the property of their enemies. On the day appointed for the slaughter, the Jews gather their weapons and kill more than seventy-five thousand Persians. To honor this day when they were rescued from certain destruction, the Jews established the festival of Purim. This festival is celebrated in Jewish synagogues to the present day.

Though the book is set during the time of the Persian king Ahasuerus (another name for Xerxes, who ruled from 485 to 465 B.C.E.), virtually all scholars agree that the book is a piece of religious fiction that was written a century or more after the events that it claims to narrate. The author is familiar with some aspects of Persian court life, but the book also contains a number of factual errors that would not have occurred if the story was based on actual events. For example, if Mordecai and Esther had been deported to Babylon at the time stated in Esther 2:6, they would have been well over a hundred years old when Xerxes came to power. Moreover, Persian records indicate that Xerxes' queen during the period covered by the book of Esther was a woman named Amestris who came from an old Persian family, not a Jewish woman named Esther. The fictional nature of the story is also apparent from the inclusion of many incredible details of the type that one sees regularly in tales and legends, such as the requirement that Esther undergo a full year of beauty treatments before being seen by the king; the repeated (and historically inaccurate) assertion that the decrees of Persian kings could not be changed; the poetic justice of Haman being hanged on his own (seventy-five-foot-tall!) gallows; the Jews being allowed to kill seventy-five thousand Persians with impunity; and so forth. None of this can be taken seriously as history.

Viewing the book of Esther as a work of fiction does not diminish the religious value of the book. Anyone who has read a novel or short story knows that fiction can be a powerful tool for communicating insights concerning the central issues of life. The book of Esther presents a message that would have been highly relevant to the many Yahwistic communities that had grown up across the ancient Near East by the time the book was written, probably in the late fourth century B.C.E. Unlike their fellow believers in Palestine, these people lived as minorities in the middle of foreign civilizations where their unusual beliefs and practices aroused the suspicions of their neighbors, including the religious and political authorities. Periodically these suspicions flared up into anti-Jewish violence. To Jews who lived daily with these fears, the book of Esther brought a message similar to that of Ruth: Yahweh does care for his people, but he prefers to work through the hands of humans who are prepared to act when the right moment comes along. Yahweh's people must be ready for action—including self-defense if necessary—since the governing authorities cannot be trusted to do what is right.

Esther differs from Ruth, however, in the fact that Yahweh has receded entirely into the background. Neither the name of Yahweh nor the generic title God appears anywhere in the book. This is a marked change from the earlier narrative traditions in which Yahweh routinely performs stupendous miracles to rescue and aid his people. The apparent absence of the deity led later editors to insert new episodes into the book to make Yahweh's activity more apparent. Some of the leading Jewish rabbis of second-century (and later) Palestine debated whether the book of Esther even belonged in the canon of Scripture. To the people who created and used this story, however, the hidden nature of Yahweh's activity was consistent with their experience of living as a minority group within a foreign culture. To them, the story offered assurance that Yahweh was always watching out for them, even when his activity could be seen only by the eyes of faith.

EXERCISE 52

Read Esther 3:1—4:17; 7:1-10; and 8:7—9:4, and answer the following questions.

(a) What do these verses say about the status of the Jews within the Persian Empire?

(b) How do you think these passages might have affected Jewish audiences who lived as minorities within a foreign culture?

DANIEL 1–6

The book of Daniel is a composite work consisting of two very different parts. The first six chapters contain a series of stories about a man named Daniel who is said to have been brought to Babylonia with the first group of exiles from Judah. The last six chapters describe a series of apocalyptic dreams and visions that Daniel is reported to have experienced while living in Babylonia. The apocalyptic chapters were probably a later addition to an earlier narrative work about Daniel (Daniel 1–6). Since the present chapter is concerned with narrative texts, our

Fig. 21.6. Peter Paul Rubens, *Daniel in the Lions' Den*

investigation of the apocalyptic chapters (Daniel 7–12) will be postponed until later (see chapter 36).

The story of Daniel takes place in Babylonia during the Exile. The narrative is structured as a series of loosely related tales with a set of common themes. The stories begin with Daniel as a young man and end with him a very old man. Nothing is said about his life in Judah before the Exile or his death.

In all of the stories, Daniel is depicted as a devoted follower of Yahweh who has a special gift for interpreting dreams and other mysteries. The narrative begins with Daniel and three other young men from the aristocracy of Judah being groomed for service in the courts of King Nebuchadnezzar of Babylon. Daniel and his friends refuse to eat the ritually impure food of the Babylonians,

preferring to eat only vegetables and water. At the end of their training, they are found to be healthier and wiser than any of the other trainees and are appointed to serve in the king's court. The wisdom of this appointment soon becomes apparent when Daniel proves to be the only person in all of Babylonia who can interpret a dream that is troubling King Nebuchadnezzar. As a result, the king acclaims Daniel's god (Yahweh) as the greatest of all the gods and elevates Daniel to the position of "ruler over the whole province of Babylon and chief prefect over all the wise men of Babylon" (Daniel 2:48). His three friends are given high positions as well.

Sometime later, however, Daniel's three friends find themselves in trouble when they refuse to bow down to a massive golden statue that King Nebuchadnezzar has erected. In his anger, the king has them thrown into a blazing furnace. To his surprise, they are not harmed by the fire. After telling them to come out of the furnace, he issues a decree stating that anyone who speaks badly of their god is to be torn limb from limb.

In the next episode, Nebuchadnezzar himself tells about a dream that Daniel had interpreted for him and how the dream was fulfilled. The dream foretold a time when Nebuchadnezzar would be reduced to the status of a beast and driven out of his city for seven years to humble him for his arrogance. This is precisely what Nebuchadnezzar says happened to him. At the end of seven years, Nebuchadnezzar was restored to his right mind, leading him to offer praise to "the King of heaven" (4:34-37), presumably Daniel's god, whose will no human can resist.

The final two episodes take place decades later, near the end of the Exile and the beginning of the Persian period. In the first story, King Belshazzar commands that the sacred gold and silver vessels from the Jerusalem temple be brought out and used in a drinking party. In the middle of the party, a disembodied hand appears and writes a mysterious message on the wall. Daniel is called in to interpret the message, which says that the Most High God has decided to take the kingdom away from Belshazzar as a punishment for his arrogance. That very night Babylonia is overrun by the Medes.

The last episode tells the famous story of Daniel in the lions' den. When Darius, king of the Medes, decides to make Daniel the chief official over his realm, the other officials conspire to find a way to bring him down. First they entice the king to sign an irrevocable order forbidding the worship of any deity but the king for thirty days. Then they have Daniel arrested for continuing to pray to the god of Israel. His punishment is to be thrown into a den of lions to be killed. But Daniel's god shuts the mouths of the lions, and Daniel emerges unharmed. The officials who conspired against him are then thrown into the lions' den along with their families, and all are eaten by the lions. The story ends with the king issuing a decree calling his people to "tremble and fear before the God of Daniel" (6:25-28).

Historians who have studied these stories disagree about whether they have any basis in history or should be taken as works of fiction. Apart from these stories, there is no clear evidence that a man named Daniel lived in Babylonia during the exilic period. The Babylonian and Persian records make no mention of him, even though the biblical account describes him as a high official in both empires. The name appears three times in the book of Ezekiel (14:14, 20; 28:3), but all three texts seem to be speaking about a figure from the distant past, not a man who was living in Babylonia at the same time as the prophet. Earlier Mesopotamian texts refer to a mythical figure named Daniel (or Danel) who is renowned for his wisdom. Many scholars think that the biblical figure named Daniel was based on this mythical personage.

More troubling is the fact that the book of Daniel contains a number of serious historical errors: Belshazzar was the son of Nabonidus, not Nebuchadnezzar, and he never became king of Babylonia; the conqueror of Babylon was Cyrus the Persian, not Darius the Mede, who is unknown outside the book of Daniel; the assertion that the decrees of the Medean kings could not be revoked (Daniel 6:9, 16; compare Esther 8:8) has no basis in fact; and so on. No educated person living in Babylonia during the period of the Exile could have made such errors. The supernatural quality of the narrative also betrays its legendary character: Daniel interprets dreams that accurately foreshadow the future; his friends walk out of an overheated furnace unscathed; Daniel survives a bout with hungry lions. Equally improbable are the repeated proclamations by the kings of Babylonia and Persia acknowledging the god of Israel as the lord of the universe. In fact, the account of king Nebuchadnezzar becoming like a wild beast and later being restored to health seems to be an exaggerated version of a story about King Nabonidus that is known from other sources.

For these and other reasons, most scholars have concluded that the stories in Daniel 1–6 are yet another example of religious fiction such as we saw in the books of Ruth and Esther. As with those books, the message of the stories does not require that the characters be historical figures. Throughout the narrative, Daniel is depicted as an ideal role model for the members of the many Yahwistic communities that had sprung up in towns and cities across the ancient Near East by the time the stories were written. In this sense Daniel resembles the book of Esther, though the present version of Daniel 1–6 was probably composed later than Esther, since Daniel's interpretation of the king's dream in chapter 2 implies that the story was written after the conquest of the Persians by the Greeks in the late fourth century B.C.E. The overall message of the book also echoes that of Esther: remain loyal to Yahweh no matter how great the challenge, and he will protect you from all harm. Daniel moves beyond Esther, however, in suggesting that Yahweh will use miracles if necessary to rescue his faithful servants from dire threats.

As we saw earlier, this kind of message would have been especially comforting to followers of Yahweh who had experienced abuse at the hands of their neighbors or the local authorities. But it would have been equally pertinent to those who struggled daily with subtler pressures to conform to the values and practices of their pagan neighbors. To these people, the book of Daniel says that there is no reason to abandon their devotion to Yahweh in order to advance in a pagan society, since Yahweh blesses and prospers those who stay faithful to him. Stories such as these would have found a ready audience among the socially elite but religiously conservative members of many of the Yahwistic communities outside of Palestine.

EXERCISE 53

Read Daniel 1:1-21 and 6:1-28 and answer the following questions.

(a) What do these passages say about how the followers of Yahweh should conduct themselves in a non-Yahwistic society?

(b) What do the stories imply about Yahweh's own relationship to non-Yahwistic cultures?

OTHER NARRATIVES

As we saw in chapter 4, the Writings section of the Hebrew canon remained open to some degree until the second century C.E. in Palestine, and possibly later

in other areas. The reasons certain narrative texts were included in the canon and others were rejected are largely lost to history. What is clear is that the creation of religious narratives did not cease with the books that were eventually included in the Hebrew canon (third to second century B.C.E.). The period between the second century B.C.E. and the second century C.E. saw the production of a host of narrative texts by Yahwistic authors. Some of these books were regarded as Scripture by one Jewish group or another, though none of them was finally included in the Hebrew canon. A few made their way into various Christian canons. A brief overview of some of the more important narratives from this era will highlight the continuing importance of stories within the Yahwistic tradition.

Fig. 21.7. Unknown Lombard painter (seventeenth century), *The Archangel and Tobias*

Tobit

The book of Tobit is a peculiar but entertaining folk tale that tells how Yahweh used an angel, a young man, and a bit of magic to bring healing and deliverance to two righteous Jews who were suffering from grave afflictions. One is a man named Tobit who had lost his sight when bird droppings fell in his eyes. The other is a woman named Sarah who had lost seven husbands to a ferocious demon who attacked and killed them just before their marriage was consummated. The story is set in Mesopotamia during the time of the Assyrian Empire (seventh century B.C.E.), though there are enough historical and geographical errors to convince scholars that the book is a fictional narrative written centuries later than its purported setting, probably in the late third or early second century B.C.E. This would make it roughly contemporary with Daniel 1–6.

Where Daniel and Esther embody the struggles of Jews who lived at the elite level of Babylonian society, Tobit represents the beliefs, attitudes, and experiences of ordinary Jews who lived well outside the corridors of power. The values and actions that are commended in the story are familiar to Jews everywhere: faithfully observing the laws of Torah, ensuring that the dead are properly buried, obeying one's parents, caring for the needy, and so on. The story recognizes that living in this manner might lead to conflicts with the authorities, but it assures the faithful that Yahweh will rescue them from any troubles that might come upon them if they pray for his help, though he sometimes works in unexpected ways. The fact that Tobit was included in the early Christian canons of the Old Testament despite the absence of any link to Christian teachings suggests that the book was highly regarded in at least some Jewish circles prior to the rise of Christianity.

Jubilees

The book of Jubilees claims to report things that Yahweh revealed to Moses during the forty days that he spent on Mount Sinai when he received the laws of Torah (Exodus 24:18). This "revelation" is basically a retelling of the story that runs from Genesis 1 through Exodus 20, modified and enhanced at various points to paint the ancient ancestors of Israel as holy men and women who adhered to the laws of Torah centuries before they were given to Moses. The ancestors are also shown using a 364-day solar calendar rather than the 354-day lunar calendar that has been followed by most Jews from ancient times to today. The book's emphasis on the value of the solar calendar indicates that the book was written during the second century B.C.E., a time when certain groups of Palestinian Jews were agitating for the adoption of a calendar that more closely followed the seasons and cycles of the sun.

At several points Jubilees suggests that too many Jews in the author's day were following the ways of the Gentiles and not properly observing the laws of Torah. The author is fearful that this kind of behavior will bring down Yahweh's judgment upon his people. The book includes an implicit call for repentance and renewed devotion to Yahweh's commandments, including observance of the proper solar calendar. The book of Jubilees was apparently treated as Scripture by the community that produced the Dead Sea Scrolls, but it is unclear whether any other Jews valued it to this extent.

Judith

The book of Judith tells the story of a Jewish woman named Judith who rescues her people by beguiling and then beheading the leader of the Assyrian forces that had invaded Israel as part of a sweeping military campaign. The story takes place during the time of the monarchy, but it appears to have been written during the second century B.C.E. when the Jews of Palestine were engaged in an extended battle to free themselves from the power of Syrian Greek rulers who had been oppressing them and attempting to stamp out their religion. The narrative contains so many historical and geographical errors that some scholars have suggested that the author may have deliberately mixed up material from different times and places in an effort to signify that the book was meant to apply to the present situation and was not simply a record of the past.

The story of Judith assures the audience that Yahweh will help them if they act boldly but wisely in the face of

Fig. 21.8. Cristofano Allori, *Judith with the Head of Holophernes*

a nickname that was given to one of the brothers who led the revolt, Judas Maccabeus (possibly "the hammerer").

Both books are similar in style to the Historical Books of the Hebrew Bible, with accounts of battles interspersed with bits of dialogue, speeches, prayers, letters, treaties, and other types of material. The narrative of 1 Maccabees is marked by a strong bias in favor of the family that led the revolt and subsequently ruled as kings and high priests over an independent Jewish state for nearly a century. This suggests to scholars that the book was written as a piece of political propaganda. In 2 Maccabees, by contrast, events are interpreted through the lens of a Deuteronomic theology that views history as a pattern of sin—punishment—repentance—salvation.

Fig. 21.9. A second-century B.C.E. coin showing the Seleucid king Antiochus IV Epiphanes in the guise of the Greek god Zeus.

Both books were written in the late second or early first century B.C.E. using events of the recent past to commend a particular course of action: submission to the God-given rule of the Maccabees on the one hand, faithfulness to Yahweh and his Torah on the other. The late date of the books is the chief reason neither was included in the Hebrew Bible; apparently the canon of the Former Prophets was considered closed by the time they were written. Both books remained popular with Jews in Palestine and elsewhere as reminders of Yahweh's commitment to aid his people in their fight against abusive foreign rulers. From here they eventually found their way into the list of books adopted by the early Christians as their Old Testament.

danger, regardless of how powerless they might seem to themselves or the people around them. The fact that the hero was a woman might also have helped to inspire the women in the audience to support the resistance effort. The book's message would certainly have been welcome during a time of persecution and national trial. The fact that Judith was included in early Christian canons of the Old Testament suggests that at least some Jews continued to find inspiration in the book long after it was written.

1 and 2 Maccabees

The two books called 1 and 2 Maccabees present overlapping accounts of the successful military revolt by which the Jews of Palestine gained independence from their Syrian Greek overlords in the middle of the second century B.C.E. This victory is celebrated each year in the Jewish festival of Hanukkah. The title Maccabees was based on

CONCLUSION

The postexilic period witnessed a flowering of narrative literature among the literate members of Yahwistic communities both within and outside of Palestine. Most of these texts are concerned with the question of how the followers of Yahweh should conduct themselves in the changed social and political environment of the postexilic era. In the eyes of the people who produced these texts, the answer is to be found by looking back at key periods in or great individuals from the past to uncover models for behavior in the present.

Not surprisingly, the values and conduct that are commended in these stories are rooted in the traditional faith of the Yahwistic communities, including loyalty to Yahweh and his covenant, devotion to the Jerusalem temple, and obedience to the laws of Torah. Most of the stories also make an effort to relate these values to the changed circumstances of the postexilic period, encouraging their audiences to resist the pressure to conform to the broader culture, remain strong and courageous under persecution, and uphold their fellow believers. A few stories, like Ruth, adopt a tolerant attitude toward people from outside the community, but most reflect a more defensive and conservative position.

The decision to include some of these books and not others in the Hebrew canon was motivated by a variety of factors that are difficult for us to reconstruct since there are no records indicating when or how such matters were decided. Some of the books that did not make it into the canon appear to have been honored and used as Scripture in particular Jewish communities. In the end, however, most of these books owe their preservation not to the Jewish groups that produced them but to Christians who adopted them into their Scriptures or copied them for Christian devotional use.

EXERCISE 54

Imagine that you were suddenly transported to another country where the people followed beliefs and practices that were radically different from your own and you had no idea when you would be able to return home.

(a) How do you think you would feel in this situation?

(b) What might you do to avoid losing touch with the beliefs, values, and practices of your home country? How might you pass them on to your children?

(c) What role might stories play in this process? What kinds of stories do you think might prove most valuable in the long run?

Fig. 22.1. A Torah scroll is displayed as part of a Jewish celebration in the city of Jerusalem.

The Laws of Torah

Moses came down from Mount Sinai. As he came down from the mountain with the two tablets of the covenant in his hand, Moses did not know that the skin of his face shone because he had been talking with God. When Aaron and all the Israelites saw Moses, the skin of his face was shining, and they were afraid to come near him. But Moses called to them; and Aaron and all the leaders of the congregation returned to him, and Moses spoke with them. Afterward all the Israelites came near, and he gave them in commandment all that the LORD had spoken with him on Mount Sinai. (Exodus 34:29-32)

This very day the LORD your God is commanding you to observe these statutes and ordinances; so observe them diligently with all your heart and with all your soul. Today you have obtained the LORD's agreement: to be your God; and for you to walk in his ways, to keep his statutes, his commandments, and his ordinances, and to obey him. Today the LORD has obtained your agreement: to be his treasured people, as he promised you, and to keep his commandments; for him to set you high above all nations that he has made, in praise and in fame and in honor; and for you to be a people holy to the LORD your God, as he promised. (Deuteronomy 26:16-19)

You shall put these words of mine in your heart and soul, and you shall bind them as a sign on your hand, and fix them as an emblem on your forehead. Teach them to your children, talking about them when you are at home and when you are away, when you lie down and when you rise. Write them on the doorposts of your house and on your gates, so that your days and the days of your children may be multiplied in the land that the LORD swore to your ancestors to give them, as long as the heavens are above the earth. (Deuteronomy 11:18-21)

In the last seven chapters we examined how the followers of Yahweh used stories to communicate their beliefs, values, and practices to members of their own and other groups in ancient Palestine. Like other religious communities, they valued stories for their ability to express profound insights in a memorable and appealing manner that could be understood even by the illiterate masses. Many of the stories that they found attractive were never written down and were thus lost to the dustbins of history. Some, however, were enshrined in the books that make up the Hebrew Bible, so that they not only survived but ultimately transcended their original cultural setting.

Another type of material that played a central role in the religious world of the people who formulated the Hebrew Bible centers on the laws, or rules for conduct. These legal materials, also called *commandments* or *regulations* in the Hebrew Bible, fill much of the books of Exodus, Leviticus, Numbers, and Deuteronomy. Later Jewish rabbis counted 613 divine commandments in these books—248 positive ("do this") and 365 negative ("don't do that"). The importance of these materials, however, lies not in their number but in the belief that they came directly from Yahweh. According to the Hebrew Bible, Yahweh dictated all of these laws to Moses either at Mount Sinai or at other times during the forty years that the Israelites spent wandering in the desert. Thus the laws are presented not as human products but as the very words of God, to be obeyed without question.

The next three chapters are devoted to exploring the content and importance of the laws. The present chapter provides an overview of the content of the laws and examines their historical origins. Chapters 23 and 24 offer a more detailed review of two of the major categories of laws, purity laws and social laws. Since earlier chapters have already discussed the contents of the individual books of the Torah, the legal materials will be considered here as a class, without regard to the books in which they appear.

RELIGION AND RULES

Every religion has rules or guidelines that spell out how individual believers should behave in relation to fellow group members, people outside the group, and the supernatural realm. Many also have regulations that define how the group and/or the broader society should be structured and operate. Some of these rules and guidelines are very specific in nature, while others are broad and general. A few examples from different religions will illustrate how rules provide guidance for specific situations.

> If any monk who has taken upon himself the monks' system of self-training and rule of life and has not after that withdrawn from the training, or declared his weakness, shall have sexual intercourse with anyone, down even to an animal, he has fallen into defeat; he is no longer in communion. *(Parajika Dhamma 1—Buddhism)*

> (The initiation) of a Brahmana who desires proficiency in sacred learning should take place in the fifth (year after conception), (that) of a Kshatriya who wishes to become powerful in the sixth, (and that) of a Vaisya who longs for (success in his) business in the eighth. The (time for the) Savitri (initiation) of a Brahmana does not pass until the completion of the sixteenth year (after conception), of a Kshatriya until the completion of the twenty-second, and of a Vaisya until the completion of the twenty-fourth. After those (periods men

of) these three (castes) who have not received the sacrament at the proper time, become Vratyas (outcasts), excluded from the Savitri (initiation) and despised by the Aryans. *(Laws of Manu 2.37-39—Hinduism)*

> The elders of the congregation shall lay their hands on the head of the bull before the LORD, and the bull shall be slaughtered before the LORD. The anointed priest shall bring some of the blood of the bull into the tent of meeting, and the priest shall dip his finger in the blood and sprinkle it seven times before the LORD, in front of the curtain. He shall put some of the blood on the horns of the altar that is before the LORD in the tent of meeting; and the rest of the blood he shall pour out at the base of the altar of burnt offering that is at the entrance of the tent of meeting. *(Leviticus 4:15-18—Judaism)*

Most religious rules are fairly general in character, leaving room for the individual or the group's leaders to determine how the rules apply to daily life. The following verses exemplify this kind of general guidance.

> Be kind to parents, and the near kinsman, and to orphans, and to the needy, and to the neighbor who is of kin, and to the neighbor who is a stranger, and to the companion at your side, and to the traveler, and to [slaves] that your right hands own. *(Qur'an 4:36—Islam)*

> Manifest plainness, embrace simplicity, reduce selfishness, have few desires. *(Daode Jing 19—Taoism)*

> "You have heard that it was said, 'You shall love your neighbor and hate your enemy.' But I say to you, Love your enemies and pray for those who persecute you, so that you may be children of your Father in heaven; for he makes his sun rise on the evil and on the good, and sends rain on the righteous and on the unrighteous." *(Matthew 5:43-45—Christianity)*

Religious rules can cover a wide range of subjects. Of the six dimensions of religion that we examined in chapter 10, three are often linked to the use of rules.

1. *The social dimension.* Rules play a key role in defining how religious groups are organized and how they operate. Social rules are used to regulate the distribution

of power within a group and to ensure that institutions function in a consistent manner over time. Questions that are commonly addressed by social rules include who holds positions of leadership within the group; how group leaders are chosen; how women and men should relate to one another; how the poor should be treated; and how violations of group norms should be addressed. Where a single religion is followed by most of the people in a society, social rules can include matters that secular societies normally address through criminal and civil laws, such as murder, theft, property damage, and divorce. In most cases social rules serve to uphold the status quo and preserve the power of those in authority.

2. *The ritual dimension.* Rules are also important for structuring the ritual life of religious groups. Some religions give more importance to religious rituals than others, but every religion that practices rituals has rules about how they are to be performed. Ritual rules cover such topics as how a public worship service should be conducted; what priests should do with the statue of the deity in a temple; how an animal sacrifice should be killed and butchered; and what kinds of prayers should be said on various occasions. Rules pertaining to public rituals are normally supervised and enforced by priests or other religious experts, while rules for private rituals are commonly passed on and monitored within the family. Some religions believe that the rules must be followed precisely in order for the ritual to be effective.

3. *The ethical dimension.* Most people today associate rules with the ethical side of religion. Ethical rules define what counts as proper and improper conduct within a particular religion or society. The purpose of ethical rules is not simply to ensure that people live in a certain way, but to shape those who follow them into moral individuals as defined by that religion. Issues that are commonly addressed by ethical rules include sexual morality, relations with family members, personal honesty and integrity, and the use of material possessions. Some religions have different ethical rules for people who belong to different religious categories, such as laypeople, clergy, and monks, or people from different social levels, as with the caste system in Hinduism.

On the whole, the ideals for individual and societal conduct that lie behind most systems of religious rules do not differ markedly from those that guide secular societies. What distinguishes religious rules from others is not their content but their motivation. Most religions link their rules in some way to the supernatural realm. Some claim that their rules were created by supernatural beings, while others insist that following their rules is the best way to ensure positive relations with the supernatural. Many teach that one's future fate in this world and the next is somehow tied to how well one obeys the group's rules. Beliefs such as these provide a powerful incentive for people to live by the rules. They also help to ensure the continuation of the prevailing societal system and the power of those who benefit from it, since such claims elevate the rules of the group to a status beyond question.

THE RULES OF TORAH

Several different terms are used in the Hebrew Bible to describe the set of rules that Yahweh is said to have given to Moses in the desert, including *mitzvoth* (commonly translated "commandments" or "commands"), *mishpatim* ("laws" or "ordinances"), *huqqoth* ("decrees," "statutes"), and *toroth* ("laws," "regulations"). The most common term for the entire body of materials is *Torah*, a Hebrew word that is translated as "law" in some contexts and "teaching" or "instruction" in others.

Both senses of the word *Torah* are important for grasping the way in which these materials were understood and used by the people who produced the Hebrew Bible. On the one hand, the legal sections of the Torah are presented as Yahweh's instructions to his people concerning what it means to live in a covenant relationship with the almighty ruler of the universe. The Torah explains how the people of Israel should conduct themselves in order to enjoy Yahweh's blessings and avoid his curses. Without this revelation, the text suggests, Israel would have remained like the other nations, not knowing how to please Yahweh and suffering the consequences of their disobedience. The Hebrew Bible contains many verses that voice gratitude to Yahweh for giving the Torah to his people, along with others that describe the joy that comes from studying and obeying his laws (see Psalm 119).

On the other hand, the provisions of Torah are not simply helpful guidelines or wise advice that can be followed or ignored as people choose. They are the commands of Israel's god, a powerful deity who expects to be obeyed without question. The rules of Torah spell out Israel's obligations under the covenant with Yahweh. In this sense they function as laws that regulate the conduct of Yahweh's people.

When we think of laws today, we envision a series of rules created by a group of people to define and punish forms of behavior that they believe are detrimental to their society. The laws are enforced by authorities who have the power to impose penalties upon those who violate societal norms. The Torah is not a law code in this sense. The Torah is a multifaceted literary composition that offers a vision for what society ought to be like under the rule of Yahweh. The range of issues addressed in the Torah is far broader than any modern law code, embracing not only the everyday operation of society but also such issues as the performance of religious rituals and the moral and religious conduct of individuals. Almost nothing is said about how the laws are to be enforced; in fact, most of the laws contain no penalties for violation. Clearly such a legal system is inadequate for directing the affairs of a society.

How widely these laws were known and followed at any given point in time is an open question. In their present form, the laws date to the postexilic period, though most scholars believe that they include materials drawn

Fig. 22.2. A Jewish teenager reads from a Torah scroll under the supervision of a rabbi.

from earlier oral and written collections. Determining what these earlier collections contained and how they were viewed and used in the preexilic period is one of the most difficult and controversial problems in modern biblical scholarship. But there is substantial evidence to indicate that the sources upon which the Torah is based addressed many of the same issues as the present collection, even if the laws themselves changed over time. Both the earlier and the later collections aspired to regulate the social, ritual, and ethical aspects of the lives of the followers of Yahweh.

1. *The social dimension.* Unlike in modern societies, there was no separation of church and state in the ancient Near East. Religion permeated both the public and the private spheres of life. The king was viewed as the gods' representative on earth, and legal codes routinely appealed to the gods as the ultimate guardians of justice. This helps to explain why so many issues that are viewed as matters of personal freedom or individual conscience in modern societies are treated as social or religious violations in the Torah. Next to laws addressing the standard problems of social life (assault, killing, rape, theft, property damage, civil disputes), we find laws that criminalize various kinds of religious activity (blasphemy, witchcraft, worship of gods other than Yahweh, and so on) and laws that seek to uphold the traditional order of the family (adultery, incest, rebellious children, and so on).

When someone steals an ox or a sheep, and slaughters it or sells it, the thief shall pay five oxen for an ox, and four sheep for a sheep. The thief shall make restitution, but if unable to do so, shall be sold for the theft. *(Exodus 22:1)*

Anyone who kills a human being shall be put to death. Anyone who kills an animal shall make restitution for it, life for life. Anyone who maims another shall suffer the same injury in return: fracture for fracture, eye for eye, tooth for tooth; the injury inflicted is the injury to be suffered. *(Leviticus 24:17-20)*

Any of the people of Israel, or of the aliens who reside in Israel, who give any of their offspring to Molech shall be put to death; the people of the land shall stone them to death. *(Leviticus 20:2)*

If a man is caught lying with the wife of another man, both of them shall die, the man who lay with the woman as well as the woman. So you shall purge the evil from Israel. *(Deuteronomy 22:22)*

As can be seen in these examples, many of the social laws are framed as cases that offer instruction about how various situations should be handled ("if this should happen, then this is what should be done"). Some include statements indicating how violators should be punished (normally by death, mutilation, or some kind of financial compensation), while others simply prohibit or require a particular type of action and leave the penalty for violations unspecified. Many of the laws appear designed to offer practical guidance to people who were engaged in settling disputes and administering justice in ancient Palestine (judges, village elders, or priests). Again and again the Torah calls for honesty and justice in the courts while condemning false testimony, bribery, and preferential treatment of the rich.

You shall not pervert the justice due to your poor in their lawsuits. Keep far from a false charge, and do not kill the innocent and those in the right, for I will not acquit the guilty. You shall take no bribe, for a bribe blinds the officials, and subverts the cause of those who are in the right *(Exodus 23:6-8)*

If a malicious witness comes forward to accuse someone of wrongdoing, then both parties to the dispute shall appear before the LORD, before the priests and the judges who are in office in those days, and the judges shall make a thorough inquiry. If the witness is a false witness, having testified falsely against another, then you shall do to the false witness just as the false witness had meant to do to the other. So you shall purge the evil from your midst. *(Deuteronomy 19:16-19)*

2. *The ritual dimension.* The Torah also contains many rules that aim to regulate the performance of rituals and other aspects of the religious life of the group. Many of these rules pertain to the conduct of priests and other religious officials, such as verses describing who can and cannot serve as a priest; how various kinds of sacrifices should be handled; and what kinds of activities should be performed on various occasions. Others concern the ritual activities of private individuals, including texts that spell out which foods should and should not be eaten; what kinds of activities render a person **unclean** and thus in need of ritual purification; and how religious festivals are to be observed. Few of these ritual laws specify any penalties that should be imposed upon a person who fails to follow the rules; punishment is generally left to the deity.

When you offer a bull as a burnt offering or a sacrifice, to fulfill a vow or as an offering of well-being to the LORD, then you shall present with the bull a grain offering, three-tenths of an ephah of choice flour, mixed with half a hin of oil, and you shall present as a drink offering half a hin of wine, as an offering by fire, a pleasing odor to the LORD. *(Numbers 15:8-10)*

The LORD spoke to Moses and Aaron, saying: When a person has on the skin of his body a swelling or an eruption or a spot, and it turns into a leprous disease on the skin of his body, he shall be brought to Aaron the priest or to one of his sons the priests. The priest shall examine the disease on the skin of his body, and if the hair in the diseased area has turned white and the disease appears to be deeper than the skin of his body, it is a leprous disease; after the priest has examined him he shall pronounce him ceremonially unclean. *(Leviticus 13:1-3)*

Remember the sabbath day, and keep it holy. Six days you shall labor and do all your work. But the seventh day is a sabbath to the LORD your God; you shall not do any work— you, your son or your daughter, your male or female slave, your livestock, or the alien resident in your towns. *(Exodus 20:8-10)*

Set apart a tithe of all the yield of your seed that is brought in yearly from the field. In the presence of the LORD your God, in the place that he will choose as a dwelling for his name, you shall eat the tithe of your grain, your wine, and your oil, as well as the firstlings of your herd and flock, so that you may learn to fear the LORD your God always. *(Deuteronomy 14:22-23)*

Most of the rules pertaining to ritual conduct reflect the viewpoint and concerns of the priests and other religious officials. For this reason scholars believe that the ritual laws originated in priestly circles, where they were used to train and guide the religious experts who were responsible for overseeing the public religious rituals of the followers of Yahweh. Not until much later were they adapted into a tool for teaching the broader populace about ritual matters. At this point they became part of the public domain and eventually found their way into the Torah.

3. *The ethical dimension.* Yet another kind of material that appears often in the Torah is ethical instruction. The Torah contains many statements that prescribe how people should behave toward one another without identifying any consequences for those who fail to behave as recommended. Most of these statements sound more like moral guidelines than legal requirements. Many are so broad and general as to be unenforceable in any practical sense.

> Honor your father and your mother, so that your days may be long in the land that the LORD your God is giving you. *(Exodus 20:12)*

> You shall not covet your neighbor's house; you shall not covet your neighbor's wife, or male or female slave, or ox, or donkey, or anything that belongs to your neighbor. *(Exodus 20:17)*

> You shall not take vengeance or bear a grudge against any of your people, but you shall love your neighbor as yourself: I am the LORD. *(Leviticus 19:18)*

> You shall not watch your neighbor's ox or sheep straying away and ignore them; you shall take them back to their owner. . . . You shall not see your neighbor's donkey or ox fallen on the road and ignore it; you shall help to lift it up. *(Deuteronomy 22:1, 4)*

Most of the laws in this category seem designed to train individuals to think and act in a manner that embodies the fundamental moral principles of Yahwism. The goal was to produce a society that reflected the authors' understanding of the character and will of Yahweh. Obedience was procured by insisting that the laws came directly from Yahweh and thus expressed divine standards of good and bad behavior. In reality, such moral guidelines were probably developed and passed on within families and enforced informally by village elders, religious officials, or family members. Persistent violations would have been handled on a case-by-case basis.

EXERCISE 55

Read Exodus 22:16-31; Leviticus 19:1-37; and Deuteronomy 24:1-22. As you read, make note of whether each law pertains to the social dimension, the ritual dimension, or the ethical dimension of the religious vision of the Torah. When you are done, look back over the list of laws in each category and summarize what is included under each heading.

THE RELIGIOUS VISION OF THE TORAH

In both form and substance, the laws that were included in the books of Torah resemble materials that are known from other societies in the ancient Near East. One obvious parallel is the famous Mesopotamian Code of Hammurabi, a collection of case laws framed in the same kind of "if-then" format that is employed repeatedly in the social laws of the Torah. Many of the problems cited in the two texts are identical, and the manner in which the problems are treated is often similar as well. The same is true for ethical rules: both Mesopotamia and Egypt produced many works that explore the nature of right and wrong behavior, and their conclusions often echo those found in the laws of Torah. Rituals vary more widely among religious groups, but the people of the surrounding nations composed numerous texts that address the same kinds of issues as the ritual materials in the Torah, such as rules for the performance of animal sacrifices.

What makes the Torah distinctive is not so much the way it handles particular issues and cases, but the fact that such different kinds of material—rules for social, ritual, and ethical conduct—have been combined to form a unified literary composition. Other religious communities typically treat these issues in separate texts. By molding them together into a single literary work, the Torah presents a more sweeping and all-inclusive vision for personal and societal conduct than one typically sees in ancient Near Eastern texts.

The distinctiveness of the Torah becomes even more apparent when we recall that its rules are embedded in a narrative framework that ties them closely to the origins of the people (the Exodus story). According to this narrative, the entire collection of laws was dictated by the deity to Moses within a fairly brief period of time. Such a claim is unusual in the ancient Near East, where legal practice was based on age-old traditions, though rules pertaining to rituals were sometimes attributed to the gods. Collections of case law addressing social problems were issued periodically in the names of kings, but these collections were produced by legal scholars based on long-standing traditions and could be revised and edited at any time. Not until the rise of Islam in the seventh century C.E. do we encounter a similar claim that a group possesses a set of laws that was delivered to them directly by the deity, as evidenced by the Muslim belief that Allah dictated the Qur'an to Muhammad over a period of twenty-two years.

The significance of this observation is easy to overlook. By insisting that this entire collection of laws was issued by Yahweh at a single moment in the distant past, the editors of the Torah effectively placed the contents of the collection beyond question or challenge. People can mistrust or even ignore the pronouncements of a human judge or religious official, but who would dare to argue with Yahweh? Linking the laws to Yahweh also created a strong incentive for people to follow the rules, since those who failed to do so were threatened with judgment by the same almighty god who spoke his laws to their ancestors from a cloud of smoke and thunder at Mount Sinai and revealed his awesome power through miracles of deliverance and judgment in the Exodus story. In a similar way, the belief that the laws came directly from Yahweh served to strengthen the faith of those who followed the laws when they were challenged by outsiders who questioned or rejected their way of doing things. This applied to followers of Yahweh who did not accept their laws as much as to followers of other gods.

Another noteworthy point about the Torah is its insistence that social, ritual, and ethical behaviors are equally important to Yahweh. By mixing these different types of laws together and attributing them all to the deity, the Torah presents a grand vision of religious life that encompasses the whole person and the entire society. Not all aspects of individual and social conduct are mentioned in the Torah, but the catalogue of issues is broad enough to suggest that there is no area of life that lies outside of Yahweh's

Fig. 22.3. (left) A column containing the Code of Hammurabi, a Babylonian king who lived in the eighteenth century B.C.E.; (right) a portion of the Ur-Nammu law code from Sumeria (twenty-first century B.C.E.).

Fig. 22.4. (above) William Blake, *God Writing on the Tables of Covenant*; (below) Thoth, the Egyptian god of wisdom, dictates messages to a scribe.

with material success and prosperity. As Yahweh's chosen people, Israel promises to serve Yahweh above all other gods and to live in a way that pleases him. The kind of life that Yahweh desires for his people is spelled out in the laws of Torah. These laws are not arbitrary pronouncements; they are rooted in the very character of Yahweh and are meant to make his people more like him. This point comes through clearly in the book of Leviticus, where Yahweh repeatedly calls on his people to "be holy, for I am holy" (11:44-45; 19:2; 20:7-8, 26; 21:8). Living by these rules is not a condition for earning or retaining their status as Yahweh's covenant people; that was secured forever when Yahweh chose their ancestors out of all the people of the earth to be his partners. But a persistent failure to live as Yahweh wishes will cause the deity to withhold the many blessings that he has promised and eventually bring them under his disciplinary judgment.

THE HISTORY BEHIND THE LAWS

The Torah as we know it is a product of the postexilic period. Little imagination is required to see how its vision for a society united under a common religious program would have appealed to many of the people of Judah at a time when they had lost their political identity as a nation under decades of rule by the Babylonians and the Persians. The fact that the priests stand at the pinnacle of this system as overseers of the covenant and its laws also fits the postexilic situation, when the Persian authorities looked to the priestly class, under the direction of the high priest, to administer the day-to-day affairs of the people. The growing stature of the priests in the postexilic period is epitomized in the story of Ezra the priest, who according to the book of Ezra was commissioned by the king of Persia to appoint judges throughout the land of Judah and to teach the laws of Yahweh to the people (Ezra 7:1-28). Later Ezra is shown reading aloud from "the book of the law of Moses, which the LORD had given to Israel" (Nehemiah 8:1), then leading the people in a prayer of repentance and a renewal of their commitment to the covenant (Nehemiah 9:38—10:39). The story says little about what might have been included in the "book of the law" that Ezra is said to have read, though the nar-

care. Implicit in these materials is the message that the people of Israel should live their daily lives as an expression of devotion to Yahweh, the covenant deity of Israel.

At the heart of the Torah lies the conviction that the people of Israel—those who claim descent from Abraham and the Exodus generation—stand in a special covenant relationship with Yahweh. As in all meaningful relationships, this covenant involves commitments by both parties. As the initiator and guarantor of the covenant, Yahweh promises to guide Israel in the proper way to live, to protect them from harm, and to bless them rator implies that it included both stories and laws as in the present version of the Torah. But the story gives the clear impression that the authority of the priests and the laws of Torah were both on the rise in postexilic Judah.

When we ask about the status of the laws in earlier periods, on the other hand, we find broad disagreement among scholars who have investigated the question. As we have seen in other cases, the principal alternatives can be identified by examining the viewpoints of minimalist, conservative, and maximalist scholars.

Minimalists tend to view the laws of Torah as a purely postexilic production that bears little or no relation to the earlier history of Israel. In their view, the laws are part of a larger effort by a group of literate elites to unite the diverse population of postexilic Judah (Persian period or later) under a religious program that gave central authority to the priestly class. These laws were imbued with an aura of antiquity and authority by embedding them in a mythical narrative that portrayed them as the direct commands of the deity delivered to the people's ancestors at a specific moment in the distant past. With the possible exception of some of the social laws, these laws were neither known nor followed in Israel until they were created as part of a literary work in the postexilic period. From the standpoint of the minimalists, scholars who claim to find evidence of earlier collections of laws within the Torah are allowing themselves to be misled by the literary artistry of the composition. The Torah is fundamentally a piece of social and political propaganda, not a historical document.

Conservative scholars, by contrast, prefer to follow the biblical narrative and attribute most or all of the laws, together with the idea of the covenant, to the period of the Exodus. Some would allow for the possibility that the laws might have been refined or edited in minor ways over time, but most find little reason to question the story as it is presented in the Torah. In the eyes of these scholars, the postexilic period was a time when the people of Judah committed themselves once again to follow the ancient laws that Yahweh had given to their ancestors at Mount Sinai, not a period when laws were being created for the first time.

Maximalist scholars view the present version of the Torah as the product of a long history of compilation, revision, and editing that brought together materials from different sources to form a coherent collection of laws that was joined at some point to the narrative tradition that now serves as the backbone of the Torah. How and when this happened is a matter of debate, since maximalists interpret the limited evidence in different ways. The answer that dominated biblical scholarship from the late nineteenth to the late twentieth century is known as the **Documentary Hypothesis**. This theory proposes that the Torah was created by combining material from four earlier written sources. Two of these sources are dated to the early days of the monarchy (tenth to ninth century B.C.E.), one to the latter part of the monarchy (seventh century B.C.E.), and one to the postexilic era (sixth to fifth century B.C.E.). The first two sources are called *J* and *E*, shorthand for the name of the deity that is typically used in each source (J for Jahweh, the German spelling of Yahweh, and E for Elohim). The last two sources are labeled *D* (shorthand for the book of Deuteronomy, which was largely complete before it entered the collection) and *P* (a reference to the Priestly material in the Torah).

All of these sources are hypothetical; none of them exists outside the present version of the Torah. Scholars use various kinds of evidence to identify the presence of earlier source material within the Torah.

(a) Sometimes the Torah includes more than one version of the same story or law, such as the two accounts of creation in Genesis 1 and 2. Most scholars take these duplications as evidence that the editors found different versions of the same story in their sources and decided to include both stories so as not to lose important material.

(b) Some sections of the Torah show a strong preference for one divine name over others, especially the names Yahweh and Elohim. The patterns of usage are consistent enough in many passages to convince scholars that the names mark the use of earlier sources that employed different names for the deity.

(c) In still other places the language of the text shifts suddenly in the middle of a passage or between two passages, creating awkward transitions in the language, plot, or ideas of the text. Scholars view these awkward spots as places where material from two earlier sources has been brought together.

(d) Sometimes scholars find inconsistencies and contradictions within a single story, as when Yahweh tells Noah to take two of every type of animal into his ark and then a few verses later instructs him to take seven of every ritually pure animal (animals that can be offered as sacrifices) and two of every unclean animal. Scholars view these inconsistencies as indications that two earlier versions of the same story have been woven together to create a single account.

(e) Less visible in translations are the many differences in linguistic usage that can be observed at various points in the Torah. Differences in vocabulary, grammar, and style from one section to another are commonly viewed as signs that the editors have taken over material from earlier sources that used distinctive linguistic styles.

These and other lines of evidence have convinced the great majority of scholars that the Torah was created by combining material from earlier sources, though not all agree that the material can be categorized into as few as four discrete sources. Those who accept the Documentary Hypothesis have developed various criteria for dividing the laws in Exodus, Leviticus, and Numbers among the four source texts. According to this theory, the laws that were taken from J and E are the earliest, while the laws in Deuteronomy represent a later revision of these laws. The P material, with its focus on priestly concerns, was inserted by a postexilic editor to bring the preexilic laws into line with the more ritualistic religion of the postexilic era. Earlier versions of the theory viewed the postexilic preoccupation with ritual as a decline from the focus on moral and ethical conduct that characterized the earlier period, but this interpretation has been rightly rejected as anti-Jewish by more recent scholars.

Over the last few decades, the Documentary Hypothesis has come under fire from a variety of directions. Most of the criticisms are too technical for an introductory textbook, but the critics are in agreement that the theory is an oversimplification of a much more complex process, not a completely mistaken approach. Virtually all of the competing theories view the composition of the Torah as a gradual process involving the blending of materials from a wide range of oral and written sources and traditions. Some of these earlier traditions may have been combined into smaller units before they were incorporated into the broader collection that became the Torah, but the history of these earlier collections is difficult to trace. Examples of early collections include the Ten Commandments (Exodus 20:1-17; Deuteronomy 5:6-21), which many regard as the essence of the Torah; the Book of the Covenant (Exodus 20:22—23:33), a unit that focuses primarily on social conduct; and the Holiness Code (Leviticus 17:1—26:46), a series of chapters that addresses matters of purity and other ritual concerns. Even the book of Deuteronomy, which the Documentary Hypothesis regards as a single source, is viewed by its challengers as a compilation of material from earlier sources. Many of the critics also reject the claim that the so-called priestly materials reflect a postexilic viewpoint, arguing instead that rituals were vital to Yahwistic religion from its earliest days, though the precise form of the rituals changed over time. Most believe that the Exile played a key role in motivating the literate elites to compile and edit these earlier traditions, though their work continued well into the postexilic period. In short, critics of the Documentary Hypothesis view the laws of Torah as the selective distillation of a living tradition that grew and changed as long-standing legal traditions were applied to a variety of new situations at diverse times and places.

With so many different theories about the origins and development of the Torah, it is impossible to speak with confidence about the status of the laws in Israelite society prior to the exilic period. Depending on whose reconstruction one accepts, the ancient people of Israel possessed either (a) a full complement of laws that regulated their individual and social lives (the conservative view), or (b) a series of localized laws and traditions that changed and developed over time (the maximalist position), or (c) no coherent system of social and religious laws that can be discerned at this time (the minimalist approach). All three interpretations of the evidence have strengths and weaknesses.

(a) Conservative scholars have been criticized for placing too much trust in the biblical narrative and ignoring evidence that points to the use of earlier sources and a long history of development for the Torah. On the other hand, their insistence on an early date for the laws of Torah has forced other scholars to grapple with the question of how these laws came to be associated so strongly with Moses and the Exodus saga if they did not in fact originate at that time. Many maximalists would now agree that at least some of the laws might go back to the time of Moses.

(b) Maximalist scholars have come under fire for devoting their energies to the quest for earlier sources and neglecting the exilic and postexilic contexts that led to the production of the present collection. At the same time, their rigorous linguistic and historical studies have uncovered a formidable body of evidence that has convinced the majority of scholars that the Torah was indeed compiled from earlier source materials. Both conservatives and minimalists have found it necessary to develop arguments to counter their observations and conclusions.

(c) Scholars who interpret the data through a minimalist lens have been charged with misreading or ignoring evidence that points to the presence of preexilic material within the Torah. At the same time, their efforts to situate the Torah within the social and political contexts of the postexilic era have prompted their opponents to pay more attention to the social factors that led to the compilation and editing of the Torah instead of focusing so heavily on the earlier sources that they believe lie behind the Torah.

Whatever we conclude about the nature and content of Israelite legal traditions during the preexilic period, we can be certain that there were many people who neither accepted nor followed Yahwistic legal traditions during this era. This is apparent both from the grand narrative of the Hebrew Bible, which speaks of times when Yahwism was actually a minority religion within Palestine, and from the sayings of the preexilic prophets, who repeatedly condemn the people of Israel and Judah for rejecting Yahweh and

living contrary to his ways (see chapters 32–33). There were also many followers of Yahweh who held different ideas about what the deity wanted for his people. Perhaps some of them had legal traditions of their own that have not survived.

For these reasons it makes more sense to view the legal traditions that lie behind the Torah as the intellectual property of a particular group or movement of Yahwists rather than as the accepted law of the land. The group could have been large or small, but it must have been led by members of the literate elite who were able to ensure that the group's ideas would be written down and compiled to form the collections that most scholars believe were used in the production of the Torah. Unfortunately for them, they lacked the power to impose their laws upon the entire nation. Not until the coming of the Exile (or

Fig. 22.5. (top) The oldest known fragment of a Torah text, a small silver scroll from the seventh century B.C.E. that contains the priestly blessing from Numbers 6:24-26; (bottom) one of the oldest Torah scrolls in existence, a copy of the book of Leviticus that was found among the Dead Sea Scrolls (second century B.C.E.).

NUMBERS 6:24-26

English text	Hebrew text
The LORD bless you and keep you; the LORD make his face to shine upon you, and be gracious to you; the LORD lift up his countenance upon you, and give you peace.	יברכך יהוה וישמרך יאר יהוה פניו אליך ויחנך ישׂא יהוה פניו אליך וישׂם לך שלום

later) did the people who developed and maintained these traditions gain enough influence among the social and religious elites to ensure that their ideas would become the norm for the people as a whole.

One benefit of this way of viewing the materials is that it explains why some of the laws in the Torah strike modern readers as too idealistic to be implemented in the real world. The people who developed these laws were laying out their vision of an ideal Yahwistic society, not issuing prescriptions that carried the force of law. Clearly they hoped that their vision would one day be realized, but they were not engaged in writing legislation for an existing social group.

Another advantage of this understanding of the origins of the Torah is that it suggests an explanation for why the laws came to be linked to Moses and the Exodus tradition. If the people who formed these collections of laws were seeking to convince other followers of Yahweh to accept their views, it is easy to see why they might have found it effective to frame their traditions as commands issued by Yahweh during the time of the Exodus. As far as they knew, some of the laws in their collections were so ancient that they might well go back to Moses' time. If this view is correct, it suggests that the decision to link together the Exodus story, the ideology of the covenant, and the laws of Torah may have arisen out of a conflict between groups of Yahwists who had different ideas about what it meant to be a follower of Yahweh.

EXERCISE 56

Read the following sets of verses from the Torah and note where they agree and where they disagree. How might you explain the differences?

- Exodus 20:1-17 and Deuteronomy 5:1-21
- Exodus 21:1-6 and Leviticus 25:39-46
- Leviticus 17:1-9 and Deuteronomy 12:13-18
- Numbers 18:21-24 and Deuteronomy 14:22-29

CONCLUSION

The laws and regulations that fill the books of Exodus, Leviticus, Numbers, and Deuteronomy are embedded in a narrative that depicts them as divine commandments given by Yahweh to Moses during the forty years that the Israelites spent wandering in the wilderness. While conservatives continue to defend the validity of this story, most contemporary scholars view this part of the Exodus narrative as a literary fiction that obscures the actual historical process by which the laws developed.

Nonetheless, there is little agreement among scholars about when and how the laws of Torah might have originated. Some think that the present version of the Torah was crafted out of four earlier written sources, while others argue that the process was more complex and used a broader range of oral and written materials. Still others view the laws of Torah as a vital part of a postexilic program for establishing an ideal society under the rule of Yahweh and his priests. Whatever their prior history, it was not until sometime after the Exile that the laws of Torah came to be widely acknowledged as the standard upon which the lives of the followers of Yahweh should be based.

In its present form, the Torah includes laws that address the social, ritual, and ethical dimensions of life. The sheer breadth of the materials suggests that the editors were seeking to promote a religious vision in which all of life would be lived as an act of devotion to Yahweh. This vision finds its fullest expression in the idea of a covenant between Yahweh and his people in which Yahweh promises to care for his people and they commit themselves to obey his laws. This program is reinforced by assurances of divine blessings for those who live as Yahweh wishes and curses for those who do not. Such a view of Yahweh's relationship with his people would have served as a powerful incentive for those who accepted its basic premises to comply with the laws of Torah.

EXERCISE 57

Review the following list and circle those items that you think might have been (a) required or (b) prohibited under the laws of Torah. Then read the verses below the list and match them up with the relevant items on the list. (The verses do not follow the same order as the list.) Those that do not match up with a verse are not in the Torah.

When you are done, look back at the list and make note of anything that surprises you. Which items were you expecting to find in the Torah that were not there? Which ones were you surprised to see included? Explain your answers.

Required

1. Going to church
2. Killing adulterers
3. Standing when older people approach
4. Animal sacrifices
5. Women to obey their husbands
6. Killing witches
7. Marrying one's brother's widow
8. Draining all the blood from meat
9. Baptizing one's children
10. Women to be virgins when they marry
11. Loving your neighbor as yourself
12. Keeping away from foreigners
13. Leaving land unplanted every seven years
14. Killing idol worshippers
15. Confessing one's sins to a priest
16. Woman to marry a man who rapes her
17. Resting on Sundays
18. Loving God with your whole heart
19. Capital punishment for murder
20. Prayer before meals

Prohibited

1. Eating shellfish
2. Gambling
3. Touching a corpse
4. Wearing tattoos
5. Owning slaves
6. Working on Saturdays
7. Lending money at interest
8. Masturbation
9. Divorce
10. Mistreating animals
11. Getting drunk
12. Homosexuality
13. Lying about other people
14. Abortion
15. Mistreating foreigners
16. Eating insects
17. Marrying one's niece
18. Swearing at one's parents
19. Taking oaths
20. Cross-dressing

Deuteronomy 19:11-13; 24:17
Leviticus 18:10
Deuteronomy 6:5
Deuteronomy 22:5
Exodus 22:18
Exodus 20:8-11; 23:12; 31:14-17; 35:1-3
Deuteronomy 5:12-15
Numbers 19:11-21
Leviticus 19:32
Leviticus 18:22; 20:13
Exodus 22:25
Deuteronomy 23:19-20
Leviticus 20:10-12
Deuteronomy 22:22
Exodus 21:17

Leviticus 20:9
Leviticus 19:28
Deuteronomy 22:13-21
Deuteronomy 13:6-11
Exodus 23:12
Deuteronomy 22:6-7; 25:4
Exodus 23:10
Exodus 22:21; 23:9
Leviticus 11:9-12
Exodus 23:1
Deuteronomy 25:5-10
Leviticus 17:10-14
Deuteronomy 22:28-29
Leviticus 19:18

Fig. 23.1. An ancient Jewish ritual bath; the person wishing to be cleansed would walk down one side of the steps as "unclean" and return on the other side as "clean."

Purity Laws

You shall keep all my statutes and all my ordinances, and observe them, so that the land to which I bring you to settle in may not vomit you out. . . . You shall therefore make a distinction between the clean animal and the unclean, and between the unclean bird and the clean; you shall not bring abomination on yourselves by animal or by bird or by anything with which the ground teems, which I have set apart for you to hold unclean. You shall be holy to me; for I the Lord am holy, and I have separated you from the other peoples to be mine. (Leviticus 20:22, 25-26)

The Lord spoke to Moses, saying: When any of you commit a trespass and sin unintentionally in any of the holy things of the Lord, you shall bring, as your guilt offering to the Lord, a ram without blemish from the flock, convertible into silver by the sanctuary shekel; it is a guilt offering. And you shall make restitution for the holy thing in which you were remiss, and shall add one-fifth to it and give it to the priest. The priest shall make atonement on your behalf with the ram of the guilt offering, and you shall be forgiven. (Leviticus 5:14-16)

Those who touch the dead body of any human being shall be unclean seven days. They shall purify themselves with the water on the third day and on the seventh day, and so be clean; but if they do not purify themselves on the third day and on the seventh day, they will not become clean. All who touch a corpse, the body of a human being who has died, and do not purify themselves, defile the tabernacle of the Lord; such persons shall be cut off from Israel. (Numbers 19:11-13)

People who know nothing about the laws of Torah often feel overwhelmed upon their first exposure to these texts. Some of the laws sound vaguely familiar due to their influence on the sacred texts of Christianity and Islam, while others have parallels in the legal systems followed by most Western societies. Many, however, seem utterly foreign to contemporary readers who are unfamiliar with the vision of reality and the religious sensibility presupposed in these texts. The fact that the laws are not organized into any obvious pattern only adds to the impression that the texts are hard to understand. The present chapter aims to counter that impression by highlighting some of the patterns and principles that underlie the individual laws of Torah and examining one major category of laws within the Torah, the purity laws.

TORAH AND LAW

Before we move into a closer examination of the laws of Torah, we would do well to pause for a moment and reflect on the nature of the collection as a whole. The term *laws*, though steeped in tradition, is less than adequate as a description of the hundreds of guidelines for individual and social conduct that fill the Torah. The term has its roots in the biblical image of Yahweh as a mighty king who reigns unchallenged over his people and issues decrees that must be obeyed. But the actual content of the Torah is more complex and diverse than this image suggests. The Torah does contain many laws that identify certain behaviors as wrong and prescribe severe penalties for violations. Most of these verses are related to the Torah's vision for creating a society that reflects the character and will of Yahweh. But the Torah also includes instructions for the performance of rituals and guidelines for the ethical and religious conduct of individuals. Neither of these types of material can be described as laws in the strict sense, since there is no apparent mechanism for enforcement and most carry no penalties other than those that might be imposed by Yahweh himself.

Labeling all of these materials as laws can be misleading unless we realize that the term is being used figuratively in conjunction with the image of Yahweh as the king of Israel. Failure to acknowledge this point can lead to serious misunderstandings. For example, Christians have a long history of deriding Judaism as a "works religion" (that is, a religion that claims people can earn their way to heaven by their good deeds) that was superseded by the "faith religion" that was introduced by Jesus and embodied in the Christian church. This negative evaluation of Judaism and the Torah was one of several arguments used by Christians to justify centuries of anti-Semitism that led finally to the Holocaust. Such mistaken interpretations can only occur when people read the laws of Torah in isolation from their broader context as the terms of the covenant between Yahweh and his chosen people. Within the covenant, there is no distinction between faith and works—obeying Yahweh's decrees is the primary means of expressing one's faith in Yahweh.

Unfortunately, there is no single English word that encompasses the legal and relational imagery that lies behind and gives meaning to the individual rules for living that are contained in the Torah. Since the Torah itself uses legal terminology when referring to its provisions (laws, commandments, regulations, and the like), we will continue to use such language in our analysis of the material, but with the understanding that these terms must be understood within the context of Yahweh's covenant with Israel.

CATEGORIZING THE LAWS

The people who compiled the Torah into its present form did not organize the laws into any overall pattern. In some passages the laws are grouped according to a common theme (Exodus 21:12-27; 22:1-15; Leviticus 1:1—7:38; 23:1-44; Numbers 28:1—29:4; Deuteronomy 12:1—13:18), while in others the order seems entirely random, with little or no continuity or link between the verses (Exodus 22:16-31; 34:10-28; Leviticus 19:1-37; Deuteronomy 23:15—25:16). Additionally, not all issues are treated equally—some are addressed in a verse or less, while others fill a chapter or more of text (Exodus 25:1—30:38; Leviticus 13:1—14:57; 16:1-34; Numbers 30:1-16; Deuteronomy 20:1-20). Some subjects are mentioned only once, while other topics (the Sabbath, the festivals, the rituals for animal sacrifice) are addressed repeatedly. Clearly the people who compiled these materials did not share our modern concerns for topical arrangement or balanced treatment.

Some scholars have claimed to discern a literary purpose behind the distribution and arrangement of the laws, but most believe that the haphazard and uneven nature of the collection points to the use of earlier collections. Instead of reorganizing the laws into a more usable format, the editors felt compelled, presumably out of respect for their sources, to preserve the earlier materials in their original order. This does not explain why the laws were arranged in a particular order in the first place, but it does help us to understand the nature of the finished product.

Scholars who study the rules and regulations of the Torah have developed their own systems of categorization to reduce the complexity of the materials and make them easier to analyze. Most of these systems reflect the common scholarly desire to identify earlier sources within the Torah or to trace the historical development of the collection.

One way of categorizing the laws is by their linguistic features. For instance, some of the laws are framed in an "if-then" case format, while others (the majority) are presented as direct commands of the deity ("do this" or "don't do that"). The case law format resembles the law codes of Mesopotamia, while the command form is relatively uncommon outside the Torah. Some scholars have suggested that the case laws might have been created or edited by a group of legal scholars (priests?) as in Mesopotamia, while the direct commands might have originated with the same class of teachers that produced the wisdom literature, where similar modes of expression can be seen (see chapter 37). This kind of analysis, while helpful for historical purposes, does not take us very far toward understanding either the content of the laws or the ideology that lies behind them.

Other scholars have catalogued the materials according to the types of problems that they address. Some divide the laws into broad categories like public offenses and private offenses, while others choose a recurring theme like property damage, sexuality, or the worship of other gods, then investigate how the issue is treated in different passages. Where comparative materials are available, scholars also look at how the subject was handled in the law codes of Mesopotamia in order to determine which of the biblical laws represent common approaches to problems and which are distinctive. In most cases the goal is to retrace the development of the legal materials contained in the Torah. Studies such as these are helpful for highlighting the many inconsistencies in the Torah that point to a complicated history for the collection. But the piecemeal nature of their approach does not shed much light on the nature of the collection as it now stands.

` A more fruitful and less technical way of analyzing the materials for beginning students is to divide them into two broad categories, purity laws and social laws. In shorthand form, purity laws aim to regulate and channel the people's interactions with the supernatural realm (that is, their "vertical" relationships with the deity), while social laws define how people should relate to one another both individually and as a society (that is, their "horizontal" relationships). Purity laws pertain primarily to issues that were identified as part of the ritual dimension in the previous chapter, while social laws relate to the social and ethical dimensions of Yahwistic religion. Not all of the laws of Torah fit easily into one of these two categories, and some could be fruitfully analyzed under either heading. But organizing the laws in this way does have the advantage of exposing many of the central ideas that lie behind the collection as it now stands. Most of these concepts are older than the present collection, though purity concerns clearly became more important during the era of the Exile and beyond.

EXERCISE 58

Read the following passages and make note of any words or phrases that appear repeatedly in different passages or that seem to play a central role within a particular passage. What do these words tell you about the belief system that lies behind the texts?

- Leviticus 11:41-45
- Leviticus 12:1-7
- Leviticus 16:29-33
- Leviticus 18:24-30
- Leviticus 21:16-23
- Numbers 19:11-13
- Deuteronomy 23:9-14

THE SACRED AND THE PROFANE

Many of the laws of Torah reflect a strong interest in the subject of ritual purity. Pairs of adjectives like clean/unclean, pure/impure, and holy/profane dominate these passages. Some passages are preoccupied with identifying actions that defile a person, while others focus on ways to be purified from defilement. **Impurity** is not limited to people; animals, crops, buildings, household utensils, even a piece of ground can be classified as clean or unclean. Most forms of impurity can be cleansed by following certain rituals, but some can only be removed by executing the offender.

The worldview presupposed in these passages is foreign to most contemporary readers. Centuries of Christian influence have led religious people in the West to view reality through a moral lens. Sin, not impurity, is the term that is commonly used to describe deviations from the will of the deity. Sin is viewed as a conscious choice; there is no such thing as unintentional sin. Such a view of reality has no place for a belief that one's relations with the deity might be affected by physical contact with an unclean person or object. In fact, many people today would regard such beliefs as a form of superstition.

Nevertheless, there are millions of people in the world today who view reality through the same kind of lens that we see in the Torah. Native Americans and African tribal groups in particular have many ideas and practices that resemble the biblical purity laws. People outside these groups are often unfamiliar with their views because many of their beliefs and practices are passed on orally

Fig. 23.2. (top) Native Americans often use smoke for ritual purification; (bottom) Muslims wash in a prescribed manner to purify themselves before praying.

rather than in written form and they tend to live apart from other groups. Other religions that take ritual purity seriously include Shinto (Japan), Zoroastrianism (Iran), and some forms of Hinduism (India). Islam, too, requires the avoidance of certain types of impurity and the use of ritual cleansings before prayer.

At the heart of all purity systems lies a belief that the universe is permeated by supernatural forces that are not always friendly or accessible to humans. Interactions with these forces must be handled with care if one is to avoid being harmed by them. Rituals play a central role in the maintenance of such a system. Certain kinds of actions (commonly called taboos) are thought to offend or interfere with the workings of the supernatural and must therefore be avoided in order to maintain positive relations with the divine realm. Various forms of ritual purification are provided for individuals who violate these taboos. Purification is also required in the case of natural occurrences that are viewed as either out of the ordinary or mysterious, such as menstruation, childbirth, disease, and death. People who have physical contact with impure people or objects are also deemed impure and in need of cleansing under most purity systems. If impurities are not properly handled (and removed), the rituals that open up channels of communication with the divine realm will eventually become ineffectual. Some groups even believe that untreated impurities can result in physical harm to the affected individuals or the community.

Many ideas about what makes a person pure or impure are consistent from culture to culture. Virtually all purity systems hold that physical contact with blood, bodily fluids, or corpses makes a person impure. Many also use ritualized forms of washing and periods of isolation to cleanse people from impurity. Yet no two groups have exactly the same beliefs about purity issues. Eating pork is viewed as impure in Judaism and Islam, while pork is acceptable and beef is unclean for Hindus. Similarly, fire is used as a form of purification in Zoroastrianism but not in Judaism. Most of the agreements among different groups involve universal human experiences, while the differences usually reflect local customs or adaptive responses to diverse environments.

Contemporary anthropologists have identified several purposes that purity systems serve for the people who follow them. First, they help to make sense of the world and bring it under control. Humans everywhere have an innate longing for a sense of meaning, order, and safety in the face of a universe that frequently appears inexplicable and threatening. Purity systems are basically a prescientific way of organizing the bewildering variety of the universe into a limited set of manageable categories. Familiar objects, people, and experiences are considered pure (that is, normal) and associated with the hidden order that lies behind the visible universe. Things that are unfamiliar or strange are deemed impure (that is, abnormal) and linked to the forces of chaos and evil. The same is true for people and objects that do not fit the culture's mental map of the universe, whether because they are in some sense out of place (by being located in a place where they do not ordinarily belong) or out of the ordinary (lacking some of the characteristics commonly associated with a particular category of reality). Of course, few people in antiquity actually thought about the laws in this way; most simply accepted them as divine commands. Nonetheless, we can see in hindsight that many purity rules are rooted in astute observations about the nature of humans and their physical environment.

Second, purity systems reinforce societal norms and institutions. The claim that a particular type of action will elicit the favor or disfavor of the gods by influencing the balance between purity and impurity in a society is a more effective motivator than the command of a fallible human authority. This is especially true when people have been taught to believe that the actions of each individual affect the group's relations with the supernatural realm. In these cases peer pressure becomes a powerful tool for persuading people to conform to the rules of the system and accept the judgments of its leaders. Those who control the definitions of purity and the means of purification (usually a small priestly class) invariably wield substantial power in a society framed around purity concerns.

Finally, purity rules can help a group of people to maintain their identity in the presence of cultural diversity. Most purity systems require their followers to distance themselves to some degree from people outside the group, since outsiders do not follow the group's purity rules and are therefore potential sources of contamination. This pattern of thinking can produce strong psychological and social barriers against close contact (especially sexual contact) with outsiders. In some cases, purity rules are defined in explicit opposition to the practices of another group in order to diminish the possibility that the members of the two groups might mix. By associating purity with "us" and impurity with "them," purity systems reinforce the pride and cohesiveness of group members while making it harder for them to consider defecting to another group or adopting their practices.

PURITY AND THE TORAH

The purity system of the Torah is most visible in the book of Leviticus, though examples can be found in other books as well. The biblical system is similar to what we see in other religions. The similarities can be difficult to discern, however, because the Torah contains only the rules by which the system operates; almost nothing is said about the broader rationale behind those rules. Clearly the editors assumed that their ancient audience already understood why the system was needed.

At the heart of the Torah's purity system lies a single defining concept: Yahweh is a holy god who requires a holy people to serve as his covenant partners. As we saw in chapter 12, the word *holy* refers to something that has been "set apart" from other people, places, times, or objects of a similar type. To call Yahweh holy is to say that he is fundamentally unlike any other living being, whether divine (the gods honored by other peoples), human, or animal. Yahweh is the only being in the universe who is inherently holy; everything else is by nature unholy or **profane**. (The heavenly council that appears in some other biblical texts is not present in the purity system of the Torah.) By definition, that which is holy must be set apart from that which is unholy in order to preserve its holiness. The diagram on page 308 illustrates the key elements of this worldview using adjective pairs that the Torah employs to describe each sphere.

Out of the category of profane humanity, Yahweh has graciously chosen one group of people, the descendants of Abraham (later narrowed to the descendants of the people whom he led out of Egypt), to be his covenant partners. This choice makes them holy, since by it they are set apart from other nations for a unique relationship with Yahweh.

YAHWEH

holy
sacred
pure
clean

HUMANS

unholy
profane   **buildings**   **animals**
impure
unclean   **nations**

                    implements   **crops**

In the worldview of the Torah, Yahweh is the only being in the universe who is inherently "pure" or "holy."

Out of all the people of Israel, Yahweh has chosen certain families to serve as his priests. This divine choice elevates these families to a position of holiness above other Israelites, since they will interact directly with the deity and manage the rituals by which people and objects are made holy to Yahweh. Yahweh has also selected a special building where he will reside in the midst of his people. This building (in the Exodus narrative, the tabernacle; in later texts, the Jerusalem temple) is to be set apart for the service of Yahweh alone. Other sites can be made holy by the temporary presence of the deity, but the holiness of this building exceeds that of any other spot on earth. The innermost part of the building, called the Holy of Holies, is the most sacred place of all, since it is the dwelling place of a holy god. Nothing impure is to enter Yahweh's house; people and objects must be purified before they can come near to the holy presence of Yahweh. Those who violate this requirement are subject to death.

People and objects can be made holy and thus suitable for association with Yahweh by the performance of certain rituals. Priests who serve in the temple must undergo special purification ceremonies when they are installed into office and must follow stricter purity rules than ordinary Israelites. When performing their duties, they must wear special clothing that can be worn on no other occasion and eat only food that has been dedicated to the deity in sacrifice. Animals that are sacrificed to Yahweh must be physically flawless and must be slaughtered and cooked according to special rules. Other food products that are used in temple ceremonies (oil, incense, bread) must be made from a special formula that is reserved exclusively for the temple. Even the tools and implements used by the priests must be purified by special rituals and used nowhere else. Everything associated with the temple must be protected from contact with any form of impurity. The diagram on page 309 shows these additional elements of the Torah's purity system.

If Israel is to have a holy god living in its midst, the people and the land must be kept holy as well. The way to do this is spelled out in Yahweh's laws. Following these laws will set Israel apart from the sinful and impure ways of the people around them, as Yahweh intended when he chose their ancestors to be his holy nation. Some of the laws provide guidelines for moral or ethical conduct,

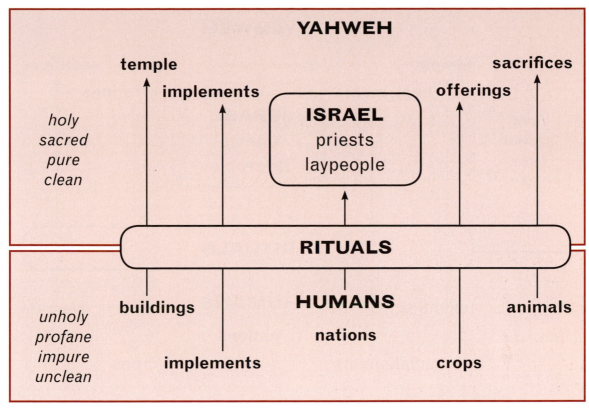

People and objects that are inherently "impure" or "unholy" can be set apart as holy through the use of rituals.

while others identify impure acts that should be avoided. Still others seek to prevent the mixing of things that Yahweh designed to remain separate. Obedience to these laws will ensure that the physical and moral order that Yahweh embedded in the universe is preserved intact. Disobedience, by contrast, threatens the people and the world with chaos and dissolution.

Fortunately, Yahweh does not require perfect obedience. His laws include a variety of rituals designed to cleanse his people from their sins and restore them to a state of holiness when they violate any of his commandments. Rituals are also crucial for removing other forms of impurity that people contract in the ordinary course of living, such as the touching of a corpse, which brings people into contact with the fearsome powers of death; menstruation, an inexplicable occurrence associated with the power of blood; and skin diseases, which threaten not only the person who is afflicted but also others whom they happen to touch. The precise ritual to be followed

in each case varies with the nature and cause of the impurity. Options include immersion in water, isolation, animal sacrifices, prayers, and the passage of time. Not all impurities can be cleansed by rituals. Some acts are so dreadful that the offender must be removed from the land, whether by exile or death.

Holy objects that become impure (for example, through contact with an impure person or object) can be purified in most cases by rituals, though there are some cases in which the object must be destroyed. The temple and its altar must be cleansed of impurities once a year through the performance of special sacrifices and the application of sacred blood to the temple precincts. Even the land can become impure and require cleansing if the people's sins and impurities are allowed to accumulate without purification. To be accurate, then, the diagram that we have been using to illustrate the purity system of the Torah should include arrows that point in *both* directions between the sphere of the pure and the impure as,

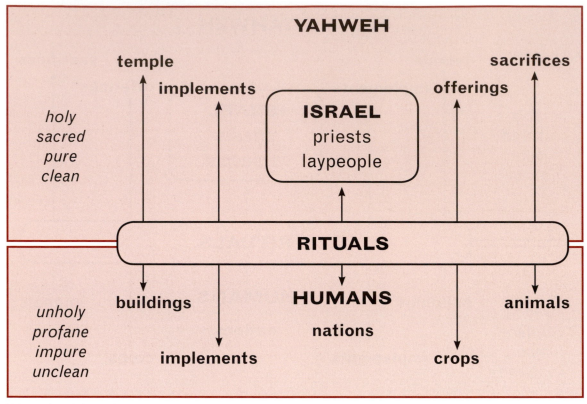

Holy people and objects that become "unclean" can often be restored to a state of purity through rituals.

as indicated above, since anything in the pure category (apart from Yahweh) can be rendered impure under certain circumstances and can be made pure again through the proper performance of rituals.

As long as the people of Yahweh make a serious effort to follow his laws and perform the proper rituals when needed to cleanse them from impurity, Yahweh will remain with Israel and continue to provide for their needs. If his people persist in disobeying his laws, however, or if they fail to follow the proper cleansing rituals, then impurity can spread to the entire land, including the temple, making it unsuitable for a holy god. Eventually Yahweh will remove his protective presence and abandon his people, leaving them to be overcome by disease, famine, and foreign invaders. The desire to retain Yahweh's presence among his people appears to have been one of the central motivations for obeying the purity laws.

Two other points are worth noting about the Torah's purity system. The first concerns the power of blood.

Blood was a potent substance in the eyes of the people who created the purity laws. As far as they were concerned, blood carried the power of life for people and animals alike, since they could see that the uncontrolled emission of blood invariably led to death. Thus the purity laws include special provisions for the handling of blood. Blood must be drained from all meat before it is eaten, and special rituals must be used whenever blood is spilled, including childbirth and menstruation. On the positive side, the blood of an animal that has been ritually dedicated to Yahweh can be sprinkled upon people and objects to cleanse them from impurity. In fact, the blood of a sacrificed animal is the most potent of all cleansing forces, since it is both powerful and holy.

The final point that should be noted is that the purity system described in the Torah operates under the oversight of the priests. Ordinary Israelites are not allowed to enter Yahweh's holy temple. They can bring animals and crops to the temple precincts to be offered to Yahweh,

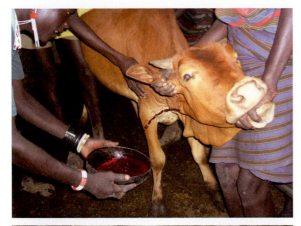

Fig. 23.3. (top) Members of a Ugandan tribe collect blood from a bull for ritual use; (bottom) a Hindu priest in Bali offers incense to the gods.

should be considered impure and segregated from the community. If the disease goes away, a priest is supposed to perform special cleansing rituals to remove any lingering impurity from the person's house and possessions (Leviticus 13–14). Priests also oversee a ritual that is used to determine whether a wife has been unfaithful to her husband (Numbers 5:11-31). According to the book of Deuteronomy, difficult cases of legal interpretation are to be brought to the priests for resolution, and their rulings are to be accepted as final (Deuteronomy 17:8-12). In summary, the purity laws envision a society in which priests play a key role in managing the social and religious lives of the people.

EXERCISE 59

Read Leviticus 12:1-8; 16:1-34; 22:1-16; and Numbers 6:1-21. Then write a paragraph explaining how the ideas and practices described in one of these passages relate to the purity system that we have been studying in this chapter.

WHY PURITY?

As we saw earlier in the chapter, purity systems represent an effort to establish and maintain a sense of psychological and social order in the midst of the confusion and dangers of everyday life in a prescientific society. In this sense, the purity system of the Torah is simply a localized expression of a broader cross-cultural phenomenon. Thus the many biblical laws that prohibit the mixing of dissimilar substances (for example, no sowing of two types of seed in a field, no wearing of garments made of two types of material) can be understood as a symbolic means of reinforcing the importance of maintaining purity (understood here as avoiding mixtures) in every area of life. Concerns about mixing also lie behind some of the food laws, which forbid the eating of animals that violate the Torah's mental map of the animal world by having qualities commonly associated with different groups of animals. Thus the eating of pork is disallowed on the grounds that pigs have split hooves like cattle but do not chew cud like other split-hooved animals, while

but the priests, aided by their assistants, the Levites, perform the sacrifices and direct the prayers and songs that are offered in conjunction with the sacrifices (see chapter 30). The priests also receive a portion of most of the sacrifices and offerings as their food. In addition to overseeing the offerings of individuals, the priests offer daily sacrifices on behalf of the entire nation and special sacrifices at festival times and other sacred occasions.

The priests also supervise the practical implementation of some of the laws. For example, it is the duty of the priests to decide when a person with a skin disease the eating of rabbits is prohibited for the opposite reason (that is, they chew cud but do not have a split hoof; see Leviticus 11:6-7). The eating of shellfish is likewise banned because shellfish do not have fins and tails as fish do (Leviticus 11:9-12). Similar concerns lie behind many other biblical laws. Anything that does not fit the societal understanding of normality can potentially be declared unclean.

Cross-cultural parallels are also evident in the concern for bodily integrity that appears in many of the purity laws. For example, illnesses or other conditions that result in the emission of fluids from the body (blood, pus, semen, and so forth) render a person unclean in a way that sicknesses affecting only the inner parts of the body do not. Even such natural occurrences as menstruation and childbirth fit into this category, since they result in the emission of blood (Leviticus 12:1-8). These and similar laws appear to reflect a cross-cultural concern for protecting the wholeness of the body, a concern that some anthropologists see as a symbolic representation at the microlevel of a broader concern for preserving the integrity of the social group. Just as the boundaries of the group must be rigidly defined and protected in order to preserve it from dissolution by the chaotic forces that surround it, so also the integrity of the physical body must be guarded against similar threats. Similar reasoning probably lies behind the biblical prohibitions against bringing physically defective people or animals into Yahweh's presence (Leviticus 21:16-23; 22:17-25): either their bodily integrity has been compromised, or else they lack characteristics that would qualify them as normal or whole.

Cross-cultural comparisons such as these are helpful for understanding the logic behind the biblical purity system, but they do not explain why a purity system emerged among some of the followers of Yahweh, nor why it took the particular form that it did. Unfortunately, the texts give us few direct answers to these questions. Hardly any of the purity rules are accompanied by an explanation or rationale; most are simply presented as the commands of Yahweh, the holy god of Israel, whose words must be obeyed without question. A few exceptions can be observed: the care required in the handling of blood is justified by the assertion that "the life of the flesh is in the

blood" (Leviticus 17:11); sacrifices are to be performed in order to atone for the people's sins (though the manner in which they operate is never specified) and to offer a "pleasing odor to the Lord" (Leviticus 1:9, 13, 17; 2:2, 9, 16); and the fatty portions of a sacrificial animal are to be burned on the altar and not eaten because "all fat is the Lord's" (Leviticus 3:16). Yet statements such as these tell us little about how the various practices originated. The Exodus narrative claims that the entire collection of laws goes back to the earliest days of the nation. But only conservative scholars would accept this account as a historical record, as we noted in the previous chapter.

One possible clue to the historical origins of the purity system can be found in several passages that contrast the behaviors required by the Torah with the customs of the surrounding peoples. For example, Leviticus 17 requires the people to bring their sacrifices "to the priest at the entrance of the tent of meeting" (that is, the tabernacle, later replaced by the Jerusalem temple) "so that they may no longer offer their sacrifices for goat-demons, to whom they prostitute themselves" (17:5, 7). In other words, animal sacrifices are restricted to a specific site so that the priests can make sure that the people are offering them to Yahweh and not to other gods. The same idea is expressed more explicitly in texts like Leviticus 18:24-30:

> Do not defile yourselves in any of these ways, for by all these practices the nations I am casting out before you have defiled themselves. Thus the land became defiled; and I punished it for its iniquity, and the land vomited out its inhabitants. But you shall keep my statutes and my ordinances and commit none of these abominations, either the citizen or the alien who resides among you (for the inhabitants of the land, who were before you, committed all of these abominations, and the land became defiled); otherwise the land will vomit you out for defiling it, as it vomited out the nation that was before you. For whoever commits any of these abominations shall be cut off from their people. So keep my charge not to commit any of these abominations that were done before you, and not to defile yourselves by them: I am the Lord your God.

According to this passage, the prior inhabitants of Palestine (the Canaanites) who worshipped gods other than Yahweh had defiled the land (that is, rendered it impure) by their practices, and Yahweh had removed them from his territory as a result (an act of purification). Now Yahweh is warning his people to obey his laws and avoid Canaanite religious practices in order to avoid a similar fate. The passage presupposes a situation in which the target audience is familiar with non-Yahwistic religious practices and at least some of them have found these practices attractive.

A careful study of the purity laws reveals that many of them require conduct that is the direct opposite of the social and religious practices of the non-Yahwistic residents of Palestine. This suggests that the purity laws were designed to create a psychological and social barrier between the people of Yahweh and the followers of other gods. From a psychological standpoint, the purity laws promote a feeling of disgust at the practices of people outside the group and encourage the audience to take pride in the beliefs and practices of their own group. From a social standpoint, the laws challenge the audience to stay away from people outside the group in order to avoid the temptation to follow their religious beliefs and practices. This segregationist agenda is especially prominent in the book of Deuteronomy.

> When the LORD your God brings you into the land that you are about to enter and occupy, and he clears away many nations before you—the Hittites, the Girgashites, the Amorites, the Canaanites, the Perizzites, the Hivites, and the Jebusites, seven nations mightier and more numerous than you—and when the LORD your God gives them over to you and you defeat them, then you must utterly destroy them. Make no covenant with them and show them no mercy. Do not intermarry with them, giving your daughters to their sons or taking their daughters for your sons, for that would turn away your children from following me, to serve other gods. Then the anger of the LORD would be kindled against you, and he would destroy you quickly. But this is how you must deal with them: break down their altars, smash their pillars, hew down their sacred poles, and burn their idols with fire. For you are a people holy to the LORD your God; the LORD your God has chosen you out of all the peoples on earth to be his people, his treasured possession. *(Deuteronomy 7:1-6)*

Fig. 23.4. Both the Amish people (top) and the Hare Krishnas (bottom) follow distinctive social and religious practices that set them apart from other Americans; the biblical purity laws would have done the same for their followers.

> When the LORD your God has cut off before you the nations whom you are about to enter to dispossess them, when you have dispossessed them and live in their land, take care that you are not snared into imitating them, after they have been destroyed before you: do not inquire concerning their gods, saying, "How did these nations worship their gods? I also want to do the same." You must not do the same for the LORD your God, because every abhorrent thing that the LORD hates they have done for their gods. They would even burn their sons and their daughters in the fire to their gods. You must diligently observe everything that I command you; do not add to it or take anything from it. *(Deuteronomy 12:29-32)*

When we ask what this segregationist impulse might tell us about when and where the purity laws originated, the answers are less than clear. Most scholars believe that the purity laws originated in priestly circles, since they represent the concerns and viewpoints of the priestly class and depict the priests as the leading authorities within Israelite society. The earliest collections were probably oral and might even have been limited to the priests. If this is correct, then the question arises as to when and why the collection was first written down and expanded for use by non-priests. Scholars have been unable to reach agreement on this question. Some believe that an earlier version was available in the preexilic period, while others attribute the initial collection to the Exile or the postexilic era (see chapter 22). Whenever it originated, it seems clear that the development and circulation of such a collection would have served to enhance the social status of the priests and elicit support for their religious agenda.

Scholars also disagree about whether the purity laws represent a new vision for the relationship between Yahweh and his people or whether they reflect long-standing beliefs and practices that were only later compiled into a written collection. The social and religious turbulence of the exilic and postexilic eras provided a natural climate for the production of such a collection, but so did the eighth century B.C.E., when the kingdom of Israel fell to the Assyrians and the kingdom of Judah was threatened with a similar fate. The presence of purity laws in the book of Deuteronomy, a book whose roots go back to at least the seventh century B.C.E., has led many scholars to associate purity concerns with the kingdom of Israel, where the legal sections of Deuteronomy are believed to have originated (see chapter 19). But the presence of a powerful priestly class at the Jerusalem temple suggests that an ideology framed around ritual purity might have developed within the kingdom of Judah as well.

Behind these diverse historical reconstructions lies a broad scholarly consensus that the purity system depicted in the Torah represents a vision for the way in which a Yahwistic society ought to work rather than a picture of the way people actually lived in ancient Palestine. Even conservative scholars agree that the people of Israel did not follow these laws during the preexilic period, since

the prophets repeatedly condemn them for following the religious practices of their Canaanite neighbors. During this era, most people probably encountered purity concerns only when they made a trip to one of the shrines of Yahweh, where the priests told them what they needed to do to purify themselves before approaching the deity. The idea of an entire society organized around purity concerns probably originated with a group of devout Yahwists, led by priests, who wanted to uphold a strict version of Yahwism in the face of the persistent religious diversity of the kingdoms of Israel and Judah. This would explain why the purity laws place so much emphasis on avoiding practices associated with Canaanite religions, as well as other preexilic features that scholars have noted in the collection. It also fits well with the presumed preexilic date of Deuteronomy.

As far as we know, however, it was not until the Babylonian exile or later that these ideas began to gain broad support within the broader Yahwistic community. The Babylonians made no effort to convert their conquered subjects to their religious beliefs, but the experience of living in a foreign culture would have caused the exiles to feel a persistent internal pressure to adopt the social and religious practices of their Babylonian neighbors. No doubt many were worried about how they were going to preserve their culture and identity in the midst of such an alien environment. It is thus no wonder that many of the exiles would have been attracted to a plan that called for the people of Yahweh to organize themselves as a separatist religious community under the guidance of a set of purity rules that embodied the will of Yahweh. This is especially true if the plan was reinforced by a claim that faithful obedience to Yahweh's laws would cause Yahweh to renew his concern for his people and restore them to their land. Tying the purity system to the emerging Exodus narrative would have added yet more weight to this claim, since the Exodus story likewise insisted that Yahweh cared for his people and would in due time rescue them from foreign domination.

In the long run, this concern for ritual purity helped to secure the survival of the people of Judah in Babylonia by giving them a social and ideological alternative to assimilation. But the idea was slower to take root in Palestine. During the decades of the Exile, the residents of Judah who had not been deported to Babylonia continued to follow the religious practices of their ancestors. The differences between these people and the Babylonian community became apparent when the exiles began returning to Palestine. Some of the returning exiles married people who had remained in the land and adopted their religion, while others followed the Babylonian purity model and set themselves apart from the people of the land, whom they regarded as a threat to the true religion of Yahweh. The books of Ezra and Nehemiah hint at the tensions that existed between the two communities (see Ezra 9:1-2; Nehemiah 13:23-31).

Eventually the purity system became the dominant form of religion among the followers of Yahweh in Palestine, whether through the influence of leaders like Ezra (as depicted in the book of Ezra-Nehemiah) or through other processes that have been lost to history. The fact that the purity laws were linked to the Exodus story, which held a key position in the increasingly influential grand narrative of Israel's past, no doubt helped to reinforce their validity. By the time the canon of the Torah was closed around the third century B.C.E., the purity laws had become such an integral part of Yahwism that few would have questioned their authority.

CONCLUSION

The concern for ritual purity that we find in certain portions of the Torah has parallels in many other religions. But the Torah model also contains many distinctive elements that reflect the cultural environment in which it arose.

The Torah's purity system is based on the belief that Yahweh is a holy god who requires a holy people to serve as his covenant partners. Yahweh has chosen Israel for this purpose and has given them a series of laws that defines what it means to be holy, or set apart for the deity. Included in these laws are provisions relating to their social, ethical, and ritual conduct. Violations of these laws render the people unclean. If they do not make use of the purification rituals described in the Torah, Yahweh will eventually leave them, since a holy god cannot live among an unholy people.

The idea of ritual purity is rooted in the thought-world of priests whose power derives from their position as mediators between the impure world of humans and the holy and awesome presence of the deity. The Torah's vision of a society framed around a system of purity laws probably originated with a group of priests and lay supporters who wished to strengthen their people's devotion to Yahweh at a time when religious diversity was the norm in the kingdoms of Israel and Judah. The separatist orientation of this system made it popular with the Babylonian exiles who faced daily pressures to conform to the social and religious systems of their Babylonian neighbors. With their support, it became the standard for proper religious behavior among the followers of Yahweh during the postexilic period.

EXERCISE 60

Read the following passages from the narrative books of the Hebrew Bible and explain how each passage relates to the purity issues discussed in this chapter.

- Joshua 7:1-26
- 2 Samuel 6:1-19
- 2 Chronicles 29:1-36
- Nehemiah 13:1-31

Fig. 24.1. To be poor, elderly, and alone is to live a very vulnerable life. The Qur'an, like the Bible, tells its followers to give generously to the poor.

Social Laws

If you lend money to my people, to the poor among you, you shall not deal with them as a creditor; you shall not exact interest from them. If you take your neighbor's cloak in pawn, you shall restore it before the sun goes down; for it may be your neighbor's only clothing to use as cover; in what else shall that person sleep? And if your neighbor cries out to me, I will listen, for I am compassionate. (Exodus 22:25-27)

If a man dies, and has no son, then you shall pass his inheritance on to his daughter. If he has no daughter, then you shall give his inheritance to his brothers. If he has no brothers, then you shall give his inheritance to his father's brothers. And if his father has no brothers, then you shall give his inheritance to the nearest kinsman of his clan, and he shall possess it. It shall be for the Israelites a statute and ordinance, as the LORD commanded Moses. (Numbers 27:8-11)

You shall not spread a false report. You shall not join hands with the wicked to act as a malicious witness. You shall not follow a majority in wrongdoing; when you bear witness in a lawsuit, you shall not side with the majority so as to pervert justice; nor shall you be partial to the poor in a lawsuit. (Exodus 23:1-3)

Alongside the purity laws, the Torah contains many laws that talk about how Yahweh wants the people of Israel to behave toward one another and how their society should be structured. The list of subjects addressed in these laws is quite broad, though not comprehensive. Some of the laws focus on the handling of specific social violations, while others speak more generally about the way in which societal institutions should operate and how people should treat one another. This chapter presents an overview of these laws and their place in the lives of the followers of Yahweh.

RELIGION AND SOCIETY

Residents of the United States are accustomed to living in a society with a strong legal wall of separation between church and state. Most Americans would also agree that societal institutions that are not explicitly religious (businesses, clubs, sports teams, and so forth) should follow a secular model of operation that either ignores the religion of their members or treats all religions alike. The idea of a society in which most or all of the citizens belong to a single religion and the government and other institutions base their policies on the teachings of that religion sounds odd and even threatening to many Americans. This is clear from the way in which Americans view Muslim nations such as Iran or Saudi Arabia that seek to base their laws on the Qur'an and the principles of Islam. Polls suggest that most Americans believe that these nations would be better off with a secular system of government.

Many Americans are surprised to learn that their vision of a society that is not tied to a particular religion is a relatively recent development in the history of civilization. At the time of the American Revolution, Europeans were convinced that the American proposal to eliminate state support for religion and allow people to follow their own consciences in matters of religion could not possibly succeed, since a common religion was necessary to preserve the unity of society and to provide moral guidance for its leaders. To this day most European nations have an official state church that is supported by the tax system, even though Europeans in general are less religious than Americans.

In spite of a long-term global trend toward secularization, there remain many countries where daily life is dominated by a single religion that shapes the way the society operates. Most of the nations of Latin America are heavily Roman Catholic; Israel is a Jewish society; India is predominately Hindu; Thailand is culturally Buddhist; and dozens of nations are committed to following the path of Islam. In the United States, Protestant Christianity has shaped the values and institutions of society for most of the nation's history, despite a constitutional amendment prohibiting the establishment of a national church. Indeed, religion is such a vital element of human existence that it cannot be kept out of public life unless there is a deliberate effort to repress it, as in the Soviet Union and other Communist countries.

The role of religion was even more significant in ancient societies. Gods in the ancient Near East were associated with territories and groups of people from the level of the nation down to the city, town, or village. Everyone was expected to honor and obey the local deities in order to ensure their protection and avoid their displeasure. Individuals might perform special acts of devotion to a particular god or goddess, but they knew better than to neglect or offend the deities who watched over their locality. No one

would have imagined that it was either possible or desirable to have a society that did not honor the gods.

As we observed in the last chapter, rituals played a crucial role in maintaining a positive relationship between gods and humans. But the gods also had expectations for how their people should treat one another and how their societies should be structured. Not surprisingly, these expectations usually supported the status quo. At the top of every society stood the king, who was thought to have a special relationship with the gods, whether as the agent through whom they exercised their rule on earth or as a divine being himself. His decrees were to be honored and obeyed as divine law; to challenge the word of the king was to court punishment from the gods. Priests and other religious leaders also held a prominent position in society due to their familiarity with the gods and their ability to perform vital rituals on behalf of the people. Kings regularly turned to them for guidance, especially in times of trouble. Virtually all of the formal positions of honor and authority were held by men, since the gods had decreed that men should rule over women and children in both

Fig. 24.2. (left) A Babylonian king consults with an enthroned deity; (right) an Egyptian priest offers prayers to the god Ra-Horakhty.

the society and the home. In short, things were the way they were because the gods had made them so. As long as people accepted this view, the basic structures of society were regarded as fixed and beyond question. The result was a conservative social order that valued continuity and conformity and discouraged originality and independent thought.

At the everyday level, societies were regulated primarily by custom. Ideas about right and wrong and norms for social conduct were passed on within the family, rooted in traditions that had been inherited from the ancestors. While it would have been unusual for someone to claim that a particular ancestral tradition had come directly from the gods, the moral standards upon which these traditions were based would have been justified by reference to the will of the gods. This gave the accepted norms for social behavior a decidedly religious tenor, even when the religious element was not explicitly stated.

Within the broader community, interpersonal disputes and violations of social norms were handled by village elders or judges who relied on local precedent and their own sense of justice to figure out an equitable solution or a fitting punishment. Occasionally legal scholars or priests would compile a collection of rulings indicating how various social problems should be handled (as in the Code of Hammurabi), but these were useful only to people who could read. The relation between these collections and the actual distribution of justice in the towns and villages of the ancient Near East remains unclear due to the limited nature of our sources.

EXERCISE 61

Read the following passages and make note of any patterns that you observe among them. What can you infer from these passages about the moral and legal principles upon which the social laws of the Torah were based?

- Exodus 21:18-27
- Exodus 22:1-8
- Numbers 35:16-28
- Deuteronomy 15:12-18
- Deuteronomy 21:18-21
- Deuteronomy 24:19-22

SOCIAL LAWS AND THE TORAH

The Torah includes a host of laws aiming to regulate the everyday lives and social relationships of the people of Israel. These laws are scattered throughout the Torah, though they are concentrated in certain passages more than others (Exodus 21:1—23:9; Leviticus 19:1-37; Numbers 35:1—36:13; Deuteronomy 19:1—22:30). The sheer breadth of the issues addressed in these laws is remarkable for a religious text. Their inclusion in the Torah suggests that the people who compiled these laws believed that Yahweh's covenant relationship with Israel carried implications for all aspects of social life, from the behavior of individuals to the manner in which society was organized. According to their vision, all of life was to be lived as an act of devotion to Yahweh, and everyone was responsible for developing and maintaining a society that reflected and nurtured this ideal.

Social Organization

For a book that is so full of laws, the Torah has surprisingly little to say about how the people of Yahweh are to be governed. Most of the verses on this subject relate to the conduct of the local courts. Judges are the primary arbiters of justice in these texts, though village elders and priests are also presumed to have judicial authority in certain cases (Deuteronomy 19:11-12; 21:1-9, 18-21; 22:13-18; 25:5-10), and at least one passage calls for the congregation to serve in a judicial role (Numbers 35:22-25). Most of the laws relating to the handling of court cases are quite general, directing judges to issue impartial rulings and avoid bribery and telling witnesses to speak the truth at all times. A few verses go into more detail, requiring careful investigation of the facts, the use of multiple witnesses, and severe penalties for false testimony (Deuteronomy 17:2-7; 19:15-21). Punishments are to be executed swiftly, whether they are performed by the judges (Deuteronomy 25:1-3), the elders (Deuteronomy 22:18-19), or the entire congregation (Leviticus 24:13-16; Numbers 15:32-36; Deuteronomy 21:18-21; 22:20-21).

Outside the judicial context, references to governing officials are sparse. Only one passage mentions the king

(Deuteronomy 17:14-20), while a few texts speak about elders and officials who play some sort of leadership role among the tribes (Exodus 3:16-18; 18:13-27; Leviticus 4:13-15; Numbers 11:16-17; Deuteronomy 1:15; 16:18; 20:5-9; 29:10). The Torah claims that these secondary positions of leadership, together with the office of the priests, were established by Moses under the guidance of Yahweh. In this way the Torah elevates the later occupants of these offices to a lofty position in society. On the other hand, the relative lack of laws pertaining to the conduct of these officials (apart from the priests) suggests that the people who created these laws were not in a position to regulate the behavior of societal leaders, whether because they lacked the necessary influence or because the offices no longer existed at the time when the laws were written (if they originated during the exilic period or later).

Social Problems

Closely related to rules for social organization are laws that prescribe how to handle various problems that disrupt the social order. Many of these laws pertain to acts that would be covered by criminal laws in modern secular societies—theft, rape, murder, manslaughter, assault, kidnapping, and so on. Others provide guidance for resolving interpersonal disputes that would be settled today through civil lawsuits, including loss of or dam-

age to property, negligence, fraud, and similar issues. Still other laws address problems that are peculiar to the value systems and practices of ancient societies, such as escaped slaves, violations of female chastity, and disrespect to parents. Finally, the Torah contains laws designed to prohibit and punish various religious practices that would be protected in today's world under laws guarding freedom of religion: idolatry (worship of gods other than Yahweh), blasphemy, false prophecy, consultation of the dead, witchcraft, and the like.

Virtually all of these laws contain instructions for the punishment of wrongful acts, with the more serious violations, including most of the religious offenses, carrying a penalty of death. Only rarely, however, is there any indication of who is to carry out these punishments. Perhaps the punishment system was so well known to the original audience that no further explanation was needed. At the same time, such a glaring omission raises questions about whether these laws reflect actual practice or offer a blueprint for handling problems in an ideal society.

Social Practices

Another category of laws aims to define how the primary institutions of society should operate under normal conditions. Some of these laws are framed in positive terms, identifying behaviors that should be followed, while others

Fig. 24.3. (left) A group of village elders from Afghanistan; (right) the Hebrew Bible speaks of judicial hearings taking place at the city gates, possibly in rooms like this one from the gate complex at Beersheba in southern Palestine.

Fig. 24.4. The Torah's vision for social justice includes provisions for the use of honest weights in the marketplace (top) and for farmers to leave some of their crops in the field so that poor people can gather them for food (bottom).

divorce, husbands are to oversee the legal obligations of their wives and daughters, daughters may inherit when there are no sons.

Most of the laws in this category are designed to prevent people from abusing or taking advantage of others. Farm animals and agricultural property are also protected under these provisions. Almost none of the laws in this category include any provisions for identifying or punishing violations. As in the previous section, scholars disagree about the implications of this observation. Many think that violators were punished by local judges who had the freedom to determine the nature of the penalty. Others view the omissions as evidence that the laws were designed to function as general guidelines that carried no penalties or as model provisions for an ideal society.

Social Relationships

Not all of the social laws pertain to the institutional side of life. The Torah also contains many laws that seek to encourage positive attitudes and relationships with people inside and outside of the group. On the positive side, the audience is told to respect the elderly, fulfill their promises, help those who are in need, protect others from harm, watch over other people's property, and "love your neighbor as yourself" (Leviticus 19:18; note that this verse originated in the Torah, not with Jesus). On the negative side, they are directed to avoid lying, slander, hatred, vengeance, cursing people in authority (parents and societal leaders), and abusing the weak and the powerless (widows, orphans, the disabled, and foreigners who live in their land). Less attention is given to conduct within the family: children are commanded to honor and obey their parents, but nothing is said about how parents should treat their children or how husbands and wives should relate to one another, apart from the broad requirement that wives must limit their sexual activity to their husbands (but not vice versa).

are cast in negative language, spelling out acts that should be avoided. Here, too, the laws cover a broad range of issues. Some of the laws pertain to economic transactions: sellers are to use honest weights for their goods, workers are to be paid each day, fraud is to be avoided. Others relate to the practice of agriculture: fields are to be left fallow every seven years, oxen are not to be muzzled while they are treading grain, portions of the crop are to be left in the field for the poor. Still others address the legal aspects of family life: women are to be protected in case of

The inadequacy of the term *law* is especially apparent in these cases, since all of the provisions under this heading are too broad to function as legal guidelines and none specifies any penalty for violation. While it is possible that someone might have cited one of these laws as a basis for bringing a complaint before the local authorities, their chief purpose was to provide moral instruction for individuals concerning the proper way to relate to others.

Social Stratification

One of the most interesting categories of laws centers on relationships between people who have power and resources and people who do not. Some of these laws have been cited already, but their distinctive nature calls for special treatment.

Several laws place limits on what people can do with their personal property, including some that require people to share their wealth with others. Landowners, for example, are not to harvest all of their crops; they are to leave some in the fields so that poor people can enter their property and gather food. People who have money are to lend to others without charging interest, since most borrowers were poor people who had exhausted their limited resources. Anyone who has needy relatives is to take care of them, including buying and returning to them any lands that they might have been forced to sell in order to survive and purchasing them out of slavery if they should be compelled to give up their freedom in order to pay off their debts. Perhaps the most remarkable provision calls for the cancellation of all debts every fiftieth year and the return of all lands to the families that originally owned them (Leviticus 25:8-13).

Other laws seek to protect the weak and powerless from abuse. Judges are to refrain from giving special treatment to the rich, avoid taking bribes, and protect the rights and property of widows and orphans. Men who divorce their wives must take care of them until the women marry again. Israelite slaves are to be treated as hired hands and freed after six years with enough provisions to enable them to start a new life. Slaves who are injured by their owners are to be compensated, and slaves who escape are not to be returned.

As with most of the other social laws that we have examined, few of these laws include any instructions for the investigation or punishment of violations. Some of the provisions are so unrealistic that it is hard to imagine that anyone ever followed them, though we cannot rule out that possibility. Certainly many people who had money and power would have found ways to avoid obeying the laws that obligated them to spend their resources on others. Once again we must be alert to the possibility that these laws represent someone's vision of the way things ought to be rather than a set of rules that was actually obeyed.

> ### EXERCISE 62
>
> Based on what you have learned so far, what would you see as some of the positive and negative aspects of living in a society that followed the social laws of the Torah? Would your answer be affected by your social status within the community?

THE SOCIAL VISION OF THE TORAH

In its present form, the Torah presents a particular vision of what life could be like if the people of Israel were committed to live in a manner that reflects the character and expectations of Yahweh. The society envisioned here is not perfect; if it were, there would be no need for atoning sacrifices or criminal punishments. Instead, the Torah depicts a society in which the majority of the people are making a serious effort to live by Yahweh's standards. To create a society based on this vision would require people to lay aside many of their selfish inclinations. The Torah clearly assumes that this is within the capacity of ordinary humans, as we see in the following passage from the book of Deuteronomy:

Surely, this commandment that I am commanding you today is not too hard for you, nor is it too far away. It is not in heaven, that you should say, "Who will go up to heaven for us, and get it for us so that we may hear it and observe it?" Neither is it beyond the sea, that you should say, "Who will cross to the other side of the sea for us, and get it for us so that we may hear it and observe it?" No, the word is very near to you; it is in your mouth and in your heart for you to observe. *(30:11-14)*

In its overall structure, the social world envisioned in the Torah is quite similar to other societies in the ancient Near East. The reins of power are held by a small group of elite males, and a significant proportion of the property is concentrated in the hands of a small number of families. But there are notable differences as well. Most obvious is the virtual invisibility of the king. Only one passage in the entire Torah (Deuteronomy 17:14-20) mentions the conduct of the king, and the image there is highly idealized—a ruler who is devoted to Yahweh and his Torah, treats all people as equals, and refrains from accumulating both possessions and wives. On the whole, the society envisioned by the Torah operates without input or direction from the king. Power is vested in the priests, the judges, and the village elders, who share the responsibility for identifying and addressing threats to the social order, whether from criminal violations, disputes among individuals, or ritual impurities. People who own land and resources also wield a form of power in the world of the Torah, but they are expected to use their wealth for the common good and not for selfish gain. Again and again the Torah commands those who hold power to avoid exploiting the powerless and to help those who are in need.

At the heart of the Torah lies a vision for a society in which all of the citizens respect and care for one another as they would their own families. This vision was reinforced by a set of stories that portrayed the people of Israel and Judah as distant relatives who had descended from a common set of ancestors (Abraham and the Exodus generation). Those who accepted these stories were implicitly challenged to extend to their neighbors the same level of care that they would give to members of their extended family. As with real-life families, a family-based society would still have inequities, since people begin life with varying amounts of power and resources and are affected in different ways by the vagaries of life in a traditional agricultural society (location and fertility of farmland, exposure to insects and diseases, sickness or death of farm animals and family members, and so forth).

Unlike in modern families, however, the values of traditional societies dictate that the members of an extended family must come to the aid of a family member who is in need. Defining everyone in the society as kin was thus an effective strategy for motivating people who owned more resources to give generously to the poorer members of the society. Acts of personal generosity are vitally important for maintaining the stability of traditional societies, since there is no government safety net to care for the poor.

Such a system of benevolent **patriarchy** sounds antiquated and perhaps even oppressive to modern ears. In its own day, however, the social vision of the Torah was remarkably enlightened. Where the laws of the surrounding nations sought to uphold the status quo and defend the prerogatives of the wealthy, the Torah challenged those who controlled the power and resources of society to voluntarily limit the exercise of their privileges in order to help those at the bottom of the social ladder. Many of the people to whom this message was addressed (the wealthier members of society) would have viewed it as an unwelcome intrusion into their personal affairs.

Even more remarkable is the way in which the Torah links this message to the will of Yahweh. Where other nations claimed that the gods stood on the side of the rich and powerful, giving them what they had and defending it against challenge, the Torah places the god of Israel firmly on the side of the poor and the powerless. Those who abuse the needy are repeatedly threatened with divine retribution.

> You shall not abuse any widow or orphan. If you do abuse them, when they cry out to me, I will surely heed their cry; my wrath will burn, and I will kill you with the sword, and your wives shall become widows and your children orphans. *(Exodus 22:22-24)*

> If you lend money to my people, to the poor among you, you shall not deal with them as a creditor; you shall not exact interest from them. If you take your neighbor's cloak in pawn, you shall restore it before the sun goes down; for it may be your neighbor's only clothing to use as cover; in what else shall that person sleep? And if your neighbor cries out to me, I will listen, for I am compassionate. *(Exodus 22:25-27)*

You shall not revile the deaf or put a stumbling block before the blind; you shall fear your God: I am the LORD. *(Leviticus 19:14)*

A number of verses tie Yahweh's concern for the helpless directly to the Exodus story. These passages insist that the god who rescued his people from the oppression of the Egyptians stands ready to aid and defend those who are oppressed in later times.

You shall not oppress a resident alien; you know the heart of an alien, for you were aliens in the land of Egypt. *(Exodus 23:9)*

If any who are dependent on you become so impoverished that they sell themselves to you, you shall not make them serve as slaves. They shall remain with you as hired or bound laborers. They shall serve with you until the year of the jubilee. Then they and their children with them shall be free from your authority; they shall go back to their own family and return to their ancestral property. For they are my servants, whom I brought out of the land of Egypt; they shall not be sold as slaves are sold. You shall not rule over them with harshness, but shall fear your God. *(Leviticus 25:39-43)*

Passages such as these enhance the moral weight of the Torah's social vision by tying it to the central religious story from which the community derives its identity. No one who knew the Exodus story could have missed the underlying message: those who oppress Yahweh's people have aligned themselves with the Egyptians who experienced Yahweh's terrible judgment rather than with the poor and marginalized whose cause Yahweh supports.

VISION AND REALITY

As we have seen, even a cursory reading of the Torah raises questions about how far the social laws were actually followed. Some of these laws, especially those framed in an "if-then" case format, sound as though they might have been derived from real-world court proceedings. Among the many examples that could be cited are rules that explain what to do when an individual causes bodily harm or death to another person or inflicts damage upon another person's property. Mingled together with these laws are others that sound so unreasonable or unrealistic that it is hard to think that anyone ever tried to implement them. Did wealthy people really write off all of their debts, free their Israelite slaves, and restore their accumulated lands to the previous owners every fifty years (Leviticus 25:8-55)? Were children who cursed, struck, or failed to obey their parents actually punished by execution (Exodus 21:15, 17; Deuteronomy 21:18-21)? Did jealous husbands ever compel their wives to drink a potentially lethal liquid in order to prove that they were innocent of adultery (Numbers 5:11-31)? Did military officers tell their soldiers that they should leave the field prior to battle if they felt afraid or had unfinished business at home (Deuteronomy 20:1-9)? Laws such as these sound more like wishful thinking than actual practice.

Additional problems arise when we compare the laws of Torah with other books in the Hebrew Bible. Both the narrative books and the books of the prophets indicate that the people of Israel and Judah worshipped other gods alongside Yahweh and followed religious practices forbidden by the Torah during the era of the monarchy. Yet there is no indication that any of these people were executed or even disciplined; in fact, they probably constituted the majority at certain points in Israel's history. Similarly, many verses in the prophetic books denounce the rich and powerful for exploiting the poor and powerless. Yet nowhere do we hear of any of these people being prosecuted for their failure to live by the social laws of Torah. In fact, many passages in the books of Psalms and Proverbs imply that the rich followed an alternate theology that interpreted their success as a mark of divine approval for their behavior.

How are we to explain these facts? As we saw in our discussion of the purity laws, the answer depends on how we understand the history of the Torah. Conservatives argue that this discrepancy between theory and practice is consistent with their belief that the people of Israel and Judah knew the laws of Torah but failed to follow them. Maximalists insist that the mixed evidence favors their own view that the laws of Torah were only partially developed and little known among the broader populace during the era of the monarchy. Minimalists point to the rarity of legal references in the narrative and prophetic books as proof that most or all of the laws originated during the postexilic period and therefore could not have been used to regulate the lives of people before that time.

As we saw in chapter 22, there are many reasons to believe that the maximalist position is closer to the truth when we consider the Torah as a whole. Further support for this conclusion comes from the observation that the books of the preexilic prophets (those who lived before the Babylonian conquest of Judah) routinely presuppose that their audiences are familiar with the social norms that were later enshrined in the laws of Torah. Otherwise their criticisms of the social behaviors of the people of Israel and Judah would have carried no weight. Precisely what they expected their audiences to know is unclear, since references to specific laws are hard to find (see chapters 32–33). But the presence of social laws in the book of Deuteronomy strongly suggests that such laws existed in some form during the preexilic period (see chapter 19). In short, there is substantial evidence to indicate that the Torah's postexilic collection of social laws is based on earlier materials that were known in oral or written form by at least some of the people of Israel and Judah during the preexilic period.

Whether the more idealistic and visionary parts of the Torah also date from this period is unclear. If they arose in the preexilic era, we might infer that they reflect the views of a fairly radical group of Yahwists who hoped that their alternative model of society would eventually replace the prevailing social system. If they originated in the exilic or postexilic era, we might see in them the hopes and dreams of a community that has lost its traditional framework and is trying to figure out what it might mean to create a society that is rooted in rigorous devotion to Yahweh. In the end, the evidence is too sparse to make any reliable judgments.

EXERCISE 63

Read the two versions of the Ten Commandments that appear in Exodus 20:1-17 and Deuteronomy 5:1-21. How do these laws compare with the others that we have studied thus far? Which of the laws would you categorize as purity laws and which as social laws?

THE ESSENCE OF THE TORAH?

So far we have not talked explicitly about the passage that many people would regard as the most important part of the Torah, and perhaps of the entire Bible: the Ten Commandments, also known as the **Decalogue** (meaning "ten words" or "ten sayings"). These materials, which Yahweh supposedly gave to Moses on two stone tablets at Mount Sinai, appear in two versions in the Torah, one in Exodus 20:1-17 and the other in Deuteronomy 5:1-21. The language of the two passages is different, reflecting the complex textual history of the collection, but their general content is the same. The first four laws would be classified as purity laws under the terms that we have been using, while the last six would qualify as social laws.

Most people who refer to the Ten Commandments today know little about their original cultural setting and therefore misinterpret many of the verses. A brief review of the individual commands will show what these statements might have meant to the people who created and used them.

1. *You shall have no other gods before me.* Both Exodus and Deuteronomy link this commandment to the story of the exodus from Egypt. Implicit in this command is the idea that Yahweh has chosen the people of Israel as his covenant partners and that he deserves their heartfelt devotion in return. The existence of other gods is not denied, but the verse insists that Israel should honor no other gods above Yahweh. Whether this means that they should worship Yahweh alone is unclear. At a minimum, such a statement would have drawn a dividing line between those who saw Yahweh as the chief god of Israel and those who honored him as one god among many, or not at all.

Fig. 24.5. Lucas Cranach the Elder, *The Ten Commandments*

2. *You shall not make for yourself an idol.* The use of the English word *idol* here is unfortunate, since most people today interpret this term to mean something like "statue of a false god." The behavior that is being criticized in this commandment is not the worship of other gods besides Yahweh, but the use of a visible image to mark the presence of a deity. The Torah does not depict Yahweh as inherently invisible—various texts show him walking in the garden with Adam, appearing in human form to Abraham, and allowing Moses to see his "back" but not his "face" (Exodus 33:12—34:10). But the Torah does insist that Yahweh's appearance is too awesome to be captured in any physical image. The ultimate aim of this command is to set Yahweh apart from all other gods—to underline his holiness. Archaeological discoveries have suggested that some people did in fact make images to represent Yahweh and use them in their worship alongside the statues of other gods. This commandment rejects all such practices as a diminishment of Yahweh's distinctive glory.

3. *You shall not make wrongful use of the name of the* Lord *your God.* Ancient people were impressed by the power of words. In the proper ritual context, words could be used to exert control over other people or the forces of nature. Names were thought to carry special power, since it was believed that they conveyed the essence of a person.

Names were often used in rituals to manipulate the gods or other humans. The use of divine names in oaths is a natural extension of this practice. The commandment against using the name of Yahweh in a wrongful manner seems to have had these kinds of activities in mind. As in the previous verse, the text suggests that using Yahweh's name in oaths or magical rituals cheapens his dignity by reducing him to the level of other gods who can be manipulated by the application of certain techniques or rituals. The god of Israel is ultimately beyond human control.

4. *Remember the Sabbath day, and keep it holy.* The historical roots of the practice of resting from work on the last day of the week (Saturday) in honor of Yahweh are obscure. The Genesis creation story explains it as a commemoration of Yahweh's rest on the seventh day of creation (Genesis 2:1-3), but this explanation lies outside the realm of history. The practice appears to be unique to Israel. Interestingly, the Torah does not mandate any kind of worship on this day, only rest. Perhaps the intent was to provide a break from the backbreaking work of farm life in antiquity. If so, it could be interpreted as having a humanitarian purpose.

5. *Honor your father and your mother.* The Torah is addressed to adults, so this law probably refers to the honor and material provision that are due to elderly parents from their adult children. In a society with no social

security system, this verse implies that people who are too old to work should not be discarded as useless but should be given respect and support by their offspring. This kind of respect does not arise overnight; it requires training beginning with the earliest days of childhood. Thus the law applies indirectly to younger children as well as adults. The inclusion of the mother suggests that both parents were valued and honored in the world of the Bible, despite the fact that men held ultimate authority in the home.

6. *You shall not murder.* The Hebrew language has many different words for killing. The word that is used here refers to the premeditated taking of an individual's life by another person without legitimate cause. Both capital punishment and killing in warfare appear to lie outside this prohibition, since both are permitted and even required in other parts of the Torah. In fact, murder is one of the many violations for which the Torah prescribes capital punishment, apparently as a means of avoiding perpetual blood feuds within the society.

7. *You shall not commit adultery.* Marriage was valued quite highly in the Yahwistic community, but the obligations that were imposed upon the two parties were unequal. Women were expected to have no sexual partners besides their husbands, while men could have sex with slaves or prostitutes without penalty. Thus the term *adultery* technically refers to sexual contact between a married woman and a man who is not her husband, whether he is married or single. While chauvinism no doubt played a role in this double standard, placing limits on women's sexuality also ensured that everyone would know the identity of a child's father when the time came to pass on property within the family or to fulfill other familial obligations.

8. *You shall not steal.* Virtually all wealth in the ancient world was tied up in farmland or movable items. There were no banks where excess funds could be stored for safekeeping, though the Jerusalem temple sometimes fulfilled this purpose for the wealthier members of society. As a result, a successful burglary or robbery could lead to the loss of everything that a person owned. This command aims to keep people from engaging in this socially destructive act. The Hebrew word used here could also refer to

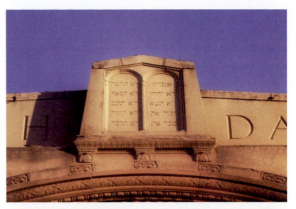

Fig. 24.6. The Ten Commandments hold a place of honor in both Jewish synagogues (top) and Christian churches (bottom).

kidnapping, or the "stealing" of a human being for the purpose of sale or slavery.

9. *You shall not bear false witness against your neighbor.* As the term *witness* implies, this verse refers primarily to testimony given in court. Again and again the Torah reminds its audience to tell the truth when they

are called to provide testimony about possible criminal or civil violations. While this might suggest that people lied routinely to judges, the repetition was probably meant to underline the seriousness of legal testimony as compared with other forms of speech. The term *neighbor* may have been chosen to indicate that the obligation applies not only to fellow Israelites or Yahwists but also to non-Israelites who lived in Palestine. In this way the command promotes a sense of social responsibility to people outside of one's family or clan.

10. *You shall not covet.* This commandment is different from the others in that it refers to an inner attitude rather than an outward action. The intent, of course, is not merely to prevent a bad attitude but also to ensure the security of private property by teaching people to respect one another's possessions and to be content with their own. In a society where rich and poor often lived in close proximity, such a law could apply as much to the poor who might be tempted to steal as to the rich who might use subtler means to gain control of others' possessions. The listing of the wife among the items that "belong to your neighbor" reflects the male orientation of the passage.

The history of this collection is murky. Some scholars see it as one of the earliest parts of the Torah, perhaps even the basis for the entire collection. Certainly that is the impression that the Torah gives by placing it first among the laws that Yahweh gave to Moses at Mount Sinai. Others view it as a late summary that was created to distill the central principles of the Torah. All agree that the list functioned more as a teaching tool than as a legal code, since the statements are all quite general and none includes any penalty for violation.

While the Ten Commandments clearly occupy a central position in the Exodus story, their role in the lives of the people of ancient Israel is less clear. Many scholars have noted that the laws are framed in simple, repetitive language that would have been easy for ordinary people to remember. The presence of ten rules also makes the list more memorable, since it matches the number of fingers on a person's hand. These factors have led many scholars to conclude that the Ten Commandments were formulated as a functional summary of some of the key laws of Torah for the illiterate masses.

On the other hand, there are few verses in the Hebrew Bible that refer explicitly to any of the Ten Commandments, apart from the narrative texts that describe how they were given to the people by Yahweh. Some of the other laws of Torah contain ideas or wording that are similar to what we see in the Ten Commandments, but the points of contact are so broad that it is difficult to say whether they reveal an awareness of this collection or simply the use of a common vocabulary. Even if the collection arose early in Israel's history, the Ten Commandments say nothing about a number of issues that are considered important elsewhere in the Torah, such as ritual purity, the annual festivals, and the obligation to care for the poor. Thus while it might be correct to say that the Ten Commandments summarize some of the basic principles that underlie the individual laws of the Torah, it would be historically inaccurate to describe them as the core or essence of the Torah.

CONCLUSION

The inclusion of social laws alongside the purity laws of the Torah sends a clear message that Yahweh cares as much about how his people treat one another as about how they follow the ritual aspects of his laws. Similar ideas can be found in the words of the preexilic prophets, who repeatedly criticize the people of Israel and Judah for abusing and mistreating one another, especially the poor and the marginalized. While there are questions about whether the prophets actually knew the social laws, it seems clear that they based their pronouncements on principles similar to those found in the Torah.

Social laws define not only how people are to treat one another as individuals but also how their society should be structured and how violations of the social order should be handled. While some of the laws were designed to uphold the status quo, others place Yahweh firmly on the side of those at the bottom of the social ladder. Few of the laws in this category include any penalties for violation; instead, they claim that Yahweh himself will act to aid the oppressed, as he did long ago when he rescued their ancestors from Egypt. Such a message would have been somewhat countercultural in its day.

While some of the laws of Torah might reflect actual practice, the collection as we know it presents a vision for society that was never fully realized within the bounds of history. Much of this vision probably originated with a group of dedicated Yahwists who lacked the power and influence to implement their views in society, though their ideals seem to have been taken more seriously in the postexilic period. The fact that these laws were eventually included in the sacred Scriptures of Judaism suggests that the people of Israel continued to be inspired by their vision long after the laws were formulated.

EXERCISE 64

Look back over the list of laws at the end of chapter 22, focusing on the ones that were actually included in the Torah. Make a list of which laws from the list would qualify as purity laws, which are social laws, and which could be placed in either category. Be prepared to explain your answers.

Fig. 25.1. Personal prayer is a vital means of contact with the supernatural world in many religious traditions.

CHAPTER
25

Encountering the Holy

Moses said, "Show me your glory, I pray." And he [the LORD] said, "I will make all my goodness pass before you, and will proclaim before you the name, 'The LORD' [Yahweh]; and I will be gracious to whom I will be gracious, and will show mercy on whom I will show mercy. But," he said, "you cannot see my face; for no one shall see me and live." And the LORD continued, "See, there is a place by me where you shall stand on the rock; and while my glory passes by I will put you in a cleft of the rock, and I will cover you with my hand until I have passed by; then I will take away my hand, and you shall see my back; but my face shall not be seen." (Exodus 33:18-23)

In the year that King Uzziah died, I saw the Lord sitting on a throne, high and lofty; and the hem of his robe filled the temple. Seraphs were in attendance above him; each had six wings: with two they covered their faces, and with two they covered their feet, and with two they flew. And one called to another and said: "Holy, holy, holy is the LORD of hosts; the whole earth is full of his glory." The pivots on the thresholds shook at the voices of those who called, and the house filled with smoke. And I said: "Woe is me! I am lost, for I am a man of unclean lips, and I live among a people of unclean lips; yet my eyes have seen the King, the LORD of hosts!" (Isaiah 6:1-5)

O God, you are my God, I seek you, my soul thirsts for you; my flesh faints for you, as in a dry and weary land where there is no water. So I have looked upon you in the sanctuary, beholding your power and glory. Because your steadfast love is better than life, my lips will praise you. So I will bless you as long as I live; I will lift up my hands and call on your name. My soul is satisfied as with a rich feast, and my mouth praises you with joyful lips. (Psalm 63:1-5)

As we have seen in the last three chapters, the Torah is rooted in a vision of Israel as the special covenant people of Yahweh, a people who express their devotion to the deity by obeying the terms of his covenant as spelled out in the laws of Torah. According to this vision, Yahweh's people should obey his laws not out of a wooden sense of duty, but out of hearts filled with love and gratitude for his gracious choice of Israel and his constant care for his people above all the nations of the earth.

Obeying the laws of Torah is not the only form of religious expression that we find in the Hebrew Bible. Other texts, along with materials uncovered in archaeological excavations, reveal a rich variety of individual and group religious activities in ancient Palestine. The next six chapters will examine the many channels by which these people attempted to experience, control, and respond to the supernatural realm. The present chapter will introduce a number of important terms and concepts that scholars use when analyzing this key aspect of religious life. Chapters 26–28 will explore how the people of ancient Palestine sought to interact with the supernatural realm in the overlapping spheres of the family, the local community, and the nation. Chapters 29 and 30 will focus more narrowly on two key aspects of religious devotion in ancient Palestine, the practice of bringing offerings and sacrifices to the deity and the use of songs and prayers at public worship centers.

THE RITUAL DIMENSION

As we saw in chapter 12, virtually all religions believe that there is some kind of invisible reality behind, above, or beyond the visible universe. This belief carries with it the expectation that humans should orient their lives toward the unseen realm instead of focusing exclusively on the world of sensory experience. One way of doing this is to make a serious effort to live by a set of moral standards that is believed to reflect the character of the invisible world. Another is to engage in various kinds of formalized actions that are thought to have the power to link humans in some way to the world beyond. These actions are commonly called rituals.

The nature of rituals and their anticipated effects vary from religion to religion. Some religions place more stress on the ritual life of the individual, while others value group rituals more than personal acts. Some prescribe the same activities for every member of the group, while others have different expectations for different classes of people (men and women, religious experts and laypeople, and so forth). Some require that rituals be performed frequently (daily or more often), while others believe that direct contacts with the supernatural realm should be limited to specific occasions. Some engage in ceremonies that are highly ornate and carefully orchestrated, while others value simplicity, leaving substantial creative freedom to the individual. Some believe that the effectiveness of the ritual depends on the intention or attitude of the person who performs it, while others insist that the act can achieve its purpose as long as it is properly performed.

Religions also vary widely in the kinds of rituals that they expect their members to perform. Almost any kind of action can serve as a religious ritual under the proper circumstances. All that matters is that people believe that the action somehow links the performer and/or the community with the unseen realm. Many rituals are essentially formalized versions of ordinary activities such as cooking, washing, and eating. Others involve special actions that were designed for use in a particular ritual context, such as a public worship ceremony or a wedding. Still others require behaviors that would be considered unacceptable in another context, as when young boys are left alone in the woods for days during a puberty ritual or married

Fig. 25.2. (top) Young Buddhist monks meditate before statues of the Buddha; (bottom) Native Americans engage in a ritual dance.

Fig. 25.3. (top) A baby is baptized by a Christian priest; (bottom) a Chinese parade includes ritualized images of supernatural beings.

men engage in prohibited sexual activity as part of a fertility ritual.

Because rituals are so diverse, scholars have developed different ways of organizing them for the purpose of study and discussion. One system that is especially pertinent to the Hebrew Bible centers on when the rituals are performed. At the most basic level are rituals that are integrated into the daily activities of the group or the individual. Some, like saying a blessing before meals or chanting at sunrise, are associated with a specific activity or time of day. Others, such as bowing before an image of a deity or reciting a personal prayer, can be performed at any time. Rules that prescribe how to avoid ritual impurity in the ordinary course of life could also be included under this heading.

A second type of ritual is associated with specific dates or transition points on the group's calendar. Most religions have certain days or periods that they set apart as religious holidays involving special rituals. Often these observances are tied to the agricultural seasons or the movement of the heavenly bodies. Many groups also use rituals to mark key dates in the history or mythology of the group.

A third class of ritual is performed at key points in the individual's life cycle. Birth, naming, puberty, marriage, divorce, retirement, and death are all marked by rituals in various religious traditions. Some regard these rituals as little more than symbolic acknowledgments of the person's passage from one stage or status to another within the community. Others believe that such rituals serve as channels of supernatural power that provide protection from harmful forces during a vulnerable period of transition and enable participants to fulfill the duties of their new status.

A fourth category of ritual is reserved for times of crisis or change in the life of the group or the individual. Rituals of this type usually seek to tap into the power of the supernatural realm in order to bring about a change in circumstances. Events that might require the use of such rituals include personal illness, a prolonged shortage of rainfall, the installation of a new king, or the initiation of war.

WHY RITUALS?

Despite their diversity, rituals fulfill a number of common purposes for the people who practice them. First, rituals help to sustain the belief system of the group by recalling key elements of that system to the minds of its members. Without such an interpretive framework to give them meaning, rituals would be no different than any other act.

Second, rituals serve to bring order and meaning to the community's world. Nearly all groups have rituals that are thought to give access to a higher reality where order and stability prevail in the midst of the often chaotic appearance of ordinary life. This experience helps people to put the troubles of life into perspective.

Third, rituals help to sustain the group's existence by enhancing its sense of identity and unity. The repetitive nature of rituals means that group members are constantly

Fig. 25.4. A Shinto religious ceremony in Japan.

overcome in the unity of the ritual. Some groups believe that the proper practice of rituals can even transform the physical universe and/or the supernatural realm.

HOW RITUALS WORK

At the most basic level, rituals derive their power from the belief that they open up channels between the ordinary world and the supernatural. Since the supernatural world is usually envisioned as a sphere of sacred power, rituals must be handled with great care. Virtually all groups insist that rituals must be performed according to a set of precise guidelines in order to be effective. Some believe that errors or omissions can render the ritual useless; a few contend that mistakes can actually cause the ritual to have the opposite effect from the one intended.

Fig. 25.5. A religious shrine in Togo, Africa, where individuals can present offerings as part of a healing ceremony.

reminded of what binds them together and what distinguishes them from other groups. In this way the identities of the individual members are knitted ever more tightly to the identity and survival of the group.

Fourth, rituals provide a degree of structure to the group. Rituals that take place on a regular basis help to shape the community's awareness of time. Rituals that are held at particular locations help to structure the group's sense of space. Rituals that require the expertise of special personnel help to reinforce accepted beliefs about who should receive honor and respect within the community.

Finally, rituals serve as channels of transformative power. The belief that one has been in direct contact with the supernatural realm can offer important psychological, emotional, and physical benefits to individual worshippers. Transformation can also occur at the group level as differences and problems within the group are temporarily

To ensure that rituals are performed properly, most groups have a set of rules or guidelines that is recorded in sacred books or passed on by word of mouth. These rules explain who can perform each ritual, how it is to be conducted, where and when it should take place, what kinds of implements are needed to perform it, and so on. The primary purpose of these rules is to preserve the holiness of the interaction between the human world and the supernatural. Special conditions are required to convert an ordinary act into a holy action.

(a) *Holy people.* People who participate in rituals are often expected to engage in some sort of cleansing ritual to make them holy before they can interact with the supernatural realm. Cleansing rituals can take a variety of forms: washing of bodily parts, changing of clothes,

Fig. 25.6. An Orthodox Christian priest, dressed in special clothing and wearing a sacred cross, pronounces a ritual blessing upon his congregation.

confession of sins, application of sacred substances, and so forth. Most groups also have a special class of holy people (priests, shamans, and the like) who are believed to have unique knowledge and/or skills that enable them to interact safely with the supernatural realm and mediate its presence and power to others. Rituals that require close or extended contact with the supernatural world are often limited to such people, who must be properly prepared for their duties. Ordinary people could be harmed by such close contact with the supernatural, or they might foul up the process and render the ritual ineffective.

(b) *Holy places.* Encounters with the supernatural often require a special place that has been ritually prepared to handle the divine presence. Sometimes an entire building is set aside for this purpose (for example, a church, mosque, or temple); at other times a dedicated space within a building is sufficient, such as a portable shrine or prayer site within a home. Outdoor sites are more common in traditional societies: a hilltop, a grove of trees, a secluded pond, a river bank. Even ordinary public spaces can be set apart as holy through the use of appropriate rituals and visual markers. Special preparations are usually required before an ordinary person can enter a holy place. Entrance to some holy places is restricted to professional holy people.

(c) *Holy times.* Some rituals can be performed at any time, while others are linked to particular calendar dates, seasons, or life-cycle events. Virtually any time can be set aside as holy by the performance of special rituals. Some rituals last for only a few moments, while others can continue for hours or even days. The entire period of time during which a ritual is being performed is typically regarded as holy. Many ordinary activities are prohibited during this period. Some groups believe that the performance of certain rituals transfers people into a special holy time that lies outside the sphere of ordinary time.

(d) *Holy objects.* Many rituals require the use of special objects in order to be effective. Some holy objects are created specifically for use in religious rituals, such as statues of deities, magical **amulets**, or trance-inducing drugs. Others are items from ordinary life that have been set apart for ritual purposes and are no longer available for other uses, such as the jars and pots in which sacrificial offerings are cooked and stored. As with the other

Fig. 25.7. The columns of Stonehenge, a sacred site in England where religious rituals were performed in ancient times.

in the latter category are groups that place more emphasis on the community than on the individual, as well as groups that believe that focusing on extraordinary experiences distracts people from the truly significant elements of religion, which might involve obeying the group's rules, caring for the needy, or spreading the message to others.

Groups that pay more attention to personal religious experience vary widely in the kinds of experiences that they seek to promote. For some, the goal is a profound sense of oneness with the universe. For others, the aim is a trance state in which the believer is overcome by a supernatural spirit. Still others search for a feeling of peace and contentment, or the power to control others or to perform miracles. However the experience is defined, rituals play a key role in helping people to achieve their desired ends. Among the more popular techniques that people use to experience the presence of the supernatural world are controlled breathing, meditation on a particular word or syllable, repetitive body movements, frenzied dancing, the recitation of magical words, and the ingestion of hallucinogenic substances.

EXERCISE 65

Read the following passages from the Hebrew Bible and make a list of the holy people, places, times, and objects that are mentioned in each passage.

- Leviticus 23:33-43
- Joshua 8:30-35
- 2 Chronicles 5:1-14
- Ezra 6:13-22
- Psalm 116:12-19

categories, virtually any item can be converted into a holy object through the performance of rituals that imbue it with the proper degree of sanctity.

One final point that should be noted concerns the link between rituals and personal religious experience. Religions have different ideas about the importance of individual encounters with the supernatural. Some see such experiences as a vital part of religious life, while others regard them as peripheral and unimportant. Included

THE HEBREW BIBLE AND ISRAELITE RELIGION

A person reading the Hebrew Bible for the first time might think that it would be fairly easy to identify the religious rituals and practices of the ancient Israelites, since the text refers again and again to activities that we would describe as religious. But the issue is not as simple as it appears. In the first place, the biblical narrative indicates clearly that the religious practices of the people who came to be known as Israelites changed over time. They also varied by location (north or south, city or country), gender, and probably social class as well. Some of these changes and differences are mentioned by the biblical authors, but others must be teased out of the text through careful analysis.

A second set of problems arises from the fact that the Hebrew Bible was written and edited into its present form centuries after most of the events that it narrates. This observation has caused scholars to question how much the biblical authors and editors really knew about the religious practices of people who lived centuries before the texts were written. The fact that the narrative books depict Israel's ancient ancestors worshipping in ways that were discouraged or even forbidden later in Israel's history (for example, erecting stone pillars and pouring oil over them) suggests that the stories might indeed preserve reliable memories of earlier practices. The books of the prophets also contain sporadic references to the religious practices of the people of Israel and Judah. But the data are sketchy and selective at best, and there is much that we will never know, especially about the religious lives of women and the poor.

Another problem that limits our ability to reconstruct the religious practices of people in ancient Palestine relates to the difficulty of dating particular laws within the Torah. The Torah is filled with statements that require, encourage, or prohibit various religious practices. If we knew when a particular statement was formulated, then we could presume that there must have been people in Palestine at that time who were following the practices that it prescribes or prohibits, though we would still know little about the popularity of many of the practices. Unfortunately, however, none of the laws are dated (apart from the legendary claim that they were all written during the time of Moses), and scholars disagree about the history of their development (see the discussion in chapter 22). Thus, it is hard to know how far we can rely on the laws of Torah for information about the religious practices of the people of ancient Palestine.

Finally, the Hebrew Bible provides only limited information about many of the rituals and other religious practices that it mentions. This is especially true for acts that were regarded as idolatrous by the Yahwists whose traditions lie behind the Hebrew Bible. For example, we know that people worshipped Yahweh and other gods at shrines scattered around the countryside despite occasional efforts by the Jerusalem authorities to centralize the worship of Yahweh in their temple. But the Hebrew Bible offers only sporadic hints about what was actually done at these shrines. This is true even for the royal shrines at Dan and Bethel that functioned as the national worship centers for the northern kingdom. We know even less about the many rituals that were conducted within the family, since the Hebrew Bible offers only tantalizing glimpses of private religious devotion in ancient Palestine. The biblical silence about family practices is especially glaring when we compare the scanty biblical materials with the findings of archaeology, which has uncovered numerous objects that were used in family worship (see chapter 26). We know more about the rituals that were performed at the Jerusalem temple, since the Hebrew Bible was produced by temple supporters, but even here the texts leave many details ambiguous or unstated. The limited nature of the evidence makes it hard to speak with confidence about many aspects of religious life in ancient Palestine.

Despite these problems, scholars have been able to formulate a broad outline of the ways in which the residents of ancient Palestine expressed their devotion to Yahweh and other gods. The next three chapters will investigate what we can know about these practices at the level of the family, the local community, and the nation. Before we look at what people actually did, however, we should take a few minutes to examine how the materials in the Hebrew Bible relate to what we learned earlier about the role of rituals in religious communities.

RITUALS IN THE HEBREW BIBLE

Rituals played an important role in the religious life of the people of ancient Palestine. This is evident not only from the many references to rituals in the Hebrew Bible but also from comparisons with the neighboring cultures, which likewise made frequent use of rituals. Across the ancient Near East, people believed that they were surrounded by supernatural powers that controlled the awesome and unpredictable forces of nature. Since most people earned their living by farming or shepherding, it was vitally important to them to do whatever they could to influence the deities who directed the agricultural cycle. The most common way of doing this was through the performance of rituals that would attract the attention of gods or spirits who had the power to bring them what they wanted and turn away any forces that might harm them. Some of these rituals were performed on a routine basis, while others were reserved for special occasions. Rituals were also used to ensure divine protection at transitional moments in the lives of individuals and at key stages in the agricultural cycle. Certain rituals were conducted by religious officials at national or regional shrines on behalf of the entire nation, while many others were initiated by individuals seeking assistance for their family or clan.

Since people had differing views of the supernatural, the details of their rituals varied, though certain practices were common across all ancient Near Eastern cultures (public and private prayers, singing and dancing, animal sacrifices, and the like). In some cases the practices of a particular group were distinctive enough to provide a basis for group identity and unity. This seems to have been the case for the followers of Yahweh whose ideas are encapsulated in the Hebrew Bible. Their exclusivist attitude toward other groups, including Yahwists whose methods or places of worship differed from their own, led them to develop rituals and practices that distinguished them from people who followed other paths. The book of Deuteronomy in particular emphasizes the importance of following certain forms of religious devotion and avoiding others. The book overflows with statements that encourage hostile attitudes and actions toward people who practice other forms of religion, even calling for them to be executed and their places of worship destroyed (Deuteronomy 7:1-6, 22-26; 12:1-3; 13:1-18; 17:2-7). Statements like these show how religious rituals and practices can be used to mark the boundaries between different groups while simultaneously promoting solidarity among the members of a group.

Still, this does not tell us what rituals the biblical authors had in mind as markers of group identity. This question will be addressed in the next several chapters. In the meantime, it can be useful to conduct an inventory of the people, places, times, and objects that were identified as holy by the people who compiled the Hebrew Bible.

(a) *Holy people.* Individuals who serve as mediators between Yahweh and his people play an important role in the religious system of the Hebrew Bible. The most important holy people are the priests and their assistants, the Levites, who manage the shrines (including but not limited to the Jerusalem temple) where people come to seek divine assistance or to give thanks to Yahweh. The king is also viewed as a holy person who can intercede with Yahweh on behalf of the nation. Prophets and seers functioned as holy people when they spoke messages from Yahweh to his people, but their status is more ambivalent, since some of them challenged the practices of other holy people, including priests, rulers, and other prophets. More mundane forms of interaction with the deity (for example, personal or familial prayers) could take place without the mediation of a holy person, but even these activities would have been marked by a deep sense of awe and respect.

(b) *Holy places.* Holy places were also vital to the religious lives of the people of ancient Palestine. People in the ancient world associated gods with territories, and most believed that the divine presence could be further concentrated in physical objects such as stones or statues. Places where the gods were thought to live, or at least to visit fairly often, were regarded as holy. The most popular holy places were hilltop shrines, where worshippers could draw nearer to the heavenly dwellings of the great gods, and sites containing groves of trees or water, which stood out against the general dryness of the land. The Hebrew Bible also tells stories of divine appearances at specific sites that were regarded as holy from then onward (Genesis 22:13-14; 35:1-7; Exodus 3:1-12; 19:10-13; 24:4-6). Some of the kings and priests of Judah sought to advance the idea that Yahweh lived in concentrated essence within the inner sanctum of the Jerusalem temple (the so-called Holy of Holies), thus making it the holiest spot on earth (see chapter 28). Only rarely, however, did a king try to stop people from worshipping Yahweh at other holy places besides the temple.

(c) *Holy times.* The Hebrew Bible indicates that the people of ancient Palestine observed a rich variety of holy times. From their earliest history, the people known as Israel seem to have celebrated a series of annual festivals that coincided with key phases in the agricultural cycle. Yahwists eventually linked some of these festivals to episodes from the Exodus story, such as Passover and **Booths**. Each festival was marked by a series of rituals that signified the presence of holy time. Some of these rituals were conducted in the village square or at the local shrine (for example, offering up the **firstfruits** of the harvest to the deity), while others were carried out in the home (for example, preparing and eating a celebratory meal). Rituals were also used by families to mark transitional moments in the lives of family members, such as **circumcision** (for infant boys), puberty, marriage, sickness, and death. Perhaps the most distinctive holy time mentioned in the Hebrew Bible is the Sabbath (the Hebrew word for "rest"), which required people to rest from work on Saturdays. This practice probably arose fairly late in their history. The Torah also identifies every seventh year and every fiftieth year as holy times in which fields were to be left unplanted and debts forgiven, but there is little evidence that these laws were actually observed.

(d) *Holy objects.* The Hebrew Bible contains numerous references to objects that were viewed as holy by at least some of the people of ancient Palestine. Virtually any objects could be made holy through the performance of a ritual that dedicated them to the deity, such as the pots and implements that were used in the service of the Jerusalem temple (see chapter 28). Objects that were commonly associated with a particular ritual could also take on a holy quality, such as unleavened bread (a key element of the Passover ritual) and certain types of incense (offered regularly to the deity). Still other objects were seen as inherently holy due to their close connection with supernatural power, such as the blood that was thought to carry the life force of animals and humans or the **Ark of the Covenant** that served as Yahweh's symbolic throne. Holy objects were supposed to be treated with special care due to their close links with the divine realm. Holy objects that came into contact with nonholy objects or were used for ordinary purposes usually lost their holiness, though some items, like sacrificial blood, were thought to be capable of transmitting their holiness to other objects or people (see chapter 29).

RITUALS AND EXPERIENCE

Despite all of the attention given to rituals in the Hebrew Bible, the cultivation of personal religious experience was not a high priority for the people who compiled these materials. This might not seem obvious at first, since the narrative books depict people having firsthand encounters (including conversations) with Yahweh, and the prophets claim to be hearing from Yahweh on a regular basis, including having occasional visions of his heavenly throne room. Most of these passages, however, involve people who could be viewed as holy in some sense, not ordinary men and women. Nowhere in the Hebrew Bible is there any encouragement for ordinary individuals to pursue what we today would call spiritual experiences— no invitations to seek enlightenment, no provisions for lengthy periods of meditation, no lectures on the benefits of self-denial, no instructions for achieving trance states, no system for soliciting dreams or visions. Instead, the Hebrew Bible encourages people to follow Yahweh's instructions and to care for one another as family. The positive outcomes that it promises are social and public in nature—justice, peace, prosperity—not momentary private experiences.

The closest that the Hebrew Bible comes to any celebration of personal religious experience is in the book of Psalms, where the authors pour out their hearts to Yahweh in cries of deep need or exultant joy. Clearly the people who crafted these poems felt that Yahweh was accessible and concerned about his people. As we will see in chapter 30, however, most of these materials were associated with the Jerusalem temple, where people came to address their prayers to Yahweh on special occasions. In their present form, they reflect the concerns and insights of the literate elites, not the ordinary worshippers. Even those that are less clearly tied to the temple show little interest in religious experience for its own sake. The authors' goal is to motivate Yahweh to intervene in their circumstances or to thank him for what he has already done, not to achieve a particular spiritual state. The profound emotions that the speakers express in the Psalms are a by-product, not the goal, of their prayers to the deity. In short, the religion of the Hebrew Bible was more practical than mystical in its orientation.

A TEST CASE: 1 SAMUEL 9:1—10:13

Many of the concepts that we have been discussing in this chapter are fairly abstract. A careful examination of a specific text can help to make things clearer. For the remainder of this chapter, we will investigate a sample passage from the Hebrew Bible in an effort to uncover some of the key elements of the religious system that it presupposes. Most of the analysis will follow the categories identified earlier in the chapter. The question of the historical reliability of the passage will be left to the side for the purposes of this study.

> ### EXERCISE 66
>
> Read 1 Samuel 9:1—10:13 at least twice and list all of the examples that you can find of the following items: (a) holy people; (b) holy places; (c) holy times; and (d) holy objects. As you read, make a list of any holy actions (rituals) that are mentioned in the story. When you are done, check your answers against the materials presented below.

(a) *Holy people.* The primary holy person in this passage is Samuel, described here as a "man of God" (9:6-7, 10) and a "seer" (9:9, 18-19). In the latter capacity he serves as a channel for people who want to "inquire of God" (9:9) and receives messages from God about things that he could not have discovered by his reasoning faculties alone (9:15-20), including future events (9:16-17, 24; 10:1-7). He also plays a key role in the sacrificial system: his blessing is required before the people will eat the sacrificial meal (9:13), and he promises Saul that he will meet him at Gilgal after seven days and offer sacrifices (10:8).

The prophets whom Saul meets near Gibeah are also marked as holy people by their association with the sacred high place at Gibeah and their divinely inspired ability to prophesy (10:5-6, 10-11). The three men whom Saul encounters near Bethel should probably be understood in the same way, since the food offering that they are carrying seems to identify them as priestly figures (10:3-4).

By the end of the passage, Saul, too, could be viewed as a holy person, since the coming of God's spirit upon him not only enables him to prophesy (10:10-11) but also makes him in some sense "a different person" (10:6). The fact that he is given some of the sacred food that the three men were carrying to God at Bethel (10:4) also supports this conclusion. Empowered by the presence of God (10:7), Saul has now been set apart for the God-given mission of liberating the Israelites from their Philistine oppressors and ruling over them on God's behalf (9:16-17; 10:1).

In a loose sense, we might even describe the character called God (Elohim in Hebrew) (9:6-10, 27; 10:3, 5, 7, 9-10) or less often, Yahweh (9:15-17; 10:1, 6) as a holy person. His role in the story is limited to two lines of dialogue (9:15-17) and one brief, overwhelming appearance (10:9-10). Yet his shadow hangs over all that happens. Three characteristics of the deity are noted in this passage: hearing and responding to prayers (9:16); knowing and ordering future events (9:16-17, 27); and empowering people to prophesy (10:6, 10).

(b) *Holy places.* The most obvious holy places in this story are the high places where much of the action takes place. At least four such places are mentioned in the passage: one at an unidentified town "in the district of Zuph" (9:5, 12-14, 19, 25), where Samuel lives; one at Bethel, where Samuel says Saul will meet three men bringing offerings to God (10:3); one near Gibeah, from which a group of prophets is processing when Saul encounters them (10:5, 10); and one at Gilgal, where Samuel plans to offer sacrifices in a few days (10:8). Where the location is specified, the high place seems to be located on an elevated site near a town rather than in the town itself (9:13, 19, 25; 10:5). Each of these places serves as a center for worship. Since animal sacrifices are mentioned at three of the four centers, we can surmise that some sort of altar was present at each site. The one near Samuel's house

Fig. 25.8. The large round altar in the center of the photograph marks this site (Megiddo in northern Palestine) as a "high place."

that Samuel set apart and gave to the cook to prepare for Saul (9:23-24). The same is true for the young goats, bread, and wine that the three men are carrying to God at Bethel (10:3) and the sacrifices that Samuel intends to offer at Gilgal (10:8). Nothing is said about the implements that were used to perform the sacrifice, but they would surely have been regarded as holy also. Whether the musical instruments employed by the prophets should be viewed as holy objects or as ordinary instruments used for a holy purpose cannot be determined from the passage (10:5). The same is true for the oil that Samuel uses to anoint Saul (10:1).

(e) *Holy actions.* A variety of holy actions is mentioned or implied in this passage. All of the actions associated with the presentation of sacrifices at the high places would qualify as holy, including the killing of the animal, the preparation of the carcass for the altar, and the cooking of the meat. Each of these acts would have been performed according to established ritual procedures. The eating of the sacrificial meat is also portrayed as a holy action involving the entire community (9:13, 24), though its ritual significance cannot be deduced from the passage. Saul's act of giving money to Samuel to obtain a word from God (9:8) could be viewed as a holy action if the giver was following an established procedure rather than making a spontaneous gesture. Samuel's anointing of Saul's head with oil (10:1) is likewise a holy act, since the action sets Saul apart for a divine purpose. Finally, all of the deeds of the prophets at Gibeah (marching in procession, playing musical instruments, prophesying) (10:5, 10) are by definition holy actions, as is Samuel's prophecy over Saul (10:1-8),

also has a banquet hall large enough to seat thirty people, along with a cook to prepare the sacrificial food (9:22). Prophets and other holy people seem to have played a significant role in the activities of these holy places, though in this account they are portrayed as regular visitors rather than as fixed residents.

(c) *Holy times.* At least two verses in the passage could be taken as referring to holy times. In the initial scene, the people insist on waiting for Samuel to arrive and bless the sacrificial food before they will eat (9:13). Since the meat has already been declared holy through the act of offering it to God in sacrifice, it seems likely that the people are waiting on Samuel's blessing to mark the beginning of the special time in which they are permitted to eat the holy meal. The same idea probably lies behind Samuel's command to Saul to wait until he arrives at Gilgal in seven days to offer sacrifices (10:8).

(d) *Holy objects.* All of the holy objects mentioned in this passage are used in some way in the worship of the deity. Certainly the meat that is offered to God at the high place is deemed holy (9:13), particularly the piece since they involve direct interaction with the supernatural realm.

From this brief analysis we can see that this rather quaint tale about the selection of Israel's first king is literally saturated with indicators of holiness. Why might this be? What reason might a storyteller have for surrounding such a story with holy people, places, objects, and actions? The answer becomes clear when we look at the literary and historical context in which the story is situated. Immediately before and after this story (1 Samuel 8:1-22; 10:14-27), we read about a nation that is deeply divided over the prospect of being ruled by a king. These stories anticipate the ambivalent experiences of the people of Israel and Judah with the actual holders of the royal office. Samuel's prophecy in 1 Samuel 8:10-18 paints a bleak picture of the abuses that the people can expect from kings, and the ensuing narratives blame the fall of Israel and Judah on the behavior of their kings. Yet many of the people who crafted these stories following the Babylonian conquest were still looking for the restoration of a monarchy. For them, it was important to show that the office of kingship was endorsed by the deity from the beginning and not a violation of Yahweh's intentions, as some would later claim. As it now stands, the story serves to uphold the institution of the monarchy at a time when many people were questioning its validity.

For now, we need not be concerned about the details of these debates over the value of the monarchy. What matters is to note how a story that seems fairly innocent upon first reading can veil a hidden agenda that lurks just beneath the surface, shaping the way the story is told. One of the marks of a good storyteller is the ability to tell a story so artfully that the hearers are led to adopt the viewpoint of the narrator without raising questions. The use of religious symbols is a powerful tool for playing on the feelings and attitudes of an audience.

CONCLUSION

Virtually all religions use rituals as a way of bringing their followers into contact with the supernatural realm. Some rituals can be practiced at any time, while others are reserved for particular occasions. Because rituals recall or enact the fundamental beliefs of a religious community, they play a vital role in sustaining the identity, cohesiveness, and continuity of the group. Rituals can also have powerful transformative effects on the individuals who perform or participate in them. The power associated with rituals requires that they be handled with care. Many are accompanied by strict guidelines that explain how, when, where, and by whom they are to be performed.

Rituals also play an important role in the religion of the Hebrew Bible, though the connection between the biblical text and the actual religious practices of people in ancient Palestine is not always clear. According to the Hebrew Bible, rituals are vital for maintaining the relationship between

Fig. 25.9. Samuel anoints (that is, pours holy oil on the head of) Saul, thus setting him apart for the sacred office of kingship.

Yahweh and his people, since Yahweh is a holy and awesome god whose holiness must be protected from violation. The performance of rituals requires special people, places, times, and objects that have been set aside for this purpose.

The Hebrew Bible does speak of individuals having spontaneous encounters with Yahweh or approaching the deity in prayer, but the text shows little interest in the inner religious experience of the individual. What matters is the relationship between Yahweh and the people as a whole. Many of the rituals prescribed in the Hebrew Bible also serve to distinguish the followers of Yahweh from their neighbors, thus reinforcing the identity and cohesion of the group.

EXERCISE 67

Read the following passages from the Hebrew Bible, paying careful attention to the presence and purpose of holy items in each passage. Then choose one of the passages and prepare an analysis similar to the one that you just read for 1 Samuel 9:1—10:13. Be sure to include comments about what you learned from the passage as a whole concerning encounters with the holy in the Hebrew Bible.

• Exodus 29:1-46
• Leviticus 1:1-17
• 1 Kings 12:25-33
• 2 Chronicles 30:1—31:1

Fig. 26.1. Melishipak I, king of Babylonia (twelfth century B.C.E.), presents his daughter to the goddess Nannaya for healing. The symbols above the figures represent heavenly deities who watch over the transaction.

Family Religion

Jacob said to his household and to all who were with him, "Put away the foreign gods that are among you, and purify yourselves, and change your clothes; then come, let us go up to Bethel, that I may make an altar there to the God who answered me in the day of my distress and has been with me wherever I have gone." So they gave to Jacob all the foreign gods that they had, and the rings that were in their ears; and Jacob hid them under the oak that was near Shechem. **(Genesis 35:2-4)**

Tell the whole congregation of Israel that on the tenth of this month they are to take a lamb for each family, a lamb for each household. . . . You shall keep it until the fourteenth day of this month; then the whole assembled congregation of Israel shall slaughter it at twilight. They shall take some of the blood and put it on the two door-posts and the lintel of the houses in which they eat it. They shall eat the lamb that same night; they shall eat it roasted over the fire with unleavened bread and bitter herbs. **(Exodus 12:3, 6-8)**

Then all the men who were aware that their wives had been making offerings to other gods, and all the women who stood by, a great assembly, all the people who lived in Pathros in the land of Egypt, answered Jeremiah: "As for the word that you have spoken to us in the name of the LORD, we are not going to listen to you. Instead, we will do everything that we have vowed, make offerings to the queen of heaven and pour out libations to her, just as we and our ancestors, our kings and our officials, used to do in the towns of Judah and in the streets of Jerusalem. We used to have plenty of food, and prospered, and saw no misfortune. But from the time we stopped making offerings to the queen of heaven and pouring out libations to her, we have lacked everything and have perished by the sword and by famine." **(Jeremiah 44:15-18)**

In the last chapter we used a comparative model to investigate how the Hebrew Bible depicts people interacting with the supernatural realm. We also noted a number of problems that hinder any effort to use the biblical materials to reconstruct the actual religious practices of the people of ancient Palestine. Fortunately, the problems are not insurmountable. Many of the practices mentioned in the Hebrew Bible are similar to what we see in the surrounding cultures. Others appear in such diverse time periods and literary contexts that we can be fairly confident that they reflect historical reality.

Archaeological excavations have also yielded numerous finds that have expanded our knowledge about religious practices in ancient Palestine.

The chief value of using outside sources is that it helps scholars to balance out and correct the one-sided picture of religious life that we see in the Hebrew Bible. Even a cursory reading of the books that were included in the biblical canon reveals that they were produced by people who viewed their own brand of Yahwism as right and others as wrong. This conviction led them to produce highly disparaging portraits of people whose beliefs and practices differed from their own. Careful study is required to free ourselves from this bias and analyze the materials in a more neutral light.

Today scholars have a fairly good idea of the kinds of things that people in ancient Palestine did to maintain positive relations with the supernatural realm and to restore those relations when things went wrong. Many of the details of these practices have been lost to history, but there is still much that can be learned from such a study. After a few comments about methodology, this chapter will investigate what scholars have been able to learn about the nature and role of religious rituals at the level of the family. The next two chapters will examine how religion was practiced at the level of the local community and the state.

IDEALS AND REALITY

For most of the period covered by the Hebrew Bible, the religious practices of the people of ancient Palestine were highly diverse. This is not always apparent when one is reading the text, since the Hebrew Bible was produced by people who wanted to give the impression that their beliefs and practices had been the norm for Yahweh's people since the time when Moses delivered the laws of Torah to their ancestors. From their point of view, those who followed other paths were simply rejecting Yahweh's clear commands. But a careful reading of the texts reveals a different story. The narrative books show clearly that the people of Israel and Judah worshiped other deities besides or instead of Yahweh throughout their history. Consider the following passages from very different places in the biblical story line.

> Then the Israelites did what was evil in the sight of the LORD and worshiped the Baals; and they abandoned the LORD [Yahweh], the God of their ancestors, who had brought them out of the land of Egypt; they followed other gods, from among the gods of the peoples who were all around them, and bowed down to them; and they provoked the LORD to anger. They abandoned the LORD, and worshiped Baal and the Astartes. *(Judges 2:11-13)*

Judah did what was evil in the sight of the LORD; they provoked him to jealousy with their sins that they committed, more than all that their ancestors had done. For they also built for themselves high places, pillars, and sacred poles on every high hill and under every green tree; there were also male temple prostitutes in the land. They committed all the abominations of the nations that the LORD drove out before the people of Israel. *(1 Kings 14:22-24)*

> The people of Israel secretly did things that were not right against the LORD their God. They built for themselves high places at all their towns, from watchtower to fortified city; they set up for themselves pillars and sacred poles on every high hill and under every green tree; there they made offerings on all the high places, as the nations did whom the LORD carried away before them. They did wicked things, provoking the LORD to anger; they served idols, of which the LORD had said to them, "You shall not do this." *(2 Kings 17:9-12)*

If we ignore the value judgments that identify various practices as evil, we see that all of these passages testify to the diversity of religious practice in ancient Palestine. The books of the prophets paint a similar picture. In fact, some of them even suggest that the devout followers of Yahweh were a minority in their day.

> My people consult a piece of wood, and their divining rod gives them oracles. . . . They sacrifice on the tops of the mountains, and make offerings upon the hills, under oak, poplar, and terebinth, because their shade is good. Therefore your daughters play the whore, and your daughters-in-law commit adultery. . . . The men themselves go aside with whores, and sacrifice with temple prostitutes; thus a people without understanding comes to ruin. *(Hosea 4:12-14)*

> I will stretch out my hand against Judah, and against all the inhabitants of Jerusalem; and I will cut off from this place every remnant of Baal and the name of the idolatrous priests; those who bow down on the roofs to the host of the heavens; those who bow down and swear to the LORD, but also swear by Milcom; those who have turned back from following the LORD, who have not sought the LORD or inquired of him. *(Zephaniah 1:4-6)*

Do you not see what they are doing in the towns of Judah and in the streets of Jerusalem? The children gather wood, the fathers kindle fire, and the women knead dough, to make cakes for the queen of heaven; and they pour out drink offerings to other gods, to provoke me to anger. . . . For the people of Judah have done evil in my sight, says the LORD; they have set their abominations in the house that is called by my name, defiling it. And they go on building the high place of Topheth, which is in the valley of the son of Hinnom, to burn their sons and their daughters in the fire—which I did not command, nor did it come into my mind. *(Jeremiah 7:17-18, 30-31)*

Other texts show that even those who worshipped Yahweh as their principal deity did things to honor Yahweh that are prohibited in the Torah.

And his mother said, "I consecrate the silver to the LORD [Yahweh] from my hand for my son, to make an idol of cast metal." . . . His mother took two hundred pieces of silver, and gave it to the silversmith, who made it into an idol of cast metal; and it was in the house of Micah. This man Micah had a shrine, and he made an ephod and teraphim, and installed one of his sons, who became his priest. *(Judges 17:3-5; see Exodus 20:4-6; Deuteronomy 5:8-10)*

Three times a year Solomon [who was a king, not a member of a priestly family] used to offer up burnt offerings and sacrifices of well-being on the altar that he built for the LORD, offering incense before the LORD. *(1 Kings 9:25; see Numbers 3:5-10; 18:1-7)*

He [King Manasseh] also restored the altar of the LORD and offered on it sacrifices of well-being and of thanksgiving; and he commanded Judah to serve the LORD the God of Israel. The people, however, still sacrificed at the high places, but only to the LORD their God. *(2 Chronicles 33:16-17; see Deuteronomy 12:2-14)*

The laws of Torah, too, bear witness to the diversity of religious practice in ancient Palestine. The very fact that certain religious acts are prohibited suggests that someone was in fact acting in the prohibited manner and the peo-ple who crafted these laws were afraid that others would follow them, as described in Deuteronomy 13:1-18.

You shall not make for yourself an idol, whether in the form of anything that is in heaven above, or that is on the earth beneath, or that is in the water under the earth. You shall not bow down to them or worship them; for I the LORD your God am a jealous God. *(Exodus 20:4-5)*

You shall not eat anything with its blood. You shall not practice augury or witchcraft. You shall not round off the hair on your temples or mar the edges of your beard. You shall not make any gashes in your flesh for the dead or tattoo any marks upon you: I am the LORD. *(Leviticus 19:26-28)*

You shall not plant any tree as a sacred pole beside the altar that you make for the LORD your God; nor shall you set up a stone pillar—things that the LORD your God hates. *(Deuteronomy 16:21-22)*

No one shall be found among you who makes a son or daughter pass through fire, or who practices divination, or is a soothsayer, or an augur, or a sorcerer, or one who casts spells, or who consults ghosts or spirits, or who seeks oracles from the dead. For whoever does these things is abhorrent to the LORD. *(Deuteronomy 18:10-12)*

Whether the acts prohibited by the Torah were being performed by Yahwists as an expression of their devotion to Yahweh or by people who worshipped other gods is not always clear. But the sheer breadth of the religious acts condemned in the Torah testifies to the rich diversity of religious practice in ancient Palestine.

In short, the idea of a unified pattern of religious belief and practice among the people of ancient Palestine, or even among the followers of Yahweh, is an illusion. For the people whose traditions dominate the Hebrew Bible, it was a desirable ideal—the land of Yahweh should be occupied by people who worship Yahweh as he wants to be worshipped, and all others should be either converted or eliminated. For those who held different religious beliefs, on the other hand, the implementation of this dream would have been a repressive nightmare.

The biblical texts cited above suggest that toleration was the norm in ancient Palestine throughout most of its history, despite the wishes of the people whose ideas are embedded in the Hebrew Bible. Not until the postexilic period did those who argued for a more exclusivist position gain enough power to enforce their standards upon others, and even then religious diversity was by no means abolished.

SPHERES OF RELIGIOUS ACTIVITY

Every religion has both a public face—what people do when they are gathered together—and a private face—what they do when they are alone or with their family. Some religions place more emphasis on one or the other of these two spheres, while others seek to maintain a balance between them. Most religions have different rituals and practices for the public and the private spheres, though some can be performed in either setting. Sometimes the two spheres overlap, as when a person goes alone to a public worship center (church, temple, synagogue, mosque) to pray, meditate, or otherwise interact with the supernatural realm.

Within these two broad spheres, one finds tremendous variety from culture to culture. Some religions expect their members to gather together on a regular basis, while others gather more infrequently or sporadically. Some have a large number of local meeting places, while others center on a few regional sites or even a single central shrine. Some stress the importance of individual acts of devotion, while others place more emphasis on the family, the tribe, or the people as a whole. Some spell out in detail how people must interact with the unseen world, while others allow more freedom of expression.

Scholars who have analyzed the religious practices of people in ancient Palestine have identified three institutional contexts in which religious rituals were practiced.

1. *Family religion.* Most of the ordinary practice of religion took place at the family level. Religious rituals were embedded in many aspects of daily life. Special rituals were performed as needed to deal with specific problems or to celebrate key religious festivals.

2. *Community religion.* Rituals were also performed at public sites within the towns and villages and at shrines scattered around the countryside where people went when they wanted to interact more directly with the supernatural realm. Some were associated with particular families or tribes, while others served a geographic region.

3. *State religion.* Certain religious institutions were established and maintained by the political and religious authorities and supported by a system of taxation (the **tithe**). Rituals in these institutions usually focused on the relationship between the nation and the deity.

Relations between these three spheres of religious activity were complex and fluid. Some forms of activity involved more than one sphere: families often traveled together to regional or national shrines to express their devotion or seek help from the deity, while some of the regional shrines were established and maintained by national leaders. At the institutional level, however, the three spheres operated independently of one another throughout most of the period covered by the Hebrew Bible, since there was no centralized religious authority to enforce uniformity of belief or practice, even among the followers of Yahweh. Most people probably regarded this as a virtue, since it gave them a variety of channels for interacting with the supernatural realm.

Those who held more exclusivist beliefs, however, saw this as a serious problem. Occasionally they gained the upper hand and tried to suppress certain aspects of family and community religion that they thought were contrary to the will of the deity. Many of their ideas were framed into laws that eventually found their way into the Torah. In a few cases they used force to shut down or destroy regional places of worship and to eliminate people whose religious practices they regarded as wrong. The Hebrew Bible mentions such actions during the reigns of Asa (2 Chronicles 14:1-5), Hezekiah (2 Kings 18:1-6; 2 Chronicles 31:1), and Josiah (2 Kings 23:4-20, 24; 2 Chronicles 34:1-7). Most of the time, however, people were left alone to follow their own religious paths, despite the complaints of those who wished for more uniformity of belief and practice (that is, the people who produced the Hebrew Bible).

FAMILY RELIGION

Much of our information about family religious practices in ancient Palestine is fragmentary and open to different interpretations. The Hebrew Bible says relatively little about religious actions that were performed by ordinary individuals and families. The laws of Torah refer often to such activities, but scholars are unsure about the dates of many of these laws and whether they were actually followed. Many scholars think that the ancestral narratives in Genesis and some of the stories in Judges reflect the religious practices of ordinary families, but others discount these stories as late fictions whose picture of the past cannot be trusted. Most of the references in the books of the prophets are brief and one-sided, leaving scholars to speculate about the precise nature of the practices to which they refer. Archaeologists have uncovered objects that seem to have been used in family worship, but their meaning and functions are often unclear.

One of the peculiar results of these debates is that scholars feel more confident about their knowledge of the religious practices that were rejected by the authors and editors of the Hebrew Bible than about those that they approved. As we saw in the last chapter, the fact that the laws of Torah prohibit certain actions implies that people were in fact performing these acts at some point in Israel's history. Similar conclusions can be drawn from a number of stories in the books of Genesis and Judges where Israel's ancestors are shown engaging in ritual activities that were later prohibited by the laws of Torah (setting up stones in honor of Yahweh, offering animal sacrifices in the open country, and so forth). The fact that these incidents were included and not suppressed suggests that the people who crafted the stories were aware that such acts of devotion had been performed in the past among their people, even if they were no longer permitted by the laws of Torah. The material from these books, together with scattered references in the books of the prophets and the discoveries of archaeologists, have enabled scholars to piece together a broad outline of family religious practice in ancient Palestine.

EXERCISE 68

Read the following passages from the Hebrew Bible and make a list of the rituals and other religious practices that are mentioned or implied in each text.

- Genesis 28:10-22
- Exodus 12:1-20
- Numbers 30:1-15
- Deuteronomy 12:20-27
- Judges 17:1-13
- Jeremiah 44:15-19

As we saw in chapters 23 and 24, the Torah contains hundreds of rules that offer guidance for the daily conduct of the followers of Yahweh. The Torah insists that obedience to these rules is essential for maintaining the people's relationship with the deity. Other forms of religious expression are minimized or rejected. Within the narrative texts, by contrast, we see a much richer picture of religious life in ancient Palestine. The stories of the patriarchs (Abraham, Isaac, and Jacob) suggest that individual families or clans were devoted to a particular deity whom they believed was watching over them, ensuring the fertility and health of their crops, their animals, and their families. Farmers would have associated the deity with the territory where their family lived, while shepherds seem to have thought that the divine presence traveled with them from place to place. Everyone in the family or clan was expected to honor the family god; the modern idea of pursuing one's own religious path was unknown.

The family's devotion to a particular deity was traced back to the days of their ancestors, as reflected in titles like "the God of Abraham" (Genesis 28:13; 31:42; Psalm 47:9), "the Fear of Isaac" (Genesis 31:42, 53), "the bull [or possibly the Mighty One] of Jacob" (Genesis 49:24; Isaiah 49:26; 60:16; Psalm 132:2-5), and "the God of Nahor" (Genesis 31:53). The same idea lies behind generic terms like "the God of your father" (Genesis 31:5, 29; 43:23; Exodus 3:6) and "the God of your ancestors" (Exodus 3:13, 16; 4:5; Deuteronomy 1:11, 21; 4:1; 6:3). The leading male of the family or clan was responsible for performing or overseeing ceremonial acts of devotion to the deity and praying to the deity for help or guidance in times of trouble. Many of these activities would have involved the entire family.

Unfortunately, the Hebrew Bible only hints at the various ritual activities that were performed at the family level. But careful examination of texts and artifacts can give us some idea of the kinds of things that people did as individuals and families to honor the deity and to channel supernatural power into their daily lives.

1. *Prayers.* The Torah speaks of Israel crying out to Yahweh for help during times of suffering (Exodus 2:23-25; 3:7-10; Leviticus 26:40-42), but there are no rules or guidelines for voluntary personal prayer by ordinary individuals. The narrative books depict leaders offering prayers to Yahweh on behalf of the people (1 Samuel 12:19-23; 1 Kings 8:22-53; 2 Kings 19:14-19; Nehemiah 9:6-37), and even engaging in dialogue with the deity (1 Samuel 3:2-14; 23:2-4; 1 Kings 3:5-14), but private prayers by individuals are mentioned only rarely (2 Samuel 7:18-29; Nehemiah 1:4-11; Daniel 6:10-13). Most of the references to prayer by ordinary people involve requests for divine assistance in times of trouble (as in 1 Kings 8:33-53) or prayers for other people (Jeremiah 29:7; Job 42:8-9; Psalm 109:4), though a few are more general in tone (Job 16:17; Proverbs 15:8, 29). The book of Psalms is full of prayers for divine assistance and songs of thanksgiving, but most are more polished and poetic than one would expect from ordinary people. Some of these prayers might have been used in family or clan ceremonies, especially those seeking healing from sickness. Most, however, appear to have been composed for use in the Jerusalem temple (see chap-

Fig. 26.2. Nakhthorheb, a high Egyptian official (sixth century B.C.E.), kneels in prayer.

Fig. 26.3. The inscription on this ancient Egyptian monument pronounces a curse on anyone who misuses or appropriates a piece of land that had been donated to the temple.

ter 29). Whether similar prayers were recited at the family level can no longer be determined.

2. *Blessings and curses.* As in other traditional societies, the people of ancient Palestine believed that certain people had the ability to impart good or ill fortune to others by the power of their words. At the family level, the power to bless or curse was ordinarily vested in the male head of the family. At the societal level, it was associated with societal leaders such as priests and rulers, though prophets and **sorcerers** were also credited with the ability to wield such power. People who possessed the authority to bless or curse were thought to stand in a special relationship with the deity or to have special skills or knowledge that enabled them to channel the power of the supernatural to other people. Some believed that the deity had to approve

 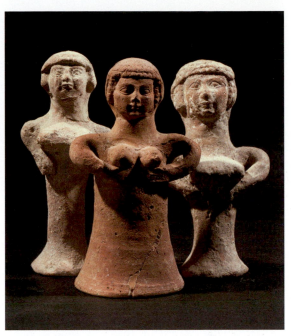

Fig. 26.4. (left) A small household shrine from Megiddo in northern Palestine, modeled after a temple, that likely contained images of deities; (right) female figurines such as these are found in archaeological excavations of residential areas throughout Palestine; many scholars believe they were linked with fertility rituals.

the words of blessing or cursing before they could take effect, while others thought that the words had a power of their own as long as they were pronounced by the appropriate person in the proper ritual context.

The Hebrew Bible contains many stories that refer to blessings or curses at the family level. Most of the blessings and many of the curses are pronounced by fathers upon their children or grandchildren (Genesis 9:24-27; 25:11; 27:18-40; 28:1-4; 31:55; 48:8-22; 49:1-28; 2 Samuel 13:23), though other people are also shown issuing blessings from time to time (Genesis 24:59-61; Judges 17:2; compare Ruth 4:13-15). Cursing one's parents, by contrast, is expressly forbidden by the Torah (Leviticus 20:9). Nearly all of the blessings and curses mentioned in the Hebrew Bible involve the long-term material prosperity of the person who is targeted, sometimes extending into future generations. The Hebrew Bible attributes great power to words of blessing and cursing, including a few instances where it is claimed that such words are irreversible once pronounced (Genesis 27:34-37; Numbers 22:6; 23:11; Judges 21:18; compare Deuteronomy 27:11-26).

3. *Offerings and sacrifices.* The Torah places strict limits on the presentation of ritual offerings and sacrifices to Yahweh. All offerings must be brought to a central shrine (the temple in Jerusalem), and all animal sacrifices must be performed by priests (Leviticus 17:8-9; Deuteronomy 12:13-14; contrast Exodus 20:22-26). Outside these texts, however, the picture is quite different. Several stories tell of families offering sacrifices to Yahweh without mentioning either priests or shrines (Genesis 8:20; 31:51-54; Judges 6:19-24; 11:30-3; 13:15-23; 1 Samuel 20:6, 29). Other texts indicate that families made regular offerings of bread, wine, and incense within their homes to honor the deity, to seek forgiveness for sins, and to request divine blessings upon the family (Jeremiah 7:17-18; 44:15-19; Job 1:5). Flat rooftops were used for presenting offerings to deities who were believed to live in the sky (2 Kings 23:12; Jeremiah 19:13; 32:29; Zephaniah 1:5).

Archaeological excavations have also found widespread evidence of ritual offerings by individual households. As many as half of the homes in some sites include objects that appear to have been used in household worship, including stone figurines (mostly modeled on humans, but some representing animal forms), incense altars and stands, libation vessels (for liquid offerings), rattles, and other animal-shaped objects.

The role of the figurines is unclear. Many scholars believe that some of them might represent the **teraphim**, or family gods, that are mentioned several times in the Hebrew Bible (Genesis 31:19, 30-35; 1 Samuel 19:13; Judges 17:1-5; 18:17; 2 Kings 23:24). Others think that they were employed in fertility rituals, since most of the figurines are female and appear to be holding out their breasts to the viewer. The frequency with which such ritual objects are found in the ruins of ancient houses suggests that many homes maintained domestic shrines that served as the focal point for family offerings and prayers to the deity, much like the household shrines that are found in many other religions. Some of these shrines would have been devoted to Yahweh, some to other deities, and some to a combination of the two.

4. *Protective rites.* The worldview of the Hebrew Bible has no place for a devil or demons such as we find later in Judaism and Christianity. But various texts do suggest that many people believed in other kinds of supernatural beings who they feared could harm them if not properly handled. Such ways of thinking were common in premodern agricultural societies where people were dependent on the unpredictable forces of nature, especially when coupled with a belief in many gods or spirits. The Hebrew Bible refers several times to people called **witches** or sorcerers who were thought to have the power to manipulate supernatural forces through the use of spells, incantations, and other ritual practices in order to inflict harm upon others (Leviticus 19:26; Deuteronomy 18:11; Isaiah 3:3; Jeremiah 27:9; Ezekiel 13:17-23; Malachi 3:5). The presence of these people evoked such fear that the Torah mandated that they be executed (Exodus 22:18; Leviticus 20:27). References to their activities are sparse in the Hebrew Bible, perhaps because they held a different worldview than that of the biblical authors and editors.

Various means were used to gain protection from harmful forces. A few verses from the Hebrew Bible refer to special objects that people may have worn to fend off dangerous spirits (Judges 8:21; Isaiah 3:18, 20). Evi-

dence for this practice can be seen in the many amulets (protective necklaces) that archaeologists have dug up in Israelite cities. In cases where harm had already occurred, family members could appeal to a religious specialist to reverse the effects (2 Kings 4:17-37; 5:1-14). Some of these people would have qualified as witches or sorcerers by the standards of the Hebrew Bible. Circumcision and death rituals may have been performed in part to ward off dangerous powers that might attack the child or the mourners (see Exodus 4:24-26). At least some of the residents of ancient Palestine seem to have performed special rites for the spirits of dead ancestors in order to prevent them from harming the living (see Deuteronomy 26:14). Scholarly reconstructions of these practices are invariably speculative, since our only evidence in many cases comes from the partial and one-sided observations of the authors and editors of the Hebrew Bible, who rejected most such activities as contrary to their understanding of Yahwism.

Fig. 26.5. This ancient Egyptian amulet would have been worn around the neck to ward off potentially harmful forces.

5. *Special times.* The Hebrew Bible divides time into distinct segments that are marked by ritual observances. Most include rituals to be performed by the family. The shortest period (other than the day) is the week, which

Fig. 26.6. Contemporary Jewish families continue to celebrate the festivals described in the laws of Torah: (top) a temporary shelter used in the Festival of Booths (Sukkoth); (bottom) a table prepared for a Passover meal.

ends on Saturday. This day is called the Sabbath, from the Hebrew word for "cease" or "stop," because all people and animals are supposed to cease from work on that day. Unlike in later Jewish practice, the Sabbath was not a time for people to gather together and worship, but simply a day to rest from the hard labor that was required for survival in an agricultural society. On the other hand, the very act of taking a day off from work for religious reasons reveals an attitude of honor and devotion to the deity. How and when the practice began are unknown, though it predates the Exile.

The Hebrew Bible also refers to a special observance at the beginning of each month, called the "new moon" festival (Numbers 10:10; 1 Samuel 20:5; 2 Kings 4:22-23; Ezra 3:4-5; Isaiah 1:13; Hosea 2:11). Most of the people of ancient Palestine followed a lunar calendar, with a new month beginning when the new moon became visible in the evening sky. Many traditional cultures view this as a time to give thanks for the return of the moon and to seek the blessing of the gods upon the coming month. The Hebrew Bible speaks only of state rituals on this date, but it seems likely that there would have been family observances as well.

Key phases in the agricultural cycle are also marked by religious festivals in the Hebrew Bible. Passover (also called the Festival of Unleavened Bread) coincides with the beginning of the barley harvest in the spring. The **Festival of Weeks** (also called the Festival of Harvest or **Pentecost**) occurs at the time of the summer wheat harvest. The **Festival of Booths** (also called the Festival of Ingathering) coincides with the season for harvesting olives, grapes, and other fruits in the fall. The Torah has absorbed all three festivals into the state religion by linking them with the Exodus story and requiring all Israelite males to travel to the Jerusalem temple during these times to bring offerings to Yahweh (Exodus 23:14-17; 34:18-24; Leviticus 23:4-8, 15-21, 33-43; Numbers 28:16-31; 29:12-38; Deuteronomy 16:1-17). Originally, however, they were family festivals that were accompanied by special rituals. The Torah records a few of these family rituals: lambs were to be sacrificed at home and eaten along with unleavened bread during the Passover festival (Exodus 12:1-20, 46), and the entire family was to live together in temporary shelters and perform special celebrations while holding leafy branches and fruits during the Festival of Booths (Leviticus 23:39-43; Deuteronomy 16:13-15). For the most part, however, the family dimension of these festivals has been lost, since it would have been passed on through oral traditions, not in writing. As with most other agricultural societies, family observances probably included prayers of thanksgiving or concern for the progress of the crops and rituals designed to ensure divine protection and proper weather for the remainder of the growing season.

The Torah also mentions other festivals and holidays that were supposed to be observed by the people of Israel, including the festival of trumpets (Leviticus 23:23-25; Numbers 29:1-6) and the presentation of the firstfruits of the harvest (Leviticus 23:9-14). Whether any of these festivals included rituals that were performed by the family is impossible to say at this point. On the other hand, we can be fairly confident that family rituals were used to mark key moments in the life cycles of individuals (birth, puberty, marriage, death, and so forth), even though the

Hebrew Bible says virtually nothing about what was done on these occasions.

6. *Other rituals.* As we saw in chapter 23, most of the purity laws of the Torah were designed to keep Yahweh's people in a proper ritual state to host the presence of the deity. Many of these laws pertain to family activities, such as rules regulating the kinds of foods that one could eat, the people whom one could have as sexual partners, and the kinds of seed that one could plant in a field. How widely these laws were known and followed in the pre-exilic period is a matter of dispute. If those who were aware of them ever reflected on the meanings behind these rules, they would have been reminded that Yahweh was near and cared about them. The Torah also refers occasionally to other types of rituals that may have been performed at the family level, though it is unclear how widely any of them were followed, or even what some of them mean (Leviticus 15:1-33; 19:27; Deuteronomy 15:19-20; 18:10; 23:21-22). Despite these ambiguities, it seems certain that religious rituals played an important part in the lives of families in ancient Palestine, giving them a ready means of interacting with and showing their devotion to the inhabitants of the supernatural realm.

CONCLUSION

The people of ancient Palestine held different ideas about the nature of the supernatural world and used a variety of ritual practices to bring them into contact with that realm. Even those who honored Yahweh as their chief deity performed ritual acts that did not agree with the laws spelled out in the Torah. The people who compiled the laws of Torah sought to counter this pattern by claiming divine sanction for their own beliefs and practices and calling for the elimination of other religious systems and the destruction of their symbols. Most of the time, however, theirs was only one voice among many in the religiously diverse climate of ancient Palestine.

Since the Hebrew Bible focuses primarily on state or national religion, it offers only brief and biased glimpses of the many religious practices that were carried out at the family level. Critical investigation is required to develop a more nuanced view of these practices. Archaeological discoveries and cross-cultural studies have helped scholars to flesh out the little that we find in the Hebrew Bible.

Scholars now know that religious rituals played a more important role in the daily lives of families in ancient Palestine than one might guess from the Hebrew Bible. Some, like prayers, blessings, and curses, involved ritualized uses of language. Others, like offerings, sacrifices, and protective rites, involved special types of actions. Virtually all of these rituals were designed to bring supernatural powers to the aid of the family and to protect it against harmful forces.

EXERCISE 69

Look back at the passages listed in the previous exercise. For each of the family religious practices that you identified, indicate whether it seems consistent with or contrary to what you learned about the laws of Torah. What do these results tell you about the relation between the laws of Torah and family religion in ancient Palestine?

Fig. 27.1. Ritual stands were used to offer incense to the gods in ancient Palestine.

Community Religion

Now, the fifteenth day of the seventh month, when you have gathered in the produce of the land, you shall keep the festival of the LORD, lasting seven days; a complete rest on the first day, and a complete rest on the eighth day. On the first day you shall take the fruit of majestic trees, branches of palm trees, boughs of leafy trees, and willows of the brook; and you shall rejoice before the LORD your God for seven days. (Leviticus 23:39-40)

When you come into the land that the LORD your God is giving you, you must not learn to imitate the abhorrent practices of those nations. No one shall be found among you who makes a son or daughter pass through fire, or who practices divination, or is a soothsayer, or an augur, or a sorcerer, or one who casts spells, or who consults ghosts or spirits, or who seeks oracles from the dead. . . . Although these nations that you are about to dispossess do give heed to soothsayers and diviners, as for you, the LORD your God does not permit you to do so. (Deuteronomy 18:9-11, 14)

Then you shall go on from there further and come to the oak of Tabor; three men going up to God at Bethel will meet you there, one carrying three kids, another carrying three loaves of bread, and another carrying a skin of wine. They will greet you and give you two loaves of bread, which you shall accept from them. After that you shall come to Gibeath-elohim, at the place where the Philistine garrison is; there, as you come to the town, you will meet a band of prophets coming down from the shrine with harp, tambourine, flute, and lyre playing in front of them; they will be in a prophetic frenzy. (1 Samuel 10:3-5)

In the last chapter we explored some of the ways in which the people of ancient Palestine sought to interact with the supernatural realm in the context of family life. Relying on the fragmentary information provided by the Hebrew Bible and material supplied by archaeologists, we were able to gain a glimpse of how thoroughly religion was integrated into the daily lives of ordinary people.

The next two chapters seek to situate those materials within a broader context by examining what people did outside the framework of the family. The present chapter examines the nature of religious practice within the towns and villages of Palestine; the following chapter does the same at the national level. As we review these materials, however, we should keep in mind that we are not leaving the family behind. When people engaged in religious activities outside the home, they usually did so as families, not as isolated individuals. When we read about people visiting a regional or national shrine to offer a sacrifice to the deity, we should envision them traveling in family groups. When we hear of people consulting a seer or a diviner for assistance with a problem, we should be aware that it was probably a family difficulty that motivated them to seek help. When we encounter people celebrating a religious festival, we should recall that such events usually included rituals that were performed within the family. The modern idea of religion as a personalized expression of one's inner spirituality would have been foreign to most of these people.

THE NATURE OF COMMUNITY RELIGION

People from Jewish or Christian backgrounds typically presume that the residents of the towns and villages of Palestine must have gathered together on a regular basis, as in a modern synagogue or church service, to engage in religious activities like singing, praying, reciting creeds, reading Scripture, and listening to sermons. Most are surprised to learn that this was not part of their culture. As far as we know, there were no weekly religious gatherings of any type in ancient Palestine. The Hebrew Bible describes the Sabbath day as a time for rest and recuperation, not for communal religious activities (Exodus 20:8-11; 31:12-17; 35:2; Leviticus 23:3; Deuteronomy 5:12-15). Only in Jerusalem do we hear of any religious rituals on the Sabbath, as the priests were commanded to offer special sacrifices to Yahweh on this day (Leviticus 24:5-9; Numbers 28:9). The earliest synagogue meetings did not take place until fairly late in the postexilic period, near the end of the era covered by our biblical texts.

This does not mean, however, that there was no communal religious activity. The local community offered a variety of opportunities for people to come into contact with the supernatural realm. Three broad spheres of activity can be identified: community rituals, religious experts, and local shrines.

EXERCISE 70

Read the following passages and make a list of what the passages say about (a) what people did collectively to pay their respects to the inhabitants of the supernatural world; (b) who performed any ritual acts that are mentioned; and (c) what kinds of objects are associated with the ritual. Not every passage will contain all of these elements.

- Exodus 20:22-26
- Leviticus 23:39-43
- Deuteronomy 21:1-9
- Deuteronomy 26:12-15
- Judges 8:22-27
- Hosea 4:10-14

Community Rituals

Since the population of most towns and villages was small and virtually all of the residents were related to one another in some way, people would have known each other quite well and interacted on a daily basis. When one of their neighbors encountered a situation that called for a religious ceremony, people from across the community would have gathered for the event. Important family occasions like birth or marriage would have been marked by religious rituals, including prayers of gratitude to the deity and rituals that aimed to protect the participants from harm during this period of transition. Painful experiences like illness or death would have brought families and neighbors together to lament and pray and to perform rituals designed to drive away any harmful powers that might be causing the problem. Annual religious festivals provided opportunities for people to participate in organized ritual activities from time to time, including animal sacrifices, singing, and group dancing. In short, while there were no regularly scheduled religious gatherings in the towns and villages of ancient Palestine, the social calendars of the local residents would have been sprinkled with events that included a religious element.

Religious Experts

Every community also had certain residents who were viewed as religious experts to be consulted in times of need. Some, like priests and prophets, appear often enough in the Hebrew Bible to give us a fairly good sense of their activities. Others are less known, usually because their activities were condemned by the people who produced the Hebrew Bible.

One class of experts, whom we might call *power brokers*, was believed to possess special skills or knowledge that enabled them to channel supernatural power to others, whether for good or for ill. Little is said about their activities in the Hebrew Bible, but comparisons with the surrounding cultures suggest that much of their effort would have been devoted to helping people with problems such as illness, bad fortune, relational conflicts, and oppression by evil spirits. Some would have operated rather like physicians, prescribing various kinds of remedies and charms

Fig. 27.2. (top) A communal healing ceremony in a village in Benin, Africa; (bottom) sacred objects used in Native American healing rituals.

the future or to know other things that lay beyond the awareness of ordinary humans. People came to them with questions about the weather, the outcome of an illness, the location of a lost item, or any other matters about which they desired knowledge. Practitioners of this art, sometimes called **divination** in the Hebrew Bible, employed a variety of techniques to gain their information. Some performed rituals that they believed gave them direct access to the supernatural world, such as casting lots, conjuring up the spirits of the dead, or working themselves into a trance and surrendering their minds to the control of a superhuman spirit. Others engaged in rational analysis of occurrences by which the gods were thought to reveal their will and intentions to humans, such as dreams, **omens** (for example, the flight patterns of birds or the entrails of a slaughtered animal), or the movements of the heavenly bodies.

The Hebrew Bible is deeply ambivalent about the practice of divination. The narrative and prophetic books portray the priests and prophets of Yahweh using many of these techniques. Yet most are expressly prohibited by the laws of Torah (Leviticus 19:26; Deuteronomy 18:9-14), and other texts condemn them as well (1 Samuel 15:23; 2 Kings 17:17; 21:6). The reason for this prohibition is never made clear. A few verses suggest that the problem lies not with the techniques themselves but with the accuracy or the source of their predictions (when it comes from gods other than Yahweh). This is especially evident in passages where diviners are lumped together with false prophets (Isaiah 3:1-3; 44:24-26; Jeremiah 27:9-11; 29:8-9; Micah 3:6-7; Zechariah 10:2). Since virtually all of these latter texts are found in the books of the prophets, it seems probable that the negative view of divination in the Hebrew Bible reflects a conflict between two groups of people who used similar techniques but came to different conclusions about the future, or in some cases credited their knowledge to different supernatural powers.

to address different types of problems, while others were more like priests, relying on rituals to drive away harmful spirits or elicit the help of more beneficial powers. Some would have credited their powers to Yahweh, while others would have looked to other gods for assistance. Those who relied on other gods would have been rejected as witches or sorcerers by the people who compiled the Hebrew Bible. In the places where they lived and worked, however, opinions about such people would have varied widely, ranging from honor and respect to suspicion and fear.

A second class of religious experts, whom we might label *knowledge brokers*, was believed to be able to foretell

Fig. 27.3. (top) An African diviner examines the organs of a sacrificed chicken for signs from the gods; (bottom) a Chinese woman consults a fortune teller outside a Taoist temple.

Local Shrines

The Hebrew Bible indicates that local and regional shrines (places where people went to interact more closely with the deity) played an important role in the religious lives of the people of ancient Palestine, including the followers of Yahweh. The Hebrew Bible commonly refers to these shrines as high places, since many of them were located on hilltops or other elevated sites. As in other cultures, the choice of an elevated spot reflects the belief that such sites bring the worshiper into closer proximity to the chief deities who are thought to reside in the sky (also called "heaven" or "the heavens").

The term *high place* is misleading, however, when applied to the many shrines that dotted the countryside

of Palestine, since they could be located in virtually any spot. Sites containing a grove of trees, or even a single outstanding tree, were common places of worship, perhaps because green trees symbolized life and fertility in a land that was often quite dry. Places where ancestors were supposed to have encountered a deity were also honored with shrines. Small shrines were often located immediately inside the gates of walled towns where people could pay tribute to the local guardian deity as they passed. Collections of ritual objects have also been found at other sites inside towns and villages, though some of these may have been used by a single clan rather than the entire populace. By the end of the monarchy, shrines were so common that virtually everyone could have reached one after a few hours of walking, and many after only a few minutes.

Shrines varied widely in size, construction, personnel, furnishings, and rituals. Some were little more than open areas in a field or under a tree, while others were large enough to host scores of worshippers. Some were exposed to the elements, perhaps marked off by a ring of stones or some other physical marker, while others included a building that could be used for various ritual activities. Most were probably open to anyone who chose to visit, though some were managed by a particular family or clan. Larger shrines might have been staffed by priests or prophets who interacted with the deity on behalf of the worshippers, while smaller ones were usually unstaffed.

Three ritual objects could be found at virtually all shrines: an altar, a stone pillar, and a wooden pole. The altar was used for making offerings and sacrifices to the gods, but the significance of the other two objects is debated. Most of the references in the Hebrew Bible associate the pillar and the pole with non-Yahwistic religious practices, though their meaning and purpose are never specified (Exodus 23:23-24; Deuteronomy 7:1-5; 12:2-3; Judges 6:25-32; 1 Kings 14:22-24; 16:31-33; 2 Kings 3:2; 17:9-16; 21:2-3; 2 Chronicles 24:17-18). Following the lead of the biblical authors, many scholars have interpreted both objects as abstract images of Canaanite deities that were worshipped at the shrine. This interpretation is supported by the observation that the Hebrew word for the wooden poles is *asherim*, a term that is very similar to the name of Asherah, a Canaanite goddess of fertility who was popular in ancient Palestine. It would also explain why the objects are viewed so negatively in much of the Hebrew Bible, as well as why Hezekiah (eighth century B.C.E.) and Josiah (seventh century B.C.E.), two of the "good kings" of Judah, are said to have made a point of destroying these objects when they attempted to shut down the high places of Judah (2 Kings 18:1-4; 23:14-15). On the other hand, this theory cannot explain why the ancestors of Israel are depicted using pillars to mark the presence of Yahweh (Genesis 28:18-22; 35:9-15), nor why so many of the "good kings" of Judah (that is, those who exhibited solid devotion to Yahweh) should have left the high places untouched if they were leading people astray from Yahweh (1 Kings 15:11-14; 22:41-43; 2 Kings 12:1-3; 14:3-4; 15:3-4, 34-35).

Most scholars today recognize that this interpretation gives too much credit to the ideological viewpoint of the biblical authors who believed that all forms of worship

Fig. 27.4. (top) A line of stone pillars at Gezer in southern Palestine that might have been part of a sacred shrine or "high place"; (bottom) a sacred pillar forms part of a gate shrine at the entrance to the ancient city of Geshur in northern Palestine.

outside the Jerusalem temple were inherently idolatrous. A more careful reading of the Hebrew Bible suggests that most of the larger shrines were probably devoted to Yahweh (as in 1 Samuel 9:11-19; 10:3-6; 1 Kings 3:2-3; 2 Kings 18:21-22; 2 Chronicles 33:17; and other texts), though their practices clearly diverged from what was considered acceptable by the people who produced the Hebrew Bible. Many of the shrines would have allowed for the worship of other gods alongside Yahweh, while others (probably a small minority in most periods) would have been dedicated primarily to the worship of non-Yahwistic deities. Shrines that had no staff could have been used to worship whatever deity one wished. The books of the prophets indicate that people did indeed worship a variety of gods and goddesses at the many shrines that dotted the territories of Israel and Judah (see chapters 32–33).

Interestingly, the pillar and pole seem to be present regardless of which deity was worshipped at a given site. If these objects somehow represented the presence of the deity, as seems likely, then we must acknowledge that Yahweh, too, could be represented by such symbols, despite the rule prohibiting such images in the Ten Commandments (Exodus 20:4-5). This fact has been obscured by the editors of the Hebrew Bible, whose depiction of the past has been shaped by their belief that the worship of Yahweh should be performed in the Jerusalem temple without the use of such images.

In addition to the pillar and pole, every shrine would have had an altar that was used to present sacrifices to the deity. Objects that might be offered on the altar include sheep, goats, birds, grain, oil, and incense. Most of these items would have been brought to the shrine by people who wished to request help from the deity or to express gratitude for help that they had received. Problems that might cause a person to travel to the local shrine to offer a sacrifice include serious or ongoing illnesses (whether of family members or animals), crop diseases, insect infestations, and drought. People who offered sacrifices of thanksgiving were often fulfilling vows they had made as part of a prayer for assistance (as in, "If you help me, I will give you my best sheep").

At the larger shrines, the sacrificial rituals would have been performed by the priestly staff of the center;

otherwise, the male head of the family would have conducted the sacrifices. Portions of the offerings would have been burned up on the altar, while the rest would have been used to feed the worshippers or the shrine personnel, if any were present. In addition to the usual items of sacrifice, several verses in the Hebrew Bible speak of rites in which children were "passed through the fire" (Leviticus 18:21; 20:1-5; Deuteronomy 12:31; 18:10; 2 Kings 16:2-3; 17:16-7; 21:6; 23:10; Jeremiah 7:30-31; 19:4-6; 32:35; Ezekiel 20:31). While it is possible that this expression refers to a ritual in which a child is dedicated to a deity by being held momentarily over a fire, many scholars believe that it refers to human sacrifice.

The reason for the act is never stated, though a few passages suggest that children might have been sacrificed as a supreme expression of devotion to the deity, perhaps in a time of great need. The practice is harshly condemned by the authors of the Hebrew Bible.

Other than the offering of animal sacrifices, little is known about what was done at these centers. Passing references in the Hebrew Bible suggest that families may have traveled to the major shrines to observe religious festivals, bringing sacrifices and offerings from their herds and fields to offer to the deity (Judges 21:19; 1 Samuel 1:3; 20:6; 1 Kings 12:32-33; Hosea 2:13). While camped around the shrine, they would have had occasion to engage in other types of business for which the presence of the deity might have been desirable, such as arranging marriages or settling disputes. The local shrine was also a natural place for people to congregate in times of distress, such as locust infestations or invading armies to seek assistance or protection from the deity (as in 1 Samuel 7:7-10).

Another common reason for visiting the larger shrines was to consult with the resident staff (usually priests or prophets) in an effort to obtain supernatural guidance for handling personal problems (Judges 18:2-6; 1 Samuel 1:9-18; 9:5-10; 1 Samuel 21:1-6). Most of the techniques used at the shrines for receiving messages from the deity were probably the same as those of the local diviners, but they also seem to have offered the seeker the option of sleeping at the shrine in order to receive revelations directly from the deity through a dream (1 Samuel 3:21—4:1; 1 Kings 3:3-15; compare Genesis 28:10-22; 31:10-13; Job 33:14-18). As in other traditional cultures, the people of ancient Palestine believed that the gods spoke to people through dreams, telling them what to do or offering insights into the future (Genesis 15:12-16; 31:10-13; 1 Samuel 28:6; Job 33:13-18; Daniel 7:1-28; 8:18-19; Joel 2:28). Some dreams were clear enough for anyone to understand, but others required interpretation by a person with special skills in this area, a role that was presumably filled at the shrines by priests or prophets (Genesis 40:1—41:36; Daniel 2:1-45; 4:1-27).

Fig. 27.5. (top) A modern replica of a four-horned altar that was excavated at Beersheba in southern Palestine, where it was used for conducting animal sacrifices; (bottom) a Roman image of a bull being led to an altar for sacrifice.

WOMEN'S RELIGION

Thus far we have said little about the role of women in the religious life of the family or the community in ancient Palestine. For the most part this is due to the limitations of our sources. Not only was the Hebrew Bible written by, for, and about men, but much of what it does say about the religious lives of women concerns practices that were rejected by the authors of the Hebrew Bible. Only in recent years have scholars begun to pore through the literary and archaeological sources in an effort to understand what women did to express their relationship with the supernatural realm.

Family Religion

Most of our texts seem to presuppose that women will follow the religion of their husbands, though foreign women at the highest levels of society seem to have been allowed to retain their native practices. In a few cases a royal husband is shown embracing the religion of his wife (for example, Solomon and Ahab). What roles women might have played in the performance of family rituals is difficult to say, though they clearly participated in group activities along with the rest of the family.

Descriptions of women engaging in religious practices in the home are rare in the Hebrew Bible. Here and there women are shown engaging in prayer, making vows (Numbers 30:3-15), and pronouncing blessings upon other people (Genesis 24:59-60; Judges 17:2; Ruth 2:20; 4:11-12). One passage tells of a woman who paid for the construction of a silver image for the family shrine (Judges 17:3-4), though this woman was obviously wealthy. Most of the religious activities of women were probably tied to their domestic duties. Women prepared the food that was used in ritual offerings or sacred meals, and women ensured that their families complied with ritual food taboos. Women may also have cleaned and tended any objects that were kept in the family shrine. In some cases this might have involved ritualized acts of devotion such as burning incense and pouring out drink offerings to the deity (Jeremiah 44:19).

Whether women engaged in religious activities that were exclusive to their gender is unclear. Many scholars have argued that the small carved female figurines that have been discovered in homes throughout Palestine (as shown on page 351) were used by women in the performance of fertility rituals designed to aid them in childbirth and protect their children, though others have interpreted them differently. The Torah's requirement that women must present special sacrifices at the temple after giving birth (Leviticus 12:1-8) might be rooted in rituals that were once performed within the family, but if so, their original form has been lost to us.

Community Religion

As with family religion, women would have participated in community rituals along with the rest of their family, including village celebrations and trips to local and regional shrines. Within the village, women played a prominent role in life-cycle rituals. When a child was born or a couple married, the women of the village gathered together to celebrate the event and pray for divine blessings. When a neighbor was sick or died, the women cried out to the deity for healing or lamented the loss. At least one text suggests that there were special rituals for young women who were approaching puberty (Judges 11:36-40), though what was done at these times is no longer apparent. All of these activities served a religious purpose within the community.

Women also played special roles at other times of communal celebration. Several times the Hebrew Bible depicts women engaging in joyous singing and dancing at the receipt of good news from outside the village (Judges 11:34; 1 Samuel 18:6-7; Jeremiah 31:13; compare Exodus 15:20-21). Other verses suggest that women engaged in similar activities during the festivals that were held at local shrines (Judges 21:20-23; compare Psalm 68:24-25).

The Hebrew Bible also depicts women filling the role of religious experts within the local community. At least some of the people described as sorcerers and diviners are women (Exodus 22:18; Ezekiel 13:17-23), including some who served as mediums and consulted the dead for guidance (1 Samuel 28:1-5). Most such women are portrayed negatively in the Hebrew Bible, since it was believed that they received their powers from gods other than Yahweh. On the positive side, a handful of verses speak about women who served as prophets of Yahweh. Some of these women were consulted by people who were seeking guidance from the deity, including royal officials (Judges 4:4-7; 2 Kings 22:13-20; Nehemiah 6:14). Whether women also served as prophets at the regional shrines is unknown.

Some scholars have argued that women in ancient Palestine preferred to worship female deities such as Asherah and the "Queen of Heaven" rather than the male warrior-god Yahweh. Evaluating such claims is difficult, since we know almost nothing about the percentage of the population that was devoted to a particular deity at a given time. While there are verses in the Hebrew Bible that speak of women worshipping female deities (1 Kings 15:13; 18:19; 2 Kings 23:7; Jeremiah 7:18; 44:17), men are also credited with honoring these goddesses (1 Kings 11:5; 2 Kings 23:4; Jeremiah 7:18; 44:15-18). As a result, it is hard to know whether gender played a role in people's decisions about which deity to worship. Comparisons with other cultures suggest that women do tend to be attracted to female deities, but the textual evidence is too sparse for us to discern

Fig. 27.6. (top) Women playing instruments and dancing; (bottom) women engaged in a mourning ritual. Both scenes are from Egyptian tomb paintings.

how far the women of ancient Palestine conformed to this pattern.

CONCLUSION

Religion played a vital role in the community life of the towns and villages of ancient Palestine. Though people did not gather together regularly for worship, the culture was rich with religious rituals that were performed as circumstances demanded. Some of these rituals were linked to events in the lives of individual community members, such as birth, circumcision, marriage, illness, and death. Others were performed as needed to respond to developments that affected the entire community, such as famines or military victories.

Religious experts were also important for maintaining the community's links with the supernatural realm. Some were thought to have special access to supernatural powers that could assist people with problems such as illness, bad fortune, relational conflicts, and affliction by evil spirits. Others were believed to be able to see into the future or to know things that lay beyond the awareness of ordinary humans. The Hebrew Bible is deeply ambivalent about these kinds of activities, crediting their powers to Yahweh in some cases and to other gods in other instances.

Many people traveled to local shrines to beg the deity for assistance or to give thanks for help received. Larger groups gathered at the shrines during the major religious festivals. People also came to the shrines to seek guidance from the deity, whether by consulting with priests or prophets or seeking revelation through a dream. A variety of gods were honored at these shrines, but most were at least nominally dedicated to Yahweh.

Women participated in all aspects of the religious life of the community, though certain roles and activities were probably limited to men and others to women. Activities that were specific to women revolved around the home and the life cycles of the members of the local community. Some women also served as religious experts within their communities, though as a rule these women were viewed negatively by the authors and editors of the Hebrew Bible. Whether women might have found female deities more attractive than the male god Yahweh remains unclear.

EXERCISE 72

Read the following passages and make a list of the kinds of religious activities that women are shown performing. How do these compare with the activities that we have seen men doing in other passages?

- Leviticus 12:1-8
- Numbers 30:3-15
- Judges 21:20-23
- 1 Samuel 18:6-7
- 2 Kings 22:11-20
- Ezekiel 13:17-23

Fig. 28.1. Most scholars believe that the temple of Solomon was located on the site presently occupied by the Dome of the Rock (the gold-domed building in the foreground), an important Muslim shrine.

State Religion

*When you cross over the Jordan and live in the land that the L*ORD *your God is allotting to you, and when he gives you rest from your enemies all around so that you live in safety, then you shall bring everything that I command you to the place that the L*ORD *your God will choose as a dwelling for his name: your burnt offerings and your sacrifices, your tithes and your donations, and all your choice votive gifts that you vow to the L*ORD*. And you shall rejoice before the L*ORD *your God, you together with your sons and your daughters, your male and female slaves, and the Levites who reside in your towns (since they have no allotment or inheritance with you). Take care that you do not offer your burnt offerings at any place you happen to see. But only at the place that the L*ORD *will choose in one of your tribes—there you shall offer your burnt offerings and there you shall do everything I command you.* (Deuteronomy 12:10-14)

*Then Jeroboam said to himself, "Now the kingdom may well revert to the house of David. If this people continues to go up to offer sacrifices in the house of the L*ORD *at Jerusalem, the heart of this people will turn again to their master, King Rehoboam of Judah; they will kill me and return to King Rehoboam of Judah." So the king took counsel, and made two calves of gold. He said to the people, "You have gone up to Jerusalem long enough. Here are your gods, O Israel, who brought you up out of the land of Egypt." He set one in Bethel, and the other he put in Dan.* (1 Kings 12:26-29)

*The king [Josiah] commanded the high priest Hilkiah, the priests of the second order, and the guardians of the threshold, to bring out of the temple of the L*ORD *all the vessels made for Baal, for Asherah, and for all the host of heaven; he burned them outside Jerusalem in the fields of the Kidron, and carried their ashes to Bethel. He deposed the idolatrous priests whom the kings of Judah had ordained to make offerings in the high places at the cities of Judah and around Jerusalem; those also who made offerings to Baal, to the sun, the moon, the constellations, and all the host of the heavens. . . . He brought all the priests out of the towns of Judah, and defiled the high places where the priests had made offerings, from Geba to Beer-sheba; he broke down the high places of the gates that were at the entrance of the gate of Joshua the governor of the city, which were on the left at the gate of the city.* (2 Kings 23:4-5, 8)

Most of what we have learned so far about family and community religion has been pieced together from brief passages and passing references scattered throughout the Hebrew Bible. When we ask about the ritual aspects of the national or state religion of Israel and Judah, on the other hand, we find a wealth of data. This observation shows where the interest of the Hebrew Bible lies. From the standpoint of the people who compiled these texts, personal experience of the deity by ordinary individuals is relatively unimportant; what matters is the relationship between Yahweh and the people of Israel as a whole (that is, their covenant with Yahweh). At the core of this relationship lies the proper conduct of rituals at state-sponsored shrines.

Before we can talk about the kinds of rituals that were performed at the national shrines, we need to critically examine what the Hebrew Bible says about the history of state religion in ancient Palestine. Most scholars believe that the pro-Jerusalem bias of the people who crafted the Hebrew Bible has produced a distorted depiction of the history and function of Israel's national religious institutions.

THE MYTH OF CENTRALIZED WORSHIP

According to the Hebrew Bible, it was Yahweh who commanded that a central shrine be set up to serve as his place of residence among the people of Israel. The book of Exodus contains detailed plans that Yahweh is said to have given at Mount Sinai for the construction and operation of the tabernacle, a portable tent shrine where Moses was to meet with Yahweh on a regular basis (thus its alternate title, the tent of meeting) (Exodus 25–31). The amount of space lavished on the construction and dedication of the tabernacle (Exodus 35–40) also testifies

Fig. 28.2. An artist's depiction of the tabernacle that the book of Exodus claims the Israelites used as a worship center during their forty years in the desert.

to its importance in the eyes of the people who framed the narrative. The same can be said for its physical location, which is described as being either in the center of the Israelites' desert encampments (Numbers 2:1-34) or far outside their camp, separated from its impurity (Exodus 33:7-11). The Torah also devotes many chapters to descriptions of the animal sacrifices and other activities that were supposed to be performed in or around the tent shrine (Leviticus 1:1—7:38; 16:1—17:9; 22:1—24:9; Numbers 15:1-31; 18:1-22).

The tabernacle becomes the focal point of Yahweh's interactions with Moses and his people for the remainder of the story. The tent is considered so holy that anyone other than a priest and Levite who approaches it is to be put to death (Numbers 1:51). This concern for the holiness of the tabernacle is rooted in the belief that Yahweh was present in concentrated essence in the innermost part of the tent, enthroned above the gold-plated box (the Ark of the Covenant) that held the Ten Commandments and other souvenirs of the desert wanderings (Exodus 25:22; 30:6; Leviticus 16:2; Numbers 7:89). Only the high priest could enter this part of the shrine, and he only once each year on the **Day of Atonement** after offering special sacrifices for his and his family's sins (Leviticus 16:1-14).

Interestingly, Moses and his assistant Joshua seem to have been exempt from this requirement (see Exodus 33:8-11).

This concentration on the central shrine is taken a step further in the book of Deuteronomy, where Moses announces that Yahweh intends to choose a single place in the land of Canaan to which all sacrifices and offerings must be brought (Deuteronomy 12:5-18, 26-27; 14:22-26; 15:19-20; 26:1-3). All male Israelites are expected to travel to this site three times a year to observe the major festivals (Deuteronomy 16:1-17). The presentation of sacrifices and offerings at any other place in Palestine, even to Yahweh, is expressly forbidden (Deuteronomy 12:13, 17; 16:5). All other places where ritual activities might be conducted are to be destroyed (Deuteronomy 7:5; 12:2-4; compare Exodus 23:23-24; Numbers 33:30-52).

As the story progresses, however, this insistence that all ritual activity must be concentrated at a single location appears to be forgotten. Not until the construction of Solomon's temple in Jerusalem (1 Kings 6–8) does it emerge once again as a concern of the narrator. Even by biblical chronology this is a period of several hundred years in which the people of Israel are shown worshipping at many different places across the land without being criticized for it. The tabernacle recedes into the background once the people settle in Canaan; even its location is unclear, since it is associated with two different towns, Shiloh and Gibeon, and nothing is said about a move. (For Shiloh, see Joshua 18:1; 19:51; Judges 18:31; 1 Samuel 1:3; 2:22; 4:3; Psalm 78:60; Jeremiah 7:12; for Gibeon, see 1 Kings 3:3-4; 1 Chronicles 16:39; 21:29; 2 Chronicles 1:3-6). The picture is clouded further by reports that the Ark of the Covenant resided for a time in Bethel (Judges 20:26-28) and later spent twenty years in Kiriath-Jearim (1 Samuel 7:1-2; 1 Chronicles 13:5), attended by priests who have no evident links to the tabernacle. Not once in these stories does anyone claim that the tabernacle is the only valid place of worship. Again and again people are shown building altars and making sacrifices to Yahweh at various places across the land, including such God-ordained leaders as Samuel and Saul (1 Samuel 7:17; 9:12-13; 10:8; 11:15; 14:35; 16:1-5). In several instances these acts are explicitly commanded or approved by Yahweh or an angel (Judges 6:24-26; 13:15-23; 2 Samuel 24:18-25).

The presence of such conflicting materials within the Hebrew Bible suggests to most scholars that the idea of centralizing all ritual activity in a single location arose at some point after the construction of the Jerusalem temple (that is, during the monarchy) and not in the time of Moses as the book of Deuteronomy claims. Scholars are divided, however, over when this drive toward centralization began. Some think that such an outcome was inevitable once the decision was made to build a royal temple that would serve as a national shrine. Others see the move as a response to the construction of competing national shrines at Dan and Bethel in the northern kingdom after the death of Solomon (tenth century B.C.E.). Still others believe that the move toward centralization was initiated by one of the kings of Judah, whether Hezekiah (eighth century B.C.E.) or Josiah (seventh century B.C.E.), perhaps under the influence of the Jerusalem priests. Some insist that there was no concern for a central shrine until after the Exile. Good arguments can be made for all of these positions.

The text is also unclear about what happened to the tabernacle after the Ark was reportedly moved to the Jerusalem temple. Many scholars believe that the tabernacle is a literary fiction that was patterned on the later Jerusalem temple, so that questions about its ultimate fate are irrelevant. Others acknowledge the similarity between the two shrines but suggest that the influence ran in the opposite direction; namely, the temple was based on an earlier tent shrine that may or may not have served as the focal point of Israelite religion prior to the temple. Among those who view the tabernacle as a real historical entity, some identify it with the tent of meeting

Fig. 28.3. Illustration from the *Christ-Herre Chronik*, ca. 1375–80.

that the Hebrew Bible says was carried with the Ark of the Covenant into Solomon's newly constructed temple (1 Kings 8:4; 2 Chronicles 5:5; compare 1 Chronicles 6:31-32), where it was either stored away or erected inside the temple to house the Ark. Others, however, argue that this text refers to a separate tent that David had set up in Jerusalem to house the Ark (2 Chronicles 1:3-6). A few texts suggest that the tabernacle may have remained at Shiloh until it was destroyed by invading armies, most likely the Assyrians (Psalm 78:56-64; Jeremiah 7:12-15; 26:4-6). The narrative books say virtually nothing about either the operation of the tabernacle or its destruction. In the end, we simply do not know what happened to the tabernacle, or whether it existed at all. Archaeological excavations are unlikely to turn up any evidence that could aid in answering this question, since the text describes the tabernacle as being made of materials that would have long since decayed.

These disputes about the relation between the tabernacle and the Jerusalem temple are important because the answers that scholars give to these questions lead to very different understandings of the nature of state religion in ancient Palestine.

1. Conservative scholars see the tabernacle as the historical predecessor of the Jerusalem temple, with similar rites being performed in both facilities as specified by the laws of Torah. The building of the temple simply transferred this system to a more permanent home. The existence and operation of a central shrine was thus vital to the state religion of the people of Israel from their earliest history, despite the practices of certain kings who tolerated or even promoted more diverse forms of worship. The performance of sacrifices and other rituals at sites other than the central shrine was a violation of state religion and thus illegitimate. To make matters worse, most of these other sites followed deviant forms of Yahwism or honored gods other than Yahweh. Kings like Hezekiah and Josiah who acted to stamp out these other worship centers were simply enforcing the historic norms of state religion.

2. Maximalist scholars vary widely in their reconstructions of Israel's state religion. Most view the move toward centralization as an attempt by certain kings, especially Hezekiah and Josiah, to enhance their control over the religious and political lives of their subjects during periods of crisis. If the tabernacle existed at all prior to the construction of the Jerusalem temple, it functioned as one shrine among many, not as a central shrine that served the entire nation. The building of the Jerusalem temple did not change this pattern; it was erected to serve as a royal shrine alongside other worship centers, not to replace local sites of communal religious life. The same is true for the royal shrines at Dan and Bethel in the north.

Apart from those limited periods when the kings were seeking to extend their control over the regional worship centers, most people's lives would have been little affected by expressions of state religion. Their encounters with the royal shrines would have been entirely voluntary, as when one of them decided to travel to one of these sites during a religious festival or on some other occasion to present an offering or sacrifice to the deity. Many who made such trips would have been motivated by the belief that this site was especially powerful due to its close association with the deity and/or the king.

3. Minimalist scholars emphasize the religious diversity of Palestine in the preexilic period. Some acknowledge the existence of royal shrines that functioned apart from the regional shrines that were visited by ordinary people, while others insist that all such stories are myths—there was no such thing as a state religion in preexilic Palestine, only diverse local and regional forms of religion that involved the worship of many different gods. The stories of the tabernacle and possibly even Solomon's temple were created to lend ideological support to the efforts of a group of priestly elites who were seeking to unite the people of postexilic Judah around a temple-centered religion that would ensure priestly control over the lives of the ordinary inhabitants of Palestine. Passages in the Hebrew Bible that speak of activities in the tabernacle or the Jerusalem temple were created during this period to give a sense of antiquity to practices that did not actually begin until the postexilic period. Only during this later

---

EXERCISE 73

Read the following passages that describe the events that the Hebrew Bible says led to the founding of the Jerusalem temple and the northern shrines. What reasons are given for the founding of these shrines? How credible do these reasons seem to you? Why does the narrator express such different opinions of the northern and southern shrines?

• 2 Samuel 7:1-17
• 1 Kings 12:1-33
• 1 Kings 16:29-33
• 2 Chronicles 3:1—5:14

era can one speak of any real state religion among the people of Palestine.

THE CREATION OF ROYAL SHRINES

The Hebrew Bible contains detailed stories about the establishment of the royal shrines at Jerusalem in the southern kingdom of Judah and at Dan and Bethel in the northern kingdom of Israel. The narrative is heavily biased in favor of the Jerusalem temple and against the northern shrines, a point that has led many scholars to doubt the historical validity of the accounts. Most, however, find at least the core of the stories plausible, especially since archaeological excavations have uncovered the remains of a massive worship complex at Dan that dates to the period of the monarchy. Excavations at the presumed site of the Jerusalem temple have been impossible due to the presence there of the Dome of the Rock, the third holiest shrine of Islam.

The Royal Shrines of Judah

According to the Hebrew Bible, the idea of building a temple for Yahweh in Jerusalem originated with King David, who envisioned it as a fixed home for the Ark of the Covenant, the sacred box from the Exodus period that David had recently brought to his new capital and placed in a special tent. Prior to that time, the Ark had been housed for most of its existence in the tabernacle,

Fig. 28.4. James Tissot, *The Ark Passes over Jordan*

though its most recent home had been in Kiriath-Jearim, where it was lodged apart from the tabernacle, as we noted earlier.

The story does not explain why David moved the Ark to Jerusalem without the tabernacle, so we can only speculate about what the narrator might have had in mind. According to the Torah, the Ark is the earthly symbol of Yahweh's presence, the place where he comes to meet with his people. The Ark is also a potent channel of Yahweh's power—the Jordan River splits in its presence (Joshua 3:9—4:18); the armies of Israel carry it into battle to ensure that Yahweh fights on their behalf (Joshua 4:1-4; 6:1-21; 1 Samuel 14:16-18; 2 Samuel 11:11); and anyone other than a priest or Levite who gets too close to it can become sick (1 Samuel 5:6-12) or even die (2 Samuel 6:6-10). The place where the Ark rests, by contrast, is invariably blessed by Yahweh (2 Samuel 6:12).

Whatever the truth behind these claims of supernatural power, the story of David moving the Ark to Jerusalem is at least plausible in light of the biblical depiction of David's reign. With the end of David's wars (2 Samuel 7:1) and the establishment of a relatively stable monarchy, David would have wanted to have this powerful object under his control. He could not afford to entrust it to a group of priests who might not support his newly united kingdom. Possession of this sacred relic would also reinforce his claim to the throne against the surviving members of Saul's family. So it makes sense that David might have ordered the Ark to be brought to Jerusalem and placed in a tent, recalling the story of Yahweh's presence in the desert tabernacle (2 Samuel 6:1-19). Here the king offered animal sacrifices (2 Samuel 6:17-18; compare 24:25) and appointed his sons to serve as priests (2 Samuel 8:18; compare 2 Samuel 15:12; 1 Kings 1:9; 8:62-64; 9:25), thus solidifying his family's position as the religious and political leaders of Israel. From a political standpoint, the plan was a stroke of genius.

Sometime later, according to the narrative, David proposed to build a glorious new temple in Jerusalem to house the Ark. But Yahweh rejected this plan, insisting that Yahweh could not be contained within a fixed building (2 Samuel 7:5-7). It thus comes as a surprise when Yahweh proceeds to give permission for David's son Solomon to build him a temple (2 Samuel 7:12-13; 1 Kings 5:5).

The book of Chronicles attempts to resolve this problem by having Yahweh explain that David is a warrior who has

shed much blood, though why this should disqualify him from building the temple is never explained (1 Chronicles 28:3; compare 1 Kings 5:3-4). On the other hand, it is easy to see why Solomon and his supporters might have wanted to claim that he was simply following the orders of Yahweh and his esteemed father when he undertook to build for Yahweh a temple that was modeled on the facilities normally used to worship Canaanite deities, as archaeological excavations have shown. At the narrative level, this transition from a portable tent shrine to a fixed temple represents a major new departure in the state religion of Israel.

The Jerusalem temple was not the only place where the state religion of Judah was carried out. Archaeologists have uncovered the ruins of several other sanctuaries scattered strategically around the land of Judah that seem to have operated under royal control (see chapter 29). None of these temples is mentioned in the Hebrew Bible, so we know almost nothing about why they were built or what kinds of activities were performed in them.

Fig. 28.5. Bulls and calves were often associated with deities in the ancient Near East: (top) a gilded bull that was given to a Canaanite temple as a votive offering; (bottom) a stela showing the Canaanite god Hadad standing on a bull with a thunderbolt in his hand.

In form they resemble the biblical descriptions of the Jerusalem temple, though scholars disagree over whether animal sacrifices were performed at these sites as at the central temple. Their very presence, however, suggests that the state religion of Judah was more complex and less centralized than the texts indicate.

The Royal Shrines of Israel

The establishment of royal shrines in the northern kingdom of Israel had an equally political motivation, if the story in the Hebrew Bible can be trusted. According to 1 Kings 12:26-33, King Jeroboam, who had recently rebelled against Solomon's son Rehoboam and set up his own kingdom in the north, established major shrines at Dan and Bethel (the northern and southern ends of his kingdom) and lesser ones at other locations so that his subjects would not have to travel to the temple in Jerusalem to offer sacrifices. The narrative attributes a political motive to Jeroboam's actions: since there was no separation of church and state in the ancient world, participation in the ritual life of the Jerusalem temple would inevitably bring his subjects under the influence of southern religious and political leaders and thus undermine his shaky authority. His solution, according to the Hebrew Bible, was to create new shrines within his own kingdom where his people could carry on their traditional forms of worship.

Here and elsewhere the narrator implies that Jeroboam's shrines honored gods other than Yahweh, using images of calves to represent their presence. But this makes no sense in the context of the narrative, since the story only works if the people of Israel are seen as devout followers of Yahweh who can be enticed to bring their sacrifices to a northern site instead of the Jerusalem temple. In fact, the Hebrew Bible includes several stories that suggest that both Dan and Bethel had long served as centers for the worship of Yahweh (for Dan, see Judges 17:1-5; 18:27-31; for Bethel, see Genesis 28:18-22; 35:1-15; Judges 20:18-28; 21:19). Most scholars believe that Jeroboam's golden calves were actually statues of bulls that symbolized the throne of Yahweh, not images of gods that were worshipped at the shrines. They served essentially the same role as the Ark and the cherubim did in the Jerusalem temple. Both types of throne imagery were associated with kingly deities in the ancient Near East.

Other aspects of the biblical depiction of the religious system of the north suggest that it was formulated in direct opposition to the state religion of Judah. The reference to the Exodus saga in the account of Jeroboam's founding of the shrines ("Here are your gods, O Israel, who brought you up out of the land of Egypt"; 1 Kings 12:28) recalls similar language in the books of Amos and Hosea, the only two biblical prophets who preached to the northern kingdom (Amos 2:10; 3:1; 4:10; 5:25; 9:7; Hosea 2:15; 9:10; 11:1-5; 13:4-6). Many scholars have suggested that the northern shrines may have given special prominence to the Exodus story as a paradigm for Israel's experience of liberation from the oppressive rule of Solomon, with Jeroboam, the founding ruler of the nation, playing the part of Moses. The ordination of priests from outside

Fig. 28.6. A platform from the royal shrine at Dan where one of Jeroboam's calf shrines may have stood.

the traditional priestly families (1 Kings 12:31; 13:33; 2 Chronicles 11:14-15), if it reflects actual practice, would likewise have distinguished Israel from the south, though the practice may have begun as a political expedient due to a shortage of priests loyal to Jeroboam. Finally, the choice of a different date for celebrating the Festival of Booths (in the eighth month rather than the seventh) would have created a difference in the ritual calendars of the two states. Though the Hebrew Bible paints all of these practices as innovations, many scholars believe that

the changes were motivated by a concern to return to older traditions that had been set aside in the south.

FROM ROYAL SHRINES TO STATE RELIGION

In both north and south, the forms of state religion changed over time. In the south, the temple was originally built as a royal shrine to be used primarily by the king and the priests to offer sacrifices and praises to Yahweh on behalf of the nation. Apart from the festival times, participation in this vital element of the state religion of Judah was effectively limited to the Jerusalem elites. The Jerusalem temple appears to have coexisted with the regional shrines for over two centuries with no effort by the kings to control what was done at the shrines or to otherwise incorporate them into any kind of coordinated religious system. Over the years, many people came to view the Jerusalem temple as the central shrine of the nation due to its close ties with the king and the royal claim that Yahweh was present there in a unique way. Some people began to travel to the temple rather than to the regional shrines to offer sacrifices or observe the major religious festivals.

Not until the time of Hezekiah (715–687 B.C.E.), however, did the kings of Judah act to bring the regional shrines under royal control, unless Chronicles' account of a similar action by King Asa a century earlier is deemed credible (2 Chronicles 14:2-5). According to the Hebrew Bible, Hezekiah ordered all of the high places to be closed and their altars, poles, and pillars destroyed (2 Kings 18:4; 2 Chronicles 31:1). The only reason given for these radical acts is the king's personal devotion to Yahweh. The book of Chronicles suggests that his actions were an effort to undo his father, Ahaz's, practice of promoting the worship of other gods (2 Chronicles 28:1-4, 22-27; 29:5-7). Many scholars doubt the story of Hezekiah closing the regional shrines, though others think that the action makes sense as part of a broader strategy to consolidate the king's control over Judah as he was pre-paring to fight the Assyrians (2 Kings 18:7).

The next two kings of Judah also seem to have con-cluded that it was in their best interest to exert control over the regional shrines. Hezekiah's son Manasseh is reported to have rebuilt the high places as part of a pro-gram to encourage the worship of gods other than Yahweh (2 Kings 21:1-7, 11), while Manasseh's son Josiah destroyed these same shrines as part of a broader "pro-Yahweh" centralization campaign (2 Kings 23:5, 8-9, 13-15, 19-20; 2 Chronicles 34:3-7). Nothing is said about the policies of the kings who came after Josiah, but the prophets Jeremiah and Ezekiel, who lived through the end

of the monarchy, speak often about people worshipping at different sites across the land (Jeremiah 3:6-13; 17:1-3; Ezekiel 6:1-7; 16:20-24) and honoring deities other than Yahweh (Jeremiah 2:23-28; 7:17-18, 30-31; 11:9-13; Ezekiel 20:30-32; 22:1-5). These statements suggest that the kings after Josiah reverted to their ancestors' policy of toleration, though it is unclear whether they sought to control the shrines.

Less is known about relations between the royal shrines and other places of worship in the north. The Hebrew Bible states that Jeroboam founded other shrines besides the ones at Dan and Bethel, but the extent of any such activity is unknown. The books of Judges and Samuel indi-cate that there were shrines in the north prior to the com-ing of Jeroboam, so the later editors may have mistakenly attributed to Jeroboam the establishment of shrines that existed long before his time. By the time of Amos and Hosea (eighth century B.C.E.), additional major shrines could be found at Gilgal, a site with a long history of Yahweh wor-ship prior to Jeroboam's time (Joshua 4:19-24; 1 Samuel 7:16; 10:8; 13:8-10; 15:20-21), and Samaria, where Ahab is said to have built a temple to Baal (1 Kings 18:32; com-pare Hosea 8:6). Both proph-ets indicate that there were many other places of wor-ship in Israel (Amos 2:8; 7:9; Hosea 4:13, 19; 8:11; 10:1), some of which were used to honor deities other than Yah-weh (Hosea 2:8, 13; 4:12-13, 17; 8:4-6; 10:5-8).

The nature of the relationship among these various shrines is unknown.

Fig. 28.7. James Tissot, *Solomon Dedicates the Temple at Jerusalem*

Since the major shrines appear to have been founded by the kings of Israel, we can assume that they continued to operate under royal patronage and control. In addition to maintaining the nation's relationship with the supernatural realm, these shrines would have served to reinforce and justify the authority of the king. The lesser shrines might have functioned independently of the royal shrines, like the ones in Judah during the same period, or they might have operated under the control of the kings. In the end, our knowledge about the state religion of Israel is simply too scanty to permit many solid judgments.

ONE GOD OR MANY?

In the eyes of the people who compiled the Hebrew Bible, the nations of Israel and Judah were judged by Yahweh because their kings failed to uphold and promote the worship of Yahweh at a single central shrine. In reality, the state religion of both kingdoms appears to have been broadly polytheistic for much of their history. In the southern kingdom, the practice emerges as early as King Solomon, who is said to have built shrines outside Jerusalem where his foreign wives could worship the gods of their homelands (1 Kings 11:7-8). The text says nothing about Solomon actively promoting the worship of foreign gods among his people, but his shrines were reportedly still in use at the time of King Josiah some three centuries later (2 Kings 23:13-14). Solomon's example was taken a step further by his grandson Abijam, who is said to have erected an image of the Canaanite goddess Asherah for his wife in Jerusalem (1 Kings 15:13).

For several years in the mid–ninth century B.C.E., Judah was ruled by kings (and one queen) who were allied by marriage with the kings of Israel. According to the Hebrew Bible, these rulers followed their Israelite relatives in worshipping the Canaanite god Baal (2 Kings 8:16-18, 25-27), even erecting a temple for Baal in Jerusalem (2 Kings 11:18). After these kings were deposed, their immediate successors, Joash and Amaziah, are accused by the author of Chronicles of shifting their allegiance from Yahweh to other deities later in their lives (2

Chronicles 24:17-19; 25:14-16). Nothing is said about any of these kings encouraging the worship of other gods besides Yahweh as a matter of policy, but at the very least the king's example was certain to influence others.

No such ambiguity clouds the stories of Kings Ahaz (742–727 B.C.E.) and Manasseh (687–642 B.C.E.), both of whom are said to have built shrines and altars to various deities throughout the land of Judah (2 Chronicles 28:25; 2 Kings 21:3). Apparently they also appointed priests to serve at these sites, since the author refers later to "the idolatrous priests whom the kings of Judah had ordained to make offerings in the high places at the cities of Judah and around Jerusalem . . . who made offerings to Baal, to the sun, the moon, the constellations, and all the host of the heavens" (2 Kings 23:5). All of these texts point to a conscious royal policy of promoting polytheistic forms of worship. A similar picture emerges from the books of the prophets, who repeatedly denounce the people of Judah for worshipping other gods during this period (see chapter 33).

The polytheistic character of the state religion of Judah in the latter decades of the monarchy is especially evident in the way the kings handled the Jerusalem temple. The book of Chronicles claims that Ahaz closed the Jerusalem temple and removed its furnishings, thus rendering it unusable (2 Chronicles 28:24). His grandson Manasseh is said to have built altars to "the host of heaven" in the courts of the temple and placed an image of Asherah inside its walls (2 Kings 21:4-7). The story of Josiah's reforms (640–609 B.C.E.) mentions a number of objects that had been placed in and around the temple for the worship of other gods, including implements that were sacred to Baal, Asherah, and "the host of heaven"; an image of Asherah; statues of horses and chariots that had been dedicated to the worship of the sun; and a series of altars probably used in the worship of various deities (2 Kings 23:4-12). In the latter days of the monarchy, the prophet Ezekiel has a vision in which he sees the leaders of Judah offering incense in front of statues and paintings of various unnamed deities inside the temple, as well as women and men worshipping the Mesopotamian fertility god Tammuz and the rising sun at the temple gates (Ezekiel 8:5-18).

If these narratives are even partially grounded in history, they testify to a state religion in Judah that was not only polytheistic to the core but also actively promoting the worship of other gods alongside Yahweh. The efforts of kings like Hezekiah and Josiah to purge Judah of polytheistic religion and centralize worship in the Jerusalem temple offered a revolutionary challenge to this system. We should not be surprised that their innovations did not last long after their deaths.

Less is known about religious developments in the north. Presumably the shrines that Jeroboam built at Dan and Bethel continued to center on the worship of Yahweh, though other gods may have been worshipped there as well. According to the Hebrew Bible, a major change occurred with the accession of King Ahab (874–853 B.C.E.), whose wife, Jezebel, was a Phoenician princess. Jezebel is portrayed as a fierce partisan of the Canaanite god Baal, the local equivalent of the Phoenician deity Melkart. Like Solomon in the south, Ahab built a temple for his wife's favored deity in Samaria, the new city that his father had built to serve as his capital. The book of Kings claims that Ahab worshipped Baal along with his wife (1 Kings 16:32-33), but the book also includes several scenes in which Ahab listens to the words of Yahweh or his followers (1 Kings 18:41-42; 20:13-22, 28-30; 21:1-4), and the names of his sons include shortened forms of the name of Yahweh. Most likely Ahab worshipped Baal alongside Yahweh, as did many other people in ancient Palestine.

The lengthy account of Ahab's reign focuses primarily on his interactions with the prophet Elijah, a man depicted as the champion of the "Yahweh-only" party. The book of Kings presents Jezebel as an evangelist for Baal who seeks to kill the prophets of Yahweh (1 Kings 18:3-4) while supporting 450 prophets of Baal and 400 prophets of Asherah, Baal's female consort, with her own funds (1 Kings 18:19). Somewhat later, however, her husband, Ahab, is shown seeking advice from 400 prophets who speak in the name of Yahweh, not Baal (1 Kings 22:5-12). Similar stories are reported for Ahab's children, who seem to have worshipped both Baal and Yahweh. Gauging the historicity of these stories is difficult, but taken together they suggest that Baalism enjoyed the official support of the rulers of Israel during this period, while the status of Yahwism was more precarious. How any of this might have affected worship at the local shrines is unknown, though it seems reasonable to think that those that operated under royal patronage would have elevated Baal to greater prominence without neglecting the worship of Yahweh.

According to the book of Kings, the temple, the priests, and all of the followers of Baal in the land of Israel were wiped out by Jehu, a general who overthrew Ahab's son and killed his entire family under the direction of Elisha, a prophet of Yahweh who had earlier served as Elijah's assistant (2 Kings 10:18-31). The story claims that Jehu called the followers of Baal to gather inside their temple and then commanded his soldiers to kill them all. The idea that all of the priests and worshippers of Baal could have been squeezed into a single building and slaughtered at one time is incredible in light of the author's earlier claim that only seven thousand worshippers of Yahweh remained in the entire land (1 Kings 19:18). Most likely any actions that Jehu took against the devotees of Baal would have been limited to the area around Samaria. This accords better with the author's later claim that Yahweh sent the Assyrians against Israel in part because they "worshiped all the host of heaven, and served Baal" (2 Kings 17:16). The narrator is also aware that the people of the north continue to worship a variety of gods in his own day (2 Kings 17:32-34). Together these passages suggest that the state religion of the northern kingdom of Israel included provisions for the worship of other deities alongside Yahweh throughout much of its history.

CONCLUSION

The people who crafted the Hebrew Bible wanted their readers to believe that Yahweh had established a centralized system of worship for his people as far back as the Exodus generation, when he ordered the construction of the Ark of the Covenant and the tabernacle. This system was to operate under the control of the priests (and later the kings) of Israel and was to revolve around a central shrine to which the people of Israel were to bring their sacrifices and offerings to Yahweh—first the tabernacle, then later the Jerusalem temple. Deviations from this system were to be punished, since Yahweh would eventually inflict judgment upon his people if they were not corrected.

Unfortunately for the authors, some of the stories that they included in their collection undermine this thesis. The books of Judges and Samuel show the followers of Yahweh worshipping at a variety of sites around the land without criticism, and many of the "good kings" of Judah are said to have allowed such activities to continue during their reigns. The book of Kings indicates that many of the kings of Israel and Judah supported and even encouraged the worship of other gods besides Yahweh, making the state religion of both nations polytheistic for much of their history. Only rarely do we hear of anyone trying to create a centralized religious system that limited the worship of Yahweh to a single site and rejected other gods.

This idea, which appears to have been a minority position among the elites of Judah, was a genuine innovation in the religious life of ancient Palestine.

EXERCISE 74

Read the following passages and summarize what they say or imply about the way the kings of Judah viewed and used the Jerusalem temple in the years following its founding.

• 1 Kings 15:9-22
• 2 Kings 12:1-18
• 2 Kings 16:10-18
• 2 Kings 21:1-9
• 2 Kings 23:1-20

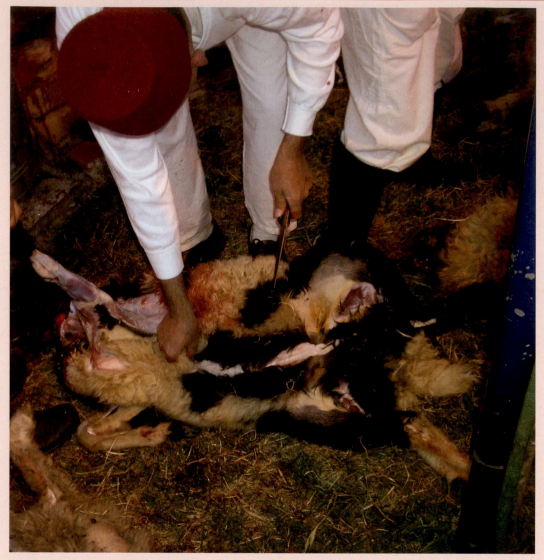

Fig. 29.1. A goat being ritually sacrificed in a contemporary Samaritan religious ceremony.

The Sacrificial System

*If you unintentionally fail to observe all these commandments that the L*ORD *has spoken to Moses—everything that the L*ORD *has commanded you by Moses, from the day the L*ORD *gave commandment and thereafter, throughout your generations—then if it was done unintentionally without the knowledge of the congregation, the whole congregation shall offer one young bull for a burnt offering, a pleasing odor to the L*ORD*, together with its grain offering and its drink offering, according to the ordinance, and one male goat for a sin offering. The priest shall make atonement for all the congregation of the Israelites, and they shall be forgiven; it was unintentional, and they have brought their offering, an offering by fire to the L*ORD*, and their sin offering before the L*ORD*, for their error.* (Numbers 15:22-25)

*Then the king, and all Israel with him, offered sacrifice before the L*ORD*. Solomon offered as sacrifices of well-being to the L*ORD *twenty-two thousand oxen and one hundred twenty thousand sheep. So the king and all the people of Israel dedicated the house of the L*ORD*. The same day the king consecrated the middle of the court that was in front of the house of the L*ORD*; for there he offered the burnt offerings and the grain offerings and the fat pieces of the sacrifices of well-being, because the bronze altar that was before the L*ORD *was too small to receive the burnt offerings and the grain offerings and the fat pieces of the sacrifices of well-being. So Solomon held the festival at that time, and all Israel with him—a great assembly, people from Lebo-hamath to the Wadi of Egypt—before the L*ORD *our God, seven days.* (1 Kings 8:62-65)

*What shall I return to the L*ORD *for all his bounty to me?*
*I will lift up the cup of salvation and call on the name of the L*ORD*,*
*I will pay my vows to the L*ORD *in the presence of all his people. . . .*
*I will offer to you a thanksgiving sacrifice and call on the name of the L*ORD*.*
*I will pay my vows to the L*ORD *in the presence of all his people,*
*In the courts of the house of the L*ORD*, in your midst, O Jerusalem.*
*Praise the L*ORD*!* (Psalm 116:12-14, 17-19)

In the last chapter we examined what can be inferred from the Hebrew Bible about the general shape of state religion in ancient Israel and Judah. In the next two chapters we continue our focus on state religion with an examination of the types of activities that were conducted at the national shrines. Many of these activities were the same as those that were done at the regional shrines, since the functions of the national shrines were similar in many respects to those of the regional shrines. But some rituals were performed differently at the national shrines, and the national shrines also developed their own distinctive practices.

OVERVIEW OF ACTIVITIES

The Hebrew Bible gives us a fairly good picture of the kinds of activities that were performed at the Jerusalem temple, since the authors regarded it as the earthly palace of Yahweh and the focal point of the state religion of Judah. Unfortunately, we have no similar source of data concerning what was done at the national shrines in the northern kingdom. As we noted earlier, the people who crafted the Hebrew Bible viewed these shrines as idolatrous due to their use of images to represent the deity. As a result, their sporadic references are highly disparaging and provide little information about the activities at these sites. Archaeological excavations have expanded our knowledge of the shrine at Dan, and the books of Hosea and Amos offer passing glimpses of religious practices in the north, but the data are still fairly meager. For this reason our discussion of the national shrines will focus disproportionately on the temple in Jerusalem, with information about the northern shrines being inserted where appropriate.

Fortunately, the available evidence suggests that similar ritual acts were performed at the national shrines of Israel and Judah. Most can be subsumed under one of two broad headings.

1. *Sacrifices and offerings.* Animal sacrifices played a central role at all of the shrines, along with offerings of oil, wine, grain, and incense. Some were offered on a routine basis on behalf of the nation, while others were performed for individuals who traveled to the shrine to request assistance from the deity or to express thanksgiving for help received. Special sacrifices and offerings were prescribed for the major festivals when people came to the shrines to celebrate the goodness and blessings of the deity, as well as for lesser occasions like new moon festivals and Sabbaths. Sacrifices were also presented at times when the nation was facing great perils or had experienced notable successes. Sacrifices and offerings were usually performed by a special group of priests, but kings also filled this role on ceremonial occasions.

2. *Prayers and praise.* Since the presence of Yahweh was thought to be particularly accessible at the national shrines, priests and other religious leaders offered prayers on behalf of the nation at these sites, whether for ongoing protection or assistance with a particular problem. Shrine personnel also sang or chanted songs of praise and thanksgiving to Yahweh (and possibly other deities) as part of their duties. Individuals and families traveled regularly to the shrines to express their concerns and needs to the deity or to offer thanks when they had experienced what they regarded as a special blessing from the deity. Some of the worshippers also consulted the resident priests or prophets in an effort to find supernatural guidance for the resolution of their problems. People also congregated at the national shrines during festival times to celebrate the goodness of the deity with singing, music, and dancing.

The remainder of this chapter is devoted to a study of the role of sacrifices and offerings at the national shrines. The next chapter will examine how prayers and praise were integrated into the sacrificial system. Before we go further, however, we need to investigate the physical layout of the national shrines, since they were designed to facilitate certain kinds of interactions with the divine and to restrict others.

EXERCISE 75

Read 1 Kings 5:1—8:66 and draw a rough diagram of the temple and its furnishings as they are described here. (A cubit is approximately 18 inches.) Then compare your picture with the artist's rendition that appears on page 381. In what ways does your picture differ from that of the artist? Can you point to any places where the artist seems to have interpreted the biblical text differently than you did?

SACRED ARCHITECTURE

No formal archaeological excavations have been conducted at the site where the Jerusalem temple is thought to have stood, since that space has been occupied for more than thirteen hundred years by a Muslim shrine called the Dome of the Rock. Scholars must therefore depend on the Hebrew Bible for their understanding of the temple's appearance. A few scholars have argued that the biblical materials are untrustworthy at this point, with some regarding them as religious fantasies and others insisting that they reflect the authors' experience with the postexilic temple. The great majority of scholars, however, take the materials as serious depictions of a real building that stood in Jerusalem.

The fullest description of the First Temple (the one built by Solomon) and its furnishings appears in 1 Kings 6:1-38 and 7:15-51. A somewhat different version is found in 2 Chronicles 3:1—5:1, but the late date of this book leads scholars to prefer the description in 1 Kings. Subsequent passages refer to repairs and minor changes that were made to the building (2 Kings 12:1-16; 15:35; 16:17-18; 22:3-7; 2 Chronicles 29:3), but the basic layout and function of the structure seem to have remained the same until it was destroyed by the Babylonians in 586 B.C.E. The book of Ezra-Nehemiah narrates the construction of a replacement temple following the Exile, but virtually nothing is said about its appearance. The writings of Jewish authors who were familiar with this Second Temple suggest that it followed the same basic pattern as the First Temple, though it was less ornate.

The narrative also mentions several occasions when the interior furnishings of the temple were changed, with certain kings adding new features (1 Kings 15:15; 2 Kings 12:18; 16:10-16; 21:4-5, 7; 22:11-12) and others taking them away, whether to pay off foreign armies (1 Kings 15:18-19; 2 Kings 12:18; 16:8; 18:15-16) or to eliminate additions that were deemed contrary to the true spirit of Yahwism (2 Kings 22:4, 6-7, 11-12; 2 Chronicles 29:16). On a few occasions foreign armies sacked the temple and removed its treasures and furnishings (1 Kings 14:25-28; 2 Kings 14:14; 24:13; 25:13-17). For the most part, however, the types of furnishings and implements that were used in the temple appear to have remained the same over the centuries.

According to the biblical narrative, the temple building was roughly 105 feet long, 30 feet wide, and 45 feet

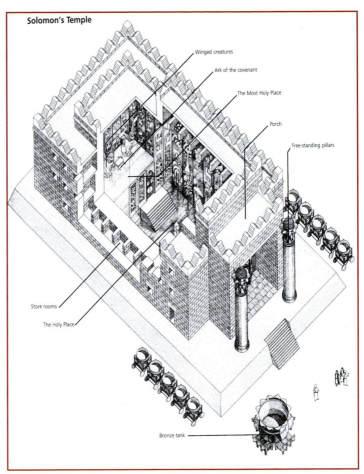

Fig. 29.2. An artist's rendition of the temple of Solomon. Note the panels separating the two chambers labeled "The Holy Place" and "The Most Holy Place" (also called "The Holy of Holies").

high, or about the size of a small four-story apartment building. Attached to each side of the building were a pair of three-story structures containing rooms that were used for storage. The exterior of the building was made of finished stone blocks. The temple had only one entrance that was flanked by two huge bronze columns. The inside of the building was divided into three rooms from front to back: a vestibule at the entrance (fifteen by thirty feet); a large open room in the middle, sometimes called the Holy Place (thirty by sixty feet); and a smaller room toward the back called the inner sanctuary, the Most Holy Place, or the Holy of Holies (thirty by thirty feet). Each room was entered by a set of elaborately carved wooden doors, and the inner walls were also covered with ornate woodwork. Everything inside the building was coated with gold.

The central room of the temple was furnished with a small golden altar for offering incense to the deity, a golden

Fig. 29.3. (top) Most scholars believe the cherub images that resided in the central chamber of the Jerusalem temple resembled this winged bull that guarded the temple of the Assyrian king Sargon II (eighth century B.C.E.); (bottom) this image of a Phoenician or Cananite god seated on a cherub-like throne recalls biblical depictions of Yahweh being enthroned between the wings of the cherubim in the Jerusalem temple.

table upon which fresh bread was placed every Sabbath, and ten lampstands (the Jewish **menorah**) that burned continually to light the room, perhaps as a symbol of the divine presence. The innermost room housed the Ark of the Covenant (the golden box that supposedly contained the Ten Commandments and other items from the Exodus period), overshadowed by the wings of two large gold-plated figures called cherubim. In the world of the Bible, a **cherub** (the singular of *cherubim*) was not a chubby little angel as depicted in Western paintings, but a huge winged beast—fifteen feet tall with eight-foot wings—that served as a symbolic guard (or possibly a throne) for the deity. Here, above the Ark and between the wings of the cherubim, is the place where Yahweh was believed to be present in concentrated essence. This explains why the inside of the building, which was visible only to the priests, was decorated in such an ornate manner: Should not a deity have a home that is at least as sumptuous as that of an earthly king? It also explains

why the temple is called *the house of God* or *the house of Yahweh*. Yahweh might visit other places, but it was here, according to the Hebrew Bible, that he had chosen to set up his earthly throne.

The temple complex also included a series of fixtures that stood in the courtyard in front of the building. At one corner stood a huge brass basin (eight feet high and fifteen feet across) called *the sea* that was probably used by the priests for ritual washings in connection with the animal sacrifices that took place in the courtyard. The sacrifices were presented to the deity in the courtyard and cooked by fire on a large bronze altar that functioned somewhat like a modern barbecue grill. The altar is not described in 1 Kings, but the author of Chronicles claims that the altar measured thirty feet on each side and stood fifteen feet high. This sounds too large for a bronze altar, especially when compared with the altar attributed to the tabernacle (eight feet on each side and five feet high), though the size is not vastly larger than that of the stone altar uncovered at the shrine in Dan (see below). Whatever its size, the altar would have been large enough to cook several whole animals at a time, and the priests probably had to climb a set of steps to reach its top. On each side of the temple stood a series of wheeled stands (five on each side) holding basins that were used along with the larger sea for ritual washings.

In its overall structure, the Jerusalem temple was similar to many Canaanite temples that have been uncovered in recent years by archaeologists. Common features include the division of the building into three rooms leading to an inner sanctuary; the inclusion of an altar inside the building to offer incense to the deity; and the presence of a courtyard around the building with altars and other implements for animal sacrifice. The key difference lies in the innermost sanctuary, where Canaanite temples typically held statues, stone columns, or other objects that were regarded as embodiments of the presence of the deity. In its initial form, the Jerusalem temple held no such images; the Ark and the cherubim represented the throne of Yahweh, not the deity himself, who was regarded as present in invisible form. This difference disappeared in later times as the kings of Judah introduced physical representations of various Canaanite deities into the Jerusalem temple (see chapter 28).

Less is known about the physical appearance of other national shrines. A temple uncovered by archaeologists in the town of Arad on the southern border of Judah seems to have functioned as part of the national religious system, since it was situated inside a military fortress. The temple layout is similar to that of the Jerusalem temple and the Canaanite shrines, though the building is much smaller. Like the Jerusalem temple, it was built on an east-west axis with an open courtyard and a large altar to the east of the building. The temple consisted of a larger room in the front where two incense altars were found and a smaller room at the back that held two standing stones, one bigger than the other, which may have represented two deities who were worshipped at the site. The temple had no vestibule leading into the building, but the biblical description of the Jerusalem temple suggests that this was not an essential part of the design. The site was modified several times over the years, but its basic structure remained intact until it was buried in the seventh century B.C.E., perhaps as part of an effort to eliminate competitors to the Jerusalem temple.

In the north, a different style of temple architecture can be seen in the royal shrine at Dan. Archaeological excavations have uncovered two large stone platforms, one twenty by sixty feet and the other sixty by sixty feet, that served as the focal point of ritual activity at the site. Whether the larger platform was built to replace the smaller one or to serve a different purpose is unclear. A wide staircase led to the top of the larger platform. The platform was surrounded by an open courtyard that included at least two altars, one large and one small. A nearby complex of buildings contained one room that held an incense altar, but no identifiable inner room where the deity might be thought to live. Instead, a number of images, presumably of gods and goddesses, were found scattered across the site. The location of Jeroboam's calf images (1 Kings 12:28) is unclear—they might have stood atop one of the platforms or inside a nearby room, or even in a temple building that has not yet been discovered.

The apparent absence of a secluded room for the deity suggests that the people who built the shrine at Dan may have held a different view of the relationship between the people and the divine realm than the people who designed the Jerusalem temple. The structure of the Jerusalem temple implies a vision of the deity as mysterious and rather inaccessible to ordinary citizens (that is, holy). The shrine at Dan, by contrast, suggests a deity who is more approachable and available to the common people. The prophet Hosea's complaint that "people are kissing calves" at Dan and Bethel (Hosea 13:2) encapsulates this difference; one

Fig. 29.4. (top) The temple at Arad—the stone altar can be seen in the right foreground, while the inner sanctum with its two stone pillars is barely visible beyond the altar; (bottom) the "high place" at Dan—a wooden model of the ancient stone altar stands in front of the platform where the calf images representing the deity would have stood.

Fig. 29.5. Worshippers present a food offering in a Chinese temple.

could hardly imagine such a thing being said about the temple in Jerusalem, at least not in connection with the worship of Yahweh.

OFFERINGS AND SACRIFICES: AN OVERVIEW

The principal activity at the national shrines was the presentation of offerings and sacrifices to the deity. Some were brought voluntarily by individuals, while others were presented by temple personnel on behalf of the entire nation. Nearly all consisted of food items (animals, grain, oil, and so forth). Individuals gave from what they grew or raised, while the regular offerings were supported by religious taxes and the produce of royal lands. Special offerings were prescribed for religious festivals and other occasions. An elaborate symbolism developed around these gifts, including special rituals that were used to dedicate the gifts to the deity.

Most contemporary people can relate to the idea of offering gifts to God, though they usually think in terms of giving money, not agricultural produce. But the idea that someone might pour food on the ground or burn it up in a fire in order to present it to the deity is foreign to modern ways of thinking. Even more troubling to many people is the practice of killing and cooking an animal as a form of religious devotion. What do such acts have to do with the worship of God?

Offering food items to the gods has been a popular form of interaction with the supernatural realm since the earliest days of human culture. Long before the invention of writing, people were devoting a portion of their daily food to the gods, whether by performing symbolic actions (such as special prayers or rituals at meals) or by placing the food in a location deemed holy to the gods (for example, a family shrine). In times of trouble or at key points in the agricultural cycle, people carried a portion of their crops and livestock to special sites and offered them to whatever supernatural beings were thought to have influence over their lives. Non-food items could also be presented as gifts to the gods, but food was the most common offering. Rituals were performed to make the offerings holy and thus suitable for contact with the divine realm. Depending on the culture, such offerings might be left at an unattended open-air shrine or entrusted to a priest or other official who presented them to the gods.

While most traditional cultures allow offerings of fresh crops or processed food, the most important rituals are marked by the presentation of a live animal. When such a gift is presented to the gods, custom usually dictates that it be ritually slaughtered (or sacrificed) so that its life force can return to the supernatural realm and its meat and blood be used for various ritual purposes. Special dedicatory rituals are used to render the animal holy to the deity. As a result, even its dead carcass is considered

Fig. 29.6. Two goats are prepared for sacrifice during the Muslim festival of Eid al-Ad'ha, which recalls Allah's call to the prophet Ibrahim (Abraham) to sacrifice his son (see Genesis 22).

holy and must be handled with care. The precise treatment of the carcass varies from culture to culture. Some rituals require that part of the meat (or occasionally the entire carcass) be burned to ashes over a fire on an altar, converting it into smoke that rises to the heavenly realm of the gods. Meat that is not burned is usually cooked and eaten as part of a sacred meal, whether by the family that brings the sacrifice or the religious officials who oversee the process. The consumption of sacred meat is often thought to enhance the eater's link to the supernatural realm. The blood of the sacrificial animal is also treated with special caution, since premodern people have generally believed that the power of life resides in the blood. Some cultures require that this holy substance be poured out in a special place as a drink offering to the gods, while others mandate that it be smeared on people or objects as a form of ritual cleansing. In some instances the blood is drunk, whether alone or mixed with other liquids, in an effort to gain benefit from its power.

Scholars of religion have identified a number of reasons people offer food products to the gods. Often the reasons intertwine so that several explanations can be given for the same ritual act.

1. *Honor of the gods.* Traditional cultures often use giving as a means of showing honor to people who are worthy of respect. In agricultural societies, animals and crops are the most common objects of exchange, since most people own few other movable possessions. Giving an item of food to a superior as a gesture of respect is costly to such people, since it takes away from their own limited food stocks. When offered to a deity, such a gift not only honors the recipient but also represents a genuine sacrifice on the part of the worshipper.

2. *Exchange for favors.* Mutual exchange plays a far greater role in traditional societies than in contemporary cultures. A person who receives a good deed or a gift from another is expected to respond in kind, often by giving more than was received. When applied to a deity, this social principle leads to the belief that people who receive special benefits from the deity (for example, a good crop year or a healthy child) should give something valuable to the deity in return. Often this principle is extended to include the idea that people can motivate the gods to come to their assistance or protect them from harm by offering them lavish gifts. Special sacrifices and offerings are usually prescribed for times of great trouble (famine, invasion, disease, and the like).

3. *Food for the gods.* In some cultures, food offerings are considered a method of feeding the gods, who are thought to require food in the same manner as humans. This is especially evident in the case of offerings that are burned to ashes, poured out on the ground, or placed in front of a symbol of the deity. Humans in these systems are envisioned as servants or caretakers of the gods who have a duty to provide for the deities' daily needs as they would for a human master. Often this includes taking care of their physical images (by washing, clothing, and feeding them) and their houses (that is, their temples). If humans do their job well, their divine masters will bless them with prosperity in their daily lives. If they fail in their duty, negative consequences can result for the irresponsible individuals or the people as a whole.

4. *Ritual cleansing.* Virtually every culture has defined certain kinds of acts as offensive to the supernatural realm. At a minimum, such acts are thought to distance or separate the individual from communion with the divine world. Some offenses are considered so serious that they can threaten the well-being of the entire group. Usually some sort of **reparation** is required to cleanse or remove the offense and restore proper relations with the supernatural. Gifts of food are a common form of payment, with the most serious offenses often requiring the sacrifice of a valuable animal. Some groups consider the death of the

animal as a substitute for the execution of the offender, while others regard it as a form of compensatory payment that somehow makes up for the offense. Still others focus on the power of the animal's blood or other body parts to cleanse the offender by physical application.

5. *Enactment of stories.* Many traditional cultures tell stories of a great ancestor (or sometimes a supernatural being) whose act of self-negating sacrifice brought the people into existence or rescued them from a potentially deadly threat. Some of these groups use rituals to symbolically reenact the events recounted in the ancient stories, often in the context of an annual festival. One common way of recalling the self-sacrifice of the hero is through the presentation of offerings and sacrifices to the deity. In this way the events of the story are made real to the worshippers and its message is imprinted once again upon their minds. The result is a deepening of their loyalty to the values of the story and the people who produced it.

6. *Mystical participation.* Many groups believe that sacrifices and offerings open up special channels of communication with the supernatural world. According to this view, the presentation of a sacrifice causes the deity to draw near to receive the offering. Humans who are present at the time can experience the presence of the divine in a way that transcends ordinary reality. Some groups speak of the worshippers sharing a ritual meal with the gods. Such experiences strengthen the faith and devotion of those who participate in the ritual, thus reinforcing their commitment to the religion as a whole.

OFFERINGS AND SACRIFICES IN THE HEBREW BIBLE

Offerings and sacrifices played a central role in the religious life of the people of ancient Palestine. This was true not only for the followers of Yahweh but also for those who served other gods and goddesses. The character and timing of the offerings may have varied from one deity to another, but the meanings attributed to the ritual were similar across the region.

The Hebrew Bible contains four types of material pertaining to offerings and sacrifices: (a) laws that spell out precisely how certain sacrifices were to be conducted; (b) stories that depict people presenting offerings and sacrifices to the deity; (c) poetic texts (primarily in the book of Psalms) that mention offerings and sacrifices as part of a broader expression of devotion to Yahweh; and (d) prophetic sayings that critique the ways in which the people of Israel and Judah viewed and used the sacrificial system. Teasing a coherent system of belief and practice out of these diverse texts is virtually impossible, since the texts come from different times and places and reflect divergent theological interests and literary genres. Even within the laws of Torah there is less consistency than we might expect from a collection that devotes so much attention to the subject. Uncertainties concerning the origins of individual laws become especially troublesome here, since it is difficult to know which periods are reflected in the various laws that pertain to sacrifices and offerings. Some scholars have argued that the entire system dates to the postexilic period, leaving us with few specifics about the practices of the preexilic temple.

While there are clearly problems associated with taking the laws of Torah as descriptions of actual practice, the many references to offerings and sacrifices outside the Torah tend to confirm the broad outlines of the Torah's description of the sacrificial system. Thus we will not be too far misled if we use the Torah materials as a heuristic tool for organizing our discussion of the role of offerings and sacrifices in the worship of Yahweh. Where possible, these materials will be supplemented by data drawn from other parts of the Hebrew Bible. Most of the available material pertains to the activities of the Jerusalem temple, though here and there we gain passing glimpses of what was done at other shrines. The few bits of information that we possess concerning activities in the northern kingdom suggest that similar practices were followed in both regions of Palestine.

EXERCISE 76

Read the following passages and make a list of the names and purposes of the various sacrifices and offerings that they mention. As you read, pay attention to the similarities and differences in the rules for the various rituals.

- Exodus 29:1—30:16
- Leviticus 1:1—7:38
- Leviticus 16:1-34
- Numbers 28:1—29:40

LAWS OF SACRIFICE

According to the Torah, the sacrificial system was directed by a hereditary clan of male priests, assisted by a group of male temple servants called Levites. At the Jerusalem temple, both of these offices were limited to families who could trace their lineage back to Jacob's son Levi, the ancestor for whom one of the twelve tribes of Israel was named. The priests, who were permitted closer access to the deity than the Levites, formed a subgroup within this broader lineage. At the northern shrines, on the other hand, priests were chosen without regard to tribal origin, if the Hebrew Bible is to be believed (1 Kings 12:31-32). In both nations, the kings and their sons are said to have

Fig. 29.7. An artist's rendition of Leviticus 8:14, which speaks of the high priest Aaron and his sons laying their hands on the head of a bull prior to sacrificing it.

presided over the sacrificial ritual on special occasions, even though they were not from the traditional priestly families (2 Samuel 6:17-19; 8:18; 15:12; 24:25; 1 Kings 1:9; 3:4; 8:62-64; 9:25; 12:33; 2 Kings 16:12-13).

Priests performed regular sacrifices and offerings on behalf of the nation in addition to preparing and presenting the offerings that were brought by individuals to the deity. The Torah contains lengthy accounts of the sacrifices that were to be offered on various occasions and the manner in which each sacrifice was to be performed. The care lavished on these subjects is one of the reasons scholars believe that at least some of the materials in the Torah originated in priestly circles.

The Torah uses several different systems to classify the laws pertaining to sacrifices and offerings. One model catalogues the sacrifices according to the purpose or motive of the one making the offering (for example, a sacrifice of well-being or a sin offering). Another relates the sacrifices to specific times of the month or year (daily sacrifices, various festivals, and so forth). Yet another approach associates sacrifices with particular circumstances (ordination of priests, purification after childbirth, and the like). Finally, there are offerings and sacrifices that are not part of any system. There is no way to do justice to the many different ways in which the Torah categorizes the offerings and sacrifices in an introductory textbook.

For the sake of simplicity, we will focus here on six broad types of offerings that most scholars agree were performed at the national shrines in ancient Palestine. These include the majority of sacrifices and offerings that are described in the Torah.

1. *Burnt offerings.* The term *burnt offerings* refers to animal sacrifices that were entirely burned up on the altar. The type of animal used in this ceremony (bull, sheep, goat, or bird) varied according to the economic status of the person making the offering (Leviticus 1:1-17). Once the animal was ritually dedicated to the deity, it became holy and could only be handled by the priests who controlled the sacrificial offerings. The priests slaughtered the animal and arranged its carcass on top of the altar for cooking. They also splashed some of the animal's blood on the sides of the altar, presumably as an act of ritual cleansing.

The primary purpose of the burnt offering, according to the Torah, was to offer a "pleasing odor to the Lord" as the scent of the sacrifice wafted upward from the altar to the heavens (Exodus 29:17-18, 41-42; Leviticus 1:8-9; 8:18-21; Numbers 28:27; 29:7-8). Similar language is used elsewhere in the ancient Near East to express the hope that the rising smoke, which would have smelled like a modern barbecue, would draw the deity to the site of the offering and dispose him to act favorably toward the one offering the sacrifice.

According to the Torah, burnt offerings were presented at the Jerusalem temple on behalf of the people every morning and evening and on special occasions. Prophets such as Hosea and Amos indicate that burnt offerings were performed in the northern kingdom as well (Hosea 6:6; Amos 5:22). In addition to these regular offerings, anyone could bring an animal to the temple and request that it be sacrificed as a burnt offering in order to seek the deity's favor prior to making a request or to give thanks for benefits received.

Fig. 29.8. Priests in Bali throw food and other items into a smoking cauldron as offerings to a deity.

2. *Grain and drink offerings.* Many passages in the Torah indicate that the burnt offering was regularly accompanied by offerings of grain and wine. Grain (primarily wheat, barley, and oats) and wine were the most common food staples throughout the ancient Near East, so it was only natural that they should be included in the rituals of sacrifice. The northern shrines also included grain and drink offerings in their rituals (Hosea 2:8; 3:1; 9:4; Amos 5:22).

As with burnt offerings, the actual presentation of the gifts was performed by the priests, but the rules governing grain offerings were more flexible than those for burnt offerings. Grain could be presented raw in the ear or as finely ground flour, or it could be cooked into flatbreads that resembled modern pita bread. Grain offerings were to be mixed with olive oil and salt (further staples of the Mediterranean diet), but no honey or leavening agent (that is, yeast) could be used. If the grain was presented raw, a small amount of frankincense, an aromatic resin that released a fragrant scent when burned, was to be added to the offering to enhance its odor. Part of the grain was to be burned on the altar, after which the remainder could be eaten by the priests. Wine was usually poured onto the altar along with the grain offering.

As with the burnt offering, the grain and wine offerings were thought to emit a "pleasing odor to the Lord" when burned on the altar (Exodus 29:41; Leviticus 2:9; 6:15; 23:13; Numbers 15:6-7, 10). The use of the term *drink offering* for the pouring of the wine suggests that at some level these offerings were viewed as food for the deity, though that notion has been largely suppressed in the Hebrew Bible.

In addition to burnt offerings, individuals sometimes brought offerings of grain and wine to the temple as a symbolic act of thanksgiving for a good crop year (Leviticus 23:9-14; Numbers 15:17-21). Other food items could also be presented to the deity at the temple as an expression of thanksgiving, but the Torah prohibits offering them on the altar (Leviticus 2:12; Deuteronomy 26:1-11). The fact that these other items are prohibited suggests that they, too, may have been presented on the altar at some point in Israel's history.

3. *Sacrifices of well-being.* Another type of sacrifice that could be offered either on its own or in conjunction with a burnt offering or a grain or drink offering is called by a variety of names in the Hebrew Bible. The most common designation is "sacrifice of well-being." The purpose of these offerings was to celebrate the care and protection of the deity, whether toward the entire nation or an individual family. The name given to the offering reflects its focus on the state of well-being that the deity was believed to have engineered. Many sacrifices of well-being were motivated by a desire to give thanks for a specific act of divine protection or rescue, but anyone who wished to express gratitude and honor to the deity could present such an offering.

Sacrifices of well-being, like burnt offerings, involved the ritual slaughter of cattle, oxen, sheep, or goats. Sometimes bread and oil were included with the offering. As with burnt offerings, the blood of the animal was splattered against the sides of the altar. The meat, however, was treated quite differently. Whereas the meat of the burnt offering was deemed too holy for anyone but the priests to handle, the well-being ritual required the worshipper to place the fat and the breast of the animal in the hands of the priest as a symbolic gesture of gratitude. The meat was then divided among the various participants in the ritual: the fat and certain internal organs were dedicated to the deity by being burned up on the altar; the right thigh and the breast were given to the priests who officiated at the ceremony; and the remainder was returned to the worshipper for use in a celebratory meal. Presumably the worshipper brought along enough people to consume an entire animal in the day or two permitted for eating the sacrificial meat. Similar rituals were performed at the northern shrines (Amos 4:5; 5:22).

Fig. 29.9. Blood drains from a sheep that has been slaughtered as part of the Muslim ceremony of Eid ul-Fitr, which marks the end of fasting for the month of Ramadan.

4. *Purification offerings.* As we saw in chapter 23, the Torah includes an elaborate system of purity laws designed to keep people and objects in a state of ritual purity and to cleanse them if they happen to become ritually impure. The underlying premise is that Yahweh is a holy god who can only live among a people who are individually and collectively holy (or pure). If impurity is not addressed, it spreads throughout the land, eventually polluting even the temple where Yahweh lives. Purification rituals must be performed periodically to remove the impurity from the land so that Yahweh can remain with his people.

The most serious forms of impurity arise from violations of Yahweh's specific commands. For the people who produced the Hebrew Bible, this meant the written laws of Torah, but earlier generations may have viewed their oral legal traditions in a similar manner. Intentional violations produce the greatest contamination, but even unintentional violations of Yahweh's will produce impurity that must be removed by the presentation of special purification sacrifices.

Animals were normally used for this ritual, but the precise nature of the offering varied with the social status and economic resources of the person who contracted the impurity. Priests were required to offer a bull, the largest sacrificial animal, while ordinary individuals could bring a goat or a sheep, or if this was beyond their means, a pair of birds or even an offering of grain. The acceptability of the grain offering is surprising, since blood plays a vital role in this ritual.

Both the meat and the blood of these sacrifices were handled differently than in the others that we have examined. As with the sacrifice of well-being, the fatty parts and some of the internal organs were offered to Yahweh by being burned on the altar. The treatment of the rest of the carcass varied with the type of impurity that the animal's blood was supposed to cleanse. The blood of a bull, which was sacrificed to remove impurities caused by the priest or the whole congregation, was to be taken into the temple. Part of it was to be sprinkled toward the Holy of Holies and part applied to the corners of the incense altar that stood in the Holy Place. Any blood that was left over was to be poured out at the base of the altar in the courtyard. The purpose of this elaborate ritual was to cleanse the temple and the ground itself from the impurities that resulted from certain types of violations. The animal whose blood was used for such a holy purpose was considered so holy that its remains had to be taken away and burned.

The blood of sacrifices that were offered to cleanse the impurity of a ruler or an ordinary Israelite, by contrast, was applied to the corners of the altar in the courtyard, with the remainder being poured out at the base of the altar. The fact that none of the blood actually entered the temple suggests that the degree of pollution was considered less in these cases. But the meat of the sacrificial animals was still considered too holy to be consumed by ordinary people; only the priests could eat from these sacrifices.

The most important purification ritual, called the Day of Atonement (Yom Kippur in Hebrew) occurred once each year and was meant to cleanse the Holy of Holies from the effects of ritual impurity. The Day of Atonement is not mentioned outside the Torah, leading many scholars to conclude that it arose only in the postexilic period. As depicted in the book of Leviticus, the ritual was performed entirely by the high priest, whose office made him the holiest individual in the nation. The ceremony took place in three stages. In the first stage, the high priest sacrificed a bull for his own purification and a goat for the purification of the temple. Some of the animals' blood was carried into the Holy of Holies and sprinkled onto the Ark of the Covenant, and some was applied to the four corners of the altar outside the temple. The bodies of the animals were then taken away and burned. In the second stage, the high priest recited all of the people's sins while laying his hands on the head of a second goat, then sent the animal off into the desert, where it symbolically carried the people's sins far away from the presence of Yahweh. The ritual concluded with the priest offering additional burnt offerings on behalf of himself and the people.

While the primary purpose of all of these purification sacrifices was to provide cleansing from ritual impurities, the Torah insists that the process also brought divine forgiveness to those whose violations had necessitated the offerings, including their unintentional sins. The idea that a person might need to be forgiven for unknowingly violating the will of the deity sounds strange to modern ears, since we usually think of sin as a conscious moral choice. But the idea is not as foreign as it seems: even today a person who accidentally knocks over another person's drink is expected to apologize and to assist with cleaning up the mess. The consideration shown to the offended party in this example is similar to the moral logic that is implied in the purification sacrifices that we see in the Torah.

Interestingly, neither Hosea nor Amos, the two prophets who addressed the northern kingdom of Israel, makes any clear reference to purification sacrifices. But the presence of purity rules in the book of Deuteronomy, which most scholars believe has its roots in the northern kingdom, suggests that some type of purification sacrifices might have been performed there as well.

5. *Reparation offerings.* According to the Torah, ritual impurity is not the only problem that results when people commit acts that violate the will of Yahweh. Some deeds require that reparations be paid to the deity before the wrong can be forgiven. The list of violations requiring reparations is quite diverse. In some cases one can see how ancient people might have thought that the honor or rights of the deity had been offended in such a way that compensation was required. Examples include the misuse of sacred objects and the swearing of false oaths, presumably by the name of Yahweh. The reasoning is less clear in cases where it is an individual rather than the deity who has suffered loss, as when someone defrauds another person or has sex with a slave to whom another man is engaged. The logic of reparation is even more opaque in cases involving the purification of a leper or the cleansing of unintentional sins. The fact that sacrifices of reparation are not mentioned in any preexilic materials outside the Torah (including Hosea and Amos) has led many scholars to conclude that the category was created in the postexilic period to encompass a variety of originally unrelated rituals.

The manner of compensation varies with the violation, but the standard form of payment is the sacrifice of a ram or a lamb. In one case the text allows for the debt to be paid with money. If the act resulted in harm to other people, then they, too, must be compensated according to the degree of harm caused. Once the payment is made, the violation is immediately forgiven.

6. *Other offerings.* Two other types of offerings that were relatively common in ancient Israel and Judah are the tithe and the presentation of firstfruits. The tithe was an obligatory offering of 10 percent of one's crops and animals to the deity. Scholars often describe it as a form of religious taxation. The practice did not originate with the Israelites; external records show that such offerings were performed in Palestine long before the biblical

period. The prophet Amos indicates that tithes were paid in the northern kingdom in his day (Amos 4:4).

Unfortunately, the Torah's rules concerning the tithe are confused and inconsistent, so it is hard to say exactly how the tithe was handled. Some verses apply the tithe only to agricultural crops (especially wine, grain, and oil), while others include herd animals in the calculation. Some depict the tithe as a system of financial support for the Levites and/or the poor, while others state that the proceeds are to be consumed by the worshippers in a celebratory meal at the temple. Some call for an additional tithe every third year to help the poor. By the postexilic period, it had become a way of filling the coffers of the temple.

The Torah also calls for a portion of the first harvest (called the firstfruits) and the firstborn of all domestic animals to be brought to the temple and given to Yahweh as an offering of thanksgiving. Similar practices are known from many other cultures. The requirement that the offering should be taken from the firstfruits is rooted in the common agricultural recognition that the quality of crops and animals often declines after multiple bearings. The Torah insists that only the best of everything is to be offered to the deity.

The Torah requirement that such offerings should be brought to the temple is probably an attempt by the Jerusalem priests to centralize a practice that most people would have performed at home or at a local shrine. The Torah assigns the firstfruits to the priests as food, since they could not raise crops and perform their temple duties at the same time. Whether the personnel of the local shrines received similar benefits is unclear, though it seems likely.

CONCLUSION

The Hebrew Bible indicates that sacrifices and offerings played a vital role in the state religion of Israel and Judah. The Torah seeks to centralize such ritual acts in the Jerusalem temple, where Yahweh was thought to dwell in concentrated essence. At the same time, other texts show that similar acts were performed at the state shrines in the northern kingdom and at local shrines in both Israel and Judah.

All of the sacrifices and offerings depicted in the Hebrew Bible involve animals or crops that were considered acceptable as food. Unlike other cultures, however, the Hebrew Bible does not view food offerings as a means of satisfying the deity's hunger. Instead, sacrifices and offerings were performed to elicit benefits or help from Yahweh, to cleanse people or objects from ritual impurity, and to express gratitude and praise to the deity.

Because the offerings were considered holy, the Torah insists that all sacrifices must be performed and controlled by the priests, who alone maintain the proper level of ritual purity to handle the sacred food and approach Yahweh's altar. In return for their service, the Torah allots them a portion of most offerings as food.

The laws of Torah prescribe different kinds of offerings for different situations. Some were offered by the priests on behalf of the entire nation, while others could be brought by individuals who wished to approach the deity with petitions or praise. The laws include detailed regulations about how the sacrificial items should be handled in order to guard their holiness. Whether similar rules were used for offerings outside the Jerusalem temple is unclear.

EXERCISE 77

Look back over the six types of offerings discussed in the latter part of the chapter and compare them with the six reasons for offering food products to the gods that were identified earlier in the chapter. What similarities and differences do you see between the two lists? Which offerings seem to be fulfilling which purposes? Note that some of the offerings could have multiple purposes—do not assume that there is a one-to-one correlation between the items in the two lists.

Fig. 30.1. An ancient Babylonian image of a man playing a harp, an instrument mentioned several times in the book of Psalms.

Worship in the Psalms

Save me, O God,
　　for the waters have come up to my neck.
I sink in deep mire,
　　where there is no foothold;
I have come into deep waters,
　　and the flood sweeps over me. (Psalm 69:1-2)

I waited patiently for the LORD;
　　he inclined to me and heard my cry.
He drew me up from the desolate pit,
　　out of the miry bog,
and set my feet upon a rock,
　　making my steps secure. (Psalm 40:1-2)

The salvation of the righteous is from the LORD;
　　he is their refuge in the time of trouble.
The LORD helps them and rescues them;
　　he rescues them from the wicked, and saves them,
　　because they take refuge in him. (Psalm 37:39-40)

In this final chapter on the ritual dimension of the Hebrew Bible, we will examine a book that arose directly out of the worship experience of the Yahwistic communities in ancient Israel, the book of Psalms. The English word *psalm* comes from the Greek word *psalmos*, which refers to a song that is accompanied by stringed instruments. The people who compiled the Hebrew Bible preferred the term *prayers* (as in Psalm 72:20) or *praises*, the usual English translation of the Hebrew word *tehillim* that became the title of the book in the Jewish tradition. All of these designations say something important about the content of the book.

The book of Psalms is a collection of highly poetic prayers and hymns that were recited or sung by the followers of Yahweh at various times and places over the course of several centuries. The significance of this book is hard to overstate. Nowhere else in the Hebrew Bible do we gain such profound insight into the thoughts, feelings, and motives of people who grappled seriously with the personal and social implications of their faith. If the book of Psalms had not been preserved, we would know very little about the inner spiritual forces that motivated people to obey the words of Yahweh, conduct the rites of worship (including the sacrificial system), and generally keep the flame of Yahwism alive within their families and local communities. While we must be careful about generalizing from these richly stylized poems to the personal religious experience of ordinary illiterate peasants, the book of Psalms demonstrates clearly that the elaborate ritual system of the religion of Yahweh contained within it the potential for profoundly emotional encounters with the supernatural world.

PRAYER AND PRAISE

Though the book of Psalms is unique within the Hebrew Bible, parallels can be found in religious communities around the globe. In fact, the idea that one should offer prayers to superhuman forces in times of trouble and render thanks and praise when things go well lies at the heart of most religions, though it is more prevalent in religions that envision the divine in personal terms (that is, as consisting of one or many gods or spirits) than in systems oriented toward an impersonal mind or force, as in Buddhism or Taoism.

Most of the prayers in the book of Psalms revolve around the needs and joys of the individual or the larger community. Prayers of this type usually assume that the supernatural realm operates much like the hierarchical societies in which nearly all of the major religions originated. Requests for divine assistance place the worshipper in the physical and emotional posture of a deferential and self-effacing peasant seeking a favor from the local landowner, while expressions of praise and thanksgiving recall the flattery and obeisance that courtiers use when seeking favors from a king. Both types of prayer presuppose that the supernatural world exercises significant power over human affairs and must be treated with respect if humans are to enjoy happy and successful lives. Both also imply that the inhabitants of the divine realm are not always concerned with or favorably disposed toward humans and must therefore be persuaded, enticed, or cajoled into acting in a way that benefits the worshippers.

In the ancient Near East, the supernatural world was invariably defined in personal terms as a series of male and female deities who were closely associated with the forces of nature. The gods were not necessarily friendly to humans; both pleasant and unpleasant experiences were thought to originate with them. Prayers and rituals were required to motivate the various gods and goddesses to bestow favors upon their worshippers and to protect them from harm, including the hurtful or inconsiderate acts of other gods. Hymns of praise acknowledged the greatness of the gods and offered thanks for the many benefits they granted to those who honored them.

The following examples show how the people of Mesopotamia and Egypt voiced their needs and expressed their gratitude to the gods. The similarities with the book of Psalms will become apparent as we review the biblical materials.

Prayer of Lamentation to Ishtar (Babylonia)
I pray to thee, O Lady of ladies, goddess of goddesses.
O Ishtar, queen of all peoples, who guides mankind aright,
O Irnini, ever exalted, greatest of the Igigi,
O mighty of princesses, exalted is thy name. . . .
At the thought of thy name heaven and earth tremble.
The gods tremble; the Anunnaki stand in awe.
To thine awesome name mankind must pay heed.
For thou art great and thou art exalted.
All the black-headed (people and) the masses of mankind
    pay homage to thy might.
The judgment of the people in truth and righteousness
    thou indeed dost decide.
Thou regardest the oppressed and mistreated; daily thou
    causest them to prosper. . . .
I have cried to thee, suffering, wearied, and distressed, as
    thy servant.
See me, O my Lady, accept my prayers.
Faithfully look upon me and hear my supplication.
Promise my forgiveness and let thy spirit be appeased.
Pity! For my wretched body which is full of confusion and
    trouble.
Pity! For my sickened heart which is full of tears and
    suffering.
Pity! For my wretched intestines (which are full of) confu-
    sion and trouble.
Pity! For my afflicted house which mourns bitterly.
Pity! For my feelings which are satiated with tears and
    suffering. . . .
Drive away the evil spells of my body (and) let me see thy
    bright light.
How long, O my Lady, shall my adversaries be looking
    upon me,
In lying and untruth shall they plan evil against me?

Shall my pursuers and those who exult over me rage against
    me?

How long, O my Lady, shall the crippled and weak seek
    me out?

One has made for me long sackcloth; thus I have appeared
    before thee.

The weak have become strong; but I am weak.

I toss about like flood-water, which an evil wind makes
    violent.

My heart is flying; it keeps fluttering like a bird of heaven.

I mourn like a dove night and day.

I am beaten down, and so I weep bitterly.

With "Oh" and "Alas" my spirit is distressed. . . .

Forgive my sin, my iniquity, my shameful deeds, and my
    offence.

Overlook my shameful deeds; accept my prayer;

Loosen my fetters; secure my deliverance;

Guide my steps aright; radiantly like a hero let me enter
    the streets with the living.

Speak so that at thy command the angry god may be
    favorable;

(And) the goddess who has been angry with me may turn
    again. . . .

Let my prayers and my supplications come to thee.

As for me, let me glorify thy divinity and thy might before
    the black-headed (people), [saying,]

Ishtar indeed is exalted; the Lady indeed is queen.

Irnini, the valorous daughter of Sin, has no rival.

Hymn of the Seven Hathors (Egypt)

We play the tambourine for Your Ka,

We dance for Your Majesty,

We exalt You

To the height of heaven.

You are the Mistress of Sekhem,

The Menat and the Sistrum,

The Mistress of Music,

For whose Ka one plays.

We praise Your Majesty every day,

From dusk until the earth grows light,

We rejoice in Your Countenance, O Mistress in Dendera!

We praise You with song.

You are the Lady of Jubilation, the Mistress of the
    Iba-dance,

The Lady of Music, the Mistress of Harp-playing,

The Lady of Dancing, the Mistress of Tying on Garlands,

The Lady of Myrrh, and the Mistress of Leaping.

We glorify Your Majesty,

We give praise before Your Face.

We exalt Your Power

Over the Gods and the Goddesses.

You are the Lady of Hymns,

The Mistress of the Library,

The Great Seshat

At the head of the Mansion of Records.

We propitiate Your Majesty every day.

Your heart rejoices at hearing our songs.

We rejoice when we see You, day by day.

Our hearts are jubilant when we see Your Majesty.

You are the Lady of Garlands, the Mistress of Dance,

The Lady of Unending Drunkenness.

We rejoice before Your face; we play for Your Ka.

Your heart rejoices over our performance.

THE BOOK OF PSALMS

The present version of the book of Psalms is the product of a long history of composition, use, and collection.
None of the psalms is dated, but many contain references
and allusions that indicate the general time frame when
they were written. Some presuppose the existence of the
monarchy, while others can be dated to the postexilic
period. Most are too general to obtain any clear idea of
their date of origin.

Jewish and Christian tradition attributes the composition of the psalms to King David. This tradition finds little
support in the Hebrew Bible. A handful of narrative texts
refer to David making music (1 Samuel 16:14-23; 18:10;
Amos 6:5) or reciting a psalm of praise (2 Samuel 22:1-
51; 1 Chronicles 16:7-36; 2 Chronicles 7:6), but nothing
is said about him composing psalms. The origins of this
tradition are obscure, but it was well established by the
time the headings were inserted at the beginning of many
of the psalms. Some of these headings link the psalm to a
specific episode in David's life (for example, Psalms 3, 7,
18, 51, 52), while others include a simple Hebrew phrase
that is commonly translated "of David" (suggesting

that it was written by him) but is better rendered as "to" or "for" David (that is, written in his honor). Over half of the headings link the psalm with someone other

Fig. 30.2. This stained glass window from a church in Wales depicts king David playing the harp, reflecting the popular belief that David composed many of the Psalms.

than David, including Asaph, the sons of Korah, Heman, Ethan, Jeduthun, and even Solomon and Moses. Over 20 percent have no heading at all.

The problem with all of these headings is that they were inserted by Hebrew editors who lived centuries after most of the psalms were written. As a result, their historical value is low. The questionable value of the headings becomes apparent when we look more closely at the psalms that are linked to David. Some clearly presuppose an exilic or postexilic setting (for example, Psalms 14:7; 51:20-21), while others speak from the viewpoint of someone other than the king (Psalms 20, 21, 61). Whether any of the psalms were written by David is impossible to say, though many scholars believe that the ancient tradition might have some historical foundation.

The book of Psalms is divided into five smaller books, each of which ends with a brief statement of praise to Yahweh (Psalms 1–41, 42–72, 73–89, 90–106, 107–150). The headings suggest that the present book was compiled from earlier collections, including a group associated with David (as reflected in Psalm 72:20), another group linked to Asaph (Psalms 73–84; see 1 Chronicles 16:4-7), and a group labeled "songs of ascent" that may have been used by pilgrims "ascending" to Jerusalem for one of the festivals (Psalms 120–134).

The book as we have it includes only a fraction of the prayers and hymns that were used for worshipping Yahweh in ancient Israel. Many psalms never made it into any type of collection. Others were removed as the various collections were revised and edited over the centuries. The book remained open to revision well into the postexilic period—copies from the Dead Sea Scrolls community (second century B.C.E.) contain several psalms that do not appear in the Hebrew Bible, and their order is different as well. Like a modern church hymnal, the book of Psalms was a living collection of songs that was revised again and again over the centuries to make room for new compositions and to respond to the spiritual needs of the community that used it. The version that appears in the Hebrew Bible is the final product of that process.

TYPES OF PSALMS

Each of the 150 songs, prayers, and poems that make up the book of Psalms is an independent literary creation. Some were crafted by people with serious artistic skills, while others are simpler and less ornate. While it would be reasonable to suppose that the more complex works were composed by the literate elites and the simpler ones by ordinary people, we must be careful about presuming too much in this area. Some of the greatest poetic works of antiquity, including Homer's *Iliad* and *Odyssey*, appear to have been composed in oral form, while the literate elites produced ample amounts of mediocre work to go along with the great classics. Most of the time it is impossible to determine whether a given psalm originated as an oral or written composition, though it seems likely that both types are included in the book of Psalms.

Once they were cast into written form, even those psalms that began as oral compositions came under the control of the literate elites, who in some cases revised and edited them to bring them into closer alignment with their ideological and literary standards. As a result, the collection as we have it reflects the ideas, experiences, and viewpoints of the Yahwistic elites who edited the final text. Psalms representing other views (for example, songs that honored other gods alongside Yahweh, as in

Mesopotamia or Egypt) were systematically rejected and thus lost to history.

The editors who arranged the psalms into their present order did not organize them according to theme, style, or date of origin. Psalms of varying types from diverse periods are placed side by side throughout the collection, making the book seem somewhat disorganized to modern readers. Yet careful study of the collection has shown that the psalms are not infinitely variable. Most of the psalms can be categorized under one of three broad headings: psalms of lament, psalms of praise, and wisdom psalms. Psalms that do not fit these categories are so few that they can be safely ignored in an introductory textbook. Within each of these categories a fairly consistent set of compositional techniques can be discerned, suggesting either a limited circle of authors or a broad cultural consensus about what should be included in each type of psalm and how they should be structured.

Lament Psalms

Approximately 40 percent of the compositions in the book of Psalms are laments. To lament something is to mourn over it. The lament psalms describe a painful situation that the speaker is facing and plead with Yahweh for help. Most of the time the speaker is an individual, but a number of the lament psalms speak of problems that afflict the people as a whole. In some cases the nature of the problem can be inferred from the language of the psalm (illness, interpersonal conflicts, foreign invaders, and so on), but many times the description is so vague and general that it is difficult to figure out what kind of circumstance gave rise to the composition. This vagueness, far from being a disadvantage, is one of the reasons many of these psalms were preserved, since it allowed a wide variety of people to apply the psalms to their own situations.

At the heart of every lament psalm lies a cry for divine assistance. Most begin with a plea for Yahweh to intervene and rescue the speaker from a bad situation. This is followed by a description of the situation that uses vivid imagery to inform the deity of how awful things are so that he will feel compassion and take action on behalf of the worshipper. The language alternates between dark depictions of the evils that are arrayed against the speaker

and poignant accounts of the physical and emotional pain that the speaker is suffering as a result of the situation. Mingled here and there among the descriptions are confessions of trust that aim to assure Yahweh that the speaker is counting on him to help. These statements seem designed to put the deity on the spot; how could he fail to come to the aid of someone who is so devoted to him?

Fig. 30.3. This ancient Egyptian statue shows the standard posture of a seeking help from a deity.

As the psalm progresses, the speaker becomes more specific about the kind of divine assistance that is desired and spells out a variety of reasons the deity should act in this situation: the speaker is innocent and does not deserve such painful suffering; Yahweh is a merciful and compassionate god who rescues those who are in trouble; the speaker has confessed and repented of any sins that might have aroused the deity's displeasure; the enemies are so bad that Yahweh cannot possibly allow them to triumph; the speaker will offer a special sacrifice of thanksgiving and tell others about Yahweh's greatness once the problem is over; and so forth. By the end of the psalm, the speaker is convinced that Yahweh will intervene and bring deliverance to his faithful servant. Nearly all of the lament psalms end on a note of confidence and praise.

The psychological benefits of reciting or hearing one of these lament psalms are not hard to see. The vividness of the poetic language makes it easy for people who are struggling with painful circumstances to identify with the feelings and experience of the speaker. By the end of the psalm, the circumstances that gave rise to the lament remain unchanged, but the attitude of the speaker has undergone a remarkable transformation, moving from anguish and despair over the situation to confidence and trust in Yahweh. In the process, the reader or listener who has identified with the speaker's sufferings is challenged to adopt a similar mind-set. The lament psalms suggest that the therapeutic power of positive thinking was recognized by the followers of Yahweh long before the invention of modern psychology. One of the chief benefits of religion is its ability to help people cope with adversity, and the lament psalms clearly served that purpose among the ancient followers of Yahweh.

EXERCISE 78

Read Psalms 7, 38, 79, and 94, paying careful attention to the change in attitude that occurs as you progress through each psalm. Then answer the following questions about one of the psalms.

- What kind of problem does the speaker seem to be facing?
- What reasons does the speaker give to motivate Yahweh to act?
- What causes the speaker to adopt a new attitude toward the situation?

Praise Psalms

Psalms of praise celebrate the greatness of Yahweh. Roughly 40 percent of the psalms fall into this category. Two major types can be identified: descriptive praise centers on Yahweh's character and his constant concern for his people and his creation, while declarative praise recalls specific deeds that Yahweh has performed on behalf of an individual or the people as a whole. Both are scattered throughout the book of Psalms, though they are especially prominent in the latter part of the book.

Most praise psalms were designed to be recited or sung by an individual in front of a gathered audience in order to encourage the hearers to trust, obey, and honor Yahweh. Some are framed as prayers, with a speaker addressing the deity directly, while others take the form of testimonies, with a speaker telling the audience about a great deed that Yahweh has done. Most include calls for the hearers to sing and rejoice along with the speaker. The Hebrew word *hallelujah*, which appears often in these psalms, is an imperative verb that invites others to "praise Yahweh" along with the speaker.

The emotional tone of the praise psalms is the polar opposite of what we saw in the lament psalms. Instead of focusing on problems and suffering, the speaker looks at the sunny side of life and finds plenty of reasons to be happy and celebrate. Yahweh is on his throne and watching out for his people; hard times have been overcome by his power; good times can prevail if people will trust and serve Yahweh. Why shouldn't Yahweh's people rejoice?

Despite their difference in tone, there is a clear link between lament psalms and declarative psalms of praise. In many of the lament psalms, a speaker promises to give thanks to Yahweh and tell others about his goodness if Yahweh will rescue the speaker from the present dire circumstances (Psalms 22:25; 35:17-18; 69:30-31; 70:12-16; 79:11-13; 109:26-30; 140:12-13; 144:9-10). Sometimes this promise is accompanied by a pledge to go up to the Jerusalem temple (Psalms 9:13-14; 26:6-7; 43:3-4; 61:8) and offer sacrifices of thanksgiving (Psalms 27:6; 56:12-13). Many of the declarative psalms of praise appear to have been composed for use on precisely these occasions. A few state explicitly that the speaker is fulfilling vows that were made during a time of trouble (Psalms 56:12-13; 65:1-4; 66:13-14; 116:18), and several refer to sacrifices of thanksgiving (Psalms 50:14-15, 23; 54:6-7; 56:12-13; 66:13-15; 107:19-22; 116:12-19). In these cases the lament psalm and the psalm of praise could be viewed as two halves of a single expression of devotion.

Declarative psalms of praise typically begin with a simple statement of praise to Yahweh, followed by a short summary of the experience that gave rise to the speaker's offering of praise. Often this section includes a call for others to join in the celebration. The body of the psalm is devoted to a colorful description of the situation from which the speaker was rescued (including the negative

Fig. 30.4. A group of Egyptian women dancing and playing tambourines, as described in some of the biblical psalms of praise.

feelings that it aroused), the speaker's appeal to Yahweh for help, and the ensuing experience of rescue. As with the laments, the language is highly allusive and poetic, making it difficult in many cases to gain a clear picture of the problem that the author had in mind. The psalm ends with further declarations of thanksgiving and praise to Yahweh. The tone of these psalms spans the entire range of human emotions, from anger and despair to exuberant joy. The theme, however, is constant: Yahweh is ever faithful to rescue his people in time of need.

Descriptive psalms of praise are less consistent in their structure. Most begin with a call to the audience to praise Yahweh along with the speaker. From here the psalm moves into a recitation of the reasons Yahweh should be praised. Some focus on aspects of Yahweh's character (his awesome power, his devotion to his people, his willingness to forgive, his righteousness and holiness), while others recite the many wonderful deeds that Yahweh has performed on behalf of humanity and/or Israel (creating and sustaining the physical world, rescuing his people from bondage in Egypt, and so on). Where specific divine acts are mentioned, they concern the distant past, such as the exodus story, and not the recent experience of the speaker. The psalm usually ends with a repeated call to the audience to sing praise to Yahweh.

People who were present when these psalms of praise were performed could hardly avoid being touched by them. The chief purpose of these psalms was to assure the deity that his followers recognized and appreciated what he had done for them and to encourage him to maintain his care for them. Implicit in their language, however, was a call to the audience to turn their attention away from their troubles and to focus instead on the benefits they enjoyed as the people of such a god. Those who accepted this challenge would have found their faith in Yahweh renewed and strengthened and their hope restored. They might still question why Yahweh had not yet rescued them from their present circumstances, but they would be assured once again that Yahweh had not forgotten them and that he would eventually act to help them.

Like the lament psalms, the psalms of praise helped the followers of Yahweh to cope emotionally and psychologically with the many troubles that life threw at them. In a world that sometimes appeared chaotic and senseless, it was good to be reminded that one was part of a people who stood under the care of a mighty and loving god.

Wisdom Psalms

Wisdom psalms are less numerous than psalms of praise or lament, but they are distinctive enough to receive special mention. Like the wisdom literature that we will be studying in chapter 37, wisdom psalms reflect on the meaning of life and the way in which people should live in order to please Yahweh and enjoy his blessings. A handful of psalms consist entirely of wisdom teachings (Psalms 37, 49, 112, 127, 128, 133), while several others combine elements of praise or lament with substantial amounts of wisdom reflection (Psalms 33, 34, 36, 73, 90). Some scholars would also include here the so-called Torah psalms that celebrate the goodness of the Torah and the benefits that come from following its teachings (Psalms 1, 19, 119).

Wisdom psalms reflect the viewpoint of a teacher who has thought long and hard about life and is now giving instructions to others about how they should live. As a result, the teacher's comments are normally directed toward the audience, though in a few cases the speaker addresses the deity. The identity of the speaker is never specified, and the message is general enough to be relevant to any audience that honors Yahweh as the supreme deity. Most are framed as poetic speeches, though in a few cases the speaker pronounces blessings on people who live in the prescribed manner (Psalms 1, 32, 34, 112, 127, 128).

Wisdom psalms follow no regular pattern or structure; most consist of observations about life and/or recommendations for proper conduct that have been loosely strung together. Most revolve around a common theme and employ repetitive language to underline their point.

Though framed as the advice of a wise teacher, they invariably reflect traditional patterns of thought, not the creative observations of an independent thinker. As a result, their message remains fairly consistent from psalm to psalm: there is a moral order behind the universe, despite occasional appearances to the contrary; people should strive to do what is right and avoid what is wrong, even when the consequences are not immediately apparent; Yahweh watches over those who serve him and provides for their needs; Yahweh will reward the faithful and bring down those who abuse them; patience and perseverance are required until Yahweh decides to act. Messages such as these presuppose an audience whose experience with life has raised questions about the fundamental morality and justice of the universe.

In both form and content, the wisdom psalms resemble the wisdom literature of the Hebrew Bible (see chapter 37). Why they were included in the book of Psalms rather than the wisdom books is not clear. The presence of wisdom language in some of the psalms of praise and lament (Psalms 33, 34, 36, 73, 90) shows that the wisdom tradition influenced the thinking of some of the people who produced the psalms, so it seems reasonable to think that the wisdom psalms originated in similar circles. How the wisdom psalms were used is also unclear. Many imply the presence of an audience, suggesting that they might have been sung or recited on public occasions when crowds were gathered together (for example, at the temple during a festival).

Fig. 30.5. A man offers instruction to his followers in this ancient Egyptian tomb painting.

Yahwists who heard these psalms would have found comfort in their message, since the psalms reassure them that Yahweh is on his throne and everything will turn out fine for them in the end, even though it might not appear that way at the moment. Such a reminder would have been especially meaningful to people whose lives were filled with troubles, though anyone who had reflected upon the seeming unfairness of life could have found their message encouraging.

Fig. 30.6. (top) This Egyptian tomb painting shows musicians playing many of the same instruments that are mentioned in the psalms; (bottom) similar instruments are used today by a Sufi group in Cairo, Egypt.

EXERCISE 80

Read Psalms 1, 37, 49, and 112. Then choose one of them and make a list of the kinds of behavior that the speaker says the audience should follow and the kinds that they should avoid. What reasons are given to explain why they should behave in this manner?

THE PSALMS IN ISRAEL'S WORSHIP

What can we know about how the psalms were used in ancient Israel? The headings indicate that by the post-exilic period many of them were accompanied by music (Psalms 7, 18, 65–68, 75–76, 87–88, 92, 108, 120–134). A few specify the instruments that were to be used for accompaniment: Psalms 4, 6, 55, 61, and 76 mention stringed instruments, while Psalm 5 refers to flutes. Several include notations that probably indicate the tune to which they were to be chanted or sung ("The Gittith"—Psalms 8, 81, 84; "The Deer of the Dawn"—Psalm 22; "The Lily of the Covenant"—Psalm 60; and so on). Hebrew words like *maskil, miktam, higgaion,* and **selah** were probably musical notations whose meaning has been lost over the centuries.

What about earlier times? Even a cursory examination of the psalms reveals numerous references to singing and music. Similar language can be found in psalms from every period, so it appears that the psalms were linked with music throughout their history. Instruments that are mentioned in the psalms include harps and lyres (ancient stringed instruments), trumpets, horns, flutes, tambourines, and cymbals. Some of these instruments produce mellow sounds that are conducive to reflection, while others are loud and exuberant and thus more appropriate for times of rejoicing. Many of the psalms mention physical acts that were performed along with the singing, including dancing, clapping, shouting, lifting the hands, and bowing. A few refer to people marching in processions through the streets or around the temple area (for example, Psalms 42:4; 68:24-27; 118:27). In short, the book of Psalms depicts a form of interaction with the deity that involves not only the mind but also the body and the emotions. This correlates well with the common biblical view of the self as a unified being (see chapter 13): a proper response to the deity must involve the whole person, not just one part.

On the other hand, there is much that remains unclear about when, where, and how particular psalms were used. Many of the psalms are so vague and general that we can only speculate about the context in which they were employed. In fact, their generalized language may be one of the reasons these psalms were included in the collection, since it allowed them to be used by people in different times and situations, much like modern hymns. Psalm 13, for example, could be recited by a person facing virtually any kind of problem that might be caused by other people, while Psalm 145 could be sung whenever a worshipper wanted to declare the greatness of Yahweh.

Psalm 13

How long, O LORD? Will you forget me forever?
　　How long will you hide your face from me?
How long must I bear pain in my soul,
　　and have sorrow in my heart all day long?
How long shall my enemy be exalted over me?

Consider and answer me, O LORD my God!
　　Give light to my eyes, or I will sleep the sleep of death,
and my enemy will say, "I have prevailed";
　　my foes will rejoice because I am shaken.

But I trusted in your steadfast love;
　　my heart shall rejoice in your salvation.
I will sing to the LORD,
　　because he has dealt bountifully with me.

Psalm 145:1-7

I will extol you, my God and King,
　　and bless your name forever and ever.
Every day I will bless you,
　　and praise your name forever and ever.
Great is the LORD, and greatly to be praised;
　　his greatness is unsearchable.

One generation shall laud your works to another,
　　and shall declare your mighty acts.
On the glorious splendor of your majesty,
　　and on your wondrous works, I will meditate.
The might of your awesome deeds shall be proclaimed,
　　and I will declare your greatness.
They shall celebrate the fame of your abundant goodness,
　　and shall sing aloud of your righteousness.

In other cases a psalm seems to have been crafted for use in a particular set of circumstances, but the language is

broad enough to be applied to other people facing similar issues. For example, Psalm 38 represents a cry for healing in a time of sickness, while in Psalm 116 an individual who has been rescued from death comes to the temple to present a thanksgiving sacrifice to Yahweh. Anyone who encountered either of these situations could find in these psalms a helpful tool for expressing his or her thoughts and feelings to Yahweh.

Psalm 38:1-8, 21-22

O LORD, do not rebuke me in your anger,
　　or discipline me in your wrath.
For your arrows have sunk into me,
　　and your hand has come down on me.

There is no soundness in my flesh
　　because of your indignation;
there is no health in my bones
　　because of my sin.
For my iniquities have gone over my head;
　　they weigh like a burden too heavy for me.

My wounds grow foul and fester
　　because of my foolishness;
I am utterly bowed down and prostrate;
　　all day long I go around mourning.
For my loins are filled with burning,
　　and there is no soundness in my flesh.
I am utterly spent and crushed;
　　I groan because of the tumult of my heart. . . .

Do not forsake me, O LORD;
　　O my God, do not be far from me;
make haste to help me,
　　O LORD, my salvation.

Psalm 116:1-6, 12-14, 18-19

I love the LORD, because he has heard
　　my voice and my supplications.
Because he inclined his ear to me,
　　therefore I will call on him as long as I live.
The snares of death encompassed me;
　　the pangs of Sheol laid hold on me;
　　I suffered distress and anguish.

Then I called on the name of the LORD:
> "O LORD, I pray, save my life!"

Gracious is the LORD, and righteous;
> our God is merciful.
The LORD protects the simple;
> when I was brought low, he saved me. . . .

What shall I return to the LORD
> for all his bounty to me?
I will lift up the cup of salvation
> and call on the name of the LORD,
I will pay my vows to the LORD
> in the presence of all his people. . . .
I will pay my vows to the LORD
> in the presence of all his people,
in the courts of the house of the LORD,
> in your midst, O Jerusalem.
Praise the LORD!

Other psalms were designed for more specialized situations. Several contain language that suggests that they were recited in conjunction with liturgical events that took place on a periodic basis. Some might have been used only once a year, much as Christmas carols are sung for only a few weeks each year in Christian churches. Psalm 24, for example, seems to have served as part of an entrance ritual when the Ark of the Covenant was being brought back to the Jerusalem temple after being paraded through the streets at one of the annual festivals. Similarly, Psalm 79 may have been used at a ceremony recalling the destruction of the temple by the Babylonians.

Psalm 24:7-10
Lift up your heads, O gates!
> and be lifted up, O ancient doors!
> that the King of glory may come in.
Who is the King of glory?
> The LORD, strong and mighty,
> the LORD, mighty in battle.
Lift up your heads, O gates!
> and be lifted up, O ancient doors!
> that the King of glory may come in.

Who is this King of glory?
> The LORD of hosts,
> he is the King of glory.

Psalm 79:1-7
O God, the nations have come into your inheritance;
> they have defiled your holy temple;
> they have laid Jerusalem in ruins.
They have given the bodies of your servants
> to the birds of the air for food,
> the flesh of your faithful to the wild animals of the
> > earth.
They have poured out their blood like water
> all around Jerusalem,
> and there was no one to bury them.
We have become a taunt to our neighbors,
> mocked and derided by those around us.

How long, O LORD? Will you be angry forever?
> Will your jealous wrath burn like fire?
Pour out your anger on the nations
> that do not know you,
and on the kingdoms
> that do not call on your name.
For they have devoured Jacob
> and laid waste his habitation.

While many of the psalms are broad enough to be recited virtually anywhere, a sizable number contain language that links them specifically to the Jerusalem temple. Some state that the speaker is present in the temple or engaging in activities that were normally performed at the temple, including animal sacrifices. Others presuppose that the speaker is addressing a group of people who have gathered together for prayer or worship, most likely at one of the major festivals when people traveled to Jerusalem on pilgrimage. One psalm that shows clear links to the temple is Psalm 26, in which a person who is seeking Yahweh's help mentions marching around the altar, loving Yahweh's house, and praising Yahweh "in the great congregation" (v. 12). Another is Psalm 99, which depicts Yahweh as a mighty and just king and calls on the audience to "worship at his holy mountain" (v. 9).

Psalm 26:1-8, 12

Vindicate me, O Lord,
 for I have walked in my integrity,
  and I have trusted in the Lord without wavering.
Prove me, O Lord, and try me;
 test my heart and mind.
For your steadfast love is before my eyes,
 and I walk in faithfulness to you.
I do not sit with the worthless,
 nor do I consort with hypocrites;
I hate the company of evildoers,
 and will not sit with the wicked.

I wash my hands in innocence,
 and go around your altar, O Lord,
Singing aloud a song of thanksgiving,
 and telling all your wondrous deeds.

O Lord, I love the house in which you dwell,
 and the place where your glory abides. . . .

My foot stands on level ground;
 in the great congregation I will bless the Lord.

Psalm 99:1-5, 9

The Lord is king; let the peoples tremble!
 He sits enthroned upon the cherubim; let the earth
  quake!
The Lord is great in Zion;
 he is exalted over all the peoples.
Let them praise your great and awesome name.
 Holy is he!
Mighty King, lover of justice,
 you have established equity;
you have executed justice
 and righteousness in Jacob.
Extol the Lord our God;
 worship at his footstool.
 Holy is he! . . .

Extol the Lord our God,
 and worship at his holy mountain;
 for the Lord our God is holy.

Finally, the collection contains psalms that were composed for special occasions like royal weddings or coronations. Since these events occurred only sporadically, the psalms in this category would not have been used often, but they had to be ready when the occasion demanded. Psalm 45, for example, was designed to be sung at the king's wedding, while Psalm 110 would have been used at his coronation. Both would have been pronounced by a high official, most likely a priest.

Psalm 45:1-3, 10-13

My heart overflows with a goodly theme;
 I address my verses to the king;
  my tongue is like the pen of a ready scribe.

You are the most handsome of men;
 grace is poured upon your lips;
  therefore God has blessed you forever.
Gird your sword on your thigh, O mighty one,
 in your glory and majesty. . . .

Hear, O daughter, consider and incline your ear;
 forget your people and your father's house,
  and the king will desire your beauty.
Since he is your lord, bow to him;
 the people of Tyre will seek your favor with gifts,
  the richest of the people with all kinds of wealth.

Psalm 110:1-4

The Lord says to my lord,
 "Sit at my right hand
until I make your enemies your footstool."

The Lord sends out from Zion
 your mighty scepter.
  Rule in the midst of your foes.
Your people will offer themselves willingly
 on the day you lead your forces
 on the holy mountains.
From the womb of the morning,
 like dew, your youth will come to you.
The Lord has sworn and will not change his mind,
 "You are a priest forever according to the order of
  Melchizedek."

THE TEMPLE HYMNBOOK

As we have seen, many of the compositions in the book of Psalms refer directly or indirectly to the Jerusalem temple. In fact, the collection mentions no other setting for any of the psalms while the temple was standing—no references to private homes, extended family gatherings, villages or towns, or local shrines. A few of the psalms were written or edited while the temple was in ruins (Psalms 51:18-19; 79:1-4; 102:12-17), and a few may have been composed outside the land of Israel (Psalms 106:47; 120:5). But these minor exceptions do not undermine the overall impression that the present book of Psalms was derived from materials that were used in the Jerusalem temple. This does not mean that psalms were absent from family gatherings or local celebrations; it simply means that this side of the religious life of Yahweh's followers, if it existed, has been lost to us. Some of the psalms in the present book may in fact have originated outside the temple, but they survived only because they were carried to Jerusalem and incorporated into one of the collections used at the temple.

In short, it seems that the songs and prayers contained in the book of Psalms were part of the state religion of Judah, not the personal devotional expressions of ordinary Yahwists. In fact, most of the materials in the pres-

ent collection were probably written by temple officials for use in conjunction with the daily liturgy and other activities that took place around the temple. As a result, they reflect the viewpoints and experiences of the Jerusalem elites, not the ordinary worshipper of Yahweh. Again and again the psalms mention the streets and walls of the city (that is, Jerusalem) and the activities of the temple, including but not limited to animal sacrifices. The social world of the psalms is filled with rivalries and conflicts involving powerful individuals (Psalms 7, 12, 37, 49, 52, 62) and nations (Psalms 9, 18, 44, 59, 60, 68, 74), and the king appears often as a lead character (Psalms 2, 20, 21, 33, 45, 61, 72, and others). The poor are viewed from the vantage point of the rich and powerful, who are expected to care for them (Psalms 41:1; 72:1-4, 12-14; 109:15-16; 112:9). Occasionally a speaker will refer to himself as poor in an effort to elicit Yahweh's compassion, but this is entirely figurative, as can be seen from a closer look at the rest of the psalm (see Psalms 35:10; 40:16-17; 70:4-5; 74:18-21; 86:1-2). Songs and prayers reflecting the experience of the rural poor—the physical and emotional trauma caused by abusive landlords and crop failures, the joys surrounding a family wedding or a successful harvest—are virtually absent from the psalms. If such psalms existed, they did not survive.

So how were the psalms used at the Jerusalem temple? Apart from the highly questionable descriptions of David's organization of the temple service in the book of Chronicles (1 Chronicles 23–26), we have no direct information on this point. All that we know is what can be inferred from the psalms themselves. Fortunately, there are enough references to provide at least a broad outline of their use.

Some scholars have referred to the book of Psalms as the hymnbook of the Jerusalem temple. This term is misleading if it leads us to think of a printed book that served as a guide for congregational singing as in a modern church. In fact, the current collection did not even exist until sometime in the postexilic era. In earlier times the psalms would have been part of a broader collection of oral and written materials that were utilized by the temple personnel when carrying out their duties. A careful study of the psalms suggests a variety of situations in which psalms might have been used.

1. *Routine worship.* As sacrifices were offered every morning and evening in the temple, singers sang or chanted psalms of praise to Yahweh. The psalms expressed in words what the sacrifices communicated by actions; both were done to honor the deity and to solicit his mercy and protection for the nation. Many of the descriptive psalms of praise would have been at home in this environment. A few texts imply that psalms were sung as part of the regular temple worship at other times as well, even during the night (Psalm 134:1).

2. *Annual celebrations.* Many of the psalms of praise mention large numbers of people who have gathered in the streets of Jerusalem and the temple precincts to voice their gratitude to Yahweh. Others portray a speaker calling a group of people to join together in praise and worship. The most likely setting for these psalms is one of the annual festivals when people would have come to Jerusalem to worship around the temple. A significant number of psalms appear to have been written for use during these special times of corporate celebration.

3. *National crisis.* When the nation was threatened by foreign armies or other dangers, the king (or sometimes a priest or other leader) might go up to the temple and plead for Yahweh's assistance and protection. Several of the psalms seem to have been composed for such moments of crisis. The tone of these psalms is often quite emotional, since the health and survival of Yahweh's people are at stake. Prayers were offered at the temple not only because it was the dwelling place of Yahweh, where he was most likely to hear the cries of his people, but also because it was the king's sanctuary, the place set aside for the king to approach the deity on behalf of the nation.

4. *National thanksgiving.* Once a crisis had passed, a gathering might be held at the temple to offer thanks to Yahweh for carrying his people safely through their time of danger. As before, the king or another high official would speak to the deity on the nation's behalf, using the language of a psalm to rehearse the nature of the threat

Fig. 30.7. This pedestal from the Ishtar Temple in Assur, which may have held an image of a deity, shows the Assyrian king Tukulti-Ninurta I (thirteenth century B.C.E.) bowing before a similar pedestal in prayer.

and recount how Yahweh had aided his people and rescued them from danger. Often the ceremony would be accompanied by lavish sacrifices of thanksgiving. Members of the general populace may or may not have been present for these events. The key point was to express the nation's gratitude to the deity, and this could be done with or without the presence of a gathered congregation.

5. *Personal crisis.* Ordinary people who were facing unusual difficulties could travel to the house of Yahweh at any time to bring their needs to the deity and request his help. Often they would bring a sacrifice with them to curry favor with the deity or atone for any sins they might have committed. Many of the psalms reflect this kind of situation, though it is unclear how exactly they were used. One plausible scenario is to imagine the person describing the problem to a priest, who then selects a psalm that seems appropriate for the situation and either sings it on the needy person's behalf or asks the person to repeat it after him. The vagueness and generality of many of the psalms allowed them to be applied to a variety of situations, though the priests may also have had

access to a broader repertoire of psalms than the present collection.

6. *Personal thanksgiving.* Individuals who wished to celebrate the goodness of Yahweh also came to the temple to express their gratitude to Yahweh. As in times of suffering, the worshippers often brought an animal to sacrifice to the deity. Psalms of praise seem to have played an important part in the ritual of thanksgiving. Some of these psalms describe fairly mundane blessings, such as the completion of a successful harvest, while others celebrate extraordinary occurrences, such as a family member's recovery from sickness. The ritual was probably similar to that for the personal laments: the priest selected a psalm of praise that paralleled the circumstances of the one making the offering and sang or recited it on behalf of (or along with) the person. The ritual was then followed by a celebratory meal. For an ordinary peasant, a trip to the temple with a sacrifice of thanksgiving was a time to remember.

CONCLUSION

The present book of Psalms is a collection of 150 songs and prayers that were used in and around the Jerusalem temple from the early monarchy through the postexilic period. These songs, along with many others that have been lost, played a vital role in the state religion of Judah. Their primary role was to provide proper language for the followers of Yahweh to express their needs and joys to the deity. Often they were used in conjunction with sacrifices and other rituals.

While some of the psalms may have been composed by ordinary individuals, most were probably written by temple personnel. As a result, they reflect the ideas and experiences of the city elites. In most cases, however, the language is broad and general enough to be applied to a variety of individuals and situations. The psalms reminded the worshippers that Yahweh is a mighty god who cares deeply about his people and stands ready to help them if they honor him above all other deities. This message not only brought significant psychological benefits to those who heeded it but also helped to popularize the form of Yahwistic religion that eventually came to dominate the religious life of ancient Palestine.

EXERCISE 82

Read the following psalms carefully, paying close attention to details that indicate what is being done in conjunction with the psalm. Then choose one of the psalms and indicate what kind of psalm it is and how, why, and by whom it might have been used at the Jerusalem temple.

- Psalm 27
- Psalm 44
- Psalm 65
- Psalm 68
- Psalm 83
- Psalm 118

Fig. 31.1. Antonio Cifrondi, *Elijah in the Chariot of Fire*

The World of the Prophets

Ah, you who make iniquitous decrees, who write oppressive statutes, to turn aside the needy from justice and to rob the poor of my people of their right, that widows may be your spoil, and that you may make the orphans your prey! What will you do on the day of punishment, in the calamity that will come from far away? To whom will you flee for help, and where will you leave your wealth, so as not to crouch among the prisoners or fall among the slain? For all this his anger has not turned away; his hand is stretched out still. (Isaiah 10:1-4)

"I will sanctify my great name, which has been profaned among the nations, and which you have profaned among them; and the nations shall know that I am the LORD,*" says the* LORD *God, "when through you I display my holiness before their eyes. I will take you from the nations, and gather you from all the countries, and bring you into your own land. I will sprinkle clean water upon you, and you shall be clean from all your uncleannesses, and from all your idols I will cleanse you. A new heart I will give you, and a new spirit I will put within you; and I will remove from your body the heart of stone and give you a heart of flesh. I will put my spirit within you, and make you follow my statutes and be careful to observe my ordinances. Then you shall live in the land that I gave to your ancestors; and you shall be my people, and I will be your God."* (Ezekiel 36:23-27)

Just as you have been a cursing among the nations, O house of Judah and house of Israel, so I will save you and you shall be a blessing. Do not be afraid, but let your hands be strong. For thus says the LORD *of hosts: "Just as I purposed to bring disaster upon you, when your ancestors provoked me to wrath, and I did not relent," says the* LORD *of hosts, "so again I have purposed in these days to do good to Jerusalem and to the house of Judah; do not be afraid. These are the things that you shall do: Speak the truth to one another, render in your gates judgments that are true and make for peace, do not devise evil in your hearts against one another, and love no false oath; for all these are things that I hate," says the* LORD. (Zechariah 8:13-17)

In the last several chapters we have been exploring what the Hebrew Bible tells us about the religious practices of the followers of Yahweh in ancient Palestine. In this chapter we shift our attention to a class of religious specialists called **prophets** who played a unique role in the religious life of ancient Israel and Judah. Our information about the prophets comes from two sources: (a) collections of their sayings which were eventually compiled into books that were included in the Prophets section of the Hebrew Bible, and (b) stories about prophets that are found in some of the narrative books. Only a small fraction of the prophets who lived in ancient Israel left any trace in the written record. Others appear as members of groups, but their names are unknown. As we shall see, we should not assume that all ancient Israelite prophets were like the ones who are mentioned or quoted in the Hebrew Bible.

The next six chapters are devoted to an examination of the phenomenon of prophecy in ancient Israel and Judah. The present chapter provides an overview of the prophetic movement, including comparisons with similar activities in other religions. Chapters 32 and 33 look more closely at the sayings of the prophets who lived before the Babylonian Exile, while chapters 34 and 35 examine the prophets who spoke to the people of Judah during and after the Exile. The study concludes in chapter 36 with an investigation of the apocalyptic movement, which arose out the prophetic movement toward the end of the biblical period.

While it might appear that we are devoting an excessive amount of attention to a single aspect of the religious life of ancient Israel and Judah, a quick review of the Table of Contents of any Bible will show why this is necessary. Nearly 30 percent of the text of the Hebrew Bible consists of sayings attributed to prophets, and stories about prophets appear at key points in the narrative books as well. Clearly the people who compiled and preserved these texts thought that prophets had played a vital role in their people's history. If we wish to understand the Hebrew Bible, we must pay attention to the role of prophets in the biblical texts.

PENETRATING THE VEIL

When people today hear the word *prophet*, they usually think of someone who claims to be able to foretell the future, like Nostradamus or the publicity-seekers whose predictions are used to sell tabloids at supermarket stands. This association has given the term *prophet* a bad name, since few people today believe that humans can accurately predict what will happen in the future.

In the ancient world, however, things were different. Virtually everyone thought that people with special gifts or training could attain insight into things to come. The world of the future, like the world of the gods, might be veiled, but it was not closed. Life was filled with signs and messages from the supernatural world. Those who knew how to interpret these messages could uncover many mysteries that escaped the awareness of ordinary people.

Various methods were used to discern what the gods were saying to humans. Some involved activities that anyone could perform, while others required specialized training. One of the most popular techniques was the casting of lots (for example, rolling dice or drawing sticks from a pouch), which worked on the assumption that the gods would influence the outcome and so make their will known. Another common practice was to look for hidden patterns within the world of nature, such as the flight of a flock of birds or the behavior of a sacred animal. Unusual natural events like eclipses, comets, and freak storms were invariably regarded as omens of the future, though the question of how they were to be interpreted was usually left to experts. Specialized training was also required to interpret dreams or to read the messages embedded in the organs of a sacrificed animal. Many of these practices can be found in various tribal cultures today.

At the pinnacle of specialization was a class of religious experts who sought to attain direct contact with the supernatural world by means of visions, dreams, spirit possession, and similar experiences. Scholars who study tribal cultures usually call these people **shamans**, but this term carries associations that can be misleading when applied to other types of cultures. A more neutral term is **intermediaries**, since the principal activity of these people is to mediate between the world of humans and the world of the divine.

Intermediaries employ a variety of techniques to penetrate the veil that in their view hangs lightly between the two worlds. Purification rituals are used to remove the taint of earthly associations and to prepare the person for interaction with the sacred realm. Sacred objects and sacred

Fig. 31.2. (top) The Assyrian king Shamshi-Adad V (ninth century B.C.E.) accompanied by symbols of heavenly deities, whose motions the Assyrians studied to gain insight into the will of the gods; (bottom) a Babylonian model of a sheep's liver, marked to show pupils how to discern messages from the gods in the animal's entrails.

places serve as channels through which the power of the supernatural enters the world of humans. Reciting sacred words and (in literate cultures) studying sacred texts help to usher the mind into the presence of the divine. Special kinds of music and ritualized dance serve to attune the senses to the presence of the supernatural and bring the person under the influence or control of a sacred power. Eating or inhaling sacred substances, including but not limited to items known today to be hallucinogenic, is yet another common means of opening one's mind and spirit to the world beyond.

Fig. 31.3. (top) An Indonesian shaman listens for the voices of the gods speaking through his sacred staff; (bottom) a painting created by a Mexican artist based on sacred visions triggered by eating peyote cactus buttons.

Such close encounters with the supernatural world must be handled with great care, since the forces with which the intermediaries are interacting can turn against those who approach them without proper respect. But the benefits to society clearly outweigh the risks. In addition to learning about and possibly influencing the future, intermediaries often bring back messages from the gods concerning the kinds of moral or ritual conduct that their people should perform in order to avoid future hardship and enjoy prosperity. Intermediaries also channel supernatural power to help individuals who are sick or otherwise troubled within the society.

The fact that intermediaries are able to interact safely with the supernatural realm evokes both respect and fear from their fellow citizens. It is not uncommon to observe a level of tension between these charismatic individuals and other societal leaders. As a rule, intermediaries use their influence to support the social and political status quo, serving as personal counselors to those in power and lending legitimacy to their undertakings. Some, however, become critics of the established order, whether due to personal conviction, disputes with other leaders, or membership in a marginal social group. Often their criticism is framed as a message from the gods to return to social or religious practices that prevailed during some golden age of the past, even when what they are proposing is in fact a new practice.

Whether the proposed changes are accepted depends as much on the social status of the speaker as on the content of the message. This is especially true when intermediaries are lined up on both sides of a proposal. An intermediary who has earned the respect of societal leaders might find them willing to embrace the desired change, whereas one who is viewed as an outsider or whose message threatens the interests of important leaders might be ignored, abused, exiled, or even killed. The mere assertion that one is speaking on behalf of the gods does not guarantee that the message will be accepted, especially when other intermediaries can be found to speak on the opposite side of the recommendation.

PROPHETS IN THE HEBREW BIBLE

The narrative books and the books of the prophets contain a veritable treasure trove of material pertaining to the words and actions of men and women who were viewed as prophets by the people who compiled the Hebrew Bible. Virtually all of the stories about the prophets are associated with the era of the monarchy, though we do find a few references to prophets in earlier and later periods. By contrast, the prophets whose sayings are recorded in the books of the prophets extend from the monarchy through the Babylonian Exile and beyond.

Like other elements of the Hebrew Bible, the stories and sayings of the prophets have been subjected to critical scrutiny by scholars. Before we can look at what scholars have said about the prophets, however, we must understand how prophets are depicted in the Hebrew Bible. Following the chronological framework provided by the biblical editors, the prophets can be divided into three periods: preexilic prophets (those who lived and spoke prior to the Babylonian Exile), exilic prophets (those who pronounced their messages during the period of the Exile), and postexilic prophets (those who arose after the return from Babylonia).

Preexilic Prophets

The first person to be designated a prophet in the biblical story line is Abraham, though the term appears only once, in the mouth of a non-Israelite (Genesis 20:7). The title is used more often in the Exodus story, where it is applied to Moses (Deuteronomy 18:15; 34:10), his brother Aaron (Exodus 7:1), his sister Miriam (Exodus 15:20), and two men named Eldad and Medad (Numbers 11:25-29). The only other person prior to the monarchy to be labeled a prophet is an unnamed man from the period of the judges (Judges 6:7-10).

With the rise of the monarchy, prophets become almost commonplace in the narrative books. The transition occurs with Samuel, who functions simultaneously as prophet (also called a seer; see 1 Samuel 9:9), priest, and judge. According to the Hebrew Bible, Samuel, following the leading of Yahweh, chose and anointed Saul to be the first king of Israel (1 Samuel 9:1—10:27). This meant laying aside his own political power as a judge in favor of a more limited role as religious leader of the nation and prophet to the king. When Saul repeatedly fails to obey Samuel's instructions, Samuel is told by Yah-

weh to anoint David to replace him (1 Samuel 16:1-13). During David's reign, prophets serve as advisors to the king, informing him what Yahweh wants him to do and challenging him when he fails to obey the will of the deity (2 Samuel 7:1-17; 12:1-15; 24:10-19; 1 Kings 1:22-40; 1 Chronicles 25:5; 2 Chronicles 29:25; 35:15). Scholars commonly call such people *court prophets*, since they served in the court of the king.

Beginning with David's son Solomon, the relationship between the kings and the prophets changes. Solomon receives a number of messages directly from Yahweh, but no prophets are named among his officials. Toward the end of his reign, a prophet named Ahijah arises from outside his court, pronouncing words of judgment against the king and predicting the division of the kingdom after his death (1 Kings 11:26-40). From this time forward, prophets are depicted primarily as adversaries of the kings. They appear at key points in the narrative to announce Yahweh's displeasure with the kings' conduct and to declare his intention to execute judgment against them, their families, and their people for failing to abide by his covenant, primarily by worshipping other gods (1 Kings 14:1-16; 16:1-4; 21:17-26; 2 Kings 9:1-10; 17:13-14; 21:10-15; 2 Chronicles 25:14-16; 28:8-11). The verdict is usually presented as final, with no possibility of repentance or change. In a few cases, however, the kings repent after hearing the words of the prophet and Yahweh reduces their punishment as a result (1 Kings 21:27-29; 2 Chronicles 12:5-8; 33:10-13). This description of the words and activities of the prophets coheres fairly well with the messages that are attributed to the preexilic prophets in the biblical books of the prophets (see chapters 32 and 33). As might be expected, the message of these prophets was not well-received—most were ignored, mocked, or otherwise abused.

Yet this is not the whole story. The narrative books acknowledge that at least some of the kings whom they condemn had prophets among their advisors, both prophets of Yahweh and prophets of other gods (1 Kings 18:18-19; 22:1-12; see also Jeremiah 37:17-19). The prophetic books likewise include several passages in which the biblical prophet criticizes other prophets who have more influence with the rulers and people than the person making the pronouncement (Isaiah 28:9-12;

Jeremiah 5:30-31; 23:9-40; 28:1-17; 37:17-19; Ezekiel 22:27-28; Micah 3:5-8). By contrast, none of the "good kings" is credited. On the other hand, the Hebrew Bible also contains several stories in which "bad kings" follow the advice of the prophets of Yahweh and win victories or otherwise succeed in their endeavors (1 Kings 20:13-30; 2 Kings 3:11-27; 6:8-7:20). In this they resemble the "good kings" who consistently take the prophets seriously and seek their advice in times of need (1 Kings 22:5-9; 2 Kings 3:11-20; 19:1-37; 22:11-20; 2 Chronicles 20:20; 29:25). These conflicting images suggest that the relationship between the prophets of Yahweh and the kings of Israel and Judah in the preexilic period was not as simple as some biblical texts might lead us to believe.

Exilic Prophets

With the coming of the Exile, the biblical depiction of the prophets undergoes a striking change. The narrative books say nothing about prophets during the Exile, but the prophetic books include sayings from several prophets who lived during this period (chapter 34). With no more kings to serve as their foils, the exilic prophets addressed their message to the elders of the exiled community and the people as a whole. Some of their statements recall the judgmental language used by the preexilic prophets against the leaders of the community and other prophets whose message differed from their own (Isaiah 44:24-26; Jeremiah 29: 8-9; 29:20-32; Ezekiel 13:1-23; 14:1-11; 34:1-31). More often, however, their words of judgment are directed against the foreign nations who are oppressing the people of Yahweh.

The message that they bring to their own people is primarily one of hope and encouragement. The exilic prophets assure their people that Yahweh has not forgotten them. Though he was angry with them for a time, he plans to return them to their land and bless them with peace and prosperity. Some of the prophets seem to envision a renewed Israel that has no need for kings, while others speak of Yahweh sending a new Davidic king who will rule with justice and equity (see Ezekiel 34:23-24; 37:15-28). In both cases the historical tension between prophets and kings has been replaced by the hope of a return to an idealized earlier period when the people lived

under divine rule without a king (the time of the Exodus or the judges) or when the king did what was right and did not need to be corrected by the prophets (the time of David).

Postexilic Prophets

When the story resumes in the postexilic period, the narrative books paint a picture of cooperation and respect between the prophets and the community's leaders. When the prophets Haggai and Zechariah call on the people to resume their rebuilding of the temple, the governor and the high priest act on their words, despite the fact that their Persian overlords had previously ordered them to stop (Ezra 5:1-2; 6:13-15; compare Haggai 1:1-15). This obedient response to the words of Yahweh causes the prophets to speak in glowing terms about the community's leaders and to promise Yahweh's blessings upon their actions (Haggai 2:1-5; 2:20-23; Zechariah 3:6-10; 4:1-14; 6:9-15; compare Nehemiah 6:6-7).

Yet there are still hints of trouble. Nehemiah prays for divine judgment against "the prophetess Noadiah and the rest of the prophets who wanted to make me afraid" (Nehemiah 6:14), and Zechariah mentions prophets who speak for other gods besides Yahweh (Zechariah 13:2-6). The book of Malachi and the collection that scholars call "Third Isaiah" (Isaiah 56–66; see chapter 35) criticize community leaders in language that recalls the words of the preexilic prophets (Isaiah 56:9-12; 66:6; Malachi 1:6—2:3; 2:8-9), and several passages accuse the populace of ignoring the words of the prophets as their ancestors had done in earlier times (Isaiah 57:4; 65:11-12; 66:4-5; Zechariah 1:1-6; 7:8-14). Clearly not everyone respected and followed the prophets of Yahweh in the postexilic period.

In summary, the biblical narratives and the prophetic books present a picture of the prophets that is more complex than it first appears. The people who compiled the Hebrew Bible clearly favored certain prophets over others, but they included enough references to the prophets whom they rejected to give us at least a modest sense of the diversity of the prophetic movement in ancient Palestine.

ASSESSING THE SOURCES

Despite the abundance of material in the Hebrew Bible concerning the prophets, scholars have questioned the reliability of certain aspects of the biblical depiction of the prophets. Several problems have given rise to these scholarly concerns.

1. *The questionable historicity of the narrative books.* Most of the stories involving prophets appear in the books of Samuel, Kings, and Chronicles. Discussions of the historicity of these stories cannot be separated from the ongoing debates over the historical reliability of

Fig. 31.4. This parchment fragment from the Dead Sea Scrolls contains several verses from an ancient copy of the book of Jeremiah.

the narrative books of the Hebrew Bible. Scholars who believe that the narratives are based on reliable materials tend to accept their depiction of the prophetic movement in ancient Palestine, even if they question some of the individual stories. Scholars who are more skeptical of the narratives regard much of the material about the prophets as the fictional creation of a later editor. Further problems arise from the manner in which the prophets are portrayed in the narrative books. Many of the stories show prophets predicting specific events in the future and even performing miracles. These features are largely absent from the books of the prophets. This gap has fueled doubts about the reliability of the stories, leading many scholars to view them as more legendary than historical.

2. *The editorial history of the prophetic books.* As we saw in chapter 4, the books of the prophets were compiled and edited into their present form long after the prophets are thought to have lived. Scholars have different ideas about how well the words and deeds of the prophets were preserved in the intervening years and how much freedom the editors used in preparing their books. Conservatives believe that everything in the books reflects the words and experiences of the prophets to whom they are attributed. Maximalists find evidence that some of the sayings of the prophets were updated for later audiences and materials from later periods were included in the collections, but they accept the bulk of the material as reliable. Minimalists insist that the sayings in the prophetic books have been heavily reworked or even created by later editors to reflect their own beliefs and circumstances. Some question whether the books tell us much at all about the prophets whose names are associated with the books. How one answers these questions will have a profound impact on the way one views the history of the prophetic movement as well as the lives and messages of individual prophets.

Fig. 31.5. (top) An artist's rendition of the famous "night journey" in which the Muslim prophet Muhammad is said to have been escorted to heaven by angels to meet with Allah; (bottom) Joseph Smith, founder of the Church of Jesus Christ of Latter-Day Saints, began his ministry as a prophet after receiving a vision in which he talked with God the Father and his son Jesus Christ.

3. *The selectivity of the biblical materials.* The people who compiled the prophetic books into their present form were not simply historians seeking to preserve material from the past. They were people of faith who believed that these particular prophets had spoken a message that was relevant to their own generation. The decision about which sayings and stories would be compiled into a written collection and how those materials would be organized was made by these later editors, not by the prophets or their immediate followers. Prophets whose message was deemed irrelevant or incorrect were omitted from the collection, as were those who honored Yahweh as one among many gods and those who spoke for other deities. The editors were also limited to the materials that had survived until their day. Little is known about how the words of the prophets were preserved, but most were probably passed on by word of mouth for an extended period of time (see chapter 4). Along the way, some of the prophets' sayings could have been revised and others lost. Finally, careful study of the prophetic books has convinced most scholars that the editors felt free to change or even create materials to make the words of the prophets speak more immediately to their own day. Together these factors suggest that we should be careful about generalizing from the books of the prophets to the broader social and religious movement of which they were a part.

Despite these problems, most scholars believe that a judicious and critical reading of the biblical text can give us a fairly good idea of the nature and activities of prophets in ancient Palestine, including those aspects of the tradition that the editors rejected. Debates continue over how to counterbalance the editors' obvious preference for certain types of prophets over others and how to fill in those parts of the story that they neglected. Comparisons with similar figures from elsewhere in the ancient Near East are helpful for filling in the gaps, as are studies of prophets and shamans from other cultures. In the end, however, many questions remain unanswered.

EXERCISE 83

Read the following passages from the Hebrew Bible and make a list of the thoughts, feelings, and sensory experiences that the narrator associates with a direct encounter with Yahweh. Do you see any common features among the passages?

- Isaiah 6:1-13
- Jeremiah 1:1-19
- Ezekiel 1:1-14; 1:22—3:11
- Amos 7:1-9
- Isaiah 49:1-13
- Zechariah 4:1-14

THE RELIGIOUS EXPERIENCE OF THE PROPHETS

The people known as prophets in the Hebrew Bible are both similar to and different from the intermediaries that have been observed in other cultures. The most obvious similarity is that they, like other intermediaries, claim to have direct personal experiences with the supernatural world in which they receive messages that they feel compelled to deliver to their people. The Hebrew Bible says little about the nature or content of these experiences. Several of the prophetic books describe or refer to an initial "calling" experience in which the prophet encounters the awesome presence of Yahweh and is commissioned to deliver messages to his people. Some of the books also include brief descriptions of subsequent experiences of the divine presence. Most of the time, however, the prophet's interaction with the deity is hidden behind the recurring phrase, "Thus says Yahweh." With these words the prophet asserts a divine origin for the message while giving few clues about how it might have originated.

Whether we should envision the prophets arriving at their messages through a rational process of observation and reflection or an ecstatic experience is impossible to say. Both the narrative books and the prophetic books speak of visions as a means of divine communication, though it is unclear what these visions entailed or whether they were common or extraordinary experiences. Many scholars have suggested that the texts are in fact describing dreams, since dreams were regarded as channels of divine communication throughout the ancient Near East and elsewhere around the world. Several passages state explicitly that Yahweh spoke to prophets at night or in dreams (Numbers 12:6-8; 1 Samuel 3:2-18; 2 Samuel 7:4-17; 1 Kings 19:9-18; Jeremiah 24:25-32; Zechariah 1:7-8; compare Isaiah 29:7: "like a dream, a vision of the night"), though there are also verses in which the prophet is depicted as awake and alert during the visionary experience (Numbers 22:22-35; 24:1-9; 2 Kings 6:15-17; Ezekiel 8:1-4).

More common than visions are auditory images. The frequency of expressions like "thus says Yahweh" and "the word of Yahweh came to [prophet's name]" suggests that audition (that is, the hearing of voices) was the most common mode of revelation among the prophets whose sayings are preserved in the Hebrew Bible. Whether this should be taken as implying that the prophets experienced audible sounds from outside their own consciousness is unclear. Similar language is used in prescientific cultures to describe what psychologists would regard as the reflective faculties of the human mind. The commonness of both visionary and auditory experiences among intermediaries in different cultures suggests that both types of experiences have psychological roots.

For the most part the Hebrew Bible suggests that the word of Yahweh came to the prophets without any effort on their part. A few passages even speak of the prophet being forced by the deity to proclaim a message against his will (Jeremiah 20:7-9; Amos 3:7-8; 7:14-15). Little is said about the Yahwistic prophets engaging in ritualized

Fig. 31.6. This eighth-century B.C.E. column from Syria tells how king Zakkur of Hamath received a message from his seers confirming that Baal would protect him from invading armies.

actions to generate encounters with the divine, as we see with intermediaries in other cultures. Here and there a prophet will deliver a message from Yahweh in response to a person's prayers, but there is no sign that the prophet did anything to elicit the message (2 Kings 20:1-7; 22:11-20; 2 Chronicles 20:5-17; Isaiah 37:14-35; 38:1-6; Jeremiah 21:1-7; 32:16-35; 37:3-10), apart from a single passage that mentions the use of music (2 Kings 3:13-19; compare 1 Samuel 10:5-6). Overall, the Hebrew Bible gives the impression that the prophets had a hotline to Yahweh that allowed them to speak for the deity whenever guidance was needed. By contrast, those whom the editors regarded as false prophets are shown using a variety of techniques to evoke the presence of the deity, including sacrifices (Numbers 24:1-10; 24:14-25), cutting themselves (1 Kings 18:28-29), and divination (Deuteronomy 13:1-5; Jeremiah 14:14; Ezekiel 12:24; 13:6-9; 13:23).

Whether this difference reflects a genuine historical distinction is hard to judge. It is certainly possible that the prophets whom the biblical editors regarded as true used different techniques than those whom they derided as false. The sharpness of the contrast, however, suggests that the distinction is a literary contrast created by the editors. Perhaps they decided to suppress what they knew about the activities of the prophets whom they favored because such activities would have been unacceptable in their own day. Or perhaps they knew little about what their ancient prophetic heroes had done and simply presumed that the true prophets must have been fundamentally different from those whom they considered false. Whatever their thinking, it seems clear that the theological judgments of the biblical editors concerning which prophets were true and which were false influenced the way they portrayed the prophets' activities.

THE SOCIAL CONTEXT OF THE PROPHETS

Prophets in ancient Palestine came from all walks of life. Unlike the priesthood, which was restricted to males, women could serve as prophets (Exodus 15:20-21; Judges 4:4-7; 2 Kings 22:14-20; Nehemiah 6:14; Isaiah 8:3; Ezekiel 13:17-23), though most of the prophets named in the Hebrew Bible are men. Some, like Jeremiah and Zechariah, were members of priestly families, while others, like Amos, labored at ordinary occupations and had no formal ties to the religious establishment. Some grew up in towns or cities and moved among the urban elites, while others came from rural areas and viewed the world through the eyes of farmers and peasants. Some had a good education, while others were probably illiterate. Some were married and had families, while others remained single throughout their lives.

Prophets also differed in the way they related to the religious and political systems of their day. Some spoke in the name of Yahweh alone, while others were devoted to different deities. Some served at local or regional shrines, where ordinary people would come and request a word from Yahweh. Others moved from place to place, proclaiming their message to anyone who would listen. Some spent their entire lives as prophets, while others prophesied for a time and then returned to their former occupations. Some worked in groups with other prophets, while others labored alone. Some operated at the highest levels of society, even serving as advisors to kings, while others lived far outside the corridors of power. Some spoke in favor of the status quo, while others issued words of judgment against the ruling elites.

Given all of this diversity, it should come as no surprise that the Hebrew Bible speaks repeatedly of tensions between prophets and rulers as well as conflicts among the prophets themselves. Several passages in the Hebrew Bible suggest that the kings of Israel and Judah maintained a stable of court prophets whom they consulted when they needed guidance on matters of state, particularly decisions about war and peace. In the pages of the Hebrew Bible, these prophets invariably claim to speak in the name of Yahweh. Even King Ahab, whose wife is said to have fed nine hundred prophets of Baal and Asherah at her own table (1 Kings 18:19), is shown consulting only Yahwistic prophets. Since they were supported by the king, these prophets clearly felt pressured to promise divine blessings upon whatever course of action the king wished to pursue. With few exceptions, the Hebrew Bible derides these prophets as false prophets who speak

Fig. 31.7. (top) Palma Giovane, *The Prophet Nathan Admonishes King David*; (bottom) the prophet Elijah confronts king Ahab of Israel.

Somewhat different are the individual prophets who served as personal advisors to the kings. The few who are mentioned by name in the Hebrew Bible are depicted in a positive light, though their numbers are too small to make any firm judgments about their activities. Following the reign of David, the only person who clearly fits into this category is Isaiah, who advised King Hezekiah in the eighth century B.C.E. As portrayed in the Hebrew Bible, these prophets were able to maintain a degree of independence from the kings, supporting them when they were acting properly but also challenging them when they did wrong. Their independence is attributed to their openness to the word of Yahweh, who gives them special messages for the kings as the need arises. The biblical image of these individuals is clearly idealized, but it seems likely that people like them played an important role in the royal administration of Israel and Judah, whether as prophets of Yahweh or other deities.

The Hebrew Bible also speaks of prophets who were not part of the king's court, but who were consulted by the kings in times of uncertainty or crisis. Two individuals who clearly fit this category are Elisha (ninth century B.C.E.) and Jeremiah (sixth century B.C.E.). Neither served as a close personal advisor to the king, since the kings who ruled during their days are depicted as less than faithful servants of Yahweh. Yet both seem to have been respected by their rulers as spokesmen for Yahweh, though in Jeremiah's case the content of his message (the imminent victory of the Babylonians over Judah) repeatedly aroused the king's displeasure. Several other prophets are mentioned briefly when one of the kings turns to them for guidance, including Ahijah (1 Kings 14:1-18), Micaiah (1 Kings 22:5-28), and Huldah (2 Kings 22:14-20). All of the prophets in this category are depicted as faithful servants of Yahweh who bring valid messages to the kings, though their words are not always followed. Why a king should have wanted to consult one of these prophets rather than (or in addition to) his court prophets is unclear, though in a couple of stories the text implies that the king had doubts about the words of the court prophets (1 Kings 22:1-28; 2 Kings 3:1-20). How often such outside consultations might have occurred is impossible to say.

Even further removed from the corridors of power are prophets who criticized and challenged the ruling elites.

what the king wants to hear rather than declaring the true word of Yahweh.

The narrative books tell several stories of prophets who approach one of the kings of Israel or Judah unbidden and pronounce a word of judgment in the name of Yahweh (1 Kings 13:1-10; 16:1-4; 18:17-18; 20:35-43; 21:17-24). The books of the prophets likewise include many sayings that condemn rulers either directly to their face (Isaiah 5:8-24; 10:1-4; 22:15-25; Jeremiah 22:1-17; 23:1-4; 34:1-7; Ezekiel 34:1-10; Amos 4:1-4; 6:1-7; Micah 3:1-12; Haggai 1:1-11) or indirectly in speeches addressed to the common people (Isaiah 1:21-24; 3:1—4:1; Micah 2:1-5; Zephaniah 3:1-6). All of the prophets who speak out against the ruling elites are cast in a positive light in the Hebrew Bible. Most likely there were other prophets who voiced similar concerns about leaders whom they viewed as too narrowly Yahwistic, but their words have not survived. The decision to collect and preserve the sayings of some prophets and not others implies that the elites who created these books shared their critical view of the behavior of the elites, whether they lived close to the prophet's lifetime or much later (during or after the Exile).

Finally, there were prophets who had little or no contact with the royal house. As with the other categories, there were surely more of this type than are named in the Hebrew Bible, since only prophets who attracted the attention of the literate elites had a chance of having their names or sayings enshrined in writing. Some of these prophets were associated with local shrines, where they focused on the needs of the people who came to see them and said little about the problems of the nation. Some may have been peasants who lived among the illiterate masses, where they escaped the attention of the elites. Some spoke in the name of deities other than Yahweh or offered messages that were discredited with the passing of time. In none of these cases would their words have been recorded and preserved by the people who produced the Hebrew Bible.

In short, the Hebrew Bible gives us a picture of the prophetic movement that has been filtered through the lens of a particular Yahwistic viewpoint. Whether this makes it historically or theologically inaccurate is a matter of judgment. The important point to keep in mind is that when we are reading the stories or sayings of the prophets, we are only getting one side of the story.

EXERCISE 84

Read the following passages and summarize what each one says about the social position and role of the prophet, include the prophet's relations with people who hold positions of leadership.

- 1 Kings 1:28-40
- 1 Kings 21:17-29
- 2 Kings 3:4-20
- Jeremiah 37:11-21
- Amos 7:10-17
- Micah 3:1-12
- Haggai 1:1-15
- Malachi 1:6—2:9

TRUE AND FALSE PROPHETS

In a culture that has one principal intermediary, such as a shaman or medicine man in a tribal community, people are taught to honor and trust the intermediary's words. While some individuals might have doubts about a particular pronouncement, serious questioning arises only in times of extreme crisis or when the intermediary's message threatens those who hold political power within the group.

In ancient Palestine, by contrast, there were numerous prophets who claimed to be speaking for various gods, including many who served as prophets of Yahweh. In addition to those mentioned earlier, the narrative books refer several times to bands of Yahwistic prophets who seem to have lived, traveled, and worked together, sometimes at regional shrines. Prophetic groups are associated with the towns of Gibeah (1 Samuel 10:5-13), Naioth (19:20-24), Bethel (2 Kings 2:3), Jericho (2 Kings 2:5; note that this band included more than fifty prophets, v. 7), and Gilgal (2 Kings 4:38), as well as "the hill country of Ephraim" (2 Kings 5:22) and various unidentified locations (1 Kings 20:35; 2 Kings 4:1; 9:1). The prophetic books also contain several verses that seem to refer to a similar phenomenon (Isaiah 8:16-18; Amos 2:11; 7:14; Zechariah 7:1-3).

With so many people claiming to be able to speak for the gods, including many who were devoted to Yahweh, the question of which prophet to consult and whom to believe must have been continually at the surface. At any rate that is impression that one gets from reading the Hebrew Bible. Again and again we hear of disputes among people who were regarded as prophets, with each side disparaging the other as false prophets who were speaking lies concocted out of their own minds. Even the kings appear unsure whom to trust on occasion.

So how does one decide which of several competing intermediaries is in fact speaking for the deity? The question rarely arises today in the same form, since most people (including religious believers) tend to be skeptical of anyone who claims to be hearing messages from God. Yet contemporary believers face similar problems when they hear religious or political leaders offering different ideas about how their sacred texts and traditions should be applied to current issues like war, gay rights, or abortion. Often those who hold opposing positions cannot even agree on the criteria that should be used to settle the matter. The situation was no different in ancient Palestine.

The narrative and prophetic books offer several criteria for distinguishing a true prophet from a false one. The frequency with which these criteria are cited in the books of the preexilic prophets suggests that at least some Yahwists were grappling with this problem from an early period, though it is possible that some of these references are later additions that reflect the viewpoint of the Exile. At any rate, the people who edited the Hebrew Bible accepted these criteria as valid. We can assume that those who opposed the biblical prophets had their own criteria for accepting some prophets and rejecting others, but we hear almost nothing about their point of view.

1. *Devotion to Yahweh.* While some of the biblical prophets acknowledge the existence of other gods, they invariably insist that the people of Israel and Judah should serve Yahweh alone. Not once do we hear a positive word about any other deity; some of the later prophets even mock those who worship other gods (Isaiah 40:19-20; 41:21-24; 44:9-20; Jeremiah 2:9-13; 10:1-16; Ezekiel 16:15-22; Habakkuk 2:18-20). According to the Hebrew Bible, individuals who speak in the name of other deities are by definition false prophets whose words should be ignored (Deuteronomy 13:1-5; 18:20; Jeremiah 2:8; 2:26-28; 23:13).

Behind this criterion lies the presumption that Yahweh should be the sole guide and authority for Israel and Judah. This does not mean that any prophet who speaks in the name of Yahweh must be heeded, but it does eliminate all non-Yahwistic prophets as possible sources of guidance. Even Yahwistic prophets are accused of spreading lies when they disagree with the prophets whose words are included in the Hebrew Bible (Isaiah 9:13-16; Jeremiah 14:13-16; 23:35-42; Ezekiel 22:28; Zechariah 13:2-3), so it is not surprising to see non-Yahwistic prophets being rejected without a hearing. Obviously this negative judgment would not have been shared by those who prophesied in the name of other gods.

2. *Accurate predictions.* Several of the later biblical prophets insist that true prophets must be able to make accurate predictions about the future, particularly the future of the nation (for example, Isaiah 44:7-8; compare Deuteronomy 18:21-22). The central question that divides the preexilic prophets is whether Yahweh means to protect his people from the looming threat of invaders from the north or whether he intends to send plagues and foreign armies to punish them (Jeremiah 5:12-15; 14:13-18; 23:16-22; Ezekiel 13:8-16). From the perspective of the people who compiled the prophets' sayings, the conquest of Israel by the Assyrians and Judah by the Babylonians stands as unequivocal proof regarding which prophets were in fact speaking for Yahweh (2 Kings 17:13-23; 2 Chronicles 36:15-21; Jeremiah 29:16-19; 44:1-6; Ezekiel 33:27-33; Zechariah 1:2-6; 7:8-14). Similar disputes arose during the Exile over when and how the people would be allowed to return to their land (Jeremiah 27:16-22; 28:1-18; 29:8-14; Isaiah 44:24-28; 46:8-11). The postexilic prophets also made predictions about the future of their nation, though the text says nothing about prophetic voices that opposed them (Haggai 2:7-9; 2:20-23; Zechariah 8:11-15; 9:9-17; 14:1-21; Malachi 4:1-6).

After the Exile this criterion became problematic, since many of the predictions that had been made by the preexilic and exilic prophets about the glorious conditions that would prevail when Yahweh restored his people to their land did not come to pass. Chief among these failures were the absence of a Davidic king and the continuation of foreign rule under the Persians. Rather than admitting that the earlier prophets might have been wrong—a decision that would have compromised one of their chief criteria for identifying true prophets—the postexilic prophets and religious leaders preferred to postpone the fulfillment of their words into the future and to make them contingent on Israel's faithful conduct (see chapter 35).

3. *Moral critique.* Here and there in the books of the prophets we find verses that insist that true prophets will always challenge the moral and religious failings of their people (for example, Ezekiel 2:3-5; Micah 5:8). According to this criterion, prophets who promise only divine blessings and comfort are not speaking for Yahweh. The standard by which the people's behavior is judged to be right or wrong is never clearly identified, but the problems mentioned by the prophets are consistent with what we find in many of the laws of Torah. Scholars disagree about whether the prophets might have been familiar with an early version of the Torah, since the Hebrew word *torah*, which appears fairly often in the books of the prophets, can also mean "instruction" in a more general sense. Nonetheless, it is difficult to avoid the impression that the editors of the Hebrew Bible meant to depict the prophets as defenders of Israel's covenant with Yahweh, including the laws of Torah.

This criterion is closely related to the previous one, since the biblical prophets consistently point to their people's failure to obey Yahweh as the chief reason for their predictions of impending doom. Again and again they criticize the people of Israel and Judah for their refusal to listen to the prophets whom Yahweh has sent to correct them and warn them of coming judgment (Jeremiah 7:22-26; 29:17-19; 35:15-17). Instead, they follow false prophets who overlook their faults while promising peace and prosperity (Jeremiah 23:16-17; Ezekiel 22:23-28; Micah 3:9-12; compare Lamentations 2:14). This criterion of judgment relates primarily to the preexilic prophets, since the message of the exilic and postexilic prophets in the Hebrew Bible is predominantly positive and comforting rather than challenging (see chapters 34–35). Yet their message is not devoid of moral criticism, a fact that presumably set them apart from those labeled *false prophets.*

4. *Righteous conduct.* Several times the biblical prophets criticize the personal behavior of those whom they see as false spokesmen for Yahweh. The presumption seems to be that a person who does not live according to Yahweh's standards cannot possibly be speaking for Yahweh. Prophets are criticized for drunkenness (Isaiah 28:7-8), adultery (Jeremiah 23:14; 29:21-23), greed (Jeremiah 6:13; 8:10), favoring the wicked over the righteous (Jeremiah 23:14; Ezekiel 13:22), and generally living sinful and evil lives (Jeremiah 23:11; Zephaniah 3:4; compare Lamentations 4:13). One passage even accuses them of predicting good outcomes when they are paid well and bad results when they are not (Micah 3:5-8).

Since we see these people only through the jaundiced eyes of their opponents, it is hard to know how seriously to take these statements. The accusations imply that the false prophets have deviated from a widely accepted code of conduct, but this claim is undermined by the fact that there was no universally acknowledged law code in the preexilic period. Many of the criticisms are so broad as to be useless, though some are concrete enough to suggest a factual basis. In the end, the criticisms are significant only if one accepts the assertion that there is a relation between a prophet's behavior and the validity of the message that is pronounced. The opposing side could just as easily argue that what matters is not the prophet's conduct but the ability to access the supernatural realm. In short, this criterion would be useful only to people who shared the particular set of Yahwistic moral values that it presumes to be true. Others would simply reject it as inappropriate or irrelevant.

5. *Influence with the deity.* Less obvious but equally important is the belief that a true prophet should be able to influence the gods to act on behalf of those who request their help. Several passages in the narrative books show "good" prophets praying to Yahweh and achieving immediate results, as when Elijah calls on Yahweh to send fire from heaven to burn up the sacrifices that he has laid out on an altar (1 Kings 18:36-39) or when Isaiah asks Yahweh to reverse the movement of a shadow in order to prove to King Hezekiah that his word can be trusted (2 Kings 20:8-11). Similar ideas are found in the prophetic books, as when Jeremiah challenges a group of false prophets to prove their worth by convincing Yahweh to turn aside the coming exile (Jeremiah 27:16-18) or when King Zedekiah asks Jeremiah to pray for a similar outcome

Fig. 31.8. Johann Heinrich Schoenfeld, *The Prophet Elijah Confounds the Priests of Baal*

agenda of the stories raises serious doubts about their historical value, as does the presence of the supernatural in the accounts. The fact that intermediaries in many cultures are credited with similar mysterious powers should caution us against dismissing these stories out of hand, but most contemporary scholars would regard such accounts as legendary.

In the final analysis, all such efforts to distinguish between true and false prophets are entirely subjective, reflecting the personal opinions of the people who are making the judgment. People who followed other gods or who adhered to a different version of Yahwism would have used other criteria and come to different conclusions. There is simply no way to determine with certainty the truth or falsehood of a person's claim to be speaking for God. So why does the Hebrew Bible use these criteria and not others? Because they agree with the beliefs, values, and experiences of the people who collected and edited the stories and sayings of the prophets. In the eyes of these people, Yahweh is the supreme god who established a covenant with Israel that requires loyalty and obedience on the part of his people. Those who are devoted to this covenant, as reflected above all in the laws of Torah, will enjoy the blessings of the deity, while those who disregard or ignore the covenant will be punished. Prophets who adhere to this message are speaking for Yahweh, while those who do not are proclaiming lies.

In the end, it was the experience of the Exile that demonstrated to many people which prophets were speaking for Yahweh. Prior to the Exile, according to the Hebrew Bible, the prophets were deeply divided over which course the nation should pursue in relation to the surrounding nations. Some lobbied for an alliance with Egypt to resist the Babylonian threat, others called for submission to the Babylonians, and still others insisted

(Jeremiah 37:3; compare 7:16-20; 11:14). The narrative books also contain numerous stories of the prophets Elijah and Elisha performing miracles that demonstrate their close ties to Yahweh (1 Kings 17—2 Kings 6), though such powers are rarely attributed to other prophets. For the most part, the biblical prophets do nothing more unusual than predict events that will happen in the future (for example, Isaiah 38:14-35; Jeremiah 28:12-17; Amos 7:14-17).

Behind these passages lies the assumption that Yahweh is committed to answer prayers and work miracles on behalf of his true prophets, while false prophets can perform no such works of power, whether they claim to be speaking for Yahweh or some other god. Not surprisingly, no one identified as a false prophet is ever shown performing a miracle or motivating a god to act in the Hebrew Bible, unless we count the Pharaoh's magicians in the Exodus story (Exodus 7:8-13; 7:20-22; 8:5-7). While it is possible that this reflects a genuine difference in the abilities of the prophets, the clear theological on resistance to both powers. The crushing defeat of Judah by the Babylonians, following the earlier conquest of Israel by the Assyrians, was seen by many people as a vindication of those prophets who had predicted exactly this outcome. As they saw it, this was not an ordinary military defeat; it was Yahweh's way of punishing his people for violating his covenant and refusing to listen to the prophets whom he had sent to warn them of his displeasure.

How then were they to regain the blessing of Yahweh? An obvious answer was to renew their commitment to his covenant and to follow the words and examples of the prophets whom he had sent—and would continue to send—to guide them in the right path. To do this, they had to determine which prophets had in fact been speaking for Yahweh and then collect their sayings into a format that could be preserved, taught, and studied in the future. Out of this process came the earliest books of the prophets. Other books were added to the collection as new prophets arrived bringing messages that were consistent with the central themes of the earlier prophets. The collection was revised and edited from time to time to keep the prophets' messages current.

By the third or second century B.C.E., the religious leadership had concluded that the books of the prophets were too sacred for further revision; in modern terms, the canon of the prophets was closed. Implicit in this decision was the judgment that the era of the prophets was over; Yahweh now spoke primarily through a book. Not all shared this opinion, however, and many people continued to regard popular Jewish preachers like John the Baptizer and Jesus of Nazareth as prophets. Here again we see that the decision concerning who is and is not a true prophet of Yahweh is in the eye of the beholder.

CONCLUSION

The prophets of ancient Palestine often appear strange to modern readers, but they are far from unique. Similar intermediary figures can be seen in many cultures both past and present. What distinguishes intermediaries from other people is their ability to interact safely with the awesome powers of the supernatural realm and to channel the benefits of that realm to others. Sometimes this includes bringing messages to humans about how they should live in order to avoid hardship and enjoy prosperity. Whether these messages are taken seriously depends on the status of the speaker and the content of the message.

The prophets whose stories and sayings appear in the Hebrew Bible were part of a broader movement that included many people who were labeled false prophets by the people who compiled the collection. Some of those who were rejected spoke in the name of deities other than Yahweh, while others prophesied on behalf of Yahweh but gave messages that conflicted with the words of the prophets whom the editors saw as true prophets of Yahweh. The Hebrew Bible tells us very little about the actions or messages of these other prophets.

Prophets came from a variety of social backgrounds and worked at all levels of society, from the smaller towns and villages to the regional shrines to the courts of the kings. Some carried out their missions alone, while others worked in groups or had followers who traveled with them. Many scholars believe that it was these groups of followers who preserved the sayings and stories of the prophets, though others doubt this explanation. No one, however, doubts the importance of prophets to the religious life of the people of ancient Palestine, nor their central role in the Hebrew Bible.

EXERCISE 85

Read the following passages, then choose one of them and summarize (a) the message of those labeled false prophets, and (b) the message of the true prophet of Yahweh. What does the passage say about how one can tell when a prophet is or is not speaking for Yahweh?

• 1 Kings 22:1-40
• Jeremiah 28:1-17
• Ezekiel 13:1-23

Fig. 32.1. Michelangelo's painting of the prophet Isaiah from the ceiling of the Sistine Chapel in the Vatican.

The Early Preexilic Prophets

Hear the word of the LORD, O people of Israel; for the LORD has an indictment against the inhabitants of the land. There is no faithfulness or loyalty, and no knowledge of God in the land. Swearing, lying, and murder, and stealing and adultery break out; bloodshed follows bloodshed. Therefore the land mourns, and all who live in it languish; together with the wild animals and the birds of the air, even the fish of the sea are perishing. (Hosea 4:1-3)

Alas for those who lie on beds of ivory, and lounge on their couches, and eat lambs from the flock, and calves from the stall; who sing idle songs to the sound of the harp, and like David improvise on instruments of music; who drink wine from bowls, and anoint themselves with the finest oils, but are not grieved over the ruin of Joseph! Therefore they shall now be the first to go into exile, and the revelry of the loungers shall pass away. (Amos 6:4-7)

Ah, you who make iniquitous decrees, who write oppressive statutes, to turn aside the needy from justice and to rob the poor of my people of their right, that widows may be your spoil, and that you may make the orphans your prey! What will you do on the day of punishment, in the calamity that will come from far away? To whom will you flee for help, and where will you leave your wealth, so as not to crouch among the prisoners or fall among the slain? For all this his anger has not turned away; his hand is stretched out still. (Isaiah 10:1-4)

The prophets whose words were included in the prophetic books of the Hebrew Bible span a period of some four hundred years, from the eighth century B.C.E. through the fourth century B.C.E. If we include the prophets whose stories are told in the narrative books, the era of the prophets reaches seven hundred years, from the time of Samuel to the last of the canonical prophets. Adding the second century B.C.E. book of Daniel to the list (included in the Writings in the Hebrew Bible but listed among the Prophets in Christian Bibles) extends the period to nine hundred years. Wherever we draw the line, it seems clear that prophets played an important role in the religious history of Palestine during much of the first millennium B.C.E.

As we noted earlier, historical scholars divide the biblical prophets into three broad groups according to the time when they are reported to have lived: (a) preexilic prophets, whose sayings are associated with the era of the monarchy (to be examined in chapters 32 and 33); (b) exilic prophets, who preached during the period of Babylonian rule (chapter 34); and (c) postexilic prophets, who spoke to the people of Judah after they returned from Babylonia (chapters 35 and 36). This three-part division, while oversimplified, is a useful tool for analyzing the books of the prophets, since there are many similarities in the circumstances and messages of the prophets within each of these three periods. The next five chapters will examine the common features of the prophets in each era and provide a cursory introduction to each prophet's work. For the most part the discussion will center on those elements of each book that scholars believe are authentic and ignore later editorial additions.

THE PREEXILIC PROPHETS

If we count the Hebrew book of "The Twelve" as twelve different books, as in Christian Bibles, the Hebrew Bible contains fifteen books that are attributed in some way to Hebrew prophets. In addition, all but the most conservative scholars believe that the book of Isaiah contains the sayings of at least three different prophets, and many would allocate the latter chapters of the book of Zechariah to a later prophet as well. This yields a total of eighteen different prophets whose sayings are included in the Hebrew Bible. Some scholars have sought to expand this number by attributing portions of other prophetic books to later prophets, but most have concluded that these books simply passed through more editorial activity.

As a rule, the books of the prophets begin with an introductory verse that indicates when and by whom the ancient editors believed that the words in the book had been spoken. For example, the book of Isaiah begins, "The vision of Isaiah son of Amoz, which he saw concerning Judah and Jerusalem in the days of Uzziah, Jotham, Ahaz, and Hezekiah, kings of Judah" (Isaiah 1:1). Where the editors got their data is unclear, but the dates that they assign to the prophets (that is, the kings with whom they associate each book) are generally consistent with the content of the books. In some cases, all that is given is the name of the prophet; nothing is said about when he lived. For example, the book of Joel begins, "The word of the Lord that came to Joel son of Pethuel" (Joel 1:1), and the introduction to the book of Habakkuk says simply, "The oracle that the prophet Habakkuk saw" (Habakkuk 1:1). Some of these undated books can be dated on the basis of their content—Habakkuk, for example, speaks about the behavior of the Babylonian armies, indicating that he prophesied in the late seventh century B.C.E. A few books, however, are notoriously difficult to date, including Joel, Jonah, and to a lesser extent, Obadiah and Malachi. The reasons for assigning these books to

one period or another will be stated when the books are introduced.

The books that are associated with the preexilic era cluster around two distinct periods, the latter half of the eighth century B.C.E. and the late seventh to early sixth century B.C.E. Both are periods of political anxiety—the first coincides with the rise of the Assyrian empire in the years prior to the conquest of Israel, while the second is dominated by the growing Babylonian threat that eventually led to the devastation of Judah. The first group, which includes the prophets Amos, Hosea, Isaiah, and Micah, will be discussed in the present chapter, along with the stories of Elijah and Elisha, whom the narrative books place a century earlier (ninth century B.C.E.). The second group, which comprises Zephaniah, Nahum, Habakkuk, Jeremiah, and Ezekiel, will be examined in chapter 33.

EXERCISE 86

Read 1 Kings 17:1—19:21 and 2 Kings 2:1—4:37. How would you describe the prophets Elijah and Elisha based on these two passages? In what ways do they resemble one another? In what ways do they differ?

ELIJAH AND ELISHA

The Hebrew Bible contains no collections of sayings attributed to the prophets Elijah and Elisha, but they are included here because of the extensive attention that they receive in the narrative books. Other prophets appear at various points in the books of Samuel and Kings, but none receives even remotely the amount of space that is given to these two men. Stories about Elijah fill six chapters of the book of Kings (1 Kings 17:1—19:21; 21:1-29; 2 Kings 1:1—2:12), while Elisha plays a leading role in seven chapters of the same book (2 Kings 2:1—8:15) and a lesser role in three others (1 Kings 19:19-21; 2 Kings 9:1-37; 13:14-21). As a result, the events of the period when they are reported to have lived (ninth century B.C.E.) are narrated in more detail than any other period from the time of David and Solomon to the conquest of Judah by the Babylonians. Apparently the people who compiled this narrative thought that the ninth century B.C.E. was pivotal for understanding what eventually happened to Israel and Judah. The prophets Elijah and Elisha are the heroes of their story.

Elijah

At one level, the story of Elijah is similar to many other stories in the Hebrew Bible that pit a faithful prophet of Yahweh against an evil ruler who refuses to heed his message. The story thus epitomizes one of the central themes of the book of Kings, namely, that the people of Israel and Judah were sent into exile because their rulers violated the covenant of Yahweh and rejected the messengers whom he sent to bring them back to the true way.

At a deeper level, the story aims to show the supremacy of Yahweh over Baal, the storm god who served as leader of the Canaanite pantheon of gods. This is especially apparent in the story of the contest between Elijah and the prophets of Baal, where it is Yahweh, not Baal, who sends lightning from the sky to consume the sacrifices that had been spread upon the altar on Mt. Carmel. The same theme can be seen in subtler form in the story of the drought that frames this episode: it is Yahweh, not Baal, who decides when it will rain and when it will not. Later, when one of the kings sends messengers to a shrine of Baal to ask if he will recover from a sickness, Elijah intercepts them and pronounces a word of judgment from Yahweh instead (2 Kings 1:1-18). In every case the story underlines the futility of serving any god but Yahweh, whether the alternative is Baal (if the story was known prior to the Exile), the gods of Mesopotamia (if directed toward the exiles living in Babylonia), or other deities.

At a still deeper level, the story warns against the dangers posed by too much intermixing with foreigners. The immediate enemy of Elijah in these chapters is not King Ahab but his wife, Queen Jezebel, a Phoenician princess. Instead of becoming a follower of Yahweh when she marries the king of Israel, Jezebel leads Ahab into the service of Baal, the Canaanite equivalent of her ancestral god Melqart (1 Kings 16:31-33). Later she attempts to stamp out Yahwism and establish Baal as the chief god of Israel (1 Kings 18:3-4; 19:10). Along the way, she arranges for

Fig. 32.2. (top) Lucas Cranach the Younger, *Elijah and the Priests of Baal*; (bottom) Juan de Valdés Leal, *The Chariot of Elijah*

an Israelite man to be framed and executed so that Ahab can take over his vineyard to use as a vegetable garden (1 Kings 21:1-26). The fact that Jezebel is a foreigner is no accident; numerous passages from all parts of the Hebrew Bible emphasize the religious threat posed by foreigners and their gods and promise divine retribution to those who embrace their ways (Deuteronomy 7:1-6; 12:29—13:18; 1 Kings 11:1-13; Ezra 9:1—10:17; Isaiah 2:5-22; Zephaniah 1:7-8; Malachi 2:11-12). As the homegrown champion of Yahweh, Elijah stands as the supreme model for those who are tempted to mix too closely with foreigners, whether before, during, or after the Babylonian Exile.

Elisha

Though chosen by Yahweh to be Elijah's servant and successor (1 Kings 18:15-21; 2 Kings 2:1-18), Elisha differs in many ways from his mentor. Elijah is a loner who at one point concludes that he is the only remaining prophet of Yahweh in Israel. Elisha, by contrast, is regularly accompanied by a group of prophets (2 Kings 2:1-18; 4:38-41; 6:1-7; 9:1-3). Elijah consistently opposes the rulers of Israel because of their devotion to Baal, causing King Ahab to label him "my enemy" (1 Kings 21:20) and Queen Jezebel to order his death (1 Kings 19:1-2). Elisha, on the other hand, never personally confronts any of the kings of Israel, even though they continue to be depicted as servants of

Fig. 32.3. Giorgio Vasari, *The Prophet Elisha*

Baal, and several times he uses his power to assist them in their wars (2 Kings 3:4-20; 6:8-23; 13:14-19; compare 5:1-14). Most of Elijah's supernatural deeds are related to his efforts to root out Baal worship from Israel. Elisha, however, performs the bulk of his miracles either to help other people (2 Kings 2:19-22; 4:1-37; 5:1-14) or to deal with minor problems like a poisoned pot of stew (2 Kings 4:38-41), a lost ax head (2 Kings 6:1-7), or a group of boys who were making fun of him (2 Kings 2:23-24).

Despite these differences, there are enough similarities between the two men to reveal the storyteller's view of the role and activities of a prophet. Both are radically devoted to Yahweh and opposed to the worship of other gods. Both receive regular messages from the deity, who repeatedly tells them what they should say and do. Both are courageous in proclaiming the words of Yahweh to people in authority, even when it could cost them their lives. Both are able to do amazing feats of supernatural power on their own volition, without in most cases appealing to Yahweh. Both are concerned about the needs and sufferings of ordinary people and willing to use their powers to assist them. And both are ultimately protected by the deity from harm.

The portrait of the ideal prophet that emerges from these stories is both similar to and different from what we encounter in the prophetic books. The similarities are fairly obvious: their unwavering devotion to Yahweh; their role as spokesmen for the deity; their concern for the poor and needy; their readiness to challenge the conduct of those in authority. The differences are less apparent. Where the prophetic books focus on the words that the prophets receive from Yahweh, the stories of Elijah and Elisha highlight their deeds. Only rarely do the prophetic books show their heroes doing anything that would qualify as miraculous. The role that Elijah and Elisha play in the political events of their day also finds few parallels in the prophetic books. The latter collection shows prophets speaking out against the authorities or occasionally offering them advice, but there is nothing like Elijah personally murdering the prophets of Baal (1 Kings 18:40) or Elisha inciting a member of the Syrian royal court (2 Kings 8:7-15) and later an Israelite general (2 Kings 9:1-10) to stage violent coups and set themselves up as kings. Similar deeds are attributed to other prophets in the narrative books, though nearly all are from the era prior to Elijah and Elisha (1 Samuel 9:15—10:24; 16:1-13; 2 Samuel 12:1-14; 1 Kings 1:11-31; 10:26-37).

What are we to make of these differences between the narrative books and the prophetic books? Conservative scholars have tried to explain them away by saying that the activities of the prophets changed over time, or that the prophets whose sayings are preserved in the Hebrew Bible actually performed deeds like those of Elijah and Elisha that were not recorded. Most scholars, however, have concluded that the picture of the prophets in the narrative books, particularly the stories of Elijah and Elisha, has been clouded to a greater or lesser degree by legend. As a result, scholars tend to focus more heavily on the prophetic books when seeking to understand the nature and activities of Yahwistic prophets in ancient Palestine.

AMOS

The earliest prophet whose sayings are recorded in the Hebrew Bible is Amos. Like his contemporary Hosea, Amos addressed the northern kingdom of Israel. All of the other prophets whom we know from the books of the prophets lived and preached in Judah, or in the case of some of the exilic prophets, in Babylonia.

The book of Amos offers little information about the man to whom the sayings are attributed. Unlike Hosea, Amos was a native of the southern kingdom (the town of Tekoa—Amos 1:1) who managed herds and cultivated sycamore trees for a living until he was called by Yahweh to leave his homeland and travel north to proclaim Yahweh's message to Israel (Amos 1:1; 7:14). Nothing further is said about this call experience, though a few passages indicate that Yahweh sometimes spoke to him in visions (Amos 7:1-9; 8:1-3; 9:1) and one verse suggests that he felt an inner compulsion to prophesy (Amos 3:8). Whether his status as an outsider affected people's willingness to listen to him is unclear, though it clearly bothered the authorities, who eventually ordered him to leave (Amos 7:10-13).

According to the introductory verse, Amos delivered his message around the middle of the eighth century B.C.E. At this time the kingdom of Israel was enjoying an era of peace and prosperity under a strong and capable king, Jeroboam II, whose armies had occupied substantial amounts of territory on the eastern side of the Jordan river and taken control of the major north-south trade route across the region (2 Kings 14:23-29). This act brought great wealth to Israel through increased trade and tax revenue. Most of this income went to the king and the wealthy elites, who used it to build luxurious villas filled with ornate furnishings, or else stored it away. From the standpoint of those who had benefited from the expansion, this was a great time to be alive.

EXERCISE 87

Read Amos 2:6-16; 5:10-17; 6:1-8; and 8:4—9:4. What does Amos say is wrong with Israelite society? What will happen to the people of Israel if they don't change their ways? Is there anything that they can do to avoid this fate?

The message that Amos brings to Israel in the name of Yahweh is addressed almost exclusively to the wealthy elites. According to Amos, the prevailing sense of prosperity is deceptive; closer examination reveals that Israelite society is sick to the core. At one level, the problem is economic: the rich are getting richer while the poor are getting poorer. Archaeological excavations of private homes and public buildings at Samaria and Megiddo support Amos's contention that the gap between rich and poor widened considerably during this period. According to Amos, the rich are living lives of luxury and ease while ignoring the poor and needy (4:1; 5:12; 6:1; 6:4-6). Worse yet, some of them are actually making money by abusing the poor (2:6-8; 3:10; 4:1; 5:11-12; 8:4; 8:6) and engaging in crooked business practices (8:5-6). Money is taking priority over justice as the wealthy bribe judges to rule in their favor (5:10; 5:12).

But these observations do not go to the heart of the problem; they are merely symptoms of a deeper spiritual sickness. As Amos sees it, the wealthy have lost sight of the social dimension of Israel's covenant relationship with Yahweh, reducing religion to the proper observance of public rituals. Amos acknowledges that the people whom he criticizes are faithful about bringing their sacrifices and offerings to the shrines at Bethel and Gilgal and celebrating Yahweh's festivals there (4:4-5; 5:21-23; compare 5:5; 8:10). Some may even have attributed their material prosperity to these activities, following a popular interpretation of Deuteronomic theology that viewed wealth and success as signs of divine favor. In this context, Amos's message would have sounded like the ravings of a madman. Like wealthy people in every era, the elites of Israel did not want to listen to anyone who challenged the way they made their living, especially if he came from another country (Judah). In fact, Amos was eventually ordered to stop preaching and leave the northern kingdom (2:10-12; 7:10-13).

Yet Amos persisted in his message despite this opposition. According to Amos, Yahweh is so disgusted with the conduct of the leaders of Israel that he can no longer

Fig. 32.4. (top) Assyrian armies attack the city of Lachish in Judah (701 B.C.E.) in this carved panel from the palace of the Assyrian king Sennacherib; (bottom) the excavated ruins of the city of Samaria, destroyed by the Assyrians in 722 B.C.E.

accept their sacrifices or attend their religious assemblies (5:21-23). If they continue in their present path, he will soon pour out upon them the same harsh punishments that he has been storing up for their pagan neighbors (1:3—2:5). Already he has tried to wake them up by sending famines, drought, and disease upon their land, but they refused to change their ways (4:6-11). Now he has no choice but to send foreign armies against them. These brutal invaders will wipe out their armies (2:13-16; 3:11; 5:3), tear down their expensive houses (3:15; 6:11), destroy their temples (3:14; 5:6; 7:9), slaughter their families (5:16-17; 6:9-10; 8:3; 9:1-3; 9:10), and put an end to their luxurious and carefree lifestyles (6:7). Those who survive the coming onslaught will be led away in disgrace into exile (4:2-3; 5:11; 5:27; 6:7; 7:11; 7:17; 9:4).

Fortunately, the situation is not yet hopeless, though it is rapidly approaching that point. Amos can still call on his audience to "seek good and not evil, that you may live" and hold out the possibility that "the Lord, the God of hosts, will be gracious to the remnant of Joseph" (5:14-15; compare 5:6). If they turn from their self-centered ways and devote themselves to creating a society that is just and fair to all, perhaps they can avoid the coming judgment (5:24). But Amos holds out little real hope for the people of Israel; he seems to know that they will not respond. The message of hope that ends the book (9:9-15) appears to be a later addition that reflects the circumstances and hopes of the Exile; it should not be credited to Amos.

Whether Amos lived to see the devastating invasion of the Assyrians in 722 B.C.E. is unclear. But the fact that his sayings were preserved through that disaster shows that at least some people in Israel saw this event as a fulfillment of Amos's prophecies and a vindication of his status as a prophet of Yahweh.

HOSEA

Like Amos, Hosea began his prophetic ministry to the northern kingdom of Israel around the middle of the eighth century B.C.E. The introductory verse indicates that Hosea's ministry lasted longer than that of Amos, continuing to around the time of the Assyrian invasion in 722 B.C.E. The proximity of the two prophets in time and location allows us to compare and contrast what each said about conditions in Israel around this time. As we shall see, Hosea saw the situation rather differently than Amos did.

EXERCISE 88

Read Hosea 1:1—3:5. Do you think this story tells about events that really happened to Hosea, or is it simply a metaphorical narrative about Yahweh and Israel? Give reasons to support your answer.

All that we know about Hosea's life comes from a rather cryptic and fragmentary story that fills chapters 1 and 3. Scholars disagree about whether this story is based on actual events or was created as a piece of allegorical fiction. The story tells of Hosea's marriage to an unfaithful woman, the birth and naming of his three children, his wife's apparent turn to either adultery or prostitution, and her eventual restoration to Hosea (unless chapter 3 speaks of a different woman). If the story is true, it might explain why Hosea uses so much marital imagery in his prophecies: his own experience served as a window for comprehending how Israel's conduct looked through Yahweh's eyes. If the story is fictional, we know nothing about Hosea as a person, though his strong focus on the activities of Israel's shrines and priesthood raises the possibility that he might have been a priest. If so, the symbolic value of his marriage to a woman deemed unclean would have been all the more poignant.

Whatever his personal story, the opening chapters of Hosea provide a fitting introduction to the major themes of his book. In chapter 2, Israel is depicted as a faithless wife and Yahweh as her wronged husband. Instead of being thankful for the good harvests and riches that Yahweh has showered upon her, Israel has given credit to the Canaanite god Baal and used Yahweh's gifts to worship him (2:8; compare 2:13; 2:17; 11:1). Yahweh is understandably jealous. His response is described in the disturbing imagery of domestic violence: Yahweh will cut off her food supplies, strip her naked, parade her before her lovers, destroy her property, and drive her into the desert,

where he will woo her back to him once again (2:9-23). Why any woman would consider returning to such an abusive husband is never explained. The reference to the desert recalls the story of the Exodus, which Hosea mentions again and again, often in romanticized terms (2:15; 9:10; 11:1; 12:9; 12:13; 13:4-5). Later he describes the coming exile as a return to Egypt from which Yahweh will lead them forth once again in a new exodus that will renew Israel's devotion to Yahweh (11:5-11).

EXERCISE 89

Read Hosea 4:1-14; 8:1-14; 10:1-8; 13:1-8. What does Hosea say is wrong with Israel? How does his picture compare with that of Amos?

When we turn to the passages where Hosea describes the problems of Israel in more literal terms, we get a different picture than we did from Amos. Not once does Hosea mention the social and economic injustices and abuse of the poor that stood at the heart of Amos's indictment. In fact, only one brief passage refers to wealth at all (12:7-8). In the few verses where Hosea criticizes the social conduct of the Israelites, he focuses on the behavior of individuals rather than systemic problems: violence, adultery, lying and abusive speech, drunkenness, and so on (4:2; 6:8-9; 7:1-7; 10:4; 11:12; 12:1). The only time he even comes close to the kind of social criticism that we witnessed in Amos is when he mocks Israel's kings for forming alliances with foreign nations like Egypt and Assyria or trusting in their own armies rather than relying on Yahweh for protection (5:13-14; 7:8-16; 8:9-10; 8:14; 10:13-15; 12:1).

The reason for Hosea's lack of attention to the social and economic problems of Israel is that his concern lies elsewhere. According to Hosea, the people of Israel have provoked Yahweh to anger by engaging in improper forms of worship. Part of the fault lies with their religious leaders, the priests and prophets, who according to Hosea have forgotten Yahweh's laws and failed to teach them to their people (4:4-10; 8:1; 8:12). Their contempt for Yahweh's words is evident from the fact that they have rejected the prophets whom Yahweh has sent to correct them (9:7-8; 12:10). But the problem runs deeper than particular office holders; the entire religious system is corrupt. According to Hosea, people are going to the shrines at Bethel (which Hosea derisively calls Beth-Aven, or "house of wickedness"), Gilgal, and Samaria not to worship Yahweh, but to pay tribute to worthless idols of silver and gold and to seek guidance from idolatrous priests (4:12; 4:17; 8:4; 11:6). Hosea's indictment specifically mentions the golden bull images that King Jeroboam had constructed at Samaria (8:5-6; 10:5-6; 13:2; compare 1 Kings 11:25-33). These images had served as visible symbols of the presence of Yahweh for two centuries by Hosea's time. Unlike Amos, Hosea is not simply criticizing the spirit with which people are carrying out their worship; he portrays Israel's entire religious system as a betrayal of their covenant with Yahweh.

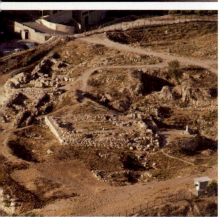

Hosea also criticizes the people of Israel for erecting altars and sacred pillars all over the land and offering sacrifices on hilltops and under trees (4:13; 8:11; 10:1-2). He does not say whether these sites are being used to worship different gods or whether the problem is their location away from the official shrines of Yahweh. He also claims that some of the Israelites are engaging in ritualized sexual activity in conjunction with their sacrifices, a practice sometimes associated with Canaanite fertility rituals (4:13-14; 4:18). Finally, an indeterminate number of people are engaging in the worship of Baal (2:8; 13:1) or "the Baals" (2:13; 2:17; 11:1-2; 13:1; possibly a collective term for Canaanite deities in general), though it is unclear how this relates to his other criticisms.

As a result of these activities, says Hosea, Yahweh is angry with his people; he is no longer listening to their prayers or accepting their sacrifices (5:6; 8:13; 9:4-6; 11:7). Once again Yahweh calls them to return to him (10:12; 12:6; 14:1-3), but unfortunately it appears to be too late; the people of Israel are too firmly set in their ways (5:4; 7:10). In response to their actions, Yahweh is going to send foreign armies to destroy their cities and fortresses (8:14; 10:14), remove their false system of worship (8:5-6; 10:2; 10:5-6; 10:8; 12:11), and slaughter both the people and their leaders (7:16; 11:6; 13:16). The kings of Israel will be removed from office (10:3; 10:7; 10:15; 13:9-11) and their nation will come to an end (1:4). Those who survive will be carried away to Assyria (9:3; 11:5; see also 9:17), where they will remain until they recognize the error of their ways and renew their devotion to Yahweh and his covenant (5:14—6:3; compare 2:16-23). What will happen at that point is unclear, since the few verses that hint at a future return from exile are thought by many scholars to be later additions (11:8-11; 14:4-7). But Hosea is certain that there is no hope for Israel unless they return to their covenant with Yahweh, which will entail among other things a radical restructuring of their present system of worship.

In the end, Hosea agrees with Amos that Israel is radically off course, despite the prosperity that has seduced many into thinking that Yahweh is pleased with them. But the two prophets have different ideas about what is wrong with Israel and what should be done about it. According to Amos, Yahweh's primary concern is the rampant social and economic injustice of the nation and its leaders. According to Hosea, the problem lies with its religious institutions. The two viewpoints are not necessarily contradictory, but they do reveal a marked difference in orientation. What holds them together is a similar understanding of Yahweh and his expectations for his people.

Fig. 32.5. (top) An Egyptian worshipper bows before the sacred bull Apis, who represented the god Ptah in the same way the calves of Samaria represented Yahweh; (bottom) the remains of a huge standing stone mark the location of a "high place," or regional worship center, in the Israelite city of Schechem.

ISAIAH

For reasons that will be explained in chapter 34, most scholars believe that the book of Isaiah is a composite work that includes the sayings of at least three prophets from different eras. Chapters 1–39 are credited to the prophet Isaiah, who lived in the eighth century B.C.E.; chapters 40–55, to an unnamed prophet who spoke near the end of the Exile; and chapters 56–66, to one or more prophets from the postexilic period. Most also believe that chapters 1–39 include materials from later prophets or editors, since several sections appear to reflect the circumstances, ideas, or language of later periods (Isaiah 13:1—14:23; 21:1-10; 23:1-18; 24:1—27:13; 34:1—35:10). Also included in these chapters are a handful of third-person stories about the prophet Isaiah (Isaiah 7:1-25; 20:1-6; 36:1—39:8) which must have been written by someone else, whether one of the prophet's immediate followers or a later editor. In this chapter we will restrict our comments to the materials that most scholars would attribute to the eighth century B.C.E. prophet Isaiah.

EXERCISE 90

Read Isaiah 6:1—8:3; 20:1-4; 36:1-10; 37:1-7; 37:21-29; 38:1-8. What was Isaiah like as a person, according to these passages? How did he understand his mission?

According to Isaiah 1:1, Isaiah delivered his messages to the people of Judah in the latter half of the eighth century B.C.E., around the same time that Amos and Hosea were preaching to the people of Israel in the north. Isaiah seems to have been a member of the Jerusalem elite, since he is shown advising Kings Ahaz and Hezekiah during times of crisis (7:1-17; 36:1—38:8; 39:1-8). He may have been a priest as well, since he claims to have seen a vision of Yahweh inside the Jerusalem temple (6:1), though it is unclear whether he was actually in the temple at the time of the vision. Isaiah was married to an unnamed woman who was known as a prophetess, by whom he had at least two sons (7:3; 8:1-4). In one passage he refers to his "disciples," possibly a group of junior prophets who

were charged with preserving his sayings (8:16; compare 30:8).

Isaiah's prophecies are set against a backdrop of recurring threats from foreign powers. First, around 734 B.C.E., the kings of Israel and Syria attacked Judah in an effort to force King Ahaz to join them in resisting the growing power of Assyria (2 Kings 16:5-9; Isaiah 7:1-13). Ahaz escaped the danger by appealing to the Assyrian king for help and paying him a massive tribute, effectively converting Judah into a vassal state of the Assyrian empire. Then in 722 B.C.E. Judah was threatened by the same Assyrian armies that brutally conquered Israel and deported its survivors to other lands (2 Kings 17:1-41). The Assyrians appear to have left Judah alone at this time, presumably because Judah did not join the resistance. Finally, in 701 B.C.E. King Hezekiah of Judah rebelled against Assyrian rule at a time when a new Assyrian monarch was busy putting down

Fig. 32.6. A series of carved panels from the palace of the Assyrian king Sennacherib depicts his assault on the city of Lachish in Judah in 701 B.C.E. (top) Soldiers deploy a battering ram against the gate of the city; (bottom) the king reviews the spoils at the end of the battle.

uprisings across his empire. This political miscalculation resulted in Assyrian armies being deployed in full force against Judah, where they devastated the land and carried off some of its inhabitants. In the end, however, they were unable to conquer the city of Jerusalem, despite a lengthy siege (2 Kings 18:13—19:37; Isaiah 36:1—37:38). Assyrian records indicate that Judah was forced to pay increased tribute after this incident, but the kingdom remained nominally independent.

These background materials are vitally important for understanding Isaiah's message. Too often Christians have ignored the historical context of Isaiah's sayings and interpreted his sayings in a manner that would have made no sense to Isaiah's eighth century B.C.E. audience. For example, Isaiah speaks in chapter 7 of the coming birth of a child who will be called "Immanuel" (Isaiah 7:14). The Christian gospel of Matthew takes this as a reference to the coming of Jesus some seven hundred years after the time of Isaiah (Matthew 1:22-23). A review of the original context, however, shows that the passage refers to a child that will be born to an unidentified woman (the king's wife?) who is already pregnant in Isaiah's day. The focus is not on the child's birth, but on Isaiah's promise that the threat from the kings of Israel and Syria will end before the child is old enough to make wise decisions (Isaiah 7:16). A similar point can be made concerning Isaiah's predictions of the coming of an ideal king who will submit to Yahweh's guidance and rule over his people with righteousness (Isaiah 9:6-7; 11:1-10). Christian tradition has long applied these verses to Jesus (see Matthew 4:12-16; Romans 15:12). In context, however, they anticipate the coming of a literal king from the lineage of David (Isaiah 11:1) who will occupy David's throne (Isaiah 9:7) and introduce an era of peace and justice that contrasts sharply with the corruption of the present era.

EXERCISE 91

Read Isaiah 1:1-31; 5:1-30; 10:1-27; 28:1-22. How does Isaiah's message compare with that of Amos and Hosea?

Isaiah views the political developments of his day through a theological lens. While most people believe that the course of human history is decided by the actions of kings and armies, Isaiah insists that Yahweh is in fact orchestrating what happens to his people, though his plans and purposes are not always clear to humans. At one point in the book he is shown protecting his people

from harm (7:1-17; 36:1—37:38), while in other places he threatens to send foreign armies against them (5:26-30; 7:18-25; 8:5-8). In still other passages Yahweh promises to punish the nations that he intends to use to discipline his people (10:5-19; 10:24-27; 31:8-9). In other words, Yahweh's mighty rule is not limited to the land and people of Israel and Judah; foreign nations, too, must do his bidding.

Similar ideas can be seen in Amos's and Hosea's predictions that Yahweh will send the Assyrians against Israel, as well as in Amos's oracles against other nations (Amos 1:3—2:3). But the idea that Yahweh is lord of history plays a more central role in Isaiah's prophecies, since he has to argue against the common belief that Yahweh will forever protect his king and his city from harm (28:14-22). At a more pragmatic level, Isaiah is also seeking to counter the ideas of people around the king who insist that Judah should form alliances with Egypt or other nations to resist the Assyrian threat (20:1-6; 30:1-7; 31:1-6). From Isaiah's standpoint, this constitutes a betrayal of trust in Yahweh, who is more than capable of protecting his people if they will only turn from their sinful ways and trust him alone. The actions of King Ahaz (7:1—8:8) and King Hezekiah (36:1—38:8) represent the opposing poles in this argument.

Like Amos and Hosea, Isaiah is sharply critical of the people of his day. Most of his criticisms are directed toward the behavior of the elites. Numerous passages speak of the wealthy, including the rulers of Judah, hoarding their riches and enjoying lives of luxury and ease while ignoring or abusing the poor and needy in their midst (1:16-17; 2:7; 3:14-15; 3:18-23; 5:8; 5:11-12; 10:1-2; 28:1-4). Rulers are also criticized for misleading the people, engaging in violence and corruption, and spending too much money on their armies (1:23; 2:7; 3:12). Violence and murder are on the rise (1:15; 1:21; 5:7), and the courts have been corrupted through bribery (1:23; 5:23; 29:21).

On the religious side, people are worshipping at places other than the holy city of Jerusalem (1:29) and using unacceptable methods to discern the will of the deity (2:6; 8:19-20). Some are honoring other gods besides Yahweh (2:8; 2:18-20; 31:7). The priests and prophets are useless, since they are usually drunk and unable to hear or proclaim the word of Yahweh (28:7-13; 29:9-12).

Fig. 32.7. Prisoners are led away into exile by Assyrian soldiers after the conquest of their city in this carved panel from the palace of king Ashurnasirpal II (ninth century B.C.E.).

Even if we allow for a fair amount of poetic license and exaggeration in Isaiah's account, it is easy to see why he might have concluded that Yahweh was unhappy with his people's behavior.

Like Amos, Isaiah declares that Yahweh is sick of his people's religious festivals and sacrifices and will not accept them as long as they continue to act in ways that are contrary to his will (1:10-17; 29:13-14). For Isaiah, Yahweh is above all the "Holy One" whose awesome power and majesty require that he be taken seriously by his people (1:4; 5:24; 6:1-5; 8:13; 12:6; 29:22-24). Elsewhere he speaks of Yahweh as a loving parent or a devoted farmer who has lavished far too much care on his people to allow them to go wild (1:2-6; 5:1-7). If they do not turn around, says Isaiah, Yahweh will be forced to discipline them by sending a foreign army to conquer and abuse them. The Assyrians will bring down their rulers, take away their riches, kill their people, and devastate their land (3:1-3; 3:16-4:1; 5:9-10; 5:25-30; 7:18-25; 8:5-8; 10:3-11; 32:9-14). Even Jerusalem will fall unless Yahweh intervenes to protect the city (1:7-9; 29:1-8). Those who survive will be carried away into exile in disgrace (5:13-15; 6:11-13).

Fortunately, it is not too late to avoid this fate. Yahweh is still willing to forgive his people if they will change their ways and do what is right (1:18-20; 30:15). Even if they do not turn around, however, Yahweh is not finished with them forever. Those who are devoted to Yahweh will be preserved as a faithful remnant when the day of judgment comes (1:27; 3:10-11). In his own time, Yahweh

will punish the Assyrians and remove them from power (10:12-19; 10:24-27; 30:27-33; 31:8-9). In that day he will make his righteous remnant the nucleus of a restored community that will enjoy peace and prosperity under the guidance of a godly king from the line of David who will follow Yahweh's direction (1:24-28; 4:2-6; 9:1-7; 10:20-23; 11:1-10; 28:5-6; 30:19-26; 32:1-5; 32:14-20). Isaiah's expectation of an ideal Davidic king is shared by other prophets from the kingdom of Judah, where David had once ruled, and sets Isaiah's message apart from those of Amos and Hosea.

MICAH

Micah preached to the people of Judah around the same time as Isaiah, so many of the issues that he faced were similar to those addressed in Isaiah's prophecies. But where Isaiah lived in the capital city and worked at the highest levels of society, Micah came from the small town of Moresheth (Micah 1:1) and spoke as an outsider to the Jerusalem establishment.

The present collection of Micah's sayings contains no personal information about the prophet's life. This probably means that the editors knew nothing more about him, since they like to include even brief episodes from the lives of the prophets when they have them, as we have observed in the books that we have studied thus far. A few hints about Micah's life can be gleaned from some of the "I" passages in the book, if these indeed go back to the historical prophet. At one point he mentions going naked and barefoot (1:8) as Isaiah is reported to have done (Isaiah 20:1-6), perhaps as a visual symbol of the coming exile. Like other preexilic prophets, he encountered opposition to his message (2:6-7), most likely from the religious and political leaders whose deeds he repeatedly criticizes (3:1-12; 6:12; 7:3-4). But he did not allow this to stop him, since he felt led and empowered by the spirit of Yahweh to proclaim his message (3:8). This is all that we can know from the book of Micah about the prophet's life and experiences with Yahweh and his people.

The book of Micah lacks the organization and structure that we find in other prophetic books. Messages from different periods follow one another in no apparent order, and each subsection is largely self-contained, with few clear links to the verses before or after it. This lack of organization suggests that the book was heavily edited over time, with materials from later periods being inserted here and there with little regard for their effect on the book's structure. In fact, many scholars believe that only the first three chapters represent the actual words of Micah, making Micah a prophet of unmitigated doom. Other scholars see parallels with Isaiah's message and accept some of the more hopeful passages as authentic.

Whatever we conclude about later additions, the book's comments about the social problems of Judah are similar enough to those of Isaiah to lend credence to the belief that it preserves the message of the eighth century B.C.E. prophet Micah. Unlike Isaiah, however, the book of Micah contains few references to current events, making it hard to relate the sayings to particular periods in Micah's lengthy ministry. As a result, we will focus here on the major themes of Micah's message without trying to link them too closely to the political events of his day.

Though Micah came from a small town, he was by no means isolated from the world around him. The book begins with a lengthy prophecy against Samaria, the capital of the kingdom of Israel (1:2-7), and later refers to the northern kings Omri and Ahab (6:16). If these verses go back to Micah, they suggest that he was at least broadly aware of events in the northern kingdom. His critical comments about the leaders of Judah (3:1-3; 3:9-12; 6:9-16) likewise indicate that he may have visited the capital city, though this is uncertain. If he did, he was not impressed.

> ## EXERCISE 92
>
> Read Micah 1:1—3:12 and 5:10—7:7 and make a list of the problems that Micah attacks in his sayings. How do these problems compare with what we saw in Isaiah?

On the whole, Micah's message reflects a rural point of view that is consistently negative toward Jerusalem as a center of oppression. While Isaiah holds out hope for the salvation of Jerusalem, Micah declares that the city will be utterly destroyed (3:12), along with the fortresses that represent Jerusalem's power in the region where Micah lives (1:13-16). According to Micah, the cities of Samaria and Jerusalem are the focal points of sinful behavior in the two kingdoms (1:5). This negative view of the cities is not simply a reaction against a culture that seems alien to people in the rural areas of Judah. It reflects the experience of small landholders who are losing their property to the wealthy elites of the cities, apparently by unjust means (2:1-2; 2:9; 3:1-3). Micah is less than clear about what the elites are doing, but he complains several times about the use of violence and bribery by the wealthy and powerful (2:8; 3:9-10; 6:11; 7:2-4). Other negative behaviors that he associates with the elites include drunkenness (2:11) and lying (6:12). He also condemns the use of dishonest weights in the marketplace, a practice that would have hurt the poor most of all (6:10-11).

Micah says less than Isaiah about explicitly religious abuses. Only one passage of uncertain origin refers clearly to the use of unacceptable forms of worship (5:12-14). Elsewhere, Micah is sharply critical of prophets and priests who expect to be paid by the people whom they serve (3:5-7; 3:11). This practice, like the other acts that Micah criticizes, would have weighed heavily on rural people whose resources were limited. Like Isaiah, Micah attacks other prophets as corrupt. In particular, he accuses them of basing their prophecies on how much payment they receive and issuing false promises of divine protection at a time when Yahweh is about to bring judgment upon his people (3:5; 3:11-12). Unlike these prophets, Micah insists that he speaks only what has been given to him by Yahweh (3:8).

As with the other preexilic prophets, Micah's vision for the future of his people is bleak. His book includes

Fig. 32.8. Byzantine pilgrims named this Jerusalem hill "Mt. Zion" in the erroneous belief that the ancient temple had been located here; the real Mt. Zion can be seen on pp. 366 and 489. Isaiah and Micah speak of a glorious future when Yahweh will rule the nations from Mt. Zion (Isaiah 2:1-4; Micah 4:1-5).

no calls for repentance and no hint that the coming divine judgment can be averted. His portrait of what will happen at that time recalls what we have seen elsewhere: invading armies will overcome their soldiers and fortresses (5:10-11), destroy their towns (5:14), take over their fields (2:4), and remove their survivors to a foreign land (1:16). Neither the city of Jerusalem nor the temple of Yahweh will be spared (3:12).

Whether there is hope beyond the coming destruction depends on whether one attributes the more positive parts of the book to Micah or a later hand. In its present form, the book speaks about a faithful remnant whom Yahweh will keep safe in their land (4:6-7; 5:7-9; 7:18). Yahweh will rule over them through his chosen king (2:12-13; 5:2-6), and they will overcome all of their enemies (4:8; 4:11-12; 5:5-6; 5:9). People from all nations will stream to Jerusalem to honor and serve Yahweh, and peace will reign forever (4:1-4; 7:12-17). This is similar to the vision that we saw in the book of Isaiah, raising the possibility that at least some of it might go back to Micah's day. In either case, it is a vision that later generations clearly found inspiring.

CONCLUSION

The Hebrew Bible contains many stories and sayings that are attributed to prophets who lived prior to the Babylonian Exile. Scholars disagree about which of these materials go back to the times of the prophets, but virtually all would agree that the books of the prophets offer a more reliable picture of the prophetic movement than the narrative books. Most also believe that the prophetic books include substantial amounts of material that go back to the person to whom the book is attributed. This means that these books can be used as a window onto the times when the prophets lived as well as the actions and ideas of the prophets themselves.

The latter half of the eighth century B.C.E. is one period when a number of prophets were active. Of the prophets whose sayings were included in the Hebrew Bible, Amos and Hosea preached to the people of the northern kingdom during this period, while Isaiah and Micah delivered their messages to the southern kingdom. In each case the prophet's message was directed toward the people and circumstances of his day; none framed his message for people living centuries after his time.

While each of the prophets from this era had a particular slant on the issues, all agreed that the people of Yahweh were radically off-track in both their social and their religious behavior. All claimed that Yahweh was displeased with his people and would soon bring judgment upon them if they persisted in their present course. In each case the anticipated judgment was the same: Yahweh would send foreign armies to depose their leaders, devastate their land, slaughter their people, and carry the survivors away into exile. Hosea and Amos may have seen their predictions come true as the Assyrian invaders brought an end to the nation of Israel, while Isaiah and Micah lived through an Assyrian invasion of Judah that caused great harm but did not ultimately end in exile. The fulfillment of their predictions would have to wait for a later day.

EXERCISE 93

Can you think of anyone in the last few decades who resembles any of the prophets described in this chapter? What do you think motivated that person to speak and act as he or she did? Who responded to the person's message and who did not? Why?

Fig. 33.1. Rembrandt van Rijn, *Jeremiah Lamenting the Destruction of Jerusalem*

The Later Preexilic Prophets

*The great day of the L*ORD *is near, near and hastening fast; the sound of the day of the L*ORD *is bitter, the warrior cries aloud there. That day will be a day of wrath, a day of distress and anguish, a day of ruin and devastation, a day of darkness and gloom, a day of clouds and thick darkness, a day of trumpet blast and battle cry against the fortified cities and against the lofty battlements. I will bring such distress upon people that they shall walk like the blind; because they have sinned against the L*ORD*, their blood shall be poured out like dust, and their flesh like dung.* (Zephaniah 1:14-17)

*They have turned back to the iniquities of their ancestors of old, who refused to heed my words; they have gone after other gods to serve them; the house of Israel and the house of Judah have broken the covenant that I made with their ancestors. Therefore, thus says the L*ORD*, assuredly I am going to bring disaster upon them that they cannot escape; though they cry out to me, I will not listen to them. Then the cities of Judah and the inhabitants of Jerusalem will go and cry out to the gods to whom they make offerings, but they will never save them in the time of their trouble.* (Jeremiah 11:10-12)

*Therefore I will judge you, O house of Israel, all of you according to your ways, says the Lord G*OD*. Repent and turn from all your transgressions; otherwise iniquity will be your ruin. Cast away from you all the transgressions that you have committed against me, and get yourselves a new heart and a new spirit! Why will you die, O house of Israel? For I have no pleasure in the death of anyone, says the Lord G*OD*. Turn, then, and live.* (Ezekiel 18:30-32*)*

In this chapter we continue our examination of the books that are attributed to prophets who lived prior to the Babylonian conquest of Judah in 586 B.C.E. All of the prophets whom we will be studying in this chapter (Zephaniah, Nahum, Habakkuk, Jeremiah, and Ezekiel) spoke to the people of Judah in the decades leading up to the Babylonian invasion. Except for Nahum, whose prophecy sounds more like the words of a court prophet, the prophets of this period attacked most of the same social and religious practices as the eighth century B.C.E. prophets and offered similar predictions of impending doom at the hands of foreign armies. Like the other prophets, they were mostly rejected as reactionaries and

crackpots, though some people clearly respected them enough to preserve their words. Not until the experience of the Exile did many people begin to change their opinions about these troublemakers.

SETTING THE STAGE

After the eighth century B.C.E., there is a gap of roughly sixty years during which the Hebrew Bible reports no prophetic messages. The reason for this gap is unclear. The Assyrian conquest of the northern kingdom and the ensuing deportation of its leading citizens had disrupted the religious life of the kingdom of Israel, so it is understandable that we would have no prophetic sayings from the north during this period. But Judah continued to function as a vassal state of the Assyrian empire in the decades after the Assyrian invasion, a status that had little impact on the nation's internal operations. Why then do we hear nothing from the prophets of Judah during this period?

According to the book of Kings, the period in question coincides with the reign of Manasseh, the son of King Hezekiah, who is reported to have ruled over Judah for fifty-five years (2 Kings 21:1). Manasseh is depicted as a bad king who actively promoted the worship of other gods and behaved worse than any other king before him—worse even than the Canaanites whom Yahweh drove out before the people of Israel (2 Kings 21:2; 21:11). Manasseh is also accused of having "shed very much innocent blood, until he had filled Jerusalem from one end to another" (2 Kings 21:16). It is tempting to imagine that the prophets of Yahweh might have been silenced during this period, whether by official decree or self-censorship, as the king used his royal power to promote the worship of other gods at the expense of Yahweh.

While this sounds plausible, the book of Kings says nothing about Manasseh suppressing the practice of Yahwism or attacking Yahweh's prophets as we saw in the story of Queen Jezebel. The author even cites a lengthy message of rebuke that Yahweh supposedly sent to Manasseh by means of "his servants the prophets" (2 Kings 21:10-15; note that the prophets are not named). The book of Chronicles likewise mentions (but does not quote) "the words of the seers who spoke to him [Manasseh] in the name of the LORD God of Israel" (2 Chronicles 33:18). Thus the Hebrew Bible implies that the prophets of Yahweh, far from being silenced, were actively confronting Manasseh over his policies. Why the words of these prophets were not preserved and included in the Hebrew Bible is a mystery. Some scholars have suggested that excerpts from their sayings might have been incorporated into the oral collections attributed to earlier prophets and thus made their way anonymously into the Hebrew Bible.

The period from the coming of King Josiah in 640 B.C.E. to the conquest of Judah by the Babylonians in 586 B.C.E. marks the rise of a number of prophets whose words are included in the Hebrew Bible: Zephaniah, Nahum, Habakkuk, Jeremiah, and Ezekiel. (The prophetic careers of Jeremiah and Ezekiel continued into the exilic period, so they will be treated in the next chapter as well.) Little imagination is required to see why so many prophetic sayings from this period were written down and preserved for future generations. From the vantage point of the Exile, these were crucial years in the history of the people of Judah as their nation spiraled slowly downward toward inevitable ruin at the hands of the Babylonians. Hindsight showed the exiles that truth has been on the side of the prophets who predicted a Babylonian victory, not those who prophesied that Yahweh would protect them from harm. This recognition led some of the literate elites to collect and write down the sayings of prophets from the recent past who had rightly anticipated these events. Over time these collections came to be honored as the words of Yahweh, which in turn led to their inclusion in the Jewish Scriptures.

ZEPHANIAH

According to Zephaniah 1:1, the prophet Zephaniah was a great-great-grandson of King Hezekiah who prophesied during the reign of King Josiah in the latter part of the seventh century B.C.E. It is difficult to know how to evaluate this claim, though it seems likely that people might have remembered if someone from the royal family had spoken such a scathingly critical message as we find in the book of Zephaniah, particularly when it singles out the political leaders of Judah for criticism (1:8; 3:3). The attention given to Jerusalem, including references to specific sites within the city (1:10-11), suggests that Zephaniah might have been a resident of the capital. Otherwise we know nothing about his personal life.

Zephaniah's condemnations of Baal-worship and other idolatrous practices (1:4-6) imply that his message should be dated to the early years of King Josiah's reign, before the enactment of his "Yahweh-only" reforms in 621 B.C.E. (2 Kings 22:1—23:25). The practices that Zephaniah criticizes recall the description of Manasseh's religious program in 2 Kings 21, so it is tempting to interpret Zephaniah's words as a prophetic response to Manasseh's success. The link is uncertain, however, since similar practices can be seen throughout Judah's history. Some scholars have suggested that the more positive parts of the book (2:5-15; 3:9-20) might reflect a later period in Josiah's reign after his reforms were implemented, while others regard all such passages in the preexilic books as the product of later editing.

EXERCISE 94

Read Zephaniah 1:1—3:8. Why do you think Zephaniah uses such extreme language to describe what Yahweh is about to do? What kind of judgment do you think he actually anticipated?

In comparison with the other prophetic books that we have examined, the book of Zephaniah does not dwell on the wrongful behaviors of the people of Judah. Instead, the book is filled with darkly poetic descriptions of the awful judgment that Yahweh is about to bring upon them. The few verses that spell out the reasons for Yahweh's anger recall what we have seen elsewhere. Apart from a few verses condemning people who worship other gods besides Yahweh (1:4-6), Zephaniah's criticisms are directed against members of the political, religious, and economic elites. Government officials and "the king's sons" are denounced for adopting foreign ways (1:8) and abusing their people through violence and fraud (1:9; 3:3). Priests and prophets are castigated for not taking Yahweh seriously and violating his laws (3:4). The wealthy are criticized for hoarding their wealth and being complacent (1:11-13; 1:18). All are guilty of ignoring Yahweh's messengers and refusing to change their ways (3:1-2; 3:7).

According to Zephaniah, Yahweh has run out of patience and will soon unleash his anger against his people. The vivid imagery and repetitive language of Zephaniah's prophecies make the looming disaster almost palpable. Unlike the earlier prophets who spoke of Yahweh using foreign armies to do his bidding, Zephaniah portrays Yahweh himself coming to carry out his judgment in a great and terrible "day of Yahweh." On that day, Yahweh will appear as a conquering warrior, crushing everything in his path; no army or fortress can stand in his way (1:14-

Fig. 33.2. One of the earliest surviving frgments of the book of Zephaniah.

16; 3:6). The city of Jerusalem will feel the brunt of his anger (1:4; 1:10-12; 3:1; 3:7), but all of the nations will be judged on that day (3:8). Even the mighty Assyrians will be brought down (2:13-15). Everything that lives will be swept from the face of the earth (1:2-3; 1:18).

Only once does Zephaniah hold out any hope for his audience: "Seek the LORD, all you humble of the land, who do his commands; seek righteousness, seek humility; perhaps you may be hidden on the day of the LORD's wrath" (2:3). A second passage that was probably added later speaks more confidently about a faithful remnant that will be preserved on that day (3:11-13). Other verses that promise a future restoration of Judah echo the language and ideas of the exilic period and are usually thought to be later additions to Zephaniah's prophecy. These verses speak of Yahweh rescuing his people from their oppressors and bringing them home to their land (3:9-20), where he will extend their control to the coastal regions of Palestine and the territories of Moab and Ammon on the eastern side of the Jordan river (2:5-11). In that day every nation will speak "pure speech" (that is, Hebrew) and honor Yahweh as their god (3:9-10). All of these expectations are inconsistent with Zephaniah's predictions of total devastation.

NAHUM

The book of Nahum is one of four prophetic books, along with Obadiah, Jonah, and Habakkuk, whose message centers on nations other than Israel and Judah. This does not mean that the residents of other nations actually read or even heard about these books; all three were spoken and/or written for the people of Judah. Unlike the other prophetic books, however, they pronounce judgment not against the people of Yahweh but against their enemies. This makes them sound like the court prophets who promised divine blessings upon the kings of Israel and Judah and pronounced curses against their opponents, though similar language can be found in many of the biblical prophets as well. For Nahum and Jonah, the enemy whom Yahweh intends to punish is Assyria. For Obadiah, it is Edom, Judah's neighbor to the southeast. For Habakkuk, it is the Babylonians.

Nothing is known about the identity of Nahum, including the location of his hometown of Elkosh (1:1). The date of the book is also uncertain, though most scholars agree that Nahum prophesied not long before the Babylonians conquered Nineveh, the capital city of Assyria, in 612 B.C.E. This date coincides with the latter years of the reign of King Josiah, perhaps two decades after his religious reforms. This might explain why Nahum's few comments about Judah are encouraging rather than critical (2:15; 3:2). In fact, it is conceivable that Nahum might have been one of Josiah's court prophets.

The bulk of Nahum's message concerns the coming destruction of the Assyrian capital. The empire of the Assyrians reached its peak in the middle of the seventh century B.C.E., when they ruled the entire Fertile Crescent from Egypt to Mesopotamia. But the residents of southern Mesopotamia, the site of the several ancient empires, did not accept foreign domination lightly. Again and again they tried to free themselves from the power of the Assyrians, until at last they succeeded under the leadership of Nabopolassar in 625 B.C.E. Over the next several years Nabopolassar, who was crowned king of a

liberated Babylonia, led his armies north against the cities and fortresses of Assyria, winning victories at every step. Finally in 612 B.C.E., he reached the Assyrian capital of Nineveh and placed it under siege. The city fell after a few months, breaking the back of the Assyrian empire, though a few more years of fighting were required to finish off the remaining resistance. Under Nabopolassar's son, Nebuchadnezzar (604–556 B.C.E.), the Babylonians succeeded in taking over all of the territories that had been controlled by the Assyrians at their height, apart from Egypt. Included among their conquests was the kingdom of Judah (586 B.C.E.). The prophecies of Nahum and the remaining preexilic prophets must be understood against this background.

EXERCISE 95

Read the book of Nahum. Why do you think this book was included in the Scriptures of Israel?

Like Zephaniah, Nahum uses vivid imagery to describe the destruction that is about to come upon the city of Nineveh. The attackers are never named; the only title that Nahum uses for them (or more likely, for their leader) is "a shatterer" (2:1). After announcing the approach of the enemy, the book dwells at length on a few scenes of conflict and eventual conquest. The scenes

Fig. 33.3. A contemporary artist's rendition of the siege of Nineveh, the Assyrian capital, by the Babylonians in 612 B.C.E.

are so artfully crafted that one can almost see and hear them happening.

Yet Nahum was not speaking simply to show off his poetic skills. Embedded in his poetry are profound messages about the character of Yahweh and what he expects from people and nations. According to Nahum, Yahweh is an awesome and powerful god who uses his might to protect those who rely on him and to punish their adversaries, whom he treats as his own enemies. Once he arises in anger, no one can stand against him; his presence is a raging fire (1:2-11).

The essence of Nahum's message is that the time has now come for Yahweh's anger to be directed against the Assyrians. Surprisingly, he says very little about the reasons for Yahweh's anger. The central idea seems to be that the Assyrians have done wrong by attacking Israel and Judah (1:12-13). Although Yahweh sent the Assyrians against his people, he still holds them accountable for the blood that they have spilled, the plunder that they have taken, and the abusive way they have treated the people whom they have conquered (3:1; 3:4; 3:19). The cruelty of the Assyrian armies, which included mutilating the bodies of survivors and impaling their corpses on stakes for all to see, was legendary throughout the region. Nahum's condemnation of the Assyrians' "sorcery" (3:4) probably refers to the practices of the diviners who traveled with their armies to discern the will of the gods. According to Nahum, the Assyrians believe that their gods have given them their victories, but Yahweh will destroy their gods to show that this is not so (1:14).

Like others who have suffered under abusive colonial rulers, Nahum gloats over the fate that he foresees for the Assyrians and dwells at length on the devastation that will accompany the fall of their capital. The scene is bleak: after massive slaughter and removal of booty, the survivors will be taken away into exile as people throw garbage at them (2:4-10; 3:2-7). Several times he depicts Yahweh taunting his fallen foes (2:11-12; 3:8-10; 3:12-13; 3:17-18).

From one point of view, Nahum's rejoicing over the fall of Assyria seems as heartless as the people whose fall he celebrates. Yet Nahum's prophecy is not simply a personal celebration of divine vengeance. Behind his message lies the conviction that Yahweh is a just and righteous deity

who directs the affairs of nations in order to show his commitment to his people. The success of a nation like the Assyrians poses a severe challenge to that belief, while their downfall reinforces it. It is therefore understandable that a Yahwistic prophet like Nahum would rejoice when such a fundamental religious conviction is upheld. In the absence of such an outcome, the entire religious system of Yahwism would be open to question.

HABAKKUK

As with Nahum, we know nothing about the personal history of the prophet Habakkuk. The introductory verse identifies neither his hometown nor the king under whom he prophesied. Scholars have speculated that Habakkuk might have served as a prophet at one of the shrines, or possibly even as a priest, since his language, especially in chapter 3, includes liturgical elements that are also found in the psalms. His concern about the might of the Babylonian armies (called by the alternate name "Chaldeans" in 1:6) shows that he lived at a time when the Babylonians presented a growing threat to Judah. Most scholars therefore date his message to the end of the seventh century B.C.E. or the beginning of the sixth, which would place him shortly after the time of Nahum and the final defeat of the Assyrians by the armies of Babylonia.

Most of the book of Habakkuk is framed as a dialogue between the prophet and Yahweh. Only the central section of the book (2:6-20), in which Habakkuk pronounces judgment against the Babylonians, diverges from this pattern. This part of the book is similar to Nahum and Obadiah in showing the prophet speaking directly to a foreign nation. The book closes with a hymn that echoes the language of the psalms.

EXERCISE 96

Read the book of Habakkuk. Why is Habakkuk unhappy about Yahweh's actions? How does Yahweh answer his concerns?

The book of Habakkuk paints an unusual picture of a prophet questioning the propriety of Yahweh's plans for

Fig. 33.4. This panel from the palace of the Assyrian king Ashurnasirpal II (ninth century B.C.E.) shows the kind of cavalry assault Habukkuk has in mind when speaking about the Babylonians.

violent and wicked nation to punish his own people when, despite their faults, they are still more righteous than the pagan Babylonians who worship the symbols of their own power (2:16-17). How can Yahweh associate with such an evil people? Yahweh replies by sending Habakkuk a prophetic vision and commanding him to write it down so that future generations can read it and understand what he is doing (2:2-3). In this vision Yahweh assures Habakkuk that he will indeed judge and bring down the Babylonians, but it will not happen soon. In the meantime his people must remain faithful (2:4).

The next part of the book (2:5-20) spells out the reasons for Yahweh's coming judgment of the Babylonians. The highly poetic language is rather obscure at points, but it appears that the Babylonians are being condemned for looting the nations whom they have conquered (2:6-11), abusing their inhabitants (2:12-17), and worshipping idols (2:18-20). Unlike these idols, Yahweh is a deity who sees and knows what is going on, and he plans to inflict upon the Babylonians the same kind of violence that they have used against others (2:7-8; 2:16-17). In that day all people will see his glory (2:14).

The last chapter of the book begins with a prayer for Yahweh to perform mighty deeds as he has done in the past (3:2). In response to this prayer, the speaker sees a vision of Yahweh coming in awesome power to rescue his people from those who are attacking them (3:3-16). Whether this experience should be understood as a second prophetic vision or an extension of the one mentioned in 2:2 is unclear. Many scholars believe that this last chapter was written separately from the rest of the book and was added here because of its obvious link with the vision theme of chapter 2. Whatever its origin, the vision's message of trusting Yahweh even when his might and power are nowhere to be seen (3:17-19) is consistent with the rest of the book. Such a message would have offered encouragement not only to those whom Habakkuk labels as the righteous in his own day (1:4) but also to the people of Judah who lived under foreign domination during the exilic and postexilic periods.

his people. Other prophets sometimes plead with Yahweh to be merciful and refrain from a particular act of punishment (see Amos 7:1-6; Jeremiah 7:16; 11:14; 14:11-12), but they rarely question the wisdom or goodness of Yahweh's actions. Jonah is the only other prophet who poses such a direct challenge to Yahweh's intentions, and the narrator implicitly criticizes him for doing so (see chapter 35). Habakkuk, by contrast, is viewed positively throughout the book that bears his name, and his questions are rewarded with answers from Yahweh.

The book begins with Habakkuk questioning why Yahweh has not acted to punish those among his people who are acting wrongly and harming others (1:2-4). Wherever the prophet looks he sees violence and injustice, and he cannot comprehend why Yahweh does not intervene to rescue those who are faithful to him and so uphold his own standards of justice. In response to this challenge, Yahweh informs Habakkuk that he plans to send the ruthless and invincible armies of the Babylonians against his people (1:5-11). He does not say what the Babylonians will do to them or when this judgment will take place, but his portrait of their character and activities is definitely menacing.

In Habakkuk's view, however, this answer only raises more questions. In the second part of the book (1:12—2:1), Habakkuk asks how Yahweh can possibly use such a

JEREMIAH

The books of Jeremiah and Ezekiel contain far more stories about the lives and activities of the prophets than any of the other prophetic books. The disproportionate amount of attention that is devoted to the lives of these two prophets cries out for an explanation. Minimalist scholars claim that most or all of the stories were created by the elites of a later period as part of a broader effort to formulate a fictional past for the people who inhabited Palestine under Persian rule. But this approach cannot explain why so many stories were created about these two prophets and not others, nor why their stories fit so well with what we know about the events of the time when they are reported to have lived.

The simplest and most reasonable explanation for the frequency of stories in the books of Jeremiah and Ezekiel is that more information was available about them than about the earlier prophets. The reason for this is obvious. The sayings of both prophets indicate that they lived and spoke in the decades immediately before and after the coming of the Babylonians. Both prophets warned repeatedly that the people of Judah would be vanquished by the Babylonian armies if they did not turn from their sinful ways. Both delivered their messages in oral form, though the book of Jeremiah claims that the prophet also had some of his earlier sayings written down during his lifetime (Jeremiah 36:32; 45:1).

When events unfolded as Jeremiah and Ezekiel had predicted, many of those who survived the Babylonian conquest would have concluded that the two men had indeed been speaking for Yahweh. Stories would have been told about their heroic efforts to convince the people of Judah to change their ways, and their sayings would have been compiled and edited for future use. Some of these materials might have come from people who knew the prophets and heard them speak. Many scholars believe that the earliest written edition of the book of Jeremiah was prepared by his scribe Baruch, whom the book claims wrote down some of his sayings during his lifetime (Jeremiah 36:4; 36:32). In the case of Ezekiel, the fact that he continued to prophesy in Babylonia well into the exilic period made it possible for people to write down some

of his later sayings and actions soon after they occurred. These early collections ultimately became the nucleus of the present books of Jeremiah and Ezekiel. Other materials were added over time, including some that originated later than the time of the prophet to whom they are attributed (for example, Jeremiah 50–51). But the core of each book seems to have been put together during or soon after the life of the prophet.

By including stories as well as sayings in their books, the editors of the books of Jeremiah and Ezekiel presented the two men not only as prophets but also as models of faithfulness to Yahweh in the face of rejection and opposition. Here we see one of the great ironies of the prophetic books: after spending most of their lives challenging the religious systems of their day, the two prophets were finally honored as paradigms of the kinds of values and actions that the religious elites hoped to inspire in their exilic and/or postexilic audiences. Of course, this did not happen to Jeremiah and Ezekiel alone; other preexilic prophets went through a similar process of rehabilitation that raised them from their original status

Fig. 33.5. (top) This statue of an Egyptian scribe gives a visual sense of what Jeremiah's scribe Baruch might have looked like while carrying out his work; (bottom) an impression made by the official seal of Baruch the scribe, discovered in the 1970s.

as social and religious outsiders to positions of honor as personifications of the religious ideals of the postexilic Jewish community. But the process is more obvious in the case of Jeremiah and Ezekiel, since we have so many stories that show how people actually responded to them during their lifetime.

EXERCISE 97

Read Jeremiah 1:1-19; 15:15-21; 18:18-23; 20:1-18; 28:1-17; 37:11—38:13. What do you learn from these passages about Jeremiah's life as a prophet? What do you think about the way he handles himself in these passages?

The book of Jeremiah contains enough information about the prophet (or at least what the editors presumed to be true about him) to allow us to construct at least an outline of his life story. Jeremiah was born to a priestly family in the village of Anathoth, a few miles north of Jerusalem. At some point he moved to the capital city, which is where his public ministry took place. How he supported himself is unclear, though he had enough money to buy a piece of property near the end of his time there (Jeremiah 32:6-12). The book makes no reference to Jeremiah officiating at the temple, and his sayings include almost none of the ideas usually associated with the priestly community, so it is unlikely that Jeremiah actually worked as a priest in Jerusalem. Perhaps he lived on inherited money or income generated by the family farm.

According to Jeremiah 1:1-3, Jeremiah was called by Yahweh to be a prophet in 627 B.C.E. when he was quite young, and he continued in this role for his entire life, even after the conquest of Judah by the Babylonians in 586 B.C.E. (Jeremiah 42–44). The story of his initial encounter with Yahweh (1:4-19) sets the tone for his public ministry. Using visions and direct speech, Yahweh commissions him to announce the judgment that he plans to bring upon his rebellious people at the hands of an unnamed kingdom from the north. Yahweh warns Jeremiah that his message will arouse fierce opposition from the people and leaders of Judah, but he also promises to strengthen him and protect him from their plots. This is exactly what happens throughout the rest of the book.

A significant number of the stories and sayings in the book of Jeremiah are dated to a particular year in the reign of one of the kings of Judah. These headings associate

the bulk of Jeremiah's ministry with two kings, Jehoiakim (609–598 B.C.E.) and Zedekiah (597–586 B.C.E.). Both of these kings faced the difficult task of jockeying between Egypt and Babylonia at a time when the two nations were fighting for control of the territory around Palestine. Both engaged in a policy of shifting alliances that eventually led to open conflict with the Babylonians, who invaded Judah twice, in 597 B.C.E. and again in 586 B.C.E. The first invasion led to the deportation of a large group of leading citizens (including the prophet Ezekiel) to Babylonia, while the second ended in the destruction of Jerusalem and the removal of the surviving elites.

Jeremiah repeatedly spoke out against the policies of both kings, insisting that nothing short of a renewal of the nation's covenant with Yahweh could save them from the coming devastation at the hands of the Babylonians (18:1-17; 22:1-10; 26:1-6). King Jehoiakim was so hostile to Jeremiah's message that he had to go into hiding (36:26), while his successor Zedekiah mostly ignored Jeremiah until it was too late, then refused to follow his advice to surrender to the invading Babylonians (21:1-10; 27:1-15; 38:14-23). Jeremiah also faced opposition from other prophets who insisted that Yahweh would protect Jerusalem from the Babylonians and return the earlier exiles to their land (14:13-16; 23:9-40; 28:1-17). Several times Jeremiah was imprisoned or abused for proclaiming a message that many regarded as treasonous, and once or twice he barely escaped with his life.

The book of Jeremiah includes many verses in which Jeremiah complains to Yahweh about the consequences of his call to be a prophet. According to Jeremiah 16, he was prohibited by Yahweh from getting married and participating in normal social relations, and he seems to have spent most of his life as a social outcast. Often he was told by Yahweh to do strange things to symbolize the coming judgment, such as wearing a wooden yoke around his neck as he preached (27:1—28:17; for similar actions, see 13:1-11; 19:1-13; 32:1-44). The abuse that he suffered from his opponents was a constant burden to him, leading him to demand that Yahweh take vengeance on them (11:18-20; 15:15-18; 17:14-18; 18:18-23; 20:1-18). Jeremiah also complains about having to bring such a negative message to his fellow citizens. Despite their many failings, Jeremiah remained deeply committed to his people, and the thought of the devastation that

Yahweh intended to bring upon them caused him great pain (4:19; 8:18—9:1). Such glimpses into the psyche of a prophet are unique in the Hebrew Bible, and indeed in the literature of the ancient world.

The book of Jeremiah says nothing about the prophet's death. After the victory of the Babylonians, he lived for a time in Israel until he was taken to Egypt by a group of fleeing exiles after the assassination of the Babylonian governor (40:1—43:7). There he continued preaching against the idolatrous practices that his people carried with them from Judah (44:1-30). Most scholars presume that he died in Egypt of natural causes.

EXERCISE 98

Read Jeremiah 2:1—3:5; 5:1-19; 7:1-20; 22:1-10; 24:1-10; 29:1-14; 30:1-9; 31:1-14; 31:31-40. Why does Jeremiah say Yahweh is angry with the people and rulers of Judah? What does the future hold for them?

At its core, Jeremiah's message is similar to that of the other preexilic prophets: Yahweh is displeased with his people's worship of other gods and their social injustice, and he is going to send foreign armies to punish them. The same verdict applies to both the people and their leaders; all have turned away from Yahweh, and all will be judged in the same manner. References to the coming invasion appear so often that they cast a dark shadow over the entire book. Here and there Jeremiah holds out the possibility that his people might repent and avoid the coming catastrophe (3:22—4:4; 4:14; 5:1; 7:5-6; 18:1-17; 22:1-10; 26:1-6), but most of his prophecies leave no doubt that the threatened judgment will come to pass. Several times Yahweh even tells him to stop praying for Judah, since his decree of punishment is irrevocable (7:16; 11:14; 14:11-12; 15:1-3).

The content of Jeremiah's preaching echoes many of the major themes of the preexilic prophetic movement as it is represented in the Hebrew Bible. His message combines language and imagery from the northern kingdom, which was just north of his ancestral home, and the southern kingdom, where he actually lived. Like the northern prophet Hosea, he identifies the worship of other gods as the central reason for Yahweh's anger with his people. Several times

he uses Hosea's image of Yahweh as Judah's husband and Judah's worship of other gods as adultery or prostitution (2:20-25; 3:1-10; 3:20; 13:26-27; 31:32). Similarities are also apparent in the prominence that both prophets give to the Exodus story and their references to Yahweh's covenant with Israel as the standard by which the behavior of the present generation is to be judged (2:1-13; 7:21-26; 11:1-13; 22:8-9; 32:20-23). The influence of Amos, another northern prophet, can be seen in Jeremiah's criticisms of the social injustices of his people (5:26-29; 6:6-7; 7:5-10; 9:3-9; 22:13-18) and his insistence that Yahweh no longer accepts their sacrifices and religious observances (6:19-20; 7:21-29; 11:15), though similar ideas can also be found in some of the southern prophets. Northern influence is also evident in Jeremiah's radical rejection of the southern belief that the presence of Yahweh's temple in Jerusalem will protect the city from harm (7:1-15; 26:1-19).

On the other hand, Jeremiah is following southern traditions when he predicts a glorious future for the royal house of David (17:24-25; 22:1-5; 23:5-8; 30:8-9; 33:14-26), and his prophecies against the surrounding nations (46:1—51:58) echo the language and ideas of southern prophets like Isaiah. The same can be said for his belief that Yahweh will one day restore his people to their land and initiate an era of peace and prosperity in which they will at last live as he desires (3:15-18; 16:14-15; 28:10-14; 30:1-8; 30:18-21; 31:1-40, 32:36—33:26). Such a message of hope is surprising in someone as persistently negative as Jeremiah, but it flows directly out of his emphasis on the importance of Yahweh's covenant with Israel. To Jeremiah, the

Fig. 33.6. Jeremiah's vision for the future of Judah includes women dancing with joy at the restoration of the nation (31:1-14), as depicted in this image from a medieval psalter.

Exodus story is not just an account of what Yahweh did in the time of Judah's ancestors; it also provides a paradigm for what Yahweh will do in the future when he restores his people to their land after a time of exile in a foreign nation (16:14-15; 23:7-8; 31:31-34; 32:36-44; 50:4-5). In a similar way, the covenant that Yahweh established with his people at Mount Sinai foreshadows a "new covenant" in which Yahweh's laws will be engraved not on stones but on the hearts of his people (31:31-34; 32:37-41; 50:4-5).

In the final analysis, Jeremiah is a prophet of hope as well as doom. He simply cannot believe that Yahweh will finally abandon his covenant people. He insists that Yahweh's intention is not to destroy the people of Judah but rather to humble them so that they will turn back to him and renew their commitment to his covenant. The near future will be painful, but a glorious reward awaits those who will lay aside their other gods and devote themselves to Yahweh alone. Messages such as this no doubt played a vital role in sustaining the hopes of the people of Judah during the long decades of the Babylonian Exile.

EZEKIEL 1–24

Ezekiel is usually considered one of the exilic prophets, since he was taken to Babylonia with the first wave of exiles in 597 B.C.E. and served as a prophet to the exiled community in Babylonia. But a sizeable number of his prophecies were issued in the last few years before Jerusalem was overrun by the Babylonians, and these messages reflect a decidedly preexilic mindset. For this reason we will look at Ezekiel's earlier prophecies in this chapter and his later ones in chapter 34.

As we noted earlier, the book of Ezekiel interweaves stories about the prophet's activities with sayings that he is reported to have delivered to his people. Unlike the book of Jeremiah, however, the stories about Ezekiel are framed in first-person speech. This format implies that the reports were recorded or dictated by the prophet himself during his lifetime, though it is possible that this is simply a literary device that was used to enhance the book's authority. Elsewhere in the prophetic books such first-person narratives are found primarily in reports of visionary interactions with Yahweh (Isaiah 6:1-13; Jeremiah 1:4-19;

18:1-11; 24:1-10; Amos 7:1-9; 9:1; Habakkuk 1:1—3:19; Zechariah 1:7—6:15; 11:4-17). A similar pattern can be seen in the book of Ezekiel: virtually all of the narratives have to do with the prophet's encounters with Yahweh. In fact, we hear more about Ezekiel's experiences of the divine than any other prophet in the Hebrew Bible.

Unlike most of the other prophetic books, the material in the book of Ezekiel appears to be arranged in chronological order. Whether this is indeed the case cannot be determined with certainty, since most of the sayings are undated. But the ones that do carry dates are presented in the order in which they were delivered, and the others seem appropriate to their present place in the book's story line. Many scholars have cited the chronological arrangement of the materials as evidence that the sayings were recorded near the time when they were delivered, while others believe that the order was supplied by later editors. The primary exception to the chronological structure is the collection of prophecies against the surrounding nations (Ezekiel 25:1—31:32), some of which mention the destruction of Jerusalem before it is actually announced in Ezekiel 33. As in the other prophetic books, these messages of divine judgment against other nations appear to have been placed together because of their common subject matter rather than their temporal proximity.

EXERCISE 99

Read Ezekiel 1:1—3:27; 8:1-18; 37:1-14; 40:1-4; 43:1-5. How does the book say that Ezekiel received the prophetic messages that he declares to his people? What do you think about these claims?

The book of Ezekiel begins with Ezekiel's account of his call to be a prophet. The book dates this event to "the fifth year of the exile of King Jehoiachin" (1:2), the young ruler whom the Babylonians carried off to Babylon with the first wave of exiles in 597 B.C.E. If this date is correct, Ezekiel began his ministry in 592 B.C.E., six years before the Babylonians conquered Jerusalem. Ezekiel was living in Babylonia at the time of his call, so he must have been part of the first wave of exiles, and he seems to have lived in Babylonia for the rest of his life. The book identifies him as a priest (1:3), which would have given him a certain amount of status within the exiled community. Several times he is consulted by the community's elders (8:1; 14:1; 20:1-3), but it is unclear whether this is due to his status as a priest or his role as a prophet. Apart from the fact that he was married (24:15-18), we know little else about Ezekiel's life, including when he died. If the dating system in the book is reliable, Ezekiel prophesied until at least 571 b.c.e. (the "twenty-seventh year" mentioned in Ezekiel 29:17).

Ezekiel's account of his initial call to be a prophet (1:1—3:15), like the stories of Isaiah and Jeremiah, tells of a visionary encounter with the deity in which Ezekiel is informed that he has been chosen by Yahweh to deliver a message to his rebellious children. Like Isaiah and Jeremiah, Ezekiel is told that the people of Judah will reject his message, but he is also assured that Yahweh will strengthen him to speak boldly despite the opposition. The description of Ezekiel's vision is far more elaborate than those of Isaiah or Jeremiah, but the language is so opaque and allusive that many later readers have found it difficult to imagine what he saw. The vision appears to portray Yahweh riding upon a heavenly chariot that is pulled or surrounded by four strange beasts, presumably some kind of heavenly beings. The appearance of Yahweh is so magnificent that Ezekiel falls on his face like a dead man (1:28). Immediately he is raised to his feet by a/the "spirit" or "wind" (2:2; the Hebrew could be translated either way) that later lifts him up and carries him back to his community (3:12-15).

This reference to being lifted up and carried by a spirit or wind introduces one of the most unusual features of the book of Ezekiel, the prophet's repeated accounts of being carried in a vision from place to place and seeing events in distant locations as though he were actually there. The language sounds very much like what people today would call an out-of-body experience. Scholars disagree about whether such reports should be taken as descriptions of real experiences or whether they reflect the use of a fictional literary device. Similar experiences have been reported by intermediaries in other cultures, so we should not rule out the possibility that the stories narrate actual occurrences, whether we attribute them to divine activity, artificially altered states of consciousness, or some other cause. On the other hand, it is also possible that Ezekiel

(or a later editor) framed the account in this way in order to enhance the authority of his pronouncements. Ezekiel's reports about what was happening in the land of Palestine might have been based on news that he had received from travelers who had recently arrived from there (Jeremiah 29:1-32; Ezekiel 33:21).

The book also claims that Ezekiel received repeated auditory messages from Yahweh, much like the other biblical prophets. Apart from the stories that describe his visionary experiences, nothing is said about how these messages came to the prophet. In most cases Ezekiel simply announces a message that he says Yahweh has given him to speak to his people. Many of these messages are quite long and detailed. On several occasions, he also performs symbolic actions that he claims Yahweh has ordered him to do in order to illustrate what Yahweh is doing or about to do with his people. Some of these acts are quite bizarre. On one occasion Ezekiel is ordered to shave off his beard and divide the hair into three parts, of which a third is to be burned, a third cut up with a sword, and a third scattered to the wind. Afterward he is to gather up a few leftover hairs and tie them into his robe, then burn some of them (5:1-4). This series of actions is intended to symbolize what will happen to the citizens of Jerusalem when their city is overcome by the Babylonians (5:5-12). Another time Ezekiel is told to pack his bags as though he is going into exile, then dig through a wall at night in front of a group of witnesses and walk through the hole into the dark with his face covered (12:1-7). Only after he has obeyed this divine command does he learn that his act was meant to illustrate the coming exile of the inhabitants of

Fig. 33.7. Ezekiel's vision of the Valley of Dry Bones (Ezekiel 37), depicted in a Byzantine icon.

Jerusalem (12:8-16). Similar acts were performed by other prophets from time to time, but Ezekiel seems to have used them far more often than previous prophets.

Most of the prophetic books follow the canons of Hebrew poetry. Whether this reflects the way the prophets actually spoke or the literary creativity of a later editor is impossible to say. Ezekiel's messages, on the other hand, are framed as prose sermons. But this does not mean that they were boring. Ezekiel's prophecies overflow with vivid imagery and symbolism that would have gripped the imaginations and emotions of his ancient audience. Of course, this does not mean that they followed his advice. Ezekiel himself notes that many people thought that he was speaking about events in the distant future, not their own time (12:21-28). He also had to compete with other prophets whose messages conflicted with his own (13:1-23; 14:9-11). Clearly Ezekiel had to

use all of the rhetorical tools at his disposal to catch the attention of his people.

Ezekiel's evaluation of Judah's conduct is similar to that of Jeremiah, his older contemporary. The similarities in language and ideas are close enough to convince many scholars that Ezekiel had either heard Jeremiah while he was living in Jerusalem or received reports of Jeremiah's prophecies after he was taken away to Babylonia. Like Jeremiah, Ezekiel points to the worship of other gods as the chief reason for Yahweh's anger with his people (6:1-14; 8:5-18; 11:21; 14:1-8; 16:17-21; 20:27-31; 23:37-39), though he does not overlook the social injustices and violence that the people have committed (7:23-24; 9:9; 22:1-13; 22:25-29; 24:6-9). His allegories of Israel and Judah as unfaithful sisters recall similar passages in Jeremiah's prophecies (Ezekiel 16:46-52; 23:1-27; compare Jeremiah 3:6-13).

Like Jeremiah, Ezekiel condemns the political decisions of Judah's kings and predicts that the Babylonians will abuse King Zedekiah after they conquer Jerusalem (12:10-14; 17:11-21; 19:1-9; 23:11-21). His descriptions of the coming devastation are also very close to those of Jeremiah, though his language is often more graphic (4:9-17; 5:9-17; 6:11-14; 7:14-27; 12:8-20; 16:35-43; 21:1-32; 23:22-30). Like Jeremiah, he insists that the coming judgment is irrevocable (14:12-23), though he agrees with Jeremiah that Yahweh will preserve a small group of the faithful to bear witness to what he has done (9:4-5; 12:16; 14:22-23). His picture of the future of the restored kingdom is virtually identical to that of Jeremiah (see chapter 34). On the whole, Ezekiel's language is more expansive than Jeremiah's, but their ideas are remarkably similar.

But Ezekiel is more than a clone of Jeremiah. His background as a priest leads him to additional insights that are clearly his own. Several times he refers to Yahweh's anger over his people's failure to follow his "ordinances" and "statutes" (5:5-8; 11:12; 20:11-21; compare 18:9; 18:17), and his vision for the future includes a people who will live by these standards (11:19-20; 36:26-27; 37:24; 43:10-11; 44:23-24). Ezekiel's language is too vague in most cases to know precisely what he meant by these terms, but scholars have

Fig. 33.8. Ezekiel's vision of the inner walls of the Jerusalem temple being covered with idolatrous images of animals (Ezekiel 8) recalls the Egyptian practice of engraving or painting images of deities onto the walls of temples, such as the one depicted here.

noted that many of his criticisms of Judah's behavior echo the language and concerns of the so-called Holiness Code that appears in Leviticus 17–26. Most of the laws in these chapters revolve around purity issues that were overseen by the priestly class.

A priestly viewpoint is also evident in the many passages where Ezekiel refers to his people being "unclean" due to their worship of other gods (20:30-31; 20:43; 22:15-16; 22:26; 36:16-17; 36:29; 39:23-24). According to Ezekiel, the deeds of the people of Judah have defiled the temple itself (5:11; 7:22; 8:5-18; 9:6-7; 23:38; 24:21), causing Yahweh to abandon his house to destruction by the Babylonians (9:3; 10:4-22; 11:22-23). Yahweh's people must be cleansed of their defilement before he can live among them again (20:38; 36:25; 37:23). Yet this is not the end of the story. As a priest, Ezekiel cannot imagine a future for Judah that does not include a restored temple and priesthood. The last seven chapters of his book are devoted to describing what this new temple will look like and how it will operate (40:1—46:24). It comes as no surprise that Ezekiel's vision for the future culminates in Yahweh returning in glory to his house (43:1-9).

At the heart of Ezekiel's message lies a concern for the holiness of Yahweh. His visions of the divine presence have sensitized him to the awesome majesty of Yahweh, and his training as a priest tells him that such a holy deity can only live among a holy people. The behavior of the people of Judah shows that they do not appreciate this fact. They have so defiled the land by their worship of other gods and their abusive conduct that Yahweh must purge the evil from their midst if he is to remain true to his covenant. His act of judgment will reveal to the people of Judah and the neighboring lands what kind of god he is. (The phrase "they will know that I am Yahweh" occurs fifty-four times in the book of Ezekiel.) In the end, however, all will be well as Yahweh's chastened but purified people once again devote themselves to his covenant and enjoy the blessings that Yahweh will shower upon them as he dwells among them in his restored temple.

CONCLUSION

The late preexilic period was a time of social, political, and religious turmoil for the nation of Judah. First the Assyrians and then the Babylonians threatened to overrun their land, depose their kings, and impose direct foreign rule. The kings of Judah were forced to engage in constant political jockeying to preserve their people's independence. Their efforts to obtain divine guidance to help them through these difficulties were hampered by conflicts among the prophets over what Yahweh wanted them to do.

The prophets from this period whose sayings were included in the Hebrew Bible were primarily outsiders who challenged the political decisions and religious activities of Judah's leaders and predicted that foreign powers would soon conquer their nation. Worse yet, they claimed that Yahweh was on the side of their enemies. According to these prophets, Yahweh was profoundly unhappy with his people's worship of other gods and the way they were treating one another, and he had finally decided to send foreign nations against them to punish them. His goal was not to destroy them, but to purge them of harmful influences and renew their commitment to his covenant. Those who returned to him could expect a bright future under divine rule.

Few people took these prophets seriously, since accepting their message would have required more personal and social change than most people were willing to make. Some were even accused of treason because of their claim that Yahweh was on the side of their enemies. When events unfolded as they had predicted, however, some people began to conclude that they had indeed been speaking for Yahweh and that their words should be preserved and followed. The efforts of these people and their descendants to collect and edit the sayings of these prophets led eventually to the production of the books that bear their names.

EXERCISE 101

Imagine that you were living in Judah during the time of the prophets who are discussed in this chapter. How do you think you would have responded to their preaching? Why? Would your response be affected by your social level? By your religious beliefs?

Fig. 34.1. A model of the Ishtar Gate, the main entrance into the city of Babylon.

The Exilic Prophets

Thus says the LORD, your Redeemer, the Holy One of Israel: For your sake I will send to Babylon and break down all the bars, and the shouting of the Chaldeans will be turned to lamentation. I am the LORD, your Holy One, the Creator of Israel, your King. . . . I, I am He who blots out your transgressions for my own sake, and I will not remember your sins. (Isaiah 43:14-15, 25)

Thus says the Lord GOD: I will take the people of Israel from the nations among which they have gone, and will gather them from every quarter, and bring them to their own land. I will make them one nation in the land, on the mountains of Israel; and one king shall be king over them all. . . . They shall live in the land that I gave to my servant Jacob, in which your ancestors lived; they and their children and their children's children shall live there forever; and my servant David shall be their prince forever. I will make a covenant of peace with them; it shall be an everlasting covenant with them; and I will bless them and multiply them, and will set my sanctuary among them forevermore. (Ezekiel 37:21-22, 25-26)

But on Mount Zion there shall be those that escape, and it shall be holy; and the house of Jacob shall take possession of those who dispossessed them. The house of Jacob shall be a fire, the house of Joseph a flame, and the house of Esau stubble; they shall burn them and consume them, and there shall be no survivor of the house of Esau; for the LORD has spoken. (Obadiah 17-18)

In this chapter we continue our study of the biblical prophets by examining the sayings of several prophets who delivered their messages in the years between the Babylonian conquest of Judah in 586 B.C.E. and the return of the first wave of exiles in 539 B.C.E. Only three prophets can be dated with certainty to this period: Ezekiel, Obadiah, and an unknown man whom scholars call "Second Isaiah." A few of Jeremiah's later prophecies also belong to this period, as does the book of Lamentations, which Jewish tradition wrongly attributed to Jeremiah. Some of the later additions to the sayings of the preexilic prophets may also have originated during the exilic era, but it is hard to know whether these additions reflect the words of later prophets or the creative activity of literary editors. Dating these editorial additions is also rather

difficult. As a result, this chapter will focus on the three prophets whose words can definitely be linked to this period, along with the book of Lamentations. Though not technically a prophetic book, Lamentations reveals the trauma of the Babylonian conquest like no other book in the Hebrew Bible.

SETTING THE STAGE

As we saw in chapter 8, the Hebrew Bible says relatively little about the lives of the people of Judah under Babylonian rule. Most of what we know about this period comes from Babylonian records, archaeological studies, and scattered references in the narrative and prophetic books, including postexilic works like Ezra and Nehemiah. None of these sources offers anything like a continuous description of the period.

This lack of hard data has led to heated scholarly debates over virtually every aspect of the period. Scholars disagree over such important questions as whether the massive deportations reported in the Hebrew Bible really occurred, how many people remained in Judah after the deportations, and what life was like for those who were taken to Babylonia and those who were left behind. All but minimalist scholars view the biblical account of the deportation of the elites to Babylonia as historically reliable, since it agrees with what we know about Babylonian policy elsewhere. But most scholars now believe that the Hebrew Bible has overstated the impact of the Babylonian conquest on the poor farmers, shepherds, and craftspeople who remained in the towns and villages of Judah after the elites were deported. For them, life probably went on much as it always had, though the effort to rebuild after the invasion would have made life difficult for a while. Life may even have been better for them with the elites gone; at worst, they would have been no more impoverished than in the past.

By contrast, the experience of being carried away to a foreign land where they were members of a displaced population was profoundly disruptive to the elites who were accustomed to being treated with respect and having substantial resources at their disposal. But there is no

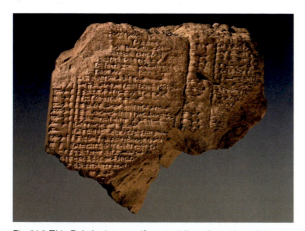

Fig. 34.2. This Babylonian cuneiform text lists the rations that were given to king Jehoiachin of Judah after he was deported to Babylon with a group of exiles in 597 B.C.E. (see 2 Kings 25:27-30).

evidence that they were mistreated once they settled into their new lives in Babylonia. In fact, Babylonian records indicate that some of them were quite successful in the ensuing decades, accumulating substantial wealth and influence. Most apparently remained faithful Yahwists as well, since we know that there was a large and thriving Jewish community in Babylonia for many centuries to come.

Yet problems remained. After the first wave of deportations in 597 B.C.E., prior to the conquest of Jerusalem, hopes remained high that Yahweh would soon restore the exiles, including King Jehoiachin, to their land (Jeremiah 22:11-12, 24-27; 27:16—28:17; 29:8-14). But the destruction of Jerusalem and the temple of Yahweh, followed by the public execution of the defeated King Zedekiah and his replacement by a Babylonian governor, seems to have dashed those hopes. Now the exiles, including a new wave brought to Babylonia after the destruction of Jerusalem, were faced with the daunting task of making sense of what had happened to their people and finding some form of hope and direction for the future. Why had Yahweh not protected them? Was he too weak to defend them, or had he abandoned them forever? How could they maintain their religious life without a temple and sacrificial system? Could Yahweh even hear them this far from their homeland? How should they order their lives in this foreign land? Should they strive to maintain their own separate community, or should they blend in with the Babylonians? Would they ever be able to return to their homes?

The words of the prophets helped them to answer these questions. Some people found guidance in the messages of the preexilic prophets who had warned them that Yahweh would send judgment against his people for their sins if they did not repent and do what he wanted. These sayings not only explained their recent sufferings but also indicated how they should live if they wished to avoid a similar fate in the future. The evident value of these insights led some people to begin collecting, writing down, and editing the words of the prophets for posterity. Other people composed narratives of their nation's past that depicted the fall of Judah as the final act in a centuries-long drama of sin and judgment. These narratives were heavily influenced by the viewpoint of the preexilic prophets. Still others focused on the messages of hope that could be found in some of the preexilic prophets. These messages promised them that Yahweh would one day restore them to their land and bless them with peace and prosperity. Messages like these would have provided comfort and encouragement to people who wondered whether Yahweh had forgotten or abandoned them forever.

But prophets were not merely a relic of the past. We have seen how Ezekiel spoke on Yahweh's behalf to the exiles of Judah in Babylonia, and Jeremiah indicates that there were other prophets among those who were taken to Babylonia in the first wave of deportations (Jeremiah 29:8-9, 15, 21-23). From much later in the exilic period we have the sayings of the prophet known as Second Isaiah, and there were undoubtedly others whose words have been lost or were mingled together with the sayings of earlier prophets. As for the people who remained in the land of Judah, it seems unlikely that prophets would have stopped speaking to them during the Exile, though our knowledge of their activities is as skimpy as the rest of our information about this dark period in the nation's history. The book of Obadiah was written in Judah soon after the Babylonian conquest, and the book of Lamentations also reveals the influence of prophetic ideas in Judah during the exilic period. Both of these books were composed by highly literate individuals, so it would appear that the Babylonians did not in fact remove all of the elites from the land of Judah. Nonetheless, there must have been many other prophets during this period whose sayings were lost due to the scarcity of people who were capable of recording their messages.

The simple fact that prophets continued to bring messages to Yahweh's people during the Exile reassured them that Yahweh had not forgotten or abandoned them. The additional fact that these prophets spoke effectively to the questions and problems of the exiles made their words especially memorable and ensured their preservation. The prophets whose words are included in the Hebrew Bible preached at the beginning or the end of the Exile, the two periods that later editors would have deemed crucial to the survival of their people. A review of their messages will show how these books sought to address the needs and concerns of their exilic audiences.

OBADIAH

The book of Obadiah, with twenty-one verses, is the shortest book in the Hebrew Bible. It is also one of the least read, since it pertains so directly to issues and questions that arose in Judah after the Babylonian conquest. Its brevity and highly poetic style have suggested to many scholars that it may have been written by the prophet himself, who then passed it on to others, but this is merely speculation. The book contains no information about the prophet Obadiah other than his name.

EXERCISE 102

Read the book of Obadiah. Can you figure out what has occurred that provoked such an outburst on the part of the prophet? What does he say is going to happen as a result?

The book of Obadiah, like the book of Nahum, consists entirely of a prophecy of doom against a foreign nation. In this case the nation is Edom, located immediately to the southeast of Judah. The book of Genesis claims that the people who lived here were descended from Esau, the brother of Jacob, the purported ancestor of the people called Israel (Genesis 36:1-43). Only conservative scholars would take this story seriously as history, but Obadiah clearly knows and accepts the tradition: twice he refers to Israel as Edom's "brother" (vv. 10, 12), and several times he implies that Edom's actions are somehow more blameworthy since they were directed toward relatives.

Obadiah is certainly not the first person in the Hebrew Bible to adopt a negative stance toward Edom. The book of Numbers claims that the people of Edom refused to allow the Exodus generation to pass through their territory (Numbers 20:14-21), and the books of Samuel and Kings tell a number of stories of conflicts between the two nations (1 Samuel 14:47; 2 Samuel 8:13-14; 1 Kings 11:14-17; 2 Kings 8:20-22; 14:10). Some of the earlier prophets also announced the coming judgment and devastation of Edom (Isaiah 34:1-17; 63:1-6; Jeremiah 49:7-22; Ezekiel 25:12-14; 35:1-15; Amos 1:11-12; compare Lamentations 4:21-22; Malachi 1:2-5). The harshness of

Fig. 34.3. A scene from the shore of the Dead Sea shows the mountains of Edom on the opposite side.

ing expressed in the book of Obadiah is consistent with the experience of someone who has lived through the experience. This sense of immediacy also poses problems for scholars who argue that the book was written decades or even centuries later when Edom was invaded and destroyed by foreign armies (see Malachi 1:2-5).

Obadiah's message is clear: Yahweh is angry with the way the Edomites treated his people, and he is going to send invaders against them to utterly destroy them (vv. 1-9). When that happens, the Edomites will be left alone with no one to help them (v. 7), just as Judah was abandoned in its day of calamity. In a stunning reversal of fortunes, the people of Israel and Judah will return to their homeland and take over the territory of Edom, destroying all of its inhabitants (vv. 17-18, 21). But Edom is not Yahweh's only target. On the day when he restores his people to their land, Yahweh will also execute judgment against all of the surrounding nations (v. 15) and give his people control over the whole of Palestine, from the Negev to Phoenicia (vv. 19-21). Through them, Yahweh will reign as king over all of this territory, ruling from his temple on Mount Zion (v. 21).

Obadiah's prophecy is not simply a reaction to a single episode of violence, but rather the product of a long history of hostility between the two nations.

Obadiah's message is usually dated to the early years after the Babylonian conquest of Judah on the basis of verses 10-14, which accuse Edom of collaborating with the Babylonians during their invasion of Judah. The prediction of the restoration of the "exiles of Jerusalem" in verse 20 also points to a date after 586 B.C.E. The book appears to been written in Judah rather than Babylonia, but there is no way to be certain.

According to Obadiah, the Edomites have incurred Yahweh's judgment because they not only refused to assist Judah against the Babylonians (v. 11) but also plundered Jerusalem (as allies of the Babylonians? vv. 13, 16) and helped to capture people who were trying to escape (v. 14). Some scholars have questioned whether Edom's role in the conquest of Jerusalem has been exaggerated, since there is no outside evidence to verify Obadiah's accusations. But negative depictions of Edom's actions can be found in other parts of the Hebrew Bible as well (Psalm 137:7-9; Ezekiel 35:5, 10, 15), and the intensity of feel-

In hindsight we can see that the latter part of Obadiah's message was wishful thinking, but he certainly was not alone. Obadiah's anger at what other nations had done to his people and his hopes for their future restoration expressed the feelings of countless people during the period of the Exile. Both were part of a larger effort to make sense of a series of tragic events that might otherwise have shattered their faith. This effort to find some kind of ultimate meaning and purpose in the destruction of Judah is typical of all of the exilic prophets.

LAMENTATIONS

The book of Lamentations is not a prophetic book, but it is included here both because it shows the influence of prophetic ideas and because, other than Obadiah, it is our only direct window onto the thoughts and feelings of people who experienced and reflected upon the events of the Babylonian conquest. The name of the book reveals its similarity to the laments that we find in the book of Psalms. The book consists of five highly artistic poems that use vivid imagery to depict the physical and emotional loss that resulted from the destruction of the city of Jerusalem and its temple. Whether the poems were composed by a single individual or by several different people is unclear. Since ancient times the book has been attributed to the prophet Jeremiah, but scholars have found no reliable evidence to support this view. The book appears to have been written by an unknown member (or members) of the Jerusalem elite who either stayed behind in Judah when the Babylonians deported most of the city's leading citizens or lived through the events that it describes before being taken away to Babylonia.

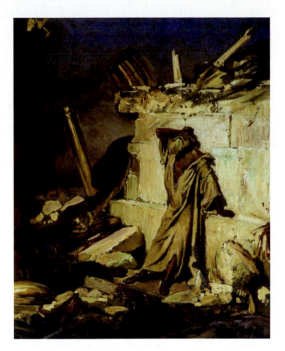

Fig. 34.4. Ilya Repin, *Cry of Prophet Jeremiah on the Ruins of Jerusalem*

> ## EXERCISE 103
>
> Read Lamentations 1:1-12; 2:1-22; and 3:21-42 and make a list of all the bad things that the speaker says have come upon Judah. What is his explanation for why these things have happened? Is there any hope for the future?

The book of Lamentations relies on the power of poetry to paint a vivid picture of the aftermath of the Babylonian conquest of Judah and Jerusalem. Using the rhythm of a funeral dirge to enhance its emotional effect, the book gives powerful expression to the thoughts and feelings of people who survived the Babylonian invasion. Parts of the book look back at the painful occurrences of the recent past; others plumb the depths of the present sufferings of the people of Judah; still others examine the possibility of hope for the future. The result is a moving depiction of the physical, mental, emotional, and spiritual pain that afflicted those who remained in Judah after the conquest.

When looking back at the past, the author draws a sharp contrast between the beauty and apparent invincibility of Jerusalem before the Babylonian invasion and its sorry state now. The loss is incalculable: the fortresses of Judah have been destroyed, the city and its walls lie in ruins, the temple has been demolished, the population has been slaughtered, and the survivors (including their king) have been taken away into exile. But the author is not content simply to describe what has happened; these awful events cry out for an explanation. For this the author turns to the ideas voiced by the preexilic prophets and the Deuteronomic tradition. Again and again the poems insist that the sufferings of Judah represent Yahweh's punishment for their sins (1:5, 8, 12, 14, 18; and others). The Babylonians fade into the background; it is Yahweh who fought as a warrior against his people and devastated their land (1:12-13, 15; 2:2-9, 20-21; 3:1-18, 43). Surprisingly, almost nothing is said about the nature of the sins that led to Yahweh's judgment. One verse might conceivably allude to the worship of other gods (1:19), and a couple of others speak about prophets who gave false messages (2:14) and priests who had innocent people killed (4:13). For the most part, however, the poems operate at the level of generality. Perhaps the author thought that Judah's sins were so obvious as to require no listing, or perhaps he simply presumed that severe sufferings should be interpreted as divine punishments, even if the nature of the sins was unclear.

The author's description of the present troubles of Judah is bleak. The poems paint a picture of desperate hunger and starvation that are especially hard on children (1:11, 19; 2:11-12, 19-20; 3:16; 4:2-10; 5:4-6, 10). Families have been left homeless (2:2; 3:19), young women have been raped (5:11), and young men have been put to forced labor (5:13). The destruction of the temple has put an end to their religious festivals and sacrifices (1:4; 2:6), and their prophets are no longer hearing messages from Yahweh (2:9). The humiliation of being defeated and ruled by their enemies is made worse by the physical abuse that they have endured at the hands of their rulers (3:34-36; 5:4-6, 12) and the verbal abuse that they hear (or imagine) from the residents of neighboring lands (2:15-17; 3:45-47, 61-63). The people weep and mourn over their fate (1:2; 2:10-11; 3:48; 5:14-15), but no comfort is to be found (1:2, 16-17, 21; 3:17).

In the face of such painful circumstances, there is only one thing that the people of Judah can do: return to Yahweh and cry out to him for forgiveness and help (2:18-19; 3:40-42). The poem assures them that Yahweh has not forgotten them. He sees their troubles (3:34-36, 59-63) and will rescue those who trust in him and wait patiently for him to act (3:25-33). His love for his people never ceases. Though their circumstances seem bleak at the moment, the time will come when Yahweh will once again shower them with mercy and compassion (3:22-24, 31-32). He will not let their oppressors rule over them forever. In due time he will answer their prayers to bring down their enemies (1:21-22; 3:64-66; 4:21-22) and restore his temple (4:22).

Despite its dark tones, the book of Lamentations is ultimately a hopeful book. That hope is rooted in Yahweh's unfailing devotion to his people. Looking back, the author insists that Yahweh had a purpose in all of the bad things that have come upon them. Looking at the present, he assures them that Yahweh has not forgotten them in their troubles and calls them to renew their devotion to Yahweh. Looking ahead, he offers hope that Yahweh will once again reveal his love for his people by rescuing them from their present circumstances. Precisely what Yahweh plans to do remains murky; the author shows little awareness of the prophetic predictions of a glorious future for the restored people of Judah. But as Lamentations shows us, speculating about what will happen in the future is not the only way to bring hope and assurance to a group that is facing difficult circumstances.

EZEKIEL 25–48

As we saw in the previous chapter, the prophet Ezekiel straddled the preexilic and exilic periods. The people who compiled his sayings into the present collection made a clear distinction between the two periods, placing the preexilic sayings in chapters 1–24 and the exilic sayings in chapters 25–48. The pattern is not followed in every case: Ezekiel 33, which speaks of the fall of Jerusalem, belongs with the earlier materials, while some of the more hopeful passages in the earlier chapters (11:14-21; 17:22-24; 20:40-44) seem to fit better in the exilic period. But the overall division into two periods of ministry is clearly intentional.

The message and tone of the exilic chapters are markedly different than those of the preexilic chapters. While the earlier materials focus squarely on the coming judgment of Judah at the hands of the Babylonians, the later materials speak about Yahweh judging the other nations of the region and restoring the people of Judah to their land under a righteous Davidic king. The earlier chapters bring a message of unremitting doom; the later chapters are filled with hope and encouragement. The shift in message and tone is consistent with what we see elsewhere as we move from the preexilic to the exilic era. Nowhere else, however, do we witness such a radical change in the message of a single prophet.

Fig. 34.5. Ruins of the city of Tyre in modern Lebanon (ancient Phoenicia). The city was destroyed by Alexander the Great in 332 B.C.E., some 250 years after Ezekiel spoke of its coming doom (Ezekiel 26–28).

EXERCISE 104

Read Ezekiel 25:1—26:14; 36:1—37:28; 43:1-12. Why does Ezekiel say that Yahweh is going to judge the nations that surround Judah? What is he going to do for Judah in that day?

The first part of Ezekiel's exilic prophecy (chapters 25–32) focuses on the coming judgment of various nations that are accused of harming Yahweh's people in the years immediately before and after the Babylonian conquest of Judah. In the case of Egypt, the criticism centers on its failure to support Judah in its hour of need (29:6-7). The other nations are condemned for taking advantage of or gloating over the fall of Jerusalem (25:3, 6, 8, 12, 15; 26:2). Egypt and Tyre bear the brunt of the attack, with seven chapters devoted to their coming downfall. Why these two nations should have been singled out for criticism is unclear. The prophecies against them list a variety of ways in which they have offended Yahweh, including their pride (27:3; 28:2, 6, 17; 29:9; 31:10; 32:2), their use of violence (28:16), and their unfair business practices (28:18).

The language that is used to describe the coming judgment of the surrounding nations is virtually identical to that used elsewhere for Israel and Judah: Yahweh will send foreign armies against them to destroy their cities, slaughter their people, take over their land and possessions, and carry the survivors away into exile. Interestingly, nothing is said about any coming judgment against the Babylonians; Ezekiel still holds firmly to the preexilic mind-set that sees the Babylonians as Yahweh's tool for bringing judgment upon his enemies (26:7; 29:18-20; 30:10-11, 24-26; 32:11-12). This omission produces a certain amount of ambiguity in Ezekiel's message to the exilic community: Yahweh has not forgotten their sufferings, and he will take vengeance against those who have harmed them—except for the Babylonians, who hurt them the most.

From chapter 34 onward, Ezekiel's message focuses on the glorious future that Yahweh has in store for his people. The message is not entirely positive: the leaders of the exilic community are criticized for ruling harshly and not showing proper concern for the needy (34:2-10), while others in the community are condemned for abusing the weak and the powerless (34:17-22). These observations explain why Ezekiel's vision of the future includes a moment when Yahweh's people will be cleansed from their sinful ways (34:17, 20; 36:31-32; 39:25-27;

compare 11:18, 21; 16:61-63; 20:35-39, 43). Ezekiel's statements about the future are not consistent, but most of his predictions assume that this cleansing will take place after the people have been restored to their land. At that time they will see how much Yahweh has done for them and how little they deserve his favors, and most will feel ashamed and turn from their evil ways to serve Yahweh. The others will be judged and removed from

Fig. 34.6. Francisco Collantes, *The Vision of Ezekiel* (see Ezekiel 37)

the community. Those who choose to follow Yahweh will receive a "new heart" and a "new spirit" that will enable them to obey his commands (36:26-27; 37:14; 39:29; compare 11:18-20). In that day Yahweh will once again live among them as their god in his restored temple, served by his holy priests (34:30; 37:26-28; 40:1—47:12; compare 20:40-41).

On the other hand, the blessings that Yahweh has in store for his people are not merely spiritual. After they return to their land, Yahweh will bless them with material prosperity—healthy animals, green pastures, ample rains, fruitful harvests, safety from wild animals, and everything else that is vital to the life of a rural population (34:13-14, 25-29; 36:8-11, 29-30). The towns and cities of Judah will also be rebuilt, and their population

will increase and spread out across the land (36:10-11, 33-38). The two nations of Israel and Judah will once again be united under the rule of a righteous king from the line of David (34:23-24; 37:15-25), and Yahweh will keep them safe from the attacks of other nations (34:28-29; 38:1—39:29). As a result of all of these acts, Yahweh's people and the surrounding nations will come to recognize that he alone is god and Israel is his people (34:30; 36:23; 39:22, 28; compare 16:62; 17:24; 20:42).

The relevance of this message to Ezekiel's audience in Babylonia is easy to see. Just as his earlier prophecies explained the meaning of the destruction of Jerusalem, so his later messages assured them that Yahweh had not forgotten them and was working in the affairs of nations to restore them to their land and renew his blessings upon them. No timetable is given, nor is there much explicit attempt to direct the people's conduct while they remain in exile. What Ezekiel offers instead is the assurance that Yahweh is with them in Babylonia and has a glorious future in store for them. This alone would have been enough to lift the spirits of his audience and motivate many of them to remain faithful to Yahweh in the midst of a polytheistic Babylonian culture.

SECOND ISAIAH (ISAIAH 40–55)

One of the great mysteries of the Hebrew Bible is why the words of an unknown prophet from late in the exilic period should have been appended to a collection of the sayings of the prophet Isaiah, who lived some two hundred years before his time. The words of this prophet, which can be found in Isaiah 40–55, represent some of the most beautiful and compelling poetry in the entire Hebrew Bible. One would think that the identity of such a prophet would have been not only preserved but also celebrated. Yet his very name was allowed to slip into obscurity, and scholars have no way of knowing who he was or anything about him other than what is revealed in his words. The fact that his words were appended to the book of Isaiah has led many scholars to presume that he spoke as a representative of a "school of Isaiah" that was devoted to the words of the eighth-century B.C.E. prophet, but this is pure speculation. We simply do not know why his words were placed where they now stand.

More than two hundred years ago, scholars came to recognize that Isaiah 40–55 could not have been written by the eighth-century B.C.E. prophet Isaiah. Not only are the language and style quite different from the first thirty-nine chapters of the book of Isaiah, but numerous verses in chapters 40–55 presuppose that the audience is living in exile in Babylonia. (Isaiah 56–66, which appears to have been added to the book in the postexilic period, will be treated in chapter 35.) Again and again the prophet identifies Babylonia as the great enemy who has conquered the people of Yahweh and will soon be brought down by Israel's god (43:14; 47:1-15; 48:14, 20-21). The sayings even name the Persian king Cyrus as the one who will conquer Babylonia, anticipating the events of 539 B.C.E. (44:28; 45:1-3, 13-14). These messages about the coming defeat of Babylonia would have made no sense to the people of Judah in Isaiah's day (eighth century B.C.E.), when the Assyrians ruled Mesopotamia and Babylonia did not exist as an independent nation. (The references to Babylonia in Isaiah 13–14 and Micah 4:10 are later additions.) Isaiah 40–55 also contains many references to the ruined buildings and walls of Judah (44:26-28; 49:16-17; 52:9) and the impending return of the people to their land (43:5-7; 48:20; 49:22-23; 55:12-13). These verses presuppose that the land of Judah has been devastated by invaders and the audience is living outside their homeland. Finally, Isaiah 40–55 is filled with hopeful messages about the future and repeated assurances of Yahweh's love and forgiveness, the polar opposite of what we find in the preexilic prophets.

EXERCISE 105

Read Isaiah 40:1-8; 42:1-9; 43:8-10; 49:1-12; 50:4-11; 52:13—53:12. Who do you think is the "servant" mentioned in these passages? Who is the "I" who speaks?

Conservative scholars have sometimes argued that the conditions of the Exile could have been revealed to the prophet Isaiah in advance of their occurrence, but there are no signs in these chapters that the prophet is speaking about an imaginary situation. The great majority of scholars agree that the prophet who spoke these words lived in Babylonia toward the end of the exilic period.

While we know nothing directly about the prophet who stands behind Isaiah 40–55, the present collection contains a number of "I" passages that sound very much like the voice of the prophet describing his own experience. Several of these verses reveal an awareness of being called by Yahweh to be a prophet to the exiled people of Judah (40:1-6; 48:16; 49:1-5, 8-9) and the nations (42:5-7; 49:6-7). At least two passages claim to report the words that Yahweh used when commissioning the speaker for his mission (40:1-6; 49:3-9). Nearly all of the sayings in Isaiah 40–55 are framed as the first-person speech of Yahweh, implying that the speaker is receiving regular messages from the deity for his people. A few verses suggest that the speaker experienced opposition and abuse as a result of his efforts to proclaim Yahweh's message (50:4-11).

In addition to these "I" passages, there are a number of verses in Isaiah 40–55 that describe someone whom Yahweh calls "my servant." The identity of this servant of Yahweh has been debated for centuries. Christians have claimed that these verses point ahead to the coming of Jesus, particularly the famous "suffering servant" passage in Isaiah 53. But there is no sign in any of these passages that the prophet was thinking of a person who would come in the future. Scholars are divided over whether the term refers to an individual (most likely the prophet) or to Israel, depicted here in figurative terms as a person. Verses can be cited in support of both positions: a number of verses directly or indirectly equate the servant with the people of Israel (41:8-10; 42:18-22; 43:10; 44:1-2, 21; 45:4; 48:20), while others just as clearly apply the term to the speaker (49:3-7; 50:10). In still other cases, the identity of the servant is ambiguous, including the lengthy text of Isaiah 53 (42:1-4; 52:13—53:12). Some scholars have seen in this latter passage a poetic description of the painful death that the prophet suffered at the hands of the Babylonians, who would have viewed his predictions of the impending defeat of Babylonia by the Persians as subversive. Others insist that the verses offer a figurative description of the sufferings that Israel has experienced as a result of the exile. In the end, there is no way to be sure what the speaker had in mind. We must therefore be careful about using these suffering servant passages as evidence for the life and ministry of the shadowy but important prophet whom scholars call Second Isaiah.

Fig. 34.7. An artist's rendition of Cyrus the Great, king of the Medes and the Persians, 550–530 B.C.E.

EXERCISE 106

Read Isaiah 43:1-13; 44:1-23; 45:1-13; 47:1-15; 55:1-13. What would you say are some of the major themes or emphases of Second Isaiah's message?

The sayings of Second Isaiah do not appear to be organized according to any overarching pattern. A loose sense of progression can be seen in the way the collection begins with an announcement of Yahweh's intention to rescue his people and ends with a depiction of their anticipated return to their homeland. But there is little evidence of chronological development or thematic arrangement in the intervening chapters. The book reads like a loose collection of oracles delivered at different times and places.

Behind the highly poetic sayings of Second Isaiah lies a message that is quite similar to that of the other exilic prophets. What the prophet offers his people is not a new vision for the future, but a new insight into Yahweh's timing. Yahweh has told him that the time has come for their hopes to be fulfilled: Yahweh is going to empower the Persian king Cyrus to defeat the Babylonians, after which Cyrus will allow Yahweh's people to return to their homeland and rebuild their homes, their cities, and their lives. Cyrus's role in Yahweh's plan is so crucial that the prophet can describe this pagan king as Yahweh's "anointed one" (45:1), the same Hebrew word that is elsewhere translated as "Messiah."

The prophet must have known that many in the audience would doubt his message, since he surrounds this essentially political announcement with religious ideas and language that aim to allay the fears and stimulate the hopes of his audience. A review of some of the book's major themes will show how closely the prophet's message is tailored to the needs of his day.

1. *Redemptive suffering.* Like other prophets before him, Second Isaiah believes that the Exile occurred as a punishment for his people's sins (42:21-25; 43:22-28; 47:6-7; 50:1-2). But how long are they to be punished? Second Isaiah claims that Yahweh has told him that the era of punishment is now at an end (40:2; 51:21-23). Yahweh's people have suffered enough; the time has come for him to forgive their sins and return to their side (43:25; 44:22-23; 45:9-11). From now on he will use his power to help them rather than to harm them (40:27-31; 41:13-14). Very soon he will use the pagan king Cyrus to bring down the Babylonians and restore his people to their land.

2. *Yahweh and Israel.* Again and again Second Isaiah underlines Yahweh's deep commitment to his people. After decades of living in Babylonia, some of the exiles had apparently begun to wonder if Yahweh had forgotten them or no longer cared for them (40:27). Second Isaiah repeatedly reminds them how Yahweh chose their

ancestors out of all the nations of the earth and made them his covenant people (41:8-10; 43:1; 44:1-2, 21; 51:1-3). He has not abandoned that commitment; he still loves Israel (43:3-4; 45:4; 46:3-4; 54:5-10). Since Yahweh is on their side, there is no reason for them to be afraid or worry about the future. He will bring down their foes, restore them to their land, and provide for their needs (41:13-20; 43:5-7; 44:1-5).

3. *The power of Yahweh.* Second Isaiah insists that Yahweh is the only god who knows the future and has the power to bring it about (41:21-29; 43:9-13; 44:6-8; 45:21; 46:8-13; 48:1-8). There is no other god like him. His mighty hand formed the universe; how can anyone question his ability to carry out his plans (45:9-14, 18-19)? Certainly the gods of the Babylonians cannot stop him (45:20; 46:1-2; 47:12-13). They are nothing but hunks of wood overlaid with gold, devoid of all life (40:18-19; 44:9-20; 46:5-7). The exiles need not worry that the Babylonian gods will be able to protect them from Yahweh's judgment. Yahweh is the only deity who has the power to shape the future.

4. *The new Exodus.* Throughout his sayings, Second Isaiah uses images drawn from the Exodus story to illustrate what Yahweh is going to do for his people. Just as he once brought Israel out of Egypt, so he now plans to lead them out of Babylonia in a new exodus that will restore them to their homeland. Like the first time, Yahweh will lead them through waters, deserts, and all manner of trials, but he will protect and take care of them (40:3-5; 43:16-21; 48:20-21; 50:2; 51:9-11). In the process, he will once again make a covenant with them as he did at Mount Sinai, but this time it will last forever (55:3). Drawing parallels between their situation and the Exodus story allowed Second Isaiah to tap into a vast reservoir of positive feelings about Yahweh and his ability to work in human history.

5. *The restoration of Zion.* More than virtually any other prophet, Second Isaiah stresses Yahweh's devotion

to Jerusalem, often calling it by its poetic name Zion, the name of the hill upon which Yahweh's temple was located. Several times Yahweh tells the prophet how much he loves Jerusalem and how he longs for it to be rebuilt (44:26-28; 46:3; 49:14-23; 51:16—52:10; 54:11-17). In fact, the first message that he receives from Yahweh is to announce to Zion the good news that its restoration is at hand (40:9-11). If Yahweh feels this strongly about Jerusalem, how can he fail to lead his people home?

6. *Israel and the nations.* Like the prophets before him, Second Isaiah insists that Yahweh controls the affairs of nations—not just of Israel, but of its neighbors as well. He alone has the power to move kings and armies to do his bidding (40:21-24; 41:2-4, 25). Just as he sent the Babylonian armies against his people, so he will bring down the Babylonians at the hand of Cyrus and the Persians (43:14; 44:28—45:7; 47:1-15; 48:14, 20).

But Yahweh's interest in other nations is not limited to their military might; he wants his people to share their knowledge of him with others so that they, too, might come to know Yahweh (45:14, 22-23; 49:6-7, 22-23; 51:4-5; 55:5). To the exiles, this meant speaking confidently about the power and goodness of their god instead

Fig. 34.8. A contemporary artist's rendition of Second Isaiah's vision of the coming destruction of Babylon.

of being cowed by their minority status. If they will only obey, their experience of punishment can bring salvation to the nations.

OTHER EXILIC PROPHETS?

Were there other exilic prophets besides those covered in this chapter? Everything that we have learned so far would lead us to suspect that there must have been prophets in the exilic communities whom the common people consulted for "words of Yahweh" in times of need, just as they did in the preexilic period. The ritual activities of the exiled priests would have been limited by their distance from the religious shrines where they carried on their duties. But prophets could work anywhere. The few prophets whose words were preserved may have been the most prominent of the exilic prophets, but it is unlikely that they were the only ones.

Any search for information about other prophets is limited by the nature of our sources, which contain no coherent narrative of the exilic period. But there are several tantalizing hints that lend credibility to the idea that there were other prophets during the exilic period besides those whose sayings were included in the Hebrew Bible. The book of Lamentations (2:9) mentions prophets in Palestine in the early days of the Exile, and prophets were clearly active there in the years after the Exile (see chapter 35). The book of Nehemiah (6:14) mentions a prophetess named Noadiah who opposed the work of the returning exiles and must therefore have been a resident of Palestine. Thus there is no reason to think that prophets ceased their activities in Palestine during the period when the elites were away in Babylonia.

As for the Babylonian community, Jeremiah refers to several prophets who were taken away like Ezekiel in the first wave of exiles and continued to preach in Babylonia (Jeremiah 29:8-9, 15, 21-23). No information is available from the middle decades of the exilic period, but the preservation of the words of Second Isaiah, who lived near the end of the exilic era, and of the messages of Haggai and Zechariah, who returned to Judah at the end of the Exile, suggests that prophecy was not a lost art among those who lived in Babylonia during the exilic period.

Additional evidence for prophecy in Babylonia comes from the books of the preexilic prophets. Several of these books contain passages from the exilic period that were apparently added when the books were being put together in Babylonia. For example, Amos 9:11-15 looks forward to a time when Yahweh will "raise up the booth of David that is fallen" (that is, install a new Davidic king) and the people of Judah will "rebuild the ruined cities and inhabit them." Both the language and the ideas of this passage reflect the aspirations of the Exile. Similarly, Isaiah 13:1—14:23 contains a lengthy oracle against Babylonia that includes a promise that Yahweh will one day restore his people to their land (14:1). This passage would have made no sense to an eighth-century B.C.E. audience, but it fits quite well in the exilic period. Passages such as these are not mere editorial updates. In both style and content, they are as "prophetic" as anything that appears in the books of the prophets. While it is possible that these added passages were created by editors who mimicked the style of the prophets, it makes more sense to see them as the sayings of exilic prophets that were incorporated into the books of the prophets at some point during the editorial process. If this is correct, Second Isaiah is not the only exilic prophet whose name and identity have been lost in the mists of history.

CONCLUSION

The Babylonian conquest inaugurated a new era in the political history of the people of Judah. The change was accompanied by a marked shift in the message of the prophets whose words were included in the Hebrew Bible. Instead of issuing threats of divine judgment, the prophets of the exilic period brought a more positive message that offered hope and assurance to a defeated and dejected people. Judgment language did not disappear, but it was directed against the surrounding nations rather than Judah.

Little is known about the prophets who lived in Palestine during the exilic era. The books of Obadiah and Lamentations are our only direct windows onto this dark period in the history of Israel. From the community of exiles in Babylonia we have the sayings of Ezekiel and Second Isaiah, but there must have been other prophets at work in both Babylonia and Palestine during this period.

The prophetic sayings that have survived from the exilic era exhibit many common themes. Both Ezekiel and Second Isaiah reassure the exiles that Yahweh has not forgotten them. Their defeat and exile at the hands of the Babylonians are not a sign that Yahweh was too weak or unconcerned to help them. Instead, Yahweh sent the Babylonians against them to purge them of their sinful ways and renew their devotion to him and his covenant. When the cleansing is complete, Yahweh will free them from Babylonian rule and restore them to their land, initiating an era of peace and prosperity. Here they will live as Yahweh desires, and Yahweh will dwell in their midst forever.

While such an idyllic vision of the future might seem unrealistic to us today, the psychological value of such a message should not be underestimated. The words of the exilic prophets gave meaning to their people's sufferings in the past, direction for their lives in the present, and hope for a better world in the future. The fact that their words were preserved and eventually incorporated into the Hebrew Bible shows that people in later periods found their message both meaningful and encouraging.

EXERCISE 107

Imagine that you lived in Babylonia during the exilic period. What kinds of religious questions and stresses might you have faced there? How might the words of the preexilic prophets have helped you to deal with those stresses?

Fig. 35.1. Ruins of the Gate of All Nations at Persepolis, the ceremonial capital of the Persian Empire in the postexilic era. The gate carries an inscription by king Xerxes (486–465 B.C.E.), who credits the Persian god Ahuramazda for assistance in building the gate and other structures in the city.

The Postexilic Prophets

For thus says the LORD of hosts: Just as I purposed to bring disaster upon you, when your ancestors provoked me to wrath, and I did not relent, says the LORD of hosts, so again I have purposed in these days to do good to Jerusalem and to the house of Judah; do not be afraid. These are the things that you shall do: Speak the truth to one another, render in your gates judgments that are true and make for peace, do not devise evil in your hearts against one another, and love no false oath; for all these are things that I hate, says the LORD. (Zechariah 8:14-17)

For thus says the LORD of hosts: Once again, in a little while, I will shake the heavens and the earth and the sea and the dry land; and I will shake all the nations, so that the treasure of all nations shall come, and I will fill this house with splendor, says the LORD of hosts. The silver is mine, and the gold is mine, says the LORD of hosts. The latter splendor of this house shall be greater than the former, says the LORD of hosts; and in this place I will give prosperity, says the LORD of hosts. (Haggai 2:6-9)

For I am about to create new heavens and a new earth; the former things shall not be remembered or come to mind. But be glad and rejoice forever in what I am creating; for I am about to create Jerusalem as a joy, and its people as a delight. I will rejoice in Jerusalem, and delight in my people; no more shall the sound of weeping be heard in it, or the cry of distress. No more shall there be in it an infant that lives but a few days, or an old person who does not live out a lifetime; for one who dies at a hundred years will be considered a youth, and one who falls short of a hundred will be considered accursed. (Isaiah 65:17-20)

The period that scholars call the Babylonian exile formally ended with the Persian conquest of Babylonia in 539 B.C.E. and the subsequent decision by the Persian king Cyrus to allow the descendants of the exiled citizens of Judah to return to their homeland. From here the Hebrew Bible shifts its attention to the people who accepted the king's offer to move back to Palestine. As a result, we lose sight of the many people (probably the majority) who chose to remain in Babylonia rather than start new lives in the land of their ancestors. Though neglected by the biblical editors, the group that stayed in Babylonia became the nucleus of a sizable Jewish community that nearly a thousand years later produced the Talmud,

the authoritative collection of rabbinic discussions concerning the meaning and application of the Torah.

There is no reason to think that prophecy suddenly died out in Babylonia with the departure of the returning exiles. We simply lack evidence for the activities and sayings of prophets in this community. From Palestine, however, we have several collections of prophetic sayings that show clearly that prophets continued to play an important role in the religious life of the postexilic community. Prophetic books that most scholars would assign to this period include Haggai, Zechariah, "Third Isaiah" (Isaiah 56–66), Jonah, Malachi, Joel, and "Second Zechariah" (Zechariah 9–14), along with the apocalyptic chapters of the book of Daniel (Daniel 7–12). The materials in Second Zechariah and Daniel 7–12 are very different from the other books in this chapter and will be discussed in chapter 36. The present chapter will examine the books of Haggai, Zechariah, Third Isaiah, Malachi, Joel, and Jonah.

When viewed as a unit, these books lack the unifying focus of the earlier periods, since they were composed in response to the changing circumstances of the Yahwistic community in Palestine over a period of nearly four hundred years. Even assigning dates to some of these books is difficult. As a result, the present chapter will probably seem more disjointed than the previous chapters. But there are still a number of common themes that run through many of the prophetic books from this period.

SETTING THE STAGE

From a political standpoint, the postexilic period includes at least three distinct eras: (a) the Persian era (539–332 B.C.E.); (b) the Greek era (332–142 B.C.E.), which includes periods of Ptolemaic/Egyptian (301–198 B.C.E.) and Seleucid/Syrian (198–142 B.C.E.) rule; and (c) the **Hasmonean** era (142–63 B.C.E.), when the Jewish people finally gained their independence and lived under their own kings for several decades. The Hasmonean era was followed by several centuries of Roman rule, but this takes us beyond the time when the books of the Hebrew Bible were being composed.

Most of our information about political developments in this period comes from outside the Hebrew Bible, since the narrative books extend only into the early Persian period (Ezra and Nehemiah). In general, the foreign nations that controlled Palestine during this era allowed the followers of Yahweh to practice their religion freely and to control their own religious affairs. This explains why the messages of the postexilic prophets contain so few references to foreign domination and the changing political circumstances of Palestine. Only two political events from the postexilic era attracted any serious attention from the biblical authors: a decree by the Persian king putting an end to the reconstruction of the Jerusalem temple in the late sixth century B.C.E. and a bout

of religious persecution by the Seleucid king Antiochus IV in the mid-second century B.C.E. In both cases messengers from Yahweh arose to offer their people guidance concerning how they should respond to the actions of the foreign rulers: Haggai and Zechariah in the Persian period, "Daniel" in the Greek period. More will be said about both of these episodes in the sections where these books are discussed.

Apart from these special situations, the religious life of the postexilic community developed along its own path, independent of changes in the political administration of Palestine. Most of what we know about this community comes from the sayings of the postexilic prophets. Unfortunately, the poetic language that was used by the prophets leaves much to the imagination, and scholars disagree about how their sayings should be interpreted. The absence of a coherent narrative for this period also makes it difficult for scholars to date the prophets' sayings, leading to numerous disagreements about the nature and history of the postexilic community. Periods of several decades cannot be linked with any written records. The further we move into the postexilic period, the more speculative our historical judgments become.

In light of these difficulties, the present chapter will not delve too deeply into the historical circumstances that gave rise to the sayings of the postexilic prophets, apart from the two periods that have already been mentioned. Nor will much attention be given to the question of when particular books or sayings were composed, since most of the arguments are fairly technical and therefore beyond the scope of an introductory textbook. In the end, there are many questions about the postexilic period that simply cannot be answered. Responsible historical scholarship can only proceed as far as the evidence will allow.

HAGGAI

The book of Haggai gives precise dates for the five units that make up the book (four prophetic oracles and one short narrative section). All five are dated to a three-month period in 520 B.C.E., the second year of the Persian king Darius. The same dating system is used in the book of Zechariah, whose prophetic ministry overlapped that of Haggai. The dates in both books are consistent with the brief references to Haggai and Zechariah in Ezra 5:1 and 6:14, though no specific dates are cited in the latter passages. Many scholars believe that the books of Haggai and Zechariah were compiled by the same editor fairly soon after the prophets delivered their messages, since both books talk about the process of rebuilding the Jerusalem temple but neither mentions its completion in 515 B.C.E.

The present collection of Haggai's sayings tells us nothing about the prophet's life or background, but the book does offer a few tantalizing clues. Haggai's focus on the Jerusalem temple and his use of "holiness" language (2:10-15) suggest that he might have come from a priestly family like his colleague Zechariah (see below). Presumably he was a member of the local elite, since he spoke his message directly to the governor Zerubbabel, a descendant of King David, and to the high priest Joshua, and both leaders took his words seriously (1:12). The sudden commencement of his prophetic ministry nearly twenty years after the first wave of exiles had returned from Babylonia might suggest that he had only recently arrived in Palestine, but his message could also be interpreted as a response to political developments in the Persian Empire around that time (see below). What happened to Haggai after the period represented by this short collection is unknown, though he probably continued to work as a prophet, perhaps at the Jerusalem temple.

EXERCISE 108

Read the book of Haggai. To what does Haggai attribute the poor economic conditions of the postexilic community in Judah? What does he say Yahweh will do if they rebuild his temple?

According to the book of Ezra, the first wave of returning exiles from Babylonia received permission from the Persian king Cyrus to rebuild the temple of Yahweh in Jerusalem, which had been destroyed by the Babylonians (Ezra 1:2-4). Their efforts to carry out this mission were opposed by the people who had stayed in Palestine during the Exile, presumably because they did not want outsiders coming in and taking over their community. Their

opponents appealed to Cyrus's successor and obtained a decree ordering the construction activity to cease (Ezra 4:6-24).

The reliability of this narrative has been challenged, not only because the story includes "official documents" that use the wrong name for Cyrus's successor but also because Haggai's initial prophecy seems to imply that no work has been done on the temple (Haggai 1:1-8). Scholars who accept the Ezra narrative find significance in the timing of Haggai's message. The Persian king Darius had recently come to the throne after several years of instability that followed the death of Cyrus's son Cambyses in 522 B.C.E. Many scholars believe that the rise of a new king from a different family might have aroused hopes for a resumption of construction activity on the temple, leading to Haggai's call to recommence the work. Those who question the reliability of the Ezra narrative, on the other hand, see no real significance in the change of rulers.

The book of Haggai gives no indication that outside political factors played any role in the prophet's thinking. Instead, his message focuses on the economic problems

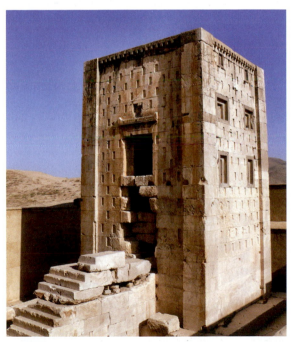

Fig. 35.2. The ruins of a Persian era Zoroastrian temple at Naqsh-e Rostam, Iran, that stands in front of the royal tombs of several ancient Persian kings.

that are plaguing his community. Like the preexilic prophets, Haggai sees a direct link between his people's obedience to Yahweh and their material prosperity. According to Haggai, the poor harvests and droughts that they have been experiencing were sent by Yahweh to motivate the people of Judah to rebuild his temple (1:3-11; 2:15-17). These circumstances will not change until they commence work on Yahweh's house (2:18-19). Haggai directs his message not to the ordinary people but to Zerubbabel and Joshua, the political and religious leaders of the nation. They are the ones who will have to coordinate this massive and costly undertaking (1:1-2, 8). A brief narrative section indicates that Haggai's message fell on fertile soil as the leaders and people started immediately to work on the temple (1:12-15).

Once the construction has begun, Haggai shifts into a predictive mode. Drawing on themes from earlier prophets, Haggai insists that Yahweh intends to do more for his people than simply give them good crops. His plans are so far-reaching that they will cause heaven and earth to shake (2:6, 21). In that day Yahweh will arise as a warrior to break the power of the nations, overthrowing their kings and shattering their armies (2:21-22). All of their wealth will be brought to Yahweh's temple in Jerusalem, giving it a splendor beyond compare (2:6-8). The people of Judah will prosper under the rule of Yahweh's chosen servant Zerubbabel, who is not only the Persian governor but also a direct descendant of King David and thus qualified to occupy the throne. Haggai may even have thought that he was the promised Messiah (2:9, 23). Everything will be glorious and wonderful in that day.

The value of such a message for the people of Haggai's day should be obvious. Earlier prophets had promised a wonderful future for the people of Judah when they returned to their land. Nearly twenty years after their return, however, times were still hard. Haggai's prophecy not only explains why the earlier predictions had not come to pass but also assures the people of Judah that Yahweh still intends to bless them as the earlier prophets had promised. Though he does not say exactly when this will happen, he seems to imply that the reversal will occur as soon as the temple is finished. Clearly it has to be soon if Zerubbabel is to play a major role in this new era.

Since the book ends before the completion of the temple, we do not how people responded when the glory that Haggai had promised failed to materialize. The fact that the book was preserved, however, suggests that later generations continued to find his message inspiring long after the passage of time had disproved his predictions about Zerubbabel. Apparently later audiences were able to find enough hope and encouragement in Haggai's vision to override the evident failure of his prophecy.

ZECHARIAH 1–8

The book of Zechariah, like the book of Isaiah, appears to contain the sayings of at least two different prophets. Chapters 1–8, which reflect the concerns and events of the early postexilic period, are usually dated to the sixth century B.C.E. and credited to the prophet Zechariah. Chapters 9–14, by contrast, contain language and ideas that seem to relate to a later period. Most scholars attribute these chapters to an unknown prophet who lived a century or more after Zechariah. This latter part of the book, sometimes called "Second Zechariah," will be discussed in chapter 36.

The prophet Zechariah was a contemporary of Haggai. Three of the prophecies in the book of Zechariah are dated (1:1, 7; 7:1). The first overlaps the ministry of Haggai (520 B.C.E.), while the latest extends to the end of 518 B.C.E., three years before the completion of the temple in 515 B.C.E. Assuming that all of the sayings were delivered between these two dates, Zechariah prophesied for approximately two years. This is consistent with references in the book of Ezra (5:1 and 6:14) that depict him working alongside Haggai to promote the rebuilding of the temple. What Zechariah did after these two years is unknown, though it seems likely that he continued to function as a prophet.

As with Haggai, the book of Zechariah offers few clues about the prophet's personal life. The fact that two generations of Zechariah's ancestors are named in the introduction to the book (1:1) has suggested to many scholars that the prophet came from a prominent family. This inference finds support in Nehemiah's designation of Zechariah's father as one of the priestly leaders who returned with Zerubbabel from Babylonia (Nehemiah 12:1-4; 12:16). The great respect that Zechariah shows for the high priest adds weight to the suggestion that the prophet came from priestly stock (Zechariah 3:1-10; 6:9-14).

On the whole, Zechariah's language and ideas place him closer to the prophets than to the priestly class. Several times he refers to earlier prophets who had warned the people of Israel and Judah to turn from their sins (1:4-6; 7:7, 12), and many of his sayings resemble those of other prophets (1:3-6, 12-17; 2:4-12; 7:5-14; 8:1-8, 14-17). The book of Zechariah differs from other prophetic books, however, in the amount of space that it devotes to descriptions of visionary experiences. Well over half the book consists of visions that Zechariah is said to have received from Yahweh (1:7—6:8). Most include conversations with angels who tell Zechariah what the visions mean. Mingled together with these vision reports are a number of more traditional passages in which the prophet speaks a message in the name of Yahweh (2:6-13; 4:8-10; 6:9-15; 7:4, 8; 8:1, 18, 20). Similar combinations of visions and direct speech can be seen in other prophetic books, but the visionary element is more prominent in Zechariah. Whether Zechariah actually experienced more visions than other prophets or whether the editors simply chose to emphasize this aspect of his experience is impossible to say.

EXERCISE 109

Read Zechariah 1:7-17; 2:6—4:14; 6:9-15; 8:1-8. What recurring themes do you see in Zechariah's message? How does his message speak to the needs of the postexilic community in Judah?

The bulk of Zechariah's message is positive and upbeat, though he includes enough criticism and instruction to show that Yahweh is not entirely pleased with his people. Several times he warns his audience not to be like their ancestors who refused to listen to the words of the prophets and ultimately suffered the consequences (1:3-6; 7:4-7, 11-14). His repeated warnings against stealing, lying in court, abusing the poor and needy, and plotting evil against others also recall the pronouncements of the preexilic prophets (5:1-4; 7:7, 17).

For the most part, however, Zechariah's message focuses on the good things that Yahweh is going to do for his people. His message is clear: Yahweh has not forgotten about his people, and he will bless them with prosperity and security if they will commit themselves fully to him (1:3-6, 12-17). The punishments that Yahweh inflicted upon their ancestors are now over, and their sins have been removed (3:9; 5:5-11; 8:14-15). From this time forward they will experience nothing but blessings. As in Haggai, the change in Yahweh's attitude is linked directly to his people's decision to commence work on his temple (8:9-13), which will be completed during the lifetimes of the community's present leaders (4:8-10; 6:12).

Now that the building process is under way, the community can count on their god to restore their cities and fill them with people (1:17). Jerusalem in particular will be blessed. Yahweh will once again live there in his restored house, and the city will overflow with returning exiles and enjoy divine blessings and protection (2:1-5, 10-12; 8:1-8). Those who have abused Yahweh's people will be punished, and the people of the surrounding nations will flock to Israel not to conquer but to honor their god (1:21; 2:8-11; 8:22-23). Such a glorious vision of the future would have served as a profound source of encouragement to the community of returned exiles, particularly those who still harbored doubts about their present course of action (see 2:9; 4:10; 8:6).

Interspersed with these visions of the coming glory of Jerusalem are three long passages in which Yahweh offers ringing endorsements of the two men who stood at the head of this small community—Zerubbabel, the Persian-appointed governor, and Joshua, the high priest (3:1-10; 4:1-14; 6:9-14). These are the same two leaders whom Haggai addressed in his prophecies. Together they are described as "the two anointed ones [in Hebrew, the two Messiahs] who stand by the Lord of the whole earth" (4:14). Unlike Haggai, however, Zechariah gives pride of place to Joshua, not to Zerubbabel. While the governor clearly has an important role to play in rebuilding the temple (4:6-10), it is the high priest who will wear the royal crown and rule over Yahweh's people (6:9-14).

Zechariah even calls Joshua "the **Branch**," a title that other prophets apply to the coming Davidic king (Isaiah 11:1-5; Jeremiah 23:5-6; 33:15-16).

This designation of the high priest as the Branch has struck most scholars as odd, since the high priest would have come from the priestly tribe of Levi, not the royal tribe of Judah. The confusion intensifies when we observe

Fig. 35.3. A nineteenth-century artist's rendition of a priest officiating in the Temple. The high priest Joshua (Zechariah 3) would have been dressed similarly.

that Joshua is distinguished from the Branch in 3:8-9 and that the Branch is supposed to have "a priest by his throne, with peaceful understanding between the two of them" (6:13). These tensions have suggested to many scholars that the Branch passages were originally applied to Zerubbabel, whose royal ancestry had led Haggai to foresee an exalted position for him over Yahweh's restored people (Haggai 2:23). Supporters of this interpretation believe that the Persians eventually became suspicious of Zerubbabel and removed him from office before the community had a chance to make him king. The prophecy that spoke of Zerubbabel wearing a crown and ruling over Yahweh's people was then transferred to Joshua, whom Yahweh had already placed in charge of his restored temple (3:1-7).

Whatever the history behind these passages, the words of Zechariah would have served to strengthen the positions of both Zerubbabel and Joshua within the postexilic community. Zechariah's declarations of divine support for the ruling elites recall the messages of some of the court prophets from the preexilic period. From his affirmation of the temple project to his insistence on the centrality of Jerusalem to his endorsement of the authority of Joshua and Zerubbabel, Zechariah played a key role in shaping the political and religious landscape of the postexilic community.

THIRD ISAIAH (ISAIAH 56–66)

As we saw in the previous chapter, the book of Isaiah includes material from prophets who lived much later than the eighth-century B.C.E. prophet for whom the book is named. The material in chapters 40–55 is clearly a unified whole that can be dated to the latter years of the Babylonian exile. The material in chapters 56–66, by contrast, is more diverse. Some of the sayings reflect the circumstances and concerns of postexilic Judah, while others seem to fit better in the exilic or even the preexilic period. Most scholars credit these materials to one or more prophets who lived in Palestine after the return from Babylonia, though they disagree about whether the speaker(s) lived near the time of Haggai and Zechariah or later. Others see these chapters as a compendium of material from different periods. Scholars commonly use the term *Third Isaiah* to refer to these chapters, with the understanding that the term may or may not refer to a single historical individual.

EXERCISE 110

Read the following passages and decide whether you think each one would fit better into the preexilic, exilic, or postexilic period: Isaiah 57:1-13; 59:1-15; 60:1-14; 61:1-7; 64:6-12; 65:6-12. Give reasons for your answers.

The problem of determining the authorship and date of these chapters is made more acute by the shortage of personal references. In one passage the prophet claims that Yahweh has told him to deliver a message of judgment to his people (58:1-2), while elsewhere the speaker asserts that Yahweh has sent him to proclaim words of joy and comfort (61:1-4; 62:1). No coherent image of a single prophet can be constructed from these passages. Most of the other first-person passages appear in prayers, where they reflect liturgical patterns and not the words of a particular speaker (59:9-15; 61:10-11; 63:7—64:12). If the prophecies in these chapters originated with a single individual, the text tells us virtually nothing about this person.

The materials in Isaiah 56–66 are not organized according to any clear thematic or chronological pattern. The sayings jump from passages that are sharply critical of the audience's behavior to oracles of salvation and restoration. Verses that condemn the people for worshiping other gods and oppressing the poor are followed by passages that assume that the audience is devoted to Yahweh and his commands. Chapters that speak of the coming restoration of Jerusalem and its temple are followed by chapters that presume that the city is inhabited and the temple is in use.

Those who attribute the bulk of Isaiah 56–66 to a single prophet see this lack of focus as a sign of division within the postexilic community. Several passages in these chapters distinguish between a group that is called "the righteous," "the humble," or "Yahweh's servants" (57:1-2, 15; 65:8-10, 13-15; 66:14; compare 59:9-15; 66:2, 5) and another group made up of "wicked" and "sinful" people who perform all kinds of evil deeds (57:3-13, 20-21; 59:1-8; 65:11-15; 66:17). The prophet, who clearly belongs to the first group, assures his audience that Yahweh plans to reward them with prosperity and inflict punishment upon those who have rejected his ways. According to this view, the haphazard organization of the material in Isaiah 56–66 reflects the dual character of the prophet's preaching, which offered comfort to the members of his own group while criticizing those outside it.

The chief problem with this theory is that it fails to do justice to the diversity of the materials in these chapters. In particular, it is hard to see how a single prophet can be credited with texts that speak of Jerusalem and its temple lying in ruins and people mourning over them (60:15; 63:18; 64:10-11; compare 58:12; 61:4; 62:4; 65:19; 66:10) as well as passages that presuppose that the temple is currently in operation (56:4-7; 57:13; 65:11; 66:6). Isaiah 56–66 also contains many verses that address Yahweh's people as a whole, not a smaller subgroup, including some that voice Yahweh's anger over their sins (58:1-4; 64:6-12) and others that announce his plans to bless and restore them (60:1-22; 62:1—63:6; 65:17-25; 66:10-13). Finally, the language and ideas in these chapters are quite diverse, including some passages that sound like Second Isaiah and others that recall Jeremiah or one of the other preexilic prophets. While there are no doubt materials in these chapters that reflect intergroup conflicts from the postexilic period, it makes more sense to view Isaiah 56–66 as a collection of prophetic sayings from a variety of times and places.

Despite (or possibly because of) their diverse origins, most of the prophecies in Isaiah 56–66 echo sayings that we have encountered elsewhere in the Prophets. Verses that highlight the sinfulness of Yahweh's people point to the same problems as the preexilic prophets, including the worship of other gods (or possibly worship Yahweh at unauthorized sites), neglect and abuse of the poor, oppression of workers, dishonesty in the courts, lying speech, and violence toward others (57:3-13; 58:1-4; 59:1-8; 65:1-12; 66:3-4, 17). The fact that Haggai and Zechariah say almost nothing about these kinds of behaviors, particularly the worship of other gods, suggests that these sayings either reflect the circumstances of a later period (possibly long after the initial return to Palestine) or represent remnants of preexilic material. The few verses that spell out the kinds of behavior that

Fig. 35.4. Several times in Isaiah 56–66 Yahweh is depicted as a warrior fighting either for or against his people, as in this image of a warrior deity from Assyria.

Yahweh expects from his people also echo the sayings of earlier prophets (56:1; 58:6-7, 9-10; 61:8), though more attention is given in these chapters to proper observance of the Sabbath (56:2-6; 58:13) and fasting (58:2-9), reflecting the growing importance of both of these practices in the postexilic period.

The vision of the future that occupies a prominent position in these chapters is also similar to what we saw in the earlier prophetic books, though the picture is less coherent than the following summary suggests. At the proper time, Yahweh will arise as a mighty warrior to judge the nations for their sins (59:16-20; 63:1-6) and punish the sinners among his own people (57:13; 65:6-7, 12-15; 66:4-6, 14-17, 24). At that time he will bring the remainder of his dispersed people back to their land (56:8; 60:4-9), where they will rebuild the ruined places (58:12; 61:4) and live in prosperity and peace (60:17-18; 65:21-22, 25; 66:12-14). The people of Yahweh will be given authority over the nations (60:3, 10-16; 61:5-6) and Jerusalem will be renowned throughout the earth (60:14-15; 62:2-7). Yahweh will reside in his holy temple (60:19-20) and his people will worship and praise him there, accompanied by visitors from other lands (56:6-7; 66:18-23). Surprisingly, nothing is said here about the restoration of the Davidic monarchy; apparently the editors did not see this as a necessary or desirable condition for the restored community.

Taken as a whole, Isaiah 56–66 offers a message of both hope and warning to the postexilic community in Judah. Those who remain faithful to Yahweh and rely on him for help are reassured that a glorious future awaits them. The current state of Yahweh's people under foreign domination may seem bleak, but the day is coming when Yahweh will fulfill all of the promises that he made to their ancestors through the prophets. On the other hand, those who are not living as Yahweh desires are threatened with divine punishment when Yahweh acts. Their only hope is to turn from their sinful ways and return to Yahweh, though the prophet offers little hope that they will actually do so. In the meantime, the faithful can only wait patiently until the time when Yahweh arises to purge the sinners from their midst and exalt the righteous to a position of honor and power among the nations.

MALACHI

The introductory verse of the book of Malachi offers no information about the identity or date of the prophet to whom the book is attributed. In Hebrew, the word *Malachi* means "my messenger," so it is possible that the book represents the words of an anonymous prophet (defined here as a messenger of Yahweh) rather than a person named Malachi (see 3:1). The content of the book implies that the prophet either came from a priestly background or worked around the Jerusalem temple, since he addresses much of his message to the priests and shows a marked interest in the proper conduct of the temple. On the other hand, the sharply critical tone of the bulk of his sayings suggests that many priests would have viewed him as an adversary. A short narrative passage toward the end of the book (3:16-18) indicates that the prophet had followers (identified here as "those who revered Yahweh"), though their identity is unclear. The language that is used to describe them suggests that they viewed themselves as the only faithful followers of Yahweh in their community. The prophet could have lived virtually anytime after the Jerusalem temple was rebuilt, but most scholars place him decades later than the time of Haggai and Zechariah (perhaps mid to late fifth century B.C.E.), since he shares none of their concern for the reestablishment of the exiled community.

The literary style that Malachi uses to frame his message is different from that of the other prophets we have studied. Instead of issuing authoritative statements in the name of the deity ("thus says Yahweh"), Malachi reasons with his audience in an effort to persuade them of the rightness of his positions. The book divides readily into six sections, each of which focuses on a different issue (1:2-5; 1:6—2:9; 2:10-16; 2:17—3:5; 3:6-12; 3:13—4:3). Each section begins with a statement or question that accuses the audience of an inappropriate pattern of behavior or thought. This is followed in most cases by a question that anticipates how the audience might respond to the accusation. From here the prophet proceeds to explain what is wrong with their current behavior and how Yahweh feels about it. But Malachi does not rely on reason alone. Several times he threatens his audience with divine judgment, using language that recalls the sayings of the preexilic prophets (2:1-3, 9, 12; 3:1-5; 4:1, 6). This combination of reasoned argument and threat gives Malachi's pronouncements a rhetorical force that would have made it hard for his audience—even the priests—to ignore him. Whether the priests actually changed their behavior after hearing his message is unclear, though the book does indicate that there were people who responded favorably to his words (3:16-18).

EXERCISE 111

Read Malachi 1:6—3:5. What kinds of behavior does Malachi criticize in these verses? What reasons does he give for his criticism in each case?

Unlike the other postexilic prophets whom we have been studying, Malachi's message is more critical than encouraging. Many of Malachi's sayings recall the legal traditions of the Torah, though he does not cite any specific provisions. According to Malachi, both the priests and the people of Judah have become lax and careless in their devotion to Yahweh. As evidence, he describes the manner in which they are fulfilling their ritual obligations to Yahweh: the priests are offering sick and lame animals on the altar instead of the pure and unblemished animals that Yahweh requires (1:6-8, 11-14), while the people are withholding the tithes and offerings that they owe to Yahweh (2:8-9). Abuse of other people is also common: people are engaging in adultery, giving false testimony, and oppressing the poor and needy (3:5). Some are even seeking divorces in order to marry foreign women who serve gods other than Yahweh (2:11-16). People are beginning to doubt the value of serving Yahweh as they see the wicked prospering and the righteous gaining no clear benefit from their devotion to the deity (2:17; 3:13-15).

According to Malachi, Yahweh is deeply upset about the way his people are behaving. Their conduct reveals their contempt for the covenant that Yahweh made with their ancestors (2:4-10). In response, Yahweh has decided to stop accepting their sacrifices and answering their prayers for help (1:10; 2:13). If they do not mend their ways, he will bring against them all of the curses promised in his covenant (2:1-3, 9, 12; 3:1-5; 4:1, 6). Yet it is not too late for them to repent and return to Yahweh (3:7). He does not want to destroy his people; he only wants to purify them so that they will honor him and bring acceptable offerings to his altar (3:2-4, 16; 4:2). If they do as he says, they can be assured of his covenantal blessings and protection (3:10-12, 17; 4:2-3). Their response to Malachi's message will determine their fate.

By the end of the book, it is clear that Malachi does not expect such a radical reversal. Instead, he anticipates a

Fig. 35.5. Malachi compares Yahweh's impending judgment of his people to a refining fire (3:2-5) and a burning furnace (4:1).

divine judgment in which Yahweh will sort out the righteous (those who respond to his message) from the wicked (those who reject his call to repentance—3:17-18). At that time the wicked will be burned up like stubble and removed from the land, while the righteous will prosper (4:1-3). Unlike the preexilic prophets, Malachi does not speak of judgment being inflicted by foreign armies, since the nation is already under foreign domination. Instead, it is Yahweh himself who will judge the wicked and reward the righteous. In this way he will make his justice known to those who have questioned the value of serving him. As we will see in chapter 36, this vision of Yahweh coming to judge the world reflects the apocalyptic mind-set that became increasingly dominant in the postexilic era.

JOEL

The book of Joel is perhaps the hardest book in the entire Hebrew Bible to date. The latter half of the book (2:28—3:21) is clearly a postexilic work, since it presumes that the Jerusalem temple has been rebuilt (2:32; 3:16-18) and looks forward to the imminent return of the remaining exiles of Judah who were sold into slavery and scattered among the nations when Judah was conquered by the Babylonians (3:2-3, 5-7). By contrast, the first part of the book (1:2—2:27) could have been written at virtually any time during the preexilic or postexilic eras. The problems that gave rise to the prophet's message (a deadly invasion of locusts combined with a drought) were so common in the ancient world that they could have occurred at any point in Israel's history, while the highly poetic language of these chapters contains no clear allusions to historical events that would allow scholars to date the sayings. The repeated references to the community's elders (1:2, 14; 2:16) coupled with the lack of any mention of a king have led most scholars to conclude that these initial chapters, too, belong to the postexilic era. The language and ideas of the two parts of the book are also similar enough to convince the majority of scholars that both parts originated with the same prophet, though not all would agree with this view.

The introduction to the book (1:1) gives no information about the prophet other than his father's name. His repeated references to the priests and the Jerusalem temple have led many scholars to suppose that he came from a priestly family and/or worked as a prophet at the temple. The fact that he could call on the entire nation, including its leaders, to engage in a fast and gather at the temple to pray for Yahweh's help suggests that he was a respected leader within the postexilic community. The power and beauty of his poetry indicate that he was a member of the educated elite class of Jerusalem. Apart from these inferences, we know nothing about the prophet or his life.

> ### EXERCISE 112
>
> Read Joel 2:1—3:3; 3:17-21. What is Yahweh like, according to these verses? How does he relate to his people?

Most of the first half of the book of Joel is consumed with the prophet's lament over the disaster that has overtaken Judah and his call for the people to weep and pray to Yahweh to rescue them from their dreadful circumstances. Behind Joel's powerful poetry lies a depiction of two devastating plagues that have come upon Judah at once: a massive swarm of locusts that has devoured the bulk of their crops (1:4-7; 2:1-11) and a severe drought that has dried up what remains of the year's harvest and hindered the growth of the next season's plantings (1:10-12, 17-20). The locusts are like an invading army that destroys everything in its path; the drought resembles a fire sweeping across their fields. Not only are the people

and animals left without food or drink, but there is not even enough grain or wine to perform the regular offerings in the Jerusalem temple (1:9, 13, 16; 2:14). Nothing like this has ever struck the land of Judah (1:2-3).

The role of the prophet in this situation is twofold: to make sense of what is happening and to tell the people what they can do to stop it. On the first point, Joel announces that such a cataclysmic series of events can only be the work of Yahweh, whom he portrays as the captain of the locust horde (2:11, 25). Like Amos and Zephaniah before him, Joel uses the term "day of Yahweh" to describe this dreadful time when Yahweh sends judgment against his people (1:15; 2:1, 11). In response to this act of divine judgment, Joel urges the priests to declare a national fast and gather the people of Judah together at the temple to cry out to Yahweh for help (1:13-14; 2:15-17; compare 1:8-9, 19). Though he gives no specific reason as to why Yahweh might have done

Fig. 35.6. Swarms of locusts, like this one from South Africa, continue to plague crops around the world.

this to them, Joel clearly sees their present suffering as a punishment for sin, since he calls on the people of Judah to repent and return to Yahweh in the hope that he will forgive them and reverse their fortunes (2:12-13).

Whether Joel's instructions were heeded is unclear, but the sayings in Joel 2:18-27 presume that the locusts have departed and the vital rains have at last come to water the ground. Once again Joel credits these acts to Yahweh, who "has done great things" (2:21-22) by removing the locusts and sending the rains that will eventually produce an ample harvest. Now the prophet urges his people to rejoice and give thanks to Yahweh for his goodness (2:23, 26) while assuring them that Yahweh will repay them for the harm that they have suffered (2:25-27). The idea that some people might have found it hard to give thanks to a deity who had inflicted so much harm upon them seems not to have entered the prophet's mind.

Beginning with 2:28, the book takes a marked turn toward an apocalyptic mode of expression (see chapter 36). The essence of the prophet's message is that Yahweh is going to judge the nations that have afflicted Judah and restore the remaining exiles of Judah to their land. The language that he uses to express this hope, however, is filled with images that place the coming judgment and restoration outside the present order of history. Where previous prophets had spoken of Yahweh using the ordinary deeds of rulers and nations to carry out his purposes, Joel describes a cosmic judgment scene in which Yahweh gathers all of the nations together to punish them for the way they have treated his people (3:2, 4, 11-12, 19, 21). This "day of Yahweh" will be so momentous that its approach will be marked by a series of signs and wonders in the heavens (2:30-31; 3:15). On that day, Yahweh will rescue his people from all of their enemies and devastate the lands of their oppressors, enabling the people of Judah to live in peace and security forever (2:32; 3:16, 20). Yahweh will dwell in his temple in Jerusalem, and his land will be blessed with prosperity and abundance (2:17, 21).

While it would be easy to dismiss Joel's predictions as wishful thinking, many of those who heard him speak would have found both comfort and encouragement in his words. Contrary to the rosy promises of the earlier prophets, the return from the Exile and the rebuilding of the Jerusalem temple had not brought an end to foreign domination nor inaugurated an era of peace and prosperity. The coming of locust plagues and lengthy droughts might have led some to think that Yahweh had forgotten his promises or even turned against his people. Over against these fears, Joel assures his people that Yahweh is a merciful and forgiving deity who hears and responds to the cries of his people. He has not forgotten them; he still has a wonderful future in store for them. Nothing is said about when this transformation might take place, but the simple fact that Yahweh was reaffirming his promises through his prophet would have provided encouragement to renew their hopes and their devotion to Yahweh.

JONAH

The book of Jonah is unlike any other book in the Prophets section of the Hebrew Bible. While the others are made up primarily of prophetic sayings with only an occasional snippet of narrative, the entire book of Jonah is a story about a particular episode in the life of the prophet for whom the book is named. From a literary point of view, it actually belongs in chapter 21 with the other postexilic narratives. Yet the book has been included in the Prophets section of the Hebrew canon since antiquity. For this reason the book of Jonah will be treated here along with the other prophetic books from the postexilic period.

The story of Jonah is set in the eighth century B.C.E., when the Assyrians were the dominant power of the ancient Near East. A brief reference in 2 Kings 14:25 mentions "Jonah, son of Amittai" (see Jonah 1:1) as a prophet from Gath-hepher who accurately predicted the expansion of Israel's borders under king Jeroboam II, but nothing else is known about him. Most scholars believe that the book was actually written centuries later in the postexilic era, since it uses language and ideas from other prophetic books and echoes many of the themes of postexilic narratives like Ruth and Tobit. Estimates of its date range from the sixth to the fourth century B.C.E. All but conservative scholars view the book of Jonah as a creative work of fiction and not a narrative of actual events. Not only does the book contain many implausible episodes, but the manner in which the prophet is portrayed shows clearly that the book was written as a satire.

EXERCISE 113

Read the book of Jonah. Why do you think Jonah is portrayed as such an unsympathetic character? What do you think is the message of the book?

The plot of the book of Jonah begins in a fairly traditional manner with Yahweh telling his prophet to deliver a message of judgment against Nineveh, the capital of the Assyrian Empire. Jonah's commission recalls the message of Nahum, whose prophecies spoke of the coming doom of Nineveh (see chapter 33). Unlike Nahum, however,

Fig. 35.7. An artist's rendition of the ancient city of Nineveh, capital of the Assyrian empire.

Jonah refuses Yahweh's call and boards a ship going in the opposite direction. Nothing is said at this point about why Jonah resists Yahweh's command. Yahweh, however, is unwilling to take no for an answer. First he sends a ferocious storm against the ship, leading Jonah to ask the sailors to throw him into the sea so that Yahweh will cease his attacks on the ship. Then he sends a great fish to swallow Jonah and carry him back to dry land. The story implies that Jonah has a change of heart while in the fish's belly, since he recites a hymn of praise to Yahweh for rescuing him (2:1-9).

Once again Yahweh tells Jonah to go to Nineveh and announce the impending doom of the city, and this time he complies. To Jonah's great astonishment, the people of Nineveh believe his message and repent, calling on God to have mercy and withhold the impending judgment. Yahweh, seeing their response, changes his plan and allows them to live. At this point Jonah unexpectedly becomes angry with Yahweh; he had been waiting eagerly for Yahweh to punish his enemies, and now Yahweh had decided to forgive them. Hoping that Yahweh will change his mind once again and carry out his judgment, Jonah goes outside the city and waits to see what Yahweh will do. As he waits, Yahweh decides to teach him a lesson. First he makes a bush grow up over the prophet's head to protect him from the hot sun; then he sends a worm to kill the bush. When Jonah complains about the loss of the bush and asks that he be allowed to die, Yahweh chides the prophet. If Jonah is so upset about the loss of a bush, should not Yahweh be concerned about the potential deaths of more than one hundred twenty thousand people in Nineveh? The question is left hanging in the air, though the fact that the question came from Yahweh means that the audience is expected to accept this as the final word.

Scholars have argued long and hard over the meaning of this strange tale. All agree, however, on the centrality of the contrast between the behavior of Jonah and that of the other characters in the story. The story is ironic from beginning to end, with none of the characters acting as the reader might expect. The prophet, who ought to be obedient to the word of Yahweh, first refuses to follow Yahweh's instruction and then criticizes his decision to be merciful. By contrast, the sailors and the people of Nineveh, who do not even know Yahweh, acknowledge his authority and honor him as God.

Most scholars see in this story a criticism of the narrow provincialism that was prevalent in certain circles of Palestine in the postexilic period, as evidenced by Ezra and Nehemiah's demands that the men of their community divorce their non-Israelite wives because they might lead them to follow gods other than Yahweh (Ezra 9:1—10:44; Nehemiah 13:23-31). The possibility that the non-Israelite wives might actually come to acknowledge the god of Israel through such contacts is never considered in these books. The book of Jonah offers a frontal challenge to that mind-set. Yahwists who regard other nations as worthy only of divine judgment are reminded that Yahweh is a merciful and forgiving god whose concern for his creation is not limited to the people of Israel. Even the animals of Nineveh evoke his compassion (4:11). Possibly the author was inspired by prophetic sayings that spoke of a time when the nations would turn to Yahweh and acknowledge him as God (Isaiah 19:18-25; 66:18-23; Micah 4:1-4; Zephaniah 3:9-10; Zechariah 8:20-23; compare Psalm 68:28-31).

In the end, this message might explain why the book of Jonah was included among the prophets despite its obvious narrative format. The story of the wayward prophet Jonah reveals the dangers that can arise from placing too much emphasis on prophetic sayings that speak of Yahweh judging the nations and neglecting passages that offer a more positive assessment of Yahweh's plans for those who are not part of his chosen people. In this way the book of Jonah offers an implicit commentary on the manner in which some of the author's contemporaries were interpreting the prophetic books that were already moving toward canonical status in the postexilic community. Clearly there were others who agreed with the author's position, since the book would not otherwise have been preserved and included in the developing canon of the Jewish Scriptures. The very existence of this book testifies to the presence of tolerant and open-minded attitudes toward other nations alongside more critical perspectives in the postexilic period.

CONCLUSION

The prophets who emerged in Judah during the postexilic period faced a series of daunting challenges. Those who prophesied in the early days after the return from Babylonia had to help their people deal with the disappointment that many must have felt at the failure of the earlier

prophets' predictions that Yahweh would inaugurate an era of peace, freedom, and prosperity when they returned to their land. Prophets like Haggai and Zechariah assured the returnees that Yahweh had not forgotten them and encouraged them to rebuild Yahweh's temple as a sign of their devotion to the deity. If they did this, said the prophets, they could count on Yahweh to fulfill his promises.

How people responded when the predictions of Haggai and Zechariah failed to materialize is unclear, though most probably shifted their focus to building a stable and fruitful community under the present reality of Persian rule. The prophecies of Third Isaiah, Malachi, and Joel suggest that over time, people began to return to many of the practices for which the preexilic prophets had condemned their ancestors. As a result, the messages of the prophets who lived later in the postexilic period are more critical and challenging than those of the prophets who spoke soon after the return from Babylonia. Much of what they said echoes the language and ideas of the preexilic prophets, though new emphases can be found here and there as well.

Despite their sometimes critical tone, the message of the postexilic prophets is ultimately one of hope. All of the prophetic books from this period speak of a future era when the glorious predictions of the earlier prophets will be fulfilled. Some even outstrip the earlier prophets in their descriptions of what Yahweh has in store for his people. Abandoning this hope was not an option, since this would have undermined their people's trust in Yahweh as their covenant deity as well as their own identity as Yahweh's chosen people. In the end, this expectation of a future restoration of Israel became the foundation for a new kind of apocalyptic thinking that will be examined in the next chapter.

EXERCISE 114

How do you think the people of Judah would have felt when the rebuilding of the Jerusalem temple was finished and their social, political, and economic circumstances remained unchanged? How might the sayings of the postexilic prophets have helped them to make sense of this situation?

Fig. 36.1. This golden ornament from the Persian period, which combines features from different animals, recalls the fantasy-like animal mixtures that appear in many apocalyptic visions.

The Rise of Apocalyptic

On that day the LORD will punish the host of heaven in heaven, and on earth the kings of the earth. They will be gathered together like prisoners in a pit; they will be shut up in a prison, and after many days they will be punished. Then the moon will be abashed, and the sun ashamed; for the LORD of hosts will reign on Mount Zion and in Jerusalem, and before his elders he will manifest his glory. (Isaiah 24:21-23)

Then the LORD my God will come, and all the holy ones with him. On that day there shall not be either cold or frost. And there shall be continuous day (it is known to the LORD), not day and not night, for at evening time there shall be light. On that day living waters shall flow out from Jerusalem, half of them to the eastern sea and half of them to the western sea; it shall continue in summer as in winter. And the LORD will become king over all the earth; on that day the LORD will be one and his name one. (Zechariah 14:5-9)

At that time Michael, the great prince, the protector of your people, shall arise. There shall be a time of anguish, such as has never occurred since nations first came into existence. But at that time your people shall be delivered, everyone who is found written in the book. Many of those who sleep in the dust of the earth shall awake, some to everlasting life, and some to shame and everlasting contempt. Those who are wise shall shine like the brightness of the sky, and those who lead many to righteousness, like the stars forever and ever. (Daniel 12:1-3)

Toward the end of the period covered by the Hebrew Bible, a new type of literature arose that drew on many of the themes and ideas of the prophetic books but developed them in new directions. Scholars refer to these materials as apocalyptic texts. The word *apocalyptic* comes from a Greek word that means "uncovering" or "revelation." The authors of these texts claimed to be "revealing" otherwise hidden information about what Yahweh is doing in the world and what he intends to do on behalf of his people. The earliest use of the term *apocalypse* appears in the opening verse of the New Testament book of Revelation ("the revelation [apocalypse] of Jesus Christ, which God gave him to show his servants what must soon take place"), but Jewish authors had been composing apocalyptic texts for over two centuries by the time the book of Revelation was written.

None of the documents in the Hebrew Bible consists entirely of apocalyptic material, but several books contain sections that would qualify as apocalyptic. The longest example is Daniel 7–12. Apocalyptic passages can also be found in the books of Isaiah, Ezekiel, Joel, Zephaniah, Zechariah, and Malachi. Some of these apocalyptic sayings may have been uttered by the prophet to whom the book is attributed, while others are probably later additions that were inserted during the editing process. Apocalyptic material can also be found in a number of Jewish books that were not included in the biblical canon, including 1 Enoch, parts of which were written before the book of Daniel and possibly before some of the other apocalyptic passages in the Hebrew Bible. By the first century C.E., apocalyptic thinking had penetrated most areas of Jewish culture, including the ideas of the early Christians.

The present chapter examines the rise of apocalyptic expectation in ancient Palestine and its presence in the Hebrew Bible. The first part of the chapter presents an overview of the key elements of apocalyptic thought. This is followed by a review of the origins and history of the apocalyptic movement, including its links to biblical prophecy. The chapter closes with an examination of Zechariah 9–14, a collection of prophetic sayings with many apocalyptic features, and Daniel 7–12, which contains the fullest expression of apocalyptic thinking in the Hebrew Bible.

WHAT IS APOCALYPTIC?

The Hebrew prophets whom we have been studying over the last few chapters shared a belief that Yahweh works in and through the forces of history to reward or discipline his covenant people. When announcing Yahweh's coming judgments, they spoke of natural disasters like locust infestations or droughts or the devastation caused by foreign armies. When predicting the future restoration of Israel, they described the people of Israel and Judah returning to their homeland and living together in peace and prosperity, often under the rule of a Davidic king. Sometimes the prophets employed symbolic or exaggerated language to depict the sorrows and joys that Yahweh's people would experience when the deity carried out his plans, but the events that they foresaw were expected to take place within the normal course of history.

Apocalyptic writings resemble prophetic texts in their concern for the future of Yahweh's people, but their vision of the future transcends the ordinary limits of history. Apocalyptic books are produced by people who regard themselves and their group as either oppressed or hopelessly disadvantaged by the system of government, economics, culture, and/or religion under which they are forced to live. They combine a highly critical attitude toward the present world order with an optimistic belief that Yahweh cares deeply for their community (often characterized as "the righteous") and hates their oppressors. They look forward to a time when Yahweh will put an end to the present system and replace it with a new world order in which those who are now suffering will be exalted to positions of honor under the sovereign rule of Yahweh.

Of course, the prophets also criticized their contemporaries and called for social change, but the future that they envisioned was basically a return to an idealized earlier version of the present corrupt system. To apocalyptic thinkers, by contrast, the entire universe must be transformed or else evil and corruption will once again raise their ugly heads. Humans are simply too corrupt for such a radical transformation to be realized through ordinary historical processes. Yahweh must intervene to eliminate all evil, pain, and suffering from the world and set up a new order in which only the righteous are allowed to live and rule. Then and only then can the long-awaited era of peace and happiness come to pass. Such a vision of the future is far more subversive than anything put forward by the prophets.

EXERCISE 115

Read the following apocalyptic passages from the Hebrew Bible. How do the images of the future in these passages compare with what we have seen in the books of the prophets?

• Isaiah 24:1-3, 17-25
• Isaiah 65:17-25; 66:18-24
• Ezekiel 47:1-12
• Joel 2:28-32; 3:9-21
• Zechariah 14:1-21

Apocalyptic literature is highly diverse in both style and substance. No two apocalyptic works paint exactly the same picture of the future, and the language and images that they use vary widely as well. Nevertheless, scholars have been able to identify a number of common features that distinguish apocalyptic texts from other types of literature in the Hebrew Bible.

1. *Visionary experiences.* As with some of the prophetic books, the authors of apocalyptic texts present reports of visionary experiences in which Yahweh (or more often, one of his angels) disclosed to a particular individual his plans for the future of humanity. As a rule, apocalyptic visions are more complex and elaborate than those in the prophetic books. Most are longer as well: a single vision and its interpretation can occupy several chapters of printed text. In fact, most apocalyptic works are little

Fig. 36.2. Hans Memling, *St. John the Evangelist in Patmos*

more than various visions and interpretations strung together by a thin line of narrative. In some cases the visions are identified as dreams, while in others the recipient claims to have been carried bodily to heaven, where he learned not only about the future but also about such secrets as the appearance of the heavenly throne room and the manner in which rain and snow fall from the sky. In most cases the visions are accompanied by interpretations that explain their significance for the audience, though sometimes the interpretation is left to the reader.

2. *Narrative framework*. As a rule, apocalyptic works include a loose narrative framework that recounts the circumstances under which the visions were supposedly received. Most scholars regard these narrative elements as literary fictions, since the visions are usually attributed to a famous person in the distant past, not to the person who wrote the text. This fictitious framework allowed the author to create visions that retroactively "predicted" events that had in fact already happened by the time of the actual author. The presence of so many accurate "predictions" was supposed to lend credibility to the author's predictions concerning events that had not yet taken place. Whether the author's own predictions arose out of personal visionary experiences or a creative literary imagination is impossible to say.

3. *Cosmic dualism*. As we observed in chapter 12, the authors and editors of the Hebrew Bible invariably depict Yahweh as the sovereign lord of the universe. All other powers—gods, kings, armies, even the natural world—are ultimately under his control, even when they cause harm to his people. There is no thought here of a devil who works to hinder the will of Yahweh or does battle with the forces of heaven. By the end of the biblical period, however, many people were beginning to question this way of viewing reality, due in part to a growing awareness of the difficulty of reconciling the reality of undeserved pain and suffering with belief in a good god. One way of getting around this problem was to assert the existence of supernatural forces that worked to frustrate Yahweh's purposes by motivating humans to do their evil bidding. Scholars call this idea "dualism," since it envisions two opposing armies doing battle over the universe, with Yahweh and his angels arrayed on one side and the personified forces of evil on the other. Apocalyptic writers view the earth as the chief battleground between these two forces and see all humans as allies of one army or the other. Most apocalyptic works insist that the forces of evil dominate the present world system, but they assure their readers that these forces will ultimately be conquered and overthrown by Yahweh. The fact that such evil powers stand behind the people who hold positions of authority helps to explain why the righteous are suffering as well as why the world needs to be radically transformed.

4. *Eschatological orientation*. The word **eschatological** comes from two Greek words that mean "the study of last things." The term is normally used to describe texts that anticipate some sort of cataclysmic intervention by Yahweh that will bring about a radical change in the present world order. Some texts speak of Yahweh creating a new heaven and earth, while most envision the introduction of a new era of human history that is qualitatively different from the current era. All apocalyptic texts have some sort of eschatological orientation, though they disagree about what is going to happen and when it will occur. All insist that the time of Yahweh's intervention is near; some even list signs by which the faithful can know when the anticipated day of judgment will take place. All agree that the forces of evil will be defeated and judged on that day, and most assert that every vestige of evil will be purged from the universe. All view this day as a time of salvation when Yahweh will rescue his faithful followers from the grip of their oppressors and usher them into a new era

Fig. 36.3. Edward Hicks, *The Peaceable Kingdom* (see Isaiah 11:6-9; 65:25)

of peace and joy where evil no longer holds any sway. Exactly when these momentous changes will occur is known only to Yahweh, but his plan is set, and his people can rest assured that he will bring it to pass.

5. *Moral strictness.* Since the battle between the forces of good and evil extends into the world of humans, apocalyptic works often advise their audiences to be careful not to associate too closely with people outside their group, since outsiders might be in league with the forces of darkness. Yahweh's enemies are forever seeking to tempt the faithful to turn away from the path of righteousness and join their side. To avoid this temptation, Yahweh's followers must obey Yahweh alone and live strictly by his laws. Occasionally this includes following distinctive interpretations of the Torah issued by the leaders of the group rather than the practices of people outside the group. Some apocalyptic texts acknowledge that this path of radical devotion to Yahweh might lead to suffering or even death at the hands of the evil forces that control the present world system. Yet they assure their readers that they have no reason to fear, since those who suffer and die for their faith will be richly rewarded by Yahweh after death. Some think that this will take place immediately after death, while others look forward to a future resurrection of the dead. Whether the idea of life after death entered Judaism through apocalyptic circles or elsewhere

is impossible to say, but it certainly proved useful for motivating people to hold on to their faith in the face of temptation or persecution.

6. *Symbolic language.* Apocalyptic texts overflow with vivid imagery and symbols that recall scenes from contemporary fantasy literature. Their pages overflow with images of beasts with many heads and horns, vines and trees that grow as high as the heavens, stars that fall from the sky, and battles that pit the armies of evil against the forces of good. Like their modern cousins, apocalyptic texts appeal to their readers' imaginations rather than their rational faculties. Yet their message is deadly serious. The meaning behind these symbols would have been apparent to anyone familiar with the world of apocalyptic thought, while outsiders would have found it difficult to grasp their subversive character. Later readers, unaware of the original significance of these images, have mistakenly associated them with characters and events far removed from the time when the texts were written. The book of Daniel in particular has been used by many Christians to calculate the precise date when the end of the world will come. Interpretations such as these miss the point of apocalyptic literature, which is to bring a message of hope and consolation to people who feel intensely threatened by the world around them.

THE ORIGINS OF APOCALYPTIC

Every attempt to trace the origin and history of apocalyptic thinking is fraught with difficulty. Historical sources for the later postexilic period are relatively limited, and scholars cannot always agree on which texts should be considered apocalyptic. Some would include virtually any passage that speaks of a universal judgment, while others look for a combination of several factors. Ascribing dates to some of these texts is also problematic, especially in the case of verses that have been inserted into the prophetic books in the course of editing.

Despite these difficulties, most scholars would agree that apocalyptic thinking has its roots in the prophetic movement. Apocalyptic texts share many features with the prophetic books. Common elements include:

- a belief that Yahweh reveals his plans to humans through episodes of prophetic inspiration;
- a conviction that Yahweh stands on the side of a faithful but oppressed minority within the people of Israel;
- a critical attitude toward those who hold positions of power and influence within the society;
- an expectation that Yahweh will act at the appropriate time to bring down the powerful and rescue those who are oppressed;
- an anticipation of a future era in which everyone will be devoted to Yahweh and righteousness and justice will prevail; and
- a reliance on symbolic and exaggerated language to describe both present and future events.

At the same time, there are also many differences between the prophetic books and full-blown apocalyptic works. Most of these have already been identified, but it can be helpful to summarize them all in one place. In contrast to the prophetic books, apocalyptic texts include:

- more frequent and more extensive reports of visionary experiences;
- more detailed descriptions of the heavenly realm and its inhabitants;
- more specific predictions about the future course of human events;
- a vital role for supernatural forces that stand in opposition to Yahweh;
- a highly pessimistic view of human nature and the present universe;
- an assurance that the day of judgment and salvation will occur soon;
- depictions of the fates of the righteous and the wicked after death; and
- scenes of a final, universal judgment that will eliminate evil from the universe and inaugurate a new era of peace and joy for the righteous.

What do these similarities and differences say about the link between prophecy and apocalyptic? While it seems fairly clear that apocalyptic thinking is rooted in the prophetic movement, it would be wrong to suppose that prophecy simply evolved into apocalyptic with the passage of time. Some of the early postexilic prophets used ideas and language that could be considered apocalyptic without adopting a full-blown apocalyptic mind-set, and people continued to function as prophets long after the rise of apocalyptic thought. There is no inherent reason why the prophetic movement should have given birth to apocalyptic views of reality.

Scholars who have examined this question have identified two factors that seem to have paved the way for the development of apocalyptic patterns of thought. The first is contact with foreign ideas. Several features of apocalyptic literature have parallels in Babylonian religious traditions, including the belief that dreams can serve as modes of revelation; the conviction that history is predetermined by the gods; and the practice of having a figure from the past "predict" events that have already occurred so as to lend credibility to genuine predictions. Other elements of apocalyptic seem to reflect Persian influence, including the vision of the universe as a battleground between supernatural forces of good and evil; the role of angels and demons in this cosmic battle;

Fig. 36.4. Much of the vivid imagery of apocalyptic literature has parallels in the ancient Near East, especially the use of strange beasts to represent the forces of good and evil. (top) An Assyrian winged demon named Pazuzu; (middle) images of animals symbolizing various Babylonian deities; (bottom) a Persian griffin.

the division of history into periods; and the expectation of a future resurrection of the dead. Taken together, these parallels suggest that at least some of the elites of Judah found the ideas of their foreign rulers more useful than their own traditions for making sense of certain aspects of their experience.

Yet foreign influences alone are not enough to explain the rise of apocalyptic thinking. The transition from prophecy to apocalyptic is also a reaction to historical developments in the postexilic period. The collected sayings of Second Isaiah, Haggai, and Zechariah indicate that the leaders of the prophetic movement viewed the Persian conquest of Babylonia and the subsequent return of the people of Judah to their land as signs that the wonderful future that was anticipated by the earlier prophets would soon come to pass. With the passage of time, however, it became increasingly clear that this expectation was unfounded. Several reactions to this disappointment can be discerned in the materials of the Hebrew Bible. Some claimed that Yahweh was unhappy with the sinful behavior of his people and would withhold his blessings until they repented and renewed their devotion to the deity. Others insisted that Yahweh was waiting until the proper time to fulfill his promises and encouraged their audience to remain patient and faithful in the meantime. Still others replaced their future hope with a focus on living faithfully by the laws of Yahweh in the present.

Finally, there were those who came to believe that their ancestors had seriously misunderstood the nature of Yahweh's plans for his people. Prophecies that spoke of Yahweh destroying the power of the nations and ruling over a people who had his laws written in their hearts implied a radical change in the present world order. Prophecies that anticipated a time when the humble would be exalted, soldiers would beat their swords into farm implements, and lions would live at peace with lambs could not possibly be fulfilled within the present era of human history. Humans were too prone to evil and corruption for anything like this to occur unless Yahweh first removed the power and presence of evil from human experience. By such reasoning, some came to believe that Yahweh's plans for his people were more wonderful than their ancestors had been able to anticipate. What Yahweh had in mind was nothing less than the restoration of the universe to the condition in which it was created, a condition in which there was no sin, no suffering, and

no death. This restored universe would be inhabited by people whose lives were wholly devoted to serving Yahweh. Those who were insufficiently dedicated to Yahweh would either repent or be destroyed. Apocalyptic visions of this sort became increasingly influential in Jewish circles from the third century B.C.E. onward, from whence they eventually entered into Christianity.

Still, apocalyptic thinking might have remained on the margins of Judaism if not for the role that it played in sustaining the faith of the Jewish people during the dark years when they were being persecuted by the Seleucid king Antiochus IV in the early second century B.C.E. The **Seleucids** were the descendants of one of Alexander the Great's Greek generals who ruled the lands north of Palestine for over a century before gaining control of Palestine in 198 B.C.E. Antiochus IV came to the Seleucid throne in 175 B.C.E. with an apparent concern to revive Alexander the Great's vision of an empire united by a common Greek language and culture. Prior to the coming of the Seleucids, the Jews of Palestine had been governed for more than a century by a relatively tolerant line of Greek kings from Egypt called the **Ptolemies**, so they were no strangers to Greek culture. But the Ptolemies showed little interest in converting others to Greek ways, so the influence of Greek culture did not progress much beyond the young Jewish aristocrats who embraced it as a way of getting ahead in the Ptolemaic administration. With the coming of Antiochus IV, however, those who wished to make Israel more Greek gained the upper hand, causing a massive rift within the Jewish community, especially in Jerusalem. The result was a series of conflicts between a conservative party that rejected much of Greek culture as incompatible with Jewish beliefs and traditions and a more liberal element (supported by Antiochus) that sought to convert Jerusalem into a thoroughly Greek city.

Finally, Antiochus became so incensed with those who opposed his plans for Jerusalem that he decided to outlaw the practice of Judaism in the land of Palestine (167 B.C.E.). Seleucid soldiers attacked places of worship, destroyed Torah scrolls, murdered babies who had been circumcised, and attempted to force Jews to eat pork. Worst of all, they defiled the altar of the Jerusalem temple by sacrificing a pig to Zeus, the head of the Greek pantheon. Some of the Jews went along with the orders of the Greek

Fig. 36.5. Franz Joseph Hermann, *The Martyrdom of the Seven Maccabean Brothers and Their Mother*

king in order to protect their families, while others stood up for their faith and endured brutal tortures that often led to their deaths. Still others took up arms. By 164 B.C.E., they had succeeded in defeating the Greek armies and cleansing the temple, an event commemorated each year in the Jewish festival of Hanukkah.

A number of important apocalyptic texts were written in the years surrounding this disastrous period, including the latter chapters of the book of Daniel. All of these works give serious attention to the question of what happens to Jews who suffer and die for their faith. As a result of these experiences, many Jews could no longer accept the traditional belief that death was the end of human existence. If there was nothing beyond death, then those Jews who had died under torture would never be rewarded for their faithfulness and their tormentors would go unpunished. This conclusion was unacceptable to many Jews who had witnessed the heroism of Jewish men and women who had chosen to endure all kinds of abuse rather than deny their faith in Yahweh. As a result, many Jews concluded that there had to be some sort of future reckoning when those who had remained faithful to Yahweh in this life would be rewarded and those who had lived wicked lives would be punished. Some thought that this settling of accounts would take place immediately after death, but most looked forward to a day when the dead would be raised with new bodies and stand before Yahweh to be judged. Those whose lives demonstrated their devotion to Yahweh would live forever in a land of bliss, while those who had resisted or denied Yahweh would face eternal torment or destruction. Thus arose one of the central

tenets of the apocalyptic worldview, the belief in life after death and a future judgment.

Over the next several centuries, Jewish authors repeatedly reconfigured the various elements of apocalyptic thought to create new apocalyptic works that spoke to the needs of their day. Yet all of these works shared the same basic concern to help the people of Israel deal with the changing social, political, and religious environment of the postexilic period.

ZECHARIAH 9–14

Like the book of Isaiah, the book of Zechariah appears to contain the sayings of at least two and possibly more prophets from different periods. As with Isaiah, the earlier and later chapters of Zechariah reflect different times and situations. The first eight chapters contain headings that date the prophet's message to the years 520–518 B.C.E. The last six chapters contain no such headings, nor is there any mention of the problems and concerns that dominate the first eight chapters. Unfortunately, the few historical references in these chapters are so ambiguous that scholars have been unable to agree on when they might have been written or whether they should be credited to a single prophet. Many believe that chapters 9–11 and chapters 12–14 contain the sayings of two different prophets, since the style and content of the two sections are considerably different and both are introduced by a Hebrew word that is often translated "an oracle" (9:1; 12:1). Most would date these chapters one to two hundred years after the time of the prophet Zechariah (fourth to third century B.C.E.).

Whether the sayings in Zechariah 9–14 include any personal information about the prophet(s) who produced them is unclear. Like other prophets, the speaker claims to have received messages from Yahweh for his people (9:1; 11:4, 13, 15; 12:1; 13:2, 7), but he says nothing about the kinds of visionary experiences that characterize the earlier chapters of Zechariah. The book includes one brief narrative section (11:4-17) in which the speaker tells about a series of actions that he supposedly took in obedience to instructions that he received from Yahweh, but the passage is so full of symbolism and ambiguity that it is hard to know how much to take literally. If the "I" in these verses is indeed the prophet and not a literary figure, it appears that he felt directed by Yahweh to engage in a series of symbolic acts in which he played the role of a shepherd in order to show Yahweh's unhappiness with the way Judah's leaders were treating his people. Other passages in the book indicate that the prophet identified with the common people rather than the ruling elites (10:3; 11:3), but this tells us little about his own social status. Apart from these tantalizing morsels, we know nothing about the prophet(s) who spoke the words that appear in Zechariah 9–14.

EXERCISE 117

Read Zechariah 9:9—10:12; 12:1-9; 14:1-21. Which of the common features of apocalyptic literature can you find in these passages? Which are missing?

The first oracle of Zechariah 9–14, which fills chapters 9–11, sounds very much like the sayings that we have encountered in other prophetic books. Like the prophecies of preexilic prophets, the materials in these chapters contain a mixture of criticism and hope. Most of the criticism is directed toward leaders who are abusing Yahweh's people (10:3; 11:3-17), though there is also a brief critical comment about people who seek guidance from divination and dreams instead of praying to Yahweh for help (10:1-2). The more hopeful portion of the message also recalls the sayings of prophets from the preexilic and exilic periods. According to these chapters, Yahweh will one day arise as a warrior to judge the nations (9:1-7) and

rescue his people from foreign domination (9:11-16). In that day, a king from the line of David will bring peace to the land (9:9-10) and Yahweh will watch over his people from his temple in Jerusalem (9:8). The scattered people of Israel will return to their land (10:6-12), and the fields will overflow with rich harvests (9:17). Everything in this vision of the future reflects the "this-worldly" orientation of the prophetic books rather than the "other-worldly" focus of apocalyptic literature.

The second oracle, which fills Zechariah 12–14, is quite different. Here the apocalyptic viewpoint clearly predominates. Fifteen times in these chapters the author uses the phrase "on that day" to refer to a future time when Yahweh will come to rescue his people and bring down their opponents. The general idea is similar to that of Zechariah 9–11, but the descriptions of what Yahweh plans to do on that day transcend the ordinary sphere of human experience. As in other apocalyptic texts, the picture of the future in Zechariah 12–14 is not entirely coherent: chapter 12 shows Yahweh leading his people to victory over their enemies (12:1-9), while chapter 14 indicates that they will initially be overcome by the nations until Yahweh arises to rescue the survivors (13:8-9; 14:1-5) and rain deadly punishments upon their enemies (14:12-15). In both cases, however, the description of future events is couched in supernatural terms. According to chapter 12, Yahweh will strike the armies of Judah's enemies with madness and their horses with blindness (12:4). The weakest among his people will become as strong as David, and they will devour all of their foes (12:6-9). According to chapter 14, Yahweh will split the Mount of Olives in two so that the residents of Jerusalem can escape from their enemies through the valley that is created by this act (14:4-5). Then he will destroy their enemies by causing their flesh to rot off their bones while they are still standing (14:12). Throughout these chapters the expectations of the earlier prophets have been translated to a supernatural plane.

The apocalyptic viewpoint is even more evident in the author's vision of what will happen after Yahweh has rescued his people. In some respects his vision recalls those of the earlier prophets: the wealth of the nations will be gathered to Jerusalem (14:14) and all of the families of the earth will travel to Jerusalem to honor Israel's god

(14:16-19). The rest of the picture, however, is new. Societal peace and prosperity are not enough; the earth itself must be transformed. In this new era there will be no more cold or night (14:6-7), and the land of Israel (except for the temple mount in Jerusalem) will be flattened into a plain (14:10). Rivers of water will flow nonstop from Jerusalem to the seas (14:8). Everything in the land will be holy to Yahweh; every source of evil or impurity will be removed (14:20-21; see also 13:1-2). On that day Yahweh will reign as king over all the earth (14:9), and Jerusalem will be made secure forever (14:11).

Such a scenario cannot be fulfilled on the ordinary plane of human existence. The final destination of Yahweh's people in this vision is not the present land of Israel, but a purified land from which everything that might trouble them has been removed. This does not mean that the righteous will be taken away to an ethereal heaven to live forever with Yahweh in a disembodied state. Such an idea is foreign to the Hebrew Bible. What we see instead is a vision of heaven coming down to earth, or better yet, the conversion of the land of Israel into a heavenly territory. However we describe it, the vision of Zechariah 12–14 is a classic piece of apocalyptic speculation. Not all of the elements found in later apocalyptic texts are present in these chapters, but Zechariah 12–14 clearly helped to lay the groundwork for future developments in this area.

Fig. 36.6. The temple mount in Jerusalem: according to Zechariah 14, all the nations will gather here to worship Yahweh on the day when he arises to rescue his people and purify their land.

dated by reference to the king who ruled over Babylonia at the time, with the latest coming during the reign of Cyrus, the Persian king who conquered Babylonia in 539 B.C.E. Most of the visions speak of political events that will take place once the people of Judah have returned to their land. The visions culminate in a resurrection of the dead and a final judgment (12:1-3). At the end of the book (12:4, 9-10; see also 8:26), Daniel is told to seal up his visions so that no one will be able to read them until the time when they come to pass.

EXERCISE 118

Read Daniel 7:1-28; 10:1-14; 11:1—12:13. As you read, make a list of all of the elements of apocalyptic literature that you find in these passages, noting where you found each element.

DANIEL 7–12

The latter chapters of the book of Daniel consist of a series of dreams and visions that were supposedly given to a man named Daniel during the era of the Babylonian exile. According to Daniel 1:1-7, Daniel was part of the first group of people deported from Judah by King Nebuchadnezzar in 597 B.C.E. prior to the conquest of Jerusalem in 586 B.C.E. Each of the visions in Daniel 7–12 is

While many conservatives accept the book's claim that Daniel's visions represent genuine predictions of future events, most scholars regard the narrative framework of Daniel 7–12 as a pious fiction. No king by the name of

"Darius the Mede" (9:1; 11:1; see also 5:30-31; 6:28) ever ruled over Babylonia, and it is at least questionable whether someone who was old enough to enter into the king's service in 597 B.C.E. would still be alive by the time Cyrus the Persian conquered the Babylonians in 539 B.C.E. (10:1; compare 1:21; 6:28). The actual date when the visions of Daniel 7–12 were composed can be determined from a careful reading of chapter 11. The vision that Daniel receives in this chapter depicts a series of conflicts that will occur between "the king of the south" and the "the king of the north" in the years leading up to the final judgment. Scholars have long recognized that this vision is actually a veiled account of events that took place between the kings of Egypt (located to the south of Palestine) and Syria (to the north of Palestine) from the late fourth to the early second century B.C.E. In fact, the vision agrees so closely with the history of the period that most scholars believe that it was created after the events took place, making the "predictions" a subtle form of literary fiction. Depicting past events as predictions is a common technique of apocalyptic literature.

The latter half of the chapter (11:20-45) describes the rise and fall of a king who can be identified as the Seleucid king Antiochus IV, who persecuted the Jews from 167 to 164 B.C.E. Here the narrative coincides with historical events until Daniel 11:40, where the vision speaks of a final series of battles that will end with the death of "the king of

Fig. 36.7. A modern artist's rendition of the four beasts that Daniel sees arising from the sea in Daniel 7; according to his angelic interpreter, each represents a kingdom that will arise after Daniel's time.

the north" (namely, Antiochus IV) while he is encamped in Palestine (11:45), followed by the resurrection of the dead and the final judgment (12:1-3). None of these latter events ever took place. The simplest explanation for this sudden loss of accuracy is that the person who created this vision was actually writing during the period when

Antiochus was persecuting the Jews (roughly 165 B.C.E.) and shifted at this point from reporting events of the recent past to (incorrectly) predicting the future. In short, the real author of this vision was not a Jewish member of the Babylonian court named Daniel who lived in the sixth century B.C.E. but an unknown resident of Palestine in the second century B.C.E.

A careful comparison of Daniel's other visions with historical events shows that they, too, describe the coming of King Antiochus IV and his mistreatment of the Jews of Palestine. Not surprisingly, each vision culminates in a prediction of the destruction of Antiochus's kingdom by Yahweh (7:7-11, 19-27; 8:9-14, 23-25; 9:27). This observation reinforces the impression that the person who crafted these visions was writing during the time of Antiochus IV, whom he viewed as a demonic threat that could be stopped only by divine intervention. His vivid depiction of the ultimate victory of Yahweh was designed to encourage his fellow Jews to hold on to their faith in the midst of a painful and seemingly hopeless situation.

But why cast this message as the visions of a Babylonian court official who lived some four hundred years before his time? Apparently the author thought that this format would lend credibility to his message of hope. After roughly two years of serious repression, many Jews were probably beginning to wonder whether Yahweh would ever rescue them from their dreadful situation. The author of these visions wished to assure his people that Yahweh had not forgotten them and that he would come to their aid in his own time. But why should anyone believe him? By framing his message as a series of visions given by Yahweh to a great wise man from the past, the author sought to show his audience that Yahweh is thoroughly aware of what will happen in human history. Nothing takes him by surprise; even the present round of Seleucid persecutions was foretold by Yahweh centuries before it occurred.

In reality, most of the events "predicted" in these visions had already occurred by the author's time, so it was easy for the author to ensure that Daniel's "predictions" were historically accurate. Those who recognized the accuracy of these visions would be more likely to accept the book's message that Yahweh would soon bring down Antiochus IV. This prediction would have given them the strength they needed to hold on to their faith and not turn away in the face of persecution. Even if they should be forced to die for their faith, Daniel's visions assured them that they would soon be restored to life and rewarded by Yahweh (12:1-3, 13).

As it turned out, the persecutions did indeed cease soon after the book of Daniel was written, but it was an armed uprising and not a supernatural judgment that broke the back of Antiochus IV's reign of terror. Another two decades of fighting and political maneuvering were required before the Jews were able to break free of Greek rule and establish their own kingdom, and their independence lasted for only eighty years, not "forever" as predicted in the book of Daniel (7:18, 27). The book's anticipation of an imminent resurrection of the dead and a final judgment also failed to materialize. The person who crafted these visions was clearly more effective at "predicting" the past than the future.

This way of decoding the visionary chapters of the book of Daniel is disturbing to many modern readers, since it makes Daniel's visions sound like a form of literary deception where the ends may or may not have justified the means. But this concern overlooks the fact that the ancient world followed different literary conventions than we do today. Virtually all apocalyptic works attribute their visions to great men from the past who are credited with predicting events that had in fact already occurred by the time the texts were being composed. Whether ancient readers thought that these books reflected the experience of the person who is portrayed as the recipient of the visions or whether they recognized them as literary fictions is impossible to say. The popularity of apocalyptic literature within both Jewish and Christian circles over the next several centuries suggests that the literary format did not pose a problem for the readers in either case. What mattered to people who read books like Daniel was the message of hope that was embedded in the apocalyptic worldview.

CONCLUSION

Apocalyptic literature developed out of the prophetic movement as a response to the concerns of Jews who felt oppressed or disadvantaged by the political, economic, social, or religious systems under which they were forced to live. Like the prophets, the authors of apocalyptic works claimed to have received divine revelations that spelled out the will and plans of Yahweh for his people. Apocalyptic thinkers looked forward to a time when Yahweh would put an end to the present world order and inaugurate a new era when the faithful followers of Yahweh would live blissful lives in a world free from the influence of evil. Virtually all apocalyptic works include scenes of judgment, but their message emphasizes hope over fear.

Apocalyptic works reassure those who feel abused or oppressed that Yahweh has not forgotten them and that he will rescue them from their present sufferings. The apocalyptic conviction that Yahweh's people are caught up in a cosmic battle between the forces of good and evil enables the audience to make sense of their experience and gives meaning and dignity to their losses. The apocalyptic assurance that Yahweh will finally triumph over his foes offers grounds for hope in times when it seems like evil is winning. The apocalyptic promise of heavenly rewards and the related threat of divine punishments provide incentives for people to remain devoted to Yahweh during times of trial. And the apocalyptic expectation that Yahweh will act very soon makes it easier for people to retain their faith when they are tempted to give up on Yahweh forever.

EXERCISE 119

Imagine that you are a member of a contemporary Jewish or Christian group in a country where people like you face serious abuse and repression. Do you think that your group might find a piece of ancient apocalyptic literature helpful in that situation? Why or why not?

Fig. 37.1. An Egyptian Pharaoh converses with the god Thoth, who was regarded by the people of Egypt as the patron deity of learning, wisdom, and scribal activities.

The Way of Wisdom

Happy are those who find wisdom, and those who get understanding, for her income is better than silver, and her revenue better than gold. She is more precious than jewels, and nothing you desire can compare with her. Long life is in her right hand; in her left hand are riches and honor. Her ways are ways of pleasantness, and all her paths are peace. She is a tree of life to those who lay hold of her; those who hold her fast are called happy. (Proverbs 3:13-18)

Where then does wisdom come from? And where is the place of understanding? It is hidden from the eyes of all living, and concealed from the birds of the air. Abaddon and Death say, "We have heard a rumor of it with our ears." God understands the way to it, and he knows its place. . . . And he said to humankind, "Truly, the fear of the Lord, that is wisdom; and to depart from evil is understanding." (Job 28:20-23, 28)

When I applied my mind to know wisdom, and to see the business that is done on earth, how one's eyes see sleep neither day nor night, then I saw all the work of God, that no one can find out what is happening under the sun. However much they may toil in seeking, they will not find it out; even though those who are wise claim to know, they cannot find it out. (Ecclesiastes 8:16-17)

In this final stage of our journey, we will examine a distinctive set of texts from the Hebrew Bible that scholars call *wisdom literature*. The term reflects the authors' preoccupation with the question of what it means to think and live as a "wise" person within the context of a Yahwistic worldview. The answers that they offer are diverse and even contradictory. What holds these works together is not the answers that they give but the kinds of questions that they seek to address.

The Hebrew Bible includes three books that are universally regarded as wisdom literature: Proverbs, Job, and Ecclesiastes (called *Qoheleth* in the Hebrew tradition). A number of the psalms also reflect the influence of wisdom thinking (Psalms 1, 19, 34, 36, 37, 49, 73, 90, 112, 119, 127, 128, 133; see chapter 30). Some would place the Song of Solomon (also known as the Song of Songs) under this heading, though its erotic love poetry is unlike anything else in the Hebrew Bible.

Wisdom material can also be found outside the Hebrew canon. Toward the end of the biblical era, the wisdom tradition gave rise to other books that were not accepted into the Hebrew Bible, including some that were eventually incorporated into Roman Catholic or Orthodox Christian Bibles (Ecclesiasticus, the Wisdom of Solomon, the Odes of Solomon) and others that were never part of any known canon. Jesus and some of the authors of the Christian New Testament were influenced by wisdom thinking, and the Qur'an likewise includes themes from the biblical wisdom tradition. The wisdom books of the Hebrew Bible are only selected examples of the abiding influence of the Hebrew wisdom tradition.

Our investigation of the wisdom literature is divided into two parts. The present chapter begins with an examination of the general phenomenon of wisdom thinking in religious communities, including ancient Israel. The latter part of the chapter focuses on the book of Proverbs, which represents the distilled essence of an important current in ancient Hebrew wisdom reflection. The next chapter will examine the books of Job and Ecclesiastes, both of which pose direct challenges to the worldview represented by the book of Proverbs, and the Song of Solomon, a book that is only tangentially related to the wisdom tradition.

THE QUEST FOR WISDOM

Humans appear to have a built-in drive to discover some kind of order or meaning within the universe. Scientists credit this tendency to the organizing capacity of the brain. Most religious traditions, however, insist that the universe has an order that precedes any human attempt to uncover it. This applies to the moral universe as well as the physical universe. Just as humans are capable of observing and predicting the patterns of the heavens and the seasons, so also religious thinkers believe that they can

determine the consequences that will follow from various kinds of human conduct.

In today's world, the task of understanding the physical universe is normally assigned to scientists, while religious and philosophical ethicists grapple with moral questions. Throughout most of human history, however, both of these tasks fell within the sphere of religion or philosophy. Religious thinkers in different cultures looked for patterns in both the physical universe and the moral universe in an effort to uncover the ordered reality that they believed lay behind both spheres. Out of their observations came guidelines that explained how humans should behave in order to align their lives with the underlying structures of reality. Those who followed the recommended course of action were assured of a fruitful and successful life, while those who deviated from this path would be crushed by the consequences of their actions.

This effort to uncover the moral order of the universe and to discover the best way to live in order to reap its

Fig. 37.2. Wisdom is represented as a deity in many religious traditions; from left, Saraswati (Hinduism), Wen Chang (Daoism), and Athena (Greek religion).

benefits and avoid its misfortunes is commonly known as the quest for wisdom. Wisdom is not the same as knowledge. Wisdom invariably includes a body of knowledge about how the universe works, but it also has a strong experiential component. Its goal is not to enable people to recite a collection of facts, but to shape their thought patterns and their character so that they will behave in a manner that agrees with the accepted definition of what it means to be wise. In this way wisdom teachings help to motivate people to live up to the moral ideals of a particular group or society.

Wisdom teachings resemble the religious rules that we discussed in chapter 22 in that they are concerned with promoting patterns of conduct that reflect the values and ideals of the group. They differ, however, in their level of specificity. Rules are usually quite specific about the kinds of behavior that they require, whereas wisdom teachings are more general, identifying broad principles that can be applied to a wide variety of situations. As a result, wisdom teachings place more emphasis on personal reflection and judgment than rules do. Rules require only that individuals know what is expected of them and comply with it. Wisdom teachings, by contrast, force people to decide which principles might be relevant to a particular situation and how those principles should be applied. At the heart of most forms of wisdom instruction is a systematic vision of how life works. This is less important in rule-based systems. One need not know the reason behind a rule in order to obey it, whereas understanding is crucial for the application of wisdom.

Wisdom teachings play a key role in traditional societies, where they serve as a vital channel for passing on the group's moral and ethical standards. The ideas behind these teachings are usually credited to wise people from the past. As a result, wisdom teachings serve to reinforce the status quo. People are taught from childhood to accept and live by the group's time-honored standards of wise conduct, not to form their own moral codes. Personal experimentation is discouraged through repeated warnings of negative consequences for those who reject the accepted standards, while adherence to the norms is encouraged by promises of a happy life. Often these norms are condensed into the form of proverbs, short wise sayings that are easy for both children and adults to remember and apply to their lives.

In most such groups the standards of wise behavior are regarded as fixed and unchanging, since they are grounded in the inherent order of the universe. But this does not mean that the standards are beyond question. People can see that the broad principles that they were taught as children do not always hold up in the real world. Those who violate the group's norms do not always suffer negative consequences, and those who follow them do not always succeed. Various explanations are developed to account for these discrepancies. Most of these explanations seek to uphold the ultimate validity of the accepted order. Some groups allow members of the religious leadership or the educated elites to question and debate the fundamental tenets of the group's view of the universe, but most strongly discourage this kind of thinking.

WISDOM IN ANCIENT ISRAEL

Wisdom teachings played an important role in framing the way people thought about moral problems throughout the ancient Near East. Both Egypt and Mesopotamia had long traditions of wisdom reflection that led to the creation of texts whose language and ideas resemble what we see in the biblical books of Proverbs, Job, and Ecclesiastes. These extrabiblical texts were composed by the literate elites, but they often drew on traditions that were popular among the illiterate masses.

Like their Egyptian and Mesopotamian counterparts, the wisdom materials of the Hebrew Bible reflect the experiences, concerns, and viewpoints of an elite class of authors and editors. The book of Proverbs includes instructions about how to behave around kings and other high officials, how to manage one's riches, and how to treat the poor. The book of Job contains some of the most elaborate poetry in the Hebrew Bible, revealing a level of literary sophistication that was present only among the educated elites. The author of Ecclesiastes places himself in the imaginary position of one of the kings of Judah (1:1, 12) and speaks from this elite perspective throughout the book. Several of the poems in the Song of Solomon imply that the author was familiar with the royal court (1:4, 12-13; 3:6-11; note the title in 1:1). The origins of the wisdom psalms are less clear, but their

poetic style and the sheer fact that they were written down suggest that they, too, were composed by the religious elites (see chapter 30).

On the other hand, it would be wrong to draw too sharp a line between elite and popular perspectives when discussing the wisdom literature. Most of the sayings in the book of Proverbs and the wisdom psalms are so broad and memorable that they could have been used by people at any level of society, regardless of their ability to read or write. In fact, many of these sayings probably

Fig. 37.3. (top) This Babylonian text, called the Instruction of Shuruppak, contains short wise sayings resembling the biblical book of Proverbs; (bottom) an Egyptian book called the Admonitions of Ipuwer reflects on the nature and presence of evil in a manner that recalls the books of Job and Ecclesiastes.

originated among the illiterate masses before they were taken up by the elites and incorporated into the present collections. Even the more sophisticated forms of wisdom reflection that we find in the books of Job and Ecclesiastes center on questions that would have troubled people across the social spectrum. A few of the wisdom psalms even contain criticisms of the wealthy elites that echo the concerns of the poverty-ridden masses (Psalms 49, 73).

Observations such as these have led most scholars to the conclusion that wisdom teachings played an important role at all levels of ancient Israelite society. Individuals used them to guide their personal decisions; families, to educate their children; village elders, to settle disputes; aristocrats, to advise the king and his top officials. Elderly people in particular were respected as sources of wisdom, and people often looked to them for wise counsel. At the upper end of society, wisdom traditions were used in the education of young aristocrats who would have been taught by their parents and tutors in the absence of schools.

The people who compiled the wisdom books into their present form would have been members of this upper stratum of Israelite society. The Hebrew Bible refers to a class of people called wise men or **sages** who served as guardians and teachers of the wisdom traditions, though their precise social setting and activities remain unclear. Some seem to have focused on the preservation and transmission of traditional wisdom materials, while others composed works of their own that engaged critically with those materials. Both incorporated popular wisdom teachings into their writings. Some of their works eventually ended up in the Hebrew Bible.

In short, the wisdom books of the Hebrew Bible were produced by elite authors who made substantial use of popular materials. As a result, the wisdom books tell us more about the views of the elites than about the common people, though they also give us an indirect window onto the moral thinking of the illiterate masses.

EXERCISE 120

Read the following verses from the wisdom books of the Hebrew Bible. What kinds of conduct does each passage label as proper or improper? Do you see anything here that might shed light on the social context of the authors?

• Psalm 73:1-20
• Psalm 112:1-10
• Proverbs 16:10-15
• Proverbs 22:22—23:8
• Ecclesiastes 2:1-11

WISDOM IN THE HEBREW BIBLE

The two related Hebrew words that are translated as "wisdom" and "wise" in English Bibles appear more than three hundred times in the Hebrew Bible. The two terms are used in a variety of senses. At the most basic level, they refer to the cleverness or shrewdness with which a person is enabled to handle a problem or challenge. Craft workers (carpenters, metalworkers, stone masons, and the like) are sometimes described as wise when they use their skills to plan and carry out their creative work. An individual who possesses unusual insight into supernatural matters can also be identified as wise.

Within the wisdom books, however, the term *wisdom* is normally used in a more specialized sense to refer to a systematic understanding of the way Yahweh has designed life to work, accompanied by a commitment to live according to that design. The wisdom books disagree over how much humans can know about what Yahweh is doing in the universe, but they all agree that Yahweh is ultimately in charge and that some forms of conduct are more consistent with his design than others. The person who lives in accordance with Yahweh's design is regarded as wise, while the person who lives a self-directed life

Fig. 37.4. An Egyptian artisan named Sennedjem honors the gods of wisdom and knowledge in this scene from the artisan's tomb (thirteenth century B.C.E.).

and refuses to take Yahweh's instructions into account is described as a fool.

Two types of wisdom material can be identified in the Hebrew Bible. Both have parallels in Egyptian and Mesopotamian texts. The first, found primarily in the book of Proverbs and some of the wisdom psalms, gives practical advice about how one should live in order to enjoy a pleasant and successful life. The tone of this practical wisdom is optimistic, with the speaker affirming confidently that certain kinds of behavior will lead to positive outcomes and others to negative consequences. Behind this teaching lies a conviction that the universe is an orderly place that operates according to a set of fixed moral standards that humans can discern through careful study and reflection.

The second type of wisdom material, which appears mostly in the books of Job and Ecclesiastes but also in a few of the wisdom psalms, is more reflective and skeptical in its orientation. Texts that flow out of this reflective wisdom tradition raise difficult questions about the view of reality presupposed by the teachers of practical wisdom in an effort to derive a more adequate and realistic understanding of the way life works. The tone of these texts is decidedly pessimistic, with the speaker often questioning how much humans can know about the character of Yahweh and the meaning of life.

From what we learned earlier about the prominence of wisdom traditions in ancient Israel, we might expect that wisdom teachings would be scattered throughout the Hebrew Bible. But that is not the case. Outside of the wisdom books, the influence of wisdom traditions within the Hebrew Bible is slight. The terms *wise* and *wisdom* appear infrequently in the narrative books apart from the story of King Solomon, whose wisdom is said to have "surpassed the wisdom of all the people of the east, and all the wisdom of Egypt" (1 Kings 4:30). Statements such as this made Solomon the "patron saint" of wisdom in later Jewish traditions (see Proverbs 1:1; 10:1; 25:1; Ecclesiastes 1:1, 12; Song of Solomon 1:1). A similar void can be seen in the legal sections of the Torah, where wisdom language is limited to a handful of appearances in Deuteronomy (1:13, 15; 4:6; 16:19; 32:29; 34:9). As we will see later, this verbal link with Deuteronomy is no accident, since the wisdom books interact repeatedly with the belief system that is embedded in the book of Deuteronomy. Within the prophetic books, the words *wise* and *wisdom* are used most often in a negative sense to refer to people who are "wise in their own eyes" and do not follow Yahweh as the prophets desire. Positive uses of the terms are rare. Among the non-wisdom books in the Writings, only the book of Daniel employs wisdom ideas and language. Like Solomon, Daniel is portrayed as a paragon of wisdom who receives supernatural knowledge from Yahweh about secrets that are hidden to ordinary mortals.

Why do wisdom traditions play such a limited role in the Hebrew Bible? Many scholars have pointed out that the basic outlook of the wisdom books stands in tension with important ideas that dominate the rest of the Hebrew Bible. Where the bulk of the Hebrew Bible emphasizes the importance of Yahweh's covenant with Israel, the terms *covenant* and *Israel* are virtually absent from the wisdom books. Also missing are any references to the patriarchs, the Exodus story, and the laws of Torah. In short, the wisdom books show little interest in the narrative traditions that lie at the heart of the Hebrew Bible. Instead, they focus on universal questions and observations that could have been raised by people in any culture. They also place more emphasis on the fate of the individual than does the rest of the Hebrew Bible. Elsewhere the future of the nation is the central concern.

Another area in which the wisdom books differ from the rest of the Hebrew Bible is in their understanding of how humans come to know the will of Yahweh. According to the Torah and the prophets, Yahweh reveals his will to chosen individuals (Moses, Isaiah, and so forth) who then transmit his words to his people. The authors of the wisdom books, by contrast, presume that humans are capable of figuring out for themselves what counts as proper and improper behavior by observing how life works. Here and there they acknowledge that wisdom is a gift from Yahweh, but this does not detract from the fact that their teachings are rooted in human observation and reasoning.

Finally, the dominant tradition in the Hebrew Bible insists that Yahweh always acts justly toward humans, though his justice is sometimes delayed or tempered by his mercy. The wisdom books, by contrast, include texts that raise fundamental questions about the justice and equity of Yahweh. The justice of Yahweh is generally upheld in the end, but many verses insist that humans are unable to comprehend the ways of the deity. The skeptical viewpoint that dominates the books of Job and Ecclesiastes (see chapter 38) is without parallel in the rest of the Hebrew Bible.

Of course, the wisdom books also have points in common with the rest of the Hebrew canon. Like the covenantal tradition, the wisdom books presume that Yahweh is lord of the universe, that humans should orient their lives around his will, and that Yahweh rewards those who follow him and punishes those who resist him. But there is no escaping the fact that the wisdom literature is grounded in a different view of reality than we find in the rest of the Hebrew Bible. Whether the two sets of ideas should be regarded as complementary or whether they represent the thinking of two (or more) groups with competing points of view is a matter of debate. The fact that the wisdom materials were eventually included in the Hebrew Bible suggests that the people who used them saw no fundamental contradiction between the wisdom books and the rest of the canon. But the tensions between the wisdom books and the rest of the Hebrew Bible are real and should not be underestimated.

THE BOOK OF PROVERBS

The book of Proverbs contains the oldest wisdom material in the Hebrew Bible, with many passages that go back to the preexilic period. Like the book of Psalms, the present book is the result of a long history of collection and editing. Headings that are scattered throughout the book indicate that the editors drew on earlier collections that were attributed to King Solomon (1:1; 10:1; 25:1), "the wise" (22:17; 24:23), an otherwise unknown man named Agur (30:1), and an equally unknown "King Lemuel" (31:1). Most of these named collections probably drew their material from even earlier collections. Whether any of the sayings attributed to King Solomon actually go back to his time is unclear. Most likely these attributions reflect Solomon's role as the "patron saint" of wisdom literature, indicating that the sayings were compiled in his honor. The attempt in Proverbs 1:1 to attribute the entire

Fig. 37.5. Nicolas Poussin, *The Judgment of Solomon* (1 Kings 3:16-28)

book to Solomon is clearly artificial, since the headings within the book indicate that its contents came from a variety of sources.

In its present form, the book of Proverbs consists of two very different kinds of material. The core of the book (Proverbs 10–31) is a collection of short, disconnected sayings that seek to encourage certain kinds of conduct and discourage others. These sayings, commonly known as proverbs, give the book its name. Some of the sayings in these chapters go back to the preexilic period, where they would have been passed on orally among both the illiterate masses and the educated elites. This collection is prefaced by a series of poems (Proverbs 1–9) that urges the reader to seek after wisdom and avoid folly. Most scholars believe that these poems were created in the postexilic era to provide an introduction to the written collection of sayings after it was compiled and edited during the exilic and/or postexilic period.

When studying the book of Proverbs, we must keep in mind that the sayings in chapters 10–31 were not created to be part of a written collection. Instead, each proverb was crafted to stand on its own and to communicate its message without reference to any broader literary context. That is how proverbs work in every culture. Proverbs summarize a culture's key values in a form that is easy for both children and adults to recall and apply to their lives when

ethical guidance is needed. Proverbs are especially popular in cultures with low levels of literacy, where they serve as one of the primary mechanisms for upholding traditional societal values. But proverbs can also play an important role in literate cultures as long as people continue to respect the wisdom of their ancestors.

The declining influence of proverbs in the modern world is the result not of increases in literacy but of a growing acceptance of value systems that honor novelty and free thought over the collective wisdom of the past. The use of proverbs has not entirely ceased—most Americans are familiar with sayings like "The early bird gets the worm" or "A bird in the hand is worth two in the bush," even if they no longer know what they mean. But the individualistic orientation of American society means that people today have little interest in the time-tested lessons that proverbs aim to teach.

EXERCISE 121

Open your Bible to the book of Proverbs and read for a few minutes from different chapters of the book. What do you notice about the style and content of the proverbs? How do they communicate their message?

THE POWER OF PROVERBS

All of the sayings in the book of Proverbs are framed as poetry. The poetic quality of the sayings adds to their effectiveness, since poetry appeals to the emotions and will of the audience as well as their intellect. Unfortunately, some of the poetic elements of the proverbs do not come through in translation. Still, readers who know nothing about Hebrew can learn to appreciate the poetic power of the proverbs.

The most obvious poetic feature of the proverbs is their use of parallelism, the Hebrew stylistic device that employs two (or sometimes more) lines to express a single thought (see chapter 3). By nature, parallelism requires a certain amount of reflection to make sense of the relation between the two lines. This moment of reflection engages the hearer's imagination, emotions, and will, drawing the entire person into the process of interpreting the proverb. In this way the parallel structure of the proverbs virtually compels a personal response to the proverb's message.

The parallelism of the proverbs is rich and diverse. A few examples of the most common types will indicate some of their breadth. In the simplest form of parallelism, the second line simply restates and refines the idea that is presented in the first line. In these cases the full meaning of the proverb is grasped by reflecting on the similarities and differences between the various elements of the two lines.

> One who spares words is knowledgeable;
> One who is cool in spirit has understanding. (17:27)

> Laziness brings on deep sleep;
> an idle person will suffer hunger. (19:15)

In other cases the two lines are framed as an antithesis, with the second line offering an observation that stands in contrast to the point of the first line. The contrast has the effect of recommending one kind of behavior while discouraging its opposite.

> Whoever walks with the wise becomes wise,
> but the companion of fools suffers harm. (13:20)

> The plans of the diligent lead surely to abundance,
> but everyone who is hasty comes only to want. (21:5)

In still other cases the second line completes the thought of the first line, so that both lines must be considered together in order to grasp the full message.

> The blessing of the Lord makes rich,
> and he adds no sorrow with it. (10:22)

> Do not withhold discipline from your children;
> if you beat them with a rod, they will not die. (23:13)

Explicit comparisons are also common in the book of Proverbs. In some cases the point of the comparison is obvious, while in others a degree of reflection is required to comprehend what is being said.

> Better to be despised and have a servant,
> than to be self-important and lack food. (12:9)

> Like a gold ring in a pig's snout
> is a beautiful woman without good sense. (11:22)

The poetic nature of the proverbs can also be seen in their extensive use of visual imagery. Virtually all of the proverbs rely on images drawn from the social experience of people in ancient Palestine, including family life, farming, the marketplace, military service, the judicial system, and the royal court. The cast of characters is equally

Fig. 37.6. The book of Proverbs contains sayings that provide guidance for virtually every aspect of daily life, from the proper care of animals (12:10) to the use of honest weights in the market (11:1; 16:11).

broad: fathers, mothers, children, husbands, wives, kings, courtiers, rich people, poor people, soldiers, farmers, strangers, craft workers, and countless others. These references to ordinary experience allowed the proverbs to speak to people of any social level, since the audience could validate the truth of the message by comparing it with their own observations. They also made the proverbs more memorable to the illiterate masses.

In addition to their poetic qualities, the proverbs employ a variety of rhetorical techniques to influence the thinking and conduct of their audience. Some list concrete examples of proper or improper conduct that should be imitated or avoided. Others identify broad principles that can be applied to a variety of situations. Some strive for clarity of expression, using images and language whose meaning is readily apparent. Others are more opaque, requiring the hearer to think about the meaning of an analogy or an example in order to grasp their message. Some are framed as commands that tell people how they should behave. Others simply describe how life works and leave it to the audience to figure out the ethical implications of their observations. The variability of the proverbs is limited only by the imaginations of the people who framed them, whether they were illiterate peasants or urban sages.

In short, the book of Proverbs reflects the insights of generations of people who used their imaginative faculties to figure out creative and meaningful ways of passing on the accepted values of their culture. The sayings that were included in the book of Proverbs offer only a sampling of the rich variety of proverbial material that circulated in the cities, towns, and villages of ancient Palestine.

EXERCISE 122

Read any two chapters from Proverbs 10–31 and make a list of the different issues that they address. Then reread the chapters and summarize what the proverbs say about how individuals should behave in each of the areas that you identified.

THE SOCIAL VISION OF PROVERBS

A sizable percentage of the sayings in the book of Proverbs offer guidelines for how people should treat one another, that is, their social conduct. Implicit in these sayings is a vision of the way society should operate. As with the social laws of the Torah, this vision was an ideal; the books of the prophets provide ample evidence that the people of Yahweh regularly failed to live up to these standards. Still, a brief review of the social world that is envisioned in the proverbs can help us to see how their vision of reality both resembles and differs from that of the Torah.

Since the proverbs are not arranged in any topical or thematic pattern, it is easy to overlook the fact that they actually address a fairly limited range of issues.

1. *Personal character.* At the individual level, the book of Proverbs stresses the importance of guarding one's personal integrity at all costs. This means avoiding all forms of dishonesty and deception. People are also instructed to keep their passions in check and to avoid anger, pride, jealousy, hatred, and similar negative attitudes. People who follow the teachings of Proverbs will be open to correction and willing to learn, not argumentative or prone to think that they have all the answers. They will listen to the advice of their parents and other wise people and avoid the company of fools. In particular, they will keep away from people who tempt them to become involved

Fig. 37.7. The book of Proverbs calls for parents to be strict in disciplining their children, including corporal punishment (13:24; 19:18; 23:13; 29:17).

with violence, excessive drinking, prostitutes, and other harmful forms of conduct.

2. *Family life.* The book of Proverbs envisions a family system in which fathers and husbands are in charge, though mothers are also accorded a degree of respect and authority. Both parents are expected to exercise strict control over the behavior of their children, applying corporal punishment on a liberal basis. The primary task of parents is to train their children to seek wisdom and turn away from foolishness, which is the natural condition of children. Husbands are supposed to love their wives and remain faithful to them at all times, and wives are expected to be loyal to their husbands and to follow their lead without nagging and complaining.

3. *Work and business.* The book of Proverbs calls on people to be diligent in their work and to avoid laziness,

Fig. 37.8. Care for the poor and needy is one of the chief social obligations of the wise person according to the book of Proverbs (11:24; 19:17; 21:13; 28:27).

whether they are working for themselves or for someone else. Planning for the future is also vital for achieving success in one's labors. Those who labor for others should be trustworthy and honest; those who employ others should treat them fairly and pay them promptly. People who sell goods to others should be scrupulously honest and fair in all of their transactions.

4. *Possessions.* According to Proverbs, wealth is a gift from Yahweh—as long as it is obtained by honest means. Those who gain riches must manage them responsibly. Wealth is not to be hoarded but to be shared generously with those in need. Giving is preferable to lending, since borrowers often fail to repay their loans, leading to the loss of God-given resources. Pledging to repay other people's loans in case they should default on their payments is also unwise, since it places one's security in the hands of another person who might prove to be irresponsible.

5. *Relations with peers.* The book of Proverbs envisions a social world in which people are loyal and devoted to their friends and do not talk about them behind their backs. Gossip, lying, and slander have no place in such a world. People speak when they have something appropriate to say; otherwise they guard their tongues. People are instructed to be kind to one another and to refrain from acts that might cause harm to others or their property. Differences are to be settled peacefully, without fighting or quarrels. Friends should encourage one another in the path of wisdom rather than plotting together to engage in sinful behaviors.

6. *Relations with superiors.* The world of Proverbs is a hierarchical society in which people know their place and defer to those above them in humility and respect. Older people and people of a higher social level are to be treated with special honor. At the highest levels of society, people must be particularly careful about observing proper standards of decorum if they hope to gain the trust and respect of those above them. Strategically timed gifts are often helpful for social advancement.

7. *Societal structures.* In the world envisioned in the book of Proverbs, kings rule justly under the guidance of wise counselors, and their subjects honor and respect the authority of the king. Judges issue fair rulings based on honest testimony, convicting the guilty and clearing the innocent. Everyone is treated equally in the courts,

Fig. 37.9. Wisdom is associated with age throughout the book of Proverbs, and younger people are repeatedly told to honor their elders (16:31; 20:29).

EXERCISE 123

Read Proverbs 1:20—3:26 and 8:1—9:18. What benefits do these passages say come to people who follow the path of wisdom? What happens to those who do not?

THE FRUITS OF WISDOM

Behind the specific provisions of Proverbs lies a worldview that divides all of humanity into two camps, the wise and the foolish. Those who are wise take Yahweh seriously and make a sincere effort to follow his instructions at all times. These people enjoy Yahweh's favor, which he expresses by providing them with riches, a healthy body, a happy family, a good reputation, and all of the other benefits that people in the ancient world considered vital to a successful life. Those who choose to live foolish lives, by contrast, place themselves under Yahweh's curse. The proverbs consistently assert that Yahweh will bring these people down in his own time, subjecting them to shame and physical punishment and transferring all of their possessions to the wise.

Little thought is required to recognize that this is the same worldview that we encountered earlier in the book of Deuteronomy and several of the prophetic books, a worldview that scholars call Deuteronomic theology. This worldview was deeply ingrained in the wisdom traditions of ancient Israel, appearing in proverbial sayings from every period. Some of the later wisdom teachers raised serious questions about this interpretation of human experience (see chapter 38), but few such questions can be heard in the book of Proverbs.

To understand why this black-and-white view of life was so popular, we should recall that proverbs played a central role in the moral education of children in ancient Palestine. Every culture tends to idealize and oversimplify reality when explaining to children how life works and how they should behave. Rare is the parent who would attempt to explain to an eight-year-old child why lying might be morally acceptable in some circumstances and not in others. Children are commonly taught that lying

whether rich or poor, weak or powerful. The rich do not take advantage of the poor; instead, they share their resources with the needy and submit to the judgments of the courts.

8. *Religion.* The book of Proverbs says very little about the ritual dimension of religion, though prayers and sacrifices are mentioned in passing. Instead, Proverbs stresses the importance of ethics. Proper behavior is the measure of one's devotion to Yahweh, not ritual activity. According to Proverbs, Yahweh is an almighty, righteous king who sees all that his people do and blesses or punishes them in accordance with their actions. In light of this reality, everyone should make a serious effort to live as Yahweh wishes; indeed, wisdom is rooted in the fear of Yahweh (1:7; 9:10; 15:33; compare Job 28:28; Psalm 111:10; Micah 6:9). To fear Yahweh means to take him seriously, to honor and respect him above everything else in life. In practical terms, it means doing what Yahweh says and avoiding what he says is evil; accepting his discipline without complaint; turning to him for help in times of need; and trusting him to take care of the future.

is bad and that people who lie will suffer for their actions, while those who are honest will do well in life. This is precisely the mind-set we see in the book of Proverbs. The world of Proverbs is a morally simple universe in which the difference between right and wrong is clear, people get what they deserve, and all is right with the world. Such a simplified view of reality serves two important purposes: it gives the young a moral compass to guide their actions, and it motivates them to behave in the manner that the society considers right and to avoid actions that the society deems wrong.

Fig. 37.10. An older Jewish man teaches a child how to pray at the Wailing Wall in Jerusalem.

On a subtler level, the worldview of Proverbs teaches children and adults alike to accept the prevailing social order by rooting it in the essential nature of reality. According to Proverbs, wealth, power, and success are gifts that Yahweh bestows on those who devote themselves to a life of wisdom. This suggests that those who have the most economic and political resources enjoy the support of Yahweh, while those who lack such blessings have only themselves to blame. To question the allocation of wealth and power in such a society is to challenge the wisdom of Yahweh and to risk his wrath. Little imagination is required to see how this ideology offers a subtle but potent legitimation of the current economic and political system.

Both of these themes are prominent in the opening chapters of the book, where a father repeatedly urges his son to pursue wisdom above everything else that life has to offer. The effect is the same whether the father-son

language is understood literally or metaphorically, that is, as the voice of a teacher speaking to a pupil. Here as elsewhere the moral universe is framed in stark, black-and-white terms: certain kinds of behavior are always bad (violence, adultery, quarreling, pride, laziness, and the like) and bring ruin to those who practice them, while other kinds are inherently good (prudence, faithfulness, self-control, devotion to one's wife, and so forth), leading to worldly success and prosperity. Such descriptions of wisdom as a means to an end (that is, as a tool for obtaining riches, long life, divine protection, and similar benefits) are typical of the kind of moral instruction that is given to children in every culture. The frequent use of parental and even sexual imagery (as when Wisdom and Folly are depicted as two women clamoring for the attention of the "son") lends added weight to this appeal.

Despite its social usefulness, this ideology ultimately carries the seeds of its own destruction. In a world with little or no social mobility, the great majority of people in ancient Palestine would have had no opportunity to enjoy the kinds of material benefits that are promised in the opening chapters of the book of Proverbs. For them, the definitions of success and prosperity were probably framed in more limited terms in order to protect the integrity of the ideology and the social system that it supports.

The problem would have been even more acute among the elites, since they were in a position to see that the link between devotion to Yahweh and material prosperity was tenuous at best. The books of Job and Ecclesiastes, together with several of the psalms, offer poignant meditations on the discrepancies between the moral theories embedded in the book of Proverbs and their authors' observations of reality. Along the way, they raise profound questions about the validity of the worldview that is presupposed in the book of Proverbs and the Deuteronomic tradition. Whether these questions ultimately undermine the dominant social system is less clear. Our final chapter will examine this subversive and skeptical strand within the wisdom tradition.

CONCLUSION

Wisdom teachings can be found in virtually all world religions. They arise out of a universal human need to discover some kind of moral order within the universe. The goal of wisdom traditions is practical: to determine how humans should live in order to align themselves with the moral structures of reality so that they can enjoy the good things of life and avoid its misfortunes.

The wisdom materials in the Hebrew Bible examine these questions through the lens of a Yahwistic world-view. The answers that they give, however, are not limited to the followers of Yahweh. Instead, they are rooted in an understanding of the universe that is thought to be valid for all humans, whether they accept it or not. As a result, the wisdom materials have a universal quality that is missing from much of the rest of the Hebrew Bible.

The sayings that appear in the book of Proverbs encapsulate the essence of the traditional wisdom teaching that could be found at all levels of ancient Israelite society. Various behaviors are classified as right or wrong, wise or foolish, and specific results are promised to those who follow each path. The biblical proverbs cite examples from daily life to instill a set of moral principles that can be used to guide the lives of people who reflect on their meaning. Visual imagery and poetic parallelism also make them easy for people to remember and apply, especially children. By challenging people to conform to the accumulated wisdom of the past, proverbs invariably help to reinforce the social, economic, and political status quo.

EXERCISE 124

Choose five sayings on different subjects from the book of Proverbs. For each saying, indicate (a) what kinds of behavior the saying identifies as right or wrong; (b) what outcomes are promised to those who pursue each path; and (c) how the saying might have served to reinforce the social, economic, or political status quo. In some cases the answers to these questions are implied rather than stated, so that a certain amount of "wise" reflection might be required to arrive at the answers.

Fig. 38.1. Leon Bonnat, *Job*

CHAPTER 38 — Other Paths to Wisdom

How can a mortal be just before God? If one wished to contend with him, one could not answer him once in a thousand. . . . He snatches away; who can stop him? Who will say to him, "What are you doing?" God will not turn back his anger. . . . How then can I answer him, choosing my words with him? Though I am innocent, I cannot answer him; I must appeal for mercy to my accuser. If I summoned him and he answered me, I do not believe that he would listen to my voice. For he crushes me with a tempest, and multiplies my wounds without cause; he will not let me get my breath, but fills me with bitterness. (Job 9:2-3, 12-18)

For the fate of humans and the fate of animals is the same; as one dies, so dies the other. They all have the same breath, and humans have no advantage over the animals; for all is vanity. All go to one place; all are from the dust, and all turn to dust again. Who knows whether the human spirit goes upward and the spirit of animals goes downward to the earth? So I saw that there is nothing better than that all should enjoy their work, for that is their lot; who can bring them to see what will be after them? (Ecclesiastes 3:19-22)

Set me as a seal upon your heart, as a seal upon your arm; for love is strong as death, passion fierce as the grave. Its flashes are flashes of fire, a raging flame. Many waters cannot quench love, neither can floods drown it. If one offered for love all the wealth of his house, it would be utterly scorned. (Song of Solomon 8:6-7)

In the previous chapter we examined the wisdom teachings of the book of Proverbs, which embodies the traditional moral worldview that dominated much of ancient Israelite society. In this chapter we will look at several books that raise questions about this traditional system. The bulk of the chapter is devoted to a review of Job and Ecclesiastes, two books that pose serious challenges to the view of reality that is presupposed in the book of Proverbs. The latter part of the chapter examines a book that stands on the periphery of the wisdom tradition, the Song of Solomon. Though it does not deal explicitly with wisdom themes, the celebration of love that fills the Song of Solomon can be read as a vivid example of Ecclesiastes' call to find enjoyment in the simple pleasures of life.

THE BOOK OF JOB

From a literary standpoint, the book of Job is the most celebrated book in the Hebrew Bible. Many people have called it one of the greatest works of literature ever produced. Like all great literature, the book of Job combines a deft literary touch with profound reflections on some of the fundamental questions of human existence. Both the literary styling and the ideas of the book are sophisticated and open to a variety of interpretations. This complexity has made the book a fruitful field for scholarly study.

The book of Job offers few clues as to when or where it was written. At the narrative level, the story appears to be set in the land of Edom (southeast of Judah) in the period prior to the rise of Israel as a people. But this setting, like the characters, is a literary fiction. From beginning to end the story bears the marks of a legend or fable, as evidenced by the book's idealized portrait of Job prior to his losses (1:1-5); the inclusion of scenes from Yahweh's heavenly throne room (1:6-12; 2:1-6); the improbability of Job losing all of his possessions and family members in a single day (1:13-19); the voice of Yahweh resounding from a whirlwind (38:1—41:34); and many similar scenes. Only the most conservative scholars would argue that Job was a historical person who actually experienced the events reported in the book that bears his name. Most believe that the book was written during the exilic or postexilic period when the people of Judah were struggling with questions about the suffering that they had experienced at the hands of the Babylonians and/or the failure of the prophets' predictions of a glorious future after their return from exile. The style and content of the book suggest that the author was a highly skilled member of the elite class of Judah who was dissatisfied with the kind of wisdom teaching that appears in the book of Proverbs. Nothing else is known about the origins of the book.

> ### EXERCISE 125
>
> Read Job 1:1—2:10; 42:10-17. What is Job like, according to these verses? Why does Yahweh allow him to experience the loss of everything that he has? What do you see as the message of these chapters?

The book of Job combines two very different types of material. The opening and closing sections of the book (1:1—2:13; 42:7-17) follow the standard format of a story and are written in prose. The central part of the book (3:1—42:6) consists of a series of poetic speeches by Job and four friends (and later, Yahweh), interspersed with brief narrative comments that do little more than indicate the identity of the speaker. Scholars have noted a number of contradictions between the narrative chapters and the speeches that make up the core of the book. The difference is especially visible in the character of Job, who accepts his losses patiently in the narrative sections but complains bitterly about his fate in the poetic chapters. The happy ending of the book also seems to undermine much of what Job has said in the poetic chapters (see

below). Most scholars believe that the author took a traditional story about a hero named Job (mentioned briefly in Ezekiel 14:14, 20) and adapted it for his own purposes, adding a series of poetic speeches that gave the account a substantially different message than earlier versions of the story. Modern writers do the same thing when they create fictionalized narratives about King Arthur or various biblical characters. The final product is based on tradition but reflects the author's own creative genius and ideas.

In the present version of the story, the narrative framework provides the interpretive context for the speeches in the poetic chapters. The book opens with a short prologue that introduces Job as a living model of the Deuteronomic worldview that infuses the book of Proverbs. Job is scrupulously righteous and faithful to God, and he enjoys vast wealth and a happy family as a result. When Yahweh expresses his pleasure at the righteous behavior of Job, a character called the Satan insists that this is not surprising, since Yahweh is actually bribing Job to be good by showering him with material blessings (1:9-11; 2:4-5).

Fig. 38.2. William Blake, *Satan Before God*

This Satan (a title that means "the accuser" or "the adversary") is not the devil of later Jewish and Christian tradition, but a heavenly being who appears in Yahweh's court along with the other "sons of God" (1:6), an unusual term that perhaps refers to members of Yahweh's heavenly council.

The suggestion that Job might be serving Yahweh out of less than pure motives highlights a problem that is inherent to Deuteronomic theology. Doesn't the promise of earthly rewards encourage people to obey Yahweh out of a selfish desire to receive the benefits that he offers? Wouldn't it be better if humans served Yahweh without regard for personal gain? Or is this beyond the capacity of humans? Is it possible for a person to remain loyal to Yahweh even when this loyalty brings no apparent rewards? The book of Job is devoted to an exploration of these questions.

At the instigation of the Satan, Yahweh sets up a test that he believes will reveal the purity of Job's motives. He allows the Satan to take away everything that Yahweh has given to Job and to strike his body with a hideous skin disease. From Job's vantage point, this goes against everything that the Deuteronomic theology has taught him. Though he is perfectly righteous, he is experiencing the curses that are supposed to fall upon the wicked. Yet Job remains faithful to Yahweh, accepting everything that has happened to him and reaffirming his devotion to the deity (2:9-10). His reaction to his suffering proves the Satan wrong: humans are indeed capable of remaining loyal to Yahweh in the absence of any reward.

In its original form, the story probably ended with Job being commended by Yahweh and receiving back double for everything that had been taken from him, as in the closing verses of the book (42:10-17). This version of the story affirms the validity of the Deuteronomic theology, since the narrative ends with the righteous Job once again enjoying the material blessings of Yahweh. The message seems to be that the sufferings that righteous men and women experience from time to time are not violations of the Deuteronomic worldview, but rather tests by which Yahweh proves the faithfulness of his servants. The character of Job serves as a model for the way Yahweh's followers should respond to these circumstances, namely, with patience and unwavering loyalty.

EXERCISE 126

Read Job 6:1-30; 8:1—9:35; 15:1—16:21; 27:1-23; 38:1-21; 40:1-14; 42:1-6. What explanations do Job's friends give for his sufferings? What is Job's view of his situation? How does Yahweh respond?

The speeches that fill the central part of the book are less optimistic about the way life works. Like the narrative chapters, they raise important questions about the Deuteronomic worldview, but their criticism is more profound and sustained. Where the narrative chapters tie up everything in a neat package by the end of the story, the speech chapters are more open-ended, leaving the reader with serious questions about the validity of the Deuteronomic explanation of human experience.

The challenge to the Deuteronomic worldview comes from three directions. The first, evident in the speeches of Job's friends, is somewhat subtle and ironic; the second, found in some of Job's speeches, is more blatant; the third, seen in Yahweh's speeches, questions the very foundations of Deuteronomic thought.

1. *Job's friends.* Job's friends seek to make sense of his experience with the aid of a classic Deuteronomic view

Fig. 38.3. William Blake, *Job Rebuked by His Friends*

of reality. Though the narrative says that they came to Job to "console and comfort him" (2:11), their words are anything but consoling. From their Deuteronomic standpoint, Job's sufferings are a mark of divine displeasure. Again and again they assert that Job must have done something horrible to offend Yahweh, since a righteous deity would not inflict such terrible sufferings upon a righteous man. In their more generous moments, they suggest that Job might have forgotten about some deed by which he or a member of his family might have provoked Yahweh to anger. They urge Job to search his memory and uncover the fatal offense so that he can confess his sins to Yahweh and seek his forgiveness. In their less charitable moments, they accuse Job of willfully hiding his sins until Yahweh at last afflicted him with suffering in order to pressure him to repent. Job's only hope now is to confess his hidden sins and that Yahweh will forgive him before it is too late.

From a literary standpoint, the content of these speeches is deeply ironic, since the reader knows that the accusations leveled by Job's friends are untrue. The opening chapters state clearly that Job is a righteous man who is suffering through no fault of his own. In fact, Job comes across as more righteous than Yahweh, who does not hesitate to treat Job as a human guinea pig in a heavenly experiment designed to prove his point to the Satan. Taken as a whole, the narrative suggests that Job's friends are wrong on two counts: Yahweh does not always treat people as their actions deserve, and human sufferings are not invariably a sign of divine displeasure. Both of these points represent a frontal attack on traditional Deuteronomic thinking.

2. *Job's speeches*. Job's speeches exhibit all of the emotions that one might expect from a person who has suffered such monumental losses in such a short time. At first he is simply consumed with grief, lamenting the day he was born and asking God to take his life. When his friends begin to raise questions about his conduct, his language shifts to angry self-defense. Again and again he protests his innocence, arguing that he has done nothing to offend the deity, either unknowingly or in secret. If anyone is to blame, he says, it is Yahweh. While his friends cling to their belief in the righteousness of God, Job argues that the deity has acted unjustly and abused

his power by sending suffering upon a righteous man while ignoring the guilt of people who deserve to be punished. The regular use of the impersonal titles "God"

Fig. 38.4. William Blake, *Job's Despair*

and "the Almighty" in place of the personal name Yahweh reinforces this image of a powerful but distant deity. Several times Job calls on "the Almighty" to come down from heaven and explain his actions. Finally, he takes a solemn oath inviting the deity to evaluate his actions and to inflict various punishments upon him if he has indeed sinned (31:1-40). Clearly Job is confident that Yahweh will find no legitimate basis for acting against him.

Like the speeches of his friends, Job's words overflow with irony. Unlike the reader, Job can only guess at the reasons for his suffering, but his guesses are more accurate than he knows. His assessment of his own conduct is correct according to the opening chapter, and his accusations of divine injustice are closer to the truth than are the speeches of his friends who are intent on defending the righteousness of Yahweh. The reader knows that there is in fact a purpose behind Job's sufferings, but that purpose cannot be deduced from a traditional Deuteronomic theology. From a Deuteronomic standpoint, Yahweh's actions do appear to be unfair and unjust. Thus Job's speeches shift the focus of the accusation from Job to Yahweh. Yahweh is on trial in the book of Job as much as Job himself.

3. *Yahweh's speeches*. The sudden appearance of Yahweh's voice out of a whirlwind in chapter 38 contrasts

sharply with the deity's silence throughout the preceding thirty-five chapters when Job and his friends were arguing over the reasons for Job's sufferings. Yahweh has clearly been listening to their conversation, since he is aware of Job's accusations against him. Yet when he finally decides

Fig. 38.5. William Blake, *The Lord Answering Job out of the Whirlwind*

to speak, it is not to explain why he has allowed so much pain to fall upon Job and his family. Instead, he assaults Job with a barrage of questions highlighting the vast gulf that exists between his supernatural power and knowledge and Job's puny humanity. Again and again he emphasizes the amount of power that is required to create and direct the universe and the amount of knowledge that he possesses as its maker. Job, by contrast, understands none of these things. Who is he to challenge his maker?

In the end, Job receives no answer to his questions about the reason for his sufferings. All he can do is admit how foolish he has been to question the conduct of such a mighty deity (42:1-6; see also 40:3-5). The message is clear: humans are incapable of understanding why things happen as they do, including why humans suffer. The

point is reinforced by Yahweh's surprising insistence that Job has spoken more rightly about him than his friends, who have incurred the deity's wrath with their attempts to make sense of Job's sufferings through the lens of traditional Deuteronomic theology (42:7-9). The author's rejection of Deuteronomic thinking could hardly be clearer.

Thus the book of Job offers a very different understanding of reality than the book of Proverbs. Where Proverbs insists that certain forms of conduct invariably lead to certain outcomes, Job argues that the ways of Yahweh are ultimately beyond human comprehension. Even the most devout servants of Yahweh experience sufferings for reasons that are known only to the deity. Those who claim that there is a consistent relationship between proper conduct and material success are misleading the people whom they hope to instruct. Humans should honor and obey Yahweh because he is an awesome deity who deserves their service, not because they might benefit from doing so. This is the true meaning of the proverbial expression that associates wisdom with the fear of Yahweh (Job 28:28; Psalm 111:10; Proverbs 1:7; 9:10; 15:33; Micah 6:9).

ECCLESIASTES

The book of Ecclesiastes claims to present the wise observations of an old man who reigned in Jerusalem as king of Israel (1:1, 12). The opening verse suggests that the author is King Solomon ("the son of David, king in Jerusalem"), who was renowned for his wisdom (see chapter 37). This impression is reinforced by a passage in chapter 2 that speaks repeatedly of the narrator's vast wealth, which also agrees with the biblical portrait of Solomon (Ecclesiastes 2:1-11; compare 1 Kings 3:20-28). Nonetheless, only the

Fig. 38.6. "So I hated life, because what is done under the sun was grievous to me; for all its vanity and a chasing after wind" (Ecclesiastes 1:14).

a term that is often translated as "preacher" or "teacher" (1:1, 2, 12; 7:27; 12:8, 9, 10). The meaning of the term is uncertain, though it comes from a Hebrew verb that means "to assemble" or "to gather." Some scholars have suggested that the term identifies the author as the head of a wisdom school who "gathered" students around him to learn, while others have speculated that it refers to his activity of "assembling" and reflecting on wise sayings that led eventually to the production of this book. All agree that the author was a member of the Jerusalem elite who was thoroughly familiar with the wisdom traditions of Israel. This fact, together with several verses that seem to offer advice to young men (9:7-10; 11:9; 12:1), has led most scholars to conclude that the book was written by a teacher who instructed young aristocrats in a form of wisdom that involved critical reflection on the traditional teaching that underlies the book of Proverbs. Apparently his unorthodox teachings attracted both supporters and critics, since the book contains later editorial additions that praise the author (12:9-10), along with sayings that attempt to give the book a more orthodox tone (12:11-14).

EXERCISE 127

Read Ecclesiastes 1:1—3:22; 6:1-12; 8:14—9:12; 12:1-8. What is the author's view of the human attempt to find meaning in life? Why does he hold this view? What kind of conduct does he recommend?

---

most conservative scholars take these references seriously. Elsewhere in the book the author speaks as a subject of the king (8:2-5; 10:4-7, 16-17, 20) who is aware of the abuses perpetrated by the wealthy and powerful but is unable to do anything to stop them (4:1; 5:8; 8:9). In addition, the Hebrew style of the book is clearly postexilic, which rules out authorship by Solomon or any other king. The depiction of the author as a king of Israel in the opening chapters of the book appears to be a literary device designed to allow the author to explore the extreme case of his thesis, just as we witnessed in the book of Job.

So when and by whom was the book written? Many of the ideas in Ecclesiastes have parallels in Greek philosophy, a fact that has led most scholars to favor a date in the fourth or third century B.C.E. when Palestine was under Greek rule. The Hebrew text calls the author *Qoheleth* (rendered as *Ecclesiastes* in the Greek version of the Hebrew Bible),

As with the book of Job, Ecclesiastes is framed around the story of a man who claims to have done precisely what the book of Proverbs recommends, devoting his life to the pursuit of wisdom and the avoidance of folly (1:13, 17; 2:3, 12; 7:23-25; 8:16). According to Proverbs, this should have brought him a life of success and happiness. At one level, this goal was realized—the author claims to have possessed vast wealth and to have used this wealth to experience all of the pleasures that money could buy (2:1-10). At a deeper level, however, the author was profoundly disappointed by the results of his quest. Nothing that he experienced brought him lasting happiness. The search for wisdom produced only trouble and sorrow (1:18), since it made him more aware of the dark side of life—its inequities, its ambiguities, its ultimate unfairness.

His effort to find pleasure in material things likewise proved futile, since even his best experiences proved to be transitory, leaving no lasting effects. Contrary to the book of Proverbs, he came to regard the search for wisdom as "an unhappy business that God has given to human beings to be busy with" (1:13). Based on his experience, all human activity is simply "vanity and a chasing after wind" (1:14; 2:1, 15-17).

This emphasis on the vanity of human activity lies at the heart of the message of Ecclesiastes. The term *vanity* is used to sum up the author's discovery that life seems to have no obvious goal or purpose. The book begins with a series of poetic reflections on the cyclical nature of the natural world, where everything that transpires is only a repetition of similar events from the past, producing no lasting change (1:2-11). From here the author turns to an examination of human experience, where he finds a similar pattern at work. No matter how hard people labor to improve their fortune in life, they cannot hold

Fig. 38.7. "For everything there is a season, and a time for every matter under heaven: a time to be born, and a time to die" (Ecclesiastes 3:1-2).

on to what they have accumulated; in the end they must die and leave their possessions for others to enjoy and possibly squander (2:18-21; 4:4-7; 6:1-2). Regardless of how wise or famous a person might have been during life, one is eventually forgotten (2:16; 9:5-6, 13-16). Even kings and rulers make no lasting impact on the world (2:12; 4:13-16). Instead, life revolves in cycles like the seasons of nature, with an appropriate time for every type of activity (3:1-8).

But this is only part of the story. To an honest observer, life is patently unfair, full of evils and injustice. Those who hold power routinely abuse those below them and experience no evident consequences, while the oppressed are unable to find a way out of their sufferings (4:1; 5:8; 8:9). Those who possess riches are never satisfied with what they have, while the poor are unable to enjoy the good things of life (5:10-12; 6:3-9). Those who pursue wisdom are rendered unhappy by what they learn, while fools are able to laugh and enjoy themselves and even obtain positions of power (7:2-6; 10:5-6). Those who live wicked lives are honored by their neighbors, while the righteous often receive no reward for their devotion to God (8:10, 14). Chance seems to be the most important factor in determining how people fare in life (9:11-12). If there is any kind of divine plan or moral order guiding the universe, it lies beyond the ability of the wisest minds to figure out (6:12; 7:14, 23-24; 8:6-7, 16-17; 11:5-6). In the end, everyone meets the same fate in death, regardless of how they have behaved in this life (9:1-3).

Despite its rather bleak view of life, the purpose of Ecclesiastes is not to promote despair. The author admits that some of his observations and experiences caused him to hate life (2:17-18; 4:2-3), but he never mentions suicide as a possible alternative, as do similar Greek texts. Instead, he seeks to provide advice for living in such a dark and troubled world. Though he believes that traditional wisdom teaching has gone too far in its claims to discern a consistent moral order behind the universe, he is not ready to abandon it entirely. Several times he commends the value of wisdom (2:13-14; 7:5-6; 8:1; 9:16—10:2; 10:10, 12), and the book includes a number of wise sayings that would have been quite at home in the book of Proverbs (2:14; 4:5-6, 9-13; 5:3, 7, 12; 7:1-13, 19-21; 8:1; 9:17—10:4; 10:8—11:4). At one point the author even claims that wisdom is a gift from God (2:26), though he also warns against being overly zealous in pursuing it (7:16). Even wisdom produces no lasting benefits and can lead to increased troubles for those who chase after it (1:17-18; 2:15-16; 6:8; 7:16).

From a practical standpoint, Ecclesiastes' advice about how to live wisely in such a dark and troubled world can be summed up in two simple yet profound statements.

1. *Enjoy the simple pleasures of life.* People who attempt to make sense of life and understand the order of the universe are simply wasting their time and energy. That path leads only to frustration and trouble. The same is true for those who work hard to get ahead in life; they can never be satisfied with what they have. Instead of striving to gain things that are beyond their ability to achieve, humans should take pleasure in the simple gifts that God supplies every day: productive labor, good food and drink, a wife and family, fresh clothes, friendships, and similar experiences (2:24-26; 3:12-13, 22; 4:9-12; 5:18-20; 8:15; 9:7-10; 11:9). Those whom God has blessed with wealth and possessions may enjoy these as well, as long as they keep in mind that all of these things are ultimately vanity

Fig. 38.8. The book of Ecclesiastes encourages its readers to find pleasure in the simple things of life, such as family and good food.

(5:19—6:2). In the end, nothing can bring lasting happiness, but life will be easier if one learns to find enjoyment in the simple things of life instead of chasing after things that cannot ultimately satisfy or dwelling on the negative aspects of human existence.

2. *Remember God.* Like the other wisdom books, Ecclesiastes recognizes that humans are ultimately accountable to God for their conduct. Like Job, the author rejects the idea that humans can understand God's ways, including the Deuteronomic belief that the judgments of God can be discerned in the material events of life. But he still clings to the belief that God is a righteous judge who will reward the righteous and punish the wicked (2:26; 3:17; 7:17; 8:12-13; 11:9), unless these verses are later additions designed to tame the author's raw skepticism. How and when he envisioned this judgment taking place are unclear, since he clearly rejects any idea of an afterlife (3:19-21; 9:1-6). But he seems to agree with other wisdom teachers that life will turn out better for those who fear God and do their best to avoid incurring his displeasure (3:14; 5:1-7; 8:12-13).

Clearly the form of wisdom that we find in the book of Ecclesiastes has little in common with what we saw in Proverbs. Its view of the universe is closer to that of Job, though the author's emphasis on the vanity of human activities and his advice about finding enjoyment in the simple pleasures of life distinguish his book from others in the wisdom tradition. Apparently the wisdom tradition in ancient Israel was broad enough to include a variety of ideas about the deity's relation to the world of humans and the way in which people should live. Such formalized explorations of diverse viewpoints were probably limited to the wisdom schools that served the elites, while the illiterate masses continued to rely on traditional proverbial wisdom. Yet the sheer presence of these diverse books in the Hebrew canon indicates that the elites of ancient Israel felt no compulsion to adopt a uniform viewpoint on matters of vital importance to their faith.

SONG OF SOLOMON

The book that Hebrew tradition identified as "the Song of Songs, which is Solomon's" (1:1) is a collection of erotic love poetry interspersed with snippets of first-person

Fig. 38.9. "Your hair is like a flock of goats, moving down the slopes of Gilead. . . . Your two breasts are like two fawns, twins of a gazelle, that feed among the lilies" (Song 4:1, 5).

narrative material that give the illusion of a loose story line. In actuality, most scholars view the text as a collection of love poems from different times and places that has little or no narrative unity.

Within the Hebrew Bible, the Song of Solomon stands in a class of its own. Most textbooks treat it together with the wisdom material because of its repeated references to King Solomon (Song of Solomon 1:1, 5; 3:7, 9, 11; 8:11-12), who was regarded as the "patron saint" of wisdom literature (see chapter 37). The book's positive view of romantic and sexual love also has parallels in some of the wisdom materials (Proverbs 4:5-9; 5:15-19; 8:17-19; Ecclesiastes 9:9). Yet nowhere else in the Hebrew Bible do we find anything like the emotionally charged expressions of physical desire that permeate the Song of Solomon. The fact that many of these love poems were written from a woman's point of view only adds to the uniqueness of the book. Apparently the prac-

tice of arranging marriages and placing strict controls on women's sexuality in ancient Palestine did not preclude the development of literary forms that gave voice to the romantic and sexual longings that stirred the hearts and bodies of women and men alike. In fact, history shows that romantic poetry often flourishes most vividly in societies where sexual fulfillment is tightly regulated.

The origins of the Song of Solomon are shrouded in mystery. The timeless ideas and language of the book offer few clues about when or by whom the book was written. The meaning of the reference to King Solomon in 1:1 is unclear, but few scholars take it seriously as evidence for authorship. Most view the book as a postexilic work due to the presence of a few words that have Persian or Greek roots, but these could have been added during the final editing of the book. In fact, the love poems on which the Song of Solomon is based could have been composed at virtually any time during the history of Palestine, and not necessarily within Yahwistic circles. Similar language is found in the love poetry of Mesopotamia and Egypt, including several poems that depict the love between a god and a goddess. The highly poetic language of the book would seem to demand an elite education, but even this presumption is hard to verify, since we have no popular love poetry from Palestine with which to compare it. Fortunately, the book is timeless enough to be understood and enjoyed by people who know nothing of its historical origins.

EXERCISE 128

Read Song of Solomon 2:3-13; 3:1-5; 4:1-15; 5:2-16; 8:1-7. What images and feelings do these poems arouse in you as you read them? What does their inclusion in the Hebrew Bible tell you about the people who compiled the biblical canon?

The Song of Solomon is a complex work that strikes many first-time readers as disjointed and confusing. The book is framed around a series of poetic speeches by a woman and a man who are deeply in love with one another. The transition from one speaker to the other is not always clear, since the Hebrew text contains no markers to indicate which lines are being spoken by which character. (The headings that are used in many contemporary translations to mark the identity of the speakers are not part of the original text.) Fortunately, the pronouns and poetic imagery are clear enough to identify the speaker in most cases.

Scholars disagree about whether the book has a coherent story line. Many view the book as a random collection of unrelated speeches that were compiled into their present form by a later editor with little or no regard for narrative unity. Others point to various features that suggest that the book was composed as a drama with the stage directions and character identifications missing. For example, the speeches of the two lovers are interrupted from time to time by the comments of an unnamed group that resembles the chorus in a Greek play (1:4; 5:9; 6:1, 13; 8:5, 8-9). The female speaker also turns aside several times to address a group called the "daughters of Jerusalem," which may or may not be the same as the "chorus" (1:5; 2:7; 3:5; 3:10; 5:8, 16; 8:4; compare 3:11).

Fig. 38.10. He Qi's *The Song of* Solomon conveys the delight and desire the two lovers express for each other in the Song of Solomon.

Many scholars have claimed to discern a rough plotline in the book that centers on the attempts of a young man and woman to see or spend time with one another and the resultant success or failure of their actions (2:8-13; 3:1-4, 6-11; 5:1-7; 6:1-3, 11-12; 8:5). Scholars disagree over whether these isolated bits of narrative constitute a genuine plotline or are simply the illusory by-product of a random linkage of diverse materials. Whatever the original intention, these narrative fragments have enticed countless later readers to make sense of the poem by filling in the gaps between the various scenes.

From a literary standpoint, the most striking feature of the Song of Solomon is the mixture of figurative language and visual imagery that runs throughout the poem. Both of the lovers use long strings of metaphors and similes to describe the physical charms of their partner (4:1-7, 11-15; 5:10-16; 6:4-7; 7:1-7). Many of these comparisons sound bizarre to contemporary readers, but ancient audiences would have understood what they meant. Metaphorical imagery is also common in passages that describe the characters' passionate longing for one another, including several that speak of real or imagined sexual encounters (1:2-4, 12-17; 2:3-6; 3:1-4; 4:16—5:5; 7:8-13; 8:1-3). Some of the narrative fragments are so dense with poetic imagery that it can be hard to decide whether the story should be taken literally or figuratively (1:5-7; 2:8-15; 5:2-7; 6:11-12). Most of the imagery in the speeches is drawn from the world of agriculture, and the bulk of the action takes place in rural settings as well. Scholars disagree over whether this means that the poems actually originated in a rural context or whether that, too, is part of the literary imagery of the poem.

Many modern readers wonder how such a frankly erotic book came to be included in the Hebrew canon. The history of the book is obscure, but its association with Solomon probably played a role in its acceptance. By the turn of the era, Jewish rabbis were reading the book as an allegorical reflection on the love that unites Israel and Yahweh, and Christians later developed a similar reading that identified the two lovers as Christ and the church. Not until the modern period did scholars rediscover the original meaning of the text.

If there is any overarching message to be found in the Song of Solomon, it lies in the poem's honest depictions of the joys and pains of romantic love and sexual desire.

Modern readers are often surprised to note that the book offers no judgment on the feelings and behaviors of the two lovers. Their deep attraction to one another, their joyous celebration of one another's bodies, and their repeated efforts to find satisfaction for their sexual desires are portrayed as perfectly normal aspects of human experience. Though the Torah does attempt to limit female sexual activity to marriage, the Hebrew Bible never portrays sex or bodily pleasure as inherently wrong or evil. The Western tradition of regarding the body as a channel of temptation and sin is rooted in Greek philosophical ideas. The Hebrew tradition, by contrast, views the body as an essential part of human identity (see chapter 13). Thus the Hebrew Bible views love and sex as inherently good, despite the aches and pains that they sometimes bring. Nowhere do we see this belief more clearly displayed than in the Song of Solomon.

In the end, the Song of Solomon is nothing more nor less than a celebration of the power of human love. The force that unites two lovers is so powerful and sacred that the prophets used it as a model for the covenant relationship between Yahweh and his people. In this book, however, it is the depth of human love that is regarded with awe and wonder. A famous passage near the end of the book (8:6-7) presents an eloquent reflection on the surpassing value and power of human love.

> For love is strong as death,
>   passion fierce as the grave.
> Its flashes are flashes of fire,
>   a raging flame.
> Many waters cannot quench love,
>   neither can floods drown it.
> If one offered for love
>   all the wealth of his house,
>   it would be utterly scorned.

CONCLUSION

The books of Job, Ecclesiastes, and Song of Solomon appear to have originated within the same elite circle of wisdom teachers that produced the book of Proverbs. Yet they offer a markedly different view of life than we saw in Proverbs. Where Proverbs envisions the universe as a tidy place that operates according to a fixed moral system, Job and Ecclesiastes question the ability of humans to know whether such a moral order exists. Where Proverbs voices confidence that those who follow its teachings will do well in life, Job and Ecclesiastes are pessimistic about the presence of any link between human behavior and material success. Where Proverbs urges its readers to pursue wisdom above all else, Ecclesiastes sees the pursuit of wisdom as a waste of time. Where Proverbs counsels self-discipline and control of one's passions, Song of Solomon depicts two lovers giving free reign to their passionate love for one another.

This brief overview of the wisdom books of the Hebrew Bible highlights one of the most important and overlooked characteristics of the wisdom movement in ancient Palestine—its openness to diversity. By encouraging people to study the universe for themselves and draw their own conclusions about the way life operates, the wisdom teachers of ancient Palestine ensured that the religion of Yahwism would remain alive and open to new insights rather than hardening into a rigid system of adherence to a fixed set of religious ideas. To this day, Judaism, the formal successor of Yahwism, has never developed any creed or statement of faith that one must affirm in order to be a Jew. Instead, Jews are taught to develop their own understanding of life through reasoned reflection on their Scriptures, their traditions, and the world around them. For this they owe a debt of gratitude to the wisdom teachers who trained their ancestors to use their God-given minds to grapple seriously with the difficult questions surrounding human existence. Without them, both Judaism and Christianity might have developed into very different religions than we know today.

EXERCISE 129

Think about people in your life whom you would regard as wise. What characteristics would you say they have in common? In what ways do they differ?

NOTES

Chapter 1

1. Robert E. Van Voorst, *Anthology of World Scriptures*, 4th ed. (Belmont, Calif.: Wadsworth, 2003), 6.

Chapter 5

1. Richard Coggins, *Introducing the Old Testament* (Oxford: Oxford University Press, 1990), 41.

2. David Robertson, *The Old Testament and the Literary Critic* (Philadelphia: Fortress, 1977), 3.

3. Elisabeth Schüssler Fiorenza, "The Will to Choose or to Reject: Continuing Our Critical Work," in *Feminist Interpretation of the Bible*, ed. Letty M. Russell (Philadelphia: Westminster, 1985), 129.

Chapter 9

1. Iain W. Provan, "In the Stable with the Dwarves: Testimony, Interpretation, Faith, and the History of Israel," in *Windows into Old Testament History*, ed. V. Philips Long, David W. Baker, and Gordon J. Wenham (Grand Rapids: Eerdmans, 2002), 171.

2. William G. Dever, *What Did the Biblical Writers Know and When Did They Know It? What Archaeology Can Tell Us about the Reality of Ancient Israel* (Grand Rapids: Eerdmans, 2001), 271–72.

3. Niels Peter Lemche, *The Israelites in History and Tradition* (Louisville, Ky.: Westminster John Knox, 1998), 165–66.

Chapter 10

1. Roger Schmidt, *Exploring Religion*, 2nd ed. (Belmont, Calif.: Wadsworth, 1988), xiii.

2. Clifford Geertz, *The Interpretation of Cultures* (New York: Basic Books, 1973), 79.

3. Paul Tillich, *Christianity and the Encounter of the World Religions* (New York: Columbia University Press, 1963), 4.

4. Niniah Smart, *Worldviews: Crosscultural Explorations of Human Beliefs*, 3rd ed. (Englewood Cliffs, N.J.: Prentice Hall, 1999).

Chapter 20

1. Translation by J. K. Hoffmeier, "The (Israel) Stela of Merneptah," in *The Context of Scripture*, ed. William W. Hallo and K. Lawson Younger (Leiden: Brill, 2000), 2:41.

GLOSSARY

Abraham A man traditionally regarded as the ancestor of the Jewish people and their **covenant** with Yahweh, the God of Israel. Abraham is also honored by Christians, who focus on his faith rather than his position as forefather of the Jews and their religion, and by Muslims, who view him as one of the greatest of the prophets sent by God to humanity.

absolutism/absolutist attitude The conviction that one's own religious beliefs are correct and any idea that contradicts them is wrong. When applied to the Hebrew Bible, it refers to the belief that Yahweh is the only true god and that all other deities are the creations of human minds and hands. Absolutism was uncommon in ancient Israel until after the **Exile**. Before that time, most Israelites seem to have had a more open attitude toward other religious systems.

Adam The first human being, according to the Hebrew Bible. The name is a play on the Hebrew word *adamah*, meaning "ground" or "earth," the substance from which Genesis 2 says that Adam was created. The Hebrew Bible uses the name Adam in both a generic sense, referring to the nongendered human being whom God created in Genesis 2:7, and a gendered sense, designating the male counterpart of the first female, as in Genesis 2:22 and 3:20.

Adonai (ad-ō-nigh') A title meaning "lord" or "master" that is often used in the Hebrew Bible to refer to the God of Israel. By the end of the biblical period, many Jews had become hesitant about pronouncing the divine name **Yahweh** out of a concern to uphold the commandment that prohibits "taking the name of Yahweh your God in vain" (see Exodus 20:7), so they used this title (among others) in its place. Most English translations have retained this practice, inserting "the LORD" in their translations where the Hebrew text contains the name Yahweh.

amulet Any kind of object that is worn on the body to ward off evil spirits and protect the wearer from harm. Archaeologists have uncovered many examples of amulets that were used by people who lived in the ancient Near East, including Palestine.

ancestral narratives A term used by scholars to describe the stories in Genesis 12–50 that tell about the ancient ancestors of the people of Israel, beginning with Abraham and Sarah and concluding with Jacob and his family. Scholars who see these stories as having a historical basis generally date their characters around 1800 to 1600 B.C.E.

animism/animistic A religious worldview that envisions the entire physical world as being alive (animated) with spiritual power, possessing a personal essence similar to humans. Specially trained people (often called **shamans**) serve as mediators to channel this spiritual power to humans and protect them from supernatural harm. Animism is commonly associated with the native cultures of Africa, Asia, and North America. The polytheistic religious systems that dominated the ancient Near East had features in common with animism, but animism itself was not common there.

annals Records kept by a government or other organization that list or describe the major events of a period in chronological order (also called **chronicles**). In Egypt and Mesopotamia, annals were maintained by court scribes. Many scholars believe that the authors of the Historical Books of the Hebrew Bible used similar annals from the royal courts of Israel and Judah as a resource for their narratives.

apocalyptic A type of literature that claims to reveal things that would otherwise be unknown to humans, particularly the future and the workings of the natural and supernatural realms. The term comes from the Greek word *apokalupsis*, which means "uncovering" or "unveiling." In the Hebrew Bible, apocalyptic materials can be found in the books of Isaiah, Ezekiel, Daniel, Joel, Zechariah, and Malachi.

apologetics The use of reasoned argumentation to defend the truth of a position (especially a religious worldview) and to point out the flaws of alternative modes of thinking. The use of apologetics is normally associated with social and religious groups that feel threatened by the presence of alternative worldviews. In the Hebrew Bible, some of the prophets employ apologetic argumentation from time to time.

Apocrypha (a-pok'-ri-fah) A Greek word meaning "hidden things," used by Protestants at the time of the Reformation (sixteenth century) to refer to a set of Jewish texts that were included in the Old Testament of Roman Catholic and Ortho-dox churches but not in the Jewish canon. The title is a mis-nomer, since the books were never hidden—they simply did not gain enough popular support to be included in the Jew-ish canon, though some of them would have been regarded as Scripture by at least some Jews. Protestants do not include these books in their canon of Scripture, while Roman Catholic and Orthodox Christians do.

Aramaic   A Semitic language, closely related to Hebrew, that was used in Syria and Mesopotamia from the tenth century B.C.E. onward. Through the influence of the Assyrian, Baby-lonian, and Persian empires, it became the primary language of literature and commerce throughout the ancient Near East, including Palestine. Portions of the biblical books of Daniel and Ezra are written in Aramaic.

archaeology   The scientific study of human cultures through the analysis of their physical remains, including tools, buildings, graves, artistic creations, and similar objects. Modern archaeol-ogy is a multidisciplinary activity that involves not only dig-ging up sites of human habitation but also carefully recording and analyzing every aspect of the site in an effort to understand when and how people lived at the site. In the past, many archae-ologists working in Palestine were seeking to prove (or some-times disprove) the truth of the Bible, but few archaeologists today share that concern.

Ark of the Covenant   The gold-covered box that Yahweh reportedly commanded Moses to build to hold the stone tablets of the Ten Commandments and other items from the Exodus era. The box was later placed in the inner sanctum (the Holy of Holies) of the Jerusalem temple. Its ultimate fate is unknown, though most scholars believe it was carried away to Babylonia at the time of the Exile and later destroyed.

Assyrians   A people group from northern Mesopotamia that used its military might to create an empire that extended as far as Egypt at its high point in the eighth century B.C.E. The Assyrians conquered the kingdom of Israel in 722 B.C.E. and deported many of its citizens to Mesopotamia. They also forced the kingdom of Judah to pay a heavy tribute in order to main-tain its nominal independence. The Assyrians were overthrown by the Babylonians in the late seventh century B.C.E.

Baal   (bāh-ahl' or bāy'-uhl)   A Hebrew word meaning "lord" or "master," commonly used by the biblical authors to refer to Hadad, the storm and fertility god who plays a leading role in many Canaanite religious texts. According to the Hebrew Bible, Baal was Yahweh's chief rival for the loyalties of the people of Israel, having many devoted followers in Israel throughout the biblical period. Some of the kings of Israel (and at least one queen, Jezebel) actively promoted the worship of Baal.

Babylonians   A people group from southern Mesopotamia that threw off Assyrian control in the latter part of the seventh century B.C.E. and fairly quickly brought an end to the Assyr-ian Empire. Babylonian armies subsequently took over most of the lands previously controlled by the Assyrians, including Palestine. They conquered the city of Jerusalem in 586 B.C.E., destroying the city and its temple and deporting many of its residents to Babylonia. Thus began the period called the Baby-lonian exile, which lasted until the Babylonians were defeated by the Persians in 539 B.C.E.

barter   An economic system in which people exchange goods or services to meet their needs rather than using money to buy and sell in an open market. Barter was the normal means of exchange in the towns and villages of ancient Israel, where most people labored to be self-sufficient and money was scarce.

B.C.E.   An abbreviation of the phrase "Before the Common Era," used in academic and interfaith circles as a neutral substitute for the Christian term *B.C.,* which means "before Christ." Despite the difference in terminology, the two terms have exactly the same meaning. The term *B.C.* carries negative connotations for many people, not only because it implies that the coming of Jesus is the focal point of human history but also because it recalls the era of Western colonialism when the Christian calen-dar (and the Christian religion) was spread around the world to the detriment of other religions and their calendars.

Bible   A term used by Jews and Christians to refer to the collec-tion of books that they regard as Holy Scripture. The title comes from the Greek word *biblia,* which means "books." The Jewish Bible includes only that collection of books that Christians call the **Old Testament**. The Christian Bible also includes a set of early Christian texts that Christians call the **New Testament**.

biblical criticism   A catchall term for the various methods that contemporary scholars use to analyze the Bible. The word *criticism* does not imply that scholars are seeking to attack or tear down the Bible, though biblical scholars do tend to raise more questions than ordinary believers. Its usage is similar to that of the term *literary criticism,* which refers to the careful and analytical study of a piece of literature using a particular set of methods.

blessings A term used in the Hebrew Bible to describe the many benefits that Yahweh provides for his people, including good crops, healthy animals, and protection from enemies. The word is often associated with the idea of **covenant**, where it refers to the good things that Yahweh promises to do for the people of Israel as long as they obey his commands. Certain individuals were also believed to have the power to pronounce blessings that would bring material benefits to the people whom they blessed.

Branch A word used in some of the prophetic books (Isaiah 4:2; 11:1; Jeremiah 23:5; 33:15; Zechariah 3:8; 6:12) to refer to a righteous king who will arise from the line of David to rule over the people of Israel and Judah at the time when Yahweh restores them to their land (similar to **Messiah**).

Canaan (kāy'-nun) An ancient name for the geographic area also known as Israel or Palestine. The origins and meaning of the term are unknown. Prior to the emergence of the people called Israelites, the land of Canaan was divided among a number of city-states and had no clear boundaries. The name appears often in the early stages of the biblical narrative, but disappears entirely after the period of the judges.

Canaanite A word used in the Hebrew Bible to refer to the diverse population of the land of Canaan. The term was applied by outsiders, not by the people who lived there; they would have identified themselves by the name of the city-site or ethnic group with which they were associated. In the Hebrew Bible, the word frequently has negative connotations, referring to non-Israelites who follow religious practices that are forbidden by Yahweh and thus incur Yahweh's judgment.

canon A list of books regarded as authoritative by a religious community. The term comes from a Greek word that refers to a standard of measurement. A canon may be either open or closed. An open canon lacks firm boundaries and is open to revision and editing. A closed canon contains a fixed set of books that cannot be revised or edited in any way.

canonical criticism A method of scholarly study that examines the books of the Bible in the context of the entire canon rather than as isolated compositions. Scholars who practice canonical criticism are concerned not only with how the canon was created but also with how the books relate to one another in their present canonical setting.

C.E. An abbreviation of the phrase *Common Era*, used in academic and interfaith circles as a neutral replacement for the Christian term *A.D.*, an abbreviation of the Latin phrase *anno domini*, meaning "in the year of the Lord [Jesus]." Despite the difference in terminology, the two terms mean exactly the same thing. The term *A.D.* carries negative connotations for many people not only because it implies that the coming of Jesus is the focal point of human history but also because it recalls the era of Western colonialism when the Christian calendar (and the Christian religion) was spread around the world to the detriment of other religions and their calendars.

Central Highlands The mountainous region that runs from north to south through the center of Palestine just west of the Jordan River and south of the Sea of Galilee. The Hebrew Bible depicts this region as the traditional heartland of the people of Israel, the place where their ancestors settled when they returned to Canaan from Egypt after the Exodus.

cherub One of two winged figures (plural, *cherubim*) that the Hebrew Bible says stood on either side of the **Ark of the Covenant** in the innermost part of the sacred tent that Moses erected in the wilderness and later in the same part of the Jerusalem temple. Their precise appearance and function are never described, but scholars think that they resembled the winged, human-headed beasts that appear in Mesopotamian royal imagery as spirit-guardians for the kings.

chronicles See the definition of **annals** above. The biblical book of Chronicles gets its name from the lengthy record of names that fills the first several chapters of the book.

circumcision The ritual removal of the loose flap of skin at the end of the penis. In the Hebrew Bible, circumcision is the primary identity marker of the male members of the covenant people of Yahweh (see Genesis 17) and is thus mandatory for any male who wishes to join the people of Yahweh. (No equivalent is prescribed for women.) According to the Torah, circumcision was to be performed on the eighth day after birth. The Bible offers no explanation as to why this particular ritual was followed (apart from divine command), but similar practices were sometimes used to identify priests in the ancient Near East, leading many scholars to think that its purpose was to symbolically mark all Israelite males as **holy** to Yahweh.

cistern A lined pit used to collect water during the rainy season for use at other times of the year. Most of Palestine is subject to long dry spells when little or no rain falls, so cisterns were an important source of water for the people of Israel during the dry season, along with wells and springs.

clan A group of families who claim to share a common ancestry. In the Hebrew Bible, the clan is a subdivision of the **tribe**. Being a member of a clan carries with it certain obligations toward other clan members, especially in the area of mutual protection. Property was also supposed to remain within the clan.

Coastal Plain The relatively flat region that runs along the coast of Palestine. One of the two major north-south routes through Palestine (the Way of the Sea) passed through this territory, making it strategically important to the nations to the north and south of Palestine. Its lack of natural harbors, by contrast, limited its value for the development of trade or fishing industries.

conservatives With regard to the Bible, scholars who seeks to defend the historicity of the biblical narratives. Conservatives generally hold the Bible in high esteem as a record of divine revelation, so they are hesitant to question its accuracy. Scholars who approach the Bible from a conservative perspective often say that the biblical narratives should be given the benefit of the doubt unless they can be disproved.

covenant A contract or agreement between two parties. In the Hebrew Bible, the term is used primarily to describe the special relationship that Yahweh established with Abraham and his descendants and later reaffirmed with the Exodus generation at Mount Sinai. In this relationship, Yahweh promises to provide for his people's needs and they commit themselves to live as he desires, primarily by obeying his laws. Faithfulness to the covenant will bring divine **blessings** upon the people of Israel, while unfaithfulness will elicit Yahweh's **curses**.

creed A formal statement of beliefs held by a religious community. Creeds typically draw much of their content from Scriptures and often serve as grids through which members of a religion interpret and apply their sacred texts.

cuneiform (koo-nay'-i-form) A form of writing that was used in many parts of the ancient Near East prior to the development of the alphabet. Cuneiform writing consists of various combinations of wedge-shaped characters representing syllables or numbers that were inscribed onto a variety of surfaces (mostly clay or wax tablets, but also stone, metal, wood, and the like; never paper). Cuneiform seems to have been used primarily for record keeping, though legal and religious texts were also preserved in this manner, including the **Enuma Elish** and the **Epic of Gilgamesh**.

curses A term used in the Hebrew Bible to describe the negative consequences that Yahweh promises to bring upon his people if they fail to abide by the terms of his covenant, including failed crops, sickly animals, and defeat at the hands of their enemies. Certain individuals were also believed to have the power to pronounce curses that would cause harm to the people whom they cursed.

Cyrus The king of Persia whose armies conquered Babylonia in 539 b.c.e. as part of a broader military campaign that established a Persian empire across most of the ancient Near East except for Egypt. Cyrus reversed the policies of the Babylonians and allowed the exiled people of Judah (along with similar exiles from other nations) to return to their homeland and rebuild their temple. In Isaiah 44:28 and 45:1, Cyrus is identified as the Anointed One (that is, the **Messiah**) whom Yahweh was sending to rescue his people, and two versions of his decree allowing the people of Judah to return home are presented in 2 Chronicles 36:23 and Ezra 1:2-4. The ideas (but not the language) of these decrees agree broadly with the contents of the Cyrus Cylinder that was discovered in 1879 in the Temple of Marduk in Babylonia.

Day of Atonement The high holy day of the Jewish calendar, often called by its Hebrew name, Yom Kippur. According to Leviticus 16, the high priest performed special sacrifices and cleansing rituals on this day, including carrying sacrificial blood into the inner sanctum of Yahweh's temple (the Holy of Holies) to cleanse it from the effects of the people's sins and impurities. The ritual is also mentioned in Leviticus 23:26-32 and Numbers 29:7-11, and similar rituals are described in Ezekiel 43:18-27 and 45:18-20. The fact that the Day of Atonement does not appear elsewhere in the Hebrew Bible suggests to many scholars that the practice should be dated in part or in full to the postexilic period.

Dead Sea A lake in southern Palestine into which the Jordan River empties. The lake has no outlet, and the intense heat of the area causes evaporation that leaves high concentrations of salt and minerals in the water and along the shoreline that were mined and exported in biblical times. These mineral concentrations make the lake uninhabitable to anything other than microscopic life, thus giving the lake its name. At 1,378 feet below sea level, the shore of the Dead Sea is the lowest point of dry land on the earth.

Decalogue A term used by scholars to refer to the **Ten Commandments**. It comes from two Greek words that mean "ten words."

deity A synonym for the generic term *god*, from the Latin word *deus* (god).

deuterocanonical A Roman Catholic term for the set of writings that Protestants call the **Apocrypha**. The term comes from two Greek words that mean "second canon," reflecting the Catholic belief that these books were approved by God for inclusion in the canon of Scripture later than the books that are viewed as canonical by Jews and Protestants.

Deuteronomic/Deuteronomistic Terms that signify that a particular text or idea has a close link with the biblical book of Deuteronomy. The two words are often treated as synonyms, though technically *Deuteronomic* should be used when describing characteristics of the book of Deuteronomy itself, while *Deuteronomistic* should be reserved for materials that have been influenced by the book of Deuteronomy, such as the narratives of the kings of Israel and Judah.

Deuteronomic theology A pattern of thinking that is common throughout the Hebrew Bible but is particularly prominent in the book of Deuteronomy. At its heart lies the belief that Yahweh will bring material rewards and prosperity to those who follow the terms of his covenant while imposing material sufferings upon those who are unfaithful to his covenant.

Deuteronomistic narrative A term used by scholars to refer to the biblical books from Joshua through 2 Kings, which tell the story of Israel from the end of the Exodus era to the end of the monarchy. The language and ideas of these books are very similar to those of the book of Deuteronomy, suggesting to most scholars that they were written or edited by someone who was familiar with the latter book. Many scholars prefer the term *Deuteronomistic History*, but this designation is problematic as it appears to prejudge the historicity of the narrative.

Divided Kingdom A designation for the period from the end of Solomon's rule (mid-tenth century B.C.E.) to the Assyrian conquest of Israel (late eighth century B.C.E.) when the Bible indicates that the people of Israel were divided into two kingdoms, Israel in the north and Judah in the south. Relations between these two kingdoms varied from close cooperation and intermarriage to hostility and open warfare.

divination The use of special techniques and practices that are thought to give insight into the future. Common methods of divination include casting lots (dice, sticks, and so forth), observing the behavior of animals, and reading the entrails of sacrifices. Such practices are common in most traditional societies. The fact that the laws of Torah prohibit divination suggests that it was performed in ancient Palestine as it was in the other civilizations of the ancient Near East.

doctrine A pattern of religious beliefs on a particular topic. The term is often (though not exclusively) used to describe the beliefs that have been formally endorsed by the leaders of a religion. Jews and Christians base much of their doctrine on the Hebrew Bible, but the text itself contains no formalized statements of belief.

Documentary Hypothesis A widely accepted theory concerning the origins of the Pentateuch (the first five books of the Hebrew Bible). In its traditional form, this theory proposed that the present version of the Pentateuch was created in the postexilic period by weaving together material from four earlier written sources that were composed from the tenth century B.C.E. to the sixth century B.C.E. The theory has been criticized and modified in recent years, but it continues to dominate scholarly discussions of the origins of the Pentateuch.

doublet Paired lines of Hebrew poetry. Such pairing of lines is one of the most common characteristics of poetic texts in the Hebrew Bible.

dualism/dualistic The belief that the universe is dominated by two supernatural powers who are competing for control over the natural world and its inhabitants. Dualism is uncommon in the Hebrew Bible, since the authors and editors see Yahweh as the sole ruler of the universe who brings both good and ill upon humans. Dualistic thinking does appear in some of the later biblical texts that were influenced by apocalyptic expectation.

Edom (ē'-dum) A territory and people group situated at the southern end of Palestine (south and east of the Dead Sea) during biblical times. In the book of Genesis, the people of Edom are portrayed as the descendants of Esau, the twin brother of Jacob, and thus as close relatives of the people of Israel. By contrast, the narrative texts and the books of the prophets speak of ongoing tensions and conflicts (including warfare) between the two peoples.

Egypt The land of Egypt in north Africa is mentioned repeatedly in the Hebrew Bible as one of the two great powers (along with the various kingdoms of Mesopotamia to the north) that struggled for control of the strategic land bridge of Palestine. The rulers of Egypt were generally content to leave the Israelites alone as long as they did not obstruct Egyptian access to trade and military routes that ran across Palestine, but they also used their influence to interfere in Israelite politics from time to time.

El   The common word for "divine being" across the ancient Near East. In Canaanite religious systems, El was the name of the creator of the universe and the head of the gods; he was best known as the father of **Baal**. The name is applied repeatedly to Yahweh in the Hebrew Bible (usually translated as "God" in English Bibles), indicating that the two gods were equated very early in the development of Israelite religious thought. The name is especially common in compounds such as "El Elyon" ("the highest God") and "El Shaddai" (possibly "the almighty God").

elites   A term used by social scientists to denote a small group of people who stand at the head of a society (also known as the upper class). Those who hold political power in a society are nearly always listed among the elites, but the title can also be applied to people who play a leading role in the economic, cultural, and/or religious life of a society. Because of their dominant position, elites have access to privileges and opportunities (including education) that are unavailable to other people, especially in traditional societies, where the gap between elites and nonelites can be quite broad.

Elohim   (el'-o-hēm)   The Hebrew plural of *El*, the generic word for deity in many ancient Near Eastern languages. While the word is sometimes used as a genuine plural to refer to "gods," it appears more often as a title for Yahweh, where it is commonly translated as "God." When applied to Yahweh, the plural is usually understood to be a plural of majesty, a Hebrew way of denoting greatness.

Enlightenment   An intellectual and philosophical movement that emphasized the use of human reason as both the pathway to truth and the standard by which all truth claims should be evaluated. The movement began in Europe in the late seventeenth century as a challenge to the common belief that ordinary people should simply accept what they were told by external authorities, including the church. Enlightenment thinkers adopted a more skeptical attitude toward the Bible, especially its miracle stories, which many of them rejected as contrary to reason. They also developed many of the methods and raised many of the questions that are included today under the term **biblical criticism**.

Enuma Elish   A Babylonian creation epic that tells how Marduk became the chief god by vanquishing Tiamat, the sea goddess, and creating the universe out of her body. Later in the story he creates humans to build homes for the gods (temples) and to provide them with food and drink (sacrifices). The title comes from the first words of the story in the Akkadian language, meaning "when on high. . . ." The present version was probably composed in the twelfth century B.C.E., but similar stories are known from earlier centuries. The story has many parallels with the Genesis creation narratives.

Epic of Gilgamesh   An ancient Mesopotamian text, sometimes called the Babylonian flood story, that narrates the escapades of a king named Gilgamesh and his friend Enkidu. One section of the epic tells the story of Utnapishtim, an ancient hero who survived a great flood by taking animals onto a boat and remaining there until the floodwaters subsided. The story contains many detailed similarities to the biblical flood story (Genesis 6–8), leading most scholars to regard the biblical narrative as a Yahwistic revision of the highly popular (and much earlier) Mesopotamian story. Fragments of the Epic of Gilgamesh are known from as early as the eighteenth century B.C.E., long before the rise of the Israelites as a people.

eschatological   An adjective that means "pertaining to the end." It comes from the Greek word *eschaton*, meaning "end." Scholars use the term to describe texts or ideas that speak about a future time when Yahweh will act decisively on behalf of his people, whether by defeating their foes and inaugurating an era of peace and prosperity (as in some of the prophetic books) or by purging the universe of evil and transforming it into a glorious place where the righteous will live and serve Yahweh forever (as in some of the apocalyptic texts).

ethnocentrism   A pattern of thinking that sees one's own people or ethnic group as the center of the universe. Often (though not always) it includes a belief that one's own group is inherently superior to others. Ethnocentrism was the norm in the ancient world, with people everywhere regarding themselves as the special objects of divine attention and favor. The biblical view of Israel as the chosen people of Yahweh is an ethnocentric notion.

Eve   The name given to the first woman in Genesis 3:20 and 4:1, the only places in the Hebrew Bible where the name appears. Genesis 3:20 suggests that the name comes from a Hebrew word meaning "living," but this is probably just a wordplay. Prior to this, she is simply called "the woman," which in Hebrew (as in English) is closely related to the word for "man." Later Jewish and Christian texts painted her (and all women) in highly negative terms as the channel by which sin entered into the world and captivated men, but this view finds little support in the text.

exclusivism/exclusivist attitude   A pattern of religious thinking that does not deny the validity of other religions but calls for people to remain loyal to their particular religious tradition. In the case of the Hebrew Bible, it refers to the belief that even though there might be other gods in the universe, Yahweh is the only deity to whom the people of Israel and Judah, as Yahweh's chosen people, should give their allegiance. Honoring other gods is deeply offensive to Yahweh, who expects complete loyalty from his people.

exegesis   The practice of analyzing and explaining a text. The word comes from two Greek words meaning "leading out," reflecting the common belief that exegesis is concerned with leading the meaning out of the text. Exegesis is performed on a regular basis by religious leaders who seek to instruct their congregations and by scholars who wish to elucidate the meaning of the text using scholarly methods.

Exile   To be forcibly sent away from one's homeland. In the Hebrew Bible, the word is used mainly to refer to the deportation of the elites of Judah to Babylonia that began in 597 B.C.E. and expanded in 586 B.C.E., when Babylonian armies overran Jerusalem. It is also used occasionally to describe the similar treatment of Israel at the hands of the Assyrians in 722 B.C.E. In biblical scholarship, the term has a narrower meaning, referring to the period from the conquest of Jerusalem (or sometimes to the earlier deportation) until the Persians conquered Babylonia in 539 B.C.E. and allowed the people of Judah to return to their homeland.

exilic   In biblical scholarship, an adjective that means "pertaining to the [Babylonian] **Exile.**" The Exile was so crucial to the history and religious development of the people of Israel and Judah that scholars use it as a reference point for dating the biblical materials and the events that they depict: *preexilic* means "before the Exile"; *exilic* means "during the Exile"; and *postexilic* means "after the Exile."

Exodus   The title commonly given to the story of the Israelites' miraculous departure from Egypt under the leadership of **Moses**, as narrated in the biblical book by the same name. The term is also used more broadly to refer to the entire complex of stories from the birth of Moses to the end of the Israelites' desert wanderings, as narrated in the books of Exodus, Leviticus, Numbers, and Deuteronomy. The term comes from two Greek words that mean "going out."

Festival of Booths   Also called the Feast of Tabernacles, one of three major religious festivals described in the Torah. Originally a harvest celebration, the eight-day festival came to be linked with the story of Yahweh providing for the Israelites during their forty years of desert wanderings after the exodus from Egypt. The Torah calls for the people of Yahweh to offer special sacrifices and live in booths, or temporary shelters, during this festival to commemorate the years that their ancestors spent living in tents in the desert (Leviticus 23:33-43; Numbers 29:12-34; Deuteronomy 16:13-15; compare Nehemiah 8:13-18). Jews call the festival *Sukkoth* (the Hebrew word for "booths") for this reason.

Festival of Weeks   One of three major religious festivals described in the Torah, linked in Exodus 34:22 with the beginning of the wheat harvest. The name comes from the requirement to count seven weeks after Passover to set the date of the festival (Leviticus 23:15-21; Deuteronomy 16:9-12; Numbers 28:26-31). It was also called "the festival of harvest" (Exodus 23:16) and later **Pentecost**, from a Greek word meaning "fiftieth." Jews call it *Shavuot*, the Hebrew word for "weeks."

firstfruits   The first portion of the harvest of a particular crop, regarded in the ancient world as being the best part. According to the Torah, the firstfruits are to be offered to Yahweh as an act of thanksgiving for the harvest (Leviticus 23:9-14; Deuteronomy 26:1-11). The term can also be used more loosely to refer to the first or best part of other food items produced from agricultural crops, such as wine, oil, or dough.

form criticism   A method of analysis that seeks to reconstruct the original form of a text or passage from the Hebrew Bible and to trace how that original form changed over time as it was passed on by word of mouth. Form critics also seek to determine the various social or religious contexts in which the text was created and used. Form criticism is often quite speculative, but it has proved useful in highlighting common literary patterns and types of material in the Hebrew Bible.

Former Prophets   A term used by the Jewish community to refer to the books of Joshua, Judges, Samuel, and Kings. These books tell about Israel's past from the conquest of Canaan to the end of the monarchy. They were included in the Prophets section of the canon due to the recognition that their point of view is similar to that found in the sayings of the prophets. The term *former* refers to their position in the canon (that is, they appear in the former half of the Prophets section), not to the time when they were written. Christians include these books in a category called "**Historical Books**."

fundamentalism A form of religion that seeks to define and defend what its followers regard as the essentials or fundamentals of the faith. The term arose in the late nineteenth century in conservative Protestant circles, but scholars now apply it to similar trends in other religions. Most fundamentalist systems include some kind of commitment to the absolute truth and supreme authority of sacred texts. This commitment leads their followers to reject modern critical study of Scripture and other ideas that run contrary to their Scriptures.

Galilee A hilly region located at the northern end of Palestine, west and north of the Sea of Galilee, that was part of the northern kingdom of Israel during the era of the *Divided Kingdom*. The religious shrine of Dan was located at the northern end of Galilee. Galilee does not appear often in the biblical narratives, since it was far from Jerusalem and lay on the periphery of the lands controlled by the Israelites.

genealogy A list of one's ancestors. Genealogies were important in ancient Israel (as in most traditional societies) for defining kin relationships that affected whom one could marry, how property was distributed, and so forth. As a rule, the genealogies in the Hebrew Bible list only male ancestors, since social rights and responsibilities pass through the male line in patriarchal societies such as ancient Israel and Judah.

genre (zhahn'-rah) A category of literature that shares common characteristics. The term comes from a French word meaning "kind" or "type." Identifying the genre of a piece of literature (short story, letter, legal text, and so forth) is a vital part of the interpretive process, since it helps readers to know what to expect from a text and how to make sense of its content. The process becomes more complicated when authors bend or mix the conventions of the genre in which they are writing.

grand narrative A term for the broad story line that forms the narrative backbone of the Hebrew Bible. This story line, which focuses on events involving the people of Israel and Judah, begins with the creation of the universe and extends (with some gaps) into the postexilic era. The preexilic portion of the story was shaped into a coherent narrative during or after the Exile to provide a religious interpretation of Israel's past. Its overarching goal is to explain why the Exile happened.

Hasmonean (haz-mo-nē'-un) A term used to designate the Jewish dynasty that ruled over Judah from the mid-second to the mid-first century B.C.E. The title derives from the name of one of their ancestors, Hashmon. The first group of Hasmoneans, who led the Jews to victory against their Greek rulers, were also called **Maccabees** based on a nickname that was given to their leader, Judas "Maccabeus," a term that probably means "the hammerer." Their story is narrated in the books of 1 and 2 Maccabees, which appear in the Catholic and Orthodox canons but not in Protestant or Jewish Bibles.

Hebrew A term used primarily in the earlier stages of the biblical narrative as an ethnic designation for the people who would later be called Israelites. The origin and meaning of the name are unclear, though it might be related to the Akkadian word *habiru*, which in some texts refers to a category of rootless wanderers who lived on the fringes of civilized society. The word is also used as a name for the language that they spoke. Most of the Hebrew Bible is written in the Hebrew language, but portions are written in Aramaic.

Hebrew Bible A religiously neutral title for the collection of ancient Israelite texts that both Jews and Christians regard as sacred Scripture. The term is used in academic and interfaith circles as an alternative to such religiously loaded terms as *the Bible* and *the Old Testament*. The term reflects the fact that most of the Jewish Bible is written in the Hebrew language.

high places A term used in the Hebrew Bible to designate various places around the territory of Palestine where people worshipped Yahweh and other gods. The name comes from the fact that many such sites were located on elevated spots (whether natural or man-made) in order to be closer to the heavenly realm of the gods. The term usually carries a derogatory meaning, since the people who wrote the Hebrew Bible regarded all worship centers except for the Jerusalem temple as illegitimate.

high priest The leader of the order of priests who served Yahweh at the Jerusalem temple. His duties appear to have included directing the worship of Yahweh and caring for the physical needs of the building. Leviticus 16 suggests that he alone was allowed to enter the innermost part of the temple, where Yahweh was believed to dwell, on the annual **Day of Atonement**, when he was charged with ritually cleansing the sanctuary.

Historical Books A term used in Christian Bibles for the collection of books that contains the **grand narrative** of the Hebrew Bible. The collection extends from the period of the judges to the postexilic era. Catholic and Orthodox Bibles have more books in this section than Protestant Bibles; see chapter 3.

historiography The practice of writing about the past. In the modern era, historians have developed systematic methods of probing and reconstructing the past that have made historiography into a quasi-scientific discipline. Ancient writers, by contrast, did not share this disciplined approach, and it is often unclear where they got their information and how reliable it is. As a result, modern historians have to critically sift through ancient narratives before they can be used for reconstructing past events. This is as true for the Bible as for any other ancient text.

holy To be set apart from other persons or objects in a class. When applied to Yahweh, it signifies that he is fundamentally unlike both humans and other gods, especially in the sense of being morally pure and perfect, and thus should not be viewed or treated as they are. When used of Israel, it refers to the belief that they have been set apart from other nations for the service of Yahweh and should therefore not imitate their practices. Virtually any person or object can be made holy through the application of various rituals that cleanse the recipient from impurity and set the recipient apart for the service of Yahweh and/or his temple.

Horeb (hor'-eb) Another name for **Mount Sinai**, the place where Moses is said to have heard the voice of Yahweh speaking to him in a burning bush and where he later received the **Ten Commandments** and many other laws from Yahweh.

idolatry In the Hebrew Bible, the use of physical objects (statues, stone pillars, and the like) to represent the presence of a deity during a ritual act of worship. Images of the gods were an essential feature of religious activity throughout the ancient Near East. The Hebrew Bible, by contrast, prohibits any worship involving such images, especially images representing Yahweh. Nonetheless, archaeological finds show that physical images of deities were in fact used in Palestine throughout the biblical period.

image of God An expression found only in the book of Genesis that refers to some kind of innate likeness of humans to their divine creator (Genesis 1:26-30; 9:6). The nature of this likeness is never defined, though it gives human life a value that sets humans apart from the animals (Genesis 9:6). The context suggests that the divine likeness is exhibited when humans rule over the created order under God's direction. Despite its vagueness, the expression has played an important role in Christian theological reflection about what it means to be human.

impurity The state of being ritually unprepared for close interaction with the divine realm. Since Yahweh alone is inherently **holy**, all people and objects must undergo ritual purification to make them "holy" before they can enter into his presence (for example, before entering his temple). The Hebrew Bible also identifies certain actions, including contact with corpses and impure people or objects, that produce a state of impurity that must be cleansed by proper rituals.

inerrancy The belief held by many conservative Protestant Christians that the Bible is absolutely accurate in all that it says, not only in its religious teachings but also in its references to matters of history, science, and so forth. Those who hold this view tend to reject most forms of biblical criticism.

inspiration The belief held by many Christians and Jews that God played a direct role in the production of the Bible, giving it a sacred quality unmatched by other books. Some take *inspiration* to mean that God actually dictated the words of the Bible to the authors, while others prefer to say that God guided the authors' thinking so that they invariably spoke the truth about religious matters. Still others would limit the term to the belief that God inspires those who read the Bible to recognize its truth and follow its teachings. The greater the authorial role that people attribute to God, the more they tend to resist the application of critical scholarship to the Bible.

intermediary Someone who stands between two parties as a messenger or agent. The chief intermediaries in the Hebrew Bible are priests and prophets. Priests represent the people before God, offering sacrifices, prayers, and songs on their behalf, while prophets represent the deity to the people by delivering his messages. The two roles are not mutually exclusive—priests can deliver messages from Yahweh to those who come to them seeking divine aid, while prophets are sometimes shown praying for their people. Some of the biblical prophets even came from priestly families.

Isaac (ī'-zek) The son of Abraham and Sarah through whose descendants Yahweh's covenant with Abraham was said to pass. Isaac was the father of Esau, whom the Bible identifies as the ancestor of the people of **Edom**, and **Jacob**, also called **Israel**, from whom the people of Israel took their name.

Israel   A name given to Jacob, Abraham's grandson, after he wrestled all night with an angel in Genesis 32:22-32. The name means "he wrestles with God." The name is subsequently applied to his descendants, whom the Hebrew Bible calls "Israelites" or "the people of Israel."

Jacob (jā'-kup)   The son of Isaac and grandson of Abraham whose descendants were regarded as the ultimate beneficiaries of Yahweh's covenant with Abraham. Jacob is also known as **Israel**, from which his descendants take their name. In the Hebrew Bible, Jacob is depicted as a trickster who mends his ways after many years of hard experience and a personal encounter with Yahweh.

Judah (joo'-dah)   The fourth son of Jacob and thus the ancestor of one of the twelve tribes of Israel. According to the book of Joshua, the tribe of Judah settled in the southern part of Palestine after the Israelites had conquered Canaan. As a result, this region came to be known as Judah during the era of the **Divided Kingdom**.

judge   As used in the book of Judges, one of a series of charismatic leaders who arose to lead the tribes of Israel to military victory against foreign oppressors in the era prior to the kings. The Hebrew Bible applies the term *judge* to these characters because some of them helped to settle disputes and ensure justice among their people in the years following their military victories.

Ketuvim (keh-too-vēm')   A Hebrew word meaning **Writings**, used by Jews as a title for the third part of the biblical canon.

lament   To mourn publicly over a situation marked by suffering or loss. Laments played an important role in funeral ceremonies throughout the ancient Near East. Some 40 percent of the book of Psalms consists of lament psalms that were sung or recited (often at the Jerusalem temple) by individuals and/or national leaders to express their unhappiness about various sufferings they were enduring and to call on Yahweh for help.

Latter Prophets   A term used by the Jewish community to designate the four books that contain the sayings of the prophets Isaiah, Jeremiah, Ezekiel, and "The Twelve" (that is, the twelve prophets whom Christians call the **Minor Prophets**). The term *latter* refers to their position in the Jewish canon (that is, they

appear in the latter half of the Prophets section), not to the time when the prophets lived. Christians list these books along with others under the broader heading of "Prophets."

laws   A common designation for the collection of rules and regulations that Yahweh is said to have delivered to **Moses** at **Mount Sinai**. The giving of the laws is an important part of the Exodus story, filling much of the books of Exodus, Leviticus, Numbers, and Deuteronomy. The laws define how the people of Israel should live in order to express their gratitude and devotion to Yahweh in response to his selection of them as his covenant people.

legalism   A negative term that Christians have sometimes applied to Judaism, reflecting the mistaken belief that Jews are excessively preoccupied with obeying laws in order to earn God's favor (or a place in heaven). In reality, the Scriptures and teachings of Judaism regard the laws of Torah as a divine gift and insist that Jews should obey them in order to express their love and gratitude for being chosen as God's special covenant partners, not as a mechanism for earning anything from God.

Levite (lē'-vite)   A member of the tribe of Levi, one of the sons of **Jacob**. According to the Torah, all priests were to come from the tribe of Levi, though not all Levites served as priests. In addition to the priests, the Hebrew Bible speaks of Levites who served alongside the priests at the Jerusalem temple, where they seem to have functioned as assistants to the priests.

literacy   The ability to read and/or write. Due to a lack of formal educational systems, most people in the ancient world were unable to read or write in any meaningful way, though some would have been able to sign their name and recognize simple symbols. True literacy was found only among the elites and their trained servants or slaves. The literary quality of the Hebrew Bible indicates that its authors and editors came from the elite level of society.

Maccabees (mak'-ah-bēz)   A term applied to the first generation of the **Hasmoneans**, derived from a nickname that was given to their first leader, Judas "Maccabeus" (probably "the hammerer"). Four ancient Jewish books have the name Maccabees in their title: 1 Maccabees, 2 Maccabees, and 4 Maccabees tell about various aspects of the Jewish struggle for freedom from Greek rule in the second century B.C.E., while 3 Maccabees contains a fanciful tale about how God rescued his people from persecution in Egypt in the late third century B.C.E. First and 2 Maccabees are included in the Roman Catholic and

Orthodox canons, while 3 and 4 Maccabees appear only in the Orthodox canon.

maximalists Scholars who believe that a sizable percentage of the narratives in the Hebrew Bible were derived from earlier oral or written traditions that contained significant amounts of historically trustworthy data. Rather than making sweeping claims about the historical reliability of the biblical stories as a whole, maximalists believe that the evidence for each story should be evaluated on its own terms.

menorah (me-nōr'-ah) A golden lampstand that formed part of the sacred furniture of both the desert **tabernacle** and the Jerusalem temple, as narrated in the Hebrew Bible. The stand held oil lamps that would have lighted the interior of the buildings. The tabernacle texts speak of a single seven-branched lampstand, while the temple texts speak of ten lampstands whose shape is not identified. In later Jewish tradition, the seven-branched lampstand became one of the key symbols of the people of Israel.

Merneptah Stela (mer-nep'-tah stē'-lah) A monumental pillar erected around the year 1210 B.C.E. by an Egyptian pharaoh named Merneptah in order to commemorate his military victories over a variety of enemies. Included on this list is a people group named **Israel**, making this the first reference to the people of Israel outside the Bible. The Merneptah Stela is one of the key pieces of evidence cited in debates over the origins of the Israelites.

Mesopotamia A generic name for the territory surrounding the Tigris and the Euphrates rivers in what is now Iraq. The name comes from two Latin words meaning "between the rivers." Middle Eastern civilization began in this area. In biblical times it served as the homeland and territorial base for the Assyrian and Babylonian empires. Residents of Israel and Judah who survived the invasion of their lands by the Assyrian and Babylonian armies were deported to various parts of Mesopotamia as part of a strategy to break the collective will of the peoples whom they conquered.

Messiah The English form of the Hebrew word *meshiach*, which means "anointed." To anoint is to pour oil over a person's head, normally as part of a ritual installing someone into a high office (mostly priests and kings). In the Hebrew Bible, the word is applied often to the kings of Judah. Some of the prophets anticipate a day when Yahweh will raise up an ideal "anointed one" (Messiah) to rule over Israel with justice and to inaugurate

an era of peace and prosperity. The Greek equivalent is *christos*, from which we get our word *Christ*.

Midian A region at the northern end of the Arabian Peninsula (south of Palestine) whose residents appear occasionally in the early stages of the biblical narrative, primarily in connection with the Exodus story. Some of the stories speak about hostilities between the Midianites and the people of Israel, while others depict a more cooperative relationship. The Midianites appear to have been a nomadic people who disappear from the biblical record by the time of the monarchy.

midrashim Ancient Jewish commentaries on biblical writings that were created to clarify ambiguities in the text or derive lessons from biblical stories. The title comes from a Hebrew word that means "to inquire, study, investigate."

minimalists Scholars who regard the biblical narratives as largely fictional works composed in the postexilic period to forge a common past for a group of people who were seeking to assert their claims to control the land of Palestine. As a rule, minimalists believe that the biblical narratives have so many historical problems that they should not be used for reconstructing the past unless they are supported by outside evidence.

Minor Prophets A term used by Christians to designate the twelve books of prophetic sayings that the Jewish canon combines into a single book called "The Twelve." The term *minor* refers to the shortness of the books, all of which could be copied onto a single scroll in ancient times, and not to the relative importance or influence of the prophets or their messages.

Mishnah An important Jewish text written around 200 C.E. that compiles centuries of Jewish discussions and rulings concerning the proper application of the Torah to the lives of the Jewish people. Its contents were later incorporated into the **Talmud**, the most important Jewish text outside the Bible. The ideas of the Mishnah have shaped the development of Judaism from ancient times to the present.

Moab (mō'-ab) A territory located on the opposite side of the Dead Sea from Judah. The Hebrew Bible paints a largely negative portrait of the Moabites, reflecting the tensions and periodic warfare that existed between Judah and Moab for much of their history. Yet the Bible also depicts them as distant relatives of the Israelites, perhaps reflecting an awareness of their common cultural characteristics.

monolatry/monolatrous The practice of serving and honoring a single deity without denying the reality or power of other gods. Monolatry resembles polytheism in its belief that the forces of nature are controlled by a series of personal deities, but it insists that one deity is more powerful or more worthy of service than others. Many of the ideas about Yahweh in the Hebrew Bible are more consistent with monolatry than with **monotheism**, which is found mostly in later biblical texts.

monotheism/monotheistic The belief that there is only one divine being in the universe. Implicit in monotheism is the claim that other deities are figments of the human imagination; the various forces of nature that **polytheists** (see above) see as the activity of many gods are in reality the work of one supreme deity. True monotheism appears only in some of the later biblical texts, particularly Second Isaiah.

Moses According to the Hebrew Bible, the man chosen by Yahweh to lead his people out of Egypt and back to the land of their forefathers in Canaan. The name Moses is Egyptian, but he is portrayed in the Exodus narrative as a member of an Israelite priestly family. Empowered by Yahweh, he leads the people of Israel out of Egypt and guides them through forty years of desert wanderings until their descendants finally enter the land of Canaan without him. Yahweh also uses him to deliver the laws of the Torah to his people at **Mount Sinai**.

Mount Sinai (sī'-nī) The sacred mountain where Yahweh is said to have appeared in awesome power to the Exodus generation after their departure from Egypt (Exodus 19) and given his laws to **Moses**. The location of Mount Sinai, if it is indeed a real place and not a legend, is unknown, though scholars have identified a number of possible candidates in the Sinai region south of Palestine.

myth As used by religious scholars, a story about the ancient past, usually involving supernatural beings, that aims to communicate a profound religious truth. Unlike popular notions that equate myth with fiction, the scholarly use of the term says nothing about the possible historicity of the story. Much of the narrative material in the Hebrew Bible would qualify as myth under this definition.

Negev (neg'-ev) The dry territory directly south of Judah that shades from grassland into desert as one moves farther south. The grassy areas are suitable for grazing, but the desert areas provide little support for long-term habitation. The Hebrew Bible appears to place much of the desert wanderings of the Exodus generation in this region or farther south.

Nevi'im (ne-vē-ēm') The Hebrew word for "prophets," used by the Jewish community as a title for the second part of the Jewish canon. The collection is divided into the **Former Prophets**, a set of four books that narrates the history of ancient Israel, and the **Latter Prophets**, four books containing the sayings of at least fifteen prophets who spoke their messages to the people of Israel and Judah over the course of several hundred years.

New Testament A term used by Christians to refer to the collection of early Christian writings that was adopted by the church as the second part of its canon of Scripture alongside the collection of Jewish books that Christians call the **Old Testament**. The term is an English translation of a Greek phrase that means "new covenant," reflecting the traditional Christian belief that God's original covenant relationship with Israel has now been supplemented or replaced by a new arrangement that is open to all humans on the basis of faith in Jesus.

Old Testament A Christian term for the sacred texts of Judaism that the early church adopted as Scripture due to its origins as a sect of Judaism. The title is an English translation of a Greek phrase meaning "old covenant," reflecting the traditional Christian belief that the Jewish Scriptures speak about an agreement between God and the people of Israel that has been supplemented or replaced by a new agreement (or new covenant) that God initiated with all of humanity through the death and resurrection of Jesus.

omen A natural phenomenon that is viewed by people in traditional societies as a message or sign from the supernatural realm concerning future events. Virtually any unusual occurrence can be taken as an omen, along with such ordinary activities as the behavior of animals or the movements of heavenly bodies. Some omens can be interpreted by ordinary people, while others require the skills of specialists. The reading of omens is discouraged by the authors of the Hebrew Bible, but the practice seems to have been fairly common in ancient Israel, as it was throughout the ancient Near East.

oral traditions Materials passed on by word of mouth within a community, usually because most of its members are illiterate. Scholars believe that the literate elites who wrote and edited the Hebrew Bible drew at least some of their material from oral traditions that circulated among the illiterate masses.

original sin The belief held by many Christians that the sin of **Adam** and **Eve** in the Garden of Eden (Genesis 3) made all of their descendants into corrupt sinners who are inherently displeasing to God and thus require a savior (Jesus) to rescue them from God's righteous judgment. This reading of Genesis 3 is not shared by Jews nor by many modern scholars, who find little evidence in the text to support such a view. Christians who accept this idea point to some of the writings of the apostle Paul in the New Testament to support their interpretation.

Palestine A common name for the ill-defined geographic territory where the people of Israel resided in biblical times. The title comes from the name of a people group that settled on the **Coastal Plain** during the era of the judges, the **Philistines**. Various forms of the name were used by Greek writers for centuries before it was incorporated by the Romans into the name of a province that included this area in the second century C.E. (Syria-Palaestina). The name reverted to Palaestina in the fourth century C.E., and variations of this name have been used off and on to the present day.

pantheism/pantheistic The belief that everything that exists is a manifestation of a single cosmic mind or presence that is the only true reality. In this view, the universe is divine and all of life is sacred. Pantheism is common in Eastern religions (for example, Hinduism), but it was virtually unknown in the ancient Near East.

pantheon The list or hierarchy of gods who are worshiped in a **polytheistic** religious system. Changes can occur in a group's pantheon as individual gods and goddesses increase or decline in popularity or as the group comes into regular contact with people who honor different deities. The Hebrew Bible indicates that there were people in ancient Palestine who wished to incorporate Yahweh into the traditional pantheon of **Canaanite** deities.

parallelism The technique, common in Hebrew poetry, of placing two (or more) lines of text back-to-back in some form of relationship so that their meaning is discerned by reflecting on the two lines together. The most common forms are synonymous, in which the second line repeats or echoes the first; antithetical, in which the second line contrasts with the first; and complementary, in which the second line completes the idea begun in the first. Parallelism is common not only in books like Psalms and Proverbs but also in the books of the prophets, which are written primarily in poetry.

Passover The most important of the three major religious festivals described in the laws of Torah. Originally an agricultural festival, the celebration came to be viewed as a commemoration of the night prior to the **Exodus** when the angel of death "passed over" the houses of the Hebrew people when he came to kill the firstborn sons of the people and animals of Egypt (Exodus 11–12). Protection was ensured by placing the blood of a sacrificed lamb on the doorposts of the house. Passover was primarily a home-based celebration, though some biblical texts require the men to travel to Jerusalem to celebrate Passover at the temple. Jews call the festival by its Hebrew name, *Pesach*.

patriarchs A common term for the early male ancestors of the Hebrew people whose lives are narrated in the book of Genesis (primarily Abraham, Isaac, and Jacob). The term comes from two Greek words that mean "high fathers." The term has fallen out of favor in scholarly circles in recent years due to a belief that it devalues the vital roles played by women (sometimes called *matriarchs*) in these stories. The more neutral term *ancestors* (as in **ancestral narratives**) is preferred.

patriarchy A social system in which men hold the dominant positions of authority in the family and the broader society and male values are regarded as normative for women and men alike. The term comes from two Greek words that mean "rule by the father." All societies in the ancient Near East were patriarchal. The influence of patriarchal beliefs and values can be seen throughout the Hebrew Bible, including a frequent tendency to play down or ignore the presence and contributions of women.

Pentateuch An alternate title for the first five books of the Hebrew Bible that Jews call the **Torah**. The name comes from two Greek words that mean "five scrolls." The term was used as early as the second century C.E. as a Christian alternative to the Jewish label for the books. Today the title is used by academic scholars as a synonym for the Jewish term *Torah*.

Pentecost A Greek title for the celebration known as the **Festival of Weeks**.

Persians The people in ancient times who inhabited the territory now known as Iran. Little is known about the Persians prior to the rise of Cyrus, the military leader and king who over the course of two decades in the mid-sixth century B.C.E. established an empire that extended from eastern Iran to western Turkey and south to Palestine. Later kings conquered Egypt and parts of Greece, giving the Persians control over the bulk of the Near East for more than two hundred years. The Persians are depicted positively in the Hebrew Bible for allowing the people of Judah to return to their homeland after conquering Babylonia and for aiding in the rebuilding of Jerusalem and its temple.

Pharaoh (fā'-rō) A title used by the kings of Egypt. The title, an Egyptian word that means "Great House," originally referred to the palace where the king lived, but it eventually came to be used as a shorthand designation for the king's administrative authority. Pharaohs are mentioned more than two hundred times in the Hebrew Bible, but only three of them are named: Shishak (1 Kings 14:25-26), Neco (2 Kings 23:29-35; Jeremiah 46:2), and Hophra (Jeremiah 44:30). The rest are identified only by title. The best-known pharaohs in the Hebrew Bible are the unnamed Egyptian kings who appear in the story of Joseph (Genesis 37–50) and the Exodus story.

Philistines (fil'-is-tēnz) A seafaring people group that settled on the southern Coastal Plain of Palestine around the twelfth century B.C.E. after being defeated by the Egyptians. Their place of origin is unknown, though they appear to have been part of a broader movement of sea peoples that conducted raids across the Mediterranean world for several decades. The Hebrew Bible depicts them as a militarily strong people whom the Israelites fought several times for control of territory in the days of the judges and the early monarchy.

plague A term used in the Exodus narrative to refer to the ten dreadful punishments that Yahweh imposed upon the land of Egypt when **Pharaoh** rejected **Moses**' demands to allow the Hebrew people to leave his land and move to **Canaan** (turning the Nile River to blood, sending infestations of frogs, flies, and locusts, and so on). According to the Hebrew Bible, the plagues were designed not only to motivate Pharaoh to act but also to demonstrate Yahweh's power over the gods of Egypt, who were believed to control the forces of nature. The plagues are mentioned repeatedly in the Hebrew Bible as a sign of Yahweh's power and his love for his people.

Poetic Books A term used in Christian Bibles for certain biblical books that have poetic qualities. The title is somewhat misleading, since the category includes the book of Ecclesiastes, which is written in prose, and excludes many other texts that were written in poetry (including most of the prophetic books). Catholic and Orthodox Bibles have more books in this section than Protestant Bibles; see chapter 3.

polygamy The practice of having more than one wife at the same time. Polygamy is accepted as normal for men in the Hebrew Bible, but not for women. The distinction is no doubt rooted in the common patriarchal concern to clarify which adult men are responsible to provide for which children. It is unclear how widely polygamy was practiced in ancient Israel, since most of the stories where it appears involve ancient ancestors or kings.

polytheism/polytheistic The belief that the universe is ruled by a number of personal deities (gods and goddesses) who are superior to human beings. In polytheistic systems, deities are commonly associated with specific aspects of nature, such as the sun, the wind, or the sea, or with a particular geographic location. Polytheistic systems stress the importance of using **rituals** (often including animal sacrifices) to maintain the favor of the gods and avoid their displeasure. All of the religious systems of the ancient Near East, apart from the more **absolutist** forms of **Yahwism**, were polytheistic.

postexilic A term applied to texts and events arising in the period after the Persians conquered the Babylonians in 539 B.C.E. and brought an end to the enforced exile of the people of Judah from their homeland. Some scholars limit the term to the era immediately after the return from Babylonia, while others use it more broadly to refer to the ensuing centuries of Persian and Greek rule.

praise In the book of Psalms, the act of giving public honor to Yahweh as the god of Israel. Some expressions of praise celebrate specific acts that Yahweh has done for an individual or the nation, while others acclaim his many wonderful qualities and characteristics. Similar expressions of praise can be seen in other religions of the ancient Near East.

preexilic A term applied to texts and events arising in the period before the conquest of Judah by the Babylonians in 586 B.C.E. In practice, most scholars limit the term to the era of the monarchy in Israel and Judah.

priests Religious officials who manage the performance of public rituals and serve as mediators between humans and the divine realm. Priests played a vital role in all of the religious systems of the ancient Near East. The Hebrew Bible limits the priestly office to males from the tribe of Levi. Some of the narrative texts indicate that the office was further restricted to particular families within this tribe. According to the Torah, only ritually pure priests were allowed to offer animal sacrifices at the temple of Yahweh in Jerusalem or to enter the building itself; entry was denied to ordinary Israelites.

profane A term used by religious scholars to denote the opposite of "sacred" or "holy." Many religions make such a distinction between the world of the gods, who must be approached cautiously, and the world of humans. The term *profane* thus refers to the inherent status of a person, place, or thing (that is, the world to which it belongs), not to the propriety of its conduct. Virtually anything can be transferred from the realm of the profane to the realm of the sacred through the proper performance of **rituals**.

prophets In the Hebrew Bible, people who served as messengers for Yahweh or other deities. Prophets associated with gods other than Yahweh used a variety of means to discern what the deity was saying; it is unclear whether the prophets of Yahweh used similar techniques. Under the monarchy, the prophets of Yahweh challenged the prevailing social and religious system and were mostly rejected as a result. Not until their predictions of doom came true were their words collected and compiled into books of the prophets and incorporated into the second section of the Jewish canon of Scripture, known as the Prophets.

proverbs Short, memorable sayings that express a profound observation concerning human conduct. Proverbs are a vital channel of moral instruction and guidance in traditional societies. The biblical book of Proverbs is a collection of such sayings. In both form and substance, it resembles the proverbial literature of Mesopotamia and Egypt, apart from its occasional references to Yahweh.

psalm A Greek term for a song that is accompanied by stringed instruments. In the Hebrew Bible, it refers to the collection of traditional songs and prayers that was compiled to form the book of Psalms. Most of the psalms appear to have been used in conjunction with the worship of Yahweh at the Jerusalem temple, though some may have originated in other settings.

Ptolemies (tol'-e-mēz) A term used to designate the Greek kings who ruled over Egypt for nearly three hundred years after the breakup of Alexander the Great's empire in the late fourth century B.C.E. All of the kings were named after the first member of their dynasty, Alexander's general Ptolemy, so that they are collectively known as the Ptolemies. The Ptolemaic Empire ruled over the land of Palestine from 302 to 198 B.C.E., when they were displaced by the **Seleucids**, another Greek empire located to the north of Palestine.

purity The state of being ritually prepared for close interaction with the divine realm. Since Yahweh is inherently **holy**, everything that comes into contact with him (for example, by entering his temple) must be made holy or pure so that it does not either contaminate his holy presence or motivate him to flee the impurity. The Hebrew Bible prescribes a variety of **rituals** that can be used for purification.

Qur'an (koor-ahn') The sacred text of Islam, also spelled "Koran." Muslims believe that the words of the Qur'an were revealed to the prophet Muhammad over a twenty-two-year period from 610 to 632 C.E. The Qur'an contains many references to biblical characters and stories, including more than five hundred verses that speak about Moses and the Israelites and more than two hundred verses pertaining to Abraham. Muslims attribute these references to the divine revelation of the Qur'an, while Jews and Christians claim that Muhammad learned about the Bible through conversations with Jews and Christians.

rabbi In modern times, the leader of a Jewish synagogue; in ancient times, a title of respect ("lofty one") given to Jewish scholars who were well versed in the contents of Scripture and tradition and thus qualified to teach others about the meaning of the text and the way they should live. The title does not occur in the Hebrew Bible, since the activity of rabbis presupposes the existence of a canon of Scripture and a body of interpretive tradition that can be consulted for guidance. There did exist, however, a class of **scribes** in ancient Israel that may have played an analogous role in the postexilic Jewish community.

redaction criticism A method of scholarly analysis that examines how the authors and editors of the various books of the Hebrew Bible edited (or redacted) their source materials to integrate them into their own compositions. Redaction criticism works best when we know something about the sources used by an author or editor. When the sources are unknown, scholars can still infer information about the motives and techniques of the authors and editors by looking for patterns in the way they organize and present their materials.

reparations The payment of compensation to make up for harm caused to others. The word is used in two different ways in the Hebrew Bible. When applied to relations between humans, it refers to the requirement that individuals who cause injury to the person or property of others, whether directly or indirectly (for example, by letting their animals stray into a neighbor's field), must pay for the damage caused, along with extra compensation in some cases. When applied to relations between humans and God, it refers to a type of animal sacrifice that is offered to atone for some kind of violation of the dignity or possessions of the deity.

resurrection In Jewish apocalyptic thought, the expectation that God will restore life to those who have died and judge them, rewarding the faithful and punishing the wicked, before inaugurating a new era in which the righteous will live forever in perfected bodies. The idea of a future resurrection appears only in a few late passages in the Hebrew Bible; the huge majority of texts see death as the end of human existence. The word is also used in a metaphorical sense in the Hebrew Bible to speak about Yahweh's future restoration of Israel as a people.

righteousness In the Hebrew Bible, the status of a person who fulfills the expectations of a relationship, whether with other individuals, the deity, or the broader society. The precise definition of righteousness can thus vary from situation to situation. Yet the Hebrew Bible also judges certain behaviors to be inherently righteous or unrighteous based on whether they coincide with the character and standards of Yahweh, who is the epitome of righteousness. No act can be deemed righteous if it violates Yahweh's standards.

rituals Formalized actions by which religious people seek to encounter, manipulate, or respond to the supernatural world. Rituals can be as simple as repeating a prayer before a meal or as elaborate as a multi-day religious festival. All of the religions of the ancient Near East placed great emphasis on rituals. The Torah describes a wide range of rituals that the editors expected the people of Israel to perform. The books of the prophets, by contrast, contain many statements criticizing the people of Israel and Judah for focusing on the performance of rituals and neglecting the social and ethical expectations of Yahweh.

Sabbath A Hebrew term for the seventh day of the week, when the Torah calls for the people of Israel to rest and do no work. The word means "stop" or "cease" (from work) in Hebrew. The origins of the Sabbath rest are unknown, as is the extent to which it was practiced, though several of the prophets condemn their audiences for not taking it seriously. The practice of gathering at the synagogue on the Sabbath for public prayers and the reading of Scripture did not begin until late in the postexilic era.

sacred A synonym for **holy**, used to describe a person, place, or object that has been set apart for association with a deity.

sacrifice The ritual slaughter, cooking, and (in many cases) eating of an animal as an act of religious devotion. Animal sacrifice was a vital part of all religions across the ancient Near East. The laws of Torah contain prescriptions for the performance of a variety of sacrifices for different occasions, all of which were to be supervised by the **priests**. Some were done to provide purification from sin or **impurity**, while others were offered to express gratitude or seek help from the deity.

sage A person known for being wise and instructing others in the ways of **wisdom**. Biblical scholars use the term to refer to a class of professional **scribes** and wisdom teachers that could be found in societies across the ancient Near East. Sages were responsible for preserving, developing, and passing on a society's traditional teachings concerning morality and social conduct. Some of them helped to guide political leaders in their decision making.

Satan A Hebrew word meaning "accuser" or "adversary." Within the Hebrew Bible, it is used to refer both to human opponents and to an angelic being who appears in a few late biblical texts as a heavenly adversary of Yahweh, accusing the deity and his people of wrongdoing. The idea of Satan as an evil supernatural being who rules over the underworld and is engaged in a cosmic battle against God and his angels is a later development, though the Satan does meddle in human affairs and cause harm to humans on a couple of occasions in the Hebrew Bible (1 Chronicles 21:1; Job 1:9-19; 2:3-8).

scribes In ancient societies, a class of educated people (normally men) who fulfilled a wide range of tasks that required literacy. The duties of scribes ranged from low-level clerical tasks (drafting letters, keeping records, copying manuscripts, and so forth) to higher-level duties such as training the children of the elites, interpreting sacred texts, and serving as counselors to kings. Scribes played a vital role in preserving the history and traditions that came to be included in the Hebrew Bible, and some may have been among the primary authors and editors of the biblical texts.

Scripture A generic term for the sacred texts of a religion, from a Latin word meaning "written." Not all religions have Scriptures, and those that do have them view and use them in different ways. While it is possible that some of the written materials that were used as sources by the biblical authors were regarded as sacred by those who preserved them (for example, materials associated with the Jerusalem temple), the religion of Israel had little place for Scriptures until the postexilic era.

selah (sā'-lah) A Hebrew word of unknown meaning that occurs seventy-one times in the book of Psalms and three times in the book of Habakkuk. It can appear at different places in a psalm, but it is normally found at the end of a verse, where English Bibles often print it in italics (for example, Psalms 3:4, 8; 4:2, 4; 7:5). Most scholars think that it is some kind of musical notation or an instruction to guide the reading of the psalm, perhaps marking a place to pause for reflection.

Seleucids (seh-loo'-sids) A term used to designate the Greek kings who ruled from Syria for more than two hundred years after the breakup of Alexander the Great's empire in the late fourth century B.C.E. The dynasty was named after its first member, Alexander's general Seleucus. At its height, the Seleucid Empire controlled most of the region extending from what is now Turkey to Afghanistan. The Seleucid Empire took over the land of Palestine from the **Ptolemies** in 198 B.C.E., but within a few decades their rule was ended by a Jewish resistance movement led by the **Maccabees**.

separatism A strategy adopted by certain social or religious groups to protect their members from the influence of alternative views of reality or competing moral systems. Separatist groups typically view the outside world as dominated by hostile forces that seek to entice their members to abandon the truth and embrace falsehood. Groups that hold **apocalyptic** worldviews are especially prone to separatist strategies, but there is a strong element of social separatism that runs throughout the Hebrew Bible.

Septuagint The first known Greek translation of the Hebrew Bible, begun in Egypt in the third century B.C.E. and completed over the next two centuries. The name comes from a legend that the Torah was translated into Greek by seventy (*septuaginta* in Latin) scholars who worked independently of one another, yet miraculously came up with identical wording in their translations. The Greek edition is also called the LXX, after the Roman numeral for seventy. Since the translation was carried out before the Jewish canon was fixed, the Septuagint contains books that are not in the Jewish canon, including those that Protestants call the **Apocrypha**.

shaman (shah'-mun) A person in certain kinds of religious systems who is believed to possess special skills for interacting with the supernatural world and channeling its power to others, whether for good or for ill (healing illnesses, controlling the forces of nature, foretelling the future, and the like). Shamans are commonly associated with tribal cultures that hold animistic worldviews. Some of the techniques used by **prophets** in the ancient Near East resemble the activities of shamans. Whether the prophets of the Hebrew Bible used similar practices is unclear.

Sheol (shē'-ōl or she-ōl') A Hebrew term referring either to the grave or what lies beyond it. As a rule, the Hebrew Bible sees death as the end for humans, leading some scholars to claim that Sheol is simply a poetic way of referring to the graves in which humans are buried. Others point to places where Sheol appears to refer to a dark, watery region beneath the surface of the earth where humans maintain a shadowy existence after death. Nowhere in the Hebrew Bible is there any mention of the righteous and the unrighteous going to different places directly after death (heaven and hell).

Shephelah (shef'-e-lah) The Hebrew name for a district marked by low, hilly terrain on the western side of the territory of Judah. The Shephelah was important to the mountain-dwelling people of Judah not only because it contained useful farmland but also because its valleys provided natural entry points to the hills of Judah that had to be defended with fortified cities. These fortifications also enabled Judah to control the key trade routes along the Coastal Plain. The Hebrew Bible speaks of many battles in this area due to its strategic importance.

shrine A place set aside for the worship of a deity. Religious shrines of various types were scattered throughout the land of Palestine in ancient times, including the sites that the Hebrew Bible calls **high places**. Shrines can take a variety of forms, from a small open-air location containing symbols of a deity to an elaborate building or temple attended by priests or prophets.

sorcerer A person who is believed to be able to manipulate supernatural forces to help or harm others. The Hebrew Bible speaks of both male and female sorcerers, but it makes no distinction between them in its condemnation of those who perform such acts. Little is known about their beliefs or practices, including whether they acted in the name of Yahweh or other deities.

soul In the Hebrew Bible, the life force that animates the bodies of humans or animals. The Hebrew Bible presumes the existence of an inseparable link between the inner self (soul) and the outer self (body), a view that is summed up in the description of humans as "ensouled bodies" or "embodied souls." The same Hebrew word can be translated as "person" or "self." The idea of an immortal soul that survives the death of the body and spends eternity in heaven or hell is foreign to the Hebrew Bible.

source criticism   A mode of analysis that seeks to uncover and reconstruct (insofar as possible) the literary sources that the authors and editors of the Hebrew Bible used when composing their works. In some instances the Hebrew Bible gives explicit indication that the authors have used earlier sources, while in others the use of sources can be inferred from a careful reading of the text.

spirit   In the Hebrew Bible, a near synonym of the word **soul**. Depending on the context, the same Hebrew word can also be translated as "wind" or "breath." Thus the term *spirit* appears to refer to the life force of humans or animals that remains present as long as they are breathing. It is not a separate or eternal part of human nature as in Greek thought. When used of Yahweh, it refers to his invisible, powerful presence at work in the world and not to a separate divine person as in parts of the New Testament.

stela   (stē'-lah)   An elongated slab of stone inscribed with an important message and then placed upright for people to see. In the ancient world, stelae (the plural of stela) were commonly used to mark the locations of boundaries or graves, to commemorate a significant military victory, or to publicize other materials considered significant by people in authority. Archaeologists have uncovered a number of important stelae that have helped scholars to better understand the historical background of the Hebrew Bible (such as the Code of Hammurabi and the **Merneptah Stela**).

stratigraphy   The technique of reading the layers of a **tell** to learn about life in ancient times at an archaeological site. Since ancient people tended to build on the same sites for many centuries, layers of debris built up over time, leaving clues as to how people lived there. By digging carefully through these layers and recording their findings, archaeologists can piece together important information about the history and living patterns at the site. The term comes from the Latin word for "layers" (*strata*) and the Greek word for "writing."

syncretism   Combining elements from two or more religions to form a new system. As a rule, syncretism presupposes that there is an underlying unity behind the visible differences that divide religious systems and seeks to facilitate interaction between their followers. Syncretism is repeatedly condemned in the Hebrew Bible, despite the fact that the Bible contains many passages that silently incorporate elements of non-Yahwistic polytheism into the depiction of Israel's god.

Tabernacle   See **tent of meeting/tabernacle**.

Talmud   A multivolume collection of materials representing several centuries of Jewish reflection and debate over the meaning and proper application of Scripture and tradition. The title is from a Hebrew word meaning "study" or "learning." There are actually two Talmuds, one produced in Palestine around the fifth century C.E. and another created in Babylonia from the fourth to sixth centuries C.E. The Talmud consists of the **Mishnah** and the Gemara, an extensive record of rabbinic debates and commentary on the Mishnah. The Talmud is second only to the Bible in its importance for traditional forms of Judaism.

Tanak   (tah-nahk')   A term used by many contemporary Jews as a title for their sacred Scriptures. The word is derived from the first letters of the three parts of the Jewish canon: *T* for **Torah**, *N* for **Nevi'im** (the Hebrew word for **Prophets**), and *K* for **Ketuvim** (the Hebrew word for **Writings**). As with most other words in the Hebrew language, the term was formed by adding vowels to this combination of three consonants (TaNaK).

tell   An artificial mound created by centuries of human habitation on a single site. In ancient Israel, towns and cities were often built on elevated sites, and later residents simply built on top of what was there before them, causing the site to grow taller over time. Today, tells are found across the land of Palestine, where they attract the attention and labor of archaeologists, though relatively few have been excavated.

Ten Commandments   A term used by Jews and Christians to refer to a set of ten laws that Yahweh gave to his people prior to his revelation of the other laws of Torah on **Mount Sinai** (Exodus 20:1-17). According to the Hebrew Bible, Yahweh first announced these laws orally to the Exodus generation, then wrote them onto two stone tablets for **Moses** to bring back to the people. Moses, however, smashed these tablets when he saw the people engaging in idolatry (Exodus 32:19). Afterward, either Yahweh or Moses rewrote the laws onto a second set of tablets (Exodus 34:1-4, 27-28), which Moses then placed into the **Ark of the Covenant** as Yahweh commanded (Exodus 40:20-21; compare 25:10-22).

tent of meeting/tabernacle   (tab'-er-nak'-ul)   An elaborate tent that the Hebrew Bible says was carried around by the Exodus generation during their years in the desert as a temporary dwelling place for Yahweh. The tent housed the **Ark of the Covenant**, where Yahweh said he would meet and talk with Moses, together with other symbols of the divine presence. Moses, his assistant Joshua, and the priests are the only ones who are shown entering the tabernacle. Animal sacrifices were offered by the priests on an altar that stood in front of the tent. Scholars disagree about whether there is any historical basis to the story.

teraphim (tehr'-ah-fim) A Hebrew term for figurines representing household gods. They are mentioned only rarely in the Hebrew Bible, so it is hard to know if they should be equated with any of the figurines that archaeologists have uncovered in homes across Palestine. It is also unclear whether they were used in the worship of Yahweh (see Judges 17:1-13; Hosea 3:4) or only the worship of other gods.

Tetragrammaton A scholarly term for the four Hebrew consonants of the divine name YHWH, which scholars believe was pronounced **Yahweh** (yah'-wā). The term comes from two Greek words that mean "four letters."

textual criticism A mode of analysis that seeks to reconstruct the original text of the various books of the Hebrew Bible. Textual criticism is necessary because the available manuscripts and ancient translations differ in many places. Textual critics study the manuscripts and apply special rules and personal judgment to determine which of the different readings is most likely to be the original one.

theology The reasoned attempt to understand and describe in a coherent manner the nature of the supernatural world and its relation to humans. The Hebrew Bible contains few texts that reflect explicitly on theological issues. Most of the theology of the Hebrew Bible is implicit; that is, it must be inferred from stories, songs, laws, and other kinds of material.

theophany The appearance of a deity to humans. Most religions regard the gods as being invisible to humans unless they choose to make themselves known to human senses. In the Hebrew Bible, theophanies of Yahweh take a variety of forms. Some are intensely awe-inspiring, as when Yahweh appears in superhuman glory on his heavenly throne or performs mighty acts of power. Others are less overwhelming, as when Yahweh takes on human form or speaks in dreams, visions, or voices. Still others are apparent only to a person who has the eyes of faith, as when Yahweh's presence is discerned in a thunderstorm or an earthquake.

tithe In the Hebrew Bible, the ritual offering of a tenth of one's agricultural produce to Yahweh. The laws of Torah regulate how the tithe is to be handled, though the rules are inconsistent. In general, it appears that the tithe was to be used to support those who had no means of their own, specifically the **Levites** and the poor, though a portion of the tithes was also to be eaten by the family as part of a ritual meal, which according to some texts must take place in Jerusalem.

Torah A Hebrew word meaning "teaching" or "instruction," used by Jews as a title for the first five books of the Bible. The Torah has traditionally been the most important part of the Bible for Jews. The term can also be used more broadly to refer to any form of teaching or instruction given by Yahweh to his people.

tradition criticism A mode of analysis that seeks to retrace the historical development of various ideas and stories that appear in the Hebrew Bible. Implicit in this method is the belief that the traditions changed over time as each generation sought to apply them to the life of their community. The goal of tradition criticism is to discern how and why this happened.

tribe A social group consisting of people who believe themselves to be related by one or more common ancestors. A tribe may function as a subunit within a society or cross societal and political boundaries. As a rule, tribes share a common identity and culture and encourage their members to marry within the tribe. According to the Hebrew Bible, the people of Israel were divided into twelve tribes that traced their ancestry back to one of the twelve sons of **Jacob/Israel**, and each tribe lived in a different part of Palestine. Tribal structures play little role in the biblical narrative from the time of the **Divided Kingdom** onward.

uncleanness A synonym for **impurity**; the opposite of being ritually clean or pure.

unleavened bread A kind of breadlike wafer made without yeast, known today by its Hebrew name as *matzah* or *matzoh* bread. The Feast of Unleavened Bread is another name for the festival of **Passover**. The eating of unleavened bread is a key part of the Passover ritual, recalling the episode in the Exodus story where the people of Israel had to flee Egypt at night before their bread dough had risen (Exodus 12:39; Deuteronomy 16:1-4; compare Exodus 12:14-20).

wisdom In the Hebrew Bible, an understanding of the way Yahweh has designed life to work, coupled with a commitment to live in accordance with that design. Wisdom is not the same as knowledge or intelligence; it comes from experience and insight, not from formal education, though it can be taught. The word also serves as a title for certain books of the Hebrew Bible that are characterized by an interest in wisdom (Job, Proverbs, Ecclesiastes, and some of the psalms).

witch In the Hebrew Bible, a synonym for **sorcerer**.

worldview A pattern of beliefs about life and the universe that shapes the way people interpret their experience. For most of human history, religion has played a vital role in the development and content of worldviews. The Hebrew Bible indicates that there were a variety of worldviews in ancient Israel, but most of its content is rooted in a worldview that centers on Yahweh and his relation with his people.

Writings A term used by the Jewish community to refer to the third section of the Hebrew canon. The Writings is a loosely defined category that includes a variety of texts that were viewed as Scripture by ancient Jews but did not fit the category of **Torah** or **Prophets**. The content of the Writings remained open-ended until at least the second century C.E.,

when discussions among the rabbis appear to have resulted in a closing of the canon.

Yahweh (yah'-wā) The personal name of the deity whom the authors and editors of the Hebrew Bible regard as the god of Israel and Judah. The actual pronunciation of the name was lost in antiquity as Jews came to regard it as too holy to be uttered, but scholars are fairly certain that Yahweh is the proper pronunciation of the Hebrew word indicated by the consonants YHWH. Both the origins and the meaning of the name are obscure, though it appears to be related to the Hebrew verb meaning "to be." The Hebrew Bible presents Yahweh as the supreme deity over all the universe, though it does not necessarily portray him as the only god.

Yahwism/Yahwistic Terms used by scholars to refer to forms of religion in ancient Palestine that centered on Yahweh. Normally the term *Yahwistic* is reserved for people who honored Yahweh to the exclusion of other gods, but it is not limited to those who saw Yahweh as the only deity. The term *Yahwistic* is also used by source critics to refer to hypothetical written sources that employ the name Yahweh as their primary designation for the deity rather than other names such as **Elohim**.

ACKNOWLEDGMENTS

Fig. 1.1a: Photo © iStockPhoto / Barbara Sauder.
Fig. 1.1b: Photo © iStockPhoto.
Fig. 1.1c: Photo © iStockPhoto / Braden Gunem.
Fig. 1.1d: Photo © iStockPhoto / Hanquan Chen.
Fig. 1.1e: Photo © Gurumustuk Singh Khalsa, www. SikhPhotos.com.
Fig. 1.1f: Photo courtesy of GNU Free Documentation License.
Fig. 1.2: Photo © DeA Picture Library / Art Resource, NY.
Fig. 1.3: Photo © Su Bayfield.
Fig. 1.4a: Photo © iStockPhoto / Michael Mogensen.
Fig. 1.4b: Photo © Jean-Philippe Marquis.
Fig. 1.5a: Photo © iStockPhoto / Alan Tobey.
Fig. 1.5b: Photo © iStockPhoto / Courtney Navey.
Fig. 1.5c: Photo © iStockPhoto / Claudia Dewald.
Fig. 2.1: Photo © Erich Lessing / Art Resource, NY.
Fig. 2.2a: Photo © iStockPhoto / Claudia Dewald.
Fig. 2.2b: Photo © Robert Kaufman.
Fig. 2.2c: Photo © Photo © iStockPhoto / Nancy Louie.
Fig. 2.3a: Photo © iStockPhoto / Roger Branch.
Fig. 2.3b: Photo © iStockPhoto / digitalskillet.
Fig. 2.3c: Photo © 123rf.com.
Fig. 2.4a: Photo © iStockPhoto / Tjui Tjioe.
Fig. 2.4b: Photo © Carl Safina.
Fig. 2.4c: Photo © Yusef Maisonet.
Fig. 3.1: Photo © iStockPhoto / Stephen Orsillo.
Fig. 3.2a: Photo © iStockPhoto / Steven Allan.
Fig. 3.2b: Photo © iStockphoto.com / Boris Katzman.
Fig. 3.3: Photo © iStockphoto.com / John Woodworth.
Fig. 4.1: Photo © Liza Rahmat.
Fig. 4.2a: Photo © Jennifer Hayes.
Fig. 4.2b: Photo from the film Captain Abu Raed.
Fig. 4.3a: Photo © DeA Picture Library / Art Resource, NY.
Fig. 4.3b: Photo © iStockPhoto / Tova Teitelbaum.
Fig. 4.4: Photo © Erich Lessing / Art Resource, NY.
Fig. 4.5: Photo © Alan Place / Flickr.
Fig. 5.1: Photo © Joseph A. Weaks.
Fig. 5.2a: Photo © iStockPhoto / Mark Goddard.
Fig. 5.2b: Photo © Donald W. Parry.
Fig. 5.3: Photo © Joseph A. Weaks.
Fig. 5.4: Photo © Avishai Weiss.
Fig. 6.1: Photo © Christopher Stanley.
Fig. 6.2: Photo courtesy of NASA and http://visibleearth.nasa.gov/view_rec.php?id=3151.
Fig. 6.3: Map from A Short Introduction to the Hebrew Bible by John J. Collins © 2007 Fortress Press.
Fig. 6.4a: Photo © PlanetObserver.com.
Fig. 6.4b: Map © Augsburg Fortress.
Fig. 6.5a: Photo courtesy of GNU Free Documentation License.
Fig. 6.5b: Photo © Ben Aronoff.
Fig. 6.6a: Photo © iStockPhoto / Bryan Lever.
Fig. 6.6b: Photo © Idan Gil.
Fig. 6.7a: Map © Augsburg Fortress.
Fig. 6.7b: Map © Augsburg Fortress.
Fig. 6.8a: Photo © iStockPhoto / Neta Degany.
Fig. 6.8b: Photo © iStockPhoto / Tim Kimberley.
Fig. 6.9a: Photo © Christopher Stanley.
Fig. 6.9b: Photo © Christopher Stanley.
Fig. 6.10a: Photo © Christopher Stanley.
Fig. 6.10b: Photo © Christopher Stanley.
Fig. 6.11a: Photo © Christopher Stanley.
Fig. 6.11b: Photo © Christopher Stanley.
Fig. 6.12a: Photo © Christopher Stanley.
Fig. 6.12b: Photo © Christopher Stanley.
Fig. 7.1: Photo © Christopher Stanley.
Fig. 7.2a: Photo © Carl Rasmussen, http://www. HolyLandPhotos.org.
Fig. 7.2b: Gold jewelry, Late Canaanite period, thirteenth century b.c.e. Photo © The Israel Museum, Jerusalem.

Fig. 7.3a: Photo © Christopher Stanley.
Fig. 7.3b: Photo © Christopher Stanley.
Fig. 7.4: Illustration from Stones and Stories by Donald C. Benjamin © 2009 Fortress Press.
Fig. 7.5a: Photo © Christopher Stanley.
Fig. 7.5b: Photo © Christopher Stanley.
Fig. 7.6a: Photo © iStockPhoto / Noel Powell.
Fig. 7.6b: Photo © Christopher Stanley.
Fig. 7.7a: Photo © Christopher Stanley.
Fig. 7.7b: Photo © Todd Patrick Quin.
Fig. 7.8a: Photo © Patrick Boyd.
Fig. 7.8b: Photo © Erich Lessing / Art Resource, NY.
Fig. 7.9a: Photo © Nickmard Khoey. Used by permission. (http://www.flickr.com/photos/nickmard/2928420059)
Fig. 7.9b: Photo © The Israel Museum, Jerusalem.
Fig. 8.1: Photo © Mazda Hewitt, http://www.flickr.com/photos/aduki.
Fig. 8.2: Photo courtesy of GNU Free Documentation License.
Fig. 8.3: Photo © Bildarchiv Preussishcer Kulturbesitz / Art Resource, NY.
Fig. 8.4: Photo © The Jewish Museum, NY/ Art Resource, NY.
Fig. 8.5: Photo © iStockPhoto / Asier Villafranca Velasco.
Fig. 8.6: Photo © Erich Lessing / Art Resource, NY.
Fig. 8.7: Photo © Werner Forman / Art Resource, NY.
Fig. 8.8: Photo courtesy of http://www.flickr.com/photos/15791740@N08/1766556489/in/set-72157602640349726.
Fig. 8.9: Photo © SEF / Art Resource, NY.
Fig. 8.10: Photo © SEF / Art Resource, NY.
Fig. 8.11: Photo courtesy of http://catholic-resources.org/Dore/Images/OT-134.jpg.
Fig. 9.1: Photo courtesy of The Megiddo Expedition of Tel Aviv University.
Fig. 9.2: Photo © SCALA / Art Resource, NY.
Fig. 9.3a: Photo by Stefan Wenger, Bern/ Switzerland; copyright © Kinneret Regional Project; www.kinneret-excavations.org.
Fig. 9.3b: Photo © Sievan Beverly.
Fig. 9.4: Chart courtesy of the Israel Antiquities Authority.
Fig. 9.5a: Photo © Jamie Barras.
Fig. 9.5b: Photo © Erich Lessing / Art Resource, NY.
Fig. 9.6: Photo © Wally Gobetz.
Fig. 9.7: Photo © Erich Lessing / Art Resource, NY.
Fig. 10.1: Fig. 10.1: Photo courtesy of GNU Free Documentation License.
Fig. 10.2: Photo © iStockPhoto / Danilo Ascione.
Fig. 10.3: Photo courtesy of GNU Free Documentation License.
Fig. 10.4: Photo © iStockPhoto / Jamie VanBuskirk.
Fig. 10.5: Photo © iStockPhoto / Gina Smith.
Fig. 10.6: Photo © Big Stock Photo.
Fig. 10.7: Photo © iStockPhoto / Juergen Sack.
Fig. 11.1: The Metropolitan Museum of Art, Rogers Fund, 1948. (48.105.2) Photo © The Metropolitan Museum of Art.
Fig. 11.2a: Photo © Gurpreet Singh.
Fig. 11.2b: Photo © Richard Flynn.
Fig. 11.3a: Photo courtesy of http://commons.wikimedia.org/wiki/Image:Baal_thunderbolt_Louvre_AO15775.jpg.
Fig. 11.3b: Photo © Isuru Senevi.
Fig. 11.4: Illustration © Joan Anderson. All rights reserved.
Fig. 11.5: Photo © Russian Academy of Sciences, Centre for Egyptological Studies.
Fig. 12.1a: Photo © Vernon Bell.
Fig. 12.1b: Photo © Institute of Nautical Archaeology.
Fig. 12.1c: Photo © Erich Lessing / Art Resource, NY.
Fig. 12.1d: Photo courtesy of http://commons.

wikimedia.org/wiki/Image:Baal_Ugarit_Louvre_AO17330.jpg.
Fig. 12.2: Found in The Social History of Ancient Israel: An Introduction (p. 29) © 2008 Fortress Press.
Fig. 12.3a: Photo © Carl Rasmussen, http://www.HolyLandPhotos.org.
Fig. 12.3b: Photo © Christopher Stanley.
Fig. 12.4a: Photo © Geoffrey Zheng.
Fig. 12.4b: Photo © Réunion des Musées Nationaux / Art Resource, NY.
Fig. 12.5: Photo courtesy of http://commons.wikimedia.org/wiki/File:Folio_62v_-_Psalm_CXXX.jpg.
Fig. 12.6: Photo © Erich Lessing / Art Resource, NY.
Fig. 12.7: Photo © iStockPhoto / Lukasz Laska.
Fig. 12.8: Photo courtesy of http://commons.wikimedia.org/wiki/Image:Ashurnasipal_with_official.jpg.
Fig. 13.1: Photo courtesy of GNU Free Documentation License.
Fig. 13.2: Photo © Erich Lessing / Art Resource, NY.
Fig. 13.3: Photo © The Trustees of The British Museum / Art Resource, NY.
Fig. 13.4: Photo courtesy of http://commons.wikimedia.org/wiki/File:Lucas_Cranach_d._Ä._002.jpg.
Fig. 13.5: Photo courtesy of http://commons.wikimedia.org/wiki/Image:William_Blake_008.jpg.
Fig. 13.6: Photo © DeA Picture Library / Art Resource, NY.
Fig. 14.1: Photo courtesy of GNU Free Documentation License.
Fig. 14.2a: Photo © Shane MacClure. Used by permission.
Fig. 14.2b: Photo © Gurumustuk Singh Khalsa, www.SikhPhotos.com.
Fig. 14.3a: Photo © Erich Lessing / Art Resource, NY.
Fig. 14.3b: Photo © Erich Lessing / Art Resource, NY.
Fig. 14.4: Photo © SCALA / Art Resource, NY.
Fig. 14.5: Photo © The Pierpont Morgan Library / Art Resource, NY.
Fig. 14.6: Photo courtesy of http://www.aoc.gov/cc/photo-gallery/images/70224_hr.jpg.
Fig. 15.1: Photo © Megan Burgess. Used by permission.
Fig. 15.2a: Photo © Barry Blackburn.
Fig. 15.2b: Photo courtesy of Joe Goldberg (Creative Commons).
Fig. 15.3a: Photo courtesy of http://commons.wikimedia.org/wiki/File:Capitoline_she-wolf_Musei_Capitolini_MC1181.jpg.
Fig. 15.3b: Photo © BigStockPhoto.
Fig. 15.4a: Photo © Jean-Pierre Dalbéra (Creative Commons).
Fig. 15.4b: Photo © Marie-Lan Nguyen (Creative Commons).
Fig. 15.5a: Photo © M. Haupt.
Fig. 15.5b: Photo courtesy of Lubuto Library Project.
Fig. 16.1: Photo © The Metropolitan Museum of Art / Art Resource, NY.
Fig. 16.2: Photo courtesy of http://commons.wikimedia.org/wiki/File:Lucas_Cranach_d._%C3%84._035.jpg.
Fig. 16.3a: Photo © The Pierpont Morgan Library / Art Resource, NY.
Fig. 16.3b: Jacob de Backer, "The Garden of Eden", © Image Asset Management Ltd / SuperStock.
Fig. 16.4a: Photo © Vanni / Art Resource, NY.
Fig. 16.4b: Photo © Alinari / Art Resource NY.
Fig. 16.5a: Photo © Réunion des Musées Nationaux / Art Resource, NY.
Fig. 16.5b: Photo © SCALA / Art Resource, NY.
Fig. 16.6a: Photo courtesy of Creative Commons.
Fig. 16.6b: Photo © V&A Images, London / Art

Resource, NY.
Fig. 16.7a: Photo © The Philadelphia Museum of Art / Art Resource, NY.
Fig. 16.7b: Photo © Erich Lessing / Art Resource, NY.
Fig. 16.8: Photo © The Trustees of The British Museum / Art Resource, NY.
Fig. 17.1: Photo courtesy of http://commons.wikimedia.org/wiki/Image:Moln%C3%A1r_%C3%81brah%C3%A1m_kik%C3%B6lt%C3%B6z%C3%A9se_1850.jpg.
Fig. 17.2a: Photo © Bildarchiv Preussishcer Kultursitz / Art Resource, NY.
Fig. 17.2b: Photo courtesy of Creative Commons.
Fig. 17.3a: Photo © Erich Lessing / Art Resource, NY.
Fig. 17.3b: Photo courtesy of GNU Free Documentation License.
Fig. 17.4: Photo courtesy of http://commons.wikimedia.org/wiki/Image:Friedrich_Overbeck_002.jpg.
Fig. 17.5: Photo courtesy of http://commons.wikimedia.org/wiki/File:Peter_von_Cornelius_005.jpg.
Fig. 17.6a: Photo courtesy of Creative Commons.
Fig. 17.6b: Photo © Erich Lessing / Art Resource, NY.
Fig. 17.7a: Photo courtesy of http://commons.wikimedia.org/wiki/File:Pieter_Pietersz._Lastman_001.jpg.
Fig. 17.7b: Photo © SCALA / Art Resource, NY.
Fig. 18.1: Photo © iStockPhoto / Neta Degany.
Fig. 18.2: Photo © Guildhall Art Library, London / HIP / Art Resource, NY.
Fig. 18.3a: Photo © Erich Lessing / Art Resource, NY.
Fig. 18.3b: Photo © The Jewish Museum, NY/ Art Resource, NY.
Fig. 18.4: Photo © Cameraphoto Arte, Venice / Art Resource, NY.
Fig. 18.5: Photo © SCALA / Art Resource, NY.
Fig. 18.6: Photo © Cameraphoto Arte, Venice / Art Resource, NY.
Fig. 18.7: Photo courtesy of http://commons.wikimedia.org/wiki/File:Jacopo_Tintoretto_024.jpg_Moses_striking_the_rock.
Fig. 18.8: Photo © iStockPhoto.
Fig. 18.9a: Photo courtesy of http://commons.wikimedia.org/wiki/File:Maler_der_Grabkammer_des_Rechmir%C3%AA_002.jpg Brickmakers_from_Egyptian_tomb.
Fig. 18.9b: Photo courtesy of GNU Free Documentation License.
Fig. 18.10: Map © Augsburg Fortress.
Fig. 19.1: Photo © Erich Lessing / Art Resource, NY.
Fig. 19.2: Photo courtesy of GNU Free Documentation License.
Fig. 19.3a: Photo © Glenn Austerfield.
Fig. 19.3b: Photo courtesy of http://commons.wikimedia.org/wiki/File:Pergamon_Museum_Berlin_2007089.jpg.
Fig. 19.4a: Photo © Stephen Brown.
Fig. 19.4b: Photo © King Josiah Cleansing The Land of Idols William Hole (1607-1624 British) / SuperStock.
Fig. 20.1: Photo © Erich Lessing / Art Resource, NY.
Fig. 20.2: Photo © The Art Archive / Egyptian Museum, Cairo / Dagli Orti.
Fig. 20.3: Photo © Christopher Stanley.
Fig. 20.4: Barak and Deborah / Private Collection / The Bridgeman Art Library International.
Fig. 20.5a: By kind permission of the Schøyen Collection, London and Oslo.
Fig. 20.5b: By kind permission of the Schøyen Collection, London and Oslo.
Fig. 20.6: Photo © The Israel Museum, Jerusalem.

539

Fig. 20.7: Photo courtesy of Creative Commons.
Fig. 21.1: Photo courtesy of http://commons.wiki-media.org/wiki/Image:Archers_frieze_Darius_palace_Louvre_AOD487.jpg.
Fig. 21.2: Photo © Finsiel / Alinari / Art Resource, NY.
Fig. 21.3: Photo © Marie-Lan Nguyen / Wikimedia Commons.
Fig. 21.4: Photo © Tate, London / Art Resource, NY.
Fig. 21.5: Photo © SCALA / Art Resource, NY.
Fig. 21.6: Photo courtesy of http://commons.wikimedia.org/wiki/File:Daniel_in_the_Lions%27_Den_1613-1615_Peter_Paul_Rubens.jpg.
Fig. 21.7: Photo courtesy of http://commons.wiki-media.org/wiki/Image:Anonimo_lombardo_(sec._XVII),_L%27arcangelo_e_Tobia.jpg.
Fig. 21.8: Photo courtesy of http://commons.wikimedia.org/wiki/Image:Cristofano_Allori_002.jpg.
Fig. 21.9: Photo courtesy of GNU Free Documentation License.
Fig. 22.1: Photo © iStockPhoto.
Fig. 22.2: Photo courtesy of Creative Commons.
Fig. 22.3a: Photo courtesy of GNU Free Documentation License.
Fig. 22.3b: By kind permission of the Schoyen Collection, London and Oslo.
Fig. 22.4a: Photo © Simone Tagliaferri.
Fig. 22.4b: Photo © Erich Lessing / Art Resource, NY.
Fig. 22.5a: Photo courtesy of Israel Antiquities Authority (www.antiquities.org.il)
Fig. 22.5b: By kind permission of the Schoyen Collection, London and Oslo.
Fig. 23.1: Photo © Christopher Stanley.
Fig. 23.2a: Photo © iStockPhoto.
Fig. 23.2b: Photo © iStockPhoto / Michael Mogensen.
Fig. 23.3a: Photo © Patricia Karner.
Fig. 23.3b: Photo © Charlie Sedanayasa.
Fig. 23.4a: Photo © Denise Kappa/123RF.
Fig. 23.4b: Photo © Bill Strong.
Fig. 24.1: Photo © iStockphoto / a-wrangler.
Fig. 24.2a: Photo courtesy of http://commons.wiki-media.org/wiki/File:Babylonian_stele_Louvre_Sb9.jpg.
Fig. 24.2b: Photo courtesy of GNU Free Documentation License.
Fig. 24.3a: Photo courtesy of Creative Commons.
Fig. 24.3b: Photo © Carl Rasmussen, http://www.HolyLandPhotos.org.
Fig. 24.4a: Photo © Dey Alexander.
Fig. 24.4b: Photo courtesy of http://commons.wikimedia.org/wiki/Image:Jean-Fran%C3%A7ois_Millet_(II)_002.jpg.
Fig. 24.5: Photo courtesy of http://commons.wikimedia.org/wiki/Image:10_Gebote_(Lucas_Cranach_d_A).jpg.
Fig. 24.6a: Photo © Anthony Lockhart.
Fig. 24.6b: Photo © Robert T. Kelley.
Fig. 25.1: Photo © iStockPhoto / Sharon Dominick.
Fig. 25.2a: Photo © iStockPhoto / Vicky Bennett.
Fig. 25.2b: Photo © iStockPhoto.
Fig. 25.3a: Photo © iStockPhoto / Terry Healy.
Fig. 25.3b: Photo © iStockPhoto / Nicolás Parodi.
Fig. 25.4: Photo © iStockPhoto / Juergen Sack.
Fig. 25.5: Photo © iStockPhoto.
Fig. 25.6: Photo © Yury Shirokov / BigStockPhoto.com.
Fig. 25.7: Photo © iStockPhoto / Alan Tobey.
Fig. 25.8: Photo courtesy of http://commons.wikimedia.org/wiki/Image:Rounded_altar_in_megiddo_temple.jpg.
Fig. 25.9: Image courtesy of FreeBibleIllustrations.com.
Fig. 26.1: Photo courtesy of http://commons.wikimedia.org/wiki/Image:Kudurru_Melishipak_Louvre_Sb23.jpg.
Fig. 26.2: Photo courtesy of Creative Commons.
Fig. 26.3: Photo courtesy of GNU Free Documentation License.
Fig. 26.4a: Photo © Erich Lessing / Art Resource, NY.
Fig. 26.4b: Photo © Erich Lessing / Art Resource, NY.

Fig. 26.5: Photo courtesy of Creative Commons.
Fig. 26.6a: Photo courtesy of http://commons.wikimedia.org/wiki/Image:A_Pleasant_Sukka.JPG.
Fig. 26.6b: Photo courtesy of http://commons.wikimedia.org/wiki/Image:A_Seder_table_setting.jpg.
Fig. 27.1: Photo courtesy of Creative Commons.
Fig. 27.2a: Photo © iStockPhoto / Peeter Viisimaa.
Fig. 27.2b: Photo © iStockPhoto / Juan Jose Gutierrez Barrow.
Fig. 27.3a: Photo courtesy of Creative Commons.
Fig. 27.3b: Photo courtesy of GNU Free Documentation License.
Fig. 27.4a: Photo © Carl Rasmussen, http://www.HolyLandPhotos.org.
Fig. 27.4b: Photo © Christopher Stanley.
Fig. 27.5a: Photo © Christopher Stanley.
Fig. 27.5b: Photo courtesy of http://commons.wikimedia.org/wiki/Image:Altar_Domitius_Ahenobarbus_Louvre_n2.jpg.
Fig. 27.6a: Photo courtesy of http://commons.wikimedia.org/wiki/Image:Nebamun_tomb_fresco_dancers_and_musicians.png.
Fig. 27.6b: Photo courtesy of http://commons.wikimedia.org/wiki/Image:Maler_der_Grabkammer_des_Ramose_001.jpg.
Fig. 28.1: Photo courtesy of http://commons.wikimedia.org/wiki/File:Jerusalem_Dome_of_the_rock_BW_14.jpg.
Fig. 28.2: Photo © Foto Marburg / Art Resource, NY.
Fig. 28.3: Photo © The Pierpont Morgan Library / Art Resource, NY.
Fig. 28.4: Photo © The Jewish Museum, NY/ Art Resource, NY.
Fig. 28.5a: Photo © Erich Lessing / Art Resource, NY.
Fig. 28.5b: Photo courtesy of Creative Commons.
Fig. 28.6: Photo © Matthew Lazor.
Fig. 28.7: Photo © The Jewish Museum, New York / Art Resource, NY.
Fig. 29.1: Photo © Ben Piven. Used by permission.
Fig. 29.2: From Introducing the Old Testament (Revised) © 2000 Lion Publishing. Used by permission.
Fig. 29.3a: Photo courtesy of http://commons.wikimedia.org/wiki/Image:Human_headed_winged_bull_facing.jpg.
Fig. 29.3b: Photo © Bildarchiv Preussishcer Kulturbesitz / Art Resource, NY.
Fig. 29.4a: Photo © Christopher Stanley.
Fig. 29.4b: Photo © Chris Robinson. Used by permission.
Fig. 29.5: Photo © istockphoto / Tan Kian Khoon.
Fig. 29.6: Photo © Hamid Khan.
Fig. 29.7: Photo © www.thebiblerevival.com.
Fig. 29.8: Photo © Lawrence Wee, 2006. Used by permission.
Fig. 29.9: Photo © Teri Khadija. Used by permission.
Fig. 30.1: Photo © Erich Lessing / Art Resource, NY.
Fig. 30.2: Photo © David Biggins. Used by permission.
Fig. 30.3: Photo courtesy of Creative Commons.
Fig. 30.4: Photo © SCALA / Art Resource, NY.
Fig. 30.5: Photo © Werner Forman / Art Resource, NY.
Fig. 30.6a: Photo © François Guenet / Art Resource, NY.
Fig. 30.6b: Photo © Neil Parekh. Used by permission.
Fig. 30.7: Photo © Bildarchiv Preussishcer Kulturbesitz / Art Resource, NY.
Fig. 31.1: Photo courtesy of GNU Free Documentation License.
Fig. 31.2a: Photo © Rares Nicusan.
Fig. 31.2b: Photo © Mary Harrsch.
Fig. 31.3a: Photo © Benjamin Peters. Used by permission.
Fig. 31.3b: Photo © Lynn Maycroft. Used by permission.
Fig. 31.4: Photo courtesy of http://commons.wikimedia.org/wiki/File:1QIsa_b.jpg.
Fig. 31.5a: Photo courtesy of http://commons.wikimedia.org/wiki/Image:Miraj_by_Sultan_

Muhammad.jpg.
Fig. 31.5b: Photo courtesy of http://commons.wikimedia.org/wiki/File:The_First_Vision_sculpture_Conference_Center.jpg.
Fig. 31.6: Photo courtesy of Creative Commons.
Fig. 31.7a: Photo © Erich Lessing / Art Resource, NY.
Fig. 31.7b: Photo © Ann Ronan Picture Library, London/ HIP / Art Resource, NY.
Fig. 31.8: Photo © Erich Lessing / Art Resource, NY.
Fig. 32.1: Photo © Erich Lessing / Art Resource, NY.
Fig. 32.2a: Photo © Bildarchiv Preussishcer Kulturbesitz / Art Resource, NY.
Fig. 32.2b: Photo © SCALA / Art Resource, NY.
Fig. 32.3: Photo courtesy of http://commons.wikimedia.org/wiki/Image:Giorgio_Vasari_001.jpg.
Fig. 32.4a: Photo courtesy of http://commons.wikimedia.org/wiki/Image:Assyrianbatteringram.JPG.
Fig. 32.4b: Photo © Todd Bolen/ bibleplaces.com. Used by permission.
Fig. 32.5a: Photo courtesy of Creative Commons.
Fig. 32.5b: Photo © Menachem Brody (photo@shechem.org).
Fig. 32.6a: Photo © Todd Bolen/ bibleplaces.com. Used by permission.
Fig. 32.6b: Photo © Todd Bolen/ bibleplaces.com. Used by permission.
Fig. 32.7: Photo © The Trustees of the British Museum / Art Resource, NY.
Fig. 32.8: Photo © Thor Sawin.
Fig. 33.1: Photo courtesy of http://commons.wikimedia.org/wiki/Image:Rembrandt_Harmensz._van_Rijn_064.jpg.
Fig. 33.2: Photo courtesy of the Ancient Biblical Manuscript Center for Preservation and Research, Claremont, Calif., and the Israel Antiquities Authority.
Fig. 33.3: Photo © Art Resource, NY.
Fig. 33.4: Photo courtesy of http://commons.wikimedia.org/wiki/File:Assyrian_Horse_Archer.jpg.
Fig. 33.5a: Photo © Wally Gobetz. Used by permission.
Fig. 33.5b: Photo courtesy of http://www.geocities.com/worldview_3/baruchseal.jpg.
Fig. 33.6: Photo courtesy of http://commons.wikimedia.org/wiki/Image:Miriams_Tanz.jpg.
Fig. 33.7: Photo courtesy of http://commons.wikimedia.org/wiki/File:Meister_der_Predigten_des_Heiligen_Gregor_von_Nazianz_002.jpg.
Fig. 33.8: Photo courtesy of Creative Commons.
Fig. 34.1: Photo courtesy of http://commons.wikimedia.org/wiki/File:Pergamon_Museum_Berlin_2007109.jpg.
Fig. 34.2: Photo © Bildarchiv Preussische Kulturbesitz / Art Resource, NY.
Fig. 34.3: Photo courtesy of GNU Free Documentation License.
Fig. 34.4: Photo courtesy of http://commons.wikimedia.org/wiki/Image:Jeremiah_by_Repin.jpg.
Fig. 34.5: Photo courtesy of GNU Free Documentation License.
Fig. 34.6: Used with kind permission of Museo Nacional Del Prado, Madrid, Spain.
Fig. 34.7: Photo courtesy of http://karenswhimsy.com/cyrus-the-great.shtm.
Fig. 34.8: Photo © The Trustees of the British Museum / Art Resource, NY.
Fig. 35.1: Photo courtesy of Creative Commons.
Fig. 35.2: Photo © Patrick Charlot.
Fig. 35.3: Photo courtesy of http://commons.wikimedia.org/wiki/File:Le_mariage_de_la_Vierge.jpg.
Fig. 35.4: Photo © Bildarchiv Preussishcer Kulturbesitz / Art Resource, NY.
Fig. 35.5: Photo © iStockPhoto / oneclearvision.
Fig. 35.6: Photo © iStockPhoto / Ruvan Boshoff.
Fig. 35.7: Image provided courtesy of Montclair State University META digital collection (http://meta.montclair.edu/disciplines/nineveh/).
Fig. 36.1: Photo © The Trustees of the British Museum / Art Resource, NY.
Fig. 36.2: Photo courtesy of GNU Free Documentation License.

Fig. 36.3: Photo courtesy of http://commons.wikimedia.org/wiki/File:Hicks_peaceable-kingom.jpg.
Fig. 36.4a: Photo courtesy of GNU Free Documentation License.
Fig. 36.4b: Photo courtesy of Creative Commons.
Fig. 36.4c: Photo © Erich Lessing / Art Resource, NY.
Fig. 36.5: Photo courtesy of GNU Free Documentation License.
Fig. 36.6: Photo © Todd Bolen/ bibleplaces.com.
Fig. 36.7: Photo courtesy of www.babylonforsaken.com.
Fig. 37.1: Photo © DeA Picture Library / Art Resource, NY.
Fig. 37.2a: Photo courtesy of Creative Commons.
Fig. 37.2b: Photo courtesy of GNU Free Documentation License.
Fig. 37.2c: Photo courtesy of http://commons.wikimedia.org/wiki/Image:Athena_Parthenos_Altemps_Inv8622.jpg.
Fig. 37.3a: By kind permission of the Schoyen Collection, London and Oslo.
Fig. 37.3b: Photo © Erich Lessing / Art Resource, NY.
Fig. 37.4: Photo © James Morris / Art Resource, NY.
Fig. 37.5: Photo © Erich Lessing / Art Resource, NY.
Fig. 37.6a: Photo © Jill Granberg.
Fig. 37.6b: Photo © 2007 Margery H. Freeman. Used by permission.
Fig. 37.7: Photo © Prashanth NS, India (prashanth.ns@gmail.com).
Fig. 37.8: Photo © iStockPhoto / Jerry Koch.
Fig. 37.9: Photo © Ashley Jonathan Clements.
Fig. 37.10: Photo © Damon Lynch.
Fig. 38.1: Photo © Erich Lessing / Art Resource, NY.
Fig. 38.2: Photo © The Pierpont Morgan Library / Art Resource, NY.
Fig. 38.3: Photo © The Pierpont Morgan Library / Art Resource, NY.
Fig. 38.4: Photo © The Pierpont Morgan Library / Art Resource, NY.
Fig. 38.5: Photo © The Pierpont Morgan Library / Art Resource, NY.
Fig. 38.6: Photo © Terry S. Amstutz.
Fig. 38.7a: Photo © iStockPhoto / giamoments.
Fig. 38.7b: Photo © iStockPhoto / Christian Vuong.
Fig. 38.8a: Photo © iStockPhoto / Studio1One.
Fig. 38.8b: Photo © Brad Hunter.
Fig. 38.9: Photo © Christian Dare.
Fig. 38.10: The Song of Solomon by He Qi (China). For more information and art by He Qi, please visit www.heqigallery.com.

SUBJECT INDEX

CITATION INDEX

Includes passages discussed substantially in the text.